Embedded System Design

Embedded System Design
Methodologies and Issues

Lawrence J. Henschen

Northwestern University, Evanston, IL, USA

Julia C. Lee

Northwestern University, Evanston, IL, USA

ELSEVIER

ISBN: 978-0-443-18470-3

For information on all Morgan Kaufmann publications visit our website at
https://www.elsevier.com/books-and-journals

Publisher: Peter Linsley
Acquisition Editor: Stephen Merken
Editorial Project Manager: Ellie Barnett
Production Project Manager: Beula Christopher
Cover Designer: Matthew Limbert

Typeset by TNQ Technologies

Printed in India

Last digit is the print number: 9 8 7 6 5 4 3 2 1

Preface

Embedded systems (ES), and more recently, cyber-physical systems (CPS), are systems involving computing devices in combination with a variety of other devices that sense and/or control the environment to serve a specific purpose. This contrasts with desktop/laptop computer systems which involve a computing element with a specific set of other devices (screen, keyboard, mass memories, etc.) and whose purpose is to provide a general computing platform for word processing, internet browsing, game playing, and many other activities pursued by humans. Examples of embedded systems include cell phones, smart appliances, appliances in general, sub-systems in cars, sensor networks (such as those used in geo-monitoring, agriculture, health monitoring, etc.), factory assembly lines, smart HVAC systems, traffic control lights, and many, many others. The Internet of Things (IoT) incorporates varieties of different kinds of embedded systems and general computing devices that form networks, often dynamically and opportunistically, for larger purposes. Examples of IoT applications include smart cities, smart power grids, smart buildings, and, again, many others. For example, in one aspect of a smart city smart vehicles dynamically connect with smart street lights and the smart city system, which in turn monitors cars across the city to better control traffic. As a vehicle moves through the city it connects with and disconnects from different devices in the smart city. The Introduction chapter gives more details about various kinds of embedded systems and references about embedded systems, the Internet of Things, and their growing importance.

There are vastly many more processing elements in embedded systems than there are in desktop/laptop systems. The number of connected devices surpassed the human population in 2008 and reached over 20 billion by 2020. Even more important from the perspective of system design, there are vastly more different kinds of embedded systems than different kinds of desktop/laptop systems. A typical modern car, alone, has anywhere from 50 to 300 sub-systems using processing technology. The bulk of human interaction with computing is through embedded systems (cars, ATMS, cell phones, appliances, etc.), not desktop/laptop computers. The design of embedded systems and Internet of Things applications will play a major role in the future of computing, and computer/electrical engineers will be a major part of that effort.

This book is aimed at computer and related engineering undergraduate or Master degree students who join companies that design and build embedded systems and Internet of Things applications. The primary goal is to prepare these students to join teams of other engineers, applications specialists (who are likely not engineers), psychologists, sociologists, and other kinds of team participants who work together to design modern products. The computer engineers should be able to contribute at all stages of the design process from modeling (behavioral modelling, internal modelling, etc.) through hardware/software design, evaluation/verification/validation/testing, and related aspects such as operating system issues like scheduling. A secondary goal is to make these students aware of issues, such as privacy and security, that they will face when designing embedded and Internet of Things systems.

This book tries to balance low-level hardware/software design issues and high-level requirement analysis/modeling issues. This book discusses the issues with examples making it easier for the students/readers to understand the issues and principles. This book provides large number of problems/exercises for the students/reader to practice the knowledge learned from the text. These important characteristics of the book will help to reach the goal — A general introduction that prepares students/readers to join teams of engineers designing real embedded systems.

Teaching ancillaries for this book, including solutions manual and image bank, are available online to qualified instructors. Visit https://educate.elsevier.com/book/details/9780443184703 for more information and to register for access.

Acknowledgements

We gratefully acknowledge the students who have taken our courses in embedded system design and microprocessor systems over many years and who have given valuable suggestions and provided feedback on early drafts.

Contents

CHAPTER 1   Introduction to Internet of Things and embedded systems 1
Lawrence J. Henschen and Julia C. Lee

1.1 Introduction.. 1
1.2 Introduction to Internet of Things (IoT)............................ 1
1.3 The Internet of Things vs. embedded systems 7
1.4 Brief history of three underlying technologies 8
    1.4.1 Microprocessors... 9
    1.4.2 Computer networks... 11
    1.4.3 Sensors and actuators... 12
1.5 The embedded system development process......................... 13
    1.5.1 What is a development process and why is it needed.. 13
    1.5.2 Existing software development processes and life cycles.. 14
    1.5.3 A development process for embedded systems 16
    1.5.4 IoT projects... 20
1.6 Summary 20
Problems... 21
References... 21

PART 1 Modeling the system under development

CHAPTER 2   First stage modeling — modeling interaction between the system and the environment.............. 25
2.1 Introduction.. 25
2.2 Actors, use cases, and scenarios..................................... 28
    2.2.1 Actors 28
    2.2.2 Use cases and scenarios... 32
    2.2.3 Use case analysis and related diagrams 34
2.3 Universal access — scenarios involving actors with disabilities or limitations... 41
2.4 UML and tools for use case development and analysis........... 42
2.5 Summary 42
Problems... 43
References... 45

CHAPTER 3   Finite-state machines..**47**
    3.1 Introduction..47
    3.2 Finite-state machines 48
        3.2.1 Acceptors and transducers — early forms of FSMs........48
        3.2.2 FSMs in embedded systems 51
    3.3 Refining and correcting FSMs 53
    3.4 Determinism versus non-determinism 55
    3.5 Timed FSMs..56
    3.6 Hierarchical FSMs..58
        3.6.1 OR super-states — states that are FSMs.......................59
        3.6.2 AND super-states — concurrency 62
    3.7 Issues with concurrency..72
        3.7.1 StateMate semantics 72
        3.7.2 Multiple signals arriving at nearly the same time...........73
    3.8 Summary 74
    Problems...74
    References..78

CHAPTER 4   Modeling physically distributed embedded systems..**79**
    4.1 Introduction..79
    4.2 Messages 80
    4.3 SDL — an example modeling language for distributed systems...80
        4.3.1 Behavioral specification in SDL...............................81
        4.3.2 Communication..82
    4.4 Determinism revisited 84
    4.5 Summary 87
    Problems...87
    References..89

CHAPTER 5   Petri Nets for modeling concurrency and shared resources..**91**
    5.1 Introduction..91
    5.2 Condition/event and place/transition Petri Nets.....................91
        5.2.1 Condition/event Petri Net.......................................92
        5.2.2 Place/transition Petri Net 94
        5.2.3 Comments..108
    5.3 Reachability 109

5.4 The incidence matrix associated with a place/transition network and proving properties................................ 113

    5.4.1 The incidence matrix for a place/transition network 114

    5.4.2 Using the incidence matrix to study reachability.......... 115

    5.4.3 Place invariants and characteristic vectors.................. 118

5.5 Predicate/transition Petri Nets and colored Petri Nets 120

    5.5.1 A brief review of the evolution of predicate/transition and colored Petri Nets... 120

    5.5.2 An example.. 121

5.6 Petri Nets with time... 124

5.7 Summary 129

Problems.. 129

References... 133

PART 2 Building robust, safe, and correct systems

CHAPTER 6 Designing systems that are safe and robust 137

    6.1 Introduction.. 137

    6.2 Definitions 137

        6.2.1 Service, failure, errors, and faults............................ 138

        6.2.2 Reliability and related concepts 139

        6.2.3 Robustness... 141

    6.3 Estimating and using failure rates..................................... 144

    6.4 Principles for designing safe and robust systems.................. 146

        6.4.1 Methods for counteracting failures in subsystems or components... 147

        6.4.2 Design principles 149

    6.5 Summary 152

    Problems.. 152

    References... 153

CHAPTER 7 Verification, validation, and evaluation................. 155

    7.1 Introduction.. 155

    7.2 Verification.. 156

        7.2.1 Properties of interest.. 156

        7.2.2 Useful reasoning techniques.................................... 157

    7.3 Validation 161

        7.3.1 Validation with respect to human actors 161

        7.3.2 Universal access... 164

        7.3.3 Installability and maintainability............................. 165

        7.3.4 Portability.. 166

        7.3.5 Esthetics.. 166

7.4 Evaluation 167
7.5 Summary 168
Problems 168
References 169

CHAPTER 8   Testing 171
8.1 Introduction 171
8.2 Simulation/emulation 171
    8.2.1 Simulation 173
    8.2.2 Emulation 174
8.3 Discrete event simulation 175
    8.3.1 Events and event queues 175
    8.3.2 Time 176
    8.3.3 Examples 177
8.4 Generating test cases 185
    8.4.1 Methods for deriving test cases 185
    8.4.2 General principles and guidelines 186
8.5 Summary 188
Problems 188
References 190

PART 3 Hardware

CHAPTER 9   Introduction and overview 193
9.1 Introduction 193
9.2 Overview of the structure of an embedded system 194
9.3 Example structure of a modest-sized system 195

CHAPTER 10   Processing elements 197
10.1 Introduction 197
10.2 Microcontroller vs. microprocessor 197
10.3 Features to consider when selecting a processing element 199
    10.3.1 Interrupt system 199
    10.3.2 Power control and sleep modes 203
    10.3.3 Timers and counters 205
    10.3.4 Internal memory 207
    10.3.5 Additional functional features 208
    10.3.6 Nonfunctional features 209
10.4 Sample processors 210
    10.4.1 The 8051 family 210
    10.4.2 The Stellaris family 212

10.4.3 Special purpose processors....................................215

10.5 A special note about start-up times..............................218

10.6 Summary 220

Problems...220

References..223

CHAPTER 11   Memories **225**

11.1 Introduction...225

11.2 Physical-level issues..225

11.2.1 Onboard vs. offboard memory 225

11.2.2 Serial vs. parallel access 226

11.2.3 Volatile vs. non-volatile memory...................228

11.3 Logical-level issues...229

11.3.1 Cache memory.......................................230

11.3.2 Scratchpad memory 231

11.3.3 Memory management units 232

11.4 Summary 232

Problems...233

References..235

CHAPTER 12   Field-programmable gate arrays **237**

12.1 Introduction...237

12.2 FPGAs and SOCs..237

12.3 Algorithms in hardware 239

12.4 Low-end FPGAs and CPLDs......................................239

12.5 Summary 246

Problems...247

References..249

CHAPTER 13   Devices, sensors, and actuators **251**

13.1 Introduction...251

13.2 Digital inputs..251

13.3 Analog inputs..255

13.4 Digital outputs 259

13.5 Analog outputs...259

13.6 Interfacing large numbers of digital inputs and outputs 261

13.7 Common output devices..265

13.7.1 Motors...266

13.7.2 Indicators and panel displays 271

13.7.3 Communications circuits...........................274

13.7.4 Device drivers.......................................275

13.8 PWM for controlling motors, LEDs, etc. 275

13.9 Sampling periodic analog signals.................................... 276
13.10 Summary.. 280
Problems.. 281
References... 282

CHAPTER 14   Energy... **283**
14.1 Introduction.. 283
14.2 Proximity to reliable energy sources 283
14.3 Batteries 285
14.4 Energy harvesting.. 285
14.5 Design strategies 288
14.6 Summary 289
Problems.. 289
References... 290

CHAPTER 15   Hardware-software mapping............................. **291**
15.1 Introduction.. 291
15.2 Task graphs, task splitting, and task merging.................... 292
15.3 Integer linear programming for finding acceptable
        solutions 296
        15.3.1 Integer linear programming 296
        15.3.2 Integer linear programming variables and
               equalities/inequalities for embedded system
               modeling.. 297
        15.3.3 Example.. 299
        15.3.4 Adding problem-specific knowledge to the
               basic equations.. 301
        15.3.5 Comments... 302
15.4 Pareto optimality 302
15.5 Summary 305
Problems... 306
References... 309

PART 4 Software

CHAPTER 16   Operating systems.. **313**
16.1 Introduction.. 313
16.2 Operating system features and support 313
16.3 Buy or build.. 315
16.4 Real-time operating system issues 319
        16.4.1 Time systems... 319
        16.4.2 Coordinating time among modules in a system........ 321

16.5 Classification of real-time applications............................ 322
16.6 Summary 323
Problems... 323
References.. 325

CHAPTER 17   Scheduling **327**
17.1 Introduction... 327
17.2 Definitions and notation.. 330
17.3 Independent periodic tasks with preemption..................... 332
    17.3.1 Rate monotonic scheduling................................... 332
    17.3.2 Earliest deadline first... 336
17.4 Dependent periodic tasks 337
17.5 Independent aperiodic tasks.. 337
17.6 Dependent aperiodic tasks.. 340
17.7 Scheduling for a fixed number of processors 344
17.8 Estimating execution times — worst-case execution time..... 346
17.9 Summary 349
Problems... 349
References.. 353

CHAPTER 18   Semaphores.. **355**
18.1 Introduction... 355
18.2 Motivation... 355
18.3 Semaphores 357
18.4 Issues with priority — priority inversion 360
18.5 Summary 366
Problems... 367
References.. 369

CHAPTER 19   Optimization and other special considerations 371
19.1 Introduction... 371
19.2 Fixed point arithmetic 371
    19.2.1 Addition, subtraction, and scalar-multiplication........ 372
    19.2.2 Multiplication with fractional parts in both
           numbers.. 374
    19.2.3 Division... 375
    19.2.4 Expressions involving fixed-point numbers.............. 376
    19.2.5 Binary vs. decimal.. 377
19.3 Optimizations for loop processing 377
    19.3.1 Simple loop unrolling, splitting, and fusion............. 378
    19.3.2 Memory organization for arrays and loop
           processing 381

19.4 Summary 382

Problems 382

PART 5 Communications

CHAPTER 20   Introduction to communications and messages ... 387

    20.1 Introduction 387

    20.2 Messages and message passing 388

        20.2.1 Messages and message formats 388

        20.2.2 Message passing 390

    20.3 Summary 392

    Problems 393

    References 393

CHAPTER 21   Networks 395

    21.1 Introduction 395

    21.2 Brief history of networking 395

    21.3 Basic network concepts 396

    21.4 Classification of networks 400

        21.4.1 Near-field communication networks 401

        21.4.2 Body area networks 402

        21.4.3 Personal area networks 403

        21.4.4 Near-me area networks 404

    21.5 Network topologies 405

        21.5.1 Linear networks 406

        21.5.2 Ring networks 406

        21.5.3 Star networks 408

        21.5.4 Tree networks 410

        21.5.5 Mesh networks 411

    21.6 Physical considerations 412

        21.6.1 Wired networks 413

        21.6.2 Wireless networks 417

    21.7 Summary 418

    Problems 418

    References 420

CHAPTER 22   The Internet 421

    22.1 Introduction 421

    22.2 The Open Systems Interconnection model 421

    22.3 Transport Control Protocol and Internet Protocol 424

        22.3.1 Transport Control Protocol 425

        22.3.2 Internet Protocol 427

22.3.3 Example..430

22.4 The ethernet protocol 431

22.5 Summary 434

Problems..435

References..436

CHAPTER 23   Low-level communication protocols....................437

23.1 Introduction...437

23.2 Common serial protocols for wired connections.................437

23.2.1 TTL serial protocols..438

23.2.2 RS232 protocol 440

23.2.3 Inter-integrated circuit (I^2C) protocol 441

23.2.4 Controller area network protocol...........................445

23.3 Common low-power wireless protocols and
technologies for computer networks...............................450

23.3.1 Wi-Fi..451

23.3.2 Bluetooth 453

23.3.3 Zigbee 456

23.3.4 Ipv6lowPAN 458

23.4 Contention and collisions..458

23.4.1 Collision detection and/or avoidance......................459

23.4.2 Priority-based arbitration...................................460

23.4.3 Carrier sense multiple access...............................461

23.4.4 Time division multiple access 462

23.5 Summary 463

Problems..463

References..467

CHAPTER 24   Cloud vs. edge vs. local computing 469

24.1 The cloud...469

24.1.1 Characteristics of the cloud 470

24.1.2 Benefits of cloud computing................................473

24.2 Issues for embedded system design................................475

24.3 Summary 476

Problems..477

References..477

PART 6 The Internet of Things

CHAPTER 25   Reference models for the Internet of Things........481

25.1 Introduction...481

25.2 The IoT World Forum model.......................................481

25.3 The INTEL model 485
25.4 Summary 488
Problems 489
References 489

CHAPTER 26   IoT issues **491**
26.1 Introduction 491
26.2 Things 491
26.3 Scale 493
26.4 Heterogeneity of things 494
26.5 Security, privacy, and trust 496
26.6 Connectivity 499
26.7 Issues regarding big data and data ownership 499
26.8 Summary 501
Problems 501
References 502

Index 503

Introduction to Internet of Things and embedded systems

Lawrence J. Henschen, Julia C. Lee

1.1 Introduction

In this chapter we introduce the notions of Internet of Things and embedded systems. Internet of Things is a broader concept, so we begin with its overview in Section 1.2, thereby setting the context for the material in Chapters 2–26. Embedded systems form the base of the Internet of Things, and in Section 1.3 we delineate what we consider the main differences between IoT projects and embedded systems projects. Readers interested in the historical perspective can find a brief review of the development of the three underlying technologies — processing elements, networks, and sensor/actuator devices — in Section 1.4. Finally, in Section 1.5 we describe a generic design process that can help embedded systems developers organize the design of embedded systems.

1.2 Introduction to Internet of Things (IoT)

The term "Internet of Things" was coined in 1999 by Kevin Ashton[1] to refer to the growing ability of ordinary devices (appliances, vehicles, shipping crates, etc.) to connect with the internet and eventually possibly with each other. Technologies in the 1980s and 1990s, such as radio frequency identification (RFID) and bar codes, allowed objects to identify themselves to corresponding "readers", which could then transmit at least the location of the object to places on the internet. As microprocessor/microcontroller and wireless communication technology developed, ordinary objects could become "smart" and do more than just identify themselves. An object could be equipped with sensors so that it could provide more information about itself and its local environment than just its identity. The addition of actuators allowed these objects to actually control their environments. Finally, the rapid advancement of networking and communication technologies allowed objects to communicate, and therefore potentially cooperate, with each other, either indirectly through the general internet through intermediate web sites or even directly with each other. Smart objects can sense and provide information, in many cases in much greater detail than human observers, and provide it continuously. They can act, allowing much greater potential control over the world and the environment.

Embedded System Design. https://doi.org/10.1016/B978-0-443-18470-3.00001-4

Technology now allows a smooth integration of a huge array of physical devices and the physical world in general into the world of computing, hence the growth of cyber-physical systems.

Figure 1.1 shows a generic format for the Internet of Things. Embedded systems form most of the lowest level of the structure. The figure shows typical "things" that occur at that level — buildings, environmental sensor networks, cars, appliances, animals fitted with sensors, infrastructure elements such as street lights, homes, etc. Many of these will have connections to the Internet and the cloud through gateways. Information from many different "things" can be collected and analyzed in the cloud, and commands sent back to the "things" so that they can interact and control the environment. More recently, IoT proponents envision different kinds of "things" communicating directly with each other. Some of these links can be permanent, such as links between smart buildings and local infrastructure, and are shown in the figure as solid lines. Others can be dynamic because one or more of the participating "things" is moving, shown in the figure as dotted lines between the car and a building or between the cow and a sensor data collector.

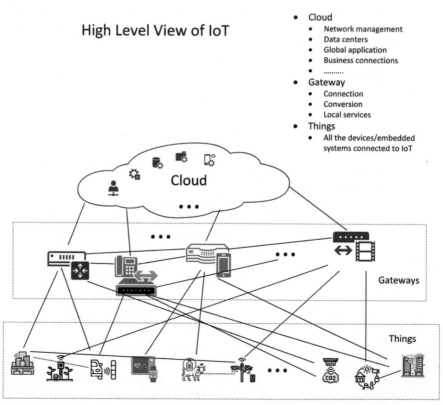

FIGURE 1.1 Generic Overview of the Internet of Things.

Drawn by authors.

An interesting viewpoint and point of contrast between IoT and the previous networks is the following. The early digital networks (see Section 1.4.2) were the web of computers. The major goal was to allow computers to work together and share resources. Later, the Internet became the web of people. The major goal of the Internet is to allow people to have access to information and resources. The new paradigm will be the web of things. The number of connected devices, or things, surpassed the human population by the year 2008,[2] and estimates for the year 2025 range from 20 billion to 50 billion connected devices.

Many people have expressed a "vision" for the Internet of Things. A typical statement is the following from Ref. [3].

"The concept goal of the Internet of Things is to enable things to be connected anytime, anyplace, with anything and anyone ideally using any path/network and any service. Internet of Things is a new revolution of the Internet. Objects make themselves recognizable and they obtain intelligence thanks to the fact that they can communicate information about themselves and they can access information that has been aggregated by other things".

Much progress has been made in many of the necessary underlying technologies, such as microprocessors, sensors, networking, low-power circuitry, and communications, but there is still much research needed to make the above vision a reality. In particular, much more research in areas like interoperability, renewable energy, and artificial intelligence is needed to reach the goal of autonomous systems coordinating and cooperating with each other without human intervention. Furthermore, there are serious social issues to be considered, such as privacy, security, and human-computer interaction. Some of these issues are discussed in Chapter 26.

Still, the IoT has great potential for improving modern society and indeed has already proven beneficial in many areas. The following are just a few of the many applications discussed in the literature and for which there are already or there likely will be commercial systems in the near future.

- Inventory control. One of the earliest applications was to use RFID tags to monitor the arrival, location, and consumption of inventory. This led to improvements in manufacturing through just-in-time (JIT) supply. Supplies were delivered just when they would be needed based on current inventory and models of consumption, as opposed to being delivered early and having to be stored. The availability of microcontroller systems with sensors and actuators allows more detailed monitoring than just location. For example, the temperature history of perishable goods in transit can be stored, and in cases where the temperature can be controlled the microcontroller can activate the cooling system to bring a rising temperature back to within acceptable limits.
- Smart agriculture. Wireless sensor networks (WSNs) are capable of monitoring crop and soil conditions continuously and at a finer granularity and more precision than human farmers. Moreover, they can sense more aspects than just temperature and moisture, for example, soil acidity and other soil features. Such

systems can make more efficient use of water by activating irrigation only when and where needed and controlling the amount of water actually used. By monitoring weather reports and local water supply conditions, a smart agricultural system can make even better decisions about when and how much to water. They can draw the farmer's attention to areas of the field that need human attention. Recent ideas include connection to the futures market to make decisions about when to fertilize and water so that crops are ready at the best time for the market.

- Smart electrical grid. Monitoring the use of electricity, both at the individual home level and the industrial level, can lead to more efficient use of energy and better pricing policies. Meters can record usage during various times of the day to promote more even usage, to help implement time-of-day based pricing, or to identify possible electrical problems such as equipment left running at times when it is supposed to be off.
- Health monitoring. Biosensors attached to a patient and connected to the internet can monitor the patient's condition 24 hours a day rather than only when the patient goes to the medical facility and can alert medical emergency resources if a health event requires attention. Motion and other kinds of sensors in the patient's home or other environments can monitor for other conditions and events, such as a fall. Medical emergency facilities can be notified even if the patient is unable to signal or phone. Smart devices in the home, such as voice-controlled appliances for people with limited dexterity, can assist the patient in activities that the patient might not be able to do alone, leading to a rich "assisted living" environment.
- Smart buildings and homes. Many of the above applications — smart energy, security, patient monitoring, etc. — plus others can be combined to make homes and buildings smart. Smart buildings/homes would include features such as smart control of temperatures (for time of day, occupancy levels of rooms, price of energy at the current time of day, etc.), identification of people at the doors (through, e.g., face recognition), and automatic notification to homeowner and/ or relevant emergency services when needed (e.g., in case of a fall, presence of strangers, housebreaking, etc.).
- Transportation. Sensors in vehicles, roads, stop lights, etc., can provide information to central control systems that can then adjust traffic patterns. Assisted driving, such as automatic parking, collision warning, and lane departure warning, is already available on cars, and systems that would take control of the car to avoid associated dangers are being developed. Driverless cars are already under development.
- Smart city. Smart buildings and transportation are just two of several areas that comprise the development of smart cities. Other aspects of smart cities include
    - Smart parking lots that report vacancies to a central site that can be accessed by drivers (or possibly even the cars themselves in the future) to optimize the search for parking spots.

- Dynamic reconfiguration of stop light operation to optimize traffic for normal time of day changes, current traffic conditions, weather, and other aspects of the environment that affect traffic flow.
- Dynamic control of community resources, such as power, police, and fire. Figure 1.2 shows a schematic of how different aspects of a city could be connected, allowing for intelligent control and coordination.

- Safety and security. Smart home monitoring systems are already commercially available and are able to communicate with outside systems such as local authorities and emergency providers. Surveillance at critical public locations such as airports can be much improved when independent monitoring systems are connected together and cooperate. Sophisticated sound recognition and tracking systems combined with information from surveillance cameras can help police identify and isolate gunshots and snipers.

These are but a few of the myriad applications being proposed, but they illustrate various ways in which cyber-physical systems and the Internet of Things can benefit people and society. The reader is referred to[4–6] for additional lists of applications. Figure 1.3, taken from Ref. [7], shows one corner of their IoT Map. The full map shows nine different service sectors and over 100 sample "Things". On the web page in Ref. [7], the different sectors of the image can be expanded for a more detailed discussion of the application and the potential for IoT in that area. The ubiquitous presence and far-reaching consequences of autonomous things coordinating

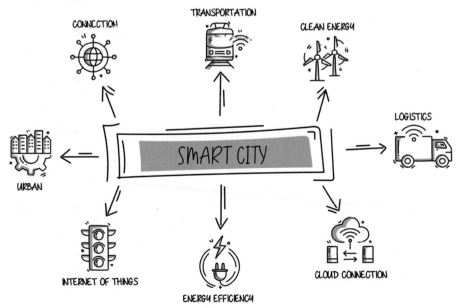

FIGURE 1.2 Schematic of Smart City Connections.

Photo purchased from iStock.

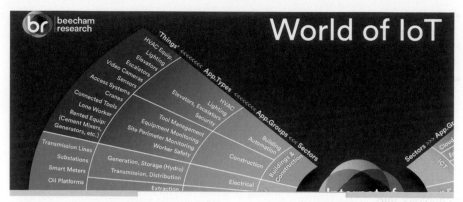

FIGURE 1.3 M2M World of Connected Services — The Internet of Things.

Photo Courtesy of Beacham Research (http://www.beechamresearch.com/article.aspx? id=4).

and cooperating with each other and controlling their environments without human intervention have led many to assert that the IoT is the next "revolution in computing".[8−11] The following quote from Ref. [12] also serves to emphasize the drastic changes expected from the IoT.

> *"In fact, after the World Wide Web and universal mobile accessibility, the IoT represents the most potentially disruptive technological revolution of our lifetime".*

As another indication of the importance placed on the IoT, most of the major computer-related companies are entering the market either in terms of concepts or products and tools (see Chapter 25).

As one might imagine from the above quote and the breadth of applications shown in Figure 1.3, the economic impact of the IoT is potentially enormous. The following information, taken from *The Internet of Things Business Index 2017: Transformation in Motion*,[13] shows how committed major business leaders are to incorporating IoT into their businesses and products. This report was prepared by the Economist Intelligence Unit (EIU), a British organization that performs research and analysis to forecast future business trends. EIU interviewed over 800 senior corporate executives around the world from a variety of industries of different sizes and half a dozen executives from major technical companies. About 20% said IoT has already had a major impact on their industry, and 30% expected major impact within the next few years. More than half expected IoT to lead to significant internal cost savings and/or generate new income within the next 3 years. Almost half "agree that the IoT will be one of the most important parts of their organization's digital transformation strategy" (Ref. [13], page 5). The report cites interesting examples of cases in which IoT concepts and technology have already made changes to an industry.

- Daimler is looking at auto-transportation as a service, with their car2go division providing cars on a need basis. This is already a reality with bicycles in the US, China, and other countries. Just swipe your card and use the bike (car) for as long as you need (usually just short trips).
- Konecranes, a Finnish company that manufactures cranes and heavy lifting equipment, says that IoT is "bringing this equipment to life, because embedded intelligence allows a crane to sense its own condition and report back on it". They can monitor their equipment and detect, or even predict, faults and problems early so that their engineers can fix those problems before they become more serious.

The report does cite current problems that are blocking rapid introduction of IoT technology into the economy. In fact, 16% said that weakness in their company's technology infrastructure was an obstacle, 35% were forced to use outside consultants for their IoT work, and 33% were implementing training programs for their staff.

1.3 The Internet of Things vs. embedded systems

Embedded systems, the main topic of this book, will form the lower level of the Internet of Things, the "things", and will thus form the foundation of the IoT. Embedded systems range from simple devices, such as sensor nodes, to complex devices with intelligence, such as security systems or smart cars or other smart devices. They include sensor networks (such as the agricultural monitoring system mentioned in Section 1.2), cyber-physical systems (such as those that may be part of smart city or smart building systems), and other kinds of systems, as illustrated in Section 1.2. Thus they span the entire range of "things" in the IoT, from the highest level of smart devices to the next-to-lowest level of dumb devices, with the lowest level of dumb devices being things like RFID tags that can do nothing more than identify themselves.

Figure 1.4 shows the generic form of a simple embedded system. A processing element and associated memory provide the computing power for the module. There may be sensors for collecting information from the module's environment. The information may be digital or analog with analog-to-digital conversion. Digital inputs are of the form ON/OFF, such as detecting whether a button is being pressed or not. Analog inputs have ranges of values, such as the range of temperature in a room. There may or may not be devices that control the environment, and again these may be digital (such as turning a motor on or off) or analog (such as varying the voltage that controls a motor's speed). There may or may not be connections to a network. A simple embedded system might be stand-alone, that is, not connected to any network. Simple appliance controls are examples of this kind of embedded system. Other embedded systems, such as those for agricultural monitoring, would be connected to some kind of network. Many embedded systems, such as sensor

Basic Components and Functions of
Embedded Systems

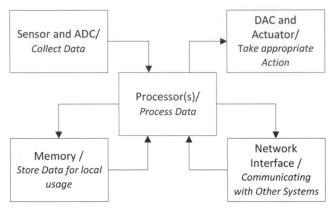

FIGURE 1.4 Structure of a Simple Embedded System.

Author drawn.

networks or systems in a modern car, consist of networks of simple modules, as shown in the figure.

Embedded systems typically involve some processing power combined with sensing and control of the system's environment, although not every embedded system will have both sensing and control. As the name "embedded" implies, they are typically part of a larger product. Examples include:

- various systems in a modern automobile, such as the brake control system and the carburation control system;
- the control unit for a smart ventilation system in a building;
- the control system for a smart stop-and-go light, one of the original uses envisioned for microcontrollers;
- health monitoring systems.

An embedded system is a system with a highly focused purpose, precisely defined internal communication channels, and relatively limited and well-defined communication channels to the world outside the system. Embedded systems are typically developed by a single team or set of teams working closely together on a well-defined product.

1.4 Brief history of three underlying technologies

Three underlying technologies are the main enablers of the IoT — microprocessors, networking, and sensors/actuators. We present a brief history of these three technologies to give the reader a sense of how the Internet of Things and embedded systems got to where they are today. This is by no means a complete history of these technologies. It is meant only to give the reader a bit of a perspective on the time-frames for the development of the aspects of the three key technologies directly relevant to embedded systems and the IoT.

1.4.1 Microprocessors

Although the earliest applications in the IoT were based on objects that merely identified themselves through technologies like RFID tags and barcodes, the real potential of the IoT lies in objects that can do more, that is, the so-called smart objects. Smart objects can sense their environments, analyze the situation, and then control some of the things in their environments. The foundation of smart objects is the ability to compute, and this requires some kind of processing element. The processing elements in embedded systems are not powerful general-purpose computing elements, like those found in desktop and laptop computers. Rather, they typically have less computing power but more features that allow interaction with the environment, features such as both digital and analog inputs for sensing and output pins that can control devices either directly for light loads or through transistors for heavier loads. Many have sophisticated features such as pulse width modulation (PWM) for controlling motors, quadrature encoding for rotation tracking, and built-in industry-standard communication protocols such as controller area network (CAN) and inter-integrated circuit (IIC).

The first processing elements not intended for use in mainframe and minicomputers began to appear by 1968; many of them were used for special products or in military applications only, for example, the 2140/2150 family from Viatron used in System 21 small computer systems.[14] The first commercially available microprocessor chip was the Intel 4004/4040 family,[15,16] a 4-bit processor. This was, in fact, a four-chip family — the processor, a ROM chip, a RAM chip, and a shift register. The RAM chip, for example, could hold 40 bytes. Instructions took either 10.8 or 21.6 microseconds operating at maximum clock speed. The processor was packaged in a 16-pin dip circuit. It was used in, among other things, desktop calculators. By 1971, Texas Instruments (TI) had joined the list of companies producing microprocessors with its TMS 1000 processor, the first complete processor with a central processing unit (CPU), program, and data memory on a single circuit.[16]

The next generation of microprocessors was developed independently by Motorola and Intel. In 1974 Motorola introduced the 6800. This was followed in 1977 by the MC 6802, which had internal program and 128 bytes of RAM. In 1985 Motorola introduced the 68HC11. Intel introduced the 8048 family, with 8-bit processors, in 1976 and followed up in 1980 with the MCS 51, also known as the 8051. The 8051 had 4K bytes of onboard ROM for holding a fixed program and 256 bytes of RAM. It also had 32 pins that could be used for general-purpose digital input/output (I/O). Two of these pins could be configured for TTL level serial communications.

Processors in these families could execute simple instructions in one or a few microseconds. These microprocessors led to the first personal computers (PCs), and the 8051 was widely used in keyboards to monitor key presses and releases and relay that information to the PC.

Along a different line, many companies were designing microprocessors meant for specific applications rather than general-purpose use. One such application area was digital signal processing. Computing elements were designed with special instruction sets that made DSP processing fast. (See Chapter 10 for examples of instructions that optimize DSP calculations.) The increased use of graphics in general computing and PCs/laptops led to the development of special-purpose processing elements for graphics calculations. Chapter 10 includes a discussion of some of the special features of these special-purpose processing elements.

Recent trends indicate the continuous development of a variety of processors. At the low end are new 8-bit processing elements with additional features like built-in analog-to-digital converters (ADCs) and digital-to-analog converters (DACs), a variety of serial interface pins, and other useful features. Many of these are now available prepackaged on small (a few square inches) circuit boards that contain additional circuitry for interface with companion boards, and these companion boards perform a variety of operations common in embedded systems, such as driving high electrical loads or sensing a variety of measurable things in the physical world. One example of this trend is the Arduino family of boards.[17] At the high end are sophisticated processors with powerful instruction sets, 32-bit arithmetic, clock speeds in the 100 MHz range, and a greater number of I/O pins, again many with secondary functions such as PWM and serial interface. Many of these processors are based on the ARM CORTEX standard.[18] A trend that is important for embedded systems and the IoT is the introduction of low-power processing elements, including ones that have one or more levels of sleep mode. In many applications some of the modules are battery operated, and in many of these cases (e.g., widespread geographical monitoring) replacing worn-out batteries is difficult or even impossible. A processing element that can "wake up" for just the few milliseconds needed to take the required measurements and send to the base station and then go back to "sleep" for a relatively long period can make the difference between a successful design and an unsuccessful one. Related to this trend is the introduction of processing elements packaged with energy harvesting circuitry, which can extend the life of the battery or even replace battery usage.

Another recent trend is the use of very large field-programmable gate arrays (FPGAs) to implement processing elements and a variety of other complex, sophisticated devices such as MP3/MP4 players, wireless communication circuits, and many others. Each of these is "implemented" by a set of equations that are used to program the FPGA circuits. By combining equation sets for different circuits (e.g., an 8051, an MP3/MP4 player, etc.), a complete application can be designed and programmed onto an FPGA chip, thus leading to a complete system-on-a-chip (SOC).

1.4.2 Computer networks

Computer networks existed and were in military and commercial use by 1960.[19] The Semi-Automatic Ground Environment (SAGE) system[20] was already in use by the US military in the radar system to connect its computers. In 1960 the Semi-Automatic Business Research Environment (SABRE) connected two mainframe computers used by the airlines for their reservation systems.[21] During the mid-1960s, the telephone industry was rapidly developing computer switches for routing phone calls, a kind of network involving computers. In 1969 the first four nodes of the ARPANET, an early network that connected research centers and which led eventually to the Internet, were connected into a computer network.[22] Wireless computer networks, a critical component of many embedded systems and IoT applications, date back to 1971, when ALOHAnet at the University of Hawaii became operational.[23] There were many other developments and much research during that period, and research into computer networking continues to the present.

In addition to general computer networking, wireless computer networking is an important technology for embedded systems and the IoT, as already noted. Applications that involve long distances, remote areas, or other situations in which wiring is difficult or impossible rely on wireless communication. Such applications include:

- Geographical monitoring in remote areas. Because of the remoteness, it is costly and/or difficult to use wire.
- Patient monitoring in mobile patients. The goal in this application is to allow the patient the freedom to move around, either around the house or even outside. Connection by a wired communication link would not allow the desired degree of mobility

WSNs form a significant portion of the embedded systems being designed nowadays.

Because of the significance of wireless communications in embedded systems and the concern for energy usage in battery-operated systems, a recent trend has been the development of various low-power wireless protocols. Bluetooth[24] and Zigbee[25] date back to the mid-1990s, and more recently, 6LoWPAN (IPv6 over Low-Power Wireless Personal Area Networks)[26] combines some of the features and advantages of IPv6 with low-power wireless transmission.

Although not normally used to connect multiple computers with each other, serial communication between processors and the devices they read or control is a major networking methodology in embedded systems. Serial communication was in use in the 1950s. The RS232 standard was introduced in 1960[27] and was used to connect mainframe computers to printers and other similar applications. In RS232 communication the "packet" size is a single byte, and the interpretation of the bytes is left completely up to the devices at the two ends of the connecting cable. In addition, RS232 connections are point to point; that is, only two devices are connected on the cable (or bus). For an application like a computer connecting to a printer, these restrictions were of no consequence; the printer received bytes one at a time and copied them to the paper. For the embedded applications that began to be developed by the 1980s, this protocol was too inefficient to be acceptable. During the 1980s, several new serial protocols were developed, aimed specifically at microcontroller applications and embedded systems. The IIC protocol was introduced in 1982.[28] The original purpose was to connect circuits on a printed circuit board with a minimum of copper traces. The CAN protocol was introduced in 1986,[29] which specifies the format of the message packet, giving each byte a particular meaning or function in the message. The Serial Peripheral Interface (SPI) bus protocol was also introduced in the late 1980s.[30] An interesting feature of this protocol is that it is not limited to an 8-bit word format. There are many other recent serial communication protocols, most notably USB. Some are designed to be general purpose, while others are designed with specific application(s) in mind.

Chapter 21 introduces some of the networking concepts and structures that are of interest to embedded systems designers.

1.4.3 Sensors and actuators

The history of sensors goes back centuries. For example, compasses were used before the early Roman times.[3] Egyptians used intricate water ducts for leveling during the construction of pyramids.[31] Thermostats and photographic film are additional examples of sensing mechanisms that have been in use for a long time.

However, to be useful for modern embedded systems and IoT applications, the sensors and actuators must be electric or electronic, must be small, and must operate on low voltage and at low power. Coils for sensing current have been in use for over 100 years, for example, in microphones. Chemical sensing dates back to the early 20th century.[3] Infrared sensing has been in use since the 1940s. Photodiodes and phototransistors were introduced during the 1950s.[3] The first self-contained digital camera was introduced in 1975 and used CMOS technology.[32,33] The 1980s and 1990s saw a vast increase in the number of low-power sensors that operated at the same voltage as the microprocessors that would use them in embedded systems. This led to, among other things, the introduction of wireless sensor networks (WSNs). WSNs typically use very small nodes consisting of a small processing element, a few sensors, and a wireless communication circuit. Sensor technology continues to be an important research area, and the number of things in the physical world that can be sensed is amazing and continues to grow.

Actuators, mechanisms that control something in the environment, depend on the use of transistors, which were invented in the early 1920s and developed into commercially useful devices in the 1950s and beyond.[34] Transistors can switch large currents and/or voltages on or off with only a very small control current and voltage. (Transistors are actually amplifiers and were originally meant to be used as such and not as digital switches. However, by far, the most common use nowadays is for digital switching — on and off.) Transistors allow a microcontroller, for example, operating at 5 or 3.3 V to control devices, ranging from other small electronic circuits to large industrial motors, the latter through a combination of transistors and relays.

The I/O pins of typical microcontrollers can switch small loads, such as other electronic circuits or LEDs. For larger loads, the pins control external transistors and/or relays. At the opposite end of the scale, recent applications are aimed at the micro- and nanoworlds. The topic of microelectromechanical systems (MEMS) is an active area of research. MEMS depends on shrinking the size of the electronic devices and the voltages and energy levels at which they run, two of the trends that make microcontrollers, embedded systems, and the IoT a possibility.

1.5 The embedded system development process
1.5.1 What is a development process and why is it needed

A development process is a method for organizing the various steps and activities needed for developing a product from the initial idea to the complete product (see, e.g., Ref. [35]). There are development processes for all major development activities, both technical and non-technical. For example, the steps in building an office building might include the following:

1. Assess the economic feasibility and expected benefit.
2. Determine requirements for the building.
3. Perhaps in parallel, request bids and seek government approval.
4. Proceed with the construction.

This is a gross simplification of the real process of designing and constructing a building, but it should give the reader an idea of what a development process may be like. Of particular interest are the various processes for software development. Wikipedia[36] describes the software development process as follows:

"In software engineering, a software development process is the process of dividing software development work into smaller, parallel or sequential steps or subprocesses to improve design, product management. It is also known as a software development life cycle (SDLC)".

This description is generic enough to be extended to the development of any kind of product, technical or otherwise, including embedded systems and Internet of Things applications.

Many, if not most, modern products are much too complex to be developed without some development process to guide the work. Individual steps are often so complex that a process just for that step is needed. For example, determining all the requirements of a major product, such as a building or a jet airplane, can take a long time and require many people and a process to guide them in their work. For most modern products, there are separate groups who participate in the various steps. For example, the management team that collects the requirements for a new product will be different from the engineering team that designs it, and that team will likely be different from the team that builds the product. In some cases there may be overlap; for example, high-level engineers may work with company management in the initial stages of the process to advise about the feasibility of ideas and proposals. But the company management is unlikely to participate in the actual manufacture of the product. A process is needed to guide and organize the steps in the development from the initial idea to end product and to define how the results of one step should be used in the next step.

To summarize then, a development process helps in the following ways:

- A development process breaks the large problem into smaller and smaller jobs until each job is manageable by a reasonable team.
- A development process allows planning ahead for the deployment of resources that will be needed at the various steps.
- A development process provides for control of workflow and the verification that the output of each step meets the needs and requirements of the following steps.
- A development process allows the definition of the proper sequencing of steps and the determination of when steps can be performed in parallel.

1.5.2 Existing software development processes and life cycles

Software plays a central role in embedded systems. Therefore we devote some attention to software development processes. It is important to note, however, that software development is significantly different from development in most other fields in the following respect. When flaws are found in software products, they are relatively easy to fix. In the worst-case scenario the software can be scrapped and completely new software developed. The same cannot be done for development in other fields. For example, a design flaw may be discovered in a building only after the building has been constructed. Scrapping the building, that is, tearing it down, and building a new one in its place, is prohibitively expensive. An error in the design of the hardware of an embedded system may or may not be easy to fix. For example, a relay to power some device may be found to be insufficient. If that relay is in an ATM or smart streetlight, it could be replaced relatively easily. But if it was part of the door security system of a building that had already been built and the actual relays were embedded into the infrastructure of the building (e.g., buried inside the walls surrounding the doorways), replacing them would be relatively expensive. Even software errors can be expensive, as witnessed by the grounding of the Boeing 737 MAX in 2019.

Software development processes or methodologies have been in use since the 1960s. We list a few here and discuss their applicability to embedded systems development.

- Prototyping. Prototyping[37] has long been used in the development of products of all kinds. A prototype gives potential users a chance to experience what the full-scale product might be like and to offer feedback to the designers. Software prototypes implement the major features of the software product, typically the user interface and the major functionalities, to a point where users can experiment with the product. Prototyping can be applied to embedded systems, even those meant to control large products. For example, a prototype of a bridge system, the common example used in Chapters 2–5, can be built using toy boats, cars, bridges, etc., in a lab setting. The software and hardware of the embedded system can then be tested in this environment. Portions of the system being designed that are not prototyped yet or are too large or complex to build in a lab (such as an entire bridge) can be simulated or emulated, as described in Chapter 8, Section 8.2.

- Continuous integration. In continuous integration[38] members of the software team work independently but frequently integrate their work into a single software package. Integration can take place as often as every day or even multiple times a day. The integrated software package is tested after each integration. This approach can be applied to the software in an embedded system. It can also be applied to combinations of hardware and the software that controls it if the hardware is also being designed incrementally.
- Incremental development. In incremental development,[39] also known as successive version development, a simple but complete version implementing the basic features is delivered to the client. While the client can use the first version and provide feedback, a second version adding more features is developed and then delivered to the client. The process is repeated until a final version satisfying all the needs of the client has been delivered. This process can be applied to some embedded systems. For example, a patient monitoring system might have a first version that implements just the monitoring and reporting of basic bodily signals. Successive versions can add additional sensors, drug delivery, artificial intelligence for predicting health issues, etc. An important key to applying incremental development to embedded systems is that early hardware decisions do not preclude future hardware additions. Software is much more easily changed, but some hardware decisions may make future hardware additions difficult.
- Rapid application development (RAD). The RAD method[40] and its later modifications, such as agile development, emphasize adaptability over planning. Initial versions are developed quickly without much planning for future versions. Clients get a product much earlier, but the product will be incomplete and may not be what the client really wanted. Because software can be modified relatively easily or even scrapped, mistakes in earlier versions can be undone, and the feedback from those first versions can be critical in designing future versions. However, as noted in the previous bullet, undoing mistakes in hardware is generally not so easy. Therefore RAD approaches may not be suitable for embedded system design.
- Waterfall development. The waterfall development method[41–43] divides the entire process into a sequence of steps. One step is completed before the following step begins. Each step produces a set of requirements for the following step. Steps might include product marketability study, requirements analysis, platform selection, software development, testing, and client evaluation. In contrast to RAD methods, waterfall development places heavy emphasis

on planning. This high-level approach could be used for embedded system design, as we describe in the following section.

- Spiral development. The spiral development process[44–46] breaks the entire process into smaller processes, or cycles, with each cycle coming closer to the final product. Each cycle contains four steps. First, the objectives for the upcoming cycle are determined. What does the team plan to learn in that cycle? Second, a prototype is built. Third, the prototype is tested and evaluated. Finally, plans for the next step in the spiral are developed. This approach allows client/user feedback from the earliest stages and thereby reduces the risk of making design mistakes early in the process that would be costly to fix later. Further, it allows different development methods to be used in different cycles. For example, RAD methods could be used in the first few cycles, but then after enough feedback had been gathered, the design team may follow a more planning-focused method. This approach can easily be applied to embedded system design, with the comments in the bullet point on prototyping above applying to the prototyping step in each cycle.

No one approach is best for all projects. Each method has its advantages and disadvantages and can be applied in different situations. Company management along with design experts would consider the company's needs, the marketing situation, the nature of the system being designed, and various other factors to determine an appropriate design process for that product.

1.5.3 A development process for embedded systems

In the preceding section we noted that no single development process is best for all situations. We also described how some of the more common software development processes could be extended to the design of embedded systems. Such extensions address the differences between simple software design and embedded system design.

- Embedded systems involve both software and hardware. Moreover, the hardware includes both electronic (e.g., circuits, sensors, etc.) and non-electronic (motors, pumps, etc.)
- Embedded systems operate in a diverse set of environments, such as outdoors or in remote areas, unlike software, which runs on a processing platform. The design of a particular embedded system may need to take into account things like weather, non-availability of reliable energy, communication across long distances, and a host of other issues that are not relevant to software alone.
- Embedded systems have more diverse forms of input and output and a more diverse range of applications than software alone.

We present an extended version of the waterfall process, shown in Figure 1.5, that accommodates the broader range of issues and problems associated with embedded system design.

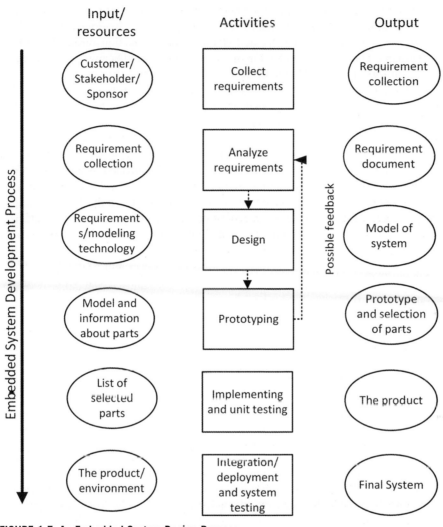

FIGURE 1.5 An Embedded System Design Process.

Author drawn.

Our extended waterfall process has six steps — collect requirements, analyze requirements, design, prototype, implement/test, and integrate/test.

Collect requirements. Like software projects, the primary set of requirements come from the client. However, for embedded systems, there are often many other stakeholders that impose additional requirements. For example, in the bridge project, the example used in Chapters 2—5, the company manufacturing the bridge has the initial set of requirements, but additional requirements come from other entities such as the local community where the bridge will be installed, the river authority, the shipping companies that use the waterway, and even groups of citizens of the city where the bridge will be located. Requirements collection must include all of these groups. Therefore the collection of requirements would be much more complicated than for a typical software project.

Analyze requirements. Like software projects, the set of informal requirements from the collection step must be analyzed to produce a formal requirements document, the document that is used later in the process to design, implement, and test the product. This analysis process is typically much more complicated than for simple software projects. Software, once installed, generally just runs until it has computed the desired output. Products that contain embedded systems are often used in differing ways. For example, the normal way for a bridge to operate is to monitor for boats and raise and then lower the bridge spans. But this behavior might have to be altered during monthly inspections or bridge maintenance (e.g., replacing bearings in a motor or even burnt-out red lights). Thus the requirements analysis phase for embedded systems has to consider a variety of issues that are not incurred in simple software. What are the different ways the product will be used? Are there timing requirements — for example, the bridge must recognize a boat within so many seconds before it reaches the bridge? Many embedded systems have modules that operate more or less independently, and the requirements analysis must consider how they coordinate. There may even be non-functional requirements. For example, a sensor system for monitoring environmental conditions in a forest must not interfere with the natural wildlife of the forest.

Design. This step generates a complete design for the system that satisfies the requirements from the previous step, just as in the software waterfall process. The difference is that the design will involve, in addition to software, the various hardware elements that will be needed for the product. Design teams will typically use modeling techniques and tools, such as those described in Chapters 3—5. The result of this step will be models of the system functions in varying levels of detail — some giving high-level overviews and some giving low-level details. These models will fully describe how each part of the system should operate, how different parts of the system cooperate, the hierarchy of the components to be used in the system, how special and error cases are to be handled, how the system should recover from faults, and how the system should interact with the environment in which it will be used. All of the interactions of the software with the various hardware components will be completely specified.

Prototype. In this step one or more prototypes of the system under development are built and tested. Different choices for specific hardware components can be made and compared with each other. Portions of the system that have not yet been built can be simulated (implemented in software) or emulated (implemented in hardware such as in field-programmable gate arrays [FPGAs]). (See Chapter 8 for a discussion of simulation and emulation.) Prototypes are tested to ensure they meet all the requirements from the requirements analysis step. Prototypes can be tested in a lab setting or in the actual environment in which the final product will perform. Clients and other stakeholders can experiment with the prototypes. Prototypes can help identify errors in the design or even in the requirements. They also allow feedback on non-functional issues from the client, stakeholders, and potential users. Errors caught at this step are immensely less costly to fix than errors discovered in the last two steps.

Implement and test. In this step the final pieces that make up the systems are prepared, and the components of the product are constructed and tested. Items like printed circuit boards, application-specific integrated circuits (ASICs), and FPGAs are manufactured and/or programmed. Each piece of software is loaded into its corresponding processing platform. Unit testing is performed. A unit could be an individual processing element with its software, that unit combined with its related hardware, or entire sub-modules of the embedded system. For example, for a dishwasher control system, the processor with its software could be tested in isolation first, then tested in combination with the relays and LEDs that would be in the control panel, and then finally in a real dishwasher. On the other hand, an actual bridge, as opposed to a toy bridge, cannot be completely constructed in a lab, but some of the components (e.g., the ground barriers that block car and pedestrian traffic) can be.

Deploy and test. The complete product is constructed or installed at the intended site of usage and tested. For example, the dishwasher control system would be attached to an actual dishwasher and tested. In this environment the embedded system will be subject to conditions not tested for in the lab, such as vibration and high temperature and humidity. The bridge control system would be installed in the actual bridge. The embedded system can then be tested in real products with real users and other actors (such as boats for the case of the bridge) and for all the various use cases. Final adjustments to sensors, motors, and other mechanisms can be made as needed.

Not every embedded system design project would use all of these steps. Each project should adapt the steps as appropriate. For example, the design of a small embedded system meant to be used indoors, such as a patient monitoring system, could combine the last two steps. In some cases there are few, if any, stakeholders other than the client, and in such cases the first two steps could be combined. Prototyping, on the other hand, would likely be useful for the design of any embedded system.

We have focused on the steps that the embedded systems designers and engineers would take. Bringing a real product to market involves many other issues that are not directly related to the system design, issues such as planning a suitable manufacturing process, planning for storage of parts and of manufactured products, and planning for delivery of products to stores or installation sites. Our goal was only to show the reader the importance of having a process to guide the design of an embedded system and the kinds of adaptations necessary to make common software design processes applicable to embedded system design.

1.5.4 IoT projects

We can differentiate two kinds of Internet of Things (IoT) projects. The first kind includes systems that are composed of a number of smaller embedded systems that operate more or less independently. For example, a smart city[47] might include smart stop-and-go lights, smart parking lots, smart traffic control, building energy conservation systems, and many more. The city might know all of the systems it wishes to incorporate into a single IoT system. The individual modules operate more or less independently but occasionally interact with each other. For example, the stop-and-go lights operate independently of the city-wide traffic control for the most part, but in certain situations they respond to signals from the traffic control system. This kind of IoT project could be considered simply as a very large embedded system composed of mostly independent simpler embedded systems with an emphasis on communications between those sub-systems. The process described in Section 1.5.3 can be applied.

The second kind of IoT project focuses on one of the important goals of IoT research — independently designed systems should be able to connect with other systems dynamically and opportunistically. For example, a smart car might be able to connect to nearby restaurants if it is near lunch or dinner time or to a nearby hospital if the car senses the driver is not well or to the smart city traffic system if the car is moving very slowly inside the city. In this case the designers of the embedded system may not know all the different kinds of systems their product should connect to in the future, and indeed some of those may not even have been thought of yet. This aspect of IoT is currently a major area of research, and it is not known yet how achieving this kind of dynamic and opportunistic behavior can be done. Therefore we cannot say much about designing an embedded system that is supposed to participate in the IoT in the future. There are some general issues and limited guidance that might help, and these are mentioned in Chapter 26.

1.6 Summary

In this chapter we illustrated the broad range of applications in the general area of the Internet of Things and discussed how the Internet of Things will play a significant role in the future of society. We discussed how embedded systems are the foundation of the Internet of Things. We gave a brief history of the three technologies underlying embedded systems — microprocessors, computer networks, and sensors/actuators — giving the reader a sense of how the computing industry arrived at a position where the Internet of Things can become a reality. Finally, we closed the chapter with a discussion of development processes, with an emphasis on software development processes. We emphasized the importance of following a development process and gave an augmented version of the waterfall development process that could be used for embedded system design.

Problems

1. Pick an application area and survey the literature and internet for articles on that application. Write a brief report describing the current state of development and future trends, making sure to include references to support the information in your report.

2. Think of some area of ordinary life. Imagine being able to monitor it continuously and in detail and to control it. Discuss the benefits and potential dangers (both technical and social) of having this participate in IoT.

3. Chapters 2—5 use a common example for illustration, a bridge over a river in a city. In a group or class setting describe the people who might participate in each of the six steps in the development process described in Section 1.5.3 for the bridge embedded system and the activities they might perform.

4. In a group or class setting discuss what kinds of feedback could be obtained from prototypes of the following products. Brainstorm the kinds of prototypes that could be built in a lab.

   a. Traffic light controller.

   b. Automated teller machine (ATM).

   c. Door security system using face recognition.

   d. Elevator control system (single and multiple cages).

References

[1] https://en.wikipedia.org/wiki/Kevin_Ashton.

[2] https://www.cisco.com/c/dam/en_us/about/ac79/docs/innov/IoT_IBSG_0411FINAL.pdf

[3] O. Vernesan, P. Friess, G. Woysch, et al., "Europe's IoT Strategic Research Agenda 2012", "The Internet of Things 2012: New Horizons", IERC — Internet of Things European Research Cluster, Halifax, UK, 2012, ISBN 978-0-9553707-9-3, pp. 22—23.

[4] https://en.wikipedia.org/wiki/Internet_of_things.

[5] *ACM Transactions on Sensor Networks*, various years.

[6] *Proceedings of SenSys*, various years.

[7] http://www.beechamresearch.com/article.aspx?id=4.

[8] http://www.businessinsider.com/iot-trends-will-shape-the-way-we-interact-2016-1.

[9] http://internetofthingsagenda.techtarget.com/blog/IoT-Agenda/The-next-Industrial-Revolution-How-IoT-will-change-our-world.

[10] https://digitaldm.com/the-internet-of-things-the-next-industrial-revolution/.

[11] http://www.bbc.com/future/bespoke/specials/the-industrial-internet-of-things/industrial-revolution.html.

[12] M. Feki, F. Kawsar, M. Bousard, L. Trappeniers, "The Internet of Things: The Next Technological Revolution", Computer Magazine, vol. 46, no. 2, pp. 24—25, February 2013.

[13] "The Internet of Things Business Index 2017: Transformation in Motion". https://perspectives.eiu.com/sites/default/files/EIU-ARM-IBM%20IoT%20Business%20Index%202017%20copy.pdf.

[14] https://en.wikipedia.org/wiki/Viatron.

[15] https://en.wikipedia.org/wiki/Intel_4004.

[16] https://en.wikipedia.org/wiki/Microprocessor.

[17] https://www.arduino.cc/.

[18] https://en.wikipedia.org/wiki/ARM_Cortex-M.

[19] https://en.wikipedia.org/wiki/Computer_network.

[20] https://en.wikipedia.org/wiki/Semi-Automatic_Ground_Environment.

[21] https://en.wikipedia.org/wiki/Sabre_(computer_system).

[22] https://en.wikipedia.org/wiki/ARPANET.

[23] https://en.wikipedia.org/wiki/ALOHAnet.

[24] https://www.bluetooth.com/.

[25] http://www.zigbee.org/.

[26] http://www.ti.com/lsds/ti/wireless-connectivity/6lowpan/overview.page.

[27] https://en.wikipedia.org/wiki/RS-232.

[28] https://en.wikipedia.org/wiki/I%C2%B2C.

[29] https://en.wikipedia.org/wiki/CAN_bus.

[30] https://en.wikipedia.org/wiki/Serial_Peripheral_Interface_Bus.

[31] M. Root, http://www.surveyhistory.org/egyptian_surveying_tools1.htm.

[32] http://www.forzasilicon.com/history-of-digital-imaging/.

[33] https://en.wikipedia.org/wiki/Digital_camera.

[34] https://en.wikipedia.org/wiki/History_of_the_transistor.

[35] https://www.tcgen.com/product-development-process.

[36] Wikipedia, Software Development Process. https://en.wikipedia.org/wiki/Software_development_process.

[37] GeeksforGeeks, Software Engineering|Prototyping Model. https://www.geeksforgeeks.org/software-engineering-prototyping-model/.

[38] F. Martin, Continuous Integration. https://martinfowler.com/articles/continuousIntegration.html.

[39] GeeksforGeeks, Software Engineering|Incremental Process Model. https://www.geeksforgeeks.org/software-engineering-incremental-process-model/.

[40] Wikipedia, Rapid Application Development. https://en.wikipedia.org/wiki/Rapid_application_development.

[41] Wikipedia, Waterfall Model. https://en.wikipedia.org/wiki/Waterfall_model.

[42] UMSL, Comparing Traditional Systems Analysis and Design With Agile Methodologies. https://www.umsl.edu/~hugheyd/is6840/waterfall.html.

[43] P. Kai, W. Claes, B. Dejan, "The Waterfall Model in Large-Scale Development". https://www.researchgate.net/publication/30498645_The_Waterfall_Model_in_Large-Scale_Development/link/555b31e208ae6fd2d829a913/download.

[44] GeeksforGeeks, Software Engineering|Spiral Model. https://www.geeksforgeeks.org/software-engineering-spiral-model/.

[45] Wikipedia, Spiral Model. https://en.wikipedia.org/wiki/Spiral_model.

[46] B. Barry, "Spiral Development: Experience, Principles, and Refinements", SPECIAL REPORT CMU/SEI-2000-SR-008, 2000.

[47] J.C. Lee, L.J. Henschen, Design interface and modeling technique, in: M. Kurosu (Ed.), HCII 2020. LNCS, 12181, Springer, Cham, 2020, pp. 97–111, https://doi.org/10.1007/978-3-030-49059-1_7.

Modeling the system under development

1

A critical mistake often made in the design of new systems is to make commitments, such as choices for hardware or data structures or algorithms, before fully understanding all the things the product is supposed to do. Products perform in many different situations beyond the ones that first come to mind. For example, the bridge system used as an example throughout this book has to perform correctly in a variety of situations: the one that first comes to mind, namely a boat arrives; situations in which more than one boat arrives at about the same time and from either the same or opposite directions; situations in which the cars and/or pedestrians don't get off the bridge in a reasonable amount of time; situations in which the monthly maintenance crew is working and boats arrive; situations in which one or more components fail to work properly, etc. Fixing operational requirements that were overlooked is expensive or even impossible.

The chapters in this part discuss techniques for determining what the product should be like from both the external and internal points of view. Chapter 2 focuses on the external point of view. What are all the ways the product interacts with its users and environment? Understanding this external behavior is the critical first step in any product design. Later chapters then focus on high-level modeling of the internal operation of the product — that is, models of internal behavior independent of later choices for actual hardware or software. Once a complete understanding of these models of the external and internal operation has been achieved, a design team can make the best choices for hardware, software, data, communication, etc.

First stage modeling — modeling interaction between the system and the environment

2.1 Introduction

Before embedded system engineers can make choices about details of the system, such as system structure or algorithms or specific hardware, it is necessary to understand exactly what the system being designed is supposed to do and what are the requirements for and restrictions on the system being developed. The emphasis is on "what", not "how", and the focus is on the boundary between the system and the environment in which it is meant to operate. Without a deep understanding of the external behavior the system is supposed to exhibit from the point of view of the environment, engineers are much more likely to make bad choices about the internal details. Such bad choices can often be very costly to fix, costlier even than bad choices in software development. It is one thing to lose the time spent writing a software module that later does not get used. It is quite another to have designed hardware components, printed circuit boards, and perhaps even purchased quantities of these, only to have to throw them away. Even if the engineer has significant experience, failure to understand the complete set of requirements at the beginning will usually lead to serious problems at later stages of the system design. Therefore the earliest stages of analysis should be directed toward understanding the interaction of the system under development with the environment in which it will operate. The requirements and restrictions are also developed and documented during this phase of the process.

The analysis at this first stage is done typically by teams. The teams will typically include representatives from the client entity. These representatives will have the basic conception of what the product is supposed to be, although it is common for the first stage of analysis to uncover issues that the client had not considered and that alter the requirements of the system being developed. (It is not uncommon for the client to not fully understand what product the client's enterprise actually needs!) Often the embedded system engineers also participate in this first stage of analysis, providing information about what is feasible or cost-effective. Other participants could include marketing personnel, who have information about what

Embedded System Design. https://doi.org/10.1016/B978-0-443-18470-3.00002-6

the product must be like to compete in the market, sociologists, who understand how people who use the product might react to features being proposed, representatives from regulatory agencies, who know the laws and regulations that apply to the product, and others. Inclusion of all these participants at this stage is crucial for the development of a complete list of requirements and specifications.

There are formal systems, such as unified modeling language (UML), described later in this chapter, for specifying the information gleaned in this first stage. However, the first documentation of this stage is typically done in a combination of diagrams and natural language using the terminology of the application so that the client and other non-engineers on the team can fully participate. Very often, the client and/or the client's representatives are not engineers, or at least not embedded system engineers, and do not understand engineering terminology. The same comment often applies to other participants, such as regulatory agents and marketing personnel. They will, of course, understand the applications for which the system is being designed. Doing the initial analyses, walk-throughs of tentative proposals, and other discussions in their own language allows them to apply their application knowledge more effectively. The engineers participating at this stage should learn the language of the application so that they may more effectively participate in the development of the requirements and translate those requirements into more formal languages, such as UML, used in later stages of the product development.

It is common for the system designers at this stage to have a very high-level understanding of the components that will make up the system being designed. For example, an ATM system will have a user interface and a data repository. A bridge may likely have a component that controls the raising and lowering of the bridge span(s), a component that detects when boats are approaching, and so on. Through the study of use cases, scenarios, and actors, as described later in this chapter, this preliminary system structure may be revised and refined.

It is crucial to consider at this stage all the ways that the system will interact with its intended environment. It is a common oversight and a serious mistake in the early stages to fail to take into account situations other than the "normal" uses. A system that cannot respond reasonably to these other situations will fail and be useless. For example, one of the two normal scenarios for a phone system is that a person picks up the handset, dials a number, talks when the other phone is answered, and then hangs up. But there are many variations of this usage — the caller hangs up before completing the number, the caller hangs up before the other end answers, the other phone is busy, the number dialed is not valid, the caller accidentally pulls the wire out of the phone set during the middle of the call, the caller presses the switch hook on a landline phone many times before dialing any numbers, the caller presses the switch hook on a landline phone after the call is connected, etc. The phone system has to work properly in all these (and many, many more) cases. Moreover, there are other uses for modern phones than just placing calls. Many phones have built-in answering machines. If the phone being designed is to have that feature, then the team has to consider how the user interacts when listening to messages. Again, there are many more cases than just listening to the messages from the first to the last —

the user listens to one message and then leaves, the user presses the "skip" button, the user presses the "delete" button, the phone rings while the user is listening to (or skipping or deleting) a message, and many more. In the case of a bridge, the normal scenario might be a boat arrives, the traffic gates are lowered, the spans go up, the boat goes through, the spans go down, and finally, the traffic gates go up. But what if two boats arrive at about the same time? What if they are coming in the same direction? What if they are coming from opposite directions? What if there are cars and pedestrians on the bridge when the boats are detected? What if there is a car stalled on the bridge? What if boats arrive during the monthly inspection? There are, of course, many, many other variations. In some cases particularly when humans do not interact with the system directly, the set of variations may be limited and could be completely understood. In other cases it may be difficult to uncover all the variations that need to be handled. Significant effort needs to be made at this early stage to uncover all the use cases, scenarios, and actors (see later section of this chapter for definitions of these).

It is also crucial, even at this early stage, to consider how the system should behave if some component fails to operate properly. For example, in the bridge system what should happen if the gates that are supposed to block the cars and pedestrians fail to go down? What should happen if the bridge span motor fails and the span does not go up or gets stuck halfway up? What if the sensors that are supposed to tell if any cars or pedestrians are still on the bridge fail and indicate all clear when there are cars or pedestrians on the span? In many cases the behavioral modelers can specify protocols for handling such situations. For example, if the span has started up but a human operator notices someone still on it, the operator should perform a sequence of operations that warn the boat and stop the span. Chapter 6 presents many concepts and techniques relating to designing systems that can continue to operate even with component failures or at least can reduce or prevent any damage from such failure.

We will use the example of a bridge across a river in a city in this and the next few chapters to illustrate a variety of modeling, specification, and design techniques. The use of a single example can better illustrate how the various techniques complement each other in the total design process. Some of the requirements for the bridge system would be known at the beginning of the design process. For example, the city may put a limit on the length of time the bridge may block car and pedestrian traffic. The government agency overseeing river traffic may have specifications about the signals that interact with the boats, such as what color lights to use, how large, how much time in advance of the boat reaching the bridge, etc. Other requirements will be uncovered as the design process continues, in our case, in the following few chapters. In fact, it is a major goal of the early stages of the design to uncover new requirements and specifications and to discover contradictory requirements and specifications. Note that some specifications and requirements are behavioral; that is, they specify how the bridge should react in various situations. Others, such as cost, are non-behavioral; they specify properties that the system should have that are not directly related to how the bridge behaves during operation.

FIGURE 2.1 A Bridge in the Partially Open State.

Purchased from iStock with Standard License Agreement.

To help the reader better visualize the example we are going to use in the next few chapters, we show a picture of a typical bridge with two spans, one emanating from each side of the river, in Figure 2.1. In this figure the spans are partially raised. Figures 2.2—2.4 show conceptual diagrams of three basic situations. In Figure 2.2, there is no boat, the spans are fully lowered, and cars and pedestrians are crossing the river. In Figure 2.3, barriers (shown as dark lines) block the cars and pedestrians in preparation for raising the spans because a boat is approaching. Finally, Figure 2.4 shows the spans raised and the boat passing through.

2.2 Actors, use cases, and scenarios

Jacobson et al.[1] introduced in 1992 a formalized methodology for studying and specifying the behavior of systems in their environments. The approach has been applied successfully to software engineering, embedded system engineering, and many other design applications. The approach is based on identifying actors, use cases, and scenarios.[3]

2.2.1 Actors

Actors are entities outside the system that provide inputs or signals into the system. Looked at another way, actors are the external entities that cause the system to react in some way. Actors may be humans; human actors are typically called users. Actors may be other systems or entities that are not human. Examples of actors for the bridge system include:

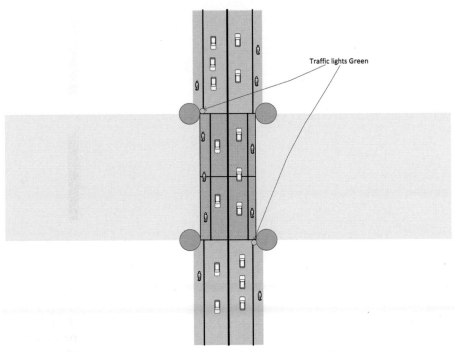

Traffic lights Green

FIGURE 2.2 A Bridge With Spans Down and Cars/Pedestrians Crossing.

Author drawn.

- Pedestrians. These are human actors, although they might include non-humans as well, such as pets. The bridge system must not raise the span when pedestrians are on it.
- Cars. Cars are non-human actors, and their presence on the span must also prevent the span from being raised.
- Boats. Boats on the river are non-human actors. Their appearance requires the bridge system to respond in some way, such as raising the span or signaling the boat to stop because the span cannot be raised.
- Bridge Operator. The bridge operator is a human (typically). The operator may operate various controls, for example, to let boats through or to override the automatic control in case of an emergency, and for other purposes, such as helping during the monthly inspection.
- Inspector. The inspector checks on a regular basis that the bridge is operating properly and within the regulatory requirements. The inspector could also monitor the structural soundness of the bridge. The inspector may interact with the bridge in many of the same ways as the operator but may also interact in ways that are special to the inspection.
- Repairmen. Humans who come to repair the bridge when something goes wrong.

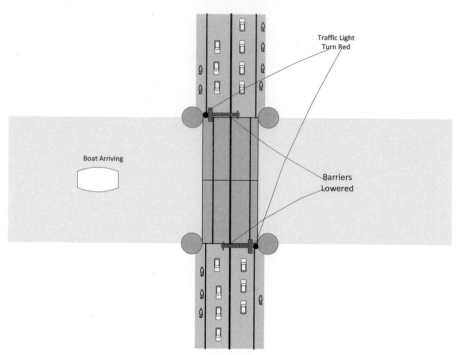

FIGURE 2.3 Bridge With Traffic Gates Down and Cars/Pedestrians Cleared for Approaching Boat.

Author drawn.

Each one of these entities, or more precisely, each instance of one of these entity classes, provides input to the bridge system that may require the system to respond in some way. The particular response may depend on the situation, or state. There may be other actors as well. It is important to develop a list of all the entities that will interact with the system being developed so that all of the use cases can be identified and studied and, in turn, all of the requirements of the system can be specified before later stages of design and development are undertaken. As another example of the variety of actors for a system, an ATM would have customers, that is, the people who come to get cash or check their accounts, as actors. But additional actors include the people who come to replenish the cash, repairmen, perhaps auditors, and possibly others. If the client (e.g., the bank that is ordering the new ATMs) wanted the system developers to try to protect against theft, the actors might even include robbers of various kinds (ones who try to steal the machine itself, ones who assault a customer right after the cash is dispersed, etc.).

Note that "actor" depends on the level of the system being studied. When considering the operation of the bridge as a whole entity, sub-modules like the span controller are internal and therefore not actors. The bridge main module may send messages to the span controller, and the span controller may send information

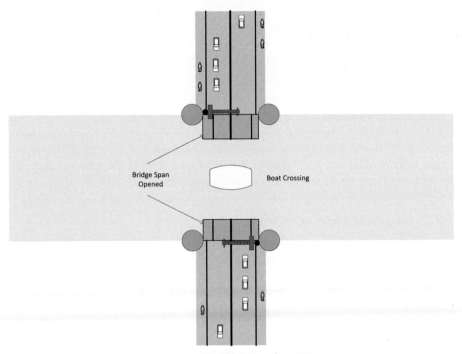

Bridge Span
Opened

Boat Crossing

FIGURE 2.4 A Bridge With Spans Raised and Boat Passing Under.

Author drawn.

back to the main module. But from the point of view of the bridge as a single entity, these messages are internal. However, a sub-contractor might design the span controller module as a separate entity that will be used inside a larger entity, the bridge system. For the sub-contractor, the bridge main module is an external entity and therefore an actor for modeling the span controller operation.

The system may generate output signals in response to inputs from actors. For example, the bridge may flash warning lights, or an ATM may dispense cash or display a message. These outputs, of course, are not actors. Outputs are generated by the system, whereas actors are entities outside the system that provide inputs to the system.

Finally, we point out that there are many other entities that can impose requirements on the system but that do not directly interact with the system. These are called stakeholders. Continuing with the bridge example, stakeholders might include the following:

- Local government officials. Local government officials would be concerned about limiting the amount of time traffic would be blocked when the bridge span is up and other similar issues. They may impose requirements on how the system behaves.

- Regulatory agencies. Regulatory agencies would be concerned with, among other issues, the system meeting standards for products similar to the one being developed.
- Merchant Marine Association. This association would suggest requirements that would ensure smooth boat traffic on the river.

Again, there would undoubtedly be many other stakeholders.

Note that an individual could belong to more than one of the classes of actors and stakeholders. For example, the inspector (actor class inspector) could also walk across the bridge to get to work (pedestrian). The mayor of the city in which the bridge is to be installed is a stakeholder when functioning in the mayoral capacity but an actor (pedestrian) when walking across the bridge.

2.2.2 **Use cases and scenarios**

A use case is one generic type of activity for which the system has a specific purpose or should accomplish a specific goal. For the bridge system, the primary use case is to handle boat traffic on the river. However, there are many other use cases — monthly inspection, regular maintenance, repair, installation, etc. For the ATM system, the primary use case is dispensing cash. But, again, there are many more use cases — deposit check, refill the cash container, weekly audit, regular maintenance, repair, alarm, etc. Each of the use cases has its own purpose or goal. The goal of handling boat traffic on the river is to let the boats pass through while not delaying road traffic too long. This is different from the goal of the monthly inspection. As will be seen in the next paragraph, different use cases may have features in common. For example, boats may approach the bridge during the monthly inspection. The bridge should handle this situation, possibly the same way as for the primary use case but possibly in a different way because the inspector is working at the bridge. The development of a relatively complete set of use cases (and scenarios, as described in the next paragraph) allows the system designers to specify the behavior in all the various situations right at the beginning of the design process rather than having new situations reveal themselves during development, implementation, or even after deployment, when the modifications and fixes could be quite expensive.

Within one use case, there can be many variations. These variations are also called scenarios in some parts of the literature. In the ATM's primary use case to dispense cash, for example, there is the normal scenario (user requests an amount that is less than the user's account balance and less than the amount of cash in the ATM). But there are also other variations — user requests more than is in the user's account, user requests more than is in the ATM machine, user makes a mistake entering the desired amount, user decides partway through to cancel the request, etc. Each of the other use cases may have variations as well. For the primary use case for the bridge, variations could include cases in which one boat arrives and goes through, two boats arrive at the same time in opposite directions, two boats arrive one after the other, etc. Some authors further classify the scenarios related to a single use case to help designers think about the possible variations. For example, Cockburn[2] mentions the main scenario, extensions, exceptions, and variations. In the bridge system, two boats arriving at about the same time in the same direction might be considered an extension of the main scenario for boat traffic, while a span failing to rise might be considered an exception.

At this stage, it is important to also consider errors that may occur, and these can be looked at as scenarios (or exceptions) within use cases. For example, what if the ATM has enough cash but, for some reason, the correct amount is not dispensed? Is this something that the client and system developers want to handle? If so, how should it be handled? Should the machine detect this by itself? If so, then later stages in the design process have to include hardware and software to do this. Or, should we provide some means for the user to indicate that not enough cash was dispensed? This approach would require a different kind of system behavior as well as means for the user to input this information into the system. In many systems failure to handle error cases can be catastrophic. It is one thing for the bank to have a disgruntled client who didn't get the right amount of cash or wasn't given cash when the account and machine had enough money. It is catastrophic and life-threatening for the bridge to signal the boat to go through when the span, for whatever reason, fails to rise. A well-designed system should handle all cases, including error situations, in ways that are both safe and reasonable. Most embedded systems need to continue to function no matter what inputs are given to the system; that is, embedded systems have to be robust. In situations in which the system does fail completely and ceases to function at all, it should "die gracefully".

For non-trivial systems, the use cases and scenarios can number in the hundreds or thousands, and the documentation of all the use cases and scenarios can be quite a large document or file. To illustrate again that the set of scenarios can be quite large, we consider two use cases of the bridge example in more detail.

- Primary use case — handle boats on the river.
  - One boat arrives, no cars or pedestrians on the bridge.
  - One boat arrives, pedestrians and/or cars on the bridge.
  - Two boats arrive from opposite directions.
  - Two boats arrive in sequence from the same direction.
  - More than two boats arrive in sequence from the same or opposite directions. This leads to the question of what the cutoff is for handling several boats at a time.
  - One boat arrives, but a car is stalled on the bridge.
  - A second boat arrives after the first boat passes through and the bridge span has started to come down. This case would help determine whether or not the motor should be able to reverse while the span is going down, which would then become part of the requirements of the system.
  - A boat arrives, but there is an emergency vehicle (ambulance) approaching on the road. Again, deciding to handle this scenario yields additional

requirements for the system that must be taken into consideration at later stages in the system-design process.

- Monthly inspection. This might contain all the scenarios in the primary use case as well as additional ones such as the following.
  - Testing the lowering of the span and a boat arrives.
  - Testing the pedestrian/car barriers when no pedestrians or cars are present.
  - Testing the pedestrian/car barriers when pedestrians and/or cars are present.
  - Testing the raising of the span (no boats present, just testing to see if the span goes up properly), and there are cars/pedestrians present.

The behavior in these scenarios may be different from the normal behavior because the inspector may be underneath the bridge or close to the mechanical parts of the gears and motor and be in communication with the operator through, for example, a cell phone. Moreover, certain tests may preclude the normal operation of the bridge in corresponding situations.

There would be many other scenarios, and the student is asked to enumerate additional ones in Problem 2. As already noted, there can be overlap in various use cases, such as in the primary use case and the inspection use cases that raise/lower the span. However, the goal of the activity being undertaken is different, which may dictate different responses from the system. For example, it may be necessary for the bridge to signal the boat to wait rather than proceed normally if the inspector is in the middle of a test that cannot be interrupted. We also note that the development of scenarios may lead to refinement of the use cases themselves. For example, in the bridge system the designers may split the inspection use case into, say, inspection of the span, inspection of the barriers, etc.

A major failure in embedded system design is not considering all the use cases and scenarios, particularly to fail to consider error scenarios. Considerable effort should be devoted to this early stage in the design process, and the team developing these should include engineers, clients, application experts, and others as relevant. Use cases and scenarios are often developed by specially trained teams of engineers and application experts.

2.2.3 Use case analysis and related diagrams

There are several kinds of analyses that can be done with information about actors, use cases, and scenarios, and there are corresponding graphs that help in the analysis. During the process, the list of actors, use cases, and scenarios is refined, and requirements and specifications are developed and refined. Individuals and teams study the various diagrams and perform "walk-throughs" and other kinds of analysis to uncover more details about the requirements and discover new requirements and specifications. The "walk-through" process has much in common with team review of software by walking through the code. Errors in the initial approximation of actors, use cases, scenarios, and behavior are discovered in much the same way that errors in software are discovered by team walk-throughs.

At this stage, there may be only a very preliminary notion of the parts of the whole system, and there needs to be no strong commitment to the tentative structure used for some of these diagrams, in particular, the sequence diagram and the activity diagram. The main goal at this stage is to gain a deep understanding of the external behavior of the system and to develop the set of requirements and specifications. However, it is not uncommon for the analyses performed at this stage to suggest internal structure, at least at some high level.

We present some of the main types of diagrams used for use case analysis. There are many other types of diagrams, and the user is referred to Refs. 2—4 for descriptions of other diagrams and their uses.

2.2.3.1 Use case diagrams

One of the first activities in use case analysis is to identify all the use cases and what actors participate in each use case. This is done in a use case diagram. This diagram has two types of nodes — use case nodes and actor nodes. There is an edge between a use case node U and an actor node A if and only if actor A participates in (at least some scenarios of) use case U. The edges may be directed to indicate the flow of information for that interaction. An example of a use case diagram for the bridge system is shown in Figure 2.5.

Although it may seem obvious which actors participate in which use cases, that is not always the case. For example, in Figure 2.5, the inspector is the only actor participating in the inspection use case. This may sound perfectly reasonable, but team review and discussion may reveal that parts of the inspection require the operator to perform some actions. Furthermore, inspections may be performed at times when there is boat and pedestrian/car traffic, so those actors may also participate during inspections. Therefore, a revised use case diagram would include additional edges, and this information would affect the development of requirements and specifications at both this stage as well as later stages of the product development. For this kind of analysis, as well as the analyses described in the next two sections, it is important that the review team include representatives from all the relevant aspects of the endeavor — engineers, local traffic officials, regulatory personnel, marine personnel, and so on. Each one of these will have their own point of view and can uncover properties and errors that others on the team cannot.

2.2.3.2 Sequence diagrams

A sequence diagram shows the sequence of interactions between actors and modules of the system for a particular scenario in much more detail than a use case diagram. The reader is referred to Figure 2.6, a sample sequence diagram for the scenario in which one boat passes the bridge, to see examples of the concepts described in the following paragraphs.

A sequence diagram is a two-dimensional diagram. The actors and system modules are listed horizontally across the top of the diagram. In Figure 2.6 these include the boat, the Before Sensor, the Control Unit, etc. The vertical axis represents the progression of time from top to bottom. Lower areas of the diagram represent

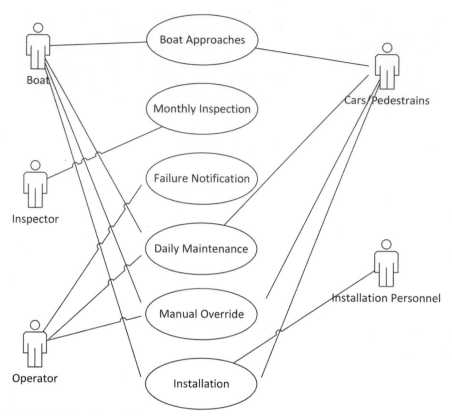

FIGURE 2.5 A Use Case Diagram for the Bridge System.

Author drawn.

information or events that happen later in time. There is a vertical line, called the life line, extending downward under each actor and system module. It is common to draw this line as a narrow rectangle during the portions of the scenario in which the actor or module is playing an active role; these portions are called, variously, activation boxes, life cycles, or execution occurrences. In the figure, for example, the boat is an active participant until the time it has passed under the bridge; after that, the boat no longer plays any role in this scenario. The remaining portions of the life line are typically drawn with dashed lines.

Horizontal arrows are drawn from the life line of one actor or module to another to represent a message being sent. The message is written above the horizontal line. In the figure, the label above the top arrow, the arrow from boat to Before Sensor, is labeled "Boat Arrives". The first action in this scenario is that the boat "sends a message" to the sensor that it has arrived. The notion of "message" in sequence diagrams is quite general. It includes information sent as a result of explicit actions by an actor or module, such as the Control Unit sending a packet to the Bridge Span over the

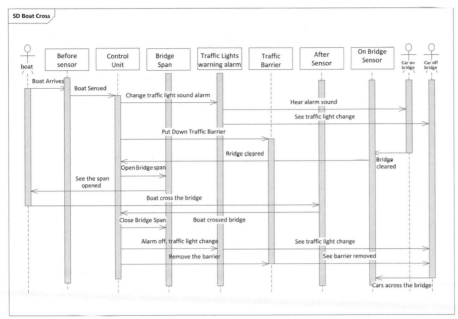

FIGURE 2.6 A Message Sequence Diagram for the Boat Crossing Under the Bridge.

Author drawn.

wired or wireless connection. It also includes information transmitted passively, such as light reflected off the boat being received by the Before Sensor. In this case the boat does not perform any action in the normal sense of that word; the boat is passive, but information is still transmitted from the boat to the Before Sensor. A return message is drawn as a dotted arrow back to the originating lifeline, and the return value from the operation is written above this dotted line. In Figure 2.6 the Bridge Span acknowledges receipt of the command to raise the span, as indicated by the dotted arrow just below the arrow with the command to raise the span. Note that this is different from a message like "span raised", which occurs later in this scenario. This latter message is a new message generated in response to an event (the span was successfully raised) and not a response *per se* to the original request to raise the span. A common use of the return message is for messages that request information. For example, the Control Unit could send a message to the Before Sensor asking how far away the boat was. The Before Sensor would respond with the distance, and this would be indicated in the sequence diagram with a dotted arrow labeled "distance". In some cases an object will need to send a message to itself. In such cases the arrow simply points back to the life line for the object sending the message.

Annotations in a sequence diagram allow the team to indicate conditions that hold for this scenario. These are typically derived from specifications and requirements that the scenario, and therefore the system, when it has been implemented, must satisfy. For example, annotations can be included in the diagram that specify specific time limits between messages or limits on how long a module can take to handle a message or that two messages occur at approximately the same time. In Figure 2.6 there could be an annotation to indicate that the acknowledgment of the raise span command happens within 10 milliseconds. One could imagine other annotations for this scenario, such as limits on how long it can take for the span to raise after the command has been given. Note that annotations contain information that holds for the given scenario. Different scenarios might have different conditions. For example, in general operation it might sometimes occur that the Bridge Span does not acknowledge within 10 milliseconds. Situations in which that occurs involve different scenarios. The design team would have to decide how the system should behave in each of these other cases. The scenario shown in Figure 2.6 is for the situation in which all the modules and actors do the expected things; in particular, in the normal case the Bridge Span *will* acknowledge within 10 milliseconds. Annotations can help with the analysis and walk-throughs of the diagram. For example, a set of annotations giving maximum times can facilitate end-to-end analysis of the timing for this scenario.

As noted, drawing a sequence diagram requires at least a preliminary notion of the modules of a system. For many systems, a first approximation to this list is obvious. For example, in our bridge system there will be warning lights for the boats, barriers for pedestrian/car traffic, bridge spans, etc. We have also made the assumption that there is some module controlling all of the actions of the bridge system. In other applications there may be only a vague notion of the modules. For example, in an ATM there is the interface, the cash dispenser, and a mass storage of some kind that stores account information. It is likely that these modules will themselves have more structure and that the ATM system as a whole will have other modules. However, the preliminary list is enough to begin studying the external behavior of the ATM system being designed. Moreover, at the very beginning stages of use case analysis, there is no commitment to the modules (or even the set of actors) tentatively proposed and certainly no concern for the internal details of those modules. Indeed, in addition to uncovering behavior and requirements, study of sequence diagrams often suggests modifications to the proposed structure of the system being designed and indicates the complete list of functions that a module must perform. When changes to the set of modules are made, all diagrams developed so far in the study must be updated.

Teams of representatives from different stakeholders would study these diagrams, perform team walk-throughs, and analyze them in various other ways until they were satisfied that each diagram accurately represented the desired behavior of the system and that all relevant requirements had been discovered. Requirements known initially, such as those imposed by regulatory agencies or the client, would be included at the beginning. The analysis would reveal others. Here are some simple examples of refinements and requirements that might be discovered through analysis of the sequence diagram in Figure 2.6.

- Study of this and related scenarios, for example, one in which the traffic control barriers fail to deploy (an error situation), would suggest that there be a message from the ground traffic module to the control module indicating success or failure to deploy the barriers, and only after that message had been received should the boat be signaled to proceed or stop. This would be indicated in the sequence charts by a new message from the Traffic Barrier module to the Control Unit module indicating success or failure and possibly an annotation indicating the time allowed for successful deployment of the barriers. Note that this modification imposes a requirement on the ground traffic barrier control module that it be able to tell if the barriers have been deployed and send messages back to the control module.
- The analysis in the preceding bullet point also suggests a new module, say Signal To Boat, that would tell the boat that the bridge was operating normally or that there was a problem. There would be a new arrow from the Control Unit to the Signal To Boat telling what signal to send to the boat. In the current scenario (i.e., the modules and actors all performing normally) the signal would be "ok to proceed".
- Representatives from the marine traffic enterprises might point out that boats are large physical devices with momentum and require certain amounts of time to stop. This would suggest a maximum time limit from the point of sensing the boat's presence until the signal (proceed or stop) is activated. For example, suppose boats take 4 minutes to get from the point of being sensed to the bridge and 1 minute to stop. Then the Control Unit must send the signal to the Signal To Boat module within 3 minutes of when the boat is first sensed. (Of course, in real life the times would depend on the size of the boat, its speed, and other factors. We present a very simplified model here just for pedagogical purposes.) This is a requirement imposed by the physical nature of an actor class.
- This, in turn, might suggest time limits for things like sensing the presence of a boat, message transmission to the control module after sensing a boat, maximum time from signaling the ground traffic barrier module until it replies success or failure to deploy, etc. In each of these cases the time would be based on the physical and operational nature of the actors/modules involved and the real-time requirements of the system. For example, it would be expected that the ground traffic barriers would be lowered in 3−5 seconds and that the module controlling them could sense their state in a matter of milliseconds. So, a time limit of, say, 6 seconds to notify the control module is both reasonable with respect to the nature of the barriers and consistent with the requirement to notify the boat within 2 minutes.
- Representative of the local government might impose a maximum time for the ground traffic barriers to be down so that traffic in the city is not affected too adversely. This is a purely human-imposed limit, not dependent on the physical nature of the boats or the nature of any hardware/software that might be used to eventually implement the design. A new requirement like this would lead to new

scenarios for cases in which the span had been up longer than the limit — no more boats sensed, more boats sensed, span module failed to lower span, etc.

Consideration of other scenarios would lead to additional specifications and requirements. See the problems for this chapter for examples.

2.2.3.3 Comments

We have already noted that use case analysis is an iterative process, just as is any design process. The team starts with preliminary ideas and through the analysis process revises the design until a satisfactory solution is reached. Along the way, new ideas are discovered and incorporated as well.

As common features among different sets of scenarios are discovered through analysis, new and/or revised organization of the use cases and scenarios is suggested. For example, the design team will notice extensive overlap among scenarios in which a single boat or multiple boats arrive but the barriers fail to deploy. This could suggest a division of a large use case into smaller ones. It might also suggest use cases to be considered when subsystems, such as the ground traffic barrier subsystem, are designed.

The analysis at this stage may suggest that options and versions of the product could be designed. A company designing a major product may wish to have alternate versions to meet the demands of many clients over an extended period. In the case of our bridge system, the company designing the bridge may in fact want many designs that will fit the needs of many different environments — urban, rural, intersecting major highways, etc. In our bridge project, for example, there could be alternatives for the repair use case as follows:

- Leave the span up and make ground traffic take a detour. This could be plausible in an urban environment, where there would be nearby alternate routes for crossing the river.
- Leave the span down and make the boat traffic stop. In a rural environment there may be no plausible detour for the ground traffic. On the other hand, this would be bad for the boat traffic but could be acceptable if it was a small river with not much boat traffic.
- Allow the repair crew to raise and lower the span. This requires more sophisticated scenarios in the repair use case because the crew must determine if and when it is feasible to interrupt the repair work and raise the span.

Note that these affect the design, and therefore the nature, of the product significantly more than alternatives, like whether to turn the flashing lights on before or after the barriers are lowered. These high-level alternatives lead to different versions of the product that can be marketed to completely different classes of customers. The bridge company could leverage the common designs derived from common use cases and scenarios and the common portions thereof in a "plug-n-play" fashion, thus being able to offer a line of products to a much wider market.

2.3 Universal access — scenarios involving actors with disabilities or limitations

In recent decades great emphasis has been placed on designing and building products that are, to the extent possible, usable by all people, including those with limitations or disabilities. This approach is called "universal design" or "design for all" in the literature. There are significant numbers of people with visual limitations (limited sight, no sight, colorblindness, etc.), limited hearing (general loss of hearing, loss of hearing in high-frequency ranges which might affect the ability to hear alarms, etc.), limited dexterity, which affects the ability to manipulate controls on products, limited mobility (general mobility, slow walking, confined to a wheelchair, etc.), and cognitive limitations. Elderly people often suffer from multiple such limitations, and the percentage of the world population that is elderly is significant and continuing to rise (see, e.g., Ref. 5). Industry should, again to the extent possible, design and manufacture products that do not put such people at a disadvantage. In fact, some governments have even passed laws supporting inclusive access to products and services. Finally, special care in the specification and behavioral modeling may be needed for users who do not have disabilities but may be limited in other ways. For example, will children interact with the product? If so, what special needs will they have?

Universal access is an issue within the scope of product specification and behavioral modeling. How will the system interact with actors with disabilities? In developing the specifications and behavioral model, the design team must consider how various disabilities might impact the way people interact with or use the product and include scenarios in which the actors have one or more disabilities. In each of these scenarios the team should consider how information is conveyed to the user and if the system might need to make some accommodation according to how the user reacts. Here are some examples relating to the bridge project.

- For any scenario in which the bridge spans go up, consider cases in which some pedestrians are blind. Will a blind pedestrian receive adequate warning that the spans are about to go up? This question would lead the design team to include both visual and audible warnings. Will such a pedestrian receive adequate notification that the bridge has gone down and it is safe to proceed? Again, the inclusion of both visual and audible signals can address this question.
- For any scenario in which the bridge spans go up, consider cases where the drivers are colorblind. Will a colorblind driver receive adequate warning that the spans are about to go up? If the system included lights that were both red and green (or other colors), the various lights would need to be made distinguishable to colorblind people. For example, the red lights might be made larger, or the standard red-yellow-green pattern used at intersections might be used.
- For any scenario in which the bridge spans go up consider cases in which pedestrians have mobility issues. For example, an elderly pedestrian might walk slowly, or a person might be in a wheelchair. In terms of the specification,

requirements for the pedestrian sensors might include being able to sense people in wheelchairs (who would not appear as tall as people standing up). In terms of the behavioral model, has the estimate of time before transitioning to an error case adequately considered that some people already on the bridge may take more time to reach safety?

- For any scenario in which the bridge spans go up, consider cases in which some pedestrians are small children. Are there issues with the pedestrian sensors sensing small people? Will children understand the warnings?

2.4 **UML and tools for use case development and analysis**

The unified modeling process (UMP) and unified modeling language (UML)[4] originated in the 1990s as a way to standardize many aspects of software design and development. It contains the diagrams mentioned in this chapter as well as others for specifying the behavior of a system – use case diagram, sequence diagram, timing diagram, state diagram (called "statechart" in UML), and others. In addition, UML contains diagrams that are used to define the structure of a system being designed – class diagram, component diagram, object diagram, package diagram, and more. These diagrams are used in many different stages of the design process and provide modeling capabilities through the entire product design process from initial consideration of use cases to specification of data structures and software components. There are a number of computer-aided design tools that implement UMP and UML, for example, Rational Rose from IBM[6] and Oracle Unified Method from Oracle. A full treatment of UML or any of the tools based on it is outside the scope of the book. We simply want to make the reader aware that the techniques presented in this book are used in real design projects and that there are tools that facilitate their use.

2.5 **Summary**

In this chapter we introduced the notion of behavioral modeling of a system and discussed why it is so important. Behavioral models show how a system being designed is supposed to interact with its environment – human users and other entities that use the system or are affected by it. We emphasized that it is crucially important to understand this external behavior before attempting to design the internal workings of the system. We described the main elements of a behavioral model – actors, use cases, and scenarios. Actors are entities that provide input to the system. Use cases describe the different ways in which the system is used or must operate. Scenarios are specific instances of use cases. We emphasized the importance of identifying all the actors and use cases and considering as many scenarios as possible. We described the basic tools for developing behavioral models – use case diagrams and message sequence charts. We described how these can be used to uncover initial errors and refine the set of requirements. Finally, we discussed the importance of considering all the potential human users, especially those with special needs that might affect their ability to interact with the system being designed.

Problems

1. For each of the following products, list actors, stakeholders, and use cases. Then draw the use-case diagram.

   a) Landline telephone with answering machine.
   b) Smartphone.
   c) Stop lights at a four-way intersection.

2. Section 2.2.2 suggests some use cases and scenarios for the bridge project. Each student individually should think of additional use cases and scenarios. Try to think of as many as you can in, say, 1 hour. Then merge the lists from all the students in the class and discuss the new use cases and scenarios.

3. The first two bullet points after Figure 2.6 suggest the addition of a module that sends signals to the boat(s) and new messages. Add the new signaling module. Then redraw the sequence diagram in Figure 2.6. Finally, draw a sequence diagram, including any timing constraints, for the case of a single boat approaching but the barriers fail to deploy.

4. The last three bullet points after Figure 2.6 suggest additional timing constraints. Redraw Figure 2.6 with these timing constraints added.

5. The fourth bullet point after Figure 2.6 fails to account for an important aspect of the ground traffic. What is the missing consideration, and how would the sequence diagram be changed to account for it?

6. In the bridge project consider the scenario in which two boats arrive from the same direction, but the second boat is not sensed until after the bridge span has started to go down. Suppose the bridge span cannot reverse direction directly but must stop for 5 seconds before starting up again. Draw a sequence diagram for this scenario.

7. A home security system includes a motion detector unit, a video camera unit, a set of door/window sensor units, a processing unit, an alarm unit, and a touchscreen man-machine interface. Assume the camera and all the sensing units can communicate with the processing unit. Draw a sequence diagram for each of the following two scenarios. Be sure to include any necessary annotations.

   a) The video camera detects motion in the yard surrounding the home because a squirrel was playing in the yard. The homeowner eventually sees that it is a squirrel and cancels the alarm.
   b) The video camera detects motion in the yard surrounding the home. One of the window sensors senses an open window event. The homeowner sees a

thief breaking the window and about to get into the house. The homeowner calls 911 to report the emergency.

8. Assume that an ATM has the following units: display, keypad, money dispenser, receipt printer, card insert slot, processing unit, and database unit. Assume that the display unit has already displayed the message, "Please, insert your card and remove quickly", when a user arrives at the ATM. The user must enter a valid pin corresponding to the card inserted into the card slot. The user gets two chances to enter it correctly; if both attempts fail, the ATM displays an error message. The user must enter a trial pin within 10 seconds of inserting the card or after the first attempt. Draw a sequence diagram for each of the following use case scenarios. Be sure to include any necessary annotations.

   a) The user inserts a card, enters the correct pin, and withdraws $100.
   b) The user inserts a card, enters an incorrect pin but then enters the correct pin on the second trial, and withdraws $100.
   c) The user inserts a card, enters an incorrect pin, then walks away from the ATM.

9. Assume a phone system has a control module (CM), a phone set (PS), an answering machine (AM), and a display module (DM). The control module counts the time that the phone is ringing. If the phone is not answered within four rings, the control module notifies the answering machine to handle the call. The phone set is connected to an outside service. It detects incoming calls, starts the ringing, and ends calls when the user hangs up, among other things. The display module shows various kinds of information such as the number of an incoming call and the number of messages in the answering machine. Draw a sequence diagram for each of the following scenarios. Be sure to include any necessary annotations.

   a) Someone calls. The homeowner answers within two rings. Later, the homeowner hangs up.
   b) Someone calls. No one answers. The caller leaves a message.
   c) Someone calls. No one answers. The caller hangs up before the beep.

10. Newer cars have lane departure warning systems. These systems detect when a car is veering too far to the left or right in the lane, warn the driver, and let us suppose also take control of the steering if the driver does not correct the situation within 3 seconds. The car has separate modules for main control (MC), lane sensing (LS), steering (S), brakes (B), throttle (T), etc. It also has a dashboard display module (DDM) that can flash yellow for warning and red to indicate that the main control module has taken control of the steering. The lane sensing module can sense when the car is approaching the left or right side of the lane. The steering module can sense the position of the steering wheel, receive commands from the main control module, and make the wheels turn left or right. Similarly for the brake, throttle, and other modules, each can sense input from the driver, receive commands from the main control module, and control the corresponding part of the car. Each module is connected to the main control module, but they are not connected to each other. Draw a

sequence diagram for each of the following two scenarios. Be sure to include any necessary annotations.

a) The car has moved too far to the right. The driver responds within 1 second by turning the steering wheel to the left.

b) The car has moved too far to the left. The driver has fallen asleep and does not respond to the warning at all.

11. Group project: pick a product and brainstorm what kinds of disabilities could impact actors and how such actors can be accommodated.

References

[1] Ivar Jacobson, Magnus Christerson, Patrik Jansson, Gunnar Overgaard, Object-Oriented Software Engineering — A Use Case Driven Approach. s.l, Addison-Wesley, 1992.

[2] Cockburn, Alistair, Write Effective Use Cases. s.l, Addison-Wesley, 2001.

[3] Alhir, Si Sinan, UML in a Nutshell: A Desktop Quick Reference. s.l, O'Reilly Publisher, 1998.

[4] Booch, Rumbaugh, Jacobson, The Unified Modeling Language User Guide. s.l, Addison-Wesley, 1998.

[5] G. Pullin, A. Newell, Focussing on Extra-Ordinary Users, in: C. Stephanidis (Ed.), Universal Access in Human Computer Interaction. Coping with Diversity. UAHCI 2007. Lecture Notes in Computer Science, vol. 4554, Springer, 2007. https://doi.org/10.1007/978-3-540-73279-2_29.

[6] IBM, Rational Rose Modeler. IBM Rational Rose Modeler. [Online] http://www-03.ibm.com/software/products/en/rosemod.

Finite-state machines

3.1 Introduction

Most embedded systems display a state-like behavior, as should be evident from the sequence diagrams in the previous chapter. A state is a situation in which the system is waiting for something to happen — waiting for an input signal or waiting for a specified amount of time. For example, most of the time, an ATM would be waiting for someone to start a transaction; this might be called the "idle" state. Once a user presses the start button, the ATM is in a new state — waiting for the user to type in the user id or swipe a credit card. Once that has been accomplished, the ATM transitions to a third state — waiting for the user to type in the password. In each state certain inputs cause the system to respond in some way and usually then assume another state. Of course, if the user does something unexpected, the system may respond with an error message or may simply ignore the user input. For example, in the idle state if the user presses a key on the keypad instead of the start icon on the screen, the ATM may simply do nothing and remain in the idle state. In our bridge system the "ground traffic" state would be the case when there were no boats approaching, the ground traffic barriers were up, there was no inspection or maintenance or repair, and the pedestrians and cars were able to cross the bridge. When a boat is sensed, the bridge system transitions to a new state in which it is waiting for the signal that the cars and pedestrians have cleared the span. After that signal is received, the bridge system transitions to a third state in which it is waiting for confirmation that the ground traffic barriers have deployed. In both of these examples some inputs require the system to generate some output or perform an action. For example, after a valid user id and password have been entered, the typical ATM will generate a new display on the screen.

The reader might contrast the state-oriented behavior of these examples with traditional compute-based programs. For example, programs that solve large sets of differential equations typically have nested loops that perform numerical computations on elements of large matrices. The process of playing a video consists of simply copying data from a large file to the display medium. In these applications the system does not stop after a few operations and waits for another input from the user. Once started, the computation just keeps going until the equations are solved or the video has completely played, and then the program terminates. In finite-state machines (FSMs) the system just waits for events (external or internal) that cause a change in state and possibly some action to be performed.

In this chapter we study internal behavior modeling using FSMs. Now the focus is on the internal behavior of the system, as opposed to the focus in the previous chapter on external behavior. The development of FSM models of the system is one of the next steps after use case analysis and modeling. We note that no single modeling technique, like FSM modeling, can handle all the design issues that require modeling, such as behavior, timing, task dependency, shared resources, distribution, etc. That is why many different modeling techniques are needed. In Chapter 2 we described a technique for modeling behavior. In this chapter we describe the main technique for modeling state-based operations. In Chapters 4 and 5 we will present two more modeling techniques that focus on modeling distributed operation and shared resources.

3.2 Finite-state machines

FSMs can be represented in either a formal set-notation fashion or as a directed graph. There are many tools for FSM development and analysis, and they can accept one or the other or both notations. The graphical form is generally easier for human understanding and analysis. Many FSM tools can automatically generate code from the model once a design team is ready to implement the model, described either formally or graphically, for testing or final deployment.

3.2.1 Acceptors and transducers — early forms of FSMs

FSMs were originally proposed in the 1960s[1-4] as a means of studying formal languages, which were used to define the grammars of programming languages. The idea was to give a procedural interpretation to reading a string of symbols to determine if that string represented a valid word in some grammar; if the grammar defined a programming language, for example, an acceptable word would be a legal program in that language. An accepting FSM F is defined formally as[2,5]

$$F = \left(\sum, S, s_0, \delta, F \right)$$

where

- $\sum$ is a finite set of input symbols.
- S is a finite set of states.
- s_0 is the start state; that is, s_0 is the state when the process is first begun. (When the FSM represents a real program or physical device, s_0 is the state when the process is started or the device is turned on.)
- δ is a partial function from $S \times \sum \rightarrow S$. This function describes the behavior of the FSM as input symbols are read. In particular, if the FSM is in state s and the

next input symbol is x and δ(s,x) is S′, then the next state is S′. If the FSM is in state s and the next symbol is not in {x | (s,x) ε δ}, the FSM stays in state s.

- F is a subset of S representing success states, or states in which the input string is a word in the grammar. If the FSM reaches a state in F and there are no more input symbols in the input string, then the input string is an acceptable word.

Figure 3.1 gives the formal definition of an FSM that recognizes or accepts strings of binary numbers in which there are an odd number of 1s. Figure 3.2 shows a graphical representation of this FSM. (The graphical notation is described in Section 3.2.2. Although we haven't yet defined the graphical formation, we suggest that the reader will already recognize that the graphical form is easier for humans to understand and study.) The motivation for how this FSM works is as follows. In the beginning, that is, in the start state s1, when no symbols have been read yet, it is false that the FSM has seen an odd number of 1s. If the FSM sees a 1 input, then the number of 1s read so far is odd; the FSM transitions to state s2. If in state s2 and a 1 is seen, the number of 1s is again even, and the FSM transitions to s1. Reading a 0 input symbol does not alter the number of 1s read so far. The reader can easily see that the state s1 corresponds to having read an even number of 1s, and state s2 corresponds to

$$F = (\Sigma, S, S_0, \delta, F) \quad \text{where}$$

$$\Sigma = \{0, 1\}$$

$$S = \{s1, s2\}$$

$$S_0 = s1$$

$$\delta = \{ (s1, 0) \rightarrow s1, (s1, 1) \rightarrow s2, (s2, 0) \rightarrow s2, (s2, 1) \rightarrow s1 \}$$

$$F = s2$$

FIGURE 3.1 Formal Definition of an FSM to Accept Strings With Odd Number of 1s.

Author drawn.

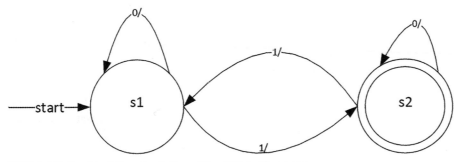

FIGURE 3.2 Graphical Representation of the FSM in Figure 3.1.

Author drawn.

the FSM having read an odd number of 1s. State s2, then, is the one and only accepting state and is indicated as such by using a double circle.

An extension to this model yields a so-called transducer FSM, a machine that in effect translates input strings into output strings. The definition given above is augmented in two ways:

1. A new element, Γ, is added to the definition of F. Γ is a set of output symbols. Γ includes a "null" symbol, meaning that no output for a given transition is to be made.
2. A new element, ω, is added to the definition of F. In the so-called Mealy transducer format, ω is a partial function from $S \times \sum \rightarrow \Gamma$. $\omega(s,x)$ is an output symbol that the FSM generates if it is in state s and the next input symbol is x. If $\omega(s,x)$ is the null symbol, then in effect the FSM produces no output for that combination of s and x.

Note that adding output elements to the FSM model increases the expressive power of the model. FSMs that represent real embedded systems almost always will have outputs.

Figure 3.3 shows a simple transducer that copies an input string to the output, except that sequences of more than one blank in the input are replaced by a single blank in the output. The second, third, etc., blanks are not copied. The FSM starts in state s1. If a non-blank character is read, it is copied to the output, and the FSM stays in state s1. If a blank is read, it is copied to the output, but the FSM transitions to s2. In s2, blanks in the input stream produce no characters in the output. The first non-blank character encountered is copied and causes transition back to s1. The input stream may be terminated with either a blank or a non-blank character, and therefore both s1 and s2 are success states. There are likely many characters in the input set. If we drew an arrow with appropriate label for each one causing a transition, the diagram would be unreadable. Therefore, in this diagram we have used an abbreviation for certain sets of arrows. The label "c not blank/c" means any acceptable character other than blank and that character is copied to the output. An arrow

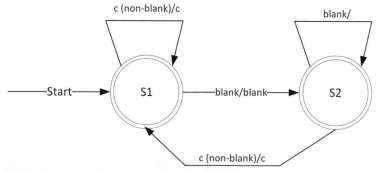

FIGURE 3.3 A Simple Transducer to Remove Extra Blanks.

Author drawn.

with that label is an abbreviation for a set of arrows, one arrow for each acceptable non-blank character.

3.2.2 **FSMs in embedded systems**

As FSMs began to be used in more and more applications, particularly in embedded system design, the basic concepts had to be adjusted in several important ways. First, embedded systems typically run until the system is turned off; there is no notion of a "final" or "accepting state". Second, the inputs are typically much more involved than simple symbols. For the ATM example, the press of a key would correspond to a simple symbol. In the bridge project, however, the "input" might be the receipt of a message from another system module, such as a sensor module. This might be a simple message, like "monthly inspection completed" in Figure 3.4 and Table 3.1; this could be thought of as a symbol. On the other hand, the "input" could be the receipt of a more complex message, such as a report. For example, the boat sensing module might contain several sensors aimed at different positions and send a report containing a number of boats sensed and the distance for each one to the main control module. This report would be an input to the current state of the main module, but it is obviously much more complex than a "symbol." Further, different sets of values may cause different transitions; for example, the main module might transition to one state if a second boat was sensed less than 200 yards away but a different state if more than 200 yards away. In addition, as we will see later in this chapter, the change in value of a shared variable among the processes and threads running in the system can also cause a state transition, that is, can also be an "input." Finally, a transition may be triggered not by a single input but by a complicated combination of signals. Although in principle the set of all these combinations could be represented as a finite set of input symbols, it is much easier for humans to understand the

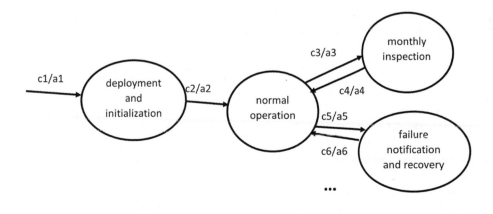

FIGURE 3.4 Top-Level FSM for the Bridge System.

Author drawn.

Table 3.1 Conditions and actions for top-level bridge system FSM.

Transition condition	Transition action
c1: true	a1: set initialization_done to 0
c2: initialization_done == 1	a2: no action needed
c3: monthly_inspection == 1	a3: prepare for inspection
c4: monthly inspection completed	a4: set monthly_inspection to 0
c5: some component failed	a5: flash red lights, warn boat, etc.
c6: failure rectified	a6: clear all warning flags, etc.
...	

behavior of an FSM if the natural descriptions of the inputs are used. Third, embedded systems take actions that are much more complex than simply outputting some symbol. In the bridge project, for example, the ground traffic barriers are deployed, the bridge spans move up and down, warning lights and horns are activated, etc. Although again, these might be represented as output symbols in some language, representing them in the language of the application facilitates the human development and analysis of the FSM. To summarize, FSMs in embedded systems do not accept streams of input symbols or translate them into another language; they monitor signals and take actions both internally and in the real, physical world. In developing the FSM model of a system, these real-world actions are abstracted into symbols. For human readability, these symbols are often descriptive, such as "traffic cleared" or "close span." From the FSM point of view, however, they are symbols, that is, elements of $\sum$, δ, and ω.

In the graphical representation, states (elements of S) are typically drawn as circles with the state name as a label inside the circle. The start state (s_0) has an arrow labeled "start" pointing to it. Accepting states are drawn as double circles. Directed, labeled arrows from one state to another represent the information in δ and ω. Labels have the form *condition/actions*. The *condition* part (often called the *guard* in some literature) is a Boolean expression involving various signals and other conditions (e.g., change in value of a shared variable). In formal definitions, the conditions are the inputs that cause the state to change. In order to maintain the property of determinism (see Section 3.4), the Boolean conditions on the outgoing arrows of any state should be mutually exclusive; that is, it must not be the case that the condition expressions on two distinct arrows leading out of the same state can be true at the same time. The *actions* part is the (possibly empty) list of actions that the system should perform if that transition is taken. In the formal definition of the FSM, the actions are the outputs. Figure 3.2 shows a graphical form of the FSM defined formally in Figure 3.1. In this case, there are no actions because the FSM is only an acceptor. In Problem 1 the student is asked to create a Mealy machine to translate text strings to all-lower-case, and in that machine, all of the transitions will have outputs, that is, actions.

To illustrate the concepts of complex real-world conditions and actions and the use of shared variables, we present a high-level FSM model of the bridge. A condition like "some component failed" in Figure 3.4 and Table 3.1 may be part of a more comprehensive report about the status of all modules. An action like "flash red lights, warn boat, etc." is obviously a complex action. Several shared variables, for example, "initialization_done," are used. This example also illustrates how the behavioral modeling described in Chapter 2 can inform and guide the development of FSM models. Figure 2.5 in Chapter 2 lists several use cases:

- Normal operation — boats arrive, the bridge opens, boats pass under, etc.
- Monthly inspection — inspectors examine and test various components of the mechanism.
- Failure notification — some part of the system is not working properly.
- Daily maintenance — checks and minor adjustments, other maintenance.
- Manual override — the system is stopped, and control is by a human operator.
- Installation — the system is deployed, adjusted and calibrated, and initialized.

Figure 2.5 indicates that there may be other use cases as well. As a first attempt at the design of a top-level FSM for the bridge, we might assume that each of these is a state. Thus, a first high-level draft of an FSM could be like that shown in Figure 3.4 and Table 3.1.

Each of the states in Figure 3.4 is itself a complex process and, as one might imagine, can be modeled as an FSM on its own. Section 3.6 is devoted to exploring the hierarchical structure of FSMs that model very complex systems.

3.3 Refining and correcting FSMs

Just as in software, the original FSM model will not likely be complete and may have errors. FSMs can be tested on the various scenarios by either simulation with a software tool or team walkthroughs. In software testing, the test cases are chosen to represent a variety of cases for the input. For example, a program that processes integers might be tested with positive integers, negative integers, zero, integers close to zero, very large positive/negative integers, etc. The test cases for an FSM are the scenarios. Walking through the behavior of the FSM on the test cases can help uncover missing states and transitions as well as errors in the behavior of the original FSM model.

Consider the FSM of Figure 3.5 and the various scenarios in Section 2.2.2 of Chapter 2. The first scenario for the primary use case, boats on the river, is for a single boat arriving and no ground traffic on the bridge. Our FSM will transition to state "prepare to open span" and then immediately transition to state "span opened" because the condition "on bridge traffic cleared" is true. After the boat passes, the FSM transitions to state "close span and resume land traffic." When the span has closed and the barriers removed and signals changed, the FSM transitions back to "span closed, on bridge traffic normal." This seems quite reasonable, assuming

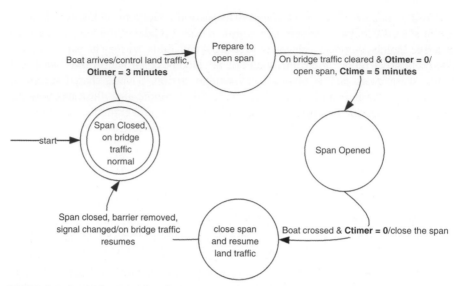

FIGURE 3.5 State Diagram With Timing Information.

Author drawn.

the actions on the transitions do their job correctly. The second scenario, one boat arrives and there is traffic on the bridge, also seems to yield the proper behavior, again assuming that conditions like "on bridge traffic cleared" are correctly done. However, the third scenario from that use case, two boats arrive, raises problems. After the first boat passes, the FSM in Figure 3.5 would transition to state "close span and resume land traffic," which we know is not correct. Thus, a walkthrough for this scenario has uncovered a flaw in the original FSM model. There needs to be a state after the boat passes that checks for more boats. The student can do walkthroughs for more of the scenarios to find other issues with the original FSM model.

Walkthroughs or simulations must take into account more than just the sequence of states. The conditions must be analyzed to make sure transitions happen only when they are supposed to. For example, in the transition back to the start state, the original model might not have included the condition "signal changed," that is, the condition that the ground traffic lights had changed back to green. A careful simulation or team walkthrough would have noticed that the red traffic lights would still be on when the "span closed, on bridge traffic normal" was reached. Similarly, if the action "close the span" had been accidentally left off in the initial FSM, walkthroughs would have revealed that the span was left open after the boat had passed. The simulations and walkthroughs must carefully follow all the conditions and actions for each of the scenarios to ensure that the proper behavior — conditions becoming true, transition to new states, actions performed — are exactly what the designers intend to happen.

3.4 **Determinism versus non-determinism**

Embedded systems should exhibit deterministic behavior. That is, the system should behave the same way if the same sequence of inputs is seen again. Both forms of FSM representation given earlier in this chapter are deterministic; for any input, the FSM either does nothing or transitions to a unique next state. Thus, for any sequence of input signals running ... end of the sequence will be the same" for better clarity. Intuitively for an FSM, if any specific sequence of input symbols always (unlimited number of repeating process) leads to a unique sequence of state transitions and result in the same final state, then the behavior of the FSM is deterministic. More formally, in the definition of an FSM in Figure 3.1, if in transition function δ, any pair of (current state input symbol) only maps to one unique next state, then the FSM is deterministic.[2] Note that some systems may make use of limited kinds of randomness. For example, the ALOHA Network system mentioned in Chapter 1 used a random number generator to distribute workloads over network channels. This kind of randomness can be considered as another kind of input symbol to the FSM; the output of the random number generator becomes one of the symbols used to define the conditions for transition. In this approach, the same sequence of messages to be transmitted plus the same random number generator *with the same starting seed* would produce the same behavior.

Some authors (e.g., Refs. [1, 2, 4–6]) describe non-deterministic FSMs. In these machines the transition function δ can produce a set of possible next states for a given state s and input symbol x. In some interpretations, when δ produces multiple states, the FSM enters all those states simultaneously. When the next input is processed, all of those states produce a next state, etc. These kinds of FSMs have interesting uses in theoretical computer science. In other interpretations, the meaning is that from state s input x will cause a transition to one of the states in $\delta(s,x)$, but the new state is not precisely determined. In some cases, a probability distribution is associated with the set $\delta(s,x)$. Note that any non-deterministic FSM can be transformed into a deterministic one (see, e.g., Refs. [2, 6]), but the deterministic one is usually very much larger than the original.

Although there are interesting theoretical results about non-deterministic FSMs (see, e.g., Refs. [2, 5, 6]), in the final implementation and deployment of an embedded system it is necessary to remove any non-determinism so that the system has precise and predictable behavior. Non-deterministic FSMs may have a place in the design process. For example, in the early stages of modeling the computation the design team may still be considering alternatives. Allowing a set of possible next states that the team can explore during simulation runs and walkthroughs facilitates the analysis of those alternatives. Ultimately, though, the system that's implemented and deployed should be deterministic.

3.5 Timed FSMs

Time is a crucial factor in most embedded systems. Real-time requirements, discussed in Chapter 16, are the most critical timing requirements. Failure to meet a real-time requirement typically means the system has failed. For example, in a modern car equipped with a front-end collision avoidance system, the sensor system has to recognize an obstacle in the vehicle path within a very short time period (a few milliseconds, probably) in order to give the brake and steering systems enough time to maneuver the car away from the obstacle. Failure of any of the three systems — sensor, brake, steering — to meet the timing limitations means collision avoidance has failed; the car will hit the obstacle. A second kind of timing requirement does not lead to catastrophic results but rather specifies requirements that affect user interaction and satisfaction with the product. For example, the designers of the system may specify that an ATM dispenses cash within 5 seconds of receipt of a valid request. This restriction is meant to keep users from getting annoyed and impatient. If the ATM took 6 or 7 seconds, it doesn't mean the ATM has failed catastrophically, as is the case for the car avoidance system failing to meet its real-time requirements. It just means the user interaction with the system may not be as pleasant. We now illustrate how timing requirements can be incorporated into the FSM model of computation.

We assume that an FSM has a means for counting time. In the abstract model considered at this stage of the design, the exact nature of the clock is not important. In later stages, when the FSM is implemented, the clock has to be part of the implementation. If the FSM is implemented on a processing element, the internal clock on that processing unit could serve as the basis for the FSM clock, although other methods such as separate clock circuits could also be considered. Some processing elements (see, e.g., Chapter 10) have programmable timers that can be set to count down and cause an interrupt when zero is reached. Other processing elements just have an internal clock, and this clock can be used as the basis for setting and testing timers. If the FSM is implemented in some kind of hardware other than a processing element, or for example, in an field programmable gate array (see Chapter 12), the clock and the related functions of setting a timer and testing when a timer has expired have to be implemented in some other way.

We assume the FSM has variables that can represent timers. There can be as many variables as needed to specify all the timing requirements. Each variable is updated as the system clock increments real time. Any timer can be set to zero at any time and independent of any other timers in the FSM. An atomic timer condition is an expression of the form x op c or $(x-y)$ op c, where x and y are timer variables, op is a comparison ($<, <=, =, >=, >, !=$), and c is a constant. Examples are $x > 3$, $y \leq 5$, and $(x-y) < 10$. Setting a timer variable is now a valid operation for the action part of a transition. An atomic timer condition can be part of the Boolean condition expression for a transition.

The FSM model is further extended by allowing each state to have a Boolean expression, called a *state invariant* in some parts of the literature, which is a combination of atomic timer conditions. The semantics defining the transition behavior is extended by the condition that a transition must be made once the Boolean expression becomes false. Note that in order to avoid non-determinism, there must be exactly one arrow whose condition becomes true when the state invariant becomes false so that exactly one state transition is possible and can be made.

We now illustrate how time can be used in specifying certain behaviors in FSMs.

Example 3.1
A simple use of timers and state invariants is to cause a fixed amount of delay. Consider a high-level state diagram for the normal operating state of the river bridge system shown in Figure 3.5. Two timers are used in this state diagram. Here we assume that it takes at least 3 minutes to stop entering traffic and clear the traffic already on bridge. So, we set Otimer to 3 when a boat is detected. Assume that it takes at least 5 minutes for the boat to pass under the bridge. We set Ctimer to be 5 when opening the bridge span. Ctimer reaching 0 will be part of the condition to close the span.

Example 3.2
It is possible to exit a state before the state invariant becomes false. A condition on an arrow out of a state may be independent of the variables in the state invariant, and therefore the condition can become true even though the state invariant is also still true. Suppose in Example 3.1 we want to provide for the span to reverse direction if a new boat is detected after the span had started down. The span should stop going down and reverse direction (i.e., go up). Suppose it is dangerous for the motor to simply reverse; perhaps the load is too great, and the motor would overheat. So, we provide an intermediate wait state of 10 seconds. However, in case of an emergency (e.g., the operator saw some big cargo pad fall off the first boat as it was going under the span), we want the operator to be able to override the 10-second delay. This could be specified in the FSM, as shown in Figure 3.6.

Example 3.3
In some cases, it is useful to have different time limits for different transitions. Consider the ground traffic barrier system for the bridge. Once a boat has been sensed, the ground traffic should be blocked from entering the spans, but any traffic (cars or pedestrians) already on the span should be given time to get off (either drive to the other end of the bridge for cars or walk to the other side or same side for pedestrians). After 5 seconds, if the ground traffic has cleared,

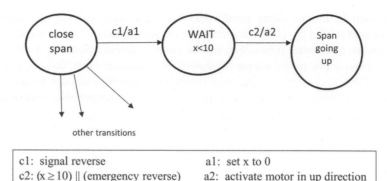

| c1: signal reverse | a1: set x to 0 |
| c2: $(x \geq 10)$ ‖ (emergency reverse) | a2: activate motor in up direction |

FIGURE 3.6 Delay With Override.

Author drawn.

then the spans can be raised. If the traffic hasn't cleared by 10 seconds, then an alarm is sounded to encourage the ground traffic to exit the bridge. The following FSM fragment illustrates one way to model this. Timer x is set to 0 when the "Clearing ground traffic" state is entered. No transition is allowed until x counts up to at least 5. If x had reached 5 but not yet reached 10 and the ground traffic has cleared, the FSM will transition to the "Ground traffic cleared" state and perform action a2. In this case the second arrow out of that state is no longer relevant. On the other hand, if x reaches 10 before the ground traffic has cleared, c3 becomes true, and the FSM transitions to the "Ground traffic warning" state. This situation is shown in Figure 3.7.

3.6 Hierarchical FSMs

The model developed so far represents processes that are a single thread and presented as a single level of processing. This would be like a software system that had no threads or concurrent processes and in which no functions were used (i.e., all functions are written inline as opposed to real function calls). Real systems, including embedded systems, are made up of modules that cooperate but operate almost independently and in parallel. For example, a car might have separate systems for the brakes, steering, engine, dashboard, etc. The bridge might have separate systems for handling the span, the ground traffic barriers, the lights, etc. Moreover, even some of these may be complex enough to have sub-modules. The hierarchical FSM model solves both of these problems by introducing two new notions — a state in an FSM can itself be a complete FSM and multiple FSMs can operate in parallel.

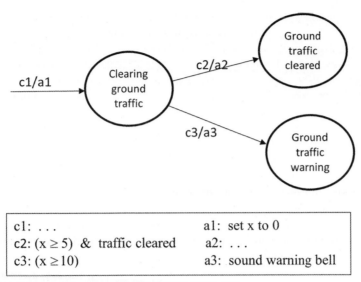

FIGURE 3.7 **Different Times Specified for Different Transitions.**

Author drawn.

3.6.1 **OR super-states — states that are FSMs**

The first new concept is that any state s can itself be a complete FSM F. State s is called an OR super-state, and the states of s are called sub-states. The term OR is used because, like a normal FSM, inside s, the machine is in one and only one state at a time — that is, in state s1 or in state s2, and so on. This is in stark contrast to the situation with AND super-state described in the next section.

Super-states can abstract out low-level details that may not be of interest in analyzing the FSM that contains s, similar to the way a function can be used in a software system to abstract out details that are not of interest to the section of code that calls the function. Consider the state "prepare to open span" in Figure 3.5. When analyzing the overall behavior of the bridge from a high-level point of view, the team may not be interested in the specific details of how the system prepares to open the span. However, the process of preparing may be sufficiently complex to warrant further detailed analysis. This can lead to an FSM representation of that process. The state "prepare to open span" then becomes an OR super-state, with an FSM as its content, as shown in Figure 3.8. The three sub-states form an FSM, with "Alarm sounded/Traffic light changes" as the start state and "On bridge traffic cleared" as a terminal state.

A transition leading into an OR super-state initiates or resumes the FSM F defined by the sub-states and their transitions. If during the operation of the system state s is entered the first time, F assumes its start state. If s has been active before, then there are two options. Either s starts in its start state or s assumes the state it was in during the last time it was active. The first of these is called variously in the

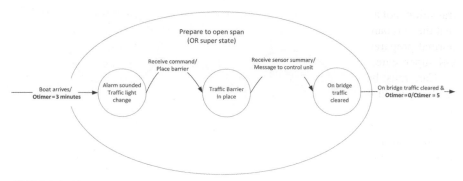

FIGURE 3.8 OR Super-State With Three Sub-States.

Author drawn.

literature a reset transition into s or a default transition into s; the second is typically called a history transition into s. There are a variety of notations for indicating the default or history transitions used in the literature and in the software tools for designing FSMs. In this book we will use a circle with letter H to indicate that there is a history mechanism associated with this sub-state. Note that the circled H is not a state itself, just a notation. Transitions into s for which the history is meant to be used must have the head of the arrow point directly to that circle. Transitions into s for which the arrowhead terminates at the boundary of s use the default mechanism.

A good example of transitions based on history is a TV set. A TV set "remembers" the channel it was on before being turned off the last time. The next time the TV is turned on, the channel displayed is the channel it remembered. Generally speaking, if a device has more than one operational option, applying the "history" transition mechanism could be a useful approach; if the user used the option last time, it is likely he/she will choose the same option the next time. Note that this implies that the system can retain memory when the system is "turned off." This could be implemented with non-volatile memory (see Section 11.2.3 of Chapter 11). Or, some parts of the system may continue to work even though from an external point of view the system is off. The latter is the case with most modern TVs. Even though the TV is turned off, some of the electronic circuitry is still active and drawing power from the wall plug or an internal battery.

A common application of the hierarchical mechanism is to provide a common response for an anomalous situation or error case. The error might arise when an FSM is in any of its states, but the response is always the same. Once the response is handled, the original process can continue. An example might be the arrival of emergency vehicles, such as an ambulance or fire equipment, when the span is preparing to go up. The design team may decide that as long as the boat has not yet reached the bridge, the boat should be told to wait and the emergency vehicles should be allowed to cross over. Once the emergency vehicles have passed, the preparation process can be started again. The team may decide that the whole process should start fresh, so the transition back into the preparation state should be a reset transition, not a history transition. This augmented FSM is shown in Figure 3.9. Note that the "prepare to open span" state is now an OR super-state with two sub-states — normal preparation and emergency vehicle. The normal operation state is itself an OR super-state, as is shown in Figure 3.8.

Care must be taken in specifying conditions on transitions out of the super-state s. There could be transitions from s itself, but there could also be transitions from sub-states that lead to states outside of s. This is illustrated in Figure 3.10. The transition labeled c_1/a_1 emanates from the boundary of state S. This is meant to indicate that if condition c_1 becomes true at any time while the system is in S the system should perform action a_1 and transition to a new state; this should happen no matter

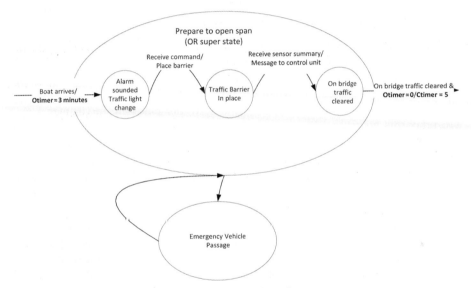

FIGURE 3.9 Emergency Case for "Prepare to Open Span."

Author drawn.

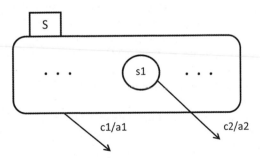

FIGURE 3.10 Transitions Out of a Super-State.

Author drawn.

what sub-state of S is currently active. This might be the case if, for example, the bridge operator could cancel the movement of the span no matter what the span was doing. On the other hand, the transition labeled c_2/a_2 emanates from a particular sub-state inside S. Condition c_2 causes a transition out of the sub-state and out of S, but only if S is currently in state s_1. The difficulty is that conditions like c_1 and c_2 might become simultaneously true. Then the questions are, (1) to which next state does the system transfer, and (2) which of a_1 and a_2 is performed? There are various definitions in the literature for the semantics of situations like this, and different tools may implement different approaches. Our goals here are (1) simply to make the reader aware of this issue and (2) to emphasize the need to either avoid such conflicts or be sure the team all agrees on which semantics is being used.

3.6.2 AND super-states — concurrency

The second new concept is that a state can consist of several FSMs that operate in parallel and communicate with each other through shared timers and other variables. Such FSMs represent concurrent activities of independent modules of a single embedded system. The use of shared variables and timers implies that all the concurrent states are implemented on the same hardware platform. In Chapter 4 we will relax this restriction, but that will require the introduction of more complex communication systems. For now, we assume a single hardware platform and shared variables and timers.

The definition of FSM given in Section 3.2.1 is augmented with the following conditions:

- Any state s in S can be a set of FSMs $\{f_1, ..., f_n\}$. Each f_i can be a simple FSM or an OR or AND super-state.
- There is a common set V of variables and common set T of timer variables associated with s. Testing the value of a variable or time is a valid condition. Setting a variable or timer is a valid action.
- The f_i all operate in parallel when s is activated.

Note that all states of the FSM see the same set of variables and timers. Therefore, setting a variable or timer in, say, one of the f_i sub-states may cause a condition in the current state of another f_j to become true and thereby cause a transition in f_j. State s is called an AND super-state. It is a super-state because it is a complete FSM and therefore has its own states. It is an AND super-state because when state s is entered, all of the f_i machines operate in parallel. Each f_i is a sub-state of s. In our notation, an AND super-state is written as a rectangle. The sub-states are separated by dashed lines.

While in state s, each f_i is also in one of its own states, say, s_i. Thus, at any given time, while in state s, the system state can be represented as a vector $(s_1, ..., s_n)$ of the states of the individual sub-states.

When an AND super-state $s = \{f_1, ..., f_n\}$ is entered, every one of its sub-states is entered. Entrance is governed by the default and history mechanisms described in

Section 3.6.1. Each f_i may have its own mechanism for entrance into f_i, independent of the entrance mechanisms of all the other f_j states in s. When one f_i exits, all f_j in s also exit. This semantics makes sense because the f_i modules are concurrent — that is, they all operate in parallel when the system is in state s. Therefore, they must all either start up or resume operation when s is entered. Moreover, if one exits, it means that not all the f_i are operating, and that in turn means the system should not be in state s.

Figure 3.11 illustrates the AND super-state concept and the use of global variables to coordinate and synchronize the sub-states. The bridge has various functional elements that are more or less independent of each other — the lights, the traffic barriers, the span, the sensors that determine if a boat is present or not, and possibly others that we do not show in this example to keep the presentation relatively simple. These various units have to coordinate in the operation of the bridge system as a whole, but the detailed operation of any one of them is separate from the operation of the others except for very specific synchronization points. For example, the spans should not be raised unless a boat has been detected and then until the traffic barriers have been lowered and any traffic already on the bridge has cleared. However, the actual control of the span motors and sensing when to stop them is independent of the traffic sensors, barrier control, or indeed any other part of the bridge. Modeling as separate FSMs also makes it easier to incorporate other use cases and scenarios. Similar to the case for the normal operation super-state, the other states in Figure 3.4 would also likely be AND super-states, allowing for the behavior

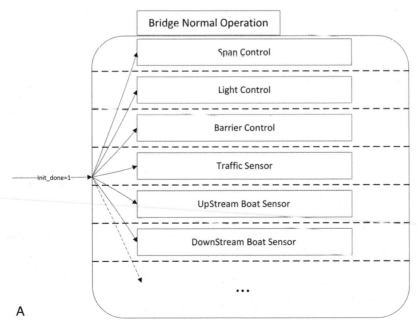

A

FIGURE 3.11A Overview of the Bridge Normal Operation AND Super-state.

Author drawn.

of the span, the lights, the barriers, etc. to be different in each of those states. For example, the lights need to respond to the approach of an emergency vehicle when no boat is present, but in this case, the barriers remain up so that the emergency vehicle can pass over the bridge. The reader can imagine how much more complicated it might be to incorporate such additional cases into a single large FSM than into the quite small FSMs in Figure 3.11. Note, separate occurrences of, say, light control FSMs from the various top-level AND super-states would eventually be merged into a single block/process in the Specification and Description Language model (described in the next chapter) for the light control module; this single block/process would then define the behavior of a single module, such as the light control module, under all the use cases.

Figure 3.11 shows a portion of an FSM for the Normal Operation state of the bridge system. (Note, this example has purposely been kept simple so the presentation can focus on the details of AND super-states. The FSMs shown here would have to be augmented to handle the other scenarios for the normal use case, such as multiple boats arriving. They would also have to be merged with the corresponding FSMs for other use cases, such as monthly inspection and failure notification.) This is an AND super-state, with individual FSMs for the various concurrently operating modules. Figure 3.11a shows the top level of the FSM, showing the various AND sub-states. Figures 3.11b—g show details of six of the sub-states. The global variables used to synchronize the various FSMs are described in Table 3.2; they start with the letter I, standing for "internal." The actions other than assignment to variables and timers performed by the FSMs start with the letter A, standing for "action." They are:

- A_sup, A_sdown — Start moving the spans up (down).
- A_green, A_yellow, A_red — Turn the green (yellow, red) light on and the other two off.
- A_bdown, A_bup — Start moving the barriers down (up).

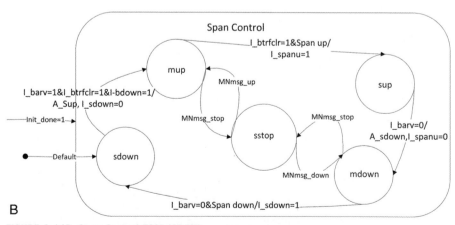

B

FIGURE 3.11B Span Control FSM (SPAN).

Author drawn.

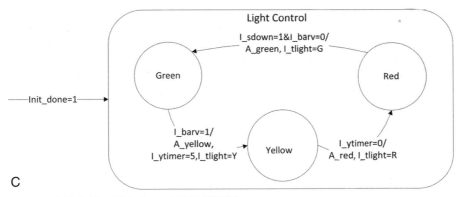

FIGURE 3.11C Bridge Light Control FSM (LIGHT).

Author drawn.

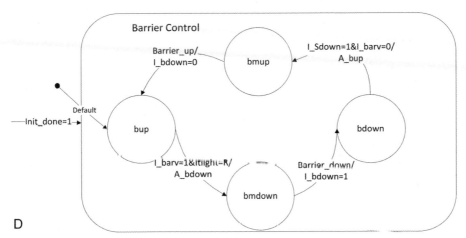

FIGURE 3.11D Bridge Barrier Control FSM (BARRIER).

Author drawn.

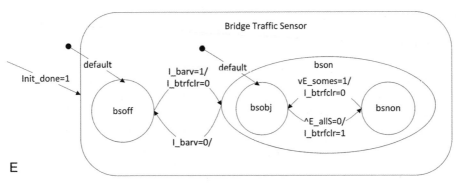

FIGURE 3.11E Bridge Traffic Sensor FSM (TrSENSOR).

Author drawn.

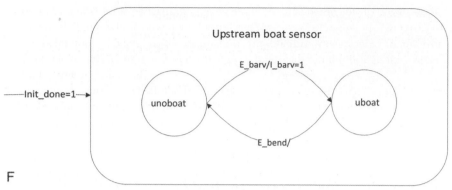

F

FIGURE 3.11F Bridge Upstream Boat Sensor (USSEN).

Author drawn.

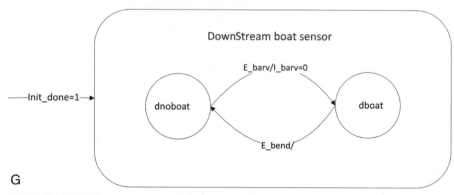

G

FIGURE 3.11G Bridge Downstream Boat Sensor (DSSEN).

Author drawn.

Table 3.2 Variables used in Figure 3.11.

Variable	Values and meaning
I_barv	1 if boat present, 0 otherwise
I_btrfcl	1 if bridge traffic cleared, 0 otherwise
I_bdown	1 if the traffic barriers are down, 0 otherwise
I_sdown	1 if the spans are in the full down position, 0 otherwise
I_spanu	1 if the spans are in the full up position, 0 otherwise
I_tlight	G/Y/R indicating lights are green/yellow/red
I_ytimer	Yellow light timer, counts down from 5 to signal when to turn red

The external events are:

- Span_up, Span_down — The spans have reached their full up (down) positions.
- Barrier_down, Barrier_up — The barriers have reached their full down (up) positions.
- E_barv, E_bend — A boat sensor has detected the arrival (end) of a boat.

All of the FSMs except Bridge Traffic Sensor are regular FSMs with only OR states. Bridge Traffic Sensor is a hierarchical FSM with two top-level states — bridge sensor off (bsoff) and bridge sensor on (bson). When Bridge Traffic Sensor is sensing (i.e., in state bson), there are two possibilities — no cars or pedestrians are on the bridge (state bsnon — bridge senses none) or there are cars and/or pedestrians on the bridge (bsobj — bridge senses objects). The Bridge Traffic Sensor system will likely include a set of sensors spread over different locations, the exact number of which would depend on the size of the bridge and the sensing range of the various sensors. The conditions on the two transitions inside bson represent all sensors detecting no objects (the "·" symbol representing the logical AND of all sensor readings) and one or more sensors detecting traffic (the "v" symbol representing the logical OR of all sensor readings).

Note the use of shared variables to allow one sub-state to provide information about its internal state to other sub-states of the AND super-state. For example, the operation of the ground traffic barriers is handled by the Barrier Control sub-state. This module raises and lowers the barriers. However, other sub-states in system need to know the position of the barriers. The variable I_bdown is used for this. The Barrier Control sub-state sets I_bdown when it has changed the position of the barriers, and then other sub-states react accordingly if barrier position is part of the condition on any transitions out of the currently active state in that module.

We now walk through the initial steps in the operation of this AND super-state on a typical scenario — one boat arrives and passes through with no other boats arriving during that time, and there are cars and/or pedestrians on the bridge when the boat is first sensed. The goal is to demonstrate how the individual FSMs operate in parallel and coordinate through the setting and testing of the global variables. Following the partial walkthrough, we make some comments about the design choices made in the development of these FSMs.

Before beginning the walkthrough, we note that specific numbers for events that occur in the scenario help guide the process. Knowledge about bridge operations and river traffic as well as estimates for actions like clearing the bridge traffic would be used to derive numbers like those used in this example. See Chapter 8 for more discussion of testing and test derivation. Our goal here is not to derive the tests but to illustrate how concurrent AND sub-states work in parallel and coordinate their operations.

Suppose it takes 3 seconds for the barriers to move up or down and 20 seconds for the spans to move completely up or down. Suppose a boat takes 2½ minutes from the time it is sensed by the Upstream Boat Sensor to reach and be sensed by the Downstream Boat Sensor. A boat takes 7 seconds to pass the upstream or downstream sensor, that is, 7 seconds from E_barv to E_bend. Suppose the system has been operating in the normal case for some time and that all initialization has already been done. The spans would be down, the traffic lights green, and the traffic barriers up. The yellow timer is not relevant yet, and although normally, I_btrfclr would be 1, its value in this state is not relevant. The values for these two variables are therefore marked as x (don't care).

STATES of the FSMs

SPAN	BARRIER	LIGHT	TrSENSOR	USSEN	DSSEN	
sdown	bup	G	bsoff	unoboat	dnoboat	

VARIABLES

I_barv	I_btrfclr	I_bdown	I_sdown	I_spanu	I_tlight	I_ytimer
0	X	0	1	0	G	x

When the boat is first detected by USSEN, that FSM transitions to the state that represents a boat sensed. It sets I_barv to 1 to indicate a boat has arrived. Call this time t = 0.

STATES of the FSMs

SPAN	BARRIER	LIGHT	TrSENSOR	USSEN	DSSEN	
sdown	bup	G	bsoff	uboat	dnoboat	

VARIABLES

I_barv	I_btrfclr	I_bdown	I_sdown	I_spanu	I_tlight	I_ytimer
1	x	0	1	0	G	x

This triggers transitions in both **LIGHT** and **TrSENSOR**. **LIGHT** transitions to yellow, and its timer is set to 5. **TrSENSOR** sets I_btrfclr to 0 and begins sensing. Note that these happen independently and in parallel.

STATES of the FSMs

SPAN	BARRIER	LIGHT	TrSENSOR	USSEN	DSSEN	
sdown	bup	Y	bsobj	uboat	dnoboat	

VARIABLES

I_barv	I_btrfclr	I_bdown	I_sdown	I_spanu	I_tlight	I_ytimer
1	0	0	1	0	Y	5

Nothing happens until the timer expires at time t = 5. Then **LIGHT** transitions to RED. There is traffic on the bridge, so **TrSENSOR** stays in bsobj.

STATES of the FSMs

SPAN	BARRIER	LIGHT	TrSENSOR	USSEN	DSSEN	
sdown	bup	R	bsobj	uboat	dnoboat	

VARIABLES

I_barv	I_btrfclr	I_bdown	I_sdown	I_spanu	I_tlight	I_ytimer
1	0	0	1	0	R	0

The light turning red causes the barriers to start moving down.

STATES of the FSMs

SPAN	BARRIER	LIGHT	TrSENSOR	USSEN	DSSEN	
sdown	bmdown	R	bsobj	uboat	dnoboat	

VARIABLES

I_barv	I_btrfclr	I_bdown	I_sdown	I_spanu	I_tlight	I_ytimer
1	0	0	1	0	R	0

At time t – 7, the boat passes the Upstream Boat Sensor. (The time it takes a boat to pass the sensor depends, of course, on the size and the speed of the boat.) USSEN transitions. I_barv is not changed and remains 1 until the boat reaches the downstream sensor. Thus, even though USSEN no longer senses the boat, the system knows that the boat is still there.

STATES of the FSMs

SPAN	BARRIER	LIGHT	TrSENSOR	USSEN	DSSEN	
sdown	bmdown	R	bsobj	unoboat	dnoboat	

VARIABLES

I_barv	I_btrfclr	I_bdown	I_sdown	I_spanu	I_tlight	I_ytimer
1	0	0	1	0	R	0

At time t = 8, the barriers reach their down position. At that time, **BARRIER** transitions to bdown and sets I_bdown to 1.

STATES of the FSMs

SPAN	BARRIER	LIGHT	TrSENSOR	USSEN	DSSEN	
sdown	bdown	R	bsobj	unoboat	dnoboat	

VARIABLES						
I_barv	I_btrfclr	I_bdown	I_sdown	I_spanu	I_tlight	I_ytimer
1	0	1	1	0	R	0

Suppose the traffic on the bridge doesn't clear for another 75 seconds. After the barriers are down, the cars would likely reach the other side in just a few seconds, but pedestrians who walk slowly would take much more than that. After 75 more seconds (t = 83), then, TrSENSOR would finally see no traffic on the bridge and transition to bsnon, setting I_btrfclr to 1.

STATES of the FSMs

SPAN	BARRIER	LIGHT	TrSENSOR	USSEN	DSSEN	
sdown	bdown	R	bsnon	unoboat	dnoboat	

VARIABLES						
I_barv	I_btrfclr	I_bdown	I_sdown	I_spanu	I_tlight	I_ytimer
1	1	1	1	0	R	0

Now SPAN can start moving the spans up. The spans are no longer fully down, so I_sdown is set to 0. However, the spans are not yet fully up, so I_spanu remains 0.

STATES of the FSMs

SPAN	BARRIER	LIGHT	TrSENSOR	USSEN	DSSEN	
mup	bdown	R	bsnon	unoboat	dnoboat	

VARIABLES						
I_barv	I_btrfclr	I_bdown	I_sdown	I_spanu	I_tlight	I_ytimer
1	1	1	0	0	R	0

Problem 2 asks the reader to continue the analysis of this scenario.

Note that there are three kinds of actions in this example — setting global variables, setting local timers, and performing actions in the physical world. An example of the third kind occurs in Barrier Control, which performs operations that interface with the physical world to make the barriers go down, most likely by turning on a motor. Similarly, there are three kinds of conditions — testing a global variable, a timer expiring or being tested, and sensing things in the physical world. An example of the third kind occurs in Barrier Control, which would contain some sensing mechanism to tell when the barriers had reached their bottom position. Each FSM deals with the physical things — action and sensing — of the items associated with that module, and no other FSM deals with those physical things. For example, the Light Control FSM does not deal with the motors that lower and raise the barriers or the sensors that tell when the barriers are fully down or fully up. Global variables are used to allow one AND sub-state to communicate with the other sub-states. This distinction between physical sensors and actuators and variable values will be especially important in the next chapter, where we consider systems in which the modules are implemented on physically separate platforms and the setting of global variables is replaced by the sending of messages over communication channels.

Finally, we note that some actions in the physical world take non-trivial amounts of time. Raising and lowering of the spans and the barriers are examples in the bridge system. In both the span control FSM and the barrier control FSM we have made states for the time during which the span or barrier is moving, that is, changing position. We did not make separate states in the light control FSM for the time during which the lights were changing. The simple justification is that lights change almost instantly, while both the barriers and the spans do not. But there are other reasons for modeling at least the span with states representing the movement. During the time the spans are moving up, an emergency situation might occur that requires the spans to stop or even reverse. For example, emergency vehicles (fire trucks or an ambulance) might suddenly appear just after the spans started moving up, and the operator might decide to halt the normal operation so the emergency vehicles could cross the bridge. After the boat passes the downstream sensor, the spans are supposed to come down. All the other systems on the bridge have to wait until the spans are all the way down. There could be a malfunction preventing the spans from getting all the way down. Without a moving down state in the Span Control FSM, we could not model this situation. In the case of the barriers, the time for moving up or down is likely too short for any emergency situation, as described for the spans moving up. However, other parts of the bridge system do require the barriers to reach their full up or full down position before proceeding with their operation. For example, the spans cannot start to move up unless both the traffic is cleared and the barriers reach their full down position. If the Barrier Control FSM had no moving down state and instead transitioned directly from bup to bdown and set I_bdown to 1 immediately, the system could not model a situation in which the barrier module malfunctioned and the barriers failed to come down all the way. On the other hand, no other part of the bridge system depends on the lights actually turning yellow or red (as opposed to the Light Control FSM being in state Yellow or Red). Failure to turn yellow or red may have impact on the cars and pedestrians, but it should not stop the bridge from continuing operation as long as the barriers do come all the way down. Note that the Light Control FSM would still be in state Yellow even if the yellow light did not light up (e.g., if the bulb was burned out). In this situation the state of the FSM and the situation in the physical world do not correspond.

3.7 Issues with concurrency

Whenever there are parallel processes using shared resources, there are issues of contention and non-determinism. In an AND super-state $s = \{f_1, \ldots, f_n\}$, multiple transitions may occur at the same time. For example, several f_j sub-states may each be in a state waiting for the same signal x. When x arrives, each of those f_j will transition at the same time. (Of course, in a real implementation they may not transition at exactly the same time depending on how the system is actually implemented. However, in the model they are supposed to transition at the same time.) The issues arise when the actions on these multiple transitions try to set or use the same resource. For example, two transitions may try to set the same variable *y*, or one may try to turn on an actuator while the other tries to turn it off. It is also possible that several different signals arrive at the same time or very close and cause multiple f_j to transition. Again, if the actions involve common resources, there could be conflicts.

3.7.1 StateMate semantics

Partial solutions to the problem of simultaneous actions affecting the same resource have been proposed in the literature. The most commonly used one is StateMate semantics.[5,7] StateMate semantics inserts an intermediate step in the performance of the set of actions for the transitions being fired. The intermediate step evaluates the expressions on all the actions but then assigns the results to temporary variables, not the real FSM variables. For each FSM variable (or timer variable) x, there is a temporary variable tempx. After all, these have been evaluated and assigned to the tempx variables; those temporary variables are copied to the real FSM variables.

We illustrate how StateMate addresses the problem with the commonly used example of a hierarchical FSM that interchanges the values of two variables, as in Figure 3.12. When signal e arrives, both transitions fire and according to FSM

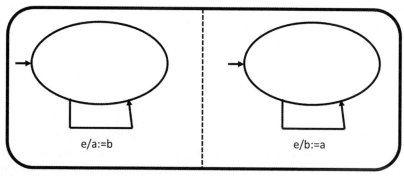

FIGURE 3.12 Conflicting Assignments a = b and b = a.

Author drawn.

semantics do so at the same time. The assignments, however, are made in two separate steps, as follows:

1. tempa = b and tempb = a
2. a = tempa and b = tempb

The end result is that variables a and b are interchanged. This will be the case no matter in what order the statements are executed as long as both assignments in step 1 are completed before the assignments in step 2 are undertaken. For example, the hierarchical FSM could be implemented as threads running on a single processing element. As long as each thread waited after the assignment to its temp variable until the other thread also completed its temp assignment, the resulting assignments in step 2 would correctly interchange the original values of the variables. Thus, the result is deterministic and predictable.

Unfortunately, StateMate semantics cannot solve all problems relating to assignment to common resources. In particular, if the resource being assigned is the same in more than one action, then the problem cannot be deterministic. For example, if in Figure 3.12, the two actions had been y = 1 and y = 2, that is, conflicting assignments to the same variable, the result after receiving signal e is indeterminable. It could also be the case that separate transitions specify conflicting actions in the real, physical world, such as telling the bridge span to go both up and down. Even if the FSMs are implemented on the same processor, perhaps as threads or even just separate objects, there may be no way to guarantee that the threads or objects will always be called in the same order each time the signal e is received. Designs that lead to such non-deterministic behavior should be avoided. Part of the team review process during the development of the FSM model should be devoted to uncovering and correcting such errors.

3.7.2 Multiple signals arriving at nearly the same time

Signals may come from a variety of different sources and may or may not be synchronized. The bridge SPAN CONTROL module, for example, may have a signal from the MOTOR module to indicate overheating. This signal would be asynchronous with other signals in other modules in SPAN CONTROL. The motor may not overheat at all, but if it does, the time at which the overheating occurs is likely random with respect to other input signals. It might occur, for example, at the same time or just about the same time as, say, input is received from the level sensors, the sensors that tell when the lowering spans are near the bottom and level with each other. The two signals might occur at exactly the same time or just a small amount of time before or after the other. There may be indeterminateness even for signals that are synchronized. For example, the motor speed signal might be scheduled to occur every half second, whereas the level sensors are scheduled to occur every quarter second. Then at the half-second time points, both signals should appear simultaneously. If they do appear exactly at the same time, then the issues discussed in Section 3.7.1 can hold. On the other hand, they may not appear at exactly the same time. One or both signals may be delayed slightly because of the nature of the signal (e.g., a sensor that may take varying amounts of time to sense the data) or the transmission into the system (e.g., shared physical wire using the CDMA protocol — see Chapter 23). Conversely, one or both signals may arrive slightly before the scheduled time due to variations in the timers in different modules in the system.

In the situation described in the preceding paragraph, the actions corresponding to the overheating and level signals are conflicting. The overheating signal should cause the spans to stop, while the level signal would be expected to cause the spans to continue lowering but at a slow speed. These two actions cannot both be done at the same time. In some cases the choice of which action to perform is obvious. In the case of the motor overheating the span should stop. In other cases the choice is not so obvious. The design team needs to study such situations carefully to identify combinations of signals that may affect each other and ensure that the design produces acceptable behavior in all cases, no matter what order in which the signals arrive.

3.8 Summary

Once the desired behavior of a system is understood, attention turns to how the system will accomplish that behavior. In this chapter we introduced one of the major techniques for modeling the internal operation of a system, the FSM model. We defined the basic concepts — state, transition, transition condition, and transition action. We discussed why the extended notions of edge conditions and actions make this model especially well suited for modeling embedded systems. We described how the study of an FSM can lead to the discovery of errors or missed cases and, thus, eventually lead to a correct and more comprehensive model. We introduced the notions of determinism and non-determinism and emphasized that embedded systems should exhibit deterministic behavior. We discussed the importance of time in the design of embedded systems and showed how to incorporate time into the FSM model. We presented the notion of hierarchical FSMs and showed how the AND super-state mechanism can be used to model concurrency in the operation of an embedded system. Concurrency is an important aspect of systems that have individual modules that operate independently. We illustrated the hierarchical concept with an extended example, the bridge system. We discussed the issue of determinism in the context of concurrent systems, particularly vis-a-vis input signals arriving at independent modules at about the same time.

Problems

1. Draw the graphical representation of a Mealy machine that translates all uppercase letters in a text to lowercase and leaves all other letters unchanged.

2. Continue the walkthrough begun in Section 3.6.2 until the boat has reached the other side and the bridge system returns to the normal operating state. Explain why the condition I_barv=1 is part of the condition on the transition from sdown to mup in the Span Control module.

3. Redraw the FSM for span control to account for the emergency stop situation described in the second paragraph of Section 3.7.2 and the added states for lowering the last short distance when the spans are nearly lined up.

4. The vowels of the English language are alphabetically ordered as a, e, i, o, u. Write an FSM that accepts strings of vowels in which the vowels are in alphabetic order. For example, the strings aaaeiioo and eiiuuuu should be accepted, but the strings eeeoaiu and aeiuo should not be accepted. Draw a graph of your machine and write the formal definition (S, Σ, δ, s0, F).

5. There are two sets of traffic lights in a major road intersection used to control the traffic in two directions, East-West (EW) and North-South (NS). Each set is controlled by its own FSM. These two FSMs are part of a larger FSM that controls the whole intersection. The top-level system has three states — normal operation, emergency state, and power-off state. In the normal situation, the traffic operates in the normal state. In the emergency state, red lights in both directions turn into flashing states and green and yellow lights are off in all directions. In the power-off state, all lights are turned off. The emergency state is caused by (1) a system error; (2) a traffic emergency triggering; or (3) manually activated by a traffic control officer. Both the normal state and the emergency state can transit to the power-off state. Transition from the emergency state to the normal operating state is controlled manually (i.e., only by activation by a traffic officer). When in the power-off state, if power goes on, the system will transition to the normal state. The following is a description of the normal operating states of the two directions.

EW direction: (major traffic)

Default initial state:	EWG	(EW green light on)
After 25 seconds	EWY	(EW yellow light on)
After 5 seconds	EWR	(EW red light on)
After NSR on for 3 seconds	EWG	(EW green light on)

NS direction: (minor traffic)

Default initial state:	NSR	(NS red light on)
After EWR on for 3 seconds	NSG	(NS green light on)
After 15 seconds	NSY	(NS yellow light on)
After 5 seconds	NSR	(NS red light on)

Draw a hierarchical FSM to model the intersection traffic light activities. Describe each of the states in words and list the conditions and actions in a table below the diagram. Describe the global variables and timers you use in your FSM.

6. A TV set has an off-on button. When the TV is turned on, both image and sound are turned on by default. There is a single change-channel button, which can be used to adjust the channel. Assume there are only five channels available for this particular TV. Pressing the change-channel button increases the channel by 1. When it reaches channel five it rolls back to 1. The sound volume of the TV can be one of only three settings — "low," "medium," or "high." A sound adjustment button cycles among these three settings, similar to the change-channel button. A mute button is provided to totally mute the sound. When pressed once, the mute button mutes the sound; when pressed again, it returns the sound to the same level as before the sound was muted. When the TV is turned on for the first time, the channel should be 1 and the sound level should be "medium." After the first time, the TV remembers the channel and sound settings when it was turned off last time.

a) Draw a hierarchical FSM for this system. Describe each of the states in words and list the conditions and actions in a table below the diagram. Describe the global variables you use in your FSM.

b) Is non-determinism a potential problem for this system? Say yes or no and explain the reason(s) for your choice.

7. One section of an automated assembly line in an auto factory has two modes of operation — normal operation and fault mode. In the first mode, normal operation, two robots cooperate to assemble four parts into a single unit. The first robot is mobile and retrieves the parts in order P1, P2, P3, and P4 from various storage areas near the working table. The second robot is stationary. When parts P1 and P2 are present, the second robot can put them together. After P1 and P2 have been assembled and when P3 is present, robot 2 can assemble P3 into the unit. Finally, after P3 has been assembled into the unit and when P4 is present, robot 2 adds P4 to the unit and places the assembled unit on a conveyer belt. At this point, robot 1 can begin collecting parts again. Robot 1 can retrieve the four parts as quickly as it can move, but it waits before retrieving parts for the next unit until the previous unit has been completed so that the working space does not become cluttered. If a fault occurs, both robots stop working until a human fixes the fault and signals the robots to continue. At this point, the robots must continue from where they were when the fault was detected. Assume that it takes 1 second for the system to initialize. Assume that it takes 9 seconds for robot 1 to get each part and put it into the common buffer area. Assume also that it takes 8 seconds for robot 2 to assemble each part onto the object. Draw a hierarchical FSM to model this system. Describe each of the states in words and list the conditions and actions in a table below the diagram. Describe the global variables and timers you use in your FSM.

8. There is an assembly line with three robots; the three robots cooperate to accomplish the assembly of circuits onto a printed circuit board. The first robot retrieves the parts in order P1 (a circuit board), P2 (a processor chip), and P3 (a memory chip) from various storage areas near the working table. The second robot is responsible for soldering the parts on the board. When parts P1 and P2 are present, the second robot can solder the chip on the board. The third robot is a tester. It tests the soldering quality of each step. That is, after robot 2

solders the processor on the board, robot 3 tests the connectivity of that soldering job. Then robot 3 puts the tested board back so that robot 2 can solder the memory chip on the board after the memory chip has been moved in by robot 1. After robot 2 finishes soldering the memory chip on the board, robot 3 tests the connectivity again, after which it puts the tested board on a transportation belt to be sent to another workshop. At this point, robot 1 can start to move in parts for next board to be assembled. To simplify the problem, let's assume the following:

1. There is no failure state to be considered.
2. There are power-on/off states, and the power-on state contains an initialization state.
3. It takes 3 seconds for robot 1 to move P1 to the workbench. It takes 6 seconds for robot 1 to move each of P2 and P3 to the workbench.
4. It takes 5 seconds for robot 2 to solder each chip on the board.
5. It takes 3 seconds for robot 3 to test the connectivity of each soldering operation.
6. Robot 1 does not need to wait for robot 2 to finish soldering P1 and P2 before starting to move P3.

Draw a hierarchical FSM to model this system. Describe each of the states in words and list the conditions and actions in a table below the diagram. Describe the global variables and timers you use in your FSM.

9. For each of the following situations, tell what actions would be warranted in response to each of the signals and which action you think the bridge system should take. Justify your choice.

   a. The variable I_tlight just changed to "red," and an emergency vehicle is approaching.
   b. The variable I_bdown just changed to 1, and an emergency vehicle is approaching.
   c. The variable I_sdown just changed to 1, and the variable I_barv just changed to 1 at (or almost at) the same time.

10. The StateMate semantics, with one phase for computing results (phase 2) and a separate phase for updating variables (phase 3), is especially well suited for modeling parallel computations that provide input for each other. Consider the following FSM system consisting of a single super-state with two AND substates.

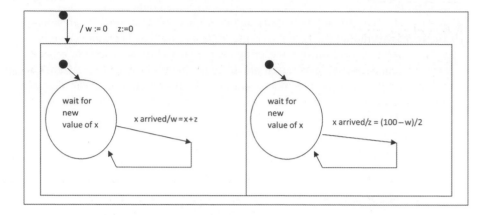

Assume the computations are done instantly so that the transitions back to the two circle states happen immediately. Trace the operation of the above machine for the following sequence of inputs for x: 0 30 60 90 108 102 100 100. For each new value of x, fill in the next row of the following table by showing all three phases of the algorithm.

Input x value	Phase 1 operation	Phase 2 operation	Phase 3 operation
0	$x = 0$, $w = 0$, $z = 0$	TempL $= x + z = 0 + 0 = 0$ TempR $= (100 - w)/2 = 100/2 = 50$	$w = 0$ $z = 50$

References

[1] Wikipedia, Finite-State Machine, [Online] Wikipedia.org, August, Sept 2001–2017, [Cited: Sept 30, 2017], https://en.wikipedia.org/wiki/Finite-state_machine.

[2] J.E. Hopcroft, J.D. Ullman, Introduction to Automata Theory, Languages, and Computation. s.l, Addison-Wesley, 1979.

[3] E.F. Moore, Gedanken-experiments on sequential machines, in: C.E. Shannon, J. McCarthy (Eds.), Annals of Mathematics Studies, vol. 34, Princeton University Press, 1956, pp. 129–153. Here: Theorem 4, p. 142.

[4] M.A. Arbib. Theories of Abstract Automata, Prentice-Hall, Inc, 1969.

[5] J. Hopcroft, R. Motwani, J. Ullman, Introduction to Automata Theory, Languages, and Computation, third ed., Addison-Wesley, 2007, pp. 55–71.

[6] E.A. Lee, S. Seshia, Modeling Dynamic Behaviors. Introduction to Embedded Systems. s.l., Part I: Modeling, 5. Composition of State Machines. https://ptolemy.berkeley.edu/books/leeseshia/structure.html.

[7] D. Harel, M. Politi, Modeling Reactive Systems With Statecharts, the Statemate Approach. s.l, McGraw-Hill, 1998.

Modeling physically distributed embedded systems

4

4.1 Introduction

While the finite state machine (FSM) model could be used at early stages to verify the correct operation of modules and correct coordination among different modules in a distributed system, the FSM model does not provide a detailed description of the communication between physically separate modules. The hierarchical FSM model implicitly assumes that the system runs on a single hardware platform because of the use of shared variables. Variables and timers can only be shared if the processes that use them are on the same processing element.

However, for many systems, the single-processor model is not feasible. Some systems are spread over distances that make shared memory infeasible. For example, parts of our bridge system, such as the sensors on the spans and the control module for the ground traffic barriers, may be physically separated by hundreds of yards. Similarly, parts of an elevator system in a high-rise building are likely to be physically separated by large distances — main control, interface at each floor, motor control module on the roof of the building, security monitor module in the lobby, and so on. Other examples where portions of the embedded system are physically distant from each other include cars, heating, ventilation and air conditioning control systems, and security systems.

It would be possible to model and implement systems like those described in the preceding paragraph as a single FSM operating on a single processing element that simply sends and receives messages from "dumb" peripherals. However, there are a variety of reasons for treating such a system as a set of cooperating processes, each with its own computing model and associated computing element and memory. First, systems may be large and complex, so modularization would be used to break a large modeling problem into manageable smaller problems, just as in software. Second, "plug-n-play" considerations make such modularization even more important. For example, in the bridge project there could be a variety of span configurations — single span, two spans, single span hinged at one end, single span in which the whole span moves vertically — each of which has its own FSM model for operation. Assuming each of these can respond to the same set of commands from a central bridge control module, treating the span control module as a separate FSM rather than an integral part of the bridge main control module allows the manufacturers to use the span configuration that best meets the needs of each bridge.

Embedded System Design. https://doi.org/10.1016/B978-0-443-18470-3.00004-X

Even if all the modules run on the same hardware platform, for example, a PC, there are other reasons for adopting a model without shared memory. For example, many embedded systems incorporate off-the-shelf software. It may be difficult (or impossible if the software is proprietary) to modify such software so that it shares variables with the system being designed. An example is the inclusion of face recognition software in a security system. This module would need the video data sent from the camera module to the PC on which the face recognition software and other modules of the system are running. If that software were proprietary, it could not be modified to use any of the system variables or timers associated with other parts of an FSM model. The face recognition software would most likely run as a separate process, and the operating system on the PC would manage its execution as one of the processes and threads comprising the portions of the whole embedded system running on that platform.

We need a modeling system that allows modeling of distributed systems that use messages to communicate with each other. In this chapter we present a method, Specification and Description Language (SDL), for modeling such distributed systems. At the lowest level of an SDL model are augmented forms of FSMs. SDL builds on top of the FSM model and adds explicit notation for modeling communication between (physically) separate modules. It makes extensions to both the computation model and the communication model.

4.2 Messages

Communication between physically separate (or distributed) modules is accomplished by sending messages. A message can be as simple as a new value for a system variable, the analog of an action setting the value of a global variable in a hierarchical FSM. A message might be a simple command; for example, in the bridge system the main control module might tell the ground traffic control module to lower the barriers. A message might contain coordination information, for example, that the receiving process(es) should reset their clocks. Messages can also be quite complex. For example, messages between two cars that both have collision avoidance systems might contain information about the car's model, speed, angle of steering, current brake pressure, current status of the autopilot control system, etc. Messages replace global variables in the FSM methodology for communication and coordination among concurrent processes, and as can be seen from the previous few sentences, they can carry much more detailed and complex information, e.g., Extensible Markup Language (XML) messages.[1] Issues related to messages and message passing are discussed in detail in Chapter 20.

4.3 SDL — an example modeling language for distributed systems

The individual modules that communicate by message passing are typically FSMs. Therefore the notation introduced in Chapter 3 could be used to model them.

However, systems have been developed that have much more sophisticated behavior modeling capabilities and explicit modeling of channels for the message-passing aspect of the model. We give a brief introduction to one of the most common ones — SDL [2–6]. SDL was first introduced in 1976 and has undergone several revisions and improvements to keep up with new developments in programming languages, such as object-oriented languages. Our goal here is only to provide a brief introduction to the concepts and issues. For a more complete treatment of SDL, see Refs. [2–6].

4.3.1 Behavioral specification in SDL

The behavioral part of an SDL model is given as a hierarchical structure. At the top level, the system is represented as a group of blocks. The blocks represent parts of the system operating in parallel with each other. These blocks may, in turn, contain subblocks and so on. Blocks are represented in SDL as rectangles. Figure 4.1 shows a high-level view of a portion of the bridge system represented now as blocks instead of AND-hierarchical FSMs. Communication channels, introduced in Section 4.3.2, are shown in Figure 4.1 as arrows between blocks. It is common to draw the hierarchical structure of the blocks as a tree, as shown in Figure 4.2.

At the bottom of the hierarchy are processes, which are finite FSMs with the complete computational power of a programming language. A process contains declarations of variables local to that process, states, and, for each state, a specification of the computation to be done in that state. The computation in a state may contain all the computational and control flow mechanisms of ordinary programming languages — expressions and assignment, branching, looping, etc. These are indicated using standard flow chart symbols such as diamonds for branching and rectangles for

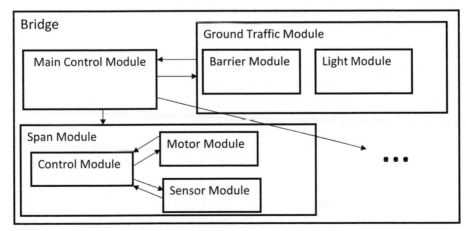

FIGURE 4.1 SDL Representation of the Top Level of the Bridge System.

Drawn by authors.

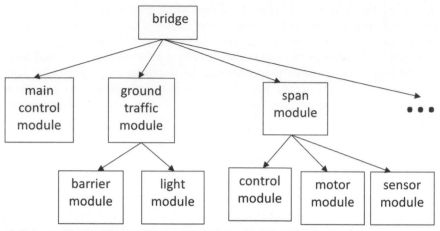

FIGURE 4.2 Hierarchical Structure of the Blocks From Figure 4.1.

Drawn by authors.

computations. A process may send messages as well as respond to messages received from other processes in the system. The notations used are as follows:

Circle — start state
Rounded-rectangle — other state
Indented rectangle — receive a message
Extended rectangle — send a message
Normal rectangle — computer code
Diamond — test and branch
Rectangles with open/closed x on left side — start/stop timer
Corner-bent rectangle (upper-right corner) — declaration

SDL supports generic data types, such as INTEGER, REAL, STRING, and STRUCT, as well as the SIGNAL type used for sending and receiving messages.

Figure 4.3 shows part of the process for the ground traffic control module. The start state waits for a command from the main control module. If the command is to deploy the barriers, the new state checks the sensors repeatedly until either there are no cars or pedestrians or 10 seconds have elapsed. In the latter case the process generates an output to activate the operator warning signal and transitions to the error state. The process would, of course, have many more states, but these two are sufficient to illustrate the format and the representational power of the SDL method.

4.3.2 Communication

Communication between blocks is modeled by communication channels. Messages are called signals, and a channel can carry one or more signals. Channels are indicated in an SDL diagram by directed arrows. A channel can have arrowheads at both

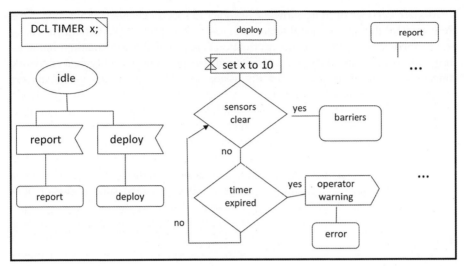

FIGURE 4.3 Portion of the Ground Traffic Process.

Drawn by authors.

ends, indicating that messages can be sent from either block to the other. However, this is essentially a shorthand notation for two separate arrows, one in each direction. The arrows typically are labeled with a channel name and a list of the signals (i.e., message types) that can be sent over that channel. (The list of messages is enclosed in brackets — "[" and "]" — and separated by commas.) There is no restriction on the specific format or content of a signal or the means of physical implementation. Message passing in SDL is nonblocking. Synchronization of processes across blocks must be handled by programming it into the processes themselves; for example, the sending process waits for a reply from the receiver as opposed to the channel itself blocking the sender.

An SDL diagram may also indicate the transmission of individual signals between processes within a single block. This kind of message passing does not require a channel. The channel notation is meant to model the transmission between physically separate pieces of hardware. On the other hand, processes within a single block would all be implemented on the same processing platform, as is the case for AND super-states in a hierarchical FSM. Therefore messages can be sent in one of two ways: either through the use of global variables as done in AND super-states in FSMs or through message queues. The latter behave very much like the First In First Outs (FIFOs) used to communicate between blocks implemented on separate platforms, but there is no physical communication channel. Therefore the only delay is the overhead for the sender to access the shared resource and copy the message into it. (See Chapter 19 for a discussion of semaphores for controlling access to shared resources.)

Modern versions of SDL allow the designer to specify channel delays, and these are important during the model simulation and testing phase. The default for channels is nondelaying — that is, the information is received at the destination immediately. However, this does not correspond to the reality of typical network connections. (See Chapter 23 for discussion of transmission delays in various communication protocols.) Messages are queued in the channel at the receiving end in FIFO fashion. This requires system designers to estimate the amount of traffic that will be sent over a channel so that implementers can provide FIFO buffers large enough to handle that traffic. These estimates can be made by considering the size and frequency of the signals to be carried on the channel and the maximum delay that the receiver can have before accepting a message from the channel. See Problem 3. Once taken inside the block, a message is directed to the subblock(s) or process(es) that will use that signal. A signal may itself indicate the specific target process or, in the cases of dynamically spawned processes, the individual instance of a process.

Table 4.1 shows some of the details of the signals carried by the various channels shown in Figure 4.1. Note that a single channel can carry more than one kind of signal. For example, the channel from the main control module to the ground traffic module carries two different kinds of messages — commands that the main control module issues to the ground traffic module (e.g., stop the traffic) and requests for reports (e.g., a status request). We also note that a complex system like the bridge would likely have many more modules and submodules and also many more message types and channels. We give only a small fragment just to illustrate the concepts.

4.4 Determinism revisited

In Chapter 3 we discussed situations in which inputs to a finite FSM can arrive very close to each other. We stressed the need for the system designers to ensure that the model performs well no matter what order the signals are used. The situation now is more complicated. In addition to the kinds of delays mentioned in Chapter 3, there are now delays introduced by the communication channels. As will be seen in Chapters 21 and 23, these delays are nondeterministic. In particular, in some communication protocols the delay depends on what other messages are being sent over the same set of wires. A serious consequence of this is that messages that were sent in a particular order by separate processes may not be received in the same order at a common destination. Consider the situation shown in Figure 4.4. Block B3 may receive message types from two separate blocks: messages of type m1 from block B1 and messages of type m2 from block B2. It may be known that B1 always sends its message before B2 sends its message, and the processes in B3 may be written in such a way that m1 must be processed before m2 can be accepted. However, delays in the channel may cause m2 to sometimes arrive at B3 before m1, while the two messages arrive in the correct order at other times. Moreover, it cannot be

Table 4.1 Messages sent between different modules.

Abbreviations:

MCM	— main control module
GTM	— ground traffic module
SM	— span module
SMCM	— span module/control module
SMMM	— span module/motor module
SMSM	— span module/sensor module

Channel names. The channel name associated with an arrow from module A to module B is abbreviated A-to-B.

Channel name	Sender	Receiver	Message type
MCM-to-GTM	MCM	GTM	GTM command
MCM-to-GTM	MCM	GTM	data request
GTM-to-MCM	GTM	MCM	GTM report
MCM-to-SM	MCM	SM	span command
...			
SMCM-to-SMMM	SMCM	SMMM	span motor command
SMCM-to-SMSM	SMCM	SMSM	span sensor command
SMMM-to-SMCM	SMMM	SMCM	status report
SMMM-to-SMCM	SMMM	SMCM	error report
SMSM-to-SMCM	SMSM	SMCM	sensor data
...			

determined *a priori* exactly when this will happen because it depends on what other inputs are arriving and being processed in other parts of the system.

One approach to this kind of nondeterminism is to allow only one signal type per channel and to require that each signal be written on only one channel. The corollary is that there must be one dedicated channel for each sender-receiver pair and message type. Within a block, each incoming signal is accepted by a single process. In Figure 4.4, then, there would be two communication channels for B3 — one leading to B1 and a second leading to B2. This kind of organization — one dedicated channel per sender-receiver pair — is a special case of a more general notion called Kahn process networks.[7] The obvious disadvantage is that more channels require more hardware (copper wires, wireless transmitters and receivers, etc.). Also, if a message is supposed to be sent to several other processes or blocks, that message must be duplicated. This, in turn, requires more energy, especially if the communication channel is wireless. Still, such duplication may be sufficient to get deterministic behavior.

Unfortunately, Kahn networks do not guarantee that messages sent over different channels arrive in the order in which they were sent. Continuing the example from

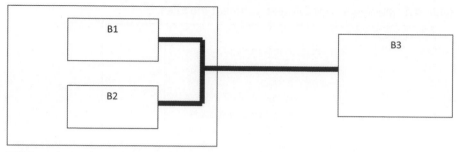

FIGURE 4.4 One Block With Two Subblocks and a Channel to Another Block.
Author drawn.

the preceding two paragraphs, messages of type m2 might be quite long or the channel over which they are sent quite slow compared to messages of type m1. Therefore the safest way to ensure proper order of processing is to use ordinary synchronization coded directly into the processes. In the example of the preceding paragraph the process receiving signal m2 can be programmed to wait until the process receiving signal m1 has written a specific value to a shared variable. Then it will not matter in what order the two signals are received. Even if channel delay causes m2 to arrive first, its process will wait until m1 has been received. The system behavior will be deterministic.

Some modeling systems and programming languages include primitives that allow the system designers to explicitly control the processing of signals from different channels. A common construct for this is the *wait* function. One form of the *wait* function includes the channel name as a parameter, e.g., *wait*(channel1). In some systems the *wait* function is blocking; that is, the function waits until there is a message in the channel before returning. In other systems the *wait* function can be nonblocking; if no message is present, the function returns NULL; otherwise, it returns the first message in the channel. To illustrate how this function can be used, we present a code snippet in which a process alternates between processing messages from two different channels. If the process is waiting for a message on channel 1, messages arriving on channel 2 will simply be queued.

```
process p( IN ch1, IN ch2) {
    while(1) {
wait(ch1, BLOCKING);
    process first message in channel 1;
    wait(ch2, BLOCKING)
    process first message in channel 2;
    }
    }
```

By contrast, if the process was simply supposed to process messages received on either channel without regard to the order of the channels, the following modified code could be used. Note that in this case it is necessary to test whether or not a channel actually has a message, whereas in the above case such testing was not necessary because of the BLOCKING aspect.

```
process p( IN ch1, IN ch2) {
    message M;
    while(1) {
M = wait(ch1, NONBLOCKING);
    if(M is not NULL) process M;
M = wait(ch2, NONBLOCKING);
    if(M is not NULL) process M;
    }
    }
```

Models with nondeterminism can be extremely difficult to analyze. System designers need to study the specific system being designed to determine if and when signal delay can cause nondeterministic behavior and whether or not such nondeterminism could cause problems and then decide whether or not to use channel splitting and/or synchronization code.

4.5 Summary

Embedded systems are typically made up of a collection of modules that are often physically separate and that have to communicate with each other. In this chapter we discussed the extension of the finite FSM model to distributed systems. The key element here is that separate modules communicate with each other through message passing. We gave examples of what information might be in a message. We described one of the major tools for defining distributed systems, the SDL, and illustrated its use. We included a discussion of the channel mechanism of SDL, a method for defining the communication links between modules and their properties. Finally, we discussed additional ways nondeterminism could affect a system over that described in Chapter 3. We also illustrated ways system designers and implementers could overcome these new kinds of nondeterminism.

Problems

1. A monitoring system for patients living at home sends hourly readings of basic bioinformation (pulse, percent blood oxygen, temperature), notifies the doctor's office immediately when one of those goes outside its acceptable range, and notifies the doctor's office immediately if it senses an emergency condition like a fall or heart attack. List the different types of messages. For each message type, tell what attributes or data is associated with that message type. For each type of data, tell what the range of values is.

2. Suppose the main control unit in a factory communicates with 16 other units in different sections of the factory. Each message sent from another unit to the main control is 128 bytes. Once a unit sends a message, it does not send another message until it has received a response from the main control unit that the previous message from that unit had been completely processed. The channel speed is 16K baud, that is, 16,384 bits per second. The main control unit can process a message in at most 200 milliseconds.

   (a) Assume the communication protocol includes 2 bits per byte — a start bit and a parity bit. (See Chapter 23 for more about data formats in communication networks.) Thus each data byte requires the transmission of 10 bits on the channel. How long does it take to send each message?

   (b) Suppose the main control unit receives a message and copies it to an internal buffer. Suppose the first byte of a second message arrives immediately after the first message has been copied. How many bytes of the second message will be received by the time the main control unit finishes processing the first message?

   (c) What is the best-case scenario for FIFO size in the main control unit? That is, in what circumstances could the FIFO be the smallest possible size?

   (d) What is the worst-case scenario? How big would the FIFO have to be to handle this scenario?

   (e) What would the worst-case scenario be if the other units did not have to wait for a response from the main control unit?

3. A modern car has the following, physically separated modules:

   A. Main control module. Communicates with modules B, C, D, E, F, G, and H.

   B. Display module. Communicates with module A.

   C. Pedal module with three separate blocks — one for monitoring the brake pedal, one for monitoring the accelerator pedal, and one for monitoring the steering wheel. The brake pedal block communicates with modules A and D. The steering wheel monitor block communicates with modules A and E. The accelerator pedal block communicates with modules A and F.

   D. Brake control module. Communicates with modules A and C.

   E. Steering control module. Communicates with modules A and C.

   F. Engine control module. Communicates with modules A and C.

   G. Autopilot module. Communicates with modules A, B, and H.

   H. GPS module. Communicates with modules A and G.

   (There may, of course, be other modules, but this list will be sufficient for this problem.)

   (a) Draw an SDL diagram for this system showing the blocks and communication channels.

   (b) Describe a set of messages that might be sent between the following blocks. Be sure to consider both normal operation and error situations. Compare your list with the lists of other students in the class and discuss the differences.

   a. Main control module and pedal module.

   b. Main control module and brake control module.

    c. Autopilot module and main control module.

(c) Draw a finite state machine for the brake control module given your answers to part (b).

(d) Is nondeterminism a potential problem for your solution? Answer yes or no and explain your choice.

4. Consider the elevator system in a building with 20 floors and 2 elevators.

    (a) Propose a list of modules for this system.

    (b) Make a list of the messages that can be sent between each pair of modules. Note that in many cases this list will be empty because those two modules don't communicate directly.

    (c) Draw a high-level diagram like the one in Figure 4.1 but with the channels labeled with their message types.

References

[1] Wikipedia, Extensible Markup Language: XML, [Online] Wikipedia.org, Nov 3, 2017, [Cited: Nov 05, 2017], https://en.wikipedia.org/wiki/XML.

[2] P. Andreas, S. Markus, S.T. Merete, A Model-based Standard for SDL, A Model-based Standard for SDL-Humboldt Universitat zu Berlin, [Online] [Cited: Oct 05, 2017], https://www2.informatik.hu-berlin.de/~scheidge/downloads/SDL07.pdf.

[3] sdl-forum.org, Specification and Description Language, Specification and Description Language — SDL Forum Society, [Online] [Cited: Oct 08, 2017], www.sdl-forum.org/SDL/Overview_of_SDL.pdf.

[4] P. Ivana, M. Branko, C. Antun, SDL Based Approach to Software Process Modeling — LSIR Group, [Online] [Cited: Oct 08, 2017], lsirpeople.epfl.ch/podnar/papers/EWSPT00.pdf.

[5] sdl-Forum Society, SDL Forum Society, SDL Forum Society, [Online] [Cited: Oct 08, 2017], www.sdl-forum.org/SDL/.

[6] P. Fonseca i Casas, SDL, a Graphical Language Useful to Describe Social Simulation Models, [Online] [Cited: Oct 08, 2017], ceur-ws.org/Vol-442/p1_Fonseca.pdf.

[7] Wikipedia, Kahn Process Networks, [Online] Sept 2017, [Cited: Oct 08, 2017], https://en.wikipedia.org/wiki/Kahn_process_networks.

Petri Nets for modeling concurrency and shared resources

5

5.1 Introduction

Embedded systems are often distributed systems, that is, parts of the system that are implemented on separate chunks of hardware. These separate modules must both communicate with each other and coordinate with each other. We present an overview of communication methods in Chapter 23. In this chapter we describe the most common technique for modeling distributed systems that have to coordinate and share resources — the Petri Net (see, e.g., any of Refs. [1-5]). Coordination is required, for example, in the bridge system between the various modules such as the traffic lights, the traffic barriers, and the span. Traffic lights should turn red first, then barriers go down, and these must happen before the span can begin to move up. Another typical case of coordination is the use of shared resources. In the bridge system one can think of the space over the river as a shared resource; only one of ground traffic and boat traffic can use that space at any given time. Other examples of shared resources include shared space in a manufacturing environment, a single wire carrying multiple signals in certain kinds of communication protocols, intersections of roads in a traffic system, and railroad tracks that carry trains in both directions. In each of these examples two or more processes are being carried out separately, and these processes coordinate at times to use a shared resource. The Petri Net is a common method for modeling the behavior of such systems.

5.2 Condition/event and place/transition Petri Nets

As with the finite-state machine (FSM) and specification and description language (SDL) modeling techniques, condition/event and place/transition nets can be represented formally or in graph form. The graph form makes it easier for the design team to visualize how the system would behave. However, the graph must satisfy a number of properties, and there are additional features of place/transition networks beyond just the graph itself. Therefore, it is convenient to also provide a formal or mathematical definition of these nets. Furthermore, such a formal definition allows the possibility of formally proving properties about the nets that embedded

Embedded System Design. https://doi.org/10.1016/B978-0-443-18470-3.00005-1

system engineer's design, for example, that two parts of the system never use a shared resource at the same time. The ability to mathematically prove such properties is rarely plausible in informal modeling methods such as Unified Modeling Language use cases.

5.2.1 Condition/event Petri Net

The first form of Petri Net, introduced in Ref. [2], was called "Condition/Event Net." The formal definition is presented as $N = (C, E, F)$. C and E are disjoint sets. C is the set of conditions, and E is the set of events. F is called the flow relation, and it satisfies $F \subseteq (C \times E) \cup (E \times C)$. Elements of F represent directed arrows from elements of C to elements of E and from elements of E to elements of C.

Figure 5.1 shows a condition/event net that models possible events occurring at an intersection of two one-way streets. We assume that the intersection allows only one car to cross at a time. Conditions are represented as circles, and events are represented as solid rectangles. Flows are represented as arrows. A condition being true is represented by a dot inside that circle. There are seven conditions:

- C1 (a car on the north-south street is waiting to go south)
- C2 (a car on the north-south street is crossing the intersection)

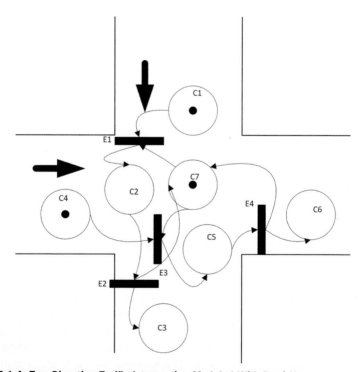

FIGURE 5.1 A Two-Direction Traffic Intersection Modeled With Petri Net.

Author drawn.

- C3 (a car on the north-south street has crossed the intersection)
- C4 (a car on the west-east street is waiting to go east)
- C5 (a car on the west-east street is crossing the intersection)
- C6 (a car on the west-east street has crossed the intersection)
- C7 (the intersection is available — not occupied by another car)

There are four events:

- E1 (a car on the north-south street enters the intersection)
- E2 (a car on the north-south street exits the intersection)
- E3 (a car on the west-east street enters the intersection)
- E4 (a car on the west-east street exits the intersection)

There are 12 flow relations — (C1, E1), (C7, E1), (E1, C2), (C2, E2), (E2, C3), (E2, C7), (C4, E3), (C7, E3), (E3, C5), (C5, E4), (E4, C6), (E4, C7).
The operation of such a Petri Net is governed by the following simple rules:

- An event can, but is not required to, fire if the conditions at the tails of all the arrows pointing into that event are true.
- If an event, t, fires, the conditions at the tails of the arrows pointing into t become false, and the conditions at the heads of arrows leading out of t become true.

Note that several events may have all their conditions true. In the model originally proposed by Petri[2] only one transition could fire at a time. Later revisions of the model do allow simultaneous firing of transitions; see Section 5.2.3 for a discussion of simultaneous firing of multiple transitions. However, in this example with the dots as shown in Figure 5.1, only one transition can fire even though two are enabled. The dots indicate that there is a car on the north-south street waiting to go south (C1), a car on the west-east street waiting to go east (C4), and the intersection is empty (C7). Thus, events E1 and E3 could fire because the corresponding conditions (C1 and C7 for E1, C4 and C7 for E3) are all true. Suppose E1 occurs. Then immediately after occurring, the two conditions C1 and C7 become false, and condition C2 becomes true. Note that at this point E3 is no longer able to fire because one of its conditions, C7, is no longer true. E1 and E3 cannot both fire at the same time because they each require a dot from C7, and C7 has only one dot.

The ability to mathematically prove properties about a Petri Net is one of the most important features of the Petri Net model because it allows designers to be sure their models actually describe what the designers want. Furthermore, if properties of the Petri Net model for an embedded system are proven, then an actual embedded system implemented in a way consistent with the Petri Net model would also be known to satisfy those same properties. In Problem 1 the student is asked to show that Figure 5.1 models the intersection in such a way that no collision will ever occur. The techniques in that problem illustrate ways in which properties about the operation of a Petri Net could be proven.

We note that the Petri Net modeling approach makes no assumptions about common initializations, where the dots come from, or start-up times for the various physical modules that may cause a dot to appear on some conditions. This is important in real-life systems, where physically separated modules may start or stop independently of each other and have no common memories, clocks, or other data. Different parts of a graph representing a net can represent different parts of a distributed system, and the Petri Net formalism provides the means for coordinating those separate modules independent of issues like start-up and initialization. For example, in Figure 5.1, a dot could "suddenly appear" in C4 because there was no car there before but a new car just arrived.

5.2.2 Place/transition Petri Net

Researchers soon discovered the need for more expressive power than was possible with the simple condition/event model. One of the first extensions to the basic model was called the "place/transition" Petri Net model. In this model the simple conditions are replaced by "places." Places can hold any number of dots, or "tokens," and can thus represent quantities such as workloads as opposed to simple true/false conditions. We now present this augmented Petri Net model and illustrate again the formal approach to defining models and their operation. The formal definition of place/transition nets is considerably more complex than that of condition/event nets.

Let N denote the natural numbers (i.e., $\{1, 2, 3, \dots\}$), N_0 denote the nonnegative integers (i.e., $N + \{0\}$), and $N^* = N + \omega$. (ω represents infinity.)

> **Definition 5.1** $PT = (P, T, F, K, W, M_0)$ is called a place/transition network if the following hold:
>
> 1. P and T are disjoint sets. P is called the set of places. T is called the set of transitions.
> 2. F is a subset of $(P \times T) \cup (T \times P)$. F is called the flow relation.
> 3. K is a mapping from P to N^*. K is called the capacity of the places in P.
> 4. W is a mapping from F to N. F defines the weight of each edge in the graph.
> 5. M_0 is a mapping from P to N_0. M_0 is called the initial marking. $M_0(p) \leq K(p)$ for all pεP.

The graph G corresponding to PT is a bipartite graph (i.e., a graph with two mutually exclusive kinds of nodes, in this case, P nodes and T nodes). Elements of P are typically drawn as open circles; elements of T are typically drawn as solid rectangles. It is common to provide annotations for elements of P and T to help the readers understand what part of the system they represent, but these are not part of the formal definition. There is a directed edge from a place node p to a transition node t if and only if (p,t) ε F. Similarly, there is a directed edge from transition node t to place node p if and only if (t,p) ε F. Note, by the definition of F there cannot be an edge from a place node to another place node or from a transition node to another transition node. A place node p can have k dots, where $0 \leq k \leq K(p)$. Each edge e in the graph is labeled by the corresponding value W(e), that is, its weight. The default weight of edges is 1, so if there is no weight specifically indicated for an edge in the graph, that edge has weight 1. M_0 represents the distribution of dots when the system first starts operating.

> **Definition 5.2** Let t be a node in T. $PRE(t) = \{p \mid (p,t) \; \varepsilon \; F\}$. $PRE(t)$ is called the preset for t.
>
> **Definition 5.3** Let t be a node in T. $POST(t) = \{p \mid (t,p) \; \varepsilon \; F\}$. $POST(t)$ is called the postset for t.
>
> **Definition 5.4** A marking is a mapping M from P to N_0 satisfying $M(p) \leq K(p)$ for all $p \varepsilon P$.
>
> **Definition 5.5** Let M be a marking representing the current state of a place/transition net. A transition $t \; \varepsilon \; T$ is said to be enabled in M if both of the following conditions are met.
>
> 1. For each $p \; \varepsilon \; PRE(t)$ $M(p) \geq W((p,t))$, that is, the current number of dots in p is greater than or equal to the weight of the edge from p to t.
> 2. For each $p \; \varepsilon \; POST(t)$ $K(p) \geq W((t,p)) + M(p)$, that is, the capacity of p is greater than or equal to the current number of dots in p plus the weight of the edge from t to p.
>
> **Definition 5.6** Let M be a marking representing the current state of a place/transition net. Let t be a transition that is enabled in M. Firing t causes a new marking M' to be reached as follows:
>
> 1. For each $p \; \varepsilon \; PRE(t)$, $M'(p) = M(p) - W((p,t))$, that is, the number of dots in p is decreased by the weight of the edge from p to t.
> 2. For each $p \; \varepsilon \; POST(t)$, $M'(p) = M(p) + W((t,p))$, that is, the number of dots in p is increased by the weight of the edge from t to p.
> 3. For all other $p \; \varepsilon \; P$, $M'(p) = M(p)$.

Transitions represent possible changes in the state of the system. Places and the current number of dots in the places, that is, the current marking, represent the actual state. The M' in Definition 5.6 represents a new state after some transition has fired.

Example 5.1

One interpretation of a transition is that it represents some kind of process that consumes resources contained in the preset and produces other resources that are passed on to the postset. Our first example in this section illustrates this and shows how capacity and dots can model real-world physical resources. Consider a particular point in an auto assembly line where the four doors are added to a partially assembled car, as illustrated in Figure 5.2. This figure shows one point for attaching doors with storage space at the side for the four doors. It also illustrates how the output of one process provides input for the next process. Installing the four doors cannot be done unless there are at least four doors and one partially assembled car at that station. Placing the four doors on the car removes four doors from the storage at the side of the assembly line. It also removes one partially assembled car from the beginning of that area of the assembly line and passes it along to the next point in the assembly line.

Figure 5.3 shows a portion of a place/transition net modeling this situation. In Figure 5.3, P1 represents the availability of a car waiting to have its four doors assembled, and P2 represents the doors available to be assembled. Suppose the

FIGURE 5.2 An Industrial Car Assembly Line.

Purchased from iStock.

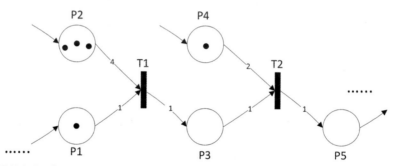

FIGURE 5.3 Petri Net Model for Part of an Automobile Assembly Line.

Author drawn.

area near the assembly line can only accommodate four doors so that the assembly line does not become too cluttered. Then the capacity of P2 would be set to four. It must be at least four because four doors are needed. It cannot be more than four because the area near the assembly line can't hold more than four doors. T1 represents the door-assembly transition. We also show P3 as the place where car(s) move to after having four doors assembled, and P4 represents the side mirror availability. T2 represents the transition of assembling the two side mirrors onto the car. Note that the marking shown would cause the assembly line to stop because neither T1 nor T2 can fire; there aren't enough doors, enough mirrors, and no car at P3. This condition (assembly line stopped) would be maintained until at least one more door was brought in from wherever doors are stored outside this particular work area.

Once four doors have been brought to the assembly line (four dots appear in P2), T1 can fire. This removes all four dots from P2 and the dot from P1. At this point new doors can be delivered to the assembly line. Note that until T1 fires no more doors can be brought to the assembly line because of the capacity of P2. This is a kind of implicit control imposed by the semantics of place-transition Petri Nets. Delivery of doors is blocked because of an internal property of one of the places in the net. Example 5.2 shows a more explicit form of control.

This example is somewhat over simplified because it does not account for the fact that the four doors on a car are different. The model would be appropriate in situations where the resources were essentially the same, for example, blocks on a disk drive or gaskets at the auto assembly line point where gaskets and valves are assembled into the motor. Problem 2 asks the reader to redo Figure 5.3 to account for the difference in doors.

Places and dots don't always have to represent physical resources. They may, instead, represent conditions. For example, in the bridge system, one condition that the span can go up is that there are no cars on the span. A place p in a Petri Net for the bridge could simply represent that condition, and having one dot could represent that the condition is true. Note that such a place p would be in PRE(t), where t is the transition that represents the span actually going up. The condition (no cars on the span) must be true before the span can go up. (Of course, there may be other prerequisites as well.) A different transition, t', could represent the change in state corresponding to the sensors detecting that no cars are present. Then p would be in POST(t'). See Figure 5.7 for more details on this example.

Example 5.2

The next example illustrates how a Petri Net can be used to model mutual exclusion of two parallel processes that share resources. This was the original motivation for the Petri Net model. We illustrate this use of Petri Nets with an example of two robots sharing a common space. Figure 5.4 illustrates one robot (in this case, the hook on the conveyer belt) moving an item into a bench, the common area. A second robot (the humanoid robot in the figure) removes items from the common

FIGURE 5.4 A Robot Moving Parts.

Purchased from iStock.

bench. Suppose that the bench is in a confined area and that only one robot can be in that area at a time. We show how a Petri Net can model this situation.

Figure 5.5 shows a Petri Net model of a two-robot system. The two robots can work autonomously and concurrently except when they need to access the common staging area. robot 1 (R1) takes a part from a storage area to the staging area, and robot 2 (R2) removes the part from the staging area and takes it to a loading dock. The staging area has room for only one robot to work inside. The staging area has only three available slots, so up to three parts can be stored at any given time. Thus, a mutual exclusion mechanism is needed for controlling entrance to the staging area. In addition, "under-flow" and "over-flow" avoidance mechanisms are needed for the available part slots. That is, the staging area cannot underflow (have less than zero parts) and cannot overflow (have more than three parts). Table 5.1 lists the meaning of each place and transition in the model. The marking shown in Figure 5.5 indicates that R1 is in the large storage area, R2 is in the loading dock area, all three slots in the staging area are available, and no robot is in the staging area. It is not hard for the reader to walk through the possible scenarios in this system. See Problems 3 and 4.

Figures 5.3 and 5.5 show two distinct ways to impose restrictions on the number of resources a place can hold. In the auto assembly line example in Figure 5.3, the blocking of delivery of more than four doors to the assembly line is implicit because the capacity of P2 is four. Implicit limits such as this may not be so easy to see in larger and more complex nets, as shown in Figures 5.6 and 5.7. Moreover, as noted in the comments section, often times capacities are discovered or imposed by analysis of a draft net. In the robot example of Figure 5.5, the control of the resources that can be put in one place is explicit. The decision in this case that the staging

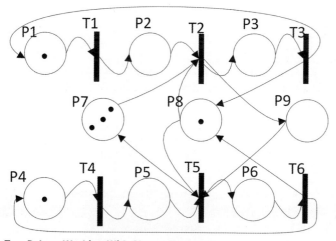

FIGURE 5.5 Two Robots Working With Shared Resources.

Author drawn.

Table 5.1 Description of places/transitions of the Petri Net in Figure 5.5.

Name	Meaning
P1	R1 is in the large storage area
P2	R1 holds a part and is outside the staging area
P3	R1 is inside the staging area and puts a part into an empty slot
P4	R2 is in dock area to put a part on the loading dock
P5	R2 is outside the staging area
P6	R2 is inside the staging area and takes out a part from a slot
P7	Number of empty slots available
P8	Staging area availability
P9	Number of parts currently in staging area
T1	R1 walks to staging area
T2	R1 enters the staging area and puts part in a slot
T3	R1 walks out of the staging area
T4	R2 walks to staging area
T5	R2 enters the staging area and removes a part from a slot
T6	R2 walks out of the staging area

area would hold up to three items was apparently made *a priori*, and the enforcement of this limit was made explicit via place P7. Although we did not give the formal definition of the Petri Net in Figure 5.5, in such a definition the capacity of P9 (number of parts in the staging area) and P7 (number of empty slots in the staging area) would be set to three. The capacity of three for P7 would preclude the need for P9. However, this small Petri Net might be part of a larger design in which other parts of the system may need to know how full the staging area is. By making this explicit through the addition of P9, representing how many empty slots there are, the modelers suggest that some additional mechanisms might be needed instead of just having R1 carry a part into the staging area, see that there are no empty slots, and go out again without leaving the part.

Example 5.3

Petri Nets can model situations in which events have to occur (i.e., transitions have to fire) in some order. Figure 5.6 shows a portion of a Petri Net model for a Time Division Multiple Access (TDMA) communication protocol. (Note, in this figure we have drawn dashed boxes around sections of the graph to help the reader identify and relate the places and transitions. These dashed boxes are not part of the net; they are only there to help the reader understand the net.) We will introduce the TDMA network protocol in Chapter 23. Briefly speaking here, a network divides its transmission time into equal-length "frames," and each frame is divided into equal-length time slots. Each device using the network gets a time slot in a preassigned order. Each device will transmit its data in its assigned slot. When a new frame is started, the device assigned to slot 1 gets a chance to place data on the network. If it has no data ready, then that slot remains unused. Then the device assigned to slot 2 gets its chance, etc.

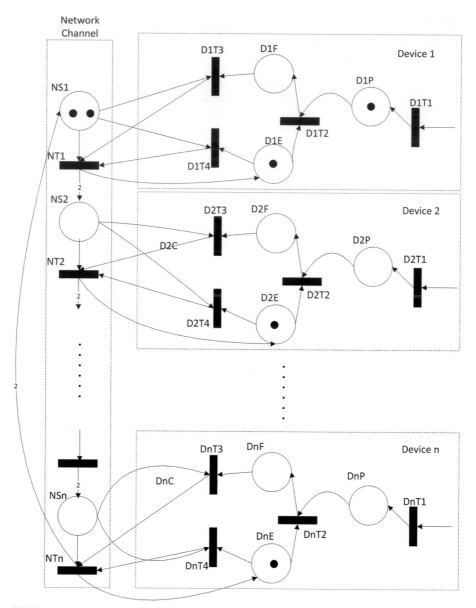

FIGURE 5.6 A TDMA Network With n Connected Devices.

Author drawn.

An individual device will have an area for holding the bytes to be transferred onto the network. We call this area the network buffer. An application running on that device generates bytes in the application's own buffer area, and when that data is ready the application transfers those bytes into the network buffer. For example, an email application may collect bytes typed by a user into the email application's own buffer. When the user clicks on the send icon, the bytes in the local buffer are transferred to the network buffer. Once in the device's network buffer, those bytes can be put out onto the network at the device's next turn.

In Figure 5.6, each device is modeled by four places and four transitions. Place DiP indicates that device i has data ready to put into the network buffer. Place DiF indicates that data has been placed into the network buffer. Place DiE indicates the network buffer does not have data ready for the network (i.e., the network buffer is empty). Place DiC indicates that the device has consumed its time slot. Each place DiE has a dot when the network starts operation. Transition DiT1 represents that an application has produced some data in its own buffer. Transition DiT2 indicates that the device has loaded its application data into the network buffer. Transition DiT3 indicates that the device has transferred the network buffer onto the network. Transition DiT4 indicates that the device consumed its time slot without sending data. The network itself is modeled with a place and a transition for each time slot. Place NSi indicates that it is the time for device i to use the network. Transition NTi indicates the change from network slot i to network slot i+1.

An individual device operates as follows. At any time, an application may generate data. The application itself is not of significance for the network operation. In Figure 5.6 we have omitted the details of how the application generates data and only shown an incoming flow into DiT1. If the application has generated data, the device may transfer that data to the network buffer (DiT2). Both of these transitions (DiT1 and DiT2) may occur at any time. The remaining two transitions (DiT3 and DiT4) may only fire when it is this device's turn to use the network, that is, when it is time for this device to use its slot. The reader may verify (see Problem 5) that at any given time exactly one of DiF and DiE has a dot. Thus, when NSi gets its two dots, exactly one of DiT3 and DiT4 is enabled. If the device has loaded data into the network buffer (DiF has the dot), then DiT3 will fire, indicating that the device has transferred the network buffer onto the network. If the dot is in DiE, then DiT4 will fire, indicating that the device is idle during this time slot, and the time slot is not used for data transferring.

The network operates as follows. Place NSi contains two dots when it is time for device i to use the network. When NSi gets its two dots, exactly one of DiT3 and DiT4 is enabled, as described in the preceding paragraph. After the enabled transition fires, DiC gets a dot indicating that the device has now consumed its time slot, either by transferring data (DiT3) or remaining idle (DiT4), and the dot that was in DiF or DiE is removed. Neither of DiT3 or DiT4 is now enabled, but NTi becomes enabled. The remaining dot in NSi and the dot in DiC are consumed by transition NTi, and two dots are placed in NS(i+1), indicating that it is now the turn for device i+1. A dot is also placed in DiE indicating that the network buffer in device i is empty again. When the last device has consumed its time slot, the network starts a new frame in which slot 1 is again the active slot. Refer to Table 5.2 for the list of Places and Transitions and their meanings for Example 5.3 — Petri Net modeling of TDMA protocol. (Note, in a real TDMA network, there would be some overhead for starting the next frame. This might be indicated by a place and transition between NSn and NS1. We have omitted this for simplicity; our goal here is to give an example of a Petri Net, not to model TDMA process in detail.)

Example 5.4

The previous examples have been quite small. We now present a slightly larger example (but still not particularly large for real-world applications) — a Petri Net model for the bridge example. The net shown in Figure 5.7 does not handle all the scenarios described in the preceding chapters, otherwise, the net would be too complicated to draw on a text book page and too complex to illustrate the points we want to make. Figure 5.7 is meant to handle the simple case of a single boat passing successfully under the bridge. Still, the example is sufficiently complex to illustrate a number of points.

Table 5.2 Place/transition list for the Petri Net in Figure 5.6.

Meaning of the places:	
Name of place	**Meaning**
NS1—NSn	Network time slots 1—n in a frame
D1P—DnP	Data produced in Device (1—n)
D1F—DnF	Device (1—n) buffer has data to be sent
D1E—DnE	Device (1—n) buffer has no data to be sent
D1C—DnC	Device (1—n) consumed time slot assigned to it

Meaning of the transitions:	
Name of transition	**Meaning**
NT1—NTn	Transit to next time slot
D1T1—DnT1	Device (1—n) generates data to be sent
D1T2—DnT2	Device (1—n) fills its network buffer
D1T3—DnT3	Device (1—n) sends data during its time slot
D1T4—DnT4	Device (1—n) consumes time slot without sending data

- Larger Petri Nets can be built up from smaller ones that model independent modules. Additional places and transitions are added to "glue" the smaller nets together.
- Many Petri Nets are FSMs, and a larger net formed by merging smaller ones often resembles an SDL model. The emphasis in FSM models is on the system's reaction to inputs from external sources. The emphasis in the Petri Net approach is on transitions, resources (capacities of places, weights of transitions), usage of shared resources, and the order of transitions in a system. In the auto assembly Petri Net, for example, the car doors come from some external source. However, the place where they enter the portion of the system modeled in Figure 5.3 has a capacity of four, meaning that place can only hold up to four of that resource (car door), and the transition that assembles the doors onto the car consumes all four of those resources.
- Capacities can be used in very interesting ways. We have seen examples in Figures 5.3 and 5.6. In this example we will see another example — a simple timer that keeps the traffic light yellow for at least 3 seconds.
- Relating to the immediately preceding bullet point, we remind the reader that the basic Petri Net model does not require an enabled transition to fire. We noted this, for example, in the intersection example of Figure 5.1. Similarly, in Figure 5.3 the Petri Net model itself does not require the doors to be assembled into the car; it only prevents assembly if there are not enough doors. However, the expectation is that in a real system enabled transitions will occur, and this can be enforced during analysis via walkthroughs or with simulation tools. In Section 5.5 we present some extensions to the basic model that can force transitions to occur.
- Performing walkthroughs on complex Petri Nets is difficult and error prone. Therefore having a formalism that can be read by computer software that can then simulate operation of the net on various initial markings is of great help in studying a draft net.

The simplified Petri Net is shown in Figure 5.7 and Table 5.3. As might be expected, the Petri Net and its corresponding graph are quite complicated because the bridge itself has many components that require nontrivial cooperation. So, at first glance, the graph may appear overwhelming. We will develop the net in Figure 5.7 in a bottom-up fashion, starting with simple nets for various modules within the bridge and showing how to merge these into the net for the whole bridge.

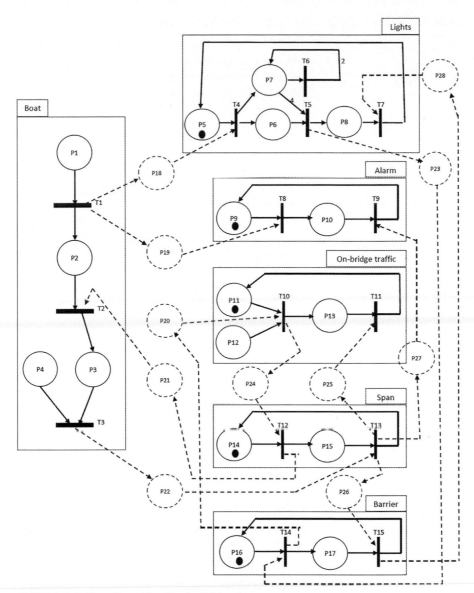

FIGURE 5.7 A Place/Transition Net for Bridge System.

Author drawn.

We begin with the timer used to make the yellow light stay on for 3 seconds. This timer is implemented by place P7 and transitions T5 and T6 in Figure 5.7. The capacity of P7 is four (see the formal definition of this net later in this section). Initially P7 has no dot. Therefore, neither of T5 or T6 is enabled. When T4 fires, changing the

Table 5.3 Place/transition list for the Petri Net in Figure 5.7.

P1	Boat is in range of the sensor
P2	Boat is proceeding toward bridge
P3	Boat is crossing the bridge space
P4	Boat sensed on other side of bridge
P5	Light is green
P6	Light is yellow
P7	Yellow light timer
P8	Light is red
P9	Alarm is off
P10	Alarm is on
P11	Ground traffic is allowed
P12	On-bridge sensor determines no traffic on span
P13	On-bridge traffic has been cleared
P14	Span is down
P15	Span is up
P16	Barrier is up
P17	Barrier is down
P18	Message sent to lights — boat has arrived
P19	Message sent to alarm — boat has arrived
P20	Message sent to on-bridge traffic — barrier is down
P21	Message sent to boat — span is up
P22	Message sent to span — boat has gone
P23	Message sent to barrier — light is red
P24	Message sent to span — on-bridge traffic cleared
P25	Message sent to on-bridge traffic — span is back down
P26	Message sent to barrier — span is back down
P27	Message sent to alarm — span is back down
P28	Message sent to lights — barrier is back up
T1	Boat has been sensed
T2	Boat has reached the bridge
T3	Boat has been sensed on other side
T4	Light has turned to yellow
T5	Light has turned to red
T6	Light timer has advanced 1 second
T7	Light has turned to green
T8	Alarm has turned on
T9	Alarm has turned off
T10	Traffic on-bridge has cleared
T11	Traffic is allowed on-bridge again
T12	Span has raised
T13	Span has lowered
T14	Barrier has come down
T15	Barrier has gone up

light from green to yellow, P7 gets one dot. T5 cannot fire until P7 has at least four dots. However, T6 can fire. T6 removes one dot from P7 but places two dots back. Thus, each time T6 fires, the number of dots in P7 goes up by one. After the first firing, P7 has two dots, after the second, three dots, etc. Assuming T6 fires at 1-second intervals (see Section 5.5 for how this might be arranged), P7 has two dots after 1 second, three dots after 2 seconds, etc. After the third firing, that is, after 3 seconds, P7 has four dots. At this point, T6 cannot fire again until the dots are removed because P7 has reached its capacity. However, T5 is now enabled, and when it fires all the dots in P7 will be consumed. Thus the yellow light will stay on at least 3 seconds, after which the timer is reset and ready for another timing event.

Now consider the boat movement on the river, represented in Figure 5.7 by places P1–P4 and transitions T1–T3. See Table 5.3 for descriptions of these places and transitions. A boat traveling on the river at some point triggers a sensor in the bridge system (P1). At that point the boat is within range of the bridge, and the bridge should start to prepare for the boat to go under the span (T1). The boat is approaching the bridge (P2). The boat cannot go under the bridge until the span is up, and so transition T2 requires both that a boat is approaching and that the span has been raised. The latter is a condition determined by the span module. In Figure 5.7 it is represented by P21. P21 is a normal place in the net, but we have drawn it as a dotted circle to distinguish this communication between separate modules from the conditions (i.e., places) inside an individual module. (Note that it is necessary to represent this communication link by a place because the Petri Net model does not allow flow from a transition to another transition. This has a side benefit that the communication link is explicit in the graph.) When both conditions are true, the boat is allowed to go under the bridge (P3). When the sensor on the other side senses the boat (dot appears in P4), a signal should be passed to the span module that it is ok to lower the span (dot appears in P22). P22 is also shown as a dotted circle because it is a communication link between separate modules.

We model the span module with two places — span is down (normal situation, ground traffic can cross bridge — P14) and span is up (P15). We could have included two additional states — span is in the process of moving up or in the process of moving down. However, the graph is already complex, so we have chosen a simplified model for this example. When a boat arrives, the span has to go up, but it cannot go up immediately. Several other things have to happen first, and the span can only begin to go up after the ground traffic has cleared the bridge (P24). As noted in the preceding paragraph, the span module has to notify the boat module that the span has successfully been raised (P21). After the boat has passed to the other side (T3), the span can be lowered, and this must occur before other parts of the bridge can return to normal operation (the alarm turns off, the barriers go up, and the lights go back to green).

The light module (P5–P8) can begin the transition to yellow (T4) as soon as the boat has been detected. The transition to yellow also initiates the timer, as described in an earlier paragraph. When the timer reaches the limit, the lights transition to red

(T5). The transition back to green could be conditioned on either the boat reaching the other side or the barriers raised or both. We have chosen to make T7 depend only on the barriers being raised. (A design team might experiment with alternate enabling conditions and firing orders to determine the design that best fits their needs.)

The reader should be able to understand the remaining modules (alarm, barriers, and on-bridge traffic) and the communications between them.

Here is the sequence of transitions for the simple scenario — one boat successfully goes through.

- Initially the bridge is open to ground traffic. The light is green (P5), the alarm is off (P9), ground traffic is allowed (P11), the span is down (P14), and the barrier is up (P16). At this point, no transition is enabled.
- When the boat finally reaches the boat sensor, a dot appears in P1. Transition T1 is enabled. After it fires, the dot in P1 is removed, and a dot appears in P2 (boat is approaching the bridge). Dots also appear in P18 and P19, indicating that messages are being sent to the other modules.
- T4 and T8 are now enabled and can fire in either order or simultaneously.
  - After T8 fires, a dot appears in P10 (the alarm sounds).
  - After T4 fires, a dot appears in both P6 (the light turns yellow) and P7 (the timer starts).
- Only T6 is enabled (T5 requires four dots from P7, and T9 requires a dot from P27). T6 has to fire three times before P7 has four dots. At that point, T5 is blocked because of the capacity limit on P7, and T5 is enabled.
- When T5 fires it puts a dot in each of P8 (light turns red) and P23 (message sent to barrier module).
- Only T14 is enabled now. When it fires, it puts a dot in P17 (barrier goes down) and P20 (message sent to on-bridge traffic module).
- At this point no transitions are enabled. Nothing happens until a dot appears in P12 (on-bridge traffic sensor determines that there is no traffic on the span).
- When the dot appears in P12, T10 is enabled. T10 fires, putting dots in P13 (on-bridge traffic cleared) and P24 (message to span module).
- T12 is enabled. It fires, putting dots in P15 (span is up) and P21 (message to boat module).
- Now T2 is the only transition that is enabled. When it fires, a dot goes to P3 (boat can go under the bridge).
- No transitions are enabled until a dot appears in P4 (boat is sensed on the other side of the bridge). At that point only T3 is enabled. T3 fires putting a dot in P22 (message to span module).
- T13 is enabled and fires, putting dots in P25, P26, and P27. The span goes to the down state.
- Transitions T9, T11, and T15 are now all enabled and can fire in any order or concurrently.
  - When T9 fires the alarm goes off.

- When T11 fires the on-bridge module stops monitoring the sensor.
- When T15 fires the barrier goes up and a message is sent to the lights module (P28).

Note, as with P1 (boat has arrived), dots appear or disappear in P12 as the sensor detects traffic on the bridge or detects the absence of traffic on the bridge. That is, the presence or absence of a dot in P12 is governed by events outside the net.

- After the barrier goes up, T7 is enabled. When it fires, the light goes back to green.
- At this point the system is back to the initial state, and nothing will happen until another boat comes along.

Here is the formal definition of the bridge Petri Net of Figure 5.7:

```
PT = (P,T,F,K,W,M₀), where
P = {P1,P2,P3,P4,P5,P6,P7,P8,P9,P10,P11,P12,P13,P14,P15,P16,P17,P18,
P19,P20,P21,P22,P23,P24,P25,P26,P27,P28}
T = {T1,T2,T3,T4,T5,T6,T7,T8,T9,T10,T11,T12,T13,T14,T15}
F = {
(P1,T1),  (T1,P2),  (T1,P18),  (T1,P19),  (P2,T2),  (T2,P3),  (P3,T3),
(P4,T3),
(T3,P22), (P5,T4), (T4,P6), (T4,P7), (P6,T5), (P7,T5), (P7,T6), (T5,P8),
(T5,P23), (T6,P7), (P8,T7), (T7,P5), (P9,T8), (T8,P10), (P10,T9),
(T9,P9),
(P11,T10), (P12,T10), (T10,P13), (T10,P24), (P13,T11), (T11,P11),
(P14,T12), (T12,P15),
(T12,P21), (P15,T13), (T13,P14), (T13,P25), (T13,P26), (T13,P27),
(P16,T14), (T14,P17),
(T14,P20), (P17,T15), (T15,P16), (T15,P28), (P18,T4), (P19,T8),
(P20,T10), (P21,T2),
(P22,T13), (P23,T14), (P24,T12), (P25,T11), (P26,T15), (P27,T9),
(P28,T7)
}
K = {
(P1,1), (P2,1), (P3,1), (P4,1), (P5,3), (P6,1), (P7,4), (P8,1),
(P9,1), (P10,1), (P11,1), (P12,1), (P13,1), (P14,1), (P15,1), (P16,1),
(P17,1) ,(P18,1), (P19,1), (P20,1), (P21,1), (P22,1), (P23,1), (P24,1),
(P25,1), (P26,1), (P27,1), (P28,1)
}
W = {
((P1,T1),1),  ((T1,P2),1),  ((T1,P18),1),  ((T1,P19),1),  ((P2,T2),1),
((T2,P3),1),
((P3,T3),1),  ((P4,T3),1),  ((T3,P22),1),  ((P5,T4),1),  ((T4,P6),1),
((T4,P7),1),
```

```
((P6,T5),1),    ((P7,T5),4),   ((P7,T6),1),   ((T5,P8),1),   ((T5,P23),1),
((T6,P7),2),
((P8,T7),1),    ((T7,P5),1),   ((P9,T8),1),   ((T8,P10),1),  ((P10,T9),1),
((T9,P9),1),
((P11,T10),1),      ((P12,T10),1),      ((T10,P13),1),      ((T10,P24),1),
((P13,T11),1), ((T11,P11),1),
((P14,T12),1),      ((T12,P15),1),      ((T12,P21),1),      ((P15,T13),1),
((T13,P14),1), ((T13,P25),1),
((T13,P26),1),      ((T13,P27),1),      ((P16,T14),1),      ((T14,P17),1),
((T14,P20),1), ((P17,T15),1),
((T15,P16),1),      ((T15,P28),1),       ((P18,T4),1),       ((P19,T8),1),
((P20,T10),1), ((P21,T2),1),
((P22,T13),1),      ((P23,T14),1),      ((P24,T12),1),      ((P25,T11),1),
((P26,T15),1), ((P27,T9),1),
((P28,T7),1)
}
```

$M_0 = (0, 0, 0, 0, 1, 0, 0, 0, 1, 0, 1, 0, 0, 1, 0, 1, 0, 0, 0, 0, 0, 0, 0, 0, 0, 0, 0, 0)$

5.2.3 Comments

Recall, the basic, original Petri Net model[2] does not specify the order of firing when more than one transition is enabled. The original model, then, is nondeterministic. There is no requirement in the definitions that a transition that is enabled must actually fire; for example, cars may be present in both directions in Figure 5.1, and both cars simply wait without entering the intersection. Furthermore, there is no specification about which transition should fire when more than one is enabled; again, in Figure 5.1 if cars are present in both directions the Petri Net model does not specify which should go first. (Note, there may well be outside requirements that determine the firing order. For example, most states have laws that determine which cars have the right of way at an intersection. This is outside the representational power of basic Petri Nets.) In real-life systems it is possible that enabled transitions in different parts of a system actually fire at the same time; that is, transitions in different parts of the net represent real-life processes in different parts of the system that can occur concurrently. Only when two (or more) enabled transitions share places in their pre- and postsets are they potentially blocked. In such potentially conflicting situations, if the simultaneous firing of several transitions would make some place exceed its capacity or require more marks than are in an element of a preset, that simultaneous firing must be blocked. When analyzing a place/transition net that is modeling some system being designed, one of the jobs of the analysis team is to consider different orders of firing, including concurrent firings of nonconflicting transitions, to be sure that the nondeterminism introduced by the selection of firing orders does not introduce unwanted behavior in the system. The reachability graph, introduced in Section 5.3, is an important tool in aiding the study of such nondeterminism.

The capacity function K should represent the real capacity in the system. In the auto assembly line, for example, the station where the doors are assembled onto the car has a finite amount of storage and can therefore hold at most a fixed, finite number of doors; in other words, it has a maximum capacity. In computer systems with processes that communicate by message passing a place may represent a communication channel and the dots represent messages. The receiving process would have a queue to receive those messages. The queue might very well be declared with a fixed length. That is, the queue can hold a fixed, finite maximum number of messages. It is tempting, especially for novice modelers, to simply put ω for the capacity of all nodes. While the definition does allow ω, every attempt should be made to determine realistic values for capacities. For example, walkthroughs or simulations could help designers determine reasonable requirements for the performance of transitions (e.g., what is the maximum allowable time for a transition to complete) and then determine what is the real capacity needed for the places. Continuing the assembly line example, the storage area for doors (P2 in Figure 5.3) would be in the postset for a different transition, a transition that moves doors from a larger storage area (not shown in Figure 5.3) to the side of the assembly line. That large storage area would be in the postset of another transition that represented the manufacture of the doors, and so on. Other parts of the assembly line would have similar sets of places and transitions for their parts. By studying the whole net and estimating how fast various processes (i.e., transitions) such as producing doors and moving them from main storage to the assembly line, can be made, designers can estimate what capacities for the places are needed, whether or not bottlenecks will exist when tentative assignments to capacities are made, check different scenarios and different orders of firing transitions to see if any of these exceed the tentative capacities, and adjust these to make the entire assembly line proceed smoothly and as fast as possible.

5.3 Reachability

An important property of place/transition nets is reachability. Given a marking (i.e., a state of the net) M, the set of markings (or states) reachable from M includes M, of course, because when the net is in state M that state has already been reached. Any state M' that can be obtained by applying a transition that is enabled in M is also reachable from M and, in fact, reachable in one step. Similarly, a state M'' that is obtained by applying a transition enabled in M' is reachable from M in two steps. The set of reachable markings is defined to be the transitive closure of this process.

> **Definition 5.7** Let PT $=$ (P, T, F, K, W, M_0) be a place/transition net. Let M be a marking that is valid for PT, that is, $M(p) \leq K(p)$ for every p in P. The set of markings reachable from M in PT, denoted by reach(PT,M), is the smallest set of markings satisfying the following two conditions.

1. M ε reach(PT,M).

2. If M′ ε reach(PT,M), and M″ can be obtained from M' by firing a transition of PT that is enabled in M′, then M″ is also in reach(PT,M).

The set of markings reachable by PT is reach(PT,M_0). When PT is understood from the context, these are often abbreviated as reach(M) and reach(M_0).

Note that when K is bounded, that is, when no place p ε P has K(p) = ω, reach(PT,M_0) is finite, although in practice it could be very large. Note also that the condition "smallest set of markings" is necessary. Without that condition, one might conclude that the set, S, of all markings, is reachable, because it also satisfies both conditions 1 and 2. S satisfies condition 1 because it contains all markings, including M. S satisfies condition 2 because M″ would also be in S. But, of course, in practice, not all markings are reachable from M through a sequence of transitions. The condition that reach(PT,M) is the smallest set satisfying conditions 1 and 2 ensures that reach(PT,M) includes all the markings that are actually reachable from M and no others.

The set of reachable markings is in general smaller than the set of all possible orderings of transition firings. In particular, two transitions t1 and t2 whose presets do not intersect and whose postsets also do not intersect will satisfy the so-called diamond property — for any marking M that enables both t1 and t2, the marking obtained by firing t1 first followed by t2 is the same as the marking obtained by firing t2 first then t1. Pictorially, this is shown as a diamond-shaped diagram.

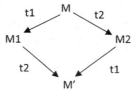

Author drawn.

reach(PT,M_0) is a set, so M′ is only included once, not twice. There are other situations in which the diamond property is satisfied, namely if all places in both presets have enough dots for both transitions, and all places in both postsets have enough capacity. In such cases t1 and t2 can operate in parallel, and the analysis of the reachability sets can help the design team discover such cases. Finally, note that reach(PT,M_0) can be explored by simulation. One could try to generate the entire set, although some cut-off point in the generation process would be needed to terminate the simulation in case reach(PT,M_0) actually was infinite.

We illustrate the reachability marking set and its corresponding reachability graph using the robot example from Figure 5.5. Note, for example, that the transition sequence T1, T2, T3, T4 leads to the same marking as the sequence T4, T1, T2, T3. This is an extended example of the diamond property. The marking at the end of these two sequences, (1,0,0,0,1,0,2,1,1), is included in the reachability graph and in the reachability set only once. There are a total of $2^8 * 4^1 = 1024$ possible markings

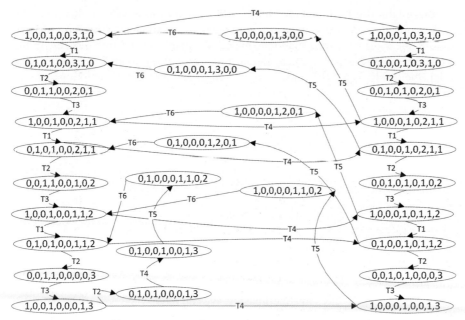

FIGURE 5.8 Reachability Graph for the Two Working Robots Example Above.

Author drawn.

(eight places that can have 0-1 tokens and one places that can have 0-3 tokens), but there are only 28 markings in the reachability set. The resulting reachability graph is shown in Figure 5.8.

From the reachability graph as well as from a careful analysis we can see potentially interesting properties of the possible transition orders. For example, R2 can wait until R1 fills in all three parts before starting to work on removing the parts. In the reachability graph this is indicated by the sequence of transitions T1 T2 T3 T1 T2 T3 T1 T2 T3. These are all transitions involving R1 and not R2. Similarly, R1 can wait until R2 removes all three parts before starting to fill in the slots. Obviously, this is not very efficient, and the design team would want to address this inefficiency in designing the final system.

Many interesting questions can be explored by studying the reachability set. For example, the design team can uncover potential inefficiencies in the operation, as indicated in the preceding paragraph. As another example, if the attempted generation of the entire reachability set does not terminate, it could be an indication of a serious problem with the design. One would not expect the set of distinct states of a real system to be infinite; the number of dots in at least one place would have to be continually increasing as the operation of the system continued. A net in which the number of dots in every place is bounded by a finite upper limit no matter what sequence of firings is followed is called bounded. In some cases boundedness can be proved formally. In other cases it must be explored through simulation.

One might also wish to know under what circumstances certain states can be reached or if there is a state that can't be reached. For example, in a net representing, say, a nuclear reactor, some markings may correspond to undesirable states. In the bridge example (Figure 5.7) there should never be a dot in both P3 (boat crossing under the bridge) and P5 (span down). If these undesirable markings are in reach(PT, M_0), then there is an error in the design that must be addressed. As another example, a robot assembly line simulation could show whether or not there is conflict for shared resources and under what circumstances conflict occurs. For example, it is easy to see potential conflict in the robot example — it is possible for one robot to be forced to wait if the other robot is occupying the staging area. In some cases that conflict can be removed or reduced by careful redesign of the system. In the robot example the motion of the robots and perhaps even the layout of the factory floor can be planned so that the time it takes for R1 to bring a part to the staging area is about the same as the time it takes for R2 to remove it to the dock. If the robots coordinate their starting times, then the staging area would always be empty when either robot approaches it.

The reachability graph can also help simplify the model, which might result in a more efficient process. In the two-robot working example, we know that the model is working correctly but has some inefficiency. We can modify the process by reducing the staging area to only one slot. This modification not only reduces the storage size but also increases the efficiency of the process. The two robots are forced to work in the common area alternately. This eliminates the two inefficiencies — R1 continues to move parts in while R2 just waits outside of the staging area doing no productive work and R2 continues to move parts out while R1 just waits. The reachability graph of the simplified process is shown in Figure 5.9.

Note that the reachability graph allows one to explore possible parallel processes. In the simplified two-robot working process, there are still possible parallel activities. When R1 is working in the staging area, R2 can move from the transportation

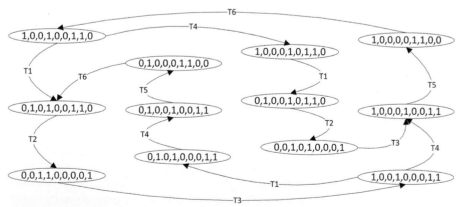

FIGURE 5.9 Reachability Graph for Simplified Two-Robot Working Process.

Author drawn.

zone to the staging area and vice versa. The reachability graph intuitively shows the parallel paths.

The study of reach(PT,M_0) might uncover a place p whose marking is always zero. In such a case, any transition containing p in its preset can never fire. Such a transition is called "dead." Again, this is an indication of problems in the design. Properties in which transitions can fire are called liveness properties.[1] There are four levels of liveness of general interest — each transition is enabled at least once, some or all transitions can fire arbitrarily often, some or all transitions can fire infinitely often, and some or all transitions must always fire. Study of the reachability graph can also verify other important properties that a Petri Net might have such as boundedness (there is a finite upper bound on the number of dots that appear in any place), conservativeness (the number of dots in the net is preserved for each firing), repetitiveness (a transition can always fire again), and others.

5.4 The incidence matrix associated with a place/transition network and proving properties

In this section we present the incidence matrix associated with a place/transition network and show how it can be used to study some formal properties of networks. For a more extensive treatment of formal properties, the reader is referred to texts such as Refs. [6, 7].

The Petri Net in Figure 5.10 is used to illustrate the concepts presented here. This net may be thought of as representing work flow. A dot in P1 means the process is

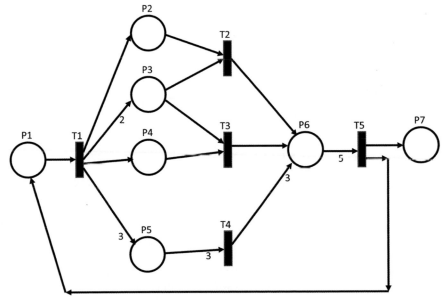

FIGURE 5.10 Sample Petri Net Representing Work Flow.

Author drawn.

ready to begin a new job. Transition T1 distributes two units of work to P3 and three units of work to P5. Place P3 should distribute the two units of work between transitions T2 and T3, and places P2 and P4 are controls that ensure this distribution. Place P6 collects dots representing finished subtasks. When all subtasks have been completed, transition T5 passes a dot representing a finished job to P7 and a dot to P1 indicating another cycle can begin. Place P7 accumulates a dot for each finished job.

5.4.1 The incidence matrix for a place/transition network

Information about the flow relation in a network can be conveniently represented as a matrix whose rows are indexed by the places and columns indexed by the transitions.

Definition 5.8 Let $PT = (P, T, F, K, W, M_0)$ be a place/transition network. The incidence matrix $N(P,T)$ associated with PT is defined as follows:

If $p \, \varepsilon \, P$ and $t \, \varepsilon \, T$, then

$\_w$, where w is the weight of flow element (p,t) and p is in PRE(t) but not in POST(t)

w, where w is the weight of flow element (t,p) and p is in POST(t) but not in PRE(t)

$N(p,t) =$

$w - w'$, where w is the weight of the flow element (t,p) and w' is the weight of the flow element (p,t) if p is in both PRE(t) and POST(t)

0 if there is no flow relation between p and t

Element $N(p,t)$ represents the net change in the number of dots in p if transition t fires. The incidence matrix for the network in Figure 5.10 is

$$
\begin{array}{c}
 & \begin{array}{ccccc} T_1 & T_2 & T_3 & T_4 & T_5 \end{array} \\
\begin{array}{c} P_1 \\ P_2 \\ P_3 \\ P_4 \\ P_5 \\ P_6 \\ P_7 \end{array} &
\left(
\begin{array}{ccccc}
-1 & 0 & 0 & 0 & 1 \\
1 & -1 & 0 & 0 & 0 \\
2 & -1 & -1 & 0 & 0 \\
1 & 0 & -1 & 0 & 0 \\
3 & 0 & 0 & -3 & 0 \\
0 & 1 & 1 & 3 & -5 \\
0 & 0 & 0 & 0 & 1
\end{array}
\right)
\end{array}
$$

The labels at the top and left are not part of the matrix; they are shown here only to emphasize the association of columns with transitions and rows with places. The first row, for example, indicates that place 1 loses one dot when T1 fires ($N(P1,T1) = -1$), gains one dot when T5 fires ($N(P1,T5) = 1$), and has no change when any of the other transitions fire.

5.4.2 Using the incidence matrix to study reachability

Recall, marking M' is reachable from marking M in a network if there exists a sequence of transitions t1, ..., t_n such that t1 is enabled in M and produces marking M_1, t2 is enabled in M_1 and produces M_2, ..., and tn is enabled in M_{n-1} and produces M'. That is,

$$M \rightarrow t1 \rightarrow M_1 \rightarrow t2 \ldots M_{n-1} \rightarrow tn \rightarrow M'$$

For example, in the network of Figure 5.10, the marking (0, 0, 0, 0, 3, 2, 1) is reachable from initial marking (1, 0, 0, 0, 0, 0, 0) via the transition sequence T1, T2, T3, T4, T5, T1, T2, T3. In this sequence T1, T2, and T3 are each used twice while T4 and T5 are each used once. The reader can easily verify reachability by simulating the sequence of transitions from the initial marking.

> **Definition 5.9** Let $PT = (P, T, F, K, W, M_0)$ be a place transition network, and let the number of transitions in T be n. Let $S = (t1, ..., tk)$ be a sequence of transitions, each ti a member of T. The count vector, C(S), for S is the sequence ($c1, c2, ..., cn$) where c1 is the number of occurrences of transition T1 in S, c2 is the number of occurrences of transition T2 in S, etc.

Let PT and S be as in Definitions 5.8 and 5.9. Let M and M' be two markings for PT. Let M(p) be the number of dots in M for place p, and similarly for $M'(p)$. A necessary, but not sufficient, condition for S to generate M' starting from M is that for each place p the sum of changes to the number of dots in p due to all the transitions in S is $M'(p) - M(p)$. For example, in the example in the paragraph preceding Definition 5.9, the number of dots in place P1 went from one to zero. Therefore the sequence mentioned in that paragraph must reduce the number of dots in P1 by one. That sequence used T1 twice for a dot reduction of two, T2 twice for no net change in dot count, T3 twice for no net change in dot count, T4 once for no net change in dot count, and T5 once for a net increase of one. Therefore the sequence would produce a total net change of dot count for place 1 of $-2 + 1 = -1$. The reader can verify that the sequence produces the required net change in dot count for places P2–P7 as well. Recall that N(p,t) is the net change to the dot count in place p when transition t fires. If S is a transition sequence and $C(S) = (c1, ..., cn)$ the count vector for S, then the net change in dot count for place p for the sequence S of transition firings is the sum of all the changes for all the firings in S, that is,

```
N(p,t1)*c1 + N(p,t2)*c2 + ... + N(p,tn)*cn,
```

that is, the vector product of row p of N(P,T) and $C(S)^T$, the transpose of C(S). Then,

$N(p1,t1)*c1 + N(p1,t2)*c2 + ... + N(p1,tn)*cn$ gives the net change in dot count for place p1,

$N(p2,t1)*c1 + N(p2,t2)*c2 + ... + N(p2,tn)*cn$ gives the net change in dot count for place p2,

and so on. Thus the matrix product $N(P,T) * C(S)^T$ produces a column vector giving the net change in dot count for all the places in P. M' is potentially reachable from M if the following condition holds:

$N(P,T) * C(S)^T = M'^T - M^T.$

For the example from the paragraph preceding Definition 5.9, $N(P,T)$, $C(S)^T$, M'^T, and M^T are as follows:

$$N(P,T): \begin{pmatrix} -1 & 0 & 0 & 0 & 1 \\ 1 & -1 & 0 & 0 & 0 \\ 2 & -1 & -1 & 0 & 0 \\ 1 & 0 & -1 & 0 & 0 \\ 3 & 0 & 0 & -3 & 0 \\ 0 & 1 & 1 & 3 & -5 \\ 0 & 0 & 0 & 0 & 1 \end{pmatrix}$$

$$C(S)^T : (2,2,2,1,1)^T$$

$$M'^T : (0,0,0,0,3,2,1)^T$$

$$M'^T : (1,0,0,0,0,0,0)^T$$

The reader can easily verify that $N(P,T)*C(S)^T$ and $M'^T - M^T$ are both $(-1, 0, 0, 0, 3, 2, 1)^T$. Thus M' is potentially reachable from M.

We can use the equation to determine if marking M' is potentially reachable from M. A necessary, but not sufficient, condition for this is that the set of linear equations given by

$$N(P,T) * U^T = M'^T - M^T,$$

where U is a vector of variables corresponding to the transitions in PT and has a nonnegative integer solution. If a sequence, S, of transitions that changes M to M' does exist, then as described in the preceding paragraph C(S) will be a solution to the equation. Conversely, if no solution exists, then M' cannot be reachable from M in the network. Note that the existence of a nonnegative integer solution does not prove reachability. It must still be determined that the transitions can be fired in some order the appropriate number of times; that is, there is some sequence t1, ..., tk such that each Ti from PT occurs the number of times indicated in the solution and at each step, the next ti is enabled.

Example 5.5

Is $(0, 0, 0, 0, 3, 2, 2)$ reachable from $(1, 0, 0, 0, 0, 0, 0)$ in the network given in Figure 5.10? The reader can verify that $(3, 3, 3, 2, 2)$ is a solution to $N(P,T) * U^T = M'^T - M^T$. So a sequence of transition firings may be possible. We must find a sequence that uses T1 three times, T2 three times, T3 three times, T4 twice, and T5 twice. Such a sequence is

  T1 T2 T3 T4 T5 T1 T2 T3 T4 T5 T1 T2 T3.

  Note, there are many satisfactory sequences, for example,

  T1 T3 T4 T2 T5 T1 T2 T3 T4 T5 T1 T2 T3

  and T1 T4 T3 T2 T5 T1 T2 T3 T4 T5 T1 T3 T2.

  Note also that not every sequence is feasible. For example, T2 is not enabled in the initial marking so no sequence starting with T2 can show reachability. It is important to examine all the possible sequences given by any solution to verify that at least one of them is feasible.

Example 5.6

Is $(0, 0, 0, 2, 3, 0, 0)$ reachable from $(1, 0, 0, 0, 0, 0, 0)$ in the network given in Figure 5.10? This would indicate place P3 had distributed both units of its work to T3. For this case, the vector $M'^T - M^T$ is $(-1, 0, 0, 2, 3, 0, 0)$. The set of linear equations is:

u5 − u1 = −1
u1 + u2 = 0
2*u1 − u2 − u3 = 0
u1 − u3 = 2
3*u1 − 3*u4 = 3
u2 + u3 + 3*u4 − 5*u5 = 0
u5 = 0

  The last equation asserts that u5 is 0. Then, the first equation forces u1 to be 1. Then, the second equation would require u2 to be −1, but negative counts are not allowed. Thus this system has no solution, and therefore $(0, 0, 0, 2, 3, 0, 0)$ is not reachable from $(1, 0, 0, 0, 0, 0, 0)$.

Example 5.7

This example illustrates that finding a solution to the equations is not sufficient to guarantee reachability. Consider the network in Figure 5.11 and the question is $M' = (1, 0, 6)$ reachable from $M = (1, 0, 0)$.

$$\begin{pmatrix} 0 & 0 \\ 0 & 0 \\ 4 & 2 \end{pmatrix}$$

$$N(P, T) \text{ is}$$

  and the difference between the beginning marking and the end marking is $(0, 0, 6)$. The transition count vector $(1, 1)$ is a solution to $N(P,T)*U = M'^T - M^T = (0, 0, 6)$. This solution would require one firing of each of T1 and T2, but T2 can never fire from initial marking $(1, 0, 0)$.

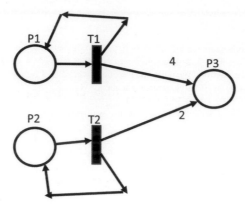

FIGURE 5.11 Petri Net for Example 5.7.

Author drawn.

5.4.3 **Place invariants and characteristic vectors**

There are many so-called structural properties, properties that depend only on the set of places, the set of transitions, and the flow, but not on any initial configuration. We describe one of these properties, place invariants, here. The reader is referred to Ref. [5] for a description of other structural properties and a more detailed discussion of their significance.

It is often important to know which sets of places in a network that the sum of all the dots in those places is preserved for all transitions. For example, if the dots represented the amount of work, then a set of places where the number of dots was always the same is a set in which the total amount of work never changes, indicating a balance between work consumed and produced by the transitions. For example, if dots accumulated in one of the places P1—P6 in Figure 5.10, it would mean work was building up at that place and not being processed fast enough; that place would be a bottleneck. On the other hand, we expect the number of dots in P7 to change, continually increasing to represent the accumulating output of the system.

> **Definition 5.10** Let PT $= (P, T, F, K, W, M0)$ be a place transition network. Let N(P,T) be the incidence matrix for PT. Let EQ be the set of linear equations obtained from the equation $N(P,T)^T * u^T = 0$, where u is a vector of variables $(u_1, \ldots, u_n)$ with n the number of places in P. A nonempty subset I of P is a place invariant subset if there is a solution V(I) to EQ satisfying the following three conditions:
>
> **(1)** The elements of V(I) are nonnegative integers.
> **(2)** The elements of V(I) corresponding to places in I are nonzero.
> **(3)** The elements of V(I) corresponding to places not in I are zero.

Solutions, if they exist, will not be unique. Because the equations are linear and the right-hand sides are all zero, any integer scalar multiple of a solution V(I) will also be a solution, and if V'(I) is another vector satisfying the equations, then

V(I) + V′(I) will also satisfy them. For the network in Figure 5.10, I = {P1, P2, P3, P4, P5, P6} is a place invariant subset and has associated vectors (10, 1, 1, 1, 2, 2, 0) and (15, 1, 2, 1, 3, 3, 0), among others.

Each vector associated with place invariant I indicates a linear relationship between the dot counts in the places in I and its reachable markings. We illustrate this with the Petri Net and initial marking is shown in Figure 5.12.

The incidence matrix for the net in Figure 5.12 is

$$N(P, T) = \begin{pmatrix} -1 & 1 \\ -1 & 1 \\ 1 & -1 \end{pmatrix}$$

The vector u = (1, 1, 2) is a solution to $N(P,T)^T * u^T = 0$. Therefore I = (P1, P2, P3) is a place invariant. If M = (m1, m2, m3) is an original marking and M′ = (m1′, m2′, m3′) any marking reachable from M, then

$$m1 + m2 + 2*m3 = m1' + m2' + 2*m3'.$$

For example, from marking M = (3, 2, 0), as shown above, M1 = (2, 1, 1) is reachable by one firing of transition T1. We can see that 3 + 2 + 2*0 = 2 + 1 + 2*1. M2 = (1, 0, 2) is reachable by a second firing of T1. Again, 3 + 2 + 2*0 = 1 + 0 + 2*2. The reader can easily verify that the equation holds for any marking reachable from M.

Place invariants often have useful interpretations in real-world applications. In the above example suppose P1 represents software engineers and P2 represents hardware engineers working for a company. When a product comes in for repair, one software engineer and one hardware engineer are assigned to fix it. That corresponds to T1 firing, and a dot in P3 represents the pair of engineers working on

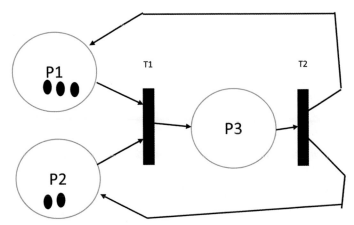

FIGURE 5.12 Petri Net With an Invariant.

Author drawn.

the repair. Each dot in P3 represents two different engineers. Thus, although after the first firing of T1, the total number of dots in the graph decreased from five to four, the total number of people working for the company remains the same. This is reflected in the linear expression because the weight assigned to the third element is two.

Of special interest are invariant subsets whose corresponding vectors have only 1s in the positions of the places in the subset. In this case the vector is called a characteristic vector. If I has a characteristic vector, then the total number of dots in all the places in I never changes from the original marking. The reader can easily verify that the network above does not have a characteristic vector and therefore does not have any such special place invariants. However, the network of Figure 5.5 does have characteristic vectors (see Problem 15). In particular, the invariant subset {P7, P9} has a characteristic vector. This means that the total number of dots in these two places is always the same as in the original marking, namely three. Thus, as indicated in the paragraph preceding Figure 5.5, the number of storage slots plus the number of parts on the loading dock is always three, and neither of those counts is ever less than zero or greater than three.

There are other kinds of invariants. In particular, a similar concept is applied to transitions and transition invariants. See Ref. [5] for details. We note that many of the properties of interest, such as number of dots not changing, can be easily studied by the eye in small networks, such as the sample networks presented here. However, such study would be difficult in the larger networks that occur in real-world problems. Algorithms based on the incidence matrix and invariants are the only feasible approach for determining whether the network has the desired properties.

5.5 Predicate/transition Petri Nets and colored Petri Nets

5.5.1 A brief review of the evolution of predicate/transition and colored Petri Nets

As we presented in this chapter, Petri Nets started with condition/event nets with places, events, and flows. Places were restricted to contain only zero or one token representing the absence or existence of that particular condition. When place/transition nets evolved, a place could contain any number of tokens. This development allowed the net to represent multiple individuals in a place, but the individual tokens were indistinguishable. Unfortunately,

> "Petri nets (in their basic form) do not scale to large systems unless the system is modeled at a very high level of abstraction."[8]

Research on Petri Net modeling for more complex systems continued. Jensen and Kristensen[8] point out:

> "The first successful step toward a common more powerful class of Petri nets was taken by Genrich and Lautenbach in 1979 with the introduction of predicate/transition, or PrT, nets."

In Genrich and Lautenbach[9] the tokens in a place in a PrT net can be individuals with distinct identities, transitions can have firing conditions labeled as true/false expressions, and flows are labeled with variables or expressions with variables that can be replaced by specific individuals. As noted in Ref. [8],

> *"The basic idea behind PrT nets was to introduce a set of colored tokens that can be distinguished from one another."*

This extension allows modeling a complex system with a relatively simple Petri Net and with scalability. Jensen and many others continued to develop the idea of "colored" Petri Nets by using programming language concepts (basic data types, records, lists, enumerations, etc.) to define the color sets. The advantages of using data types to define tokens are: (1) tokens can have structure and hence be more powerful; (2) type checking can be applied to the model using data types; and (3) well-known programming syntax and semantics can be used to define the expression guards on flows and transitions.[8]

There has been much research in the area of colored Petri Nets. Some illustrated the idea by applying it to system modeling,[10] some focused on the scalability of colored Petri Nets using application examples,[11] and some created colored Petri Net systems by formal definitions of its components.[12]

5.5.2 **An example**

We present a new model for the TDMA protocol from Example 5.3 in Section 5.2.2. As one can easily see, this model is simpler and scalable as N can be scaled to any integer number. The data types and expressions on the labels conform with commonly known programming language syntax and semantics. This new model of TDMA illustrates the scalability and programmability of colored Petri Net as we pointed out in Section 5.5.1. Figure 5.13 is the Colored Predicate/Transition Petri Net model for TDMA protocol, Table 5.4 list all place, transitions, and flows and their meanings of the model presented in Figure 5.13, and Figure 5.14 defines Token data type, Global Variables, and Defined constants for the model presented in Figure 5.13.

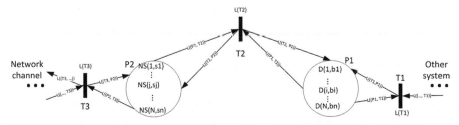

FIGURE 5.13 The TDMA Protocol Modeled by a Colored Predicate/Transition Petri Net.

Author drawn.

Table 5.4 Place/transition list for the Petri Net in Figure 5.13.

Elements	Name	Description	Label	Notes
Places	P1	Contains N tokens representing N devices connected to the network represented by array D.		
	P2	Contains N network slices in a network frame represented by array NS.		
Transitions	T1	Represents a message being sent to a device in P1. The message contains a destination ID (Did) and message size. The condition for T1 to fire is that Did matches the device id of the object selected from P1.	aMS.Did == D[k].Did	The source of the message is not shown in the model. Assume the device buffer size has no limit.
	T2	Represents the corresponding device using the network slice. The condition for T3 to fire is the device ID equals the slice ID. After T3 fires the slice status will be changed from "n" (not used) to "u" (used).	i == j	After T2 fires the number of bytes in the device buffer is reduced by the slice size (ssz) or to 0.
	T3	Represents the termination of the current network frame and the creation of a new frame. It can only fire after all N slices have been used, that is, when count exceeds N.	count > N	
Flows	(..., T1)	The message token on this flow represents	aMS	"..." means the source of the information is not

Table 5.4 Place/transition list for the Petri Net in Figure 5.13.—*cont'd*

Elements	Name	Description	Label	Notes
		information coming into a device.		represented in the example.
	(P1, T1)	The device token on this flow represents the device receiving or creating the information.	D[k]	
	(T1, P1)	The device token on this flow is the device that received/ created the new information. The device buffer content size will be increased by the message size.	D[k]ˆ D[k].csz = D [k].csz + aMS.msz	
	(P1, T2)	The device token on this flow is the device using the network slice.	D[i]	
	(T2, P1)	The device token on this flow is the device that just used the slice. The buffer content size of the device is reduced to either 0 or original size − ssz (network slice size).	D[i]ˆ D[i] = max(0,D [i].csz-ssz)	
	(P2, T2)	The slice token on this flow is the slice before being written to by the device. The slice status must be "n."	count == jˆ NS[j].Ns == "n"	The slice status will be "n," indicating that the slice has not been used yet in this frame.
	(T2, P2)	The slice token on this flow is the slice after being written to by the device. The status is changed to "u," for used. The variable count increases by 1 for the next network slice.	NS[j].Ns == "u" ˆcount++	
	(P2, T3)	The token on this flow is the array of slices.	NS	T3 only fires after all slices have been used (count > N).

Continued

Table 5.4 Place/transition list for the Petri Net in Figure 5.13.—*cont'd*

Elements	Name	Description	Label	Notes
				The array is removed from P2 in preparation for receiving a new set of slices for the next frame.
	(..., T3)	The TDMA protocol creates a new set of slices (among other things) with all status members "n" for "not used."	NS' $\wedge$ NS'[j].Ns = "n" for j = 1,...,N	
	(T3, ...)	The slices in the used frame are sent out to other parts of the system.	NS	It is possible other devices may just be listening to the bus but not writing to it. The label on this flow acknowledges the possibility that those listening devices may now do something with the information that was written during the just-completed frame.
	(T3, P2)	The new set of slices with all having state "n" is passed into P2. Variable count is reset to 1.	NS' $\wedge$ NS'[j].Ns = "n" for j = 1,...,N	

5.6 Petri Nets with time

One of the most important extensions to the original Petri Net concept is the introduction of time into the model. The real-world actions represented by transitions take real time. For example, transition T1 of Figure 5.5 (R1 walks to the staging area) does not happen instantaneously. It takes time for the robot to walk to the staging area. Moreover, the amount of time can vary over a range depending on other conditions in the area; for example, an obstacle could move into the path causing the robot to stop for a few seconds. Time can also be associated with a place, in which case the time or time range represents another condition on when transitions

Token Data Types:	Global Variables and Defined Constants:

Struct MS {
    Did;   /destination device ID
    msz;   /message size in bytes
}; /message sent to device from other systems
	const N; / number of devices
	                      /(also number of slices
	                      /in a network frame)
	const ssz; /size of one slice

Struct DV {
    Id;   /device id
    csz;   /device buffer size in bytes
}; /device assigned to a TDMA slice
	int count; /slot usage counter;
	
	Struct MS aMS; / one message

Struct NS {
    Nid;   /network frame slice ID;
    Ns;   /network slice status
}; / network slice in a frame
	Struct DV D[N]; / the devices
	                            / that are assigned
	                            /a network slice
	Struct NS NS[N]; / the network slices
	                            / in a network frame

FIGURE 5.14 Data Types, Constants, and Global Variables for the Petri Net in Figure 5.13.

Author drawn.

can fire. For example, suppose in Figure 5.5 the two robots were sharing a moving conveyor belt on an assembly line instead of a staging area. After R1 places a part on the conveyor belt (T2), R2 must act on the part (remove it, assemble it with another part, etc.) before it moves out of R2's work area. The part may have to move from where R1 drops it to within the range of R2's arm; thus there will be a minimum time before R2 can work on the part. On the other hand, if R2 waits too long, the part will have moved past R2's reach; thus there is a maximum amount of time after which the transition associated with R2 acting on that part can no longer fire. Thus a time range can be associated with the place and represent a range of times during which preconditions represented by that place can enable firing. Time ranges could even be associated with individual tokens representing individual parts in case there could be several parts on the conveyor belt. There have been a variety of extensions to the basic Petri Net model to represent the different aspects of time in real-world processes. See Ref. [3] for a survey.

The introduction of time allows several modifications and extensions to the operational semantics of the Petri Net model. In the original model there was no specification about which of several enabled transitions should fire or even whether any enabled transition should fire at all. A key concept was the reachability graph. What markings are reachable no matter what the order of firings? However, system designers often specify the order of firings so that the system displays more deterministic behavior and can be guaranteed to meet the requirements of the application or avoid bad markings. For example, in the preceding paragraph robot R2 should take care of the oldest part that is on the conveyor belt in its operational range, that is, the part that is furthest along and will pass out of range the soonest. As another example, if two transitions were enabled but one had duration time longer than the other, the one with the longest duration might be given priority so that the total time to complete all operations (i.e., all transitions) could be minimized. Or, the transition with the earliest expiration might be given the highest priority. Prioritizing based on time does not eliminate nondeterminism, but it does reduce the branching rate in the reachability graph and allows at least a rudimentary analysis of the timing behavior of the system being modeled.

We briefly describe two time-based extensions — the timed Petri Net introduced by Ramachandran[13] and the time Petri Net introduced by Merlin and Faber[14] — to illustrate the kinds of modifications to definitions and semantics that go along with the introduction of time.

Definition 5.11 A timed Petri Net is a seven-tuple (P, T, F, K, W, M_0, f), where (P, T, F, K, W, M_0) is a Petri Net
and $f{:}T \rightarrow R^+$ is a function mapping transitions to positive real numbers.

The function f is used to order transitions and to force transitions to occur. When a transition t becomes newly enabled, the value $f(t)$ is associated with t. This value represents the maximum amount of time before t must fire after it becomes enabled. As time progresses, this maximum firing time decreases (until zero). At any moment in the operation of the net, an enabled transition with the smallest associated time must be selected for firing. Thus f acts like a priority function, giving higher priority to those transitions that have lower f values. Note, there may be several enabled transitions with the same minimal value, leading to nondeterminism. These remarks lead to the following definitions.

Definition 5.12 A clock state is a pair (M, V), where
M is a marking
and $V{:}enabled(M) \rightarrow R^+$.

$V(t)$ is the amount of time left before t must fire. Note that V is defined only for the transitions that are enabled in the current marking; transitions that are not enabled in M have no associated time.

Definition 5.13 Let M be a marking. Let t be a transition that is enabled in M. Let M′ be the marking after t fires. Then a transition t′ is newly enabled after t if

t′ was not enabled in M but is enabled in M′

or t′ is t and t is enabled in M′.

The first condition covers the case that after transition t fires, another transition t′ is enabled. The second condition covers that case that t itself is enabled again after t firing — that is t′ = t. This would not be covered by the first condition because t has to be enabled in M in order to fire. Transitions that are newly enabled have their associated times set to their f value; transitions that were enabled in M (other than t) have their associated times simply continue counting down. This leads to the following definition.

Definition 5.14 Let (M, V) be a clock state, and let t be the transition that fires. Let M′ be the new marking after t fires. The new clock state is (M′, V′), where

V′(t) = f(t) if t is newly enabled (a)

V′(t) = V(t) − τ if t is enabled but not newly enabled. τ is the time elapsed since the previous transition firing (b)

The model proposed by Ramachandran[13] imposes an ordering on the firings. At any given time in the operation of the net, if t is enabled and selected for firing in clock state (M, V), then

$$V(t) \leq V(t')$$

for all enabled transitions t′. That is, t must have minimal associated time in (M, V). As noted, there may be more than one transition with minimal associated clock time, so this model still has nondeterminism. This is an example of a "strong" firing semantics. Other models relax or remove this condition, in which case they are said to have "weak" firing semantics.

Merlin and Faber[14] introduced the "time Petri Net" model in which the function f from Definition 5.11 produces a time range [eft, lft], where eft is the "earliest firing time" and lft is the "latest firing time." The general behavior is otherwise the same as that of timed Petri Nets. In particular, when a transition is newly enabled, its time range is reset, as in Definition 5.14 part (a). Time ranges count down as time progresses, as in part (b) of Definition 5.14. The new restriction is that a transition cannot fire until it's eft has counted down to 0. Figure 5.15 shows a time Petri Net. The time range [1, 2] (respectively [2, 3]) is the reset value assigned when T1 (respectively T2) becomes enabled. The operation of this Petri Net is illustrated later in this section after the introduction of discrete event simulation (DES).

Various notations have been introduced in the literature to distinguish the passage of time between transition firings. Typically, an arrow is used with a notation above the arrow. If the notation is a number, then the arrow represents the passage of time; if it is the name of a transition, it represents a firing. For example,

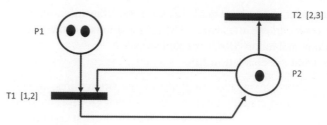

FIGURE 5.15 A Time Petri Net.

Author drawn.

$$(1)\ (M,\ V)\ \xrightarrow{1.5}\ (M',\ V')$$

$$\text{and}\ (2)\ (M,\ V)\ \xrightarrow{t}\ (M',\ V')$$

Notation (1) represents the passage of 1.5 units of time. In this case V′ is derived from V by simply subtracting 1.5 from all the times associated with enabled transitions and replacing negative values with zero. Notation (2) represents the firing of transition t. In this case V′ is derived from V according to Definition 5.14.

Time and timed Petri Nets can be tested by simulation using DES. A DES consists of pairs of sequences

```
S0 S1 ...
and t0 t1 ...
```

where each S_i is a firing of an enabled transition, called an event, and the {ti} form a monotonically increasing sequence of times. The simulation proceeds from an initial marking of the net by firing in sequence the transition specified by Si at time ti. That is, transition S0 is fired at t0, then transition S1 is fired at t1, etc. Of course, the pair of sequences must specify an acceptable sequence of events and times. That is, at time ti the transition Si must be enabled in the current marking. The behavior of the net can be studied by simulating it on different discrete event sequences. (DES is discussed in more detail in Chapter 8.)

We illustrate the operation of the time Petri Net with the simple example shown in Figure 5.15. One possible event sequence is

```
T1 T1 T2
1.5 2.7 2.9
```

The initial marking as shown in the net diagram is (2, 1) − place P1 has two tokens, and place P2 has one token. The initial clock state assigns the time range [1, 2] to T1 and [2, 3] to T2. Assuming the clock starts at zero, time proceeds in the simulation until time 1.5. During that period the time ranges associated with T1 and T2 simply count down. Thus, at the point when the first event happens, the associated time ranges are [0, 0.5] and [0.5, 1.5]. Note that the eft for T1 stopped decrementing when it reached zero. Also, note that T1 does not have to fire when its eft reaches zero. At this point in this particular event sequence, T1 fires. The new marking is (1, 1). Place P1 used one of its tokens; place P2 used its token but got a token back. Transition T1 is newly enabled, or more precisely reenabled, so its time range gets reset to [1, 2]. Transition T2 was enabled before, so its time range is not reset and remains at [0.5, 1.5]. Time continues until 2.7, that is, until another 1.2 time units have passed. Transition T1 is enabled because places P1 and P2 both have at least one token. The time range of T1 has been reduced to [0, 0.8], and the time range for T2 to [0, 0.3]. After the second firing of T1, the marking is (0, 1). Transition T1 is no longer enabled, so it no longer has an associated time range. The time range of T2 remains at [0, 0.3]. The third event occurs at time 2.9, or after an additional 0.2 time units. At that time the range associated with T2 has been reduced to [0, 0.1]. Transition T2 is enabled in the marking (0, 1), and the current time is still less than the latest firing time. So, T2 can fire. After it fires, the new marking is (0, 0). Neither transition is enabled, so neither one has an associated time range.

5.7 Summary

The modules in an embedded system operate in parallel and often use the same set of resources. In this chapter we introduced a powerful and dynamic modeling tool, the Petri Net, that is especially useful for modeling parallel and distributed systems. We introduced two major forms of Petri Net: Condition/Event and Place/Transition Petri Nets. Condition/Event Petri Nets model situations in which conditions must be true before an event can occur. Place/Transition Petri Nets model situations in which varying amounts of different resources must be present as well as some conditions be true before an event can occur. We introduced the important concept of reachability and illustrated how reachability can help designers better understand a particular Petri Net and uncover design flaws. We described the incidence matrix and discussed some of the properties, such as reachability, the incidence matrix can help determine. We mentioned some extensions to the basic Petri Net model. Finally, we discussed two ways that time can be incorporated into the Petri Net model. Through examples we illustrated ways that Petri Net models can help in the development and understanding of product designs.

Problems

1. Prove that in Figure 5.1 two cars can never occupy the intersection at the same time.
2. In Example 5.1 it was assumed that all four doors were the same. Draw a new place-transition net under the assumption that there are four different kinds of doors — left front, right front, left rear, and right rear.

3. Generate the first 10 markings for the Petri Net shown in Figure 5.5 with the initial marking as shown in that figure under the following protocols for choice of next transition.
   a) At any point if two transitions are enabled, the transition involving robot 1 is selected.
   b) At any point if two transitions are enabled, the transition involving robot 2 is selected.
   c) The two robots alternate transitions unless one of them is blocked.

4. Generate the first ten reachable markings for the Petri Net shown in Figure 5.5 with the initial marking shown in that figure assuming that at any point when two transitions are enabled they both fire simultaneously. Compare the results of this problem with those of the previous problem.

5. Consider the format for a Petri Net for the TDMA protocol, as shown in Figure 5.6.
   a) Draw a complete Petri Net for the TDMA example for four devices on the network. Recall that in the initial marking all places DiE have a dot. Suppose also that devices 2 and 3 have data ready to send but that devices 1 and 4 do not.
   b) Generate the reachable markings for the operation of this Petri Net for the first two frames. Assume that during the second frame, devices 1 and 3 have data ready to send but devices 2 and 4 do not.
   c) Prove that no marking with dots in both DiE and DiF is reachable from an initial marking in which all DiE have dots and no DiF has a dot. Hint: Prove this by induction on the number of frames. In the induction step, there are two cases — either DiE has a dot and DiF does not or DiF has a dot and DiE does not.

6. Write the formal definition of the place-transition net shown in Figure 5.3.

7. Write the formal definition of the place-transition net shown in Figure 5.5.

8. Describe in words how you would add the following features to the bridge example in Figure 5.7. Then draw the places and transitions that would have to be added and indicate how your graph would be incorporated into Figure 5.7.
   a) If the barrier does not go down within 10 seconds of being notified that the light is red, it is an error situation.
   b) The span does not move up and down instantaneously. There should be a state in which the span is moving up and a state in which the span is moving down.

9. A transportation company operates trains that run from east to west and from west to east. Most of the system has parallel tracks, one track in each direction. Eastbound and westbound trains can pass through those areas simultaneously. However, one section has just a single track. Only one train can pass this area at a time. If one train is already on this section of track, other trains must wait until the existing train has reached the other end and the single track is empty again. The following picture illustrates this situation with the single track empty, two trains waiting at the west end, and one train waiting at the east end.

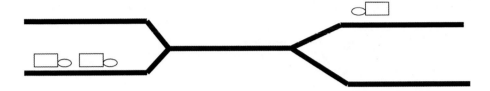

    a) Draw a Petri Net to model how the trains share the common track. Show the initial markings assuming that two trains are waiting at the west end and one is waiting at the east end. Describe in words the meaning of your places and transitions.

    b) Write the formal definition of your Petri Net, including the above initial markings.

    c) Draw the reachability graph assuming no additional trains appear.

10. A manufacturing plant has two physically separate buildings. There is a wireless data link between the two buildings. The link can handle up to four messages at a time, for example, two messages in each direction or one message from building A to building B and three messages in the opposite direction.

    a) Draw a Petri Net to model the use of these two channels. Describe in words each place and transition in your diagram. Assume Building A has two messages waiting to be transmitted initially. Show the initial marking for this situation.

    b) Write the formal definition of your Petri Net, including the above initial marking.

11. One section of an automated assembly line in an auto factory has two robots that cooperate to assemble four parts into a single unit. The first robot is mobile and retrieves the parts in order P1, P2, P3, and P4 from various storage areas near the working table. The second robot is stationary and assembles parts that robot 1 brings to the table. When parts P1 and P2 are present the second robot can put them together. Robot 1 cannot place P3 on the table until after P1 and P2 have been assembled. After P3 has been assembled into the unit, robot 1 can place P4 on the table. Finally, when P4 is present robot 2 adds it to the unit and places the assembled unit on a conveyer belt. At this point robot 1 can begin collecting parts again. Robot 1 can retrieve the four parts as quickly as it can move, but it waits before retrieving parts for the next unit until the first unit is completed so that the working space does not become cluttered.

    a) Draw a Petri Net that models the described behavior. Describe in words the meaning of the places and transitions.

    b) Define your Petri Net formally.

12. Consider the following graph of a place/transition Petri Net.

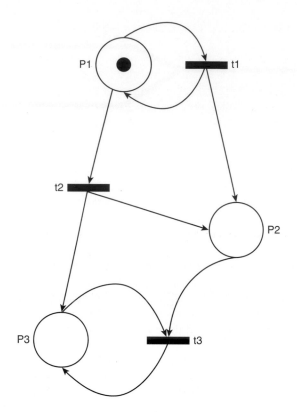

a) Write the formal definition of this net. Make plausible assumptions about the capacities.

b) Given your definition in part a), is the reachability graph given the initial marking shown finite or not? Justify your answer.

c) Suppose the capacity of P2 was 3. Draw the reachability graph under this assumption.

13. Consider the following formal definition of a place-transition Petri Net.

$N = (P, T, F, K, W, M_0)$

where

$C = \{P1, P2, P3, P4\}$

$E = \{T1, T2\}$

$F = \{(P1,T1), (T1,P2), (T1,P3), (P2,T2), (P3,T2), (T2,P1), (T2,P4)\}$

$K = (1, 1, 1, \omega)$

$W = (1, 1, 1, 1, 1, 1, 1)$

$M_0 = (1, 0, 0, 0)$

a) Draw the graphical representation of this Petri Net.

b) Prove that the capacities for P1, P2, and P3 are sufficient for any sequence of firings starting from M0.

c) Prove that starting from the initial marking the number of dots in P4 can grow infinitely large.

14. Determine that the network in Figure 5.10 does not have any place invariant whose vector has only zeros and ones. (Hint: There are two ways to approach this problem. There are only seven places, so in principle one could try all subsets of P. A better approach is to examine the equations derived from $N(P,T)^T * (a1, a2, a3, a4, a5, a6, a7)^T = (0, ..., 0)^T$ and solve for the ai variables.)

15. Write the incidence matrix for the network in Figure 5.5. Then find all the place invariants and their characteristic vectors.

16. Recall Example 5.1 — the assembly of doors into a car. Draw a colored PrT Petri Net to model the distinction between four different kinds of doors (left front, right front, left rear, and right rear) and two different kinds of cars (two-door and four-door). Specify all the data types and data structures you use in your Petri Net.

References

[1] Wikipedia, Petri Net, Petri Net — Wikipedia [Online] Apr 25, 2017, [Cited: Oct 08, 2017], https://en.wikipedia.org/wiki/Petri_net.

[2] P. Carl Adam, R. Wolfgang, Petri net, Scholapedia 3 (4) (2008) 6477.

[3] A. Cerone, Maggiolo-Schettini, A Time-Based Expressivity of Time Petri Nets, Theor. Comput. Sci. 216 (1) (1999) 1—53.

[4] S. Lafortune, C.G. Cassandras, Introduction to Discrete Event Systems, second ed., Springer, 2008.

[5] A. Zimmermann, 5 Simple Petri Net. Stochastic Discrete Event System Modeling, Evaluation, Applications, Springer, 2008.

[6] W. Reisig, Understanding Petri Nets: Modeling Techniques, Analysis Methods, Case Studies, Springer, 2016, ISBN: 9783662523070.

[7] M. Diaz (Ed.), Petri Nets: Fundamental Models, Verification, and Applications, Wiley, 2009, ISBN 9781848210790.

[8] K. Jensen, L.M. Kristensen, Colored petri nets: a graphical language for formal modeling and validation of concurrent systems, Commun. ACM 58 (July 2015) 61—70.

[9] H.J. Genrich, K. Lautenbach, System modelling with high-level petri Nets, Theor. Comput. Sci. 13 (1981).

[10] V. Gehlot, C. Nigro, An Introduction to Systems Modeling and Simulation with Colored Petri Nets, IEEE, Proceedings of the 2010 Winter Simulation Conference, 2010, pp. 104—118.

[11] J.L. Peterson, A Note on Colored Petri Nets, TR-136, Feb. 1980.

[12] A. Camurri, A. Coglio, Simple Colored Petri Nets, Nov 1997. Technical Report, Viale Causa 13 16145 Genova, Italy.

[13] C. Ramchandani, Analysis of Asynchronous Concurrent Systems by Timed Petri Nets, PhD Thesis, MIT, 1973.

[14] P. Merlin, D. Faber, Recoverability on communication protocols — implications of a theoretical study, IEEE Trans. Commun. 4 (9) (1976) 1036—1043.

Building robust, safe, and correct systems

2

Products should, to the extent possible, not harm people or the environment. Safety should be a primary consideration from the very beginning of the product design process. The behavioral modeling stage should consider how the product behaves when things go wrong, such as a user doing something wrong or a component fails, so that this can be accounted for when the design team moves to internal modeling. Can the product be designed in such a way that when bad things happen, the product can continue to provide at least some services or shut down in a way that causes minimal harm or damage?

How can the design team be sure that the product that is eventually built will do exactly what was originally intended, that is, will perform correctly? There are design techniques that can help ensure correctness, methods that can be applied to the designs to attempt to prove correctness, and methods for designing rich test cases that can uncover design and implementation errors or convince people that such errors don't exist.

This part includes guidelines for these issues.

Designing systems that are safe and robust

6

6.1 Introduction

Consideration of safety (not harming people or damaging property) and robustness (the ability to continue providing at least some level of service despite failures in some components or improper input from actors — also called fault tolerance) should be an integral part of every step in the modeling process, from early behavioral modeling to internal modeling. Embedded systems typically run continuously. Some failures may just be inconvenient. Other failures can be disastrous, for example, in the control system in an airplane or in a patient monitoring system for a critically ill patient. Classic fixes that may be acceptable in some applications, such as turning a PC that has frozen off and then on again, cannot be tolerated in many embedded systems.

Safety and robustness should be designed at every step of the modeling process, from the earliest behavioral modeling through the various internal operation modeling steps. Waiting until the system has been designed and then attempting to tack on safety and robustness is not a good approach. The earlier design steps may have imposed choices that preclude adequate safety and robustness or at least make it difficult. Behavioral modeling should include use cases and scenarios in which portions of the system fail, for example, a scenario in the bridge project in which the ground barriers fail to go down or the spans only go part way up. Finite state machine (FSM), specification and description language (SDL), and Petri models should then include corresponding states that handle the failure scenarios from the behavioral model.

There is a rich literature regarding safety and fault tolerance in a variety of fields, such as software, circuit design, computer networks, and many others (see, e.g., Refs. [1–6]). Many of the concepts and methods in those fields can be adapted to general embedded system modeling. In this chapter we present some of the major concepts and ideas.

6.2 Definitions

In this section we present definitions for the most commonly encountered terms relating to safety and reliability.

Embedded System Design. https://doi.org/10.1016/B978-0-443-18470-3.00006-3

6.2.1 Service, failure, errors, and faults

Definition 6.1 The **service** provided by a system is the behavior of the system as observed by external entities, typically the users of the system. The service is **correct** if it exactly matches the behavior intended by the designers of the system.

Definition 6.2 A **service failure**, or just **failure**, is a deviation from correct service.

Definition 6.3 An **error** occurs when an internal state of the system is different than what the designers expected it to be.

Definition 6.4 A **fault** is the cause of an error.

The distinction between failure, error, and fault allows engineers and other stakeholders to focus on different aspects of a problem that may arise during the operation of the system. For example, when a boat approaches the bridge, the ground barriers may not come down to block the cars and pedestrians. This is a failure, that is, behavior that is not correct. During behavioral modeling, the design team would consider actions to be performed if this failure was detected by the system during operation. For example, the bridge might notify the boat to stop until the ground traffic is cleared, perhaps by the bridge operator manually lowering the barrier or by a policeman who was sent to control the ground traffic. The bridge system, as a whole, could continue to provide service, albeit at a reduced level. Note, this imposes a requirement that some part of the bridge system, a human operator or possibly additional circuitry at the barrier module, be able to detect the failure and would also lead to additional states in the FSM/SDL/Petri models. Additional protocols for human actors might also be developed. For example, if there was a human operator, then consideration of this failure would lead to additional steps in the protocols for the operator, such as visually confirming that the barriers were down. Finally, consideration of failures during the modeling process can lead to analyses of how such failures can occur, that is, the errors that might occur and the faults that can cause them. These, in turn, may guide the designers toward a more robust design through various design principles, as described in Section 6.4, and may also lead to repair protocols to be used when the failure actually occurs in an operating bridge. For example, the ground traffic barriers may fail to come down because the message from the main control module didn't get through, the motor was burned out, the power to the motor was lost, something was blocking the barrier itself, etc. The design team can prepare a list of these, perhaps giving the order in which the possible faults should be checked so that the repair crew could work more quickly and efficiently.

Faults may be internal or external. For example, some components of the bridge system may cease to operate properly. On the other hand, some cars or pedestrians may remain on the bridge after the lights and warning bell sound. In behavioral modeling it is useful to consider both kinds; in particular, it is useful to consider how the system should behave if a user or some other external entity does something bad, either by accident or maliciously. Faults may or may not necessarily lead to failure or even errors. For example, if the sensor for giving the distance to the boat provides distances accurate to 1 foot but the system only considers distances at the 10-foot level, the sensor may get slightly out of calibration (or some low-order bits of the reading get garbled in transmission to the main control or ...) without affecting the behavior of the bridge.

The consequences of failures can range from simply inconvenient to catastrophic. If the bridge span fails to go up when a boat is approaching, the boat captain may observe this or see that the green light has not come on and stop the boat. This could cause disruption of traffic on the river but would not likely lead to loss of life or even property damage. Of course, the captain may not observe the failure of the bridge and crash into the bridge, which would certainly lead to property damage and possibly harm to humans. So, even this one kind of failure could have a range of consequences. If the spans go up while there are cars and pedestrians still on them (due, e.g., to a fault in the on-bridge sensors), there would almost surely be serious consequences. Some systems may not have failures that lead to life-threatening consequences. For example, an automated teller machine (ATM) is not likely to cause bodily harm, unless something really strange happens as it explodes, but it may have consequences that range from simple inconvenience (a user doesn't get the money and has to go inside the bank) to serious (the ATM transfers the user's life savings to an incorrect account). The design team should consider at each phase of the design possible failures and carefully consider each one for its likelihood and the range of consequences. In particular, failures considered during behavioral analysis can then impose restrictions and requirements on the internal design, for example leading to error states in the FSM/SDL model or requirements such as accuracy of sensors or redundancy of subsystems.

6.2.2 Reliability and related concepts

In general discourse about systems, reliability means the degree to which a system continues to operate properly over time. However, there are formal definitions for reliability and related concepts that allow more precise analyses that can be useful in selecting between system designs and, in implementation stages, the choice of system components. In this section we introduce some of those definitions.

> **Definition 6.5** The **reliability** R(t) of a system is the probability that the first failure of the system occurs at time greater than t, where t counts the time from when the system first becomes active.

Viewed another way, R(t) is the probability that the system has operated properly from the time it was turned on ($t = 0$) until time t. Note that R(t) is a monotonically nonincreasing function. The probability that the system operates correctly for t seconds is at least as big as the probability that it operates correctly for $t + \delta$ seconds for any positive δ because a failure may occur during the period from t to $t + \delta$. In physical systems parts may experience wear over time. As time proceeds, the probability that some part has worn sufficiently to cause a problem increases, and thus the probability that the system continues to operate properly decreases. In a software system there could be an error that only occurs in certain possibly rare situations. The probability that some user would have provided input corresponding to that rare situation increases over time, and again the probability that the system would never have seen that situation decreases over time.

There are various techniques for measuring reliability and the related concepts defined below, and Section 6.3 contains a discussion of some of the ones relevant to embedded system design.

> **Definition 6.6** The **mean time to failure (MTTF)** is the average time from system startup until the first system failure.
>
> **Definition 6.7** The **mean time to repair (MTTR)** is the average amount of time it takes to repair a system that has failed.
>
> **Definition 6.8** The **mean down time (MDT)** is the average amount of time from the time a system fails until the time the system is operational again.
>
> **Definition 6.9** The **mean time between failures (MTBF)** is the average time between failures.

MTBF includes both MTTF and MDT. For systems that are not repairable (or for which repairs may be too expensive to be worthwhile), MTTF measures the average useful life for a system. MDT includes both the time to actually repair the system (MTTR) plus times outside the control of the engineering team, such as delivery time for replacement parts, unavailability of workers on the weekend, etc. Figure 6.1 shows the relationship among these concepts pictorially. The relationship between MDT and MTTR is not accurately depicted because delay and repair activity can be intermingled. For example, there can be an initial delay until some parts arrive, then repair could start on a Friday and be interrupted during the weekend; repair could continue Monday and then be delayed again waiting for the remaining parts. The partitioning in Figure 6.1 was done only to make the diagram reasonably simple.

Applying these concepts to an embedded system is not a straightforward matter. Embedded systems are typically made up of many subsystems, each of which in turn has its own subsystems and components. Each component may have known reliability or MTTF data, but combining these to obtain accurate figures for the reliability and MTTF for the whole system is nontrivial. A variety of standards and tools are available to help compute reliability figures for a physical system from the corresponding figures of its components.[7–10] However, modern embedded systems typically have significant software components, for which such computations are less well developed. Moreover, failure in one subsystem may or may not affect the reliability of other subsystems and components. For example, failure of a switch that turns the warning lights on in the bridge likely has no impact on any other component of the bridge; on the other hand, certain kinds of failure in the power supply in the ground barrier subsystem may damage or destroy electronic circuits in that subsystem, making computations based on the normal reliability data for those components no longer relevant.

How can the design team make use of R(t), MTTF, etc., assuming it does have reasonable data about them? First, the team has to remember that these are only

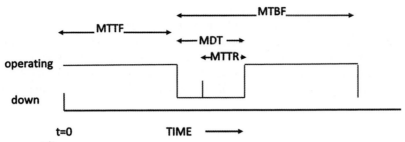

FIGURE 6.1 The Relationship Between MTTF, MTBF, MDT, and MTTR.

Author drawn.

estimates and averages. The fact that the MTTF of a component is, say, 10,000 hours doesn't mean that every system will operate correctly for 10,000 hours after being turned on. Some will fail sooner and others later. A more useful approach might be to look at a set of time to failure times or additional statistical information such as the standard deviation of times to failure if available. For example, if the MTTF of a component was 10,000 hours and the standard deviation was only 100, then a very high percentage of the components will work properly for 9900 hours or more. If, on the other hand, the standard deviation was, say, 2000, then a fair number would fail as early as 8000 hours. Depending on the consequences of failure, as described in Section 6.2.1, this may or may not be acceptable. The design team should compare the seriousness of failures against the data about reliability and time to failure to make decisions about such things as the appropriateness of the basic design and the need to add robustness (see Section 6.2.3). A 1/10 chance of failure in 10 years may be acceptable for the bridge, but it would not be acceptable for an airplane.

We close this section with one last definition, one of more theoretical interest than practical use but one which is used often in discussions of reliability.

Definition 6.10 One failure in time (FIT) is 1 failure per 10^9 hours.

Indeed, 10^9 hours is more than 114,000 years. Obviously, there is no way to test a real system for a failure rate in that range. In some industries, especially the integrated circuit industry, alternate views, such as 1 failure when 1000 devices operate for 10^6 hours or 1,000,000 devices operate for 10^3 hours, are feasible and are used instead of 1 failure in 10^9 hours.

6.2.3 Robustness

There is no formal definition of robustness. In general, the term robustness refers to the ability of an entity to continue to function in the presence of errors or other difficulties or, if unable to continue functioning, at least to fail without causing harm. For embedded systems, errors and difficulties might include environmental parameters outside the expected range for the product, higher-than-anticipated volume of service requests, incorrect inputs or sequences of inputs from users, failure of one or more components in the system, and others. Responses to such situations include issuing warnings about incorrect inputs, slowing the rate of service delivery, temporarily stopping some of the less important services while continuing more crucial ones, shutting the system down in a way that avoids harm, and others. The design team should consider such issues at all stages, starting from the very beginning of behavioral modeling. We present several examples of situations outside the normal expectations and different responses that might be adopted. The goal is not to provide definitive solutions to each example but to show that consideration of such situations during the design phases can lead to more robust systems.

Example 6.1

Environmental parameters are outside normally expected ranges. In most parts of the world where bridges would be deployed the ambient temperature would be expected to range between, say, −50 and 150°F. However, a building on fire on the river's edge close to the bridge might temporarily raise the temperature considerably higher than 150°. Operating the span motor when the temperature inside the motor compartment is, say, 250°, could cause it to burn out, causing damage to the motor and possibly disastrous damage if the span itself fell into the river because of the motor failure. The design team might propose stopping all river traffic if the ambient temperature inside the span motor compartment goes over a specified limit, whatever the cause. In this solution the bridge curtails some services (allowing boats to pass) but still maintains other services (allowing ground traffic to cross the river). Another alternative is to run the motor at half speed. The slower speed could keep the motor from overheating. In this solution the bridge continues to provide all services at a slower pace because of the extra time for the span to go up and come down. In both cases the system probably should send a warning to the operator and to local authorities. Note that both these solutions impose a new requirement on the system — that it be able to monitor the temperature at the span motor module.

Example 6.2

Pedestrians walk around the ground barriers after they have gone down and the span has started to go up. Although this may seem ridiculous, there have in fact been instances. In any case it is an extreme example of improper user behavior. Improper or incorrect user input is a common situation. The following is a list of actions that the design team might incorporate into the system. The bridge might stop the span movement or start it back down again. Stopping the span movement means the pedestrian might continue to walk to the end and fall off. Making the span move back down imposes a risk of the pedestrian losing balance because of the possibly shaky motion. Either one is better than just letting the span continue to rise, so either one is a slightly graceful degradation of service. The system almost surely should warn the boat to stop. The system could sound a loud warning horn to the pedestrian or alert the operator to warn the pedestrian over a loudspeaker. The bridge might take pictures of the pedestrian for later identification and legal action. As in Example 6.1, early consideration of abnormal situations may lead to additional requirements; in this case, it could add requirements for loudspeakers and/or cameras.

Consideration of such abnormal or unexpected behaviors and proposed actions for when they are detected cause additions and modifications to the various models. For example, an early FSM for the bridge span might have only two states — DOWN and UP. Problems like those mentioned in Examples 6.1 and 6.2 would cause the design team to propose additional states, such as GOING_UP and GOING_DOWN, and to consider additional inputs and actions. Some of the additional inputs would be determined by the requirement to be able to detect an anomaly, such as the requirement to be able to determine high temperature in the motor in Example 6.1. Other additional inputs would be determined by protocol decisions made by the design team, such as having the bridge operator visually check for pedestrians and input a clear signal (perhaps by pressing a button). In the simple FSM with only two states there might be just two actions — START_UP to start the motor for raising the span and START_DOWN to start the motor for lowering the span. Consideration of the abnormal cases might lead to additional actions, such as CHANGE_MOTOR_SPEED and STOP_MO-TOR. Problem 5 asks the reader to make choices for how to handle the situations in Examples 6.1 and 6.2 and to draw a suitable FSM for the span motor module.

Example 6.3

Handling incorrect input has long been a feature of robust software. The most common solutions were to ignore the incorrect values, ask the user if feasible to correct the input, or adjust the input somehow to make it acceptable. Similar options can be used in embedded systems. For example, suppose the bridge had a range sensor attached to the bridge structure that read the distance of an oncoming boat to the bridge every 2 seconds after the boat was detected. (This sensor is separate from the upstream boat sensor. The upstream boat sensor simply indicates that a boat is coming. The range sensor would provide distance information as the boat was approaching closer to the bridge.) Suppose the range was 0–500 yards. If the main control module received a value of 1000 or received a second value indicating the boat was further away than in the previous reading, it might ignore the value, ask the sensor to resend it, average it in with previous values, etc. In addition to specifying an action to respond to the immediate situation, the design team might also have the system report the out-of-range value to the base station to alert authorities that the sensor may be malfunctioning.

Example 6.4
The local power to the bridge fails. Obviously, the bridge cannot operate with no power. However, the design team might propose to include some backup power that would allow graceful degradation. One example would be to provide a small backup power supply for the main control module so that it could send an alert to the local authorities, which may not be aware of the power loss at the bridge site. If a boat was passing under the bridge at the time, the spans would be up and the ground barriers down. The spans must remain up and not crash down on the boat. This imposes requirements on the kinds of gearing and motor used in the span module. A more robust solution might include a second, more powerful backup power supply with enough power to lower the spans and raise the ground barriers after the boat had passed to the other side, providing an even more graceful failure.

We close this section by remarking again that robustness and safe responses to unexpected situations should be an important part of every step of the design process. Of course, a design team can't predict or consider all possible abnormal or disastrous situations, for example, a meteorite striking the bridge, a dam upriver breaking, etc. Moreover, setting operating parameter ranges, such as the motor operating temperature range, has to consider other factors such as cost or probability of need; there might exist motors that can operate at temperatures above 250°F, but they would likely be very expensive with close to zero probability of being needed. The design team would need to balance the various factors in making a final choice. Reliability, when it can be estimated, provides one of the measurements the team can use in making that balanced decision.

6.3 Estimating and using failure rates

Many devices used in embedded systems have reliable and useful data about failure rates. Some devices (e.g., integrated circuits, batteries, brushes for DC motors, etc.) have huge historical databases; for other devices, intensive and long-term testing is feasible. See Ref. [11] for a discussion of how such data is obtained and the issues

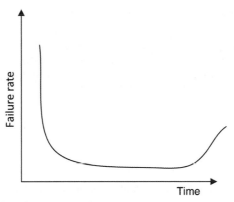

FIGURE 6.2 A Bathtub Curve Model of Failure Rate.

Author drawn.

with using that information. Also for basic information about estimating failure rates and basic formulas for R(t).

For integrated circuits, there is a wealth of historical data that gives useful information and guidance to embedded system engineers. Most families of integrated circuits display the "bathtub curve" behavior (see Figure 6.2). That is, there is a higher probability of failure during the early life of the circuit, followed by a relatively long period of low probability of failure, followed by an increasing probability of failure. The initial period is often called the "burn in" period. Power up/down and continuous usage during this period may cause minor aberrations created during the fabrication of the circuit to deteriorate to the point of failure. If a circuit makes it past the burn-in period, that circuit probably does not have any serious aberrations and will continue to work for a long time, typically hundreds of thousands of hours, until heat and other causes eventually cause failure. Other products may also follow the bathtub model. For example, the manufacturing process for heavy-duty gears may occasionally introduce small imperfections that fail quickly under the heavy usage for which the gear is intended. Gears that don't have such imperfections will perform a long time until, eventually, normal wear creates a problem.

In some cases it is feasible to do actual testing. For example, nonvolatile memory circuits are often guaranteed for 100,000 write cycles. It is quite feasible to test, say, 1000 or 2000 such circuits by writing new data every 0.01 seconds. The 100,000 write cycles would be performed in under 3 hours. For mechanical devices, for example, miniature mechanical switches, testing is also feasible. For example, testing a mechanical switch 100,000 times at a rate of once per second would take roughly 11½ days but still quite feasible.

Lifetimes and failure rates can be significantly affected by a variety of factors. For example, high storage and operating temperatures have an adverse effect on integrated circuits; humidity has an adverse effect on mechanical switches and DC motor brushes, etc. For products expected to be used in such adverse environments, the engineers will likely need to select parts designed for such environments, typically at a higher cost.

Estimates like these can be used to select components for a product or to plan scheduled maintenance and replacement operations for the product. For example, a switch with expected lifetime of only 100,000 on/off cycles would not be appropriate for the ground barrier lights of the bridge. Those lights would flash once per second or so when they were active, and they could flash for many minutes for each boat that passes under the bridge. The switch might fail after only a year or so. A more robust (and likely more expensive) switch should be chosen for the ground barrier lights. On the other hand, the green light signal to the boat only goes on once per boat crossing. It could take 10–15 years before a less expensive switch would reach its guaranteed limit. If the system recorded the number of boats that had passed, the maintenance engineers could know when to replace the switch.

Data on failure rate behavior can also be used to determine a testing protocol for newly installed products. Assuming postdeployment testing is feasible, a newly deployed product can be tested for a period longer than the burn-in period for any of its components. For example, the bridge might be tested many times overnight when both the river traffic and ground traffic are minimal. The production team may buy pretested components, usually at a higher cost. In many cases individual components or subsystems can be tested past their burn-in periods before assembly into the final product. For example, the span motor can be tested in a lab before being brought to the bridge site.

6.4 Principles for designing safe and robust systems

We present some principles that can guide design teams toward robust and safe products.

Applying some of these principles incurs additional cost per product. For example, building redundancy into a subsystem of a product almost always makes each copy of the product more expensive. Other principles might only involve extra thought during the design process. For example, designing the product to be modular and the subsystems to be insulated from each other's failures might take extra time during the design steps but may not incur much additional per-product cost. The team would need to weigh the consequences of failures against the costs of applying any of these principles. How critical is it for the system or one of its components to operate continuously? The communications module of the bridge that sends data about boat traffic to the river authority could fail with minimal consequence to the overall functioning of the bridge; boats could still pass safely. The span module, on the other hand, is fairly critical. Without it, the bridge could accommodate only ground traffic if the span remained down and no traffic if the span got stuck halfway up. Next, how likely is the failure to actually happen? The bridge communication module could fail in various ways, both internal and external. Some circuits inside the module could fail, the wireless link to the internet could fail, etc. Problems with internet transmission can occur with moderate frequency, but the consequences to the overall operation of the bridge are minimal. The span module, on the other hand, would have very low probability of failing if strong motors and gears are used. Finally, what are the possible approaches for building in robustness and what are their associated costs? For the bridge communication module, counteracting failure may only involve providing extra storage in the PC in the main control module to store all the bridge data until transmission can be resumed. Incoming information would be lost, but there appears to be no way to avoid this. At the other extreme, it would likely be very expensive or even impossible to provide a backup for the span motor. The team may then focus on ensuring that repair and/or replacement was as fast and easy as possible.

6.4.1 Methods for counteracting failures in subsystems or components

There are a variety of ways that a system could respond to failures in ways that allow the system to continue to operate, at least at some level. The three most common and widely used are redundancy, counteraction, and human intervention. We emphasize again that these need to be considered and designed from the very beginning. Waiting until the bridge is built to think about redundant pedestrian sensors or protocols for when the spans are stuck halfway up (see following paragraphs) is too late!

Redundancy means that some portion of the system is duplicated one or more times. For a subsystem or component that performs an action, this usually means providing a second way of performing the action. In the bridge, for example, the ground traffic barrier could have a hand crank in addition to the motor that raises and lowers the barrier. In some cases no additional action is needed because redundant subsystems each individually perform adequately on their own. For example, if there are both warning lights and bells for the ground traffic, then the bells will still provide suitable warning if the lights fail. Of course, if both fail, then the bridge may not be able to allow boats to go through. For a subsystem or component that provides input to the system, redundancy usually means providing three or more sources for that input. If possible, the separate sources should be different rather than simply multiple copies of the same subsystem or component. For example, the pedestrian-on-the-bridge sensor subsystem could have three separate motion detectors in the area where pedestrians walk. This may be good enough because it is unlikely that the sensors will all fail at the same time. However, some external conditions may have an equal effect on three identical sensors; for example, some birds may be flying in that area and cause all three motion sensors to give false positive readings. A better solution might be to have a motion sensor, a camera subsystem with image analysis, and a heat sensor subsystem. Minor motion that would cause a false positive reading in the motion sensor would not cause a false positive in the other two subsystems. When input subsystems are redundant, the most common way to decide what input to accept is simple voting. This decision should be made by a separate module, not one of the redundant subsystems. Continuing with the pedestrian sensor for the bridge, it would not be appropriate for, say, the camera subsystem to monitor the inputs from the other two subsystems and tally the vote because it may be the camera subsystem itself that is faulty. Of course, extra care should be taken to make the subsystem that does collect and count the input as reliable as possible, perhaps arranging for one of the redundant subsystems to take over in case a failure in the counting subsystem is detected.

Counteraction means the system itself performs some action that allows full or partial continuation of the service. We have already seen examples of how a system can counteract a failure in such a way as to continue to provide full service. For example, if the span motor overheats, the span subsystem may operate the motor at slower speed, which may in turn allow the motor to operate and cool down at the same time. In other situations the system can stop providing some services but continue to operate others. For example, if the span module fails completely, the bridge may be able to determine that the spans are down and respond by turning the red light to all boat traffic. This blocks all river traffic but allows ground traffic to continue using the bridge.

Human intervention can be applied in some situations. In some cases the human can perform actions that allow continuation of full service. For example, if the ground traffic barriers fail to go down, the human operator can lower the barrier by the crank if there is one. The boat can pass and then later the ground traffic can resume. The full service of the bridge is provided, albeit at a lower level — a delay is introduced while the human lowers the barrier. In other cases no human action may be possible to continue full or even partial service. For example, if the span motor fails completely while the spans are partially raised, no human action can move the spans. However, human intervention can allow for graceful degradation or failure. For this scenario of the bridge, the human operator may post additional warnings near the barriers to warn people nearby and can inform local authorities, such as police, who can deploy officers to nearby intersections to direct traffic away from the bridge.

In order for a system to be able to fail gracefully it has to be able to detect when some portion of it has failed. Moreover, the detection of the failure of a subsystem or component should be determined by a part of the system outside that subsystem or component. A subsystem or component can't reliably determine itself that it has failed. Care must be taken therefore in the design of detection mechanisms. For example, a failure in, say, the span motor should be detected by something outside the motor. If, say, the span motor overheats, any electronic parts inside the motor that might detect and report the situation to the span motor control module may be compromised by the excessive heat and therefore not able to operate correctly. Therefore detection should be accomplished by some mechanism(s) outside the motor itself. Heat sensors located near but outside the motor could report directly to the span motor control module. Similarly, current sensors could detect current being used by the motor and report directly to the span motor control module. For modules that communicate with each other, one approach for fault detection is regular pinging. For example, the main control module of the bridge could regularly ping the other modules, such as the span motor control module. Failure to receive an appropriate response would indicate that the entire module had failed. As with reliability and safety in general, detection should be designed into the system from the very beginning of the modeling process.

6.4.2 **Design principles**

There are many principles, both general and specific to particular areas like circuits or human-computer interfaces, for designing safe and robust systems. We present here a few of the most important general principles. Our goal is not to list as many principles as possible but rather to list the more common ones and to illustrate how those principles can be used to design more reliable and robust products. Some of these, such as making safety and reliability part of the design process from the beginning, are easy to achieve. Others are goals to strive for but whose achievement may be difficult or even impossible. Still, the more attention the design team pays to these principles, the more safe, reliable, and robust the end product is likely to be.

Safety and reliability should be part of the design process from the beginning. The behavioral model should include error cases and specify what the requirements and responses should be. For example, during behavioral modeling, the design team could uncover the need for additional use cases related to various kinds of failure, the possible need for additional modules for detection, and additional scenarios and messages related to fault detection and response. These requirements and protocols are implemented in the FSM/SDL/Petri models.

There should be no single point of failure that causes the whole system to fail. The system as a whole should continue to provide at least some services to the extent possible. We have already seen some examples in which the system can still function but at a lower level. For example, if the ground traffic barrier motor fails, the barriers can be lowered by hand; this takes more time, but the bridge still allows the boat to pass and eventually ground traffic to continue. A component may affect an entire system, in which case the design team should consider redundancy or backup. For example, failure of the power supply will remove power from the whole system. If it is really critical for the system to continue operating or at least to notify some external entity of the failure, then a redundant source of power, such as a battery, would need to be included in the design.

Isolate and limit the propagation of faults. The design team should develop a model of fault dependency and define fault-containment regions. A simple case of dependency is two circuits with wired connections. An internal electrical failure, such as a short circuit, in one could cause voltage or current to be out of range, which in turn could damage the other circuit. Limiting such fault propagation could be accomplished with diodes or opto-isolators (see Section 2, Chapter 13). Incorrect operation of the first circuit may lead to a signal which is not out of electrical range but incorrect, for example, sending a logic 0 when the correct value is logic 1. Thus this dependency has two elements in the dependency model. At a higher level in the system hierarchy, fault dependency between two separate modules typically involves the messages that flow between the two modules. For example, in Figure 4.1, the high-level SDL model of the bridge, the only way the main control module could be affected by a failure in the span module is that the message traffic between the two is inappropriate. The span module may fail to send a message. If messages are supposed to be sent regularly, the main control module may include a timer and a time-out error case. Otherwise, the main control module might ping the span module at regular intervals to see if that module is "alive." Module-to-module fault dependency also includes cases where the messages sent are incorrect. One cause for an incorrect message is corruption during transmission, which may at least be checked through the use of a check-sum or a self-correcting code. Another cause for an incorrect message is internal failure in the sending module. For this kind of potential failure, the design team could include tests for data consistency and integrity or redundant messages from several distinct modules. The more faults included in the fault dependency model, the more robust the product is likely to be. For each dependency, the team should develop a method for limiting the propagation of the fault to other parts of the system.

Identify the set of fault-containment regions. Associated with the fault dependency model is the set of fault-containment regions. A fault-containment region is a portion of the system in which faults can be isolated. Fault-containment regions can be hierarchical. For example, in the bridge system shown in the SDL model in Figure 4.1 each top-level module, such as the main control module or the span control module, would be a fault-containment region. The span control module could have its own fault-containment regions, such as the motor, the gears, the fuse box, the power supply, etc.

To the extent possible, arrange for fault handling to be internal and not interfere with normal functioning and the user interface. We have seen that this is not always possible; if the ground traffic barriers fail to go down, the most plausible solutions do involve users of the bridge and do degrade normal function. However, we have also seen that in many cases a fault need not degrade the functioning of the system or interfere in any significant way with the users if the system has been well designed. For example, the inclusion of redundant ground traffic sensors for determining if the span is clear means a fault in one will not prevent the bridge from continuing to operate at full level. A corollary to this principle is that the design team should determine which, if any, services might be continued for each kind of failure and, where plausible and useful, alert users of the service limitations. For example, in an ATM the failure of the communications link to the central bank would preclude most operations because even logging in to the user's account requires communication with the bank. However, the ATM might provide some services, such as location and hours of nearby branches, phone numbers that users can call to handle some of the curtailed services (e.g., check on a balance or report a stolen credit card), etc. On the other hand, failure of the cash dispensing unit would not preclude logging in to check balances, but users should be warned that cash dispensing cannot be performed. In both cases the user interface should continue to work and should aid the user in performing whatever services are available at that moment.

Design the system to work despite user error. In cases where the human input is active, such as entering information from a keypad, inputs should be checked to ensure they make sense and are within the range of cases handled by the system. For example, an ATM system would check that amounts entered for withdrawal from an account were at least positive (make sense) and are less than, say, $500 (are within the range of cash payouts the system should handle). The same principle applies to cases where the human input is passive. The bridge should sense when pedestrians are walking across the span, but if the sensors indicate 300 pedestrians on the span there is likely an error in the sensing module. In this case the humans are not typing on a keypad, but they are providing an input to the system. The value 300 obviously makes no sense and is out of reasonable range. The bridge can't ask the pedestrians to reenter anything; the system must be designed to handle such a situation in a different way, as indicated earlier in this chapter.

As a corollary to the above principle, design the human-computer interface to be intuitive and forgiving. The design team should seek advice from potential users of the system to ensure that the user interface meets their needs and is intuitive. The team should not just use their own ideas, which may be biased toward their own experience; the real users of the system need to provide input. The system should be designed to provide guidance to help the user avoid mistakes and checks to inform the user when a mistake has been made. An easy-to-use and intuitive user interface reduces the likelihood that the human will make an error in the first place. A forgiving interface will prevent a user error from propagating into the system. See Section 7.3.1 and the reference mentioned in that section for more on designing human interfaces.

Ensure that detected failures are reported, either to humans or to some external system that can initiate an analysis, even if the failure has been compensated for or was temporary. The check-engine light on modern cars is an excellent example. The car may continue to operate, but something inside needs attention. That something may not be noticeable to the car owner, but it still needs attention. In the case of the bridge the span motor control module may be able to compensate for the motor over-heating, but the overheating event should be reported even if it is only temporary. For example, the event may have been caused by a record hot day at the bridge site, and this was only a one-time occurrence. Still, the overheating may have caused damage to the motor, so it may need to be inspected. In addition, the design team may be interested to know that it happened so that perhaps different motors can be used for future bridges deployed in warmer climates. It is important for humans to know that the event happened so they can decide what, if any, actions might be needed.

Design the systems for diagnosis and repair. When faults and failures do occur, a repair team needs access to various internal parts of the system to determine what caused the problem and fix or replace parts as needed. Building in test points and access to parts from the earliest stages results in a product that can more easily be analyzed and repaired.

6.5 **Summary**

In this chapter we emphasized the need to design products that are safe and robust. We presented definitions of service, failure, error, and fault. These definitions help a design team understand how problems occurring during the operation of the product can impact the service provided by that product. We then presented the notion of reliability, a measure of how likely it is for a system to fail as the system operates over time. We presented concepts associated with reliability, such as MTTF and MTTR. Understanding these concepts helps the team design products that can be repaired more quickly when a failure does occur. We discussed the concept of robustness and indicated ways that products can be designed to continue providing at least some level of service even when faults occur. We discussed how failure rates for individual components can be used to estimate reliability of a system and how it might be used in selecting components to be used in the system. Finally, we presented a number of principles that can help lead to designs that are safe and robust.

Problems

1. In a group session, for each of the following products, list several service failures. For each failure, list some errors that might cause that failure. Finally, list some ways that system could be designed to continue providing at least some service when the errors occur.

   a) ATM.
   b) High-rise building elevator system.
   c) Patient monitoring system.
   d) Lane departure system in a car.
   e) Self-check-out scanner in a grocery store.
   f) Assembly line in a factory.
   g) Heating, ventilation, and air conditioning system in a smart building.

2. In Problem 1 why was it not asked to list faults?

3. For the ATM, tell for each of the following situations whether it is a failure, an error, or a fault. For each fault, tell whether it is internal or external and suggest ways the system might be designed to prevent that fault.

   a) Cash is not dispensed when requested by a user.
   b) Gears on the dispensing motor are worn, preventing correct cash from dispensing.
   c) The user has requested $100 and the ATM has begun dispensing cash even though there is not enough in the money trays.

4. In a group session, for each of the products in Problem 1, describe ways in which a human user could act in unintended ways. How likely is it that human users would actually behave in those ways? How serious would it be for the human to act in that way? How critical is it for the system designers to build in protection

against such behavior? How might the product be designed to continue providing at least some service?

5. Make choices for how to handle the situations in Examples 6.1 and 6.2 and then draw a suitable FSM for the span motor module.

6. Modern cars typically do not have direct connections between the driver controls, such as the steering wheel and brake pedal, and the corresponding mechanical systems. Submodules accept inputs from the driver control devices as well as other submodules of the car and determine how to control the mechanical system. For example, the steering control module receives input from the steering wheel as well as from other submodules, like the lane departure submodule, to determine how to control the physical direction of the car. In a group brainstorming session think of ways that a car might detect that the steering control module has failed. Then think of actions the car might take in response to such a failure. What do these suggestions imply for the design of the complete car system?

7. Consider again the ATM. For each of the following three use cases, think of ways the system could fail gracefully in case of power loss (e.g., the power company had a failure or someone pulled the plug). In each case tell what additions, if any, to the system design would be required in order to manage the graceful failure behavior you thought of.
   a) User is checking an account balance.
   b) User is transferring money from one account to another.
   c) User is dispensing cash from an account.

8. An ATM includes a power supply module, a display module, a keypad module, a cash dispensing module, and a processing module, among others. For each of those modules, which of the following might affect the MTTF of each of these modules? Explain your answer.
   a) Complete loss of power.
   b) Power brownout.
   c) The sensor that tells if the cash tray is empty fails.
   d) The gears in the cash tray that transfer bills to the dispensing slot are worn and fail from time to time.
   e) The power module overheats.

References

[1] https://en.wikipedia.org/wiki/Fault_tolerance.
[2] E. Dubrova, Fault-Tolerant Design, Springer, 2013, ISBN 978-1-4614-2112-2.
[3] N. Storey, Safety-Critical Computer Systems, Addison-Wesley, 1996.
[4] H. Kopetz, Real-Time Systems: Design Principles for Distributed Embedded Applications, Springer, 1997, ISBN 0792398947.
[5] N. Leveson, Safeware: System Safety and Computers, Addison-Wesley, 1995, ISBN 0-201-11972-2.

[6] M. Lyu (Ed.), Software Fault Tolerance, John Wiley and Sons, Inc., 1995.

[7] https://www.camcode.com/asset-tags/top-tools-in-a-reliability-engineers-toolbox/#badge.

[8] D.J. Smith, Reliability, Maintainability and Risk, eighth ed., Butterworth-Heinemann, 2011, ISBN 978-0080969022. https://www.biblio.com/book/reliability-maintainability-risk-practical-methods-engineers/d/1415295927.

[9] D. Lin, Reliability Characteristics for Two Subsystems in Series or Parallel or n Subsystems in m_out_of_n Arrangement. auroraconsultingengineering.com.

[10] https://en.wikipedia.org/wiki/Mean_time_between_failures.

[11] https://en.wikipedia.org/wiki/Failure_rate

Verification, validation, and evaluation

7.1 Introduction

Verification is the process of convincing relevant entities (clients, stakeholders, regulatory agencies, etc.) that the product satisfies a set of requirements. The requirements are typically imposed by the client and by relevant agencies such as local/regional/national governments. The product can be the final system or any of the models developed during the design process. For example, the design team may analyze the behavioral model to make sure requirements are satisfied at the earliest stages of the design process. A Finite State Machine (FSM) or Specification and Description Language (SDL) model for which timing constraints have been specified for individual modules and message transmission can be analyzed to verify end-to-end timing constraints. On the other hand, some requirements may not be verifiable until late in the design process. For example, a requirement that the warning lights be visible during all daylight hours cannot be verified until the lights have been chosen and installed into their sockets in the ground traffic barrier. Only then can it be determined (in this case by inspection) that they shine brightly enough at pedestrian eye level and don't need, for example, hoods to block out the sunlight. Verification may involve formal mathematical reasoning or a variety of informal methods such as walkthroughs and simulations.

Validation is the process of determining that the product meets the needs of the client. Validation includes verification; the product cannot meet the needs of the client if it does not even satisfy the requirements. However, there are other needs that may not be expressible as requirements that could be checked at early stages or proved in some way. Esthetic issues, such as the bridge structure "fitting in" with the surrounding architecture or the operator's console interface being intuitive and easy to use, fall into this category. There is no mathematical way of expressing either of these. A requirement like "fitting in" can be considered during the later stages of the design process, when the physical aspects of the bridge are being designed. Experts in architecture can be consulted for recommendations, but only after the bridge has been built can the clients say that the bridge meets that need.

Evaluation is the process of determining how well the product meets the needs of the client, stakeholders, and possibly others. Are the needs just barely met or met very well? What lessons were learned during the design, construction, and deployment of the product that might impact similar products in the future?

Embedded System Design. https://doi.org/10.1016/B978-0-443-18470-3.00007-5

In this chapter we describe various techniques for verification and validation and illustrate issues relating to validation and evaluation.

7.2 Verification

Each stage of the design process, from behavioral modeling to final implementation, has requirements imposed at the beginning of the stage and modifications or additional requirements discovered during that stage. Each stage produces a product, the model, which imposes initial requirements for the next stage — the model developed at the next stage must accurately implement the model just completed. Verification is the process of convincing all the relevant entities that the output of a stage satisfies the requirements given at the beginning of that stage. The convincing may be done by formal methods, such as mathematical proofs and computations, or by informal methods such as walkthroughs and simulations. The latter cannot prove that requirements are satisfied, but they can still be convincing enough to the relevant entities.

7.2.1 Properties of interest

Each requirement can be stated as a property that must be true. For example, an obvious requirement in the bridge project is that the barriers are down and the ground traffic cleared from the span before it can go up. This could be verified in the behavioral model by examining the different message sequence charts, such as the one in Figure 2.6 in Chapter 2. Requirements in the behavioral model impose related requirements in later models such as the FSM/SDL or Petri models. For example, the behavioral requirement mentioned at the beginning of this paragraph imposes a requirement on the FSM model in Figure 3.11. Barrier Control must be in state bdown, and Traffic Sensor must be in state bsnon, which leads in turn to the requirement for global variables I_bdown and I_btrfclr. Requirements for Petri Nets typically take the form of properties about the places and the number of dots they hold. For example, in the robot net of Figure 5.5 in Chapter 5 the requirement that the common space has at most one robot at a time is represented by the property that P8 never has more than one dot. The property that the total number of dots in P7 and P9 is always 3 is generated from the real-world property of the physical space, namely that it can hold only up to three items

It should be noted that there may be requirements that are not relevant to any of the models but to some other aspect of the system being designed and built. For example, there may be a requirement that the bridge system sense any approaching boat at least 3 minutes before the boat can reach the bridge. This is determined by the maximum speed of all the boats for which the bridge has to be raised and the distance at which the boat sensors can sense the boats. These are aspects outside the scope of any behavioral, FSM/SDL, or Petri model. Such requirements would be considered in the validation of the product, as described later in this chapter.

Properties of interest generally take one of the following forms:

- always — property P always holds or is always true. For example, in the bridge, it is always true that the ground traffic is cleared from the bridge before the spans are raised.
- never — property P is never true. For example, the span never goes up when there are cars or pedestrians on it.
- eventually — property P becomes true at least once, that is, eventually becomes true but may not remain true. For example, in the bridge system, it would be important to know that ground traffic is eventually allowed to cross the bridge after the system is first turned on. It would likely be the case that the ground traffic barriers were deployed until the bridge was ready to be used. When the bridge is completely installed and ready to be operated, it should be the case that ground traffic is eventually allowed to cross. Reachability properties in FSM and Petri Net models, such as a state that is reachable or the normal operating state reached after the error state, are of this form.
- eventually always/never — at some point in time, property P becomes true (false) and stays true (false) forever after that. This is a stronger condition than in the previous bullet. The property stated there is not expected to always be true after some point; ground traffic will be interrupted from time to time as boats arrive. Also note that in the case of eventually always/never, the property P may change between true and false any number of times before it settles to the target value and stays there. This kind of property is often important for embedded systems that control processes. For example, an environmental control system might have the requirement that eventually the temperature is always in the range of 68–72°F. This allows for temperatures outside the range when the system is first started.

7.2.2 Useful reasoning techniques

It is not a function of this book to train readers to be formal reasoners. However, there are several techniques used in formal reasoning that are especially useful when verifying embedded system models. We mention four of them here and illustrate these four techniques with an extended example.

- Reasoning can be either forward or backward. In forward reasoning one starts with the facts and assumptions and reasons toward the conclusion. In backward reasoning one starts with the conclusions and asks what would be required to deduce that conclusion; for each of the statements that would be used to deduce the conclusion, one repeats the backward process, ultimately arriving at facts or assumptions, which, of course, need no further justification.
- Proofs can be done by case analysis, with each case being handled separately from the others and independently in a forward or backward manner. Case analysis is particularly useful in the verification of embedded systems because the models are derived by considering different scenarios for each use case.

Studying properties of behavioral models is often done through case analysis using the different scenarios as the cases. These different scenarios lead to different message sequence charts, which in turn typically lead to different paths in corresponding FSM/SDL models or different transitions in corresponding Petri Net models. Proving properties of the FSM/SDL or Petri Net models, then, often proceeds by case analysis based on the different paths of transitions in those models, similar to the use of paths in program verification.[1-3]

- Counterexamples can be used to show that a property does NOT hold. Simulations and team brainstorming walkthroughs often uncover counterexamples. When a counterexample is discovered, of course, the model has to be fixed and the verification process repeated.
- Finally, for FSM/SDL and Petri net models, a kind of induction proof process is often used. A state S may have an associated property P that should, for example, always be true when the model is in state S. The team proves two cases − P is true the first time S is reached, and if the system is in state S and P is true, then P is true the next time S is reached. The combination of these two cases is enough to guarantee that P always holds in S. Problem 1 asks the student to conduct this kind of proof.

We illustrate these concepts with a modification of the high-level bridge control FSM, shown in Figure 7.1 and Tables 7.1 and 7.2. To simplify the illustration, this FSM is not hierarchical. However, it does include additional scenarios that represent a few of the different situations that could occur, and it does include examples of timing requirements. Suppose that after the boat is sensed, the ground traffic barriers are supposed to be lowered within 10 seconds. If they are not down within that time limit, the boat must be signaled to stop and the police called. The spans cannot begin

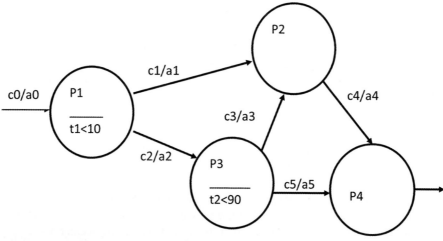

FIGURE 7.1 Modified Bridge Control FSM.

Author drawn.

Table 7.1 Meaning of states in Figure 7.1.

State	Meaning
P1	Waiting for barriers to go down after a boat has been sensed.
P2	Boat has been signaled to stop.
P3	Barriers went down, waiting for ground traffic to clear bridge.
P4	Span has been signaled to go up.

Table 7.2 Conditions and actions for Figure 7.1.

Transition condition	Transition action
c0: boat sensed	a0: set timer t1 to 0, signal barriers to go down
c1: t1>=10	a1: signal boat to stop, call police
c2: barriers down	a2: set timer t2 to 0
c3: t2>=90	a3: signal boat to stop, operator action
c4: traffic blocked and cleared from bridge	a4: signal spans to go up, signal boat to continue
c5: ground traffic cleared from bridge	a5: signal spans to go up

to move up until the police have arrived, blocked the ground traffic, and cleared any cars and pedestrians that were on the bridge. If the barriers do go down within 10 seconds, the ground traffic should be cleared within 90 seconds. If it is not cleared within that time limit, the boat must be signaled to stop and the bridge operator should go to see what the problem is. After the operator has cleared the bridge, the spans can be raised and the boat signaled to continue. For a real bridge system, there would, of course, be other error cases, such as the boat not stopping when signaled to stop or starting to move again before getting the signal to move, the span not raising properly, etc. Our goal is to illustrate the concepts in this section, so the model includes some extra cases but is kept simple enough to allow the concepts to be more easily understood.

Suppose there is a requirement that the spans must start raising at least 30 seconds before an approaching boat reaches the bridge. Proving that such a property holds for the design requires a combination of world knowledge (e.g., maximum speed of boats on the river, stopping and starting times for the boats, etc.), knowledge about other aspects of the system (e.g., how far away from the bridge the boat sensors are, how long it takes the ground traffic barriers to lower), and the information about flow and timing in the FSM model. The verification team might propose the following conjecture.

Assume an approaching boat is sensed at least 150 seconds before it can reach the bridge. Assume that a boat can stop within 5 seconds of when it is signaled to stop and takes 5 seconds to start again when it is signaled to start. Assume the pilot of the boat reacts immediately when signaled to stop. Then, the boat is at least 30 seconds away from the bridge in any situation where state P4 is reached.

(Note, assumptions like "at least 150 seconds before it can reach the bridge" would impose additional requirements on the design of the system, such as the range of the sensors and their placement in the environment of the bridge.)

One can easily see from the FSM model that there are three cases for this conjecture, each corresponding to one path from P1 to P5. Case 1 is the path P1-P3-P4. Case 2 is the path P1-P2-P4. Case 3 is the path P1-P3-P2-P4. If the conjecture holds for each of these three cases, then it holds for the FSM model. Each of the cases can be proved by forward reasoning or backward reasoning. Here is a proof by forward reasoning.

Case 1. The boat is sensed 150 seconds before it can reach the bridge. In this case the transition out of P1 happens in less than 10 seconds, so there are at least 140 seconds left when P3 is reached. The transition to P4 happens in less than 90 seconds. Therefore, at most, 100 seconds have passed before reaching P4, and the boat is still at least 50 seconds away.

Case 2. The boat is sensed at least 150 seconds before it can reach the bridge. At 10 seconds, the FSM transitions to P2. By hypothesis, the pilot sees the signal to stop and responds immediately. The boat stops within 5 seconds. So, at this point, the boat is still 135 seconds away from the bridge. In this case the police are called, and of course, they will not arrive until well after the boat has stopped. Sometime later, the police block the ground traffic and clear the bridge, at this point the FSM transitions to P4. In this case the boat is 135 seconds away from the bridge when P4 is reached.

Case 3. The boat is sensed 150 seconds before it can reach the bridge. The transition to P3 happens in less than 10 seconds, so the boat is still at least 140 seconds away from the bridge when P3 is reached. In this case 90 seconds elapse, and the FSM transitions to P2. At this point, the boat is still at least 50 seconds away from the bridge. The pilot sees the signal to stop, and the boat stops in another 5 seconds. So, at the time the boat has stopped, it is still 45 seconds away from the bridge. Sometime later, the operator clears the cars and pedestrians from the bridge. At this point, both parts of condition c4 are true — the ground traffic is blocked because in this case the barriers did go down, and the bridge has been cleared by the operator. The system transitions to P4, and the boat is still at least 45 seconds away.

An attempt to prove the conjecture by backward reasoning would start from P4 with the question of how the FSM could reach P4. In this simple FSM there are two ways — transition from P2 or transition from P3. There are now two cases, each of which would follow the same backward process. In each step the timing analysis is the same as for the forward proof, except that the arithmetic is performed in the reverse order. For example, the boat should be at least 30 seconds away from the bridge when entering P4, so it must be at least 30 seconds away when entering P3 or 35 seconds away when entering P2 (because of the 5 seconds during which the boat could move before it stops).

Finally, a search for a counterexample can be used to uncover errors. For example, if action a1 did not include signaling the boat to stop, one could easily construct a counterexample to the conjecture, that is, a scenario in which the conjecture would be false. The counterexample is the scenario in which the ground traffic barriers fail to go down and the police are called. Of course, the police would take more than 150 seconds to arrive and clear the bridge. The discovery of such a counterexample indicates there is something wrong with the model.

7.3 Validation

Validation is the process of determining that the product meets the needs of the client, users, and stakeholders. The focus is on the external behavior of the product. Validation includes verification because a product that does not satisfy all the requirements cannot meet the client's needs. However, there are many requirements that cannot be described or quantified rigorously enough to be "provable." Requirements that are qualitative or subjective fall into this category. There is a wealth of literature on designing principles that can help ensure products meet the needs of all concerned. These range from general principles, for example,[4] to principles and techniques for specific areas, such as software[5] or human-computer interaction (HCI),[6,7] many of which generalize to all product design. We describe a few of these in the context of embedded systems. A complete treatment is beyond the scope of an introductory text, so the goal here is to give the reader a flavor of the kinds of things that would fall beyond the scope of formal verification, that is, beyond the scope of things that can be formally proven.

7.3.1 Validation with respect to human actors

Many (but not all) embedded systems have human interfaces. The bridge system used as an example in this text has an operator's control PC in addition to the lights and gates that are meant to control the ground and river traffic. Other common embedded systems with human interfaces include ATMs, information kiosks, vending machines, and many, many others. Some requirements about the HCI can be verified, typically by inspection. For example, the specification may require that there be a method for the bridge operator to override the normal operation of the bridge. Inspection of the operator's PC interface could determine whether there was some method for the operator to override or not. Similarly, a requirement that pedestrians who are visually impaired are still warned that the ground barriers are being deployed could be verified by checking if the design included both visual and audible warnings. However, many requirements involving human interaction with a system are not verifiable by formal methods or even inspection because they involve nonquantifiable issues. For example, the specification may require that the operator's interface be easy to use. There are methods in the HCI literature[7] that can help design interfaces that are easy to use or that can be used to test an already implemented interface for ease of use. But "easy to use" is subjective, and there is no way to prove a theorem that a particular interface is easy to use.

A related, but broader, concept is that of usability.[7,8] Usability includes the notion of ease of use but also includes other concepts such as understandability, learnability, operability, and universal access. Figure 7.2 shows these entering into the design process, which in turn leads to products that are useable and that will therefore be accepted by the intended users. We consider the first three of these — understandability, learnability, and operability — here. Universal access is so important that we devote an entire section, Section 7.3.2, to it.

Understandability refers to the degree to which the interface makes it obvious how the controls work. Understandability must consider both the nature of the controls and their operation inside the system and also the background and experience of the users. Consider, again, the operator's PC interface in the bridge system. A red octagon-shaped icon associated with a picture of the spans might be a convenient way for the operator to cause the span motors to stop in an emergency. Red signifies emergency, and the octagon is widely used for stop signs. For bridges in most parts of the world, this would be very understandable. Put another way, there is an obvious mapping[4] from the icon to the physical world action it controls. However, there are parts of the world where red is not a color associated with alarm or the octagon is not associated with stopping. A design that easily allowed different forms of the icon for

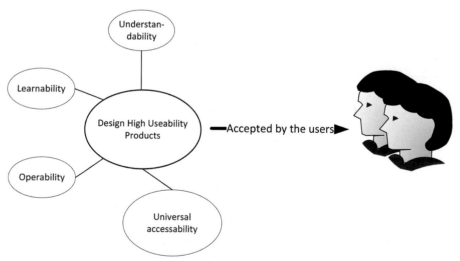

FIGURE 7.2 Factors Leading to the Design of Highly Usable Products.

Author drawn.

this action would have a higher degree of understandability because the interface could be adapted to all those other situations. Suppose, next, that the system was supposed to allow the operator to control the position of the span — have the span move up or down to any position between top and bottom. A slider bar might be considered for this. But if the slider bar were horizontal, the level of understandability would be low. Does left on the slider bar map to up or to down? A vertical slider bar would have a high level of understandability because positions on the slider (up or down) correspond to positions at the end of the span (high in the air or low to the ground).

Learnability refers to the ease with which intended users can learn how to use the system. Interfaces that are more understandable are generally easier to learn how to use than interfaces that are less understandable. Learnability must also be considered in the context of intended users. The intended users of the operator's control panel are people who will undoubtedly undergo training in many areas such as river protocols, general bridge operation, and others. Training in the use of the operator's control panel would be a part of that overall training. Moreover, if the design showed a high level of understandability, training in its use would be correspondingly easier. But what about the other users — boat pilots, car drivers, and pedestrians? The bridge interfaces for these users are fairly simple. Furthermore, the interface devices, such as red lights, alarm bells, and barriers, are already well known to most of these users, so seeing them in the context of a bridge will not require any training for those users. In fact, a general principle regarding learnability is that the more familiar the interface objects are to the intended users, the easier it is for those users to learn how to use them.

Operability refers to the ease of operating and controlling the system. An interface might be understandable and easy to learn how to use and still be difficult to use. For example, if the controls in a computer or cell phone interface are too small, then it would be difficult for some users to touch the screen in just the right spot. An operation that required touching multiple icons on the screen might again be usable and learnable but not easy to do. On the other hand, the system designers might have intended such difficulty as a safety measure to prevent accidental operation if the user accidentally touched an icon on the screen.

As with most engineering design problems, there are often tradeoffs between various competing goals. Continuing with the bridge example, there might be many controls to be placed on the PC screen. This would require individual icons to be smaller, so they all fit. The icons could be designed so that they are understandable and easy to learn to use, but the operability would be low because the screen is cluttered with many small icons. An alternative is to group related icons into a single icon which expands when clicked. For example, there could be a group for span motor operations, a group for ground barrier operations, a group for boat signals, etc. The group icons would be larger, improving the operability at the group level. However, a new user might not understand that the operations are grouped or what the grouping criteria are and therefore take longer to learn how to use the system.

7.3.2 **Universal access**

Universal access refers to the ability of all users to use the product independent of any limitations they may have. The Centers for Disease Control and Prevention (CDC) gives statistics about the number of people in the US who have disabilities and the various types of disabilities.[9] Pullin and Newell[10] give statistics about the numbers of elderly people with various disabilities as of 2007 and note that even at that time, "many countries now have legislation which makes discrimination toward people with disabilities illegal, including lack of provision of, or in-accessible, equipment and services." The World Wide Web Consortium[11] has published policies directed at increasing access to the web. The HCI literature (e.g., Ref. [12]) is rich with research and proposals aimed at making access more universal. Designing universal access to products of the future is critical.

The most common disabilities considered in product design are visual impairment, hearing impairment, and impaired manual dexterity. Other kinds of disabilities, such as cognitive issues, have received less attention to date but will become increasingly important in the future. Visual impairment can range from partial loss of sight to complete blindness and includes other impairments such as colorblindness. Hearing impairment can range from partial to complete and includes other impairments such as loss of hearing in a particular audio frequency range. Manual dexterity impairment can include a wide list of impairments such as limited or no motion in some part of the musculature, shakiness, lack of strength, and many others. The bridge project includes aspects that could limit access or usability. As already noted, visually impaired pedestrians would be at a severe disadvantage if the ground control subsystem did not contain audible warning signals. Colorblind drivers may not understand the flashing lights or even see them the same way fully sighted drivers would, and therefore they may not stop their cars as soon as they should. A colorblind human operator would find the operator's control panel harder to use if color were the main or even significant part of presenting the control information on the PC screen. Web access, including PC/laptop access and cell phone access, has until recently severely suffered in terms of universal access. These are almost exclusively dependent on visual cues. Actions such as clicking/touching icons or swiping are easily understood and learned by sighted users but are virtually useless for blind users. Touching icons on a small screen, such as on a cell phone, is difficult at best for users with low manual dexterity. Providing screen readers and voice input is an attempt by the web industry to overcome the dependency on visual cues, but simply reading the text on the screen may not serve the needs of blind users in many applications.[13]

We emphasize again that designing universal access to the product from the very beginning is crucial for future product development. Behavioral models, as discussed in Chapter 2, should include scenarios in which the human actors have various disabilities. In the bridge example this would include scenarios in which pedestrians with various types of visual impairment are present when a boat arrives, scenarios in which the operator has various types of impairment, scenarios in which the boat operator has various types of impairment, etc. The team that analyzes these scenarios should include members who have the disabilities being considered. At the very least, the team members should put themselves in a corresponding situation; for example, team members may close their eyes and imagine how they would react. If a prototype has been built, the design team can experiment by having people with the relevant disabilities (or team members simulating those disabilities) walk through the scenarios. The behavioral model should be revised if issues are found. Having the design team members "play act" leads to greater understanding by the design team, and this in turn leads to better products. Pullin and Newell[10] describe an interesting instance of play-acting by a design team producing a better product. Engineers at the Ford Motor Company wore specially designed padded suits that limited their mobility and tried to use the new car model they were designing. This resulted in design changes that made the new model more accessible and also more appealing to a wider consumer audience.

7.3.3 Installability and maintainability

To the extent possible, it should be easy to install the product and configure it for initial use. The product should also be easy to maintain and to diagnose when it is not working properly, again to the extent possible given the nature of the product. Installing an ATM, for example, is relatively easy. The device would likely be built in a factory and shipped mostly, if not completely, assembled to the intended site. Installation involves simply fastening it to the location and connecting the power line and possibly the communication link if the latter is by wire. Proper design of the interface, specifically the maintenance and configuration interface used by the technicians as opposed to the normal interface used by bank customers, should make initial setup also easy. Installing a bridge, on the other hand, is not a trivial matter, but steps can be taken to make sure installation is not harder than it has to be. For example, easily accessible cable boxes can be provided for the cables that have to run between various sections of the bridge, such as between the main control module and the various motors and lights. Positioning of the major components that need regular maintenance should allow easy access for the engineers who perform the maintenance. There should be an installation plan to guide the various work teams during installation and initial configuration. Are modules that need regular maintenance easily accessible? Are there easily accessible test points for debugging when the system does not perform properly; these would include hooks for probes used to analyze electronic circuitry and access to mechanical points for things like pressure, temperature, motor torque, etc. These issues should be addressed in the requirements and carried through during all the phases, starting from behavioral modeling and carried through all the successive design phases. Maintenance and repair scenarios should specify what tests need to be done, and validation would then use these scenarios to validate the design. Some of these requirements are verifiable, for example, the existence of test points. Others are subjective and therefore not verifiable by formal methods. Checking requirements such as "easy to access the test points" is part of the validation process.

7.3.4 Portability

Portability, or adaptability, is another feature that is important in engineering in general and embedded systems in particular but not amenable to formal analysis. To the extent possible, the design should allow the product as a whole to be used in a variety of situations and environments. For example, there should be nothing in the design of the bridge that precludes that design from being used for bridges in areas of a river that curve or bend. Are parts of the system modularized and standardized so that new components can be used in future implementations of the product? For example, is the bridge system modularized so that new, more efficient motors developed in the future can be substituted for the motors currently recommended? The credit card reader in check-out systems in physical stores is a good example of a design that allows portability and adaptability. By making the reader a separate physical device with a standardized communication link to the main cash register, the product can be easily adapted to new credit card technologies, such as chip cards and touchless cards, by replacing only a small component of the whole system. The user interface should be designed to be easily adaptable to use in different countries and in different cultures, as mentioned previously. As another example, consider the design of an ATM. How easy is it to change the size and shape of the money trays to work in different countries with their different currencies? How easy is it to alter the interface for different countries and cultures?

7.3.5 Esthetics

Finally, we mention esthetics. Esthetics is often important to the users, and products that don't look appealing may simply not be used. Norman[4] gives some interesting examples of how failure to consider esthetics leads to lower success for the product. For example, hearing aids until recently were considered unesthetic. Users often did not wear them because they drew attention to the user's disability. Much effort was spent designing hearing aids that were invisible. However, when hearing aids became decorative, for example, by being incorporated into appealing earrings, users wanted to use the product. Walkers and canes make the user look old and disabled. But decorative walking sticks can be fashionable, and walkers can be decorated to become "things of beauty" that users are proud to use (aside from also becoming functional by incorporating, say, storage capability for purses, purchased items, cell phones, etc.). Clients may also be concerned about esthetics, often for different reasons than users. For example, a governmental body that purchases bridges may want the bridges to fit into the architecture of the region or even to be amenable to decoration during holiday seasons. To the extent possible, the design of the system should accommodate such client concerns.

7.4 **Evaluation**

Verification and validation have to do with whether or not the design and the implementations meet the requirements and other needs of the client. Evaluation deals with how well those needs were met and how well the process went. There are three points of view — the client/user view, the product view, and the process view.

Client-oriented evaluation focuses on how well the client's needs were met. Optimization of quantitative requirements should have been considered during the design phase, specifically in the mapping of tasks to implementations and the corresponding analysis of alternatives, as described in Chapter 14. For example, given several alternatives for the choice of span motor and associated gearing, Pareto analysis (Chapter 14) would lead to a choice that optimized the combination of cost, energy usage, span rise time, etc., that is, the combination of quantitative requirements for the span module. However, there are aspects of the requirements that cannot be quantified. For example, the requirements may specify that bells of a certain loudness be used in addition to lights for warning pedestrians. The final design would include such bells, but their efficacy may not be determinable until the system has actually been installed. How much ambient noise is in the environment of the bridge, and how does that vary for bridges installed in different locations? Bells that are too loud may be disturbing in quiet environments but not audible in others. Similar questions can be asked about the ground traffic warning lights. Are they in positions that are easily seen by pedestrians and drivers alike? Do they shine adequately as the sun moves across the sky from morning to night? If the design included red and green lights, how well do colorblind pedestrians and drivers understand the messages being conveyed by the lights? How well are the client and users satisfied with the overall esthetics of the bridge? Client/user evaluation focuses on these kinds of nonquantifiable issues.

The company may benefit from evaluating the product independently of the client who ordered it. For example, if there are markets for similar products, the company would be concerned about issues like how easily the design can be adapted to other situations. For example, can most of the bridge design be reused for bridges with a single span hinged at one end or a single span that rotates on a central support? How easy is it to remove modules, for example, to remove the pedestrian barriers for bridges that will be installed in areas with no pedestrian traffic? These issues could have been considered during the modeling and hardware mapping phases, but if they haven't, they can be considered at the end of the project. Were there general lessons learned that can be applied to the design of future products?

Process evaluation focuses on how well the project was managed. Project management is beyond the scope of this text. However, it is important in the business model of a company, so it is important for embedded system engineers to at least know that it is needed.

7.5 Summary

In this chapter we discussed the notions of verification and validation. Verification is the process of determining whether the product meets a set of requirements. Validation includes verification but also includes consideration of other needs of the client beyond formal requirements. Evaluation examines how well the product meets all the needs of the client. We listed properties of interest that are often studied in the verification process. We presented a number of reasoning techniques that are commonly used in verification and illustrated those using our bridge example. We presented a number of additional aspects of a system that are important for the validation process as opposed to the verification process. These include aspects concerned with human usage of the system, especially by humans who may have some disabilities that impact their ability to perform operations necessary to use the system. They also include other aspects of the complete lifecycle of a system such as installability, portability, and esthetics. Finally, we discussed the importance of studying how well the system or product meets the needs of the client and how well the design process itself proceeded.

Problems

1. Consider the following FSM. S0 is the start state.

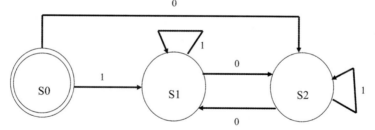

    a. Describe the paths that lead to S1 the first time.
    b. Describe the paths that lead from S1 to the next time the FSM enters S1.
    c. Prove that the following property holds for this FSM.
    P: Whenever the FSM is in state S1, the number of 0s that have been seen is even.
    (Hint: Prove that P holds the first time S1 is reached and that if P holds at some point when the FSM is in state S1, it also holds the next time S1 is reached.)

2. Review the FSM in Figure 3.3 in Chapter 3. Prove that the following statement is always true: If the FSM is in state S1, then the output string has no substring with more than one consecutive blank. (Hint: Use induction; use case analysis for the inductive case.)

3. In Chapter 3, Problem 4, you were asked to draw an FSM that accepted strings in which the vowels were in alphabetic order. Prove that your FSM is correct.

4. In a group or class setting discuss how the bridge system should accommodate people with each of the following impairments: vision impairment, hearing impairment, vision and hearing impairment, and mobility impairment (e.g., walks with a cane).

5. In a group or class setting pick a product meant to be worn, such as hearing aids or glucose monitors, and discuss how it could be made more esthetically pleasing and desirable.

6. Select some products with significant human interfaces, such as a particular cell phone app, a particular ticket vending machine, an online shopping site, the interior of a new car, etc. Discuss in class or in small groups the understandability, learnability, operability, universal access, and esthetics of the selected products.

References

[1] C. Hoare, An Axiomatic Basis for Computer Programming, Commun. ACM 12 (10) (1969) 576–580.

[2] R. Patton, Software Testing, Sams Publishing, ISBN 978-0672327988, 2005.

[3] M. Limaye, Software Testing, Chapter 3, Tate McGraw-Hill Education, 2009, ISBN 978-0-07-013990-9.

[4] D. Norman, The Design of Everyday Things: Revised and Expanded Edition, Basic Books, 2013, ISBN 0465055710.

[5] NATO RTO Task Group IST-027/RTG-009, Validation, Verification and Certification of Embedded Systems, 2005, ISBN 92-837-1146-7.

[6] A. Dix, J. Finlay, G. Abowd, R. Beale, Human Computer Interaction, third ed., Pearson/Prentice Hall, 2004, ISBN 0130-461091.

[7] M. Soares (Eds.), et al., 23rd HCI International Conference, HCII 2021, Design, User Experience, and Usability. Proceedings of the 23rd HCII International Conference LNCS 12780, Springer, 2021.

[8] M. Soares, E. Rosenzweig, A. Marcus (Eds.), Design, User Experience, and Usability: Design for Contemporary Technological Environments. Proceedings of the 10th International Conference DUXU 2021 LNCS 12781, Springer, 2021.

[9] https://www.cdc.gov/ncbddd/disabilityandhealth/infographic-disability-impacts-all.html.

[10] G. Pullin, A. Newel, Focus on extra-ordinary users, in: C. Stephanidis (Ed.), Universal Access in HCI, Part I, HCII 2007 LNCS 4554, © Springer-Verlag Berlin Heidelberg, 2007, pp. 253–262.

[11] https://www.w3.org/WAI/policies/.

[12] M. Antona, C. Stephanidis (Eds.), Universal Access in Human Computer Interaction: Design Methods and User Experience, Proceedings of the 15th International Conference UAHCI 2021, Springer (LNCS 12768).

[13] L. Henschen, J. Lee, Using Semantic-Level Tags in HTML/XML Documents, in: Proceedings of the 13th HCII International Conference, Springer, 2009, pp. 683–692.

Testing

8

8.1 Introduction

Testing is a major part of the validation process. Testing can be performed at every stage of the product development process, from the earliest behavioral modeling through internal modeling up to final product implementation and deployment. Behavioral models can be tested to ensure that they capture the operational requirements and behavior expected by the client and other stakeholders. The finite state machine (FSM)/specification and description language (SDL) and Petri models can be tested to ensure that they capture the required behavior. Final products can be tested to ensure that the manufacture and deployment capture all the aspects of the behavioral and internal models. Testing models is done by simulation. Testing a deployed product can be done by simulating inputs from actors or by real actors interacting with the system under observation by the testing team. For example, a deployed bridge can be tested by having test engineers activate the sensors or by having real boats, cars, and pedestrians approach the bridge. Test cases are driven by the use cases and scenarios. Each test should have one or more expected outcomes or results based on one or more of the requirements. The goal of running that test is to verify that the requirements are met for that scenario. (Test plan generation is, itself, a major endeavor and is well beyond the scope of this text.)

General methodologies for general test planning are beyond the scope of this text. However, we illustrate the general process in Figure 8.1. As can be seen on the right, test plans should be generated for all phases of product development, from early behavioral modeling to testing after the product has been installed. The requirements drive the creation of each test plan. For each phase, a complete plan for how the system will be tested at that stage is developed.

This chapter focuses on simulation/emulation, discrete event simulation (DES) (one of the main simulation methods), and test case development.

8.2 Simulation/emulation

Simulation can be performed at each stage in the product development process, from the behavioral modeling stage through product implementation. Simulation of a

Embedded System Design. https://doi.org/10.1016/B978-0-443-18470-3.00008-7

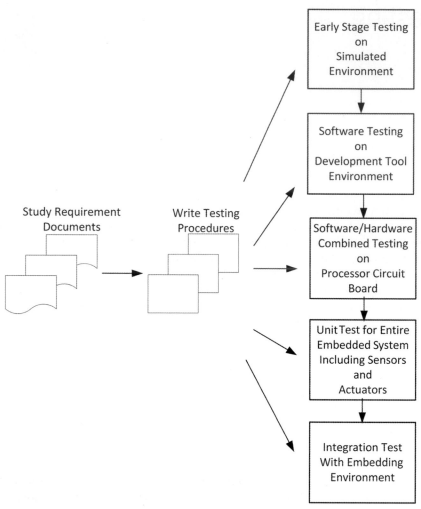

FIGURE 8.1 Embedded System Testing Procedures.

Author drawn.

behavioral model involves simulating test cases for each scenario in that model. In the case of an implementation of a product that implementation can be tested before deployment by providing artificial stimulation of inputs. Testing a model or implemented product by simulation can't prove that the model or implementation is correct. In more complex products simulation cannot even cover all possible cases. However, simulation can uncover problems and errors, and the earlier in the development process such problems and errors are found, the easier it is to correct them.

Simulation can also help convince clients and stakeholders that the model or implementation does indeed satisfy their needs, and the greater the number of scenarios tested, the more convincing the testing is. Finally, the results from simulations can be saved and compared with the actual operation of the final product to ensure that the manufacture and deployment of the product have not introduced errors in system operation.

The simulation techniques and issues we discuss here are for the simulation of discrete problems — message sequence charts, FSM/SDL systems, Petri nets, etc. Simulation for continuous systems, such as object tracking in 3D space or continuous feedback systems, is a separate topic to which an entire course could be devoted. Interested readers are referred to Ref. [1] for a brief overview and additional references.

8.2.1 **Simulation**

Simulating a model means stepping through, or "executing", the model with stimuli from actors provided by the simulation team as opposed to real actors.[2] Stepping through can mean a walkthrough by humans in which the simulation team proposes actor stimuli at specific times in the walkthrough and then describes verbally the sequence of actions that the model specifies in response to those stimuli. Simulation can also be done by special programs that allow the simulation team to input sequences of stimuli, after which the software performs all the calculations to determine the sequence of actions the model would perform in response. There are simulation tools for all the modeling techniques described in Section 1 of this text. See Refs. [3—5] for lists of simulation tools. There are also multitudes of simulation tools for programming languages and electronic circuitry. Walkthroughs by human teams can provide useful insight into the model because the humans can see all the details of the actions. This was illustrated in various examples in Chapters 3 and 5. However, human simulation can be prone to error. Software tools are accurate and allow the simulation of much more complex test cases.

Simulation can be used to test for correct behavior of the model, that is, test that the model satisfies the requirements. For example, did inputs from actors produce the correct sequence of messages in a behavioral model or the correct actions and transitions in an FSM/SDL model? Simulation can also help test for a variety of other properties and issues such as the presence of states that can never be reached, proper return and recovery after an error, if a bad state (e.g., a bad combination of actions, values, and final state in an FSM/SDL model) is reachable, robustness in the presence of faults/failures (recall from Chapter 6) or unexpected cases, and timing.

Regarding robustness, most simulation tools allow the user to stop the simulation and examine and possibly change internal values. Continuing the simulation with such altered values allows the simulation team to examine how the model behaves in unexpected situations or when some module of the system fails to perform correctly. For example, in the behavioral model of the bridge, the team might block the signal that the ground traffic had cleared the span to ensure that the system transitions to a failure case in which, say, the boat is warned and the local police are called. Or, the team might indicate that the approaching boat stops (i.e., never reaches the other side) to see how the model behaves.

Timing issues can also be studied through simulation. Examples of such issues include:

- What are minimum and maximum response times for actions to be taken or a state of interest to be reached in response to a stimulus entering the system? For example, once a boat has been detected (stimulus), what are the minimum and maximum times for appropriate messages to be received by other modules in the system? What is the maximum time before the span is ready to go up or the boat is warned to stop?
- Where are the bottlenecks in the system, especially bottlenecks due to multiple stimuli being received at about the same time? For example, in a bank kiosk with several ATMs, the communication link to the bank's database may be a bottleneck; the link may be clogged with more messages than it can handle in a reasonable amount of time.
- Do some modules in the system have to wait because other modules do not react quickly enough?
- What is the throughput of the system? That is, how many stimuli can the system receive in a given amount of time and the system still respond correctly to all of them? For example, how many boats can the bridge system handle in a given amount of time?

In order to study such issues with simulation, estimates of the amount of time each action requires or each message takes to reach its destination have to be used until prototype modules have been built or software written. Time estimates in simulations, especially simulation of early models like behavioral models, are usually made at the human level — seconds or longer. For example, in a simulation of the bridge behavioral model, the simulation team may estimate that it takes the main control module less than 1 second to recognize the arrival of a boat and send a message to the ground traffic barrier module, 5 seconds for barriers to lower, no more than 30 seconds for the spans to go up, etc., but an arbitrary amount of time for the cars and pedestrians to clear the bridge. In the case of ground traffic clearing the bridge there may be no cars or pedestrians when the boat arrives (zero time to clear), or a car might be stalled on the span (arbitrarily large amount of time to clear). As the design process continues, with some software modules written and some hardware modules implemented, more accurate estimates of the times can be made.

8.2.2 Emulation

Emulation is like simulation except that some parts of the system being tested are real, not simulated.[6] Emulation allows early testing of parts of a product in semirealistic settings. The "real" parts might be actual sub-systems that have already been built, such as a prototype of the ground traffic barrier sub-system in the example below, or lab or even toy products, such as a toy bridge span with its own toy motor to raise and lower the span. Emulation allows the test team to test implemented modules as well as see how they would behave in the completed product.

In the bridge system examples of emulations might include the following:

- The main control module of the bridge system might be implemented and then tested by linking it with various laptops that simulate the ground traffic control module, the span control module, the boat sensors, etc. Each of these laptops could have an interface that allowed a tester to see any messages sent by the main control module and to enter messages for that module to send to the main control module. Such a setup could allow the test team to check whether the main control module operates properly in all the different scenarios such as cases in which different numbers of boats arrive, ground traffic does not clear after specified wait time, span fails to go up, etc.
- A prototype of the ground traffic barrier sub-system could be tested by emulation in which a PC is used to simulate the messages between that sub-system and the main control module.

8.3 Discrete event simulation

DES[7,8] is the most common approach for the simulation of discrete systems, that is, systems in which the stimuli occur at discrete points in time. The bridge system or an ATM system is an example of a discrete system. Boats arrive at discrete times; either there are cars or pedestrians or there are no cars or pedestrians on the span, etc. Non-discrete embedded systems include, among others, continuous feedback control systems, such as in aircraft, in which the stimuli are continuous functions providing continuous input. As noted above, simulation/emulation in general, and DES in particular, provides an excellent high-level view of how a system will perform, where bottlenecks are, where errors and timing issues are, and overall system-level timing.

8.3.1 Events and event queues

Definition 8.1 An **event** is anything that causes a change in the system. New stimuli from actors are events. Internal events, such as a process finishing or a timer expiring, are also events in the DES terminology.

Definition 8.2 The **event time** (also called the **arrival time** for an event representing a stimulus from an actor) is the time at which the event should occur in the simulation.

Definition 8.3 A **discrete event sequence** is a sequence of events with corresponding times at which those events occur. The sequence is ordered by the times at which the events occur.

Event sequences are stored in a queue. The initial queue contains the events representing stimuli from actors that the design team has proposed for the test. For example, an initial event queue for the bridge might have a boat being sensed at time 0, ground traffic being cleared time 30 seconds after the barriers are down, a second boat being sensed at time 97 seconds, and so on.

During the simulation, the event at the front of the queue is processed when its time has arrived. (Note that there may be several events with the same arrival time. For example, in an AND-hierarchical FSM, separate modules may have transitions whose conditions become true at the same time. In such cases all events are processed as if in parallel.) Processing an event means that the event is given to the system being simulated, after which the system reacts to the event. The system would perform actions, some of which may create new events. Each new event will have an associated arrival time and will be inserted into the event queue in order. For example, in the behavioral model of the bridge, the arrival of a boat causes a message to be sent to the main control module. Assuming messages are not sent instantaneously (i.e., taking zero time), a new event would be created — the arrival of the "boat sensed" message with arrival time, say, 0.5 seconds after the current simulation time. The arrival of a message to lower the ground traffic barriers at the ground traffic module would cause a new event to be created — ground traffic barriers have been lowered at an estimated time based on the current clock and the estimated time it takes for the barriers to go down.

8.3.2 Time

Time is a crucial element in DES. Events are inserted into the event queue in order of their occurrence. Times for events caused by external stimuli, also called arrival times, are given by the test team and correspond to different scenarios. For example, in one scenario for the bridge system, the boat may be moving at a speed for which the boat will reach the other side of the bridge in 150 seconds, and there may be both cars and pedestrians on the bridge when the boat arrives so that it takes longer for the traffic to be cleared (pedestrians take more time to reach the other side), etc. Times for events inside the system are estimated based on knowledge about the components of the system and computations performed by the system. For example, the spans may be estimated to take 40–45 seconds to lower depending on the time needed for alignment at the end. For an example of time for computation, the upstream boat sensor might include analysis that determines the type of boat and whether it is large enough to require raising the spans. The time it takes for this would have to be included in estimating the time from boat arrival to setting of I_barv. Test teams use a variety of methods to make these estimates such as prior experience with the same or similar equipment, manufacturers' specifications, engineering knowledge (e.g., computations for raising the span based on motor rotations per minute, gear ratio, angular inertia of the span, etc.), testing/simulation of submodules, and others. When an action that is not instantaneous is performed, a new event is inserted into the queue using the time at which the action will be completed.

Actions may be instantaneous or have duration. Moreover, the notion of instantaneous depends on the time frame of interest. Sending a message in a closed communication system (e.g., a wired link between modules in the bridge system) can be an instantaneous action when simulating a behavioral model because the message would reach its destination in a time less than humans could distinguish. On the other hand, if the simulation was studying the relative arrival times of messages in an SDL model, sending a message over a link should not be considered instantaneous. For actions that are not instantaneous, the test team must make an estimate of the amount of time the action takes. This could be a single number or a time range. For example, in a closed communication network, the time that it takes for a message to go from the sender to the receiver can be determined quite accurately and would result in a single number for the simulation. On the other hand, the action of lowering the spans may take differing amounts of time depending on the process at the end, where the spans are aligned before the last few feet of lowering. The complete lowering process might take, for example, between 40 and 45 seconds.

Arrival times are determined by the test team using a variety of methods. In many cases knowledge of the application and experience imply plausible values for arrival times. For example, in the bridge application there would be extensive knowledge and experience about when boats arrive, how often more than one boat arrives, how long it takes for ground traffic to clear the span, etc. In other cases mathematical models are used to derive sets of test cases for simulation. For example, the Poisson distribution in statistics gives a good approximation of arrival times for customers at an ATM. A test case can be derived by applying the Poisson distribution to get a set of arrival times for customer arrivals, and this set of customer arrivals forms the initial event queue for a single simulation. The generation of test cases, that is, initial event queues, can be informed by various factors that affect the usage of the product. For example, the distribution of arrival times for customers is different for the lunch hour than for mid-morning or mid-afternoon because many people run errands such as banking over their lunch breaks. The weather can affect how quickly ground traffic clears the bridge or how fast the boats move or even how soon the boat sensor can "see" an approaching boat.

8.3.3 Examples

We present three examples to illustrate the concepts mentioned in the preceding sections, one for each of the modeling techniques behavioral, FSM, and Petri net. The first two examples are based on the bridge project, one using the message sequence chart in Figure 2.6 and the other using the FSM in Figure 3.11.

8.3.3.1 Simulation of a message sequence chart

Review the message sequence chart of Figure 2.6. Suppose we add the following timing information for actions performed by the bridge.

- It takes from 0.25 to 1.0 seconds after the boat arrives in a range of the sensor for the sensor to send a message to the main control. (The sensor module has to do some processing to determine if the boat is big enough to require the bridge to open.)
- It takes from 0 to 2.0 seconds for the main module to send the message to sound the alarm and change the traffic light. (The main module processor may be working on other tasks, such as updating the weather information.)
- The message to lower the barriers is sent 5 seconds later.
- It takes from 1.0 to 1.5 seconds for the barriers to go down. The traffic lights will be lit in less than 0.1 seconds.
- It takes the spans from 25 to 30 seconds to go up.
- It takes the spans from 40 to 45 seconds to go down.
- It takes from 1.0 to 1.5 seconds for the barriers to go up and the traffic lights to turn off.

Assume all other actions are performed in negligible time. For example, the main module sends the message to raise the spans immediately (i.e., 0 time) after receiving the bridge-cleared message, the main module receives the message that the boat has reached the other side (sensor senses the boat and sends the message) in 0 time, the main module sends the message to raise the traffic barriers and turn off the traffic lights immediately after receiving the message that the boat has reached the other side, etc.

For this particular scenario, we make the following assumptions about the behavior of the actors.

- Assume in this scenario that the ground traffic is cleared in no more than 50 seconds. (A different scenario is used to study cases where the ground traffic is not cleared in that time.)
- Assume that the boat will reach the bridge in from 90 to 120 seconds. (Some boats move fast, others more slowly.)
- Assume that the boat will pass under the bridge to the other side in from 5 to 8 seconds.

One situation covered by this scenario has the following times associated with internal and external events.

- The message that a boat has arrived is sent to the main module 0.4 seconds after the boat arrives.
- It takes 0.5 seconds for the main module to send the message to sound the alarm.
- It takes 1.5 seconds for the barriers to go down.
- Ground traffic on the bridge is cleared in 36 seconds.
- It takes the span of 26 seconds to go up.

- The boat arrives at the bridge in 100 seconds.
- The boat reaches the other side in 6 seconds.
- The spans arc completely lowered in 42.
- The barriers to go up and the traffic lights to turn off in 1.2 seconds.

Assume time counts from 0 when the boat first arrives. The relative times for all the events (messages sent, actions completed) are completely determined. Note that no times for things like pedestrians hearing the alarm and drivers seeing the traffic light change are given. Neither of these causes other actions in the system, and those times can be thought to be incorporated into the time for the bridge to be cleared.

Suppose there is a requirement that the spans bc fully raised at least 20 seconds before the boat reaches the bridge. One goal of the simulation for this specific scenario is to test whether or not the 20-second requirement is met.

Time	Event
0	boat arrives
0.4	message sent to main module
0.9	main module sends message to sound alarm and change lights
5.9	main module sends message to lower barriers
7.4	barriers are down and lights on
43.4	ground traffic is cleared
43.4	main module sends message to raise spans
69.4	spans fully raised
100.0	boat reaches bridge
106.0	boat reaches other side
106.0	main module receives message that boat is on other side
106.0	main module sends message to lower spans
148.0	spans are completely lowered
148.0	main module sends message to raise barriers and turn off lights
149.2	barriers are up, and lights are off

The simulation team may study the scenarios represented in this message sequence chart by specifying only a few parameters at the beginning and specifying others during the simulation. For example, the team may wish to study the consequences of longer or shorter times for ground traffic to be cleared from the span. The team may specify the same times as above, except for the time for the ground traffic to clear. This would result in the following event queue:

Time	Event
0	boat arrives
0.4	message sent to main module
0.9	main module sends message to sound alarm and change lights
5.9	main module sends message to lower barriers
7.4	barriers are down and lights on
	Filled in after team specifies time for traffic to clear.

Continued

Time	Event
100.0	boat reaches bridge
106.0	boat reaches other side
106.0	main module receives message that boat is on other side
106.0	main module sends message to lower spans
148.0	spans are completely lowered
148.0	main module sends message to raise barriers and turn off lights
149.2	barriers are up, and lights are off

The team could then make different specifications for how long it takes the ground traffic to clear the bridge, and for each such specification, the remaining lines of the event sequence would be filled in.

Problem 1 asks the student to explore this message sequence chart further.

8.3.3.2 Simulation of a finite state machine

Before presenting the second example, we formalize the general procedure and show the important data elements. Figure 8.2 illustrates a general DES procedure and the three important data elements: system clock, system state variables, and event queue. In Figure 8.2 we used the system variables of our bridge system in the FSM model represented in Chapter 3, Figure 3.11.

For a given application, there are typically many more events in the simulation of an FSM because an FSM has internal state transitions and internal as well as external actions. A message sequence chart for the same application would not have internal transitions and actions. For example, in the FSM model in Figure 3.11, there are separate states for the traffic lights (transition to yellow before transitioning to red, transitioning back to green after the spans are down) that are not of interest to the behavioral model. Similarly, Figure 3.11 shows separate states for the barriers going up or down, separate states for the spans going up or down, etc. Again, the preliminary behavioral model presented in Figure 2.6 did not model this kind of internal behavior.

However, the general simulation process is the same — some or all of the timing parameters are specified, events are processed in order of time, new events are placed in the event queue as actions are performed, and the team specifies event duration times as necessary when an event whose time has not already been given is encountered. The walkthrough presented after Figure 3.11 was, in fact, a DES with some, but not all, of the parameters specified. (Recall that the purpose of that example was to illustrate how AND super-states operated, not to illustrate simulation.) In that walkthrough specific times were specified for some of the internal parameters — barriers go down or up in 3 seconds, spans go down or up in 20 seconds. The time for a global variable to be set and the changed value to be recognized by all the modules was assumed to be zero.

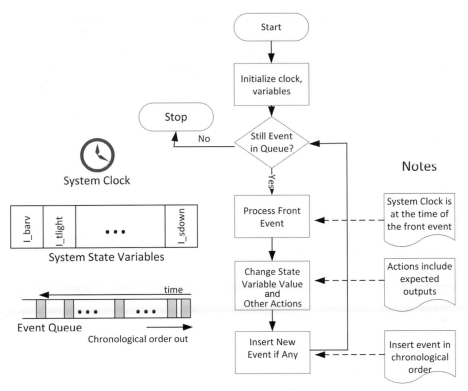

FIGURE 8.2 A General DES Simulation Procedure.

Author drawn.

For this example, we use the same time specification for barriers and spans and add the following two specifications for global variables:

- It takes 1.75 seconds from the time the boat reaches a sensor (either upstream or downstream) for the changes in the global variable I_barv to be recognized by other modules.
- It takes 0.01 seconds for all other global variable changes to take effect in other modules.

We also use the same times for external events as in the walkthrough after Figure 3.11:

- The boat arrives at the upstream sensor at time t = 0.
- Bridge traffic is cleared 75 seconds after the barriers are down.
- The boat is traveling at a speed at which it passes the upstream sensor in 7 seconds, arrives at the bridge 95 seconds after it arrives at the upstream sensor, and arrives at the downstream sensor 150 seconds after it arrives at the upstream sensor.

The goal is to verify that the spans are fully raised at least 20 seconds before the boat reaches the bridge.

The initial event queue contains three events:

Time	Event
0.00	boat arrives at the upstream sensor
7.00	boat passes the upstream sensor
150.00	boat arrives at downstream sensor

Note that the initial queue does not include the events such as the barriers reaching the down position, bridge traffic being cleared, spans reaching the up position, etc. because those times are determined during the simulation. (Of course, this FSM is simple enough that one could easily calculate all the event times without simulation. However, FSMs for real products would be so large that hand calculation would be difficult and error-prone.) The simulation clock is set to 0. The first event is simulated. The boat arrival event is removed from the queue. One new event is inserted into the queue in order — recognition of the change in global variable I_barv.

Time	Event
1.75	I_barv change to 1 recognized by other modules
7.00	boat passes the upstream sensor
150.00	boat arrives at downstream sensor

At time 1.75, LIGHT and TrSENSOR both transition. LIGHT sets its internal times to five. This timer is internal to LIGHT, so no event for other modules recognizing it is added to the queue. However, a new event corresponding to the timer expiring is added. TrSENSOR sets global variable I_btrfclr to zero. This global variable is used in other modules, so a new event at time 1.76 is entered into the queue for when the new value is recognized in those other modules. The processed event is removed from the event queue, and the two new events are inserted.

Time	Event
1.76	I_btrfclr = 0 recognized by other modules
5.75	LIGHT timer expires
7.00	boat passes the upstream sensor
150.00	boat arrives at downstream sensor

The next event occurs at time 1.76. All modules recognize that I_btrfclr is now zero. However, none of the modules has a transition whose condition is true, so nothing happens. The event is removed from the queue, and there is no new event.

Time	Event
5.75	LIGHT timer expires
7.00	boat passes the upstream sensor
150.00	boat arrives at downstream sensor

The next event occurs at time 5.75. The yellow light timer expires. LIGHT transitions to state RED and sets global variable I_tlight to R. This new value will be recognized in the other modules after 0.01 seconds, so a new event is created for t = 5.76. The processed event is removed from the queue.

Time	Event
5.76	l_tlight=R recognized by other modules
7.00	boat passes the upstream sensor
150.00	boat arrives at downstream sensor

At time 5.76, the other modules react to the new value of I_tlight. Only BARRIER has an enabled transition. BARRIER transitions to state mdown. No global variables are set, but a new event for the barriers reaching the down position 3 seconds later is created.

Time	Event
7.00	boat passes the upstream sensor
8.76	barriers reach down position
150.00	boat arrives at downstream sensor

Problem 2 asks the student to complete this simulation.

8.3.3.3 Simulation of a Petri net

Simulation of a place-transition Petri net involves moving dots from place to place. The Petri net does not itself have other actions, although of course the system being modeled would have actions associated with the transitions. These system actions would have associated times. A transition may have a constant associated time, or the real-world action it represents may take variable amounts of time at different points in the simulation. Consider, for example, the two-robot Petri net of Figure 5.5. Transition T3 may take a fixed amount of time, say 5 seconds; after robot 1 has found an empty space and placed the package, it always takes 5 seconds for it to walk out of the common storage area. On the other hand, transition T1 may take varying amounts of time. Robot 1 may have to walk to different areas of the factory to retrieve the next item and may even have to wait until a next item is available; so, T1 may take varying amounts of time. Next, recall that enabled transitions are not required to fire. The simulation team must specify if enabled transitions fire immediately or can be delayed. In the latter case the delay times must also be factored into the determination of event arrival times. Finally, multiple transitions can be enabled at the same time, and the team must specify which transitions fire in such cases. The most common choices for these are that transitions fire as soon as they are enabled and that multiple enabled transitions fire in parallel unless such parallel firing is blocked by the union of the preconditions and postconditions for those transitions.

We simulate the Petri net of Figure 5.5. Times for transitions will be assigned during the simulation. The goal of the test is to verify that P9 (number of parts in the staging area) never has more than three dots. Assume transitions fire as soon as they are enabled and that multiple enabled transitions fire simultaneously unless blocked. In the latter case one of the transitions is randomly selected to fire. When a transition fires, the markings in the preset of that transition are changed immediately. This prevents, for example, robot 2 from thinking the staging area is empty while robot 1 is in the process of entering to place a part there. An event is created for the time at which that transition is completed, and markings for the postset are changed at the time the transition completes. Assume the Petri net has the marking shown in Figure 5.5. Two transitions are enabled at time 0: T1 and T4.

Time	Event
0	T1 and T4 fire; one dot removed from each of P1 and P4

Suppose robot 1 takes 20 seconds to retrieve the next part and walk to the common storage area. Assume robot 2 takes 3 seconds to walk to the common storage area. The event at time 0 is processed, creating two new events — robot 1 arrives at the common storage area at time 20, and robot 2 arrives at the common storage area at time 3.

Time	Event
3	T4 complete; dot placed in P5
20	T1 complete; dot placed in P2

The next event is at time 3. The marking is changed. P5 gets one dot. No transitions are newly enabled, so no other actions are taken or events created.

Time	Event
20	T1 complete; dot placed in P2

The next event is at time 20. The marking is changed. P2 has one dot. T2 is now enabled and fires, removing one dot from each of P2, P7, and P8. Suppose it takes 6 seconds for robot 1 to walk into the common storage area and place the item in an empty slot. The processed event is removed from the queue, and a new event is created at current time plus 6 seconds and inserted into the event queue.

Time	Event
26	T2 complete; dot placed in P3; dot placed in P9

The next event is at time 26. The marking is changed. At this point, both P3 and P9 have dots. T3 is enabled and fires, removing one dot from P3. T5 is still not enabled because there is no dot in P8. Suppose it takes robot 1 5 seconds to walk out of the common storage area. A new event is created for time 31.

Time	Event
31	T3 complete; dot placed in P1; dot placed in P8

At time 31, T3 is complete. The marking is changed. Now both P1 and P8 have dots again. Transitions T1 and T5 both fire, removing one dot from each place in their presets. Suppose this firing of T1 takes 25 seconds, and T5 takes 7 seconds. Two new events are created. The processed event is removed from the queue, and the two new events are inserted.

Time	Event
38	T5 complete; dot placed in P6; dot placed in P7
56	T1 complete; dot placed in P2

Problem 3 asks the student to continue this example.

8.4 **Generating test cases**

Testing a model or a product by discrete even simulation means running that product with as many different test cases as is feasible. The set of test cases should cover all the use cases and as many scenarios within each use case as is feasible.

8.4.1 **Methods for deriving test cases**

Test cases can be derived by brainstorming. The test team would start with the use cases and scenarios from the behavioral analysis and create initial event sequences with times attached to the stimuli from the actors in that scenario. Some tests can also be derived directly from the requirements, for example, assuming a boat speed that allows the boat to pass from the upstream sensor to the downstream sensor within 150 seconds in normal situations (no errors or emergencies). Arrival times are determined as described in the last paragraph of Section 8.2.3.2. Estimates of the times required for the system to perform actions, like raising or lowering the span, would be determined. Where the model being tested specifies time ranges, the test set should include separate cases with event times with different values within that range. For example, the simple message sequence chart in Figure 2.6 in Chapter 2 might have included a condition that cars and pedestrians already on the bridge span reach the other side within 20 seconds. Test cases should include one with time zero (i.e., there were no cars on the span when the boat was sensed), ones with times in the middle of the range 0−10, one with a time like 9.8 seconds, and one with a time of exactly 10 seconds. Brainstorming is appropriate for generating test cases for a behavioral model.

Test case generation for models of internal operation, such as FSM/SDL and Petri net models, requires additional considerations beyond an initial brainstorming based on use cases and scenarios. These models contain additional details, conditions, and actions that are not relevant at the behavioral model level. For example, the FSM in Figure 3.11 of Chapter 3 specifies internal details of operation that do not appear explicitly in the messages sequence charts of the behavioral model. Internal timing specifications, such as the setting and expiration of timers, have impact on behavioral-level timing requirements. For example, the Light Control Module in the FSM will take a certain amount of time to reach the red state, and this may affect a time constraint in the behavioral model such as maximum amount of time for ground traffic to be cleared. Finally, internal models contain branching, much like the branching in software, that corresponds to different scenarios. For example, there would be different scenarios for situations in which the ground traffic is cleared in time and not cleared in time. If the time limit were, say, 30 seconds, then there should be test cases in which the ground traffic clears in 10 or 15 seconds (well before the limit), 29 seconds, 29.8 seconds, exactly 30 seconds, 30.1 seconds, etc. Techniques used for test case generation in software[9] can be adapted for this aspect of test generation for models.

Concurrency issues need to be studied by appropriate test cases. Concurrency issues may arise within a single module or in separate modules in a distributed system. For an example of internal concurrency, recall the example in Section 3.7.2 of Chapter 3. The span motor may overheat at about the same time as the spans reach the near bottom position. Test cases should include ones where the overheat signal occurs well before the spans reach near bottom (perhaps a few seconds), only slightly before (e.g., ½ second of 1/10 second), at exactly the same time, slightly after, and well after. For distributed systems, concurrency issues usually arise when messages are sent from one module to another. The message may arrive at about the same time as some internal change is happening. As before, test cases should include situations in which the message arrives well before, about the same time, exactly the same time, slightly after, and well after.

When an automated simulation tool is used, test cases can be generated using random number generators. For example, when a time range for a specific activity is specified, test cases can be derived by generating random numbers within that range. (Of course, the design team may generate test cases with values outside that range to see how the system behaves in unexpected scenarios.) The random number generators may use a relevant probability distribution (e.g., Poisson distribution for ATM customer arrival times) when the distribution is known or suspected. Hundreds or even thousands of test cases can be generated and run through the simulation tool. This allows meaningful statistical data about key system properties to be collected about the system. Moreover, much longer test cases can be simulated, allowing for the study of how the system behaves over extended periods of time. For example, random generation of boat arrival times over a period of 30 days gives test cases that demonstrate the behavior of the bridge over an entire month and with a variety of river traffic patterns.

8.4.2 General principles and guidelines

Here are a few principles and guidelines for generating a good set of test cases.

Test cases should always start from the initial state of the system. In a large model it may be tempting to try to test a small portion of, say, an FSM or one portion of a module in an SDL-distributed model. However, it is not easy to ensure that all the side effects of actions from other parts of the system are initialized properly. Other parts of the model may have timers that had partially expired and would affect the small portion being tested when they expired. Other parts of the system may have set global variables or sent messages that a test case looking only at a small portion of the whole system might not account for. The way to ensure that all of these things have reasonable values is to simulate from the initial state. Of course, the test case must be designed so that the portion being studied is reached. For example, in an FSM the test team would create an event sequence that caused the FSM to transition to the part being studied.

For actions performed by the system and processes outside the system that have time duration, test cases should be included with times at both boundaries and at various points in the middle of the duration. For example, in the bridge system if the span may take between 40 and 45 seconds to completely lower in normal situations, then there should be test cases in which the spans lower in 40 seconds, 40.1 seconds, 43 seconds, 44.9 seconds, and 45 seconds. There should be test cases for various possible time relationships between external stimuli. For example, a second boat may be sensed by the bridge system any time from a minimum number of seconds after the first boat is sensed (determined by laws regulating river traffic) up to the time the first boat passes under the bridge to the other side and even after. Suppose the minimum legal time for a second boat to appear was, say, 60 seconds, and suppose the time for a boat to pass under the bridge after first being sensed ranged from 120 seconds to 200 seconds. There should be test cases in which the first boat reaches the other side after 120 seconds, 121 seconds, 150 seconds, 199 seconds, etc. For each of these, there should be test cases in which the second boat is sensed 60 seconds after the first boat was sensed, 61 seconds, etc., as well as being sensed a few seconds before the first boat reaches the other side, 1 second before it reaches the other side, a fraction of a second before it reaches the other side, exactly the same time it reaches the other side, a fraction of a second after, a few seconds after, etc. Simulations tools make a large number of tests feasible, and the results of those simulations help the test team determine if the design works correctly in all those cases or there might be an issue that needs resolving.

A corollary to the principle in the preceding paragraph is that in systems in which multiple events can happen at nearly the same time, such as distributed systems and FSMs with AND super-states, test cases must be generated in which events in concurrent modules occur at or near the same time and in various orders. This allows the test team to study nondeterminism in the system. Examples in which this may be important include AND super-state FSMs in which actions may run concurrently, SDL models in which messages may be sent nearly concurrently and arrive at their destination at about the same time but in arbitrary order, and Petri nets in which transitions in different parts of the net are enabled at the same time and may fire in either order or even in parallel.

Finally, there should be test cases for error conditions. These would include at a minimum test cases for errors anticipated in the specifications and requirements for the system, such as ground traffic not clearing after a boat is sensed or the ground traffic barrier not deploying. To the extent possible, the test cases should include ones in which unexpected errors occur. For example, the bridge specifications and requirements may not have addressed what to do if a person climbs up the bridge span while it is up and a boat is going under the bridge. In the FSM model, for example, this would be indicated by an event in which the pedestrian sensor senses someone on the span after the boat has been allowed to proceed. Was the FSM designed in such a way that this stimulus would cause the span to start going down again? This could be a disaster if the span crashed onto the boat. On the other hand, even though it is illegal for a person to climb on the span in this situation, the bridge should do something safe and reasonable to the extent possible. In any case, it would be important for the client and stakeholders to know what would happen in a case like this. Of course, it is not possible for the design team to think of all the possible unanticipated scenarios, but running simulations for as many of these as feasible can help ensure that the final delivered product is safe and robust.

8.5 Summary

In this chapter we discussed ways that different models of a system could be tested. We emphasized the importance of testing as early as possible, including testing even at the behavioral modeling stage. We described simulation, the major methodology for testing designs, and discussed how emulation could be used for testing when some of the parts of the system under development had already been built but others hadn't. We then focused on the major method for simulation, DES. We discussed the importance of time in event simulation. We illustrated DES with examples in behavioral modeling, FSM modeling, and Petri net modeling. We presented some methods for deriving test cases and principles and guidelines to be used in the test generation process.

Problems

1. Continue the study of the message sequence chart begun in Section 8.3.3.1.
   a) Remember that a good set of test cases should include events with times at the low end, middle, and high end of the range of duration times for each action. Describe what a complete set of test cases would look like given the assumptions about timing given in Section 8.3.3.1.
   b) What is the minimum time for a scenario under the assumptions in Section 8.3.3.1? What is the maximum time?
   c) Are there any test cases in which the requirement that the spans be fully raised at least 20 seconds before the boat reaches the bridge is not met? If so, describe them. What does your answer imply about the timing assumptions made for this scenario?
2. Finish the simulation started in Section 8.3.3.2 using the same timing assumptions as in Section 8.3.3.1.
3. Continue the simulation begun in Section 8.3.3.3.
   a) Continue the simulation until robot 1 has added two more parts to the common storage. Make up times for the transitions as they become relevant.
   b) Create a discrete event sequence in which T2 and T5 are both enabled at the same time.
4. Consider the Petri net from Section 8.3.3.3 (Figure 5.5).

a) Suppose transitions T2, T3, T4, T5, and T6 always take less than 8 seconds, while transition T1 always takes from 30–40 seconds. Show that every time a dot is placed in P2, P5 will contain a dot, P7 will contain three dots, P8 will contain a dot, and there will be no dot in P9.

b) Assuming the timing estimates in part a are realistic, what does the result in part a suggest for the design of the system?

5. Consider an elevator system in a high-rise office building. The building has 4 elevators and 20 floors above the ground floor. There are 1200 office workers, who mostly arrive between 8 and 9 am and leave between 4 and 6 pm. Half of the workers leave the building for lunch, which occurs between 11:30 am and 1:30 pm. Between 9 am and 5 pm, there are typically between 100 and 150 customers who arrive each hour, and a similar number who depart each hour. Between 6 pm and 8 am the next morning, no more than 60 people use the elevator each hour. The building is closed from 6 pm Friday to 8 am Monday except for maintenance personnel.

a) Describe distinct time periods that have vastly different usage patterns.

b) For each time period in part a, describe a set of test cases that would provide reasonable test coverage for the elevator system. Be sure to include unusual circumstances, such as one or more of the elevators not working.

6. Consider a bank with two tellers, T1 and T2. Customers arrive in a queue. Consider the following sequence of customer arrivals and corresponding lengths of time for the transaction. Times are measured in minutes.

C1 arrives at time 0 and takes 4 minutes to complete the transaction.
C2 arrives at time 2 and takes 5 minutes to complete the transaction.
C3 arrives at time 3 and takes 1 minute to complete the transaction.
C4 arrives at time 4 and takes 6 minutes to complete the transaction.
C5 arrives at time 6 and takes 2 minutes to complete the transaction.

Assume that both tellers are available at time 0 and that customer C1 goes to teller T1. Do an event simulation for this situation until there are no more events. An event is the arrival of a customer, or a customer goes to a teller. The goal is to find the longest waiting time for any customer.

7. Modern cars are controlled by drive-by-wire systems. There are no longer direct links between driver control devices like steering wheels or brake pedals and the corresponding mechanical devices. This allows modern cars to implement features like lane-departure control or front-end collision avoidance because the car system can override what the driver is doing. Simulation tools can easily be implemented for studying the behavior of cars with these features. Further, it is easy to create test cases for individual ones of these features. However, there may be issues when two or more events happen at roughly the same time. For example, a driver could try to swerve to avoid a front-end collision, but the act of swerving causes lane departure. As a group or class exercise activity, list a set of features that a car could have. Then brainstorm different combinations of situations that could occur involving those features, discuss how the car's systems should respond, and describe test cases that could be used with a

simulator to study these cases. Discuss whether the arrival order of the external events in your test cases makes a difference and what minimum elapsed time would be sufficient to consider the external events as separate instead of nearly simultaneous.

References

1. https://en.wikipedia.org/wiki/Continuous_simulation.
2. https://en.wikipedia.org/wiki/Simulation.
3. https://en.wikipedia.org/wiki/List_of_Unified_Modeling_Language_tools.
4. https://sourceforge.net/directory/os:windows/?q=finite+state+machine+simulation.
5. https://www.informatik.uni-hamburg.de/TGI/PetriNets/tools/quick.html.
6. I. McGregor, The Relationship Between Simulation and Emulation, Winter Simulation Conference, 2002, pp. 1683−1688.
7. https://en.wikipedia.org/wiki/Discrete-event_simulation.
8. G. Fishman, Principles of Discrete Event Simulation, Wiley, 1978.
9. A. Mathur, Foundations of Software Testing, 2nd Edition, Addison-Wesley Professional, 2014.

Hardware

Once the design is complete, choices must be made for the hardware to be used in the product. Hardware includes the processing elements and related circuitry, such as memories. Hardware also includes the devices through which the product interacts with the real world, such as sensors and other input devices, actuators and other output devices, communication circuits, and others. Parts of the system might be implemented on general-purpose processing element, while other parts might be implemented on circuits specifically designed for the product under development or even implemented through software. The design team must make choices for how each part of the system is to be physically implemented. This part describes features of processing elements and other kinds of circuitry and devices that a design team would consider in selecting hardware to implement their design and then discusses techniques the team can use to make good choices among the various alternatives.

Introduction and overview

9.1 Introduction

An embedded system contains many kinds of hardware elements. This section of the book focuses on the ones the computer engineering team members would most likely need to deal with — processing elements, memory, and related circuitry, especially circuitry related to communications and to sensing and affecting the environment. Other hardware elements include motors, gears, lights, sound generation equipment, and many others. Figure 9.1 shows an overview of a generic embedded system showing the relationship between the various kinds of hardware and the environment. Sensors convey information about the environment to a processor. The

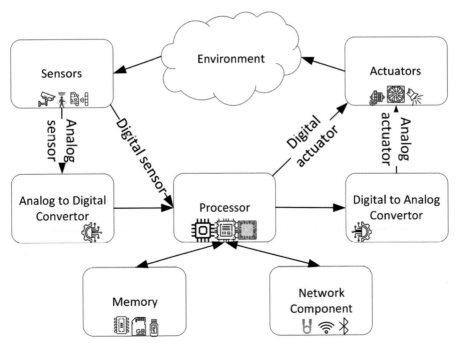

FIGURE 9.1 Overview of a Generic Embedded System and Its Hardware.

Author drawn.

Embedded System Design. https://doi.org/10.1016/B978-0-443-18470-3.00009-9

sensors can be digital (i.e., ON/OFF, 0/1, etc.) or analog. The processor controls devices, called actuators in the figure, that can affect the environment. Again, these can be digital or analog. Many embedded systems are built with small processing elements, and some of these may need extra memory, as shown in the figure. Finally, many embedded systems communicate with other entities outside that embedded system, such as nearby devices or the internet.

Larger projects, such as the bridge used as an example throughout this book, would employ engineers knowledgeable about these different kinds of hardware. In a small project with, say, only one or two engineers, the computer engineer might need to deal with these other kinds of hardware in addition to dealing with the computer-related hardware. To illustrate the difference, in the bridge project the motors that move the spans up and down are large and powerful and would require expertise well beyond that of a typical computer engineer. On the other hand, the design of a new toy car might be accomplished by a single engineer, who would deal with the processing, communication, and related circuits and also with the small motors and gears used to move and steer the toy.

Section 9.2 describes the various hardware components that make up typical embedded systems. Section 9.3 illustrates how these might be organized into a complete embedded system for our bridge example. The remaining chapters in this section of the book deal with the different hardware component types and discuss features of each that might be useful in selecting circuits to implement a design.

9.2 **Overview of the structure of an embedded system**

Hardware elements that can occur in embedded systems include the following:

- One or more processing elements and related hardware such as memory, communication, and related circuitry.
- A variety of devices that sense the condition of the environment and provide stimuli and input to the system. These can be digital (a switch that is on or off, a button that is pressed or not pressed, etc.) or analog (a quantity that takes on a [continuous] range of values such as temperature, blood oxygen level, distance, etc.).
- A variety of devices that affect the environment, such as motors, alarms, lights, etc., and electronic components that control them. These can be digital (turn a motor on or off, turn a light on or off, etc.) or analog (control the speed of a motor, control the level of a light, etc.).
- Means, such as Wi-Fi or ethernet, for communicating with other systems.
- Devices specific to the application. For example, a bridge system includes the spans that cross the river, the barrier assembly that blocks ground traffic, and other physical things associated with the bridge. An ATM would include the mechanism that actually dispenses bills and a mechanism that opens or locks the bill compartment.

- Other kinds of hardware, including but not limited to enclosures, mounting racks, and conduits for cabling.

The computer engineer on the design team may not be directly involved in the design of the parts in the last bullet points. However, the computer engineer needs to be aware of them and, indeed, be aware of the general context in which the computer and related hardware elements will operate because they may impose restrictions on those elements. For example, in a car the computer circuitry may need to be small and may need to be heat resistant if it is to be mounted in the engine compartment. The circuitry worn by a patient in a patient monitoring system needs to be comfortable and energy efficient.

An embedded system might contain subsystems that are themselves complete embedded systems operating concurrently. For example, the bridge project might have a complete embedded system for controlling the motion of the spans, another complete embedded system for controlling the ground traffic hardware (warning lights, barriers, etc.), etc. Often these correspond closely to the substates in an AND super-state.

9.3 **Example structure of a modest-sized system**

We illustrate the above remarks using our continuing example of a bridge system. Figure 9.2 shows the overall structure corresponding to the FSM model in Figure 3.11 in Chapter 3. Figure 9.3 shows a sample structure of one of the subsystems.

Figure 9.2 shows the overall structure of the system in Figure 3.11. The set of AND substates in Figure 3.11 would be implemented on the PC. The various modules, such as Span Module and Barrier Module, could be complete embedded systems themselves, as illustrated in Figure 9.3. Figure 9.2 also shows internet connections (the dashed lines) to systems outside the bridge, in this case, a weather reporting service and the local government system.

Figure 9.3 shows the embedded system for controlling the ground traffic barrier, that is, the Barrier Module in Figure 9.2. This system has a microprocessor and memory. Figure 9.3 shows two digital inputs — one for sensing when the barrier gate is fully up and one for when the gate is fully down. When the gate is fully down, for example, the button on the lower switch is pressed, closing the connection inside the switch as shown in the figure. When the gate is fully up, the other button is pressed. Figure 9.3 shows four outputs — one to turn warning bells on, one to turn on red warning lights on the barrier arms, one to control the speed of the motor that raises and lowers the gate, and one to tell the motor which direction to move. For illustration purposes, we assume the motor control is analog so that the gate can move fast or slow. The processor outputs a number (i.e., digital information) that indicates the desired speed. This has to be converted to an analog signal to actually control the motor, and the figure shows a digital-to-analog converter (DAC) that performs this

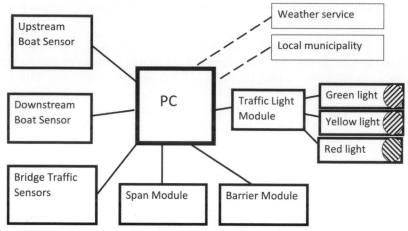

FIGURE 9.2 Sample Top-Level Architecture for the Bridge.

Author drawn.

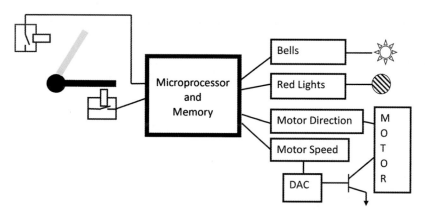

FIGURE 9.3 Sample Architecture for Barrier Control.

Author drawn.

function. The figure also illustrates a low-level detail that often has to be considered. Typical DAC circuits cannot drive heavy loads of the type required by a motor that can move the gate. Therefore a power transistor is shown between the DAC output and the motor itself.

Processing elements

10

10.1 Introduction

There are many kinds of processing elements available to choose from when implementing an embedded system. Examples of different types include ASIC (application-specific integrated circuits), FPGA (field programmable gate array), DSP (digital signal processing), MPU (microprocessing unit/microcontroller), etc. Each kind of processing element has features that make it appropriate for particular kinds of applications. Applications vary dramatically in terms of, for example, the number of inputs and outputs needed, the computational power needed, special kinds of arithmetic used, the need for parallelism (to implement finite-state machine [FSM] models with AND super-states, for example), memory requirements, and many other features. The processing element in a stop-light controller needs a modest number of I/O pins and trivial computing power. The processing elements in video and audio systems need high speed and, in many cases, special kinds of arithmetic. Digital signal processors benefit from special instructions that optimize the typical DSP calculations. The goal of this chapter is to introduce the student to a variety of the most common features so that the student can make suitable choices that will lead to robust and reliable embedded systems.

10.2 Microcontroller vs. microprocessor

Microcontrollers are processing elements designed to be used in applications where interface to and control of devices in an environment is the major concern — that is, embedded systems. Microcontroller circuits generally will have some number of pins that can be used directly for inputs and outputs, such as inputs from sensor circuits for sensing environmental conditions and outputs to controller circuits for controlling actuators that manipulate that environment. Inputs would be conditioned to match the voltage of the circuit, typically 5 volts or 3.3 volts. They may be digital or analog. Output pins will typically drive light loads, such as an LED or the input to another circuit. Figure 10.1 shows a pin layout for an Intel 8051 microcontroller.

Heavier loads require additional circuitry, such as power transistors or mechanical relays, and the microcontroller output pin controls those devices.

Embedded System Design. https://doi.org/10.1016/B978-0-443-18470-3.00010-5

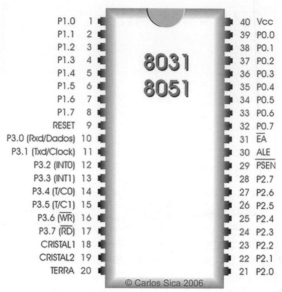

P1.0	1		40	Vcc
P1.1	2		39	P0.0
P1.2	3		38	P0.1
P1.3	4	**8031**	37	P0.2
P1.4	5		36	P0.3
P1.5	6	**8051**	35	P0.4
P1.6	7		34	P0.5
P1.7	8		33	P0.6
RESET	9		32	P0.7
P3.0 (Rxd/Dados)	10		31	$\overline{EA}$
P3.1 (Txd/Clock)	11		30	ALE
P3.2 (INT0)	12		29	$\overline{PSEN}$
P3.3 (INT1)	13		28	P2.7
P3.4 (T/C0)	14		27	P2.6
P3.5 (T/C1)	15		26	P2.5
P3.6 ($\overline{WR}$)	16		25	P2.4
P3.7 ($\overline{RD}$)	17		24	P2.3
CRISTAL1	18		23	P2.2
CRISTAL2	19		22	P2.1
TERRA	20	© Carlos Sica 2006	21	P2.0

FIGURE 10.1 Intel 8051 Microcontroller Pin Layout.

Author Carlos Sica, released to public domain, see https://en.wikipedia.org/wiki/File: Pinagem8031.jpg.

Microcontrollers have some number of built-in features beyond just computing that are useful in embedded systems. Such features include timers, counters, analog-to-digital converters (ADCs), digital-to-analog converters (DACs), various serial protocols, and many others. (See Section 10.3 for a more complete list.) On the other hand, because many embedded systems don't require extensive computing power, microcontrollers tend to have simple to moderate instruction sets; for example, few microcontrollers include floating point instructions in their instruction sets. They do, on the other hand, often include bit-manipulation instructions, which are useful for turning individual output pins on or off. Microcontrollers typically have 8- or 16-bit arithmetic, although some of the newer ones have 32-bit arithmetic. They also usually have 8- or 16-bit parallel data paths for interfacing to external circuits like memories, sensors, and other devices. Most microcontrollers have onboard program and data memory, although the lower-end controllers have very limited amounts. It is quite easy to build a simple embedded system with little more than a single microcontroller circuit.

Microprocessors, on the other hand, are designed to provide a high level of computing ability and focus less or not at all on additional features, such as the ones mentioned in the preceding paragraph. Because the focus is on computing power, microprocessors tend to have much more sophisticated and powerful instruction sets, and many do include floating point arithmetic. The pins on a microprocessor circuit are designed more to interface to general memories and devices common in personal computers and laptops, such as disk controllers and keyboard monitors, than to sensors and actuators. The pin set would typically include parallel data bus for transfer of data in and out of the processing element, address lines for accessing memory and other memory-mapped devices, and general signals for interface to memories and other similar devices. Unlike microcontrollers, microprocessor circuits rarely can operate entirely on their own but need additional circuitry, particularly memories for the program and data.

The distinction between microcontroller and microprocessor is not always clear-cut. For example, video processors may not be considered microprocessors because they are made not for general computing but rather for a specific kind of computing. On the other hand, they typically have powerful instructions and special arithmetic capabilities that are not normally found in microcontrollers. Computing elements like those in the ARM family have powerful instruction sets and 32-bit arithmetic, like microprocessors, but also typically have general-purpose I/O pins and many built-in functionalities (e.g., sophisticated timers/counters, ADCs, DACs, pulse-width modulation [PWM], and others), like microcontrollers. As circuitry shrinks and becomes cheaper, newer processing elements are likely to blur the line between microcontroller and microprocessor even further.

10.3 Features to consider when selecting a processing element

In this section we discuss the most common features that embedded systems engineers need to consider when selecting a processing element for some part of the overall design. Different processing elements implement these features in a wide variety of ways. It is the job of the computer engineer and embedded systems engineer to match the needs of the product being developed to the feature sets of different processing elements to make the best choice. In each of the following subsections we indicate typical trade-offs in the way features are implemented in different processing elements and the kinds of applications where different implementations would be more appropriate. Note that many embedded systems have more than one processing element, and it is often the case that different parts of an embedded system use different kinds of processing elements.

10.3.1 Interrupt system

We begin this subsection with an overview of the interrupt concept for the benefit of readers who have not seen this before. We then mention typical features to look for in the interrupt systems of different processing elements.

An interrupt is an asynchronous function call caused by an event external to the software that is running on the processor. See Figure 10.2 below for a conceptual illustration of interrupt process. For example, a serial byte may be received from

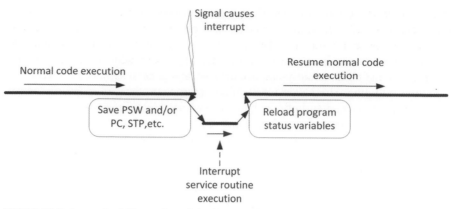

FIGURE 10.2 Conceptual Illustration of the Interrupt Process.

Autor drawn.

some other device in the system. That device would not be synchronized with the software running on the processor, and even if it were minor variations in clock speeds, delay due to the serial line being shared, or a variety of other reasons could cause the receipt of the last bit of the serial frame to occur at any point in the execution of the currently running program. Contrast this with an explicit function call in the software itself; that function call always occurs when the software reaches that point and doesn't occur at any other time. The advantage of the capability to interrupt is that the software does not need to waste time continually asking all the devices in the system if anything has happened, a process called polling. Rather, the software just performs its regular functions, and the devices in effect "notify" the processor when something has happened.

Two important concepts for interrupts are the notion of an interrupt source being enabled or disabled and the notion of an event occurring. Disabling an interrupt source means that the processor will not respond to an event from that source. Enabling an interrupt source means that the processor will respond assuming no other interrupt source of equal or higher priority is currently being handled or occurs at the same time. Most processors have the ability to disable or enable individual interrupt sources as well as to disable the entire interrupt system. Disabling interrupts is important because software often has critical sections or sections for which there are tight timing requirements; when the program is in one of those critical sections of execution it should not be interrupted. For example, the currently running program may be in the middle of executing a semaphore (see Chapter 18) or responding to a scram of a nuclear reactor. In cases like these, less urgent external events, such as a timer expiring or a press on a keypad, must wait until the more important job has been finished. When the critical job is finished, the processor can enable any interrupts that were disabled and handle any events that occurred during the critical period. The second important concept is the notion of an event occurring. For example, a byte may have been received in the serial system, the transmission of a byte in the serial system may have been completed, an input pin may have changed, a timer may have expired, etc. When an event occurs, the processor may not respond for a variety of reasons. First, as noted earlier in this paragraph, the processor may have disabled that source for interrupts. Most interrupt systems will remember an event that occurred while that interrupt source was disabled; if the processor later enables that interrupt source, the occurrence of the event will cause an interrupt request. Second, the processor may currently be handling an interrupt for an event from another source that is more urgent (i.e., has the same or higher priority — see later paragraph in this subsection); assuming the interrupt source has been enabled and remains so, when the currently executing interrupt handler completes and no other higher-priority interrupts have occurred the event will get its turn to interrupt the processor. Interrupts that are waiting to be recognized by the processor are said to be pending.

When the notification of an event (i.e., an interrupt request) occurs and the processor is ready to handle that interrupt, the processor makes a special kind of function call to a predetermined function, called an interrupt routine or interrupt handler, which will "handle" the event. Because this can happen at any point in the currently running software, the interrupt handler should affect only those parts of the processor and system that relate to the cause of the interrupt and leave everything else unchanged. This includes variables that do not relate to the source of the interrupt, registers in the CPU section, and especially the so-called program status word (PSW — the register that holds bits indicating the results of tests and other internal details during the execution of code). Consider, for example, a test in the currently running software. The following lines show pseudomachine code that might be executing.

```
compare      x,y      ; Compare variable x to variable y
jump_positive posCase ; If x > y go to another section of the program
```

Suppose an interrupt occurs between these two instructions; that is, an event occurs while the processor is executing the "compare" instruction, that interrupts source is enabled, and no same or higher-priority handlers are currently running. Then after the execution of the "compare" instruction, which sets some bits in the PSW, execution transfers to the interrupt handler. At some later point the execution returns and continues with the "jump_positive" instruction. If the interrupt handler changed the PSW, the jump instruction may not perform the correct operation based on the values of x and y. Similarly, if some section of code that was using the CPU registers got interrupted and the interrupt handler modified those registers, the regular code would compute some result different than if it had not been interrupted. For example, the current program may be adding up the values in an array and using the CPU accumulator register to collect that sum. If the interrupt handler used the accumulator register without saving and restoring it, when the system returned to the program adding the array elements, the partial sum already collected would have been lost. Therefore, in addition to the handler not changing unrelated variables in the normal code, the handler should save any registers it uses as well as the PSW, and then restore these just before exiting. The most common way to do this is to push the registers and PSW onto the execution stack at the very beginning and then pop them just before the final return.

Most processing elements implement some kind of priority scheme. This corresponds to real-world situations where some kinds of events are more critical than others. For example, responding to the nuclear core in a reactor overheating is much more important and urgent than responding to an incoming message from the power grid. In the bridge system it is likely more important to respond to an indication of the span motor overheating than to a signal from the sensor that tells the current position of the span. Part of the designers' job is to determine these priorities. Then in selecting a suitable processing element, the computer engineer would examine the interrupt system and its priority mechanism to select a processing element that could adequately accommodate the priorities of various events identified by the design team. Note that if an event associated with a higher-priority interrupt occurs while a lower-priority interrupt handler is running and the higher-priority source is enabled, the lower-priority handler will itself be interrupted by the higher-priority handler. If there are many priority levels, this situation can occur many times, delaying the completion of the handlers for the lower-level priority interrupts.

Interrupt handlers should be as fast as possible. Interrupt handlers interrupt and therefore delay the normal operation of the software. If the delays are too long, the normal software may not meet its real-time constraints. If the process required to handle the event is relatively simple, the interrupt handler can perform the operations directly. For example, in a stop-light controller, a timer expiring might cause an interrupt so that the system can change the lights. Changing the lights requires changing only a few bits in the system, a process that takes very little time. The delay would be minimal. On the other hand, when the process of handling an event is more involved or the system has other tight real-time constraints, the interrupt handler will typically just save some data to one or more variables dedicated to that kind of event. The normal parts of the software can then do the appropriate process on the new values. For example, if a multibyte message is being received through a serial port, the interrupt handler for the receipt of each byte would typically do nothing more than store the byte in a buffer and increment the counter associated with that buffer. The normal software functions would check the count value to determine when a complete message had been received and decode the message and react accordingly. In the bridge system the processor in the operator's terminal might have an interrupt handler for the sensor that tells when a boat is approaching. This handler should merely set a variable in the system to indicate the presence of a boat; the normal software that generates the display at the operator's terminal would use this variable and similar variables for other sensors in the system to generate the correct information on the display panel.

We now list some of the typical features associated with interrupts that would be of interest when selecting a processing element. We use two common processor families to illustrate the differences — the Intel 8051 family[1] and the TI Stellaris family.[2]

- Interrupt sources. Some processing elements provide for interrupts for various built-in features in that processor. For example, the 8051 has five interrupt sources corresponding to the five built-in features of that family — an interrupt for each of two timers, an interrupt for each of two external interrupt pins, and an interrupt for the serial section. Some processors have as many as 8 or 16 external interrupt pins. Other processors with more features have many sources of interrupt. For example, the Stellaris family provides interrupt capability for every pin configured as an input pin. An event occurs any time such a pin changes value, and the software can individually enable or disable the interrupt for any such pin.
- Number of priority levels. This ranges from two (e.g., the 8051 family) to eight (the Stellaris family).
- Registers automatically saved and/or restored. All processors save the value of the program counter (PC; the register that gives the address of the next instruction to be executed) so that execution can return to the place in code that was interrupted after the handler is finished. In the 8051 family that is the only register that is automatically saved; the 8051 processors do not even save the PSW, much less the general CPU registers. The Stellaris processor saves the current state of the processor (stack pointer, link register, program counter, program status register, etc.); it also allows to save application controllable registers R0—R12 via software programming.
- Location of interrupt handlers. In the 8051 family the addresses for the five interrupt sources are fixed and built into the hardware. The Stellaris family allows the software engineer to locate the interrupt handler code at any valid memory address. The addresses are placed in a table that is used by the hardware when an interrupt is processed.

10.3.2 **Power control and sleep modes**

Energy consumption is a major consideration in many embedded systems. It is always preferable to use less energy, even if the system is supplied by a reliable energy source such as normal household AC. For systems that run on batteries or get all or a portion of their energy through harvesting, energy consumption is critical. Many systems must operate unattended for extended periods of time. For example, wireless sensor nodes deployed in rural areas to monitor seismic activity cannot have batteries replaced or recharged every day or two. Even products for which recharging is the norm, such as cell phones, extending the time between recharging is a critical factor in the success of the product; imagine if cell phones required recharging every few hours!

In most embedded systems the processing element is one of the major energy consumers. In general, ASICs will use much less power to accomplish a goal than FPGAs, which will in turn use less energy for the same goal as a processor. However, ASICs require a large investment, which is impossible to justify if the expected volume of production is low. A similar comment applies to FPGAs. Therefore in many embedded systems the ability to manage energy is an important factor in selecting a processing element. Of course, other elements in an embedded system may be relatively large energy consumers. For example, the wireless transmission of data consumes large amounts of energy; in a system where data is constantly being transmitted, the energy usage of the processing element may be dwarfed by that of the wireless section. However, the processing element is still one of the major energy consumers, so being able to manage the amount of energy the processing element uses is critical. There are two major methods by which processing elements can reduce energy consumption under software control — sleep modes and voltage scaling.

In many embedded systems the processor does no useful work for large portions of the time. Consider a typical sensor application. The sensor node is supposed to take samples of the environment every, say, 5 minutes, and transmit that data to the base station. This may take a few milliseconds. In this situation the processor does nothing for 4.99 or more seconds; that is, the processor is not needed for roughly 99.9% of the time. A variation on this situation is the case of a sensor node that is supposed to react when something happens in the environment. For example, the processor in a gunshot detector node only reacts when a sudden loud noise occurs in the vicinity; the remaining 99.99…% of the time the processor does nothing.

Many processors have various levels of sleep modes. In these processors the circuitry is arranged in a hierarchical structure. At the highest level, all circuitry is powered up and running. No portion of the processor chip is in sleep mode, and the processor can perform all the functions available in the hardware. At a second level, perhaps the instruction execution section is turned off, but the timers and interrupt section remain active. Perhaps at a third level, the only circuitry remaining active is the external wake-up monitor. Three levels of sleep mode are typical, but some processors have more. At the lowest level, the "deep sleep" mode, the energy consumption might be on the order of microwatts; in contrast, energy consumption in full operational mode is typical on the order of hundreds of milliwatts. Intermediate sleep levels will have energy consumption in between, but the energy consumption at those levels will typically be closer to the deep sleep level because it is the instruction execution section that is the major energy consumer in a processing element. The data sheets for processors with sleep capability will give the energy consumption levels in each of the sleep levels.

There are several important questions to consider regarding sleep modes. First, at each level of sleep what registers and flags continue to hold their values? Usually in all but the deepest levels the registers do hold their values; this includes the PC that tells where the code was currently executing and the status register (PSW) that tells the condition after arithmetic operations and tests. The consequence of this is that the code continues execution from the point where it was when the processor entered the sleep mode. This contrasts with deep sleep modes in which those registers are not saved. In that case coming out of sleep mode requires the code to start at the same point as when the power is first turned on; the system would go through all its initialization code before returning to normal operation. A related question is how long it takes for the processor to wake up. Coming out of deep sleep mode usually takes on the order of milliseconds; not only does the circuitry have to power up, but the processor itself has to go through the same internal initialization that it does on an ordinary power-up. Waking up from shallow sleep modes is much faster, typically on the order of a few microseconds, because the circuit only needs to get the transistors in the sleeping sections ready to work again. The computer engineer needs to match these considerations with the needs of the application. A sensor node that is sampling the environment every 5 minutes can afford a long wake-up time, say 100 milliseconds. A jet plane traveling at 600 miles per hour would travel 88 feet in 100 milliseconds, and a module that was supposed to adjust the plane's flight may need to wake-up much quicker than 100 milliseconds.

Some processing elements have the ability to turn off certain sections of the chip and then turn them back on again when needed, all under software control. While the sleeping section is off the instruction execution section of the chip continues to operate. For example, a processor with a built-in wireless section might have the ability to power down the wireless section when no transmission is being done or incoming traffic is expected.

Voltage scaling is the ability of the processor to adjust the voltage supplied to the circuitry. Energy consumption is proportional to the square of the supply voltage. Cutting the supply voltage in half reduces the energy consumption by a factor of four. However, unfortunately, there is a trade-off because the circuitry cannot operate as fast at reduced voltage. (For example, at reduced voltage it takes a transistor longer to push enough current through to charge up its output line enough to change from logic 0 to logic 1.) Thus, at reduced voltage, the instructions take longer to execute. This has to be taken into account when analyzing real-time constraints. A common approach is to have the processor run at high voltage when executing sections of code that have to be fast (i.e., meet tight timing requirements) and run at lower voltage when the timing requirements are not as severe.

10.3.3 Timers and counters

Timers do exactly what the name implies — count time. Typically, they count in increments of the processor's system clock. Counters, on the other hand, count occurrences of specific events, typically a change in logic value at an input pin. In many processors, for example, the 8051, there are specific registers that can be configured to be either a timer or a counter. It is important to note that the timing or counting happens asynchronously and independently from the running software. Once the software has configured the register accordingly, the software need not further monitor or be involved with the timing or counting, at least until overflow/underflow and possibly interrupt occurs. In some applications the software does occasionally check the value of the register. For example, in a stop-and-go light the software may check the register that counts how many cars have entered the turning lane to determine if the turn light should be activated. In other applications the software simply ignores the counter until it overflows and causes an interrupt. For example, to implement a portion of a timed FSM that requires remaining in a state for a given amount of time, the software may set a timer to that time limit and configure it to count down. The software needs to do nothing more until the timer actually reaches 0.

Timers and counters are implemented as registers, which means they have a fixed range of values. For example, a 16-bit timer/counter register can have values in the range of 0 to 65,535. An important issue is what happens when a timer/counter register reaches and then passes its limit. For example, if a 16-bit timer currently has the value 65,535, what happens at the next clock increment, when the register would overflow? First, most processors allow timer/counter overflow to generate an interrupt. Second, the register can resume incrementing from 0 or can be configured to reload a specific value so that the counting continues not from 0 but from the reload value. The reload feature is useful in timer mode to program the overflow to happen at precise time intervals. For example, a 16-bit timer incrementing at 10 MHz with a reload value of 55,536 would overflow every 1 millisecond. With the indicated reload value, it takes $10{,}000 = 10^4$ increments to reach 65,535 and then overflow; $10 \text{ MHz} = 10^7$ clock cycles per second; 10^4 clock cycles therefore is 10^{-3} seconds.

Counting examples include such applications as measuring rotations in rotating devices (such as disk drives), counting cars in different lanes at intersections, and many other similar applications. In these applications the event is signaled by a digital pulse at an input pin of the processor circuit. For example, magnetic switches can be embedded in the pavement under each lane of traffic at an intersection. As cars go over a switch, it closes a circuit connected to the input pin, causing a change in the logic value at the pin. Rotating devices may have some number of activators distributed around the perimeter. These could be small magnets, optical switches, or other such devices. A sensor is placed near the perimeter of the rotating device. Each time an activator passes near the sensor, the sensor provides a pulse to the counter input pin. Using the count plus the number of activators and the system clock, the software can determine the approximate rotation speed.

Timing examples include setting a time base for serial communication, scheduling operations that need to be performed at regular intervals, implementing timers from the FSM model of the application, and many others. Consider, for example, setting the time base for TTL (transistor—transistor logic hardware protocol)/RS232 serial communication. The processor could use the reload mode to generate the appropriate time base, setting the reload value so that each overflow of the timer corresponds to the time for one bit. The timer increment time, baud rate, and reload value are related by the following equations.

BitTime = 1/BaudRate	The time per bit is the inverse of the baud rate.
OT = BitTime	The overflow time is the same as the bit time.
OT = (TimerInc * (TimerMax-Reload))	The overflow time is the clock time multiplied by the number of increments from the reload value to the register maximum.

In some cases the clock speed, that is, TimerInc in the above equations, may be set by other requirements of the system, for example, the need to run the processor as fast as possible to meet real-time requirements. This determines the set of baud rates that can be achieved by adjusting the reload value, and this in turn can be used along with other properties of the application, like the length of the wires connecting the two ends of the serial line, to select one of the possible baud rates. In other cases, it is the baud rate rather than TimerInc that is determined; for example, the application might need the serial line to be 19.2K BPS (bits per second) to match a standard RS232 baud rate or 31.25K BPS to interface to Musical Instrument Digital Interface (MIDI)[3] equipment. In these cases the equations are used to determine Timer Inc (which is then used to select the crystal or other time base to drive the processor's system clock) and Reload.

Although processor clock speeds are in the mega- or gigahertz range, time at the second/minute/hour level can be achieved by maintaining separate variables in the code that count larger units of time. For example, if the reload value is set so that timer overflow happens every millisecond, a program variable can be used to increment from 0 to 1000. Other variables could then be used to count seconds, minutes, and hours. When the millisecond counter reached 1000, the software would reset it to 0 and increment the seconds variable. When that variable reached 60, it would be reset, and the minutes variable incremented, etc.

Timer registers in a processor can also be used to implement timers from the FSM model and to control functions that must be called on a regular basis, such as every 50 milliseconds, but are not part of the normal execution sequence of the main software. One method for accomplishing this is to implement an ordered queue of tasks, ordered by increasing amount of time until the task should be executed. Tasks can include FSM timers expiring, functions that should be called at regular intervals, sensors that need to be sampled on a periodic basis, etc. When the times involved for tasks in the queue are relatively large compared to the processor's clock speed, program variables can be used as described in the preceding paragraph to count these larger time units. The processor is configured to generate an interrupt when the timer register overflows. Each time the timer register overflows, the interrupt handler checks the tasks at the front of the queue. Any task whose time has come is dispatched. In the case of a timer variable from the FSM model, appropriate transitions in the FSM model are signaled. In the case of function calls the appropriate functions are invoked.

Finally, many processors allow timers to be used to control the length of sleep modes. For example, analysis of the FSM model of the application can often determine periods when none of the super-states will be doing anything, and the processor can be put in a sleep mode to save energy.

10.3.4 Internal memory

The amount and nature of onboard memory is another important feature to consider. Random access memory (RAM) is used for storing program variables, implementing the execution call stack, etc. Some processors have relatively little; for example, the basic 8051 processor has just 256 bytes. Other processors have substantial amounts of RAM, for example, 320 KB in a typical Stellaris processor. A related question is whether or not any of the RAM is nonvolatile, that is, retains the values even when the power is off. Nonvolatile memory is useful for storing system state information, history information, and a variety of other kinds of long-term data. All RAM in the 8051 is volatile; 256 KB of the 320 KB memory of the Stellaris processors is nonvolatile. Some processors, such as the Stellaris family processors, store code in the same space as nonvolatile data. Others, like the 8051, store onboard code in a separate section of the circuit. The amount of onboard program memory in different processors ranges from zero (8031, a cut-down version of the 8051) to megabytes or more. Finally, an important consideration for onboard program memory is how the program is loaded onto the chip. Many processors provide special pins (either separate pins from the general-purpose I/O [GPIO] set or part of the GPIO pin set) for interface to device programmers and in-circuit debuggers. Others require the chip to be physically removed from the application and placed in a separate device programmer. Still others have the program hardwired at the manufacturer, a feature that could be used after the system had been completely debugged and tested and ready for mass production.

10.3.5 Additional functional features

We list here several additional features that are available in a variety of different processors. These are called functional features because they have to do with the capabilities of the processors and the ease with which systems can be built based on them.

The power of the instruction set is an obvious major feature in selecting a processor. Low-end processors have simple instruction sets and simple arithmetic (typically 8-bit integer arithmetic), while more sophisticated processors have 16- or 32-bit integer arithmetic and some even with floating point arithmetic. Some processors have bit-addressable portions of memory, useful in applications that map outputs into memory and that need to turn individual outputs (i.e., bits) on and off. Most processors have a reasonable set of test-and-branch instructions.

The number and capabilities of the GPIO pins is an important factor in selecting a processing element. The number of I/O pins ranges from 16 to more than 40. In the 8051, for example, there are 32 GPIO pins, but this count is reduced to 14 if external data or program memory is used and reduced further if some of the remaining pins are used in their alternate function, such as serial I/O or interrupt inputs. At the higher end, the Stellaris family incorporates 42 pins, but again many of these have secondary functions and when used in their secondary mode cannot be used as GPIO. Some processors allow pins configured as input to have either digital or analog inputs, while others allow only digital inputs. The major consideration for output pins is the drive capability. Pins of the 8051 family that are configured as output pins can drive only a few TTL loads. Pins of the Stellaris family that are configured as output pins can be configured to sink/source several different levels of current ranging from 2 to 8 mA, with a few pins able to drive up to 18 mA loads. The Stellaris family also allows the software to control the slew rate, configure weak/strong pull-up/down resistors, and configure pins as open drain outputs.

Many processors include at least some additional built-in features, such as ADC and DAC converters, various standard serial communications (such as TTL, I^2C, CAN [controller area network], etc.), PWM for controlling motors and the like, quadrature, and many more. There is variation even within some processor families. For example, the basic 8051 processor contains two timer/counter registers, two external interrupt pins, and TTL serial capabilities; later, more advanced members of the 8051 family include ADC, PWM, and other features plus an expanded instruction set.

The ease with which additional devices, such as wireless chips or controllers of various kinds, can be interfaced is an important consideration when such devices are part of the overall design. Processors that have mechanisms for interfacing with external memory typically also allow easy interfacing with devices that have 8- or 16-bit parallel processor interface. The devices are mapped to particular memory addresses in the data memory space, and the registers in the device are accessed as ordinary data. Processor circuits that have built-in serial circuitry can interface to devices that also support the same kind of serial protocol. In the absence of either of these processor capabilities, external device interface will be somewhat more complicated and will typically use up many of the I/O pins on the processor chip. In addition, accessing the device in software will be more complicated.

10.3.6 Nonfunctional features

There are other issues to consider when selecting a processor than the functional capabilities, issues that aren't related to the capabilities of the processors but nonetheless can affect the decision about which processor to use. We list a few of these here.

The form factor is a major consideration in applications where the hardware needs to be small. Most processors do come in surface-mount forms. However, other considerations, like the number of pins and whether the data transfer is parallel or serial, also determine the size of the chip. As an example, consider an embedded system for measuring health information in a human that is to be worn as part of a watch. A processor with only serial interface to external devices, such as the sensors and the Wi-Fi, would be preferable to one that offers parallel byte transfer because the serial interface only takes two pins whereas the parallel byte transfer requires 8 data lines plus control signals. The loss of speed because of serial data transfer is probably not a serious problem in this application. Sampling and transmission of information to a base station is likely to be at the fraction of a second level rather than millisecond or microsecond level, but this is more than adequate for most human bio-sensing applications.

For a product with expected small volume, the engineers may consider the availability of off-the-shelf single-board systems rather than incurring the cost of printed-circuit board design, fabrication, and assembly. Many companies offer single boards with processors and related additional circuits, such as ADCs and wireless communication chips.

The availability of debuggers can also be a major factor in choosing the processor. Many debugging products allow code to be downloaded into a processor and debugging to be performed while the chip is in the product. This makes debugging easier and allows the engineer to test not only the code but also the operation of the processor within the precise environment of the product.

Price is obviously a major consideration, especially on high-volume products. Saving one dollar on a part that is used in a product that will sell one million pieces a year save one million dollars a year. There is generally a positive correlation between price and capability. Higher-end processors generally cost more, although large-quantity discounts may make the price differential relatively small. In general, the design team would select the lowest-cost processing element with enough capability to do the job. However, other factors may enter into this decision. For example, the design team may be very experienced with a given processor and decide to use it to reduce product development time rather than save a small amount by using a cheaper processor. A company that makes many different products may wish not to have to stock several different kinds of processors but rather to use a single processor for all its product.

Finally, many processor families have support communities that can be accessed easily and quickly online. A generic processor with such a support community might be preferable to a less expensive but also less widely used processor.

10.4 Sample processors

In this section we present an overview of two general processors — a low-end microcontroller and a medium-to-high-end processor. Our goal is to illustrate the ranges of processing elements available and to describe how various features mentioned in Section 10.3 are implemented and programmed. We also briefly describe how special-purpose processors are designed to achieve high performance in the specific application for which they are designed. This is not a complete treatment for any of these sample processors, and the student is referred to the data sheets and other books for full discussions of the circuits and how to use them.

10.4.1 The 8051 family

The 8051 family[1] stems back to the 1980s. It was designed for the embedded systems of that time and ran at a maximum cycle speed of 12 MHz. Instructions are executed in either 12 cycles or 24 cycles, giving an instruction time of 1 microsecond for some instructions and 2 microseconds for others. It was used extensively in the keyboards that were connected to PCs and other desktop computers. Its use waned after 2000, but this family has again gained high popularity in embedded systems applications, especially with the introduction of advanced versions that have additional features and run at much higher clock speeds. The features allowed simple embedded systems to be implemented with only the processor circuit plus perhaps a few discrete components to provide extra drive power for outputs that required it. It is common nowadays to implement the 8051 architecture on large-scale FPGA circuits using off-the-shelf equations. These equations can then be combined with additional equations implementing other kinds of devices, such as MP3 controllers and similar devices so that much more sophisticated and complex embedded systems can still be implemented on a single chip. (See Chapter 12 for more on this topic.)

The basic 8051 microcontroller has the following features.

- 256 bytes of internal RAM.
- 4 KB of internal program. These are missing in the 8031. They are hardwired at the factory in the 8051 and programmable in the 8952.
- Two 16-bit timer/counter registers, each with several modes of operation, including basic counting (signal from an external source), basic timing (from the system clock), and reload mode.
- TTL serial transmit and receive.
- Five sources of interrupt (timer overflow for each of the two timer/counter registers, two external interrupt pins, and the serial section). Each interrupt source can be programmed under software control to be enabled and to have one of two priority levels — high or low. The interrupt functions are located at fixed addresses in the program space.
- Ability to directly access 64 K bytes of external data and 64 K bytes of program memory. Data and program memory are separate from each other, the so-called Harvard architecture.[4]
- 40-Pin circuit, available in several form factors.
- Four 8-bit ports providing up to 32 I/O pins.
- Two ports plus two pins in a third port are used to access external memory (program or data), thus reducing the I/O pin count to 14 when the application requires external data or program.
- Port 3 has pins for serial transmit, serial receive, external interrupt (two pins), and external input to the counters. Any pin used for its secondary purpose cannot also be used for I/O.

Configuring and using the built-in features is extremely simple and is accomplished by reading or writing certain special-function registers inside the CPU. These are accessed by normal read/write instructions, just like the bytes of internal RAM. For example, there are two special-function registers for the interrupt system, each of which has a bit for each of the five sources of interrupt. One of the registers enables or disables the individual interrupt sources, while the other sets the priority for each source. The serial section has its own set of configuration registers for setting things like the time base for serial transmission and the mode (simple 8-bit shift, TTL protocol, and two others). Sending a byte out the serial transmit pin is accomplished simply by writing to another special-function register. Reading a byte that has been received at the serial input pin is accomplished simply by reading that special-function register.

The 8051 family of processors has simple 8-bit arithmetic, including multiply (product of two 8-bit numbers is a 16-bit number) and divide (16-bit number divided by 8-bit number produces 8-bit quotient and 8-bit remainder). Bytes in a special area of internal RAM as well as in many of the special-function registers are bit address-able; that is, individual bits can be directly set or cleared without the need for mask-ing operations. This is useful for setting or clearing configuration bits or output pins in the ports.

It is common to interface 8-bit parallel devices, such as various ADCs, wireless chips, etc., as external RAM. This allows the software to read and write the registers in these devices as if they were ordinary variables in external data memory. Howev-er, as noted in the bullet list, it does reduce the set of pins that can be used for I/O to at most 14.

10.4.2 The Stellaris family

Stellaris[2] is a feature-rich family of microcontrollers introduced by Texas Instru-ments in 2007. Processors in this family operate at 50 MHz or more. The CPU is based on the ARM-CORTEX[1,5] instruction set, a set widely used in newer microcon-trollers. Figure 10.3 shows an ARM-CORTEX-M3 chip in a circuit board.

The built-in hardware features allow relatively simple software control of a wide range of devices, such as motors, as well as simple digital and analog input and output. These processors have writeable nonvolatile storage onboard.

Members of this family may include the following features as well as many others.

- 320 K bytes of onboard storage. 256 K of these are nonvolatile and may contain both data and program.
- Memory management that provides protection against accidental writing to critical sections of memory (e.g., overwriting program code or critical data).
- 32-Bit integer arithmetic.
- Four 32-bit timers, each with many modes of operation.
- Full-duplex RS232 serial, with 16-byte transmit and receive buffers.
- I^2C, CAN, and SSI (Synchronous Serial Interface) serial transmission.
- Ethernet controller.
- 36 Interrupts with 8 priority levels. Interrupt handlers can be loaded at any address in the code space. An interrupt vector table holds the addresses of the interrupt handlers.

---

[1]ARM originally stood for Acorn RISC Machine, named after the British company Acorn Computers that developed the idea. It now stands for Advanced RISC Machine. ARM forms the foundation for a set of variations on the basic instruction set and CPU architecture. These are licensed to companies that add memory, special-function units, and other computer components to produce actual microcontroller and microprocessor chips.

FIGURE 10.3 ARM Cortex-M3 Processor on a Circuit Board.

Open Grid Scheduler/Grid Engine, released to public domain, see https://en.wikipedia. org/wiki/File:ARMCortexA57A53.jpg

- Up to 42 GPIO pins organized into 7 ports. Sophisticated control of pin operation for both input and output.
- Analog inputs and analog-to-digital conversion.
- Watchdog timer. This restarts the processor if not periodically accessed. This is useful to protect against software errors such as infinite loops or invalid branches.
- PWM for controlling motors.
- Quadrature encoding for determining speed and direction of rotation for rotating devices.
- Joint Test Action Group (JTAG) interface for downloading code and debugging.
- Sleep and hibernation modes for reduced power consumption.
- Typical packages are 100 or 108 pins.

Notably absent from the list of features is external memory. The 8051 family of processors has the ability to access memory outside the chip. This is quite reasonable given the small amount of memory on the chip itself. The Stellaris family has as much onboard volatile RAM as the entire 8051 external data memory space, so additional RAM outside the chip is rarely needed. External memory can be added in one of two ways. There are many memory circuits on the market that have serial interfaces. Such a memory circuit will transfer data at a much slower rate than direct parallel access, so if high speed is critical, this may not be a viable option. Parallel external memory circuits can be added by allocating an 8-bit port on the processor chip to the data path, additional GPIO pins for addressing as needed, and yet other

GPIO pins to manipulate the standard control signals like memory chip enable, read, and write. However, this can use up the majority of the GPIO pins, so if more external memory is needed the Stellaris processor may not be a good choice. Similar remarks apply to devices that must be added as external circuits. When such devices are needed, it would be better to search for a circuit implementing the required functionality but with a serial interface so that one of the many built-in serial sections of the Stellaris processor can be used.

Not only is the set of features much larger than on typical low-end microcontrollers, but like the 8051, each feature itself is also much more sophisticated. We illustrate this with the Stellaris GPIO pins versus the I/O pins on the 8051. In the 8051 family a pin in a port can be configured by the software as either an input pin or an output pin. As an input pin, it can distinguish logic 0 and logic 1. Except for the two interrupt pins, changes in value for a pin configured as input will not cause an interrupt. As an output pin, it can drive logic 0 voltage and logic 1 voltage. No other control over the characteristics of the pin is possible. In the Stellaris processor there are 32 separate registers for configuration associated with each I/O port. We describe some of them here.

- GPIODIR. This sets the direction, input or output, of each pin in the port.
- GPIOIS, GPIOIBE, GPIOIEV, and GPIOIM. These registers configure the interrupt properties to be associated with the pins. A pin can be configured to cause an interrupt, and the interrupt event can be a change from 0 to 1, a change from 1 to 0, or both.
- GPIOAFSEL. This register is used to select the alternate function, such as I2C or PWM, for pins that have alternate functions.
- GPIODR2R, GPIODR4R, and GPIODR8R. These registers set the output drive current for pins configured as outputs.
- GPIOODR. This register is used to select the open drain option for an output pin.
- GPIOSLR. This register is used to set the slew rate for pins configured as outputs.
- GPIOLOCK and CPIOCR. These two registers provide protection against accidently reconfiguring a pin from I/O function to its alternate function or vice versa.

Finally, the Stellaris family supports the standard ARM-CORTEX thumb instruction set. Standard ARM instructions are 32 bits long. The set of 32-bit instructions provides complete access in the software to all the capabilities of the processor — all the combinations of operations with various registers and memory addresses, etc. However, many (if not most) programs in embedded systems don't use all these instructions. Rather, they use a small but very common subset of the instructions, typically using only a few of the register/operation combinations or using implicit operands or reducing the functionality of some of the operations. For example, the full 32-bit instructions for ADD include a 4-bit conditional execution field, full 4-bit register fields allowing use of all 16 registers, 12-bit immediate value fields, and two additional flags. The 16-bit thumb instruction does not have the 4-bit conditional execution field or the two flag bits, 3-bit register fields allowing use of only the first eight registers, and only 3-bit immediate values. See Refs. [6, 7] for a detailed presentation of the instruction sets. In applications where the thumb instruction set is sufficient, code size can be reduced by a factor of almost two, an important consideration because of the limit of onboard memory.

10.4.3 Special purpose processors

Many processors are designed for specific applications as opposed to general computing. Examples include processors designed for DSP, audio/video processing, image processing, and more recently artificial intelligence (AI) and machine learning (ML). High performance in the targeted application can be achieved in a number of ways, two of which are the inclusion on the processor chip of special hardware to meet the needs of the application and the inclusion of special instructions in the instruction set to match complex but common computations in that application. An example of a highly specialized hardware capability is the "raster operations pipeline" operation. This operation combines pixel information with texture information before display on the screen. In most modern graphics processing units (GPUs), this operation is performed in hardware rather than software.

An example that illustrates a combination of hardware design and instruction set enhancement is the TI 320 series C5000/6000,[8] one of many processors implementing the so-called multiply-accumulate (MAC) instruction. The MAC instruction optimizes the dot-product computation, one of the fundamental operations for DSP computations such as convolutions and filtering, video and game applications, general matrix multiplication, and many other interesting applications. In C code using pointers to access the two vectors, the dot-product computation might look like this.

```
p1 = array1; p2 = array2;      // Initialize pointers to beginning of the two
                                  arrays.
sum = 0;                       // Initialize sum to 0;
for(j=0; j<N; j++) {
sum += (*p1++) * (*p2++); // Multiply elements and add, then increment
                             // pointers after the elements have been
                                retrieved.}
```

The MAC instruction implements this entire loop with a single instruction plus, of course, the required initialization. The efficient execution of the MAC instruction depends on hardware enhancements to the address computation and memory bus architecture of the processor. If the processor has two separate address computation segments, each of which has auto-increment of the address registers, and separate memories, each with its own physical bus, the MAC instruction can execute what is called a "zero-overhead loop." Such a hardware organization is illustrated in Figure 10.4, a simplified schematic of a section of the ADSP 2100 processor. The operation is as follows. Once the two address registers, AX and AY, are loaded,

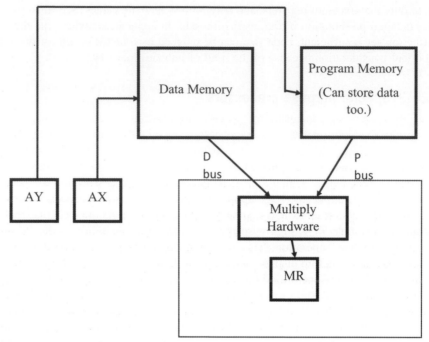

FIGURE 10.4 Illustration of the Architecture for the MAC Instruction Optimization.

Author drawn.

the MR register set to 0, and the count register set to N, the following steps are performed until the count register reaches 0.

1. Each address unit retrieves the word addressed by its register. Note that these retrievals occur in parallel along the two separate data buses − the D (data memory) bus and the P (program/data) memory bus.
2. The two words are multiplied. At the same time, the address registers are both incremented.
3. The product is added to the MR register. At the same time, the count register is decremented. If the result is not 0, the machine goes back to step 1.

In some hardware implementations the next words from memory might be retrieved during step 3, thereby increasing the parallelism and reducing the total time for execution of the loop. Note that the increment of the addresses (pointers) and decrement of the loop counter happen in parallel with the multiplication and add. Thus there is no overhead for these operations, hence the name "zero-overhead loop." See Problem 8 for an illustration of how much time this can save. When the dot-product computation is a significant part of the software, as it is in most DSP and similar applications, the use of a MAC instruction can make the difference between meeting real-time constraints or not. Note that the software engineers would need to know about the availability of the instruction on the chosen processor platform and may need to code those sections that are supposed to use the MAC instruction in assembly (or use the asm feature of a language like C/C++) if "smart" compilers are not available.

Similar hardware and instruction set enhancements are used in the more recent ML processing processor, such as the tensor processing units (TPUs)[9] introduced by Google. ML, particularly neural net training, makes extensive use of matrix and tensor operations that are more complex and sophisticated than the MAC operation illustrated in the previous paragraph. ML and AI, in general, will play an increasingly significant role in embedded systems.

Other hardware and instruction enhancements in the TS320 series and in many other processor families include saturation arithmetic and very-long instruction word (VLIW) operations. Saturation arithmetic replaces the normal overflow and underflow results by maximum and minimum values, respectively. This is useful in applications such as color blending. Consider an application in which the intensities of the three color elements (red, green, and blue) in a pixel are each represented by a 4-bit number. Thus the intensity of any color element ranges from 0 to 15. If one picture is overlaid on top of another, the intensities should add. But adding the intensities in ordinary arithmetic may produce an unexpected and incorrect result. For example, suppose the two red intensities were 10_{DEC} (1010 in 4-bit binary) and 6_{DEC} (0110 in 4-bit binary). Adding these two values in 4-bit binary produces the 4-bit result 0000 with a carry bit of 1. But 0000 represents the absence of red, that is, intensity 0, not a high level of intensity. The sum of 10_{DEC} and 6_{DEC} is 16_{DEC}, but this cannot be represented as a 4-bit binary number. Video applications would settle for the result being the maximum level of red possible, in this case, 15_{DEC} (1111 in 4-bit binary). Saturation arithmetic does produce this result. If ordinary arithmetic is used, the code must add the two intensity values and then correct the result if overflow occurred. That is, the software would require many more instructions and would thus be much slower. When the check is done in hardware as part of the add instruction itself, there is no loss of efficiency.

VLIW is a technique for allowing the specification of parallel execution of operations in a program. Instructions are fetched in longer units, for example, 64 bytes, called instruction packets. A packet can contain several instructions, and the processor executes these in parallel. Of course, the processor hardware has to allow for such parallelism. Generating code that optimizes for such parallelism for a particular piece of software is not a trivial task. Compilers have to be aware of the architecture for that particular processor platform and be able to reorder the operations given in a piece of high-level code without altering the semantics of that original code. Fortunately, such compilers do exist. The use of VLIW parallelism is not without a cost in a different aspect of performance. When one of the instructions in a packet results in a branch, some of the remaining instructions in the packet may no longer be appropriate because in the equivalent sequential version of the original code, they would come after the branch. Most VLIW processors handle this situation at some hardware level. The details would not be important in selecting a processor for a particular application, but the embedded systems engineer looking at different hardware platforms would want to make sure that candidate processors do handle the branch problem reasonably well.

The TS320 is interesting from another point of view in that it illustrates the very wide range of capabilities within a single family of processors. We have seen such ranges in processors already described, but the range was rather limited. For example, 8052 processors have just a few extra features over the basic 8051. Processors in the TS320 family range from those that have basic ARM instruction sets and hardware features similar to the Stellaris processor family to processors that implement the MAC instruction, fixed-point arithmetic for computing with fractional numbers, full floating-point instruction set, VLIW instructions, saturation arithmetic, onboard digital media hardware, and more.

These are but a few of the more common enhancements available in microcontrollers and microprocessors, but the presentation in this section does illustrate why, in part, there are so many different ones on the market. The corollary for the embedded systems engineer is that you need to search the market for processors that have capabilities matching the needs of the current project and then to be sure that the software that is eventually written for that platform does indeed use those features to advantage.

10.5 A special note about start-up times

Unlike simple digital circuits, including low-end FPGAs, which start up almost instantly once the power reaches a certain threshold, processors typically require some extra time to initialize internal registers. For example, after reaching operational voltage, the 8051 requires at least two machine cycles (0.833 ms with a 12 MHz crystal) to initialize the various special-function registers. The Stellaris processors can take up to 1 millisecond. Similarly, more sophisticated circuits, like real-time clocks or Wi-Fi chips, also take relatively long times to begin operating. In most processors the internal initialization sets the PC to the address of the first instruction that will be executed and sets most of the features inside the process to their OFF or benign state. For example, the default power-up initialization for interrupt systems is to turn all interrupts off; this is a safe choice because it prevents external circuits from accidently causing an interrupt before the processor is ready to execute instructions.

There are actually three different reasons why the circuits in an embedded system may not be ready for operation at the same time. The first is the internal initialization time required after the voltage level for that circuit has reached the operating threshold, as described in the preceding paragraph. These times can be found in the circuit's data sheet. The second reason is that different circuits have different thresholds for becoming active. Various circuits in the system may operate at different voltages, and circuits from the same technology family (e.g., CMOS [complementary metal-oxide semiconductor], HMOS [high-density metal oxide semiconductor], and TTL) operating at the same voltage may still have different thresholds. When the power is first turned on, the voltage level takes a certain amount of time to increase from 0 V to the rated voltage. This period is called the ramp-up period. Figure 10.5 shows a sample ramp-up curve, with an indication of the start-up voltages for two devices that might be in the system. T is the time during which device 2 is operating while device 1 is not. The third reason is that the software running on the processor must perform normal initialization of its own program variables as well as to override default initializations in other circuits that are not appropriate for the embedded system. For example, as noted most processors start with the interrupt system turned off. If the processor needs to use the interrupt system, the first instructions in the software will need to override the default configuration setting of the interrupt system. Thus the processor will not be ready for normal operation for some time after it comes out of its own power-up initialization.

The difference in start-up times for the various circuits in an embedded system requires careful consideration of the system (as opposed to individual circuit) initialization timing and steps. For example, the first few instructions of the software may attempt to initialize another circuit in the system. If that circuit has not started operation yet or has not come out of its own internal initialization processes, the initialization attempted by the software in the processor will be ignored, in effect leaving the other circuit in its default state rather than the intended modified state. The initialization software can account for this by inserting suitable delays before attempting to initialize devices that take longer to start up. For example, in Figure 10.5 if the processor is device 2 and the other device is device 1, then the software would have to delay a time T before attempting to access device 1. This delay can be accomplished by a combination of instructions that initialize other parts of the system and simple spin loops.

On the other hand, some devices in the system will reach operating voltage and begin operation before the processor can even execute its first instruction. The power-up state of the other circuit might be a bad state for the embedded system. For example, in a stop-and-go light device 2 in Figure 10.5 could be the transistors that drive the actual lights and device 1 the processor. The lights might turn green in all traffic directions and remain that way for at least time T plus the time it takes for the processor to reach the instructions that change the lights to an acceptable state. Because T is typically only a millisecond or two, in some situations remaining in a

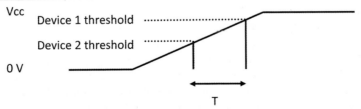

FIGURE 10.5 Ramp-up Time and Thresholds for Two Devices.

Author drawn.

bad state on power-up is not a problem. For the stop-and-go light, this is the case; the lights will be changed before any driver could see them and perhaps even before the lights themselves became illuminated. In other situations a millisecond could be disastrous. If device 2 was a pulse generator that was used to launch a nuclear missile strike, the launch signal would have been sent by the time the processor began executing instructions. In cases where it makes a difference, the design team must prevent the power-up bad state from occurring. There are a couple of options. Some circuits, such as FPGAs, allow start-up inputs to be programmed onto the circuit. A second option is to make the power to the other device be under the control of the processor. The other circuits would then have no power until the processor had started up and begun executing code.

Finally, we note that similar remarks hold for when the embedded system is turned off. Many, but not all embedded systems typically run all the time. However, others are meant to be turned on and off, and in these cases, the design team needs to do a similar analysis of when the various circuits in the system stop working as the voltage fades and whether or not this can have any bad effects.

10.6 Summary

In this chapter we described the range of processing elements available for embedded systems and discussed the major features of processing elements that a design team would use in selecting one for the system under design. Microcontrollers have components, like ADC and DAC, timers, and others, that are useful in many embedded systems, but they typically lack sophisticated instruction sets. Microprocessors are the opposite, usually containing rich instruction sets, especially for arithmetic, but few if any of the other components mentioned in the preceding sentence. We discussed major features that a design team would consider in selecting a processing element — interrupt system, power control, timers/counters, internal memory, and others. We also mentioned nonfunctional features such as form factor and the availability of development systems for the software. We illustrated the range of possibilities by describing and contrasting two popular processing elements — the 8051 family and the Stellaris family. We described several features that are present in processors designed for special applications such as graphics or DSP. Finally, we described the special start-up timing issues that must be considered in systems with several different components or modules.

Problems

1. Search for two low-end microcontrollers and compare the two devices in terms of maximum clock speed, execution time for load and arithmetic operations, internal memory, size of external memory space, number and sources of

interrupts, maximum number of I/O pins, and number of I/O pins available if external memory is used.

2. Do the same for two high-end microprocessors.
3. The following program is meant to run on a microcontroller. PORTC is an I/O pin and has an LED attached to it. When PORTC is 1 the LED is turned off, and when PORTC is 0 the LED is turned on. ISR is the interrupt service routine for external interrupt 0 (INT0). int0_init is a function that configures the INT0 pin, and sei is a system function that enables the microcontroller interrupt system.

```
int Int_flag = 0;

ISR( )
{
  Int_flag = 1;
}

int main( void )
{
  PORTC = 0x01; // Initialize LED to be off

  int0_init();   // configure INT0
  sei();         // enable global interrupts

  while (1)
  {
    if ( Int_flag )
    {
    PORTC ^= 0x01; // invert PORTC -^is logical XOR
    Int_flag = 0;
    }
  }
  return(0);
}
```

Suppose this program begins, and execution reaches the while loop. Suppose at some time after that there is an interrupt. After the interrupt is processed and some time has passed a second interrupt occurs. After the second is processed and some time has passed a third interrupt occurs. Using the following format explain what happens at each point during the operation of this program up to the complete handling of the third interrupt.

```
Event    Executing function   Variable(s) changed   LED status
```

4. Suppose a sensor node is supposed to read the temperature and humidity once every second and transmit that information to the heating, ventilation, and air conditioning control center in an office building. Reading the sensors takes 50 microseconds. Transmitting the information over the wireless link takes another 100 microseconds. The processor must remain in run mode for the entire process, that is, for 150 microseconds. The processor consumes 250 milliwatts when running in normal mode, 10 milliwatts when running in idle mode, and

200 microwatts when in sleep mode. The wireless circuit consumes 5 milli-joules to actually transmit the message, and this amount of energy is in addition to what the processor consumes. The processor takes 10 microseconds to wake up from idle mode and 100 microseconds to wake up from sleep mode. During the wake-up period, the processor consumes the same amount of energy as during normal running mode. Assume the processor can enter idle or sleep mode instantaneously, and that the lower energy usage starts immediately on entering the reduced mode.

Power and energy are related by the following equation: $W = J/t$, where W represents watts, J represents joules, and t represents time in seconds.

a) If the processor is left running 100% of the time, how much energy (i.e., joules) does the system consume each second?

b) For this application, which of the two modes, idle or sleep, should be used? Justify your answer.

c) What is the total energy consumption in joules per second for the whole system (processor plus transmission) for your choice in part 2, and how does that compare to your answer for part 1?

5. MIDI is a protocol for communication among electronic musical instruments. It is a serial protocol, and the baud rate is specified as 31,250 bits per second. RS232 is another serial protocol. RS232 allows several baud rates, but a common one is 19,200 bits per second. This problem explores the calculations necessary to use a timer with reload to set suitable time bases for these two serial protocols.

a) For each of 31,250 bps and 19,200 bps compute the time duration for one bit.

b) Suppose the system has a clock that increments the timers each microsecond. How many increments are needed for one bit in the MIDI protocol?

c) The time for one bit in the 19,200 bps RS232 protocol is not an integral multiple of 1 microsecond. What is the closest integral multiple of 1-microsecond timer increments, and what is the percentage error?

d) For each of the two serial protocols, is a 16-bit timer needed or is an 8-bit timer sufficient?

e) Given your answer to part d and assuming the timers count up, what is the reload value needed when a timer overflows?

6. A microcontroller is to be used to monitor the rotational speed of a wheel. The wheel can only rotate in one direction. The wheel has 64 magnets equally distributed around the perimeter. When one of the magnets passes by a magnetic sensor wired to the interrupt pin on the microcontroller, it causes a pulse, which in turn causes an interrupt for the microcontroller. The wheel is supposed to rotate between 100 and 200 RPM. It is impossible for the wheel to rotate faster than 256 RPM because of the machinery to which it is attached. If the rotational speed goes outside the intended range (100–200 RPM), the microcontroller is supposed to sound a warning.

a) For each of the rotational speeds 100 RPM and 200 RPM, tell what the time is in microseconds between successive interrupts.

b) Based on your answer to part a) and assuming the timer increments every microsecond, should the application use a 16-bit timer or an 8-bit timer?

c) Write an interrupt service routine that sets a variable RPM_STATUS to 0 if the rotational speed is in the acceptable range, 1 if the wheel is rotating to fast, and -1 if it is rotating too slowly. Use C or any language with which you are familiar.

7. A microcontroller is to count real time in seconds/minutes/hours. It has an 8-bit timer that increments once every microsecond.

a) How much time does it take for the timer to count from 0 to 255 and then overflow?

b) What reload value should be used to get the timer to overflow every 1/5000 of a second?

c) Write an interrupt service routine that correctly sets variables SEC, MIN, and HR to represent the seconds, minutes, and hours. Use C or any language with which you are familiar.

8. Consider the following pseudoassembly code for the loop portion of the dot-product computation.

```
// Register AX corresponds to pointer p1 in the C code.
// Register AY corresponds to pointer p2 in the C code.
// Register MR is the multiply-accumulate register.
// Register AN is an arithmetic register used to count down from N to 0.
// Assume AX and AY have already been loaded.
// Assume MR has already been set to 0.
// Assume AN has already been set to N.

loop: mov to MR from address AX
  multiply MR by value from address AY
  add MR to AR
  increment AX
  increment AY
  decrement AN
  jump to loop if 0
```

a) Suppose each instruction takes 1 microsecond to execute. What is the total execution time for the loop for a given value N?

b) What is the total time for the MAC execution assuming each step takes 1 microsecond to execute?

References

[1] https://en.wikipedia.org/wiki/Intel_MCS-51.

[2] https://www.ti.com/product/TM4C1294NCPDT.

[3] https://en.wikipedia.org/wiki/MIDI.

[4] https://en.wikipedia.org/wiki/Harvard_architecture.

[5] https://en.wikipedia.org/wiki/ARM_architecture.

[6] W. Hohl, C. Hinds, ARM Assembly Language, second ed., CRC Press, 2014, ISBN 9781498782678.

[7] ARM Developer, The Thumb instruction set. https://developer.arm.com/documentation/ddi0210/c/CACBCAAE. (Accessed 9 June 2023).

[8] https://www.ti.com/processors/digital-signal-processors/c5000-low-power-dsp/overview.html.

[9] https://en.wikipedia.org/wiki/Tensor_Processing_Unit.

Memories

11

11.1 Introduction

Unlike the case for PCs and laptops in which the main memory issue is simply how many gigabytes are available, memory requirements are an important consideration in the design and implementation of embedded systems. Standard issues include the amount of memory actually needed, how much non-volatile storage is needed, speed, cost, real estate, power consumption, etc. The computer science and computer engineering members of the embedded systems design team need to understand the options and tradeoffs available at both the physical and logical levels.

11.2 Physical-level issues

Physical-level issues for memory selection include onboard vs. offboard memory, serial vs. parallel interface, and volatile vs. non-volatile requirements.

11.2.1 Onboard vs. offboard memory

In Chapter 10 we have seen a wide range in terms of onboard memory, that is, memory that is included on the microcontroller or microprocessor chip itself. The 8051 family, for example, has a small amount of RAM and a small amount of program memory on the chip, while the Stellaris family has orders of magnitude more of both kinds. An application may need minimal computing power but more memory than is built into the low-end microcontrollers. Any processing element can be interfaced to external memory, which leads to the choice between a low-end processor with the right computational power but requiring added circuitry to meet the memory needs vs. a processing element with overkill in the computational abilities but adequate memory. Here are some of the issues the computer engineer would look at.

- Total real estate. Low-end microcontrollers typically have 32–40 pins, and memories also have relatively few pins (especially if they have serial interface — see Section 11.2.2). The total pin count and size of such a processor and memory may be less than a high-end alternative with perhaps 100 or more pins.
- Power consumption. Two small circuits, such as a low-end microcontroller and a small memory, could consume less power than a larger processor chip. On the

Embedded System Design. https://doi.org/10.1016/B978-0-443-18470-3.00011-7

other hand, larger, more sophisticated processors often have power control capability and sleep modes. If the application allows the processor to be in sleep mode for a significant portion of the time, a high-end processor may be a better choice for reduced power consumption.

- Real-time requirements. Access to offboard memory requires additional cycles. For example, in the 8051 microcontroller fetching one byte from external data memory is a separate instruction that requires 12 clock cycles; only after the byte has been brought into the processor can it be used in an operation, which itself would take 6 clock cycles. Bytes from internal RAM can be used directly as operands for instructions, like add, and the overhead for fetching the byte into the CPU is built into the instruction execution time. If the application requires significant computation using large numbers of data bytes, a processor with enough onboard RAM would perform much faster and be much more likely to meet real-time requirements.

11.2.2 Serial vs. parallel access

Parallel access means that all bits of data in the transfer (8 bits for a byte transfer, 16 or 32 for a word transfer) are transferred at the same time. Of course, for this to happen there, must be a separate wire for every data bit. In addition, there are typically separate wires for the address bits that specify which byte inside the memory chip is to be transferred. Finally, there are pins for control signals like read and write, one or two chip-enable pins, in addition to the ground pin (GND) and power pins. Figure 11.1 shows the pin-out for a particular family of 8K byte parallel memory circuits. This circuit has 32 pins in the PLCC (plastic leaded chip carrier) package format and 28 pins in the DIP (dual inline package) format. The obvious advantage of parallel transfer is speed. An entire byte or word is transferred in one processor instruction cycle; nowadays this is on the order of microseconds or nanoseconds. The disadvantages include the size of the circuit and space on the printed circuit board for multiple traces connecting the pins of the memory to the pins of the processor.

Serial access means that the bits are transferred one at a time, using one of the serial communication protocols such as Inter-Integrated Circuit (I^2C) or Serial Peripheral Interface (SPI) (see Chapter 23 for a discussion of communication protocols). This obviously reduces the pin count and therefore the size of the circuit. If the access protocol includes transferring the address of the byte(s) to be accessed in the serial interface, then the need for separate address pins is also eliminated. Thus serial memory circuits typically have very low pin counts despite storing quite large numbers of bytes. For example, the AT45DB161D memory circuit[1] holds 2 megabytes of memory, but the circuit itself has only eight pins. The pin-out is shown in Figure 11.2. Accessing a byte in the AT45DB161D memory circuit requires several steps. First, an 8-bit command (read page, read buffer, write block, etc.) followed by 3 bytes of address information followed in some cases by 4 dummy bytes is strobed into the circuit through the serial in pin. Data bits are then transferred between the processor and the memory circuit in serial fashion, either through the serial in pin for a write

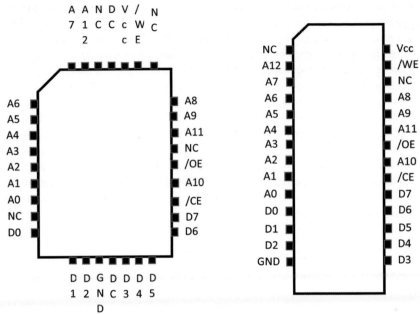

FIGURE 11.1 PLCC (Left) and DIP (Right) Pin-outs for the 2 * 64 Family of Memory Circuits.

Author drawn.

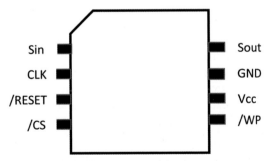

FIGURE 11.2 Pin-out for the AT45DB161D Memory Circuit.

Author drawn.

operation or the serial out pin for a read operation. Obviously, this is much slower than parallel access. Also, the overhead of 4–8 bytes of command and address information makes the time for retrieving 1 or 2 bytes extremely high. Fortunately, like most serial interface memory circuits, the AT45DB161D provides for block transfers, in which multiple bytes in the memory can be read after the initial command and address bytes have been loaded. The memory circuit can automatically increment the internal address register. So, after the 8 bits of the first data byte have been transferred, the next clock pulses transfer data to/from the next byte in the memory and so on for as long as the pulses on the clock line continue. Thus the overhead for the command and address bytes can be spread over many transferred data bytes and becomes more and more negligible as more data bytes are transferred in a single block transfer.

The choice between serial and parallel memory may be determined by the presence of other devices in the system as well as speed, cost, real estate, and so on. For example, if there are devices that are only available in parallel form, the system will already be using space for a parallel data bus and possibly a small address bus. In such a case there is no benefit in using a serial memory. On the other hand, if there are no parallel-interfaced circuits in the system and the real-time requirements can still be met, the savings in board space and power consumption would strongly suggest serial memory circuits.

11.2.3 Volatile vs. non-volatile memory

Volatile memory is memory that loses the values in the cells when power is removed from the circuit. It is used to store temporary information such as program variables, program execution stack, and the like. There are two kinds — static RAM (SRAM) and dynamic RAM (DRAM). DRAM circuits are generally cheaper and have higher densities than SRAM circuits because of the simple structure for storing each bit — just a capacitor and one transistor, as opposed to several transistors per bit in SRAM. SRAM, on the other hand, is faster and uses less power. DRAM is suitable for applications where large amounts of RAM are needed in a small space. SRAM is suitable for applications where speed is the major factor.

Non-volatile memory is memory that retains its values when the power is removed. It is used for holding boot code, look-up tables for standard math functions, configuration data that can be altered by the user, and other applications where the data must be retained even if the power is lost. There are several different kinds of non-volatile memory, each with its own special features and uses.

- ROM (read-only memory): The memory is set during the manufacturing process. The ROM option is cost-effective when the quantity used is large enough to offset the high cost of designing the chip. Bootloaders, function tables, and similar applications that are used in PCs and laptops are typically implemented in ROM. Embedded systems in cars, stop-and-go light systems, etc., also have very high volume and can benefit by using ROM to store information that is exactly the same in every instance of the system.
- PROM (programmable read-only memory): The data is programmed into the memory (typically by blowing fuses inside the circuit) by the company that is using the circuit rather than by the manufacturer of the chip. A special machine, called a device programmer, is used. Software systems allow engineers "in the field" to generate files that can be loaded into the device programmer, which the

device programmer will use to "burn" the data into the memory. Once programed, a PROM cannot be reprogramed. PROMs are useful in situations where the volume may not be so large or there are perhaps variations of the product that require the field engineers to use customized sets of data for each instance of the product.

- EPROM (erasable programmable read-only memory): These devices can be erased by placing them under suitable ultraviolet lamps and then reprogramed. Advances in technology leading to the next two memory types have made the EPROM circuits obsolete.
- EEPROM (electrically erasable programmable read-only memory): This kind of non-volatile memory is writeable "in circuit", that is, writeable directly by a processor, just like RAM. It does not require a special device programmer to load data, although initial values in an EEPROM are sometimes loaded with a device programmer. EEPROMs are suitable for small amounts of non-volatile data that can be modified as the system runs. Examples include configuration data that the user can alter, passwords, security records such as who went through a secure door and when, and other similar kinds of data.
- Flash: Flash memory is also writeable in circuit and is usually faster and cheaper than EEPROM.

For EEPROM and flash there are several special considerations that must be taken into account. First, the write time is typically on the order of 10 milliseconds, orders of magnitude slower than RAM. Second, there are limits on the number of times individual cells can be written before the cell will stop performing correctly, typically 10K–100K guaranteed write cycles with average number of write cycles normally much higher. For these reasons, EEPROM and flash are obviously not suited for normal variables in the software. Furthermore, care must be taken if it is expected that the data may change relatively frequently. One technique to manage the write-cycle limitation is to store the data in RAM and only copy to non-volatile memory under certain conditions, such as periodic back-ups or power down. (Such considerations lead to software requirements for the systems programmers.)

11.3 Logical-level issues

The memory in a processing unit of a system can be organized in several different ways. In some cases this organization can be managed under software control. We discuss three logical-level issues in this section. Figure 11.3 shows a general hierarchy of system memory. Registers, scratchpad, cache, and internal memory are all on the processor chip itself. External memory refers to integrated memory circuits that are separate from the processor chip but typically on the same or nearby printed circuit board. Mass storage refers to slower memory devices like disk drives and memory keys.

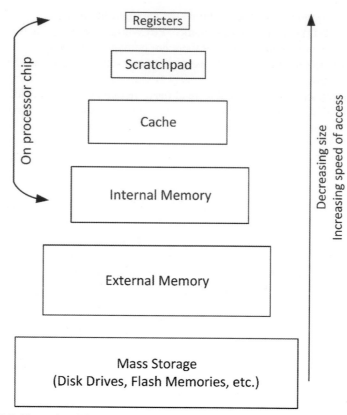

FIGURE 11.3 Hierarchy of General System Memory.

Author drawn.

11.3.1 Cache memory

Cache memory is very high-speed memory that is usually built into the processor chip. It holds recently used data from the main (and slower-speed) memory. As newer data gets used by the CPU, older data that has not been used gets removed from the cache to make room. Each time the CPU references a memory location (e.g., needs to retrieve a variable for an arithmetic operation), the cache hardware compares the memory address to the addresses of data stored in the cache. If the required data is in the cache, it is retrieved from the cache; this is called a cache hit. If the required data is not in the cache, called a cache miss, that data is retrieved from main memory, stored in the cache, and if necessary, some data already in the cache is swapped out. The precise mechanisms for determining which data get swapped out and how integrity with the main memory is maintained are beyond the scope of this book and generally not of concern to embedded systems engineers. Cache memory is generally available on high-end processors.

The major advantage of cache memory systems is speed. Cache memory is much faster than the memory circuits used for main memories. (On the other hand, cache memories are much more expensive than ordinary memory circuits, so technology would not be cost-effective for implementing the very large memories of many computer systems.) If computations are arranged so that variables that are used together in the software are clustered together in the main memory, the number of cache misses will be relatively low, and memory access will be much faster than if there were no cache. One disadvantage of cache memories is that accurate timing analysis is much more difficult because it may not be possible to accurately predict cache misses.

11.3.2 Scratchpad memory

A scratchpad memory is a small, very fast memory inside the processor chip. Unlike cache memory, data is written into or out of the scratchpad memory completely under software control, not by hardware as in cache memory. Once data is in the scratchpad, it stays there until written out under software control, so there are no "scratchpad misses". Scratchpad memories are used to bring modest amounts of data in from the slower memory circuits or where the processor can use data from external memory in only limited ways. As with cache memory, computations that use the data multiple times can be performed more quickly. For example, in matrix multiplication the elements of each row of the left-hand matrix are used in combination with each column of the right-hand matrix. The matrices may be stored in external memory circuits. Rather than bring in each element of a row of the left-hand matrix for each individual multiplication, the software can copy the entire row into the scratchpad and use that row with each column in the right-hand matrix. Thus the elements of the row are retrieved from slower memory only once. Similarly, in other applications variables that are used multiple times together inside a small block of code can be brought into the scratchpad, so the overhead for access is spread over multiple uses. Once the block of code has been completed, any variables that have changed will then be written back to the external memory. Data that is used only once in a block of code, on the other hand, need not be brought into the scratchpad because the overhead for moving to the scratchpad is the same as the overhead for the single access to external memory. Processors designed for applications that rely heavily on matrix computations, such as DSPs, typically have scratchpad memory.

The 8051 family of processors has an interesting variation on the notion of scratchpad, namely the internal memory can be thought of as a kind of scratchpad. Accessing internal memory is much faster than accessing external memory. Moreover, arithmetic and logic operations can be performed only on data in internal memory. The only operations that can access external data memory are fetch and store. To perform calculations on data in external memory, that data must first be brought into the internal memory, then the calculations performed, and finally the result written back to external memory, just as in a scratchpad.

11.3.3 **Memory management units**

Many higher-end processors provide the ability to manage and control the use of internal memory space. These processors have memory management units (MMUs), through which the software can define regions of the internal memory and restrict the use of those regions. Types of control and restrictions include the size and location of the region, whether or not code can be executed from that region, whether or not data can be written to that region, what happens when the access restrictions are violated (typically an interrupt), and a variety of other general and processor-specific features. These are useful for protecting data and for recovering in cases where the software fails and branches to locations outside the actual software. Specifying interrupts and providing suitable interrupt handlers allows the software to recover from memory usage errors and increase the chance that the system can continue to operate.

As an example, consider the Stellaris processor.[2] The default memory model has eight regions, each with its own predefined properties. Software can alter these by configuring up to eight regions. Properties that can be specified include:

- The number of software-defined regions.
- The size of each region.
- The location of each region in the internal memory space.
- Whether or not code can be executed from inside a region.
- The address of the interrupt handler to be invoked for a memory violation if there is to be such a handler.

Whether or not the bus management system can reorder memory accesses when it needs to increase the efficiency of operation, provided, of course, that the end result of the computations will not be altered. This is processor-specific feature as opposed to a general memory management feature.

Related somewhat to memory management is the instruction pair "load-exclusive" and "store-exclusive". The "load-exclusive" reads the memory location and requests exclusive access. Once the new value has been computed, the store-exclusive instruction attempts to write the value back to memory. If the write is successful, the exclusive use request is released; if the write is not successful, a fault occurs, and the system or interrupt handler can attempt to rectify the situation.[3] This is especially useful for semaphores (see Chapter 18).

11.4 **Summary**

In this chapter we discussed physical- and logical-level issues relating to memory circuits that might be used in embedded systems. One major physical issue is whether to pay more for a processing element with built-in memory or use a less expensive processing element and add external memory circuits. In the latter case there is the issue of access. Parallel access to the external memory is faster but requires more copper on the printed circuit board; serial access uses much less copper and real estate but is quite a bit slower. We discussed the issue of volatility. Which parts of the data need to be saved even if the power is lost? What kinds of memories are non-volatile? For the logical level, we discussed various levels of memory, including cache and scratchpad, and their tradeoffs. We described memory management and illustrated how this can be used in processing elements that include this feature.

Problems

1. The 8051 processor family has 256 bytes of fast RAM on the processor chip and can access up to 64 K bytes of RAM from external memory chips. The processor can access the external memory only by retrieving a byte into the accumulator (A) register or writing a byte from the A register back to the external memory circuit. If a variable from the external memory is to be used in arithmetic operations, the variable must be copied into the A register, moved to another location in internal memory, then used in the calculation, and finally, any variables that were changed copied back to the A register and then out to the external memory. Furthermore, accessing external memory requires two instructions — move the address of the variable into the data pointer (DPTR) register and then move to/from the A register. Thus the internal memory of the 8051 is somewhat, but not exactly, like a scratch pad memory. Here is a sample of code for a simple assignment statement: X = Y + Z;

```
mov    DPTR,address(Y)      ; Put address of Y in DPTR
movx A,@DPTR               ; Move Y from external to accumulator
mov    aa,A                 ; Move to an internal variable aa
mov    DPTR,address(Z)      ; Put address of Z in DPTR
movx A,@DPTR               ; Move Z from external to accumulator
mov    bb,A                 ; Move to an internal variable bb
add    A,aa                 ; Add internal copy of Y
mov    DPTR,address(X)      ; Put address of X in DPTR
movx @DPTR,A               ; Move result from accumulator to external
```

Assume the instruction that loads the DPTR register takes two execution cycles, the movx instructions take two execution cycles, and the internal mov and arithmetic instructions take only one cycle. Then the total number of execution cycles for the above sequence of code is 15.

   a. Consider the following assignment statement: Y = D*X*X + E*X + F; Write code for evaluating this statement that accesses external memory for each occurrence of a variable. For example, for the term D*X*X, there would be an external memory access for D and two external memory accesses for X. Assume there are both add and multiply instructions for the arithmetic operations. Count the number of execution cycles in your code.

b. Write code for the above expression that brings all the variables into internal memory at the beginning, then computes the right-hand side using the internal variables, then stores the result. Count the number of execution cycles in this code and compare to the number for your code in part a.

c. Under what circumstances would the execution time not be affected by the cost of accessing variables in external memory?

2. An array of N bytes is to be read into a processor.

    a. Suppose the processor uses parallel access and the access time for each byte is 2 microseconds. How much time is spent actually transferring the N bytes? (Note that in this problem you are not to consider any other program overhead, such as storing the bytes into registers or incrementing the address register.)

    b. Suppose the processor uses serial transfer. Accessing bytes in the memory circuit requires first to write a command byte plus three address bytes to the memory, then accessing the data byte itself. Assume the memory circuit has an automatic address increment feature so that accessing the next byte in memory requires only eight more pulses on the clock pin. Assume the transfer rate for one bit (either write or read) is 100 nanoseconds and there is no other overhead (e.g., start or stop bits) required. How much time is spent to read the N bytes?

    c. For which values of N is the parallel access faster? For which values of N is the serial access faster?

3. A common issue when using processors with scratchpad memories is to decide which variables to keep in the scratchpad and which to keep in the external memory. This is especially important for applications that use arrays. Consider a processor with a scratchpad memory of 1 K bytes. Accessing a byte in the scratchpad takes 1 microsecond, while accessing a byte in external memory takes 4 microseconds. Consider an application that uses the following arrays of the indicated size and number of accesses. (For example, array A has 512 bytes. Each byte is used 8 times in the application, so the number of accesses is 4096.)

Array	Number of Bytes	Number of Accesses
A	512	4096
B	1024	3072
C	128	512
D	512	1024
E	32	16,384
F	64	512

    a. What is the total time for accessing bytes if array B is stored in the scratchpad and the other arrays stored in external memory?

    b. What is the total time for accessing bytes if arrays A and D are stored in the scratchpad and the other arrays stored in external memory?

    c. What is the best organization of scratchpad vs. external memory to minimize total data access time? Show your method for deriving your answer.

4. Consider a system using a processor with a memory management system that allows sections of memory to be blocked from executing code (execution protection) and from being written to (write protection). For each of the following memory sections, which of these two should be applied and why?

  a. Code space.
  b. Configuration data.
  c. Application data.
  d. Scratchpad memory.

References

[1] https://datasheetspdf.com/datasheet/AT45DB161D.html
[2] Texas Instruments, Texas Instruments, Stellaris® LM3S811 Microcontroller DATA SHEET. https://www.ti.com/lit/ds/symlink/lm3s811.pdf
[3] ARM developer, ARM developer, ARM Architecture Reference Manual ARMv7-A and ARMv7-R edition. https://developer.arm.com/documentation/ddi0406/c/Application-Level-Architecture/Application-Level-Memory-Model/Synchronization-and-semaphores/Exclusive-access-instructions-and-Shareable-memory-regions

Field-programmable gate arrays

12.1 Introduction

Field-programmable gate arrays (FPGAs) are integrated circuits containing arrays of logic blocks. The blocks can be simple gates, such as AND, OR, and NOT gates, or more complex logic blocks, which are capable of more sophisticated logical operations. Each circuit has programmable connection layers that allow the engineer to connect circuit input pins to gate inputs, gate outputs to other gate inputs, and gate outputs to circuit output pins. Some FPGA circuits allow these connections to be programmed once, like the PROM memories that can be programmed once. Other circuits allow the connections to be erased and reprogrammed, as with EEPROMs and flash memories. This "programming" is done with a special device programmer, which reads files of equations relating inputs to outputs.

A simple subclass of FPGAs, called complex programmable logic devices (CPLDs), has the gates organized into a two-layer array, which can easily implement sum-of-product logical expressions. CPLDs are typically used to provide the "glue" to interface processors to other devices/circuits and in other applications which would require large numbers of simple AND/OR/NOT circuits for combinatorial logic. The more sophisticated and larger FPGAs are typically used to implement an entire system-on-a-chip (SOC).

A full treatment of how to use FPGA circuits is well beyond the scope of this book and would typically occupy an entire course by itself. In this chapter we describe how such circuits can be used in embedded systems. Our goal is to make the student aware of the possibility of choosing an FPGA instead of multiple circuits or even a processor plus extra circuits, that is, the possibility to implement an entire portion of the design on a single circuit.

12.2 FPGAs and SOCs

Larger-scale FPGA circuits, such as the high-end circuits from companies like Xilinx and Altera, have enough logic blocks to implement a complete microcontroller or microprocessor and have enough blocks left over to implement additional devices. Companies develop sets of equations for these processors and devices and then license the equation sets to companies that build systems using those

Embedded System Design. https://doi.org/10.1016/B978-0-443-18470-3.00012-9

237

processor/device equation sets. Equations are available for license for processors ranging from the low-end 8051 family to the high-end ARM-based families. In addition, equation sets are commercially available for a variety of devices, such as MP3/4 players, video controllers, game controllers, and many other devices and applications. Some companies provide families of equations with a variety of options that suit a large number of applications. For example, Cypress Semiconductor licenses the 8051 with a wide range of options such as 8 KB to 64 KB program memory, 3 KB to 8 KB static RAM, a variety of serial protocols, an ADC (Analog to Digital Converter), up to 4 DACs (Digital to Analog Converters), up to 72 I/O lines, and more. This leads to the possibility of building a complete system on a single chip, a system-on-a-chip, or SOC. Figure 12.1 shows a schematic for such a SOC.

The generation of the equation glue that connects the various licensed and in-house built equation sets would be accomplished by a person experienced in FPGA design. This could be a team member of the project, but it could also be done by an outside company specializing in such work. In the latter case the computer engineers and related team members would provide the specifications for how the pieces are to interact with each other, and the outside company would provide a complete set of equations for the entire FPGA.

Once the chip itself has been designed and the corresponding equation set completely implemented, the inputs and outputs of the resulting SOC can then be routed on, say, a circuit board to the actual physical inputs and outputs that the SOC will monitor and control.

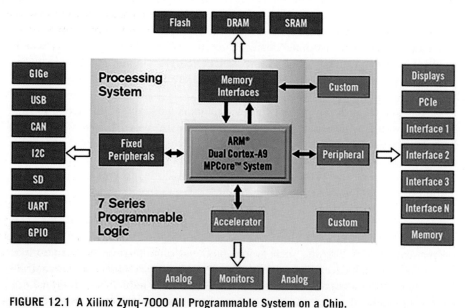

FIGURE 12.1 A Xilinx Zynq-7000 All Programmable System on a Chip.

Author: Xilinx Inc, https://en.wikipedia.org/wiki/File:Xilinx_Zynq-7000_AP_SoC.jpg.

12.3 **Algorithms in hardware**

In many applications speed is the most critical factor. In hard real-time applications failure to produce the result fast enough is the same as failing altogether. Video and audio applications and many digital signal processing applications have strong real-time constraints; imagine watching a video that displays only a few frames a second or listening to music that hesitates constantly. One common approach to achieving very high speeds is to implement in hardware functions that must be very fast or would otherwise use significant portions of the available computing power in the system. Medium- to large-scale FPGAs can be programmed to accomplish the steps of the algorithm, and these steps would proceed at the speed of the transistors, nano-seconds or less, rather than the speed of instruction execution, microseconds or fractions of microseconds. An embedded system might employ such an FPGA along with a traditional processing element. The processor would be used to collect and possibly format the data from system inputs, such as sensors or network connections, and then pass that into the FPGA. The FPGA would then produce the output without further involvement of the processor and orders of magnitude faster. An interesting extension to this idea is the use of in-circuit programmable FPGAs. The software running on the processor of the system can download different files to the reprogrammable FPGA, thus changing the function(s) that it computes. Thus a single FPGA could implement several parts of an embedded system design as long as those parts did not need to be done at the same time. Of course, the FPGA is another chip in the system, so it takes up real estate and adds to the cost. It also uses power, but that has to be compared to the power that would be used by the processor in computing the same result. The tradeoff is speed and possibly lower cost for the processor if a less powerful processor can perform the remaining tasks of the system.

Full treatment of this topic is beyond the scope of this textbook, although we present in the next section a simple example to show how an FPGA can implement a simple algorithm. The interested reader is referred to Refs. [1−3] among many others, for example, for further reading. It is sufficient for the purposes of this text that the student is aware of this alternative for implementing portions of the embedded system design.

12.4 **Low-end FPGAs and CPLDs**

Low-end FPGAs and CPLDs are used to implement Boolean logic at the circuit board level. Examples of such use are to generate chip selects from processor addresses (see Example 12.1) or other "glue" functions needed to interface the circuits on the board, generate special control signals (see Example 12.2), implement Boolean logic for system signals, and perform similar functions at the circuit board level. They can also be used to prototype and test simple application-specific integrated circuits (ASICs) before these are sent out to be manufactured in real ASIC form. In this section, we describe a typical low-level CPLD and illustrate some of these uses.

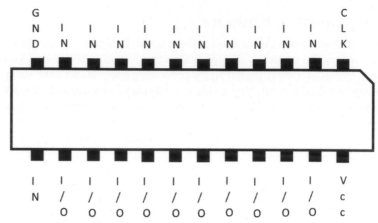

FIGURE 12.2 Pinout for the ATF 22V10 DIP Circuit.

Author drawn.

The 22v10 family of circuits typifies the low-end CPLD genre. A particular example is the ATF22V10 Ref. [4] from Atmel. This circuit has the 24-pin-DIP (double In-line) format packing and the 28-pin-PLCC (plastic leaded chip carrier) format packing. (The PLCC format has extra Ground [GND] and Voltage Common Collector [VCC] pins.) Twelve of the pins are dedicated to inputs, and one of these may be used as a clock to help implement sequential logic functions. Ten pins can be configured as either input or output during the programming process. The pinout for the standard DIP form is shown in Figure 12.2. We now present several examples to illustrate the various uses of such a circuit in an embedded system.

Example 12.1

A common use of CPLD circuits is for generating chip-select signals from processor addresses. Consider a small system containing an 8051, 16 KB of external RAM in the form of two 2064 8 KB RAM chips, 8 KB of non-volatile external data in the form of a 2864 8 KB EEPROM, a DS12887 clock circuit, and a PC16550 UART. These circuits all have 8-bit parallel data buses that connect directly to the 8051 Port 0 data bus. The three memory circuits each use the thirteen 8051 address bits $a_0 - a_{12}$ to access their 8 KB. The two remaining devices have a few internal registers, which are accessed using a few address bits. Thus low-order address bits are wired directly to the devices; in particular, 8051 address bits $a_0 - a_{12}$ are wired directly to the 2064 and 2864 address pins. That leaves address bits 13, 14, and 15 from the 8051 address bus to be used for selecting which circuit is to be active during an external data cycle. We choose the following bit patterns for these three address bits to access the individual circuits.

$a_{15}\ a_{14}\ a_{13}$	circuit	comment
0 0 0	first 2064	External data memory 0000_{HEX}-$1fff_{HEX}$
0 0 1	second 2064	External data memory 2000_{HEX}-$3fff_{HEX}$
0 1 0	2864	External data memory 4000_{HEX}-$5fff_{HEX}$
0 1 1	DS12887	
1 0 0	PC16550	

a0-a12

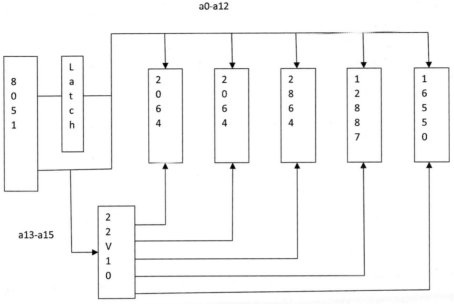

FIGURE 12.3 Diagram of the System in Example 12.1.

Author drawn.

The chip-select pins on these devices are negative true; that means that the signal must be 0 to select the device. Then, the signal for selecting the first 2064 circuit should be 0 when all 3 bits a_{13} −a_{15} are 0. This device select signal therefore is the logical OR of those 3 bits. The select signals for the other devices are, similarly, the logical OR of the top three address bits. Figure 12.3 shows a diagram of this system. For simplicity, the diagram shows only the address and chip-select signals. The system needs to generate five separate negative true (i.e., logic value 0 when active) signals corresponding to the 5-bit patterns above. With traditional logic devices, this would take several AND and NOT circuits. With the 22v10, we implement all five chip selects simply by assigning input pins to the 3 address bits, output pins to the five chip selects, and writing equations that specify when each of the five outputs should be 0 or 1. Figure 12.4 shows a complete file for specifying the solution, including the pin assignments, equations, and other information typical of what a compiler that translates the equations would use. The file shown in Figure 12.4 is "compiled" to produce a second file, which can then be read by the device programmer and used to program a 22v10 circuit.

Example 12.2

We continue Example 12.1 by specifying that the upper half of the 2864 be writable while the bottom half must not be changed by the system. Motivation for this might be as follows. The bottom half contains security codes and other permanent information of the system. The upper half is for user passwords, which can be changed by users. The 8051 emits two signals, /RD and /WR, to indicate when it is reading from or writing to external memory. The 2864 has two corresponding pins. We must ensure that the 2864 /WR pin is only active when the 8051 address is in the range 5000_{HEX} −$5fff_{HEX}$ (i.e., the upper half of the range 4000_{HEX}−$5fff_{HEX}$) and, of course, the 8051 /WR pin is

```
Name    Henschen ;
PartNo  00 ;
Date    4/2/2017 ;
Revision 01 ;
Designer Henschen ;
Company Northwestern University ;
Assembly None ;
Location ;
Device  g22v10 ;

/* *************** INPUT PINS ********************/
PIN  1  =  A15 ;
PIN  2  =  A14 ;
PIN  3  =  A13 ;

/* *************** OUTPUT PINS ********************/
PIN  23  =  RAM0 ;
PIN  22  =  RAM1 ;
PIN  21  =  EEPROM ;
PIN  20  =  RTC ;
PIN  19  =  SERIAL ;

/* *************** Logic Equations **************** */
RAM0     = A15 | A14 | A13;
RAM1     = A15 | A14 | !A13;
EEPROM   = A15 | !A14 | A13;
RTC      = A15 | !A14 | !A13;
SERIAL   = !A15 | A14 | A13;
```

FIGURE 12.4 File for the Solution for Example 12.1.

Author drawn.

active. As with the chip selects in Example 12.1, /WR is a negative true signal, so we want the 2864 pin to be logic 0 when the 8051 /WR pin is 0 and when (a_{15} a_{14} a_{13} a_{12}) is 0101. The equation is

$$WR2864 = WR8051 \mid a_{15} \mid -a_{14} \mid a_{13} \mid -a_{12}.$$

This equation and the pin assignments for the input signal WR8051 and the output signal WR2864 should be added to the file shown in Figure 12.4. All this logic can easily fit on one 22v10 or even smaller CPLD.

Next, we illustrate the use of the clock feature to implement sequential logic, that is, logic in which the outputs are gated by the clock and that can have feedback. When used in this mode, pin 1 of the 22v10 is the clock input signal, CLK. There are also internal flip-flops whose outputs are fed back to the input side of the gate array and which may or may not be gated to output pins. These flip-flops serve as memory for the value of certain signals at the previous clock period. When CLK is low, outputs and flip-flop outputs are held in their current values no matter what happens at the 22v10 input pins. When CLK goes high, the inputs and flip-flop outputs are passed through to the gate array so that new outputs and flip-flop values are created. By controlling the frequency of the CLK signal, the speed of the sequential logic can be controlled. In this mode, sequential outputs and internal flip-flops are indicated in the programming file by statements using the := operator instead of just =. Such equations are called registered equations and are illustrated in Example 12.4 below. The compiler that processes the file takes care of programming the flip-flops to achieve the desired feedback operation. Note that the 22v10 can have a mixture of combinatorial and sequential logic.

The reader will notice that the functionality described in Example 12.3 below could easily be implemented in software without straining the computational resources of the processor. Our goal is simply to show an example of sequential logic and to give a taste of how software/algorithms can be implemented in hardware, as discussed in Section 12.3.

Example 12.3

Recall the problem of aligning the spans of the bridge when they were coming down. The two spans have to be aligned in order for them to engage properly in the final few feet of travel. To accomplish this, suppose two proximity sensors, S1 and S2, are attached to one of the spans, say the right span in the pictures in Figure 12.5. Figure 12.6 shows a side view of the right-hand span lowered almost to the bottom, with two sensors at the end of the span aimed at slightly different angles shown by the dotted lines. Suppose the output of these sensors is digital — 0 if nothing is sensed, 1 if the edge of the other span is sensed. If the left span is far above the right span, as shown in the leftmost drawing in Figure 12.5, neither sensor is activated; that is the output from both sensors is 0. If the right span is stopped and the left span continues to come down, at some point S1 will sense the presence of the left span and produce an output 1. As the left span continues until the spans are relatively even, both sensors produce 1. The outputs are shown in Figure 12.5 for the various positions of the two spans. Notice that output 0 0 is ambiguous. This combination is generated when the right span is way above the left span but also when it is way below the left span. To account for this, let us suppose that the clock signal is fast enough so that the spans cannot move too far between two samples of the sensors unless there is some system or mechanical failure (e.g., the gears slip). So, if the right span is a little above the left span at one time period, short of an error condition, it cannot be a little below at the next time period; it can only remain a little above or go way above or become even.

Let us assume that the right span is started on its downward travel before the left span, so that the right span is "way below" when the two spans reach the last few

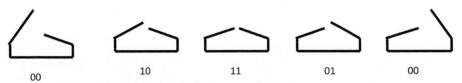

FIGURE 12.5 Sensor Outputs for Different Relative Span Positions.

Author drawn.

FIGURE 12.6 Two Sensors at the End of the Right Span.

Author drawn.

feet. Finally, suppose the processor controlling the span movement generates a signal S that becomes 1 when the right span is within a few feet of the bottom of its travel; that is, when S becomes 1, the sensors S1 and S2 are to be used to help control the final movement. This problem requires the system to remember what the previous value of S was so that it can recognize the transition from S = 0 to S = 1, that is, recognize when the spans have lowered far enough so that the sensors should be used for the last control. Also, the relative positions of the two spans in the previous clock period must be remembered so that the system can distinguish the two cases for S1 = S2 = 0 and recognize error conditions. The 22v10 should generate five separate outputs to represent the five relative positions − BB (right span way below), B (right span a little below), E (spans even), A (right span a little above), and AA (right span way above). It should also generate a signal, ERR, to indicate when the sensors sense a motion that is too large (indicating some error condition). These signals would be used by the motor controllers of the two spans to adjust the motor speed and possibly also by the bridge attendant, who would react in some way when an error occurred.

Table 12.1 shows a portion of the transitions and output values for the various combinations of inputs and previous states. The required registered equations can easily be determined from the table entries. Because the equations use the value of both the current S and the previous S on the right side of some equations, an internal variable, PS, to hold the previous value of S is also needed. Similarly, S1 and S2 have corresponding internal variables, PS1 and PS2. The first few equations are:

```
PS   := S;        Save current value of inputs for
PS1  := S1;       next clock cycle.
PS2  := S2;
BB   := (!PS * S) + (PS * S * !S1 * !S2) + ...
B    := ...
E    := ...
A    := ...
AA   := ...
ERR  := ...
```

Note that when registered equations are used, variables on the left side of the assignment represent the new values for those variables, while variables on the right side represent the flip-flop outputs for those signals, that is, the values from the previous clock period.

Table 12.1 Portion of the transition table for Example 12.3.

Previous values					Current inputs		New values	
S	S1	/S2	BB/B/E/A/AA	ERR	S	S1/S2	BB/B/E/A/AA	ERR
1	0	x/x	x/x/x/x/x	0	0	x/x	0/0/0/0/0	0
2	0	x/x	x/x/x/x/x	0	1	0/0	1/0/0/0/0	0
3	0	x/x	x/x/x/x/x	0	1	1/0	1/0/0/0/0	1
4	0	x/x	x/x/x/x/x	0	1	0/1	1/0/0/0/0	1
5	0	x/x	x/x/x/x/x	0	1	1/1	1/0/0/0/0	1
6	1	x/x	x/x/x/x/x	1	1	x/x	0/0/0/0/0	1
7	1	x/x	x/x/x/x/x	1	0	0/0	0/0/0/0/0	0
8	1	0/0	1/0/0/0/0	0	1	0/0	1/0/0/0/0	0
9	1	0/0	1/0/0/0/0	0	1	1/0	0/1/0/0/0	0
10	1	0/0	1/0/0/0/0	0	1	0/1	0/0/0/0/0	1
11	1	0/0	1/0/0/0/0	0	1	1/1	0/0/0/0/0	1

Each row of the table represents how the system should behave for one situation based on what the signals and outputs were in the previous clock cycle and what the inputs are in the current clock cycle. The x entries represent don't-care conditions, as in standard Boolean logic. For example, row 1 of the table indicates how the outputs should be computed if the S input was 0 in the previous clock cycle, ERR had also been 0 in the previous cycle, the values in the previous cycle for the other five outputs don't matter, and the current value of the S input is also 0, again without regard to the current values of the S1 and S2 inputs. Row 2 indicates that if the right span has lowered far enough to start the sensing operation (previous S was 0 but current S is 1) and both sensors are not sensing the left span, then the right span is way below the left span (BB is 1, other outputs are 0). Row 3 indicates that if the right span has lowered far enough to start the sensing operation but S1 is already sensing the left span, there is an error. For cases like row 3 and row 4, the design team would take into account the desired behavior of the spans and, perhaps, the physical aspects of the spans, motors, and other hardware, when determining the outputs. In this case, the decision was that if the left span was close enough to the right span *when first entering sensing mode*, it was an error condition. It may be the case, for example, that the spans are moving too fast in non-sensing mode and need time to slow down so that the movements can be controlled at a finer grain. Of course, the decision could have been made the other way; the design team might have just considered that the right span was still well below the left span and normal sensing operation would provide suitable control of the motors. On the other hand, row 4 would likely not correspond to a non-error situation; if the spans are just entering sensing mode but the left span is already a little below the right span (S2 is 1), then there really is an error. Finally, note that there is an implicit assumption built into row 8 that the spans cannot go from the right span far below to the left span far below in a single cycle.

Note that in this case the table describes an (hierarchical) finite state machine (FSM). The states include NOT-SENSING and SENSING. SENSING is an OR super-state with sub-states that correspond to normal sensing operation and error. Problem 3 asks the student to draw the equivalent FSM. FPGA circuits are often used to implement FSMs. See Problem 4 for another example of implementing an FSM on an FPGA. Because of the visual impact of an FSM diagram, performing the kinds of analysis described in the preceding paragraph may be easier in the FSM model than in a table defining the operation of the corresponding FPGA. It is common to use the FSM model first and then extract the equations for the FPGA from that model.

Example 12.4

FPGAs can be used to test a design or a part of a design before more costly approaches, such as ASICs, are ordered. Consider a feedback/control problem like the one in Example 12.3 — the auto-pilot in a car that is to follow the solid white line at the right edge of the road. One could easily imagine one approach that would be similar to the solution in Example 12.3 (see Problem 6). Using an FPGA allows the team to test various aspects of the design, such as different clock speeds, additional sensors to give a finer measure of how far the car is from the line, different specifications of don't-care conditions, etc. An FPGA can easily be reprogrammed to implement these various test cases, allowing the engineers to fine-tune the design and eventually pick the best solution. It also allows the team to test other parts of the system that rely on the line-following circuit, even though the final ASIC circuit to be used for that part hasn't been developed yet. After the tests have been completed and the final design chosen, the team could send the design out for fabrication as an ASIC. Because the expectation is to use millions of such circuits (the auto industry sells millions of cars each year), the high cost of designing the production process will be amortized over a large enough number of units to bring the unit cost low enough to warrant choosing the ASIC approach over the direct use of FPGAs. (Note that using an FPGA in the final product incurs not only the cost of the FPGA but the cost of having some entity program them. However, it is still much more cost effective than developing or using an ASIC if the number of final products is relatively low.) In an application like the bridge problem of Example 3, the expectation is to use perhaps only a few hundred or thousand units. That's likely too small to warrant the high cost of developing an ASIC, so for that problem, the engineers would just specify an FPGA for that part of the system.

12.5 Summary

In this chapter we described important ways in which FPGAs can be used in embedded systems. Large-scale FPGAs can be used to implement entire systems by combining relatively simple processing elements with other circuitry onto a single FPGA circuit. These SoCs typically run faster and consume less power than comparable multi-circuit designs, but they require sophisticated and more costly development. We then illustrated several ways in which lower-end FPGAs can be used to implement portions of an embedded system. The simple way is to combine all the Boolean functionality of individual AND/OR/NOT, etc. gates onto a single circuit. A more sophisticated use is to implement simple algorithms, thus avoiding the need for more expensive and power-hungry processing elements.

Problems

1. Edit the file shown in Example 12.1 to include the new features described in Example 12.2.

2. Complete the set of equations for Example 12.3.

3. Draw the FSM corresponding to the FPGA in Example 12.3.

4. Draw the FSM for the FPGA in Example 12.4.

5. Consider the FSM given in Figure 3.11c of Chapter 3. Implement this FSM in an FPGA such as the 22v10. Assume the following pins corresponding to the global variables in Figure 3.11 are to be used:

  - Init_done — an input pin.
  - I_barv — an input pin.
  - I_sdown — an input pin.
  - SG, SY, SR — three separate output pins corresponding to the FSM being in state GREEN (respectively, YELLOW or RED).

When Init_done input is 0, output SR should be 1 and SG/SY both 0, corresponding to the light being red. When Init_done turns from 0 to 1, SG should change to 1 and SY/SR to 0, corresponding to the light being green. While Init_done remains 1, the FPGA should implement the FSM in Figure 3.11c. (Note that because the outputs are digital, that is, either 0 or 1, other modules that monitor the global variable I_tlight would need to monitor the three outputs SG, SY, and SR instead of a single digital signal. In Figure 3.11, however, no other module monitors for any condition except I_tlight being R, that is, the light is red; they would need to monitor only SR. In general, however, global variables that have values other than 0 and 1 will require the use of multiple output pins in an FPGA implementation.)

To make this problem somewhat easier, assume the yellow light is supposed to stay on for 4 seconds, not 5. For that, we will need to include a counter in the FPGA. Assume that the clock input is a square wave with a frequency of 1 Hz. That means that when the yellow state is entered it must exit four clock ticks later. Because this problem assumes the yellow light stays only for 4 seconds, a 2-bit counter t1t0 is sufficient. When the yellow state is first entered, this counter should be set to 11. On each successive clock, it decrements until it reaches 00. On the next clock tick, the FSM transitions to the red state.

a) Fill in the following table. You may use x to indicate a "don't-care" value for an input or internal variable. The first two rows are filled in to show you the format. We have abbreviated the inputs I_done, I_barv, and I_sdown as ID, IB, and IS, respectively.

INPUTS			PREVIOUS VAUES						NEW VALUES				
ID	IB	IS	ID	SG	SY	SR	t1	t0	SG	SY	SR	t1	t0
0	x	x	x	x	x	x	x	x	0	0	1	0	0
1	x	x	0	x	x	x	x	x	1	0	0	0	0

b) Write the equations for the three outputs.

SG =

SY =

SR =

c) Write a file as described in Example 12.1 for your FPGA solution.

6. Design an FPGA to make a car follow a white strip in the middle of a lane. The car has three sensors at the front — left (L), middle (M), and right (R). The white strip is 2 inches wide. The distance between the left and right sensors is 1.75 inches. Each sensor produces a signal 1 when it is over the white strip and 0 when it is not. For example, the left-to-right sequence 1 1 0 means both the left and middle sensors are over the white strip, but the right sensor is no. This would indicate that the car has drifted a little bit to the right.

a) Describe in words what each of the eight 3-bit patterns indicates about the position of the car. Note that some of these patterns do not correspond to a real situation, and you should write "NA" in your list for those situations.

b) There are five output signals — steer hard left (HL), steer gently left (GL), steer straight (S), steer gently right (GR), and steer hard right (HR). Propose a set of equations that would be appropriate for determining each of the five outputs based on the three inputs L, M, and R.

c) The sensor input is to be updated every millisecond. Suppose we use a 22V10 and provide an appropriate clock signal to pin 1. Write a complete file suitable, as illustrated in Figure 12.3, to program the 22V10 for this problem.

d) After experimenting with the 22V10 defined in part c., the auto engineers may decide that three sensors are not enough and decide to use five sensors instead. Assume the decision is to put one of the new sensors between the L and M sensors and the other between the M and R sensors. Repeat parts a.−c. with this new sensor configuration.

7. In a group or class setting discuss for each of the following applications whether or some or all of the system should be implemented with FPGAs and why.

a) Fire control system on a destroyer.

b) Door security system.

c) Elevator system in a high-rise building.

References

[1] F. Bruno, FPGA Programming for Beginners: Bring Your Ideas to Life by Creating Hardware Designs and Electronic Circuits with SystemVerilog, Packt Publishing Ltd., Birmingham, 2021, ISBN-13: 978-1789805413.

[2] A. Simpson, FPGA Design: Best Practices for Team-Based Reuse, second ed., Springer, 2015, ISBN-13: 978-3319179230.

[3] S. Kilts, Advanced FPGA Design: Architecture, Implementation, and Optimization, Wiley, 1978, ISBN-13: 978-0470054376.

[4] https://www.alldatasheet.com/datasheet-pdf/pdf/56313/ATMEL/ATF22V10.html.

Devices, sensors, and actuators

13

13.1 Introduction

A typical embedded system receives input from its environment and generates output to that environment. Inputs may be digital (e.g., 0 volts vs. 5 volts, logic 0 vs. logic 1, ON vs. OFF) or analog (e.g., voltage in the range 0–5 from an analog sensor). Examples of physical world digital inputs include switches and buttons. Digital input signals may be connected directly to pins on a microcontroller, such as the General-Purpose Input/Output (GPIO) pins on the Stellaris processor described in Chapter 10. They may also be wired to interface circuits that either expand the number of inputs or protect the relatively delicate processor circuit from higher voltages, noise, and other electrical disturbances. Examples of analog inputs include the outputs from sensors, such as temperature sensors and microphones, and analog outputs from electrical devices. Analog inputs are wired to analog-to-digital converters (ADCs), which may be separate circuits or may be microcontroller pins that can be configured as ADCs, such as the ADC pins on the Stellaris processor. Similarly, outputs can be digital or analog and can be connected to the environment directly from processor GPIO pins or through subsidiary circuits such as digital-to-analog converters (DACs). Examples of digital outputs include switches or transistors that are used to turn equipment on or off; examples of analog outputs are voltages that control the speed of certain kinds of DC motors and outputs to speakers for reproducing audio signals. Finally, analog signals can be periodic (e.g., audio signals) or non-periodic (e.g., the output of a temperature sensor).

In this chapter we discuss various kinds of inputs and outputs and the most common techniques for handling them in embedded systems.

13.2 Digital inputs

Digital inputs are those inputs that assume one of two values. From an electrical standpoint, this means the input signal is either a low voltage or a high voltage. From an application standpoint, these can be logic 0 and 1, switch closed or open, device ON or OFF, etc. Low and high voltage have different meanings in different circuit families; for example, in 5 volts transistor transistor logic (TTL) and

Embedded System Design. https://doi.org/10.1016/B978-0-443-18470-3.00013-0

complementary metal-oxide semiconductor (CMOS) logic circuits, low typically means less than about a half volt, and high typically means more than about 3.5 volts. Other circuit families have different ranges for low and high. Note that there is a range in the middle where the value is not determined. For a TTL circuit, for example, a voltage level of 2 volts on the input will not lead to a guaranteed value in the circuitry interpreting the input voltage. Therefore the embedded system designers must ensure that digital inputs generate voltage levels that avoid the middle range for the circuits those inputs are wired to.

Typical digital input devices include single pole buttons and switches, that is, devices that make a single contact. Figure 13.1 shows samples of this kind of digital input device. For these to produce two clearly distinct voltage levels it is necessary to include either a pull-up or pull-down resistor, as shown in the figure. Figure 13.1a shows a button with a pull-up resistor. When the button is not being pressed, the voltage at the processor input pin is close to 5 volts; when the button is pressed, the voltage at the pin is ground (GND) (i.e., 0 volts). Figure 13.1b shows a single pole switch with a pull-down resistor. Typical values for pull-up/down resistors are in the range 10–15K ohms, but the engineer would need to consult the datasheet for the circuit receiving the input to make sure an appropriate resistance is used for that particular circuit. Many microcontrollers have internal pull-up or pull-down resistors when a GPIO pin is configured as input. For example, Figure 13.1c shows a button input to an 8051 input pin. The 8051 switches in a 15K-ohm pull-up resistor when configured as input, so no external resistor is needed.

One special kind of input device is the opto-isolator. As the name suggests, this kind of device isolates the sensitive microcontroller circuitry from the environment that is producing the signal. For example, opto-isolators might be used in situations where there are heavy motors, such as the bridge span system, that produce high levels of electrical noise and instability in the AC power supply. Figure 13.2 shows an opto-isolator sensing an input signal on the left side and producing an output on the right side which is, in turn, the input to an 8051 microprocessor. When current flows through the circuit on the input (left side in the figure) of the opto-isolator a light source (e.g., tiny LED) shines on the base of the transistor on the output side, causing the transistor to conduct current. In this case the 8051 input pin is

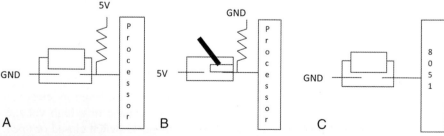

FIGURE 13.1 Single Pole Input Devices.

Author drawn.

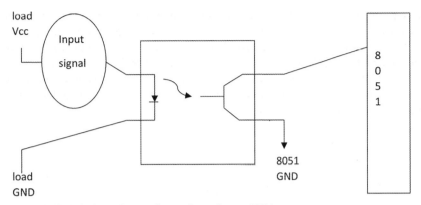

FIGURE 13.2 Opto-Isolator Generating an Input for an 8051.

Author drawn.

essentially connected to GND, and the 8051 will read the pin as logic 0. When no current flows through the input side of the opto-isolator, the light source is dark, and the transistor does not conduct current. In this case the internal pull-up resistor inside the 8051 will hold the pin at high voltage level, and the 8051 will interpret the signal as logic 1. The power system on the left side is completely separated from the power system on the right side; even the GND lines are separated. Thus effectively no noise from the input side leaks through to the output side. There are small mechanical relay devices that also accomplish this kind of electrical isolation. Figure 13.3 shows an example.

Many electronic circuits also produce a simple ON/OFF output. Examples include simple proximity sensors (something is close or not), voltage comparators,

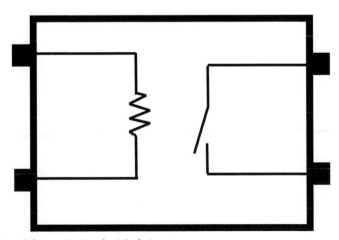

FIGURE 13.3 Miniature Mechanical Switch.

Author drawn.

etc. The embedded system engineer needs to match the output voltage and current drive capability of the circuit generating the signal with the corresponding requirements of the circuit to which that signal is wired. This will determine, for example, what kind of pull-up/down resistor is needed or whether an intermediate voltage level shifter is required.

An important issue with digital inputs, especially mechanical buttons and switches, is key bounce. Because of a variety of conditions ranging from environmental (e.g., humidity, particulate matter in the air, etc.) to mechanical (e.g., flexibility of the metal contacts), the circuit may make and break many times over a few milliseconds when the button or key is pressed or released. For example, in Figure 13.1b the contact on the left side of the switch may literally bounce when the button is pressed or may not make good contact initially because of moisture in the air and on the contact. An application that reads the switch may see multiple ON/OFF cycles for a single press by, say, a human user. If the application is counting events, the application will count many events whereas the user only intended one event. Key bounce is easily overcome by either software or hardware means. A software solution is to read the key repeatedly until the signal is steady for some number, for example, 50 or 100, of consecutive reads. This is a simple solution that can work when timing constraints are not severe. Hardware solutions typically involve simple RC circuitry possibly combined with a diode and Schmidt trigger, such as shown in Figure 13.4. In that figure diode D ensures that the capacitor is charged only through R1 and discharged only through R2. This, in turn, ensures that the voltage at point A drops more-or-less steadily when the button is pressed and rises more-or-less steadily when the button is released even if there are multiple makes and breaks. The Schmidt trigger ensures that the output at point B does not fluctuate while the voltage at point A gradually increases or decreases.

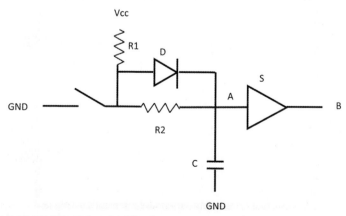

FIGURE 13.4 Simple Key Debounce Circuit.

Author drawn.

13.3 **Analog inputs**

Analog inputs are those that produce a continuous range of values. Examples include potentiometers that adjust a voltage through a range (e.g., the knobs that adjust the volume on audio devices or adjust brightness of a light) and sensors that sense inputs with a range of values, for example, temperature or humidity, and produce an output voltage in some voltage range. A microphone is a particular example of a sensor because it senses audio waves and produces a varying voltage signal in response to the pressure. For analog sensors, there are two ranges that must be considered — the range of values in the application that are the input to the sensor and the range of voltage levels that the sensor outputs.

The first is the range in the application. For example, if measuring temperature in a building, the range might be 40°F to 120°F. Of course, real temperatures can vary far outside the 40°F—120°F range, but for normal occupancy inside a building, such as a home or office building, temperatures below 40°F or above 120°F would not be expected. A sensor that sensed 120°F when the actual temperature is 130°F might be acceptable because both 120°F and 130°F are too hot for ordinary occupancy. If the embedded system that controls the air conditioning thinks the temperature is 120°F when it is actually 130°F, it's probably ok because in either case, it would likely turn the air conditioner on to maximum cooling. On the other hand, if the temperature sensor were part of a fire alarm system, the sensor might need to have a different range, say 70°F to 400°F. No sensor can handle an infinite range of application values. Part of the system requirements specification should be to determine appropriate ranges for analog inputs and to verify that the system can perform appropriately if inputs above the maximum or below the minimum value occur.

The second range that needs to be considered is the output voltage range of the sensor. Some sensors produce outputs in the millivolt range, and these normally need to be scaled and amplified before they can be processed further. Once a suitable voltage range is obtained, the next question is how values at the input side of the sensor relate to values at the output. If the sensor is linear, then there is a simple linear equation relating the input to the output. Let $A_{max} - A_{min}$ be the range of application values that the sensor handles, and let the output voltage range be 0 - V. Then for input values in the acceptable range, the real input value and sensor output voltage are related by the formula

$$A_{real} = A_{min} + V_{output} * (A_{max} - A_{min})/V.$$

When the processor inputs the analog value V_{output}, it can use this formula to compute the actual value A_{real} being sensed.

Because computers deal with bits and binary numbers, these analog voltage signals must be converted into digital form, in particular to a binary number. This is accomplished by special circuits, called, appropriately, ADCs. Some microcontrollers, such as the Stellaris series and the advanced members of the 8051 family, have built-in ADCs. Some sensors have the ADC built into the circuitry, so they can be directly interfaced to the digital inputs of a processor. When neither of these is the case, the system will require an external ADC. There are several issues to be considered when the engineer is selecting an ADC circuit. The two main issues are resolution and speed.

Perhaps the most important issue in selecting an ADC is the resolution, that is, how many bits in the binary number that is produced by the ADC. Common resolutions are 8 bits, 12 bits, 16 bits, and 24 bits. The resolution is important because it determines how closely the computer can estimate the real measured value. The output of the ADC is not a continuous function but rather a step function, with the number of steps equal to 2^R, where R is the resolution. For example, an 8-bit ADC produces outputs that are binary numbers in the range 0–255. Thus, as the application value being sensed increases through its range, the 8-bit digital output counts up from 0 to 255. For each additional increase of $\delta = (A_{max} - A_{min})/256$, also sometimes called the resolution, the 8-bit binary number increases by 1. That means that the processor cannot distinguish between inputs in the interval $[A_{min}, A_{min} + \delta)$, in the interval $[A_{min} + \delta, A_{min} + 2\delta)$, etc. That is why high-quality audio ADCs need higher resolution (at least 16 bits and preferably 24 bits) — so that the outputs can more faithfully represent the tiny nuances of sound. The embedded systems engineer must analyze the requirements of the system being designed and implemented to determine how much accuracy is needed and therefore what resolution is needed.

The second issue in selecting an ADC is the speed. For applications with tight real-time constraints, faster (and therefore costlier) ADCs need to be used. For example, video applications require high-speed ADCs, and audio applications at least medium-speed ADCs; on the other hand, conversion of body temperature in a bio-sensor application probably can use inexpensive, slow ADCs.

An issue that is not related directly to the application but is important in the design and implementation of the system is the ADC-to-processor interface. This can be either serial or parallel. ADCs with parallel output can transfer the readings to the processor at speeds comparable to ordinary memory access. On the other hand, like parallel interface memory circuits, they require multiple wires for the data bus (typically 8 or 16) plus extra wires for control like chip select, /RD, and /WR. Serial interface ADCs require only one or two wires, but the transmission of the data is slower.

The internal structure of the ADC and how the conversion is actually performed are typically not directly relevant issues in selecting an appropriate ADC. They do, however, determine many of the factors that do influence the choice. Therefore, for the sake of general understanding, we present a brief overview of the main ADC techniques. The two most widely used techniques are flash conversion and successive approximation.

In flash conversion the input analog signal is represented as a voltage in the range REF− to REF+ (typically 0–V but can be any range). An n-bit flash ADC requires 2^n resistors and $2^n - 1$ voltage comparators. The resistors are placed in series between REF+ and REF−, thus giving 2^n equally spaced voltage levels between the two reference voltages. Each of these is supplied to one side of one of the voltage comparators. The input voltage is bused to the other side of all the comparators. The structure is shown in Figure 13.5a for a resolution of 2 bits. Because the voltage levels from the resistor chain increase from one comparator to the next, a particular input voltage will produce 1s for the first m comparators and 0 for the remaining comparators. Figure 13.5b shows the comparator outputs for different ranges of input voltage. Circuitry counts the number of 1s and converts that to a regular binary number. Figure 13.5c shows the 2-bit binary outputs corresponding to the four different input voltage ranges. Because the number of resistors and comparators required is exponential in the number of bits of resolution, flash ADCs are limited to relatively lower resolutions. (Although, as circuitry shrinks and the capabilities of circuits increase, flash ADCs of higher resolution will likely become available.) Flash ADCs are also more expensive and consume more power, again because of the large amount of circuitry required. On the other hand, flash ADCs are faster because all the comparisons are done in parallel and the final conversion to the binary number is easy and fast.

The other widely used technique for analog-to-digital conversion is the successive approximation approach, or SAR. In this approach there is a single comparator that is used repeatedly to generate output bits one at a time. This method works like the standard binary chop method for searching in sorted arrays. At each iteration, one more bit of the output is determined, and the interval of uncertainty is cut in half. In the first iteration the sample voltage is compared to one-half the voltage range. If the sample voltage is greater than or equal to the mid voltage, the most significant bit is set to 1 and the new voltage range is the upper half of the starting range; otherwise, the most significant bit is set to 0 and the new voltage range is the lower half of the starting range. The process is repeated until all bits have been determined. There is a clock input that controls the iteration process. In some circuits the clock is supplied through an input pin on the ADC circuit package. The clock signal could be supplied by a separate clock circuit, the processor clock if

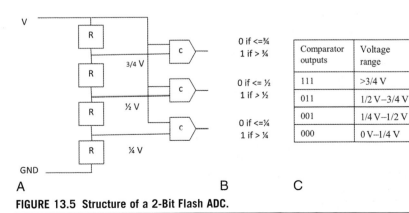

Comparator outputs	Voltage range	2-bit binary
111	>3/4 V	11
011	1/2 V–3/4 V	10
001	1/4 V–1/2 V	01
000	0 V–1/4 V	00

A   B   C

FIGURE 13.5 Structure of a 2-Bit Flash ADC.

Author drawn.

that is not too fast for the ADC, or by a GPIO pin from the processor under software control. Some SAR ADC circuits have the clock built in. Initially all output bits are estimated to be 0. Starting with the most significant bit, upper voltage $V_u = V_{max}$, and lower voltage $V_l = V_{min}$, at each clock the following steps are performed:

1. If the sample voltage is greater than or equal to the midpoint of the current range $(V_u - V_l)/2$, set the current bit to 1 and V_l to $(V_u - V_l)/2$.
2. Otherwise set the current bit to 0 and V_u to $(V_u - V_l)/2$.

Figure 13.6 shows the steps in converting a voltage by this method in a 3-bit successive approximation ADC.

Successive approximation ADCs are relatively inexpensive because there is only one comparator no matter how many bits of resolution. (Compare this to flash ADCs, in which the amount of circuitry effectively doubles for each additional bit of resolution.) Because there is relatively little circuitry, SAR ADCs also consume less power. On the other hand, they are slower, and the speed decreases as the resolution increases. There are other conversion techniques, but as of the writing of this book, they tend to have features that limit their use to particular applications. For example, there are so-called integrating ADCs, which are very low power and low cost but have sampling rates below 1 KHz. There are delta-sigma ADCs, which are capable of very high resolution but are limited to sampling rates of no more than 1 MHz and single-channel sampling.

Many ADC circuits have a track-and-hold feature. In these circuits the input voltage is latched internally, and the internal value is what is piped to the conversion circuitry. This isolates the conversion process from changes in the input signal in the middle of the conversion process. Finally, many circuit packages allow multiple input channels. The processor must write a command of some kind to the circuit indicating which channel is to be converted.

Voltage Range: 0–5		Input: 3.27		Resolution: 3 bits	
Step	Output Bit	Input Voltage	Test Voltage	Action	Tentative Output
1	2	3.27	2.5	set bit 2 to 1	100
2	1	3.27	3.75	set bit 1 to 0	100
3	0	3.27	3.125	set bit 0 to 1	101

FIGURE 13.6 Steps in Converting an Input by Successive Approximation.

Author drawn.

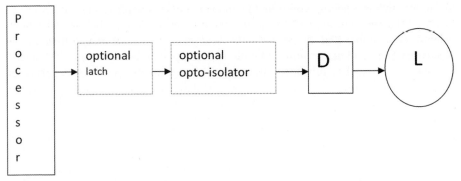

FIGURE 13.7 Generic Output From Processor to Load.

Author drawn.

13.4 Digital outputs

Digital outputs are those outputs that assume one of two values. From an electrical standpoint, this normally means the output signal is either a low voltage or a high voltage. From an application standpoint, these can be logic 0 and 1, device ON or OFF, etc. Digital outputs may simply feed other electronic parts of the embedded system, or they may control physical devices in the environment. Examples include turning on/off regular lights or indicator lights, opening or closing valves, turning motors on and off, etc. For these latter kinds of devices, the signal from a processor usually does not have the necessary electrical characteristics, such as voltage levels, current capacity, AC drive, etc. Therefore the GPIO pins drive some intermediate mechanical (e.g., small relay as shown in Figure 13.3) or electrical (e.g., power transistors or arrays of transistors) devices that do meet the needs of the item being switched on and off. Intermediate latch circuits can be inserted between the processor GPIO pins and the load to isolate the processor from electrical noise or to increase the number of digital output bits the processor can feed to the system. As with inputs, opto-isolators can be inserted between the processor and the load to further isolate the electrical systems and prevent environmental noise and fluctuation in the power supply to the load from affecting the power supply of the processor and related electronics. Figure 13.7 shows a generic schematic of the circuitry. In this figure D represents the device that takes the output from the processor and transforms it to a suitable level to drive the load. L represents the load, which could be a motor, heavy-duty switch or relay, or other heavy load.

13.5 Analog outputs

Many elements of embedded systems require analog control, that is, a signal that varies (almost) continuously through a range of values. Examples include various

DC motors whose speed is controlled by the voltage level applied, pressure controls (such as the pressure applied to the gas control in an automobile), lights whose brightness is controlled by varying the voltage, amount of magnetism in an electro-magnet, and many more. As with analog inputs, there are two value ranges to consider. First, the embedded system, probably through a processor, generates some number that is passed to a DAC (see next paragraph), which outputs a voltage in some predefined range such as 0–5 volts. Second, there is the application range, for example, how fast does the motor run or how brightly does the light shine. Part of the embedded system design is to map the first kind of value to the second kind. Additional circuitry may be required for this. For example, transistors may be needed to amplify the voltage and/or current levels produced by the converter.

DACs perform the opposite conversion from ADCs. They convert binary numbers into voltage levels. The same issues as were discussed in Section 13.4 apply here. The number of bits in the binary number, the resolution, determines how many different voltage levels the DAC can produce as output. Notice that the output of a DAC is a step function; a DAC cannot produce all the infinite number of voltages in the output range, only a discrete set of them. With fewer bits of resolution there are fewer voltage levels, and consequently, the difference between one voltage level and the next is larger. For example, if the output voltage range is 0–5 volts and the resolution of 8 bits, then each level of the output step function is $5/256 \approx 0.0195$ volts. The resolution is determined by the needs of the application. Audio applications typically require high resolution in order to generate nuanced sound. A dimmer switch for a light would not need high resolution. Speed of conversion is also an important consideration. Video and audio applications need high-speed conversion to generate results that are acceptable to the human eye and ear; a dimmer switch controller can be relatively slow. Finally, as with ADCs, the interface to the processor is an important consideration.

As with ADCs, there are several common ways to implement DACs. Again, as with analog inputs, the internal structure of the DAC is not directly important to selecting the best one for the application; the operating characteristics, such as resolution and speed, are usually the determining factors. For the sake of general understanding, again, we mention two of the main ways DACs are made. The fastest and most expensive DACs, sometimes called thermometer-coded DACs, have 2^R resistors of equal resistance, where R is the resolution in bits. Figure 13.8a shows an example for 2-bit resolution. The resistors are in series, as shown in the figure. The points between the resistors have all the voltages $kV/2^R$, where k is the position of the point counting from the bottom of the series. A decoder uses the binary number input to the DAC to select exactly one of the switches to close, thus shunting exactly one of the voltage levels to the output. The figure shows the case for input 01_{BIN}, with the second switch from the bottom being closed. These DACs can produce highly accurate output voltages and are able to generate the appropriate output in the same amount of time it takes to decode the binary number at their inputs — nanosecond speed. Another class of DACs uses one resistor for each bit of resolution. The resistors have values r, 2r, 4r, ..., $2^R r$ for some base resistor value r.

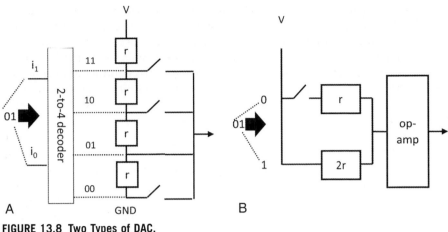

FIGURE 13.8 Two Types of DAC.

Author drawn.

Each resistor, when switched in, produces a current $V/2^i r$ that is fed into an op-amp. See Figure 13.8b for a diagram of a 2-bit DAC of this type. Each 1 bit in the input switches in the corresponding resistor, which adds a proportional current at the resistor output. The total current flows into the op-amp, which produces a corresponding output voltage. In Figure 13.8b the input is 01_{BIN}. Only the resistor with value 2r is connected to the op-amp, and therefore only current $V/2r$ flows into the op-amp. The reader can easily see that there are four possible current levels and thus four possible voltage levels on the output pin. This type of DAC also achieves high conversion rates. There are several other types of DACs as well.

We note that some circuits include both ADCs and DACs. Some advanced microcontrollers have both capabilities. Some external converters have both ADCs and DACs. For example, the Phillips 8591 circuit has four ADC input channels and one DAC channel.

13.6 Interfacing large numbers of digital inputs and outputs

As described in Section 11.2.2 for memory circuits, the interface between a device and the processor may be parallel or serial. In this section we discuss interfacing devices with parallel interface. See Chapter 23 for an extensive discussion on interfacing devices through serial connections.

When there are only a small number of inputs and outputs, the processor selected for implementation may have enough GPIO pins for both. Many applications, however, have a large number of digital inputs. For example, a piano has 88 keys, requiring 11 bytes of input. Typical synthesizers have 61 keys, requiring 8 bytes, and a variety of other controls to select the sound and various sound effects, requiring additional bits of input. An elevator system in a high-rise building might have 1 byte of input and 1 byte of output for each floor. Even high-end microcontrollers don't have that many GPIO pins and ports. A common solution is to use auxiliary circuits, such as the 573 family of gate/latch circuits shown in Figure 13.9, to gate the input bytes into a single 8-bit port on the microcontroller or to allow the outputs from a single 8-bit port to be latched into many 8-bit output devices.

The D pins of the 573 circuit are inputs to the circuit, and the Q pins are the outputs. When the L pin is held high, the 573 circuit acts like a gate, allowing the input signals to pass through to the output side when the gate is open (/OE signal low) and blocking when the gate is closed (/OE is high). When /OE is high, the output pins are in tristate mode, which means they are high-impedance and do not affect any other circuits to which they are wired. When multiple 573 circuits all have their outputs wired to the same input port on a microcontroller, the gates can be read into the processor one at a time by activating 573 /OE pins one at a time. The one circuit with active /OE pin will provide input signals to the processor input port pins, while the other 573 circuits will have their output pins in tristate mode. All that remains is to provide a means for activating the /OE pins. This can be accomplished by using pins in a second GPIO port. When there are just a few 573 circuits, each /OE pin can be assigned to a particular GPIO pin in the second port. Figure 13.10 shows the case when there are three 573 circuits. One 8-bit GPIO port is used for the input, and 3 pins of a second port are used to control the three /OE pins. This configuration uses only 11 GPIO pins instead of the 24 pins that would be required if each 573 output pin was wired directly to a separate GPIO pin. For slightly higher numbers of input gates, a decoder circuit such as the 138 3-to-8 decoder or even a complex programmable logic device like the 22V10 can be used. A 138 decoder can provide for up to 8 input gates (64 bits of input) using, again, only 11 GPIO pins (8 for data and 3 to select 1 of 8 gates) on the processor. Problem 3 asks the student to draw a detailed diagram for this situation.

If the /OE pin on the 573 circuit is tied to GND, the output pins will always be enabled. When the L pin transitions from high to low, the data at the input pins is latched into the circuit, and the output pins use these latched values for the output.

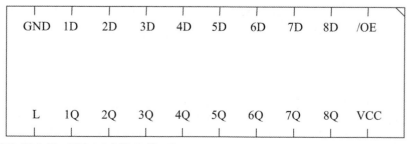

FIGURE 13.9 The 573 Latch/Gate Circuit.

Author drawn.

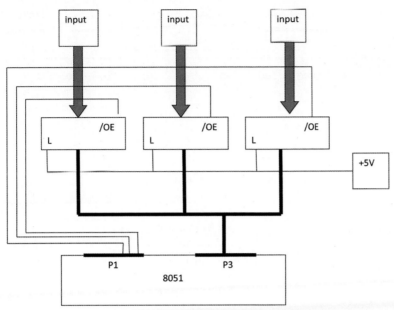

FIGURE 13.10 Three 573 Gates Attached to an 8051.

Author drawn.

In this configuration the 573 behaves like a 1-byte write-only memory. The output pins can be connected directly to the load or to transistors or relays, as discussed in Section 13.4. As for digital inputs, when external latches are used to increase the number of output pins, the processor itself needs to use eight GPIO pins to connect to the input pins of the 573 circuits. The processor also needs to control the individual L pins, either by assigning them to other GPIO pins or by using external circuits, like the 138 or 22V10. Figure 13.11 shows the configuration for when the 573 is used as an output device. Note that the processor GPIO pins are connected to the input pins of the 573, just the opposite of when the 573 is used as an input gate. When the GPIO pins can be configured under software control for input or output dynamically, it is possible to combine the data path for both input gates and output latches into a single GPIO port. See Problems 3 and 4.

When there are many bytes of digital input and/or output, such as the ventilation controls in a large building or the sensors and actuators in an assembly line, a common approach is to map the 573 circuits to the external memory space of the processor. Each input gate is a 1-byte read-only memory, and each output latch is a 1-byte write-only memory. The processor reads inputs and writes outputs using the normal instructions for accessing external data memory. These instructions will generate address information on the external address bus and also generate read and write signals. For example, the 8051 processor generates 16 bits of address information and

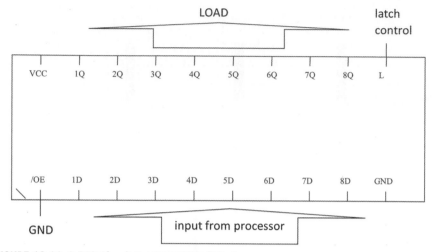

FIGURE 13.11 A 573 Circuit Configured for Output.

Author drawn.

the two signals /RD and /WR for external data access. The system designer must assign addresses to the various gates and latches and provide circuitry, typically in the form of a programmable logic device like the 22V10, to generate the appropriate signals for the /OE pins on the gates and the L pins on the latches. The data is transferred through the same port as other external data, such as data in an external RAM; in the case of the 8051 processor, for example, this is Port 0.

Figure 13.12 shows a generic configuration with eight input gates and eight output latches. Suppose the input gates are mapped to processor addresses 0x8000-0x8007 and the output latches are mapped to processor addresses 0x9000-0x9007. The /OE pin on the first input gate should be active, that is, logic 0, when the processor address is 0x8000 and the /RD signal is active, that is, logic 0. Suppose we decide to use only the top 4 and bottom 3 bits of the 16-bit address for gating inputs and latching outputs. That is, we use only address bits A0—A2 and A12—A15 and ignore the other eight address bits. (Note, this leads to a condition called aliasing — the first input gate would be activated for addresses 0x8000, 0x8010, …. If the system has no other memory or devices at these locations, no harm would be done.) Then the following equation would be suitable for controlling the /OE pin on the first input gate:

$$\text{Gate0OE} = /\text{RD} + /\text{A15} + \text{A14} + \text{A13} + \text{A12} + \text{A2} + \text{A1} + \text{A0};$$

Gate0OE will be logic 0 when all the terms on the right-hand side are logic 0, that is, when /RD is active and the top four address bits are 1000 (=0x8) and the bottom three address bits are 000 (=0x0). Equations for controlling the L pins for the output latches are obtained similarly except that the right-hand expression must be negated

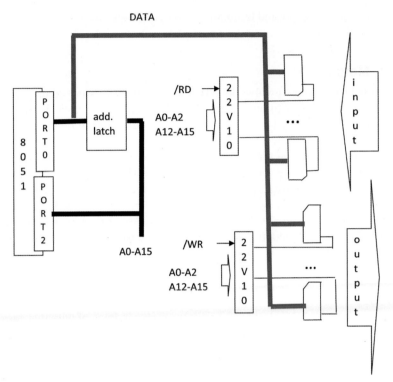

FIGURE 13.12 An 8051 Configured With Eight Input Gates and Eight Output Latches.

Author drawn.

because L is a positive-true signal, that is, L is logic 1 when active. The following equation will properly control the L pin on the first output latch:

$$Latch0L = NOT(/WR + /A15 + A14 + A13 + /A12 + A2 + A1 + A0);$$

If aliasing is a problem, it can be eliminated by adding all the address signals from A11 to A4 to the above equations. However, this would require a programmable logic device with more pins than the 22V10.

13.7 Common output devices

There are literally thousands of output devices, so we cannot survey all of them. There are a few, however, that occur in many, if not most, embedded systems and are common enough to warrant at least an introduction. As always in this text, it is not our purpose to go into deep theory or details about the electrical or other properties of these devices. Our goal is to acquaint the computer engineer or computer scientist with the concepts and terminology so that appropriate circuits and suitable code can be developed.

13.7.1 Motors

Many embedded systems involve the physical movement of some item or items in the environment. This is often accomplished by electrical motors. Large motors are not controlled directly by the microcontrollers but rather through intermediate circuitry like the relays shown in Figure 13.3. In the case of very large-scale motors, such as might be found on a manufacturing floor or assembly line, or in our open bridge example for raising/lowering the spans, there would likely be several levels of relay — small ones controlled directly by the microcontroller which, in turn, control larger ones that actually switch the heavy loads. On the other hand, many smaller systems, such as toys or small precision instruments like surgical robot arms, involve small motors that can be controlled directly by a microcontroller with at most one level of intermediate circuit. In this section we briefly describe the three most commonly used such motors — brushed DC motors,[1] brushless DC motors,[2] and stepper motors.[3]

All three types of motors involve magnets (usually permanent magnets in small motors) and the use of DC electrical current through windings of wire that surround a magnetizable material, such as soft iron, to generate magnetic fields. The direction of the current is reversed to control the polarity of the magnetic fields. From the electrical point of view, the part of the motor that contains the windings is called the armature. From the mechanical point of view, one part of the motor rotates and is called the rotor, while another part of the motor remains stationary and is called the stator. In some motor types the permanent magnet is in the rotor and the windings are in the stator, while in other motors the permanent magnet is in the stator and the windings are in the rotor. Because opposite poles of magnets attract each other and similar poles repel each other, the rotor can be forced to move by controlling the magnetic field in the windings.

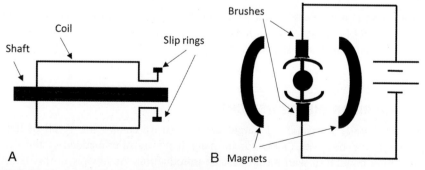

FIGURE 13.13 Schematic of a Brushed DC Motor.

Author drawn.

Figure 13.13 shows a schematic of a simple brushed DC motor. In brushed DC motors the rotor contains the coiled wire and ferrite material, while the housing in which the rotor is installed (i.e., the stator) contains permanent magnets. In this kind of motor the armature is on the rotor, and therefore the current supplied to the motor must be passed in to the rotating part. This is accomplished by attaching the two ends of the wire winding to metal plates, called slip rings, which attach to the shaft. This is shown in Figure 13.13a. Current is supplied from outside the motor by the brushes, which are conducting materials (typically graphite or some similar material). When current is applied, a magnetic field is induced in the armature, and the permanent magnets of the stator exert a force that pushes the armature, and hence the rotor, causing rotation. Eventually the armature reaches a point at which the magnetic forces of the stator are equal in both rotating directions. The slip rings are aligned so that at this point the contacts with the brushes are interchanged, thus reversing the current in the coil and reversing the polarity of the armature. The magnetic forces now continue to push the rotor around. Momentum of the rotor carries it through those points where the magnetic forces are reduced. Figure 13.13b is an end view showing the (stationary) brushes connected to a battery.

Brushed DC motors have many convenient features but also have some disadvantages. They are easy to control — the system simply supplies a voltage source; the slip rings manage the reversing of the current. However, there is friction between the slip rings and the brushes, and because the brushes are made of soft material they tend to wear out. So these motors need regular maintenance and should not be used where such maintenance would be difficult or impossible to provide. Also, if the motor is stopped with the rotor in the null position of the magnetic fields, it will likely not start when the current is applied again. Commercial brushed DC motors typically prevent this problem by providing three or more poles on the armature. The brushes sometimes cause sparks as they lose contact with one slip ring and make contact with the other ring, and if the gap between the plates in a two-pole motor is small the brushes can short circuit as they are changing from one slip ring to the other. Brushed motors are less efficient than brushless motors, the next kind of DC motor to be described. However, they are inexpensive and are a viable alternative in many applications.

In brushless DC motors the windings, that is, the armature, are on the stator, or motor housing, and the permanent magnet is on the rotor. See Figure 13.14. Closing switches A and A′ allows current to flow through the windings in one direction; closing B and B′ allows current to flow in the opposite direction. This relieves the need to supply current to a rotating part and allows much more flexible control over when the current is reversed or stopped altogether. This allows, for example, fine control of the start-up of the motor, control of the speed, and small motions of the rotor in which the rotor does not rotate completely. On the other hand, without the slip rings and their gaps, the brushless motor controller needs some other means for knowing the position of the rotor so as to activate the various poles at the appropriate time. There are a variety of mechanical (e.g., Hall effect transistors on the shaft) or electrical (e.g., measuring the back electric and magnetic fields of the coils not currently

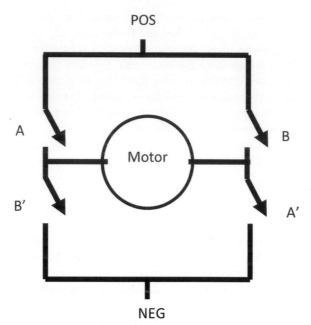

FIGURE 13.14 Schematic of a Brushless DC Motor.

Author drawn.

activated) for accomplishing this. Brushless motors can be controlled directly by a microcontroller, possibly with nothing more than some transistors to provide the current capacity to the poles of the armature. See Ref. [2] for details of algorithms for controlling brushless DC motors. Brushless motors are used in a wide range of applications such as fans and pumps that need more power and efficiency than brushed motors can provide, high-power applications such as in manufacturing, electric vehicles, and many more.

The third kind of DC motor common in embedded systems is the stepper motor, a special case of the brushless motor. The unique feature of stepper motors is that the magnet on the rotor and the magnets on the stator are cogged, as shown in Figure 13.15. (Typical stepper motors have more stator magnets and more cogs than shown in Figure 13.15, which is kept simple to make the construction easier to see.) Furthermore, the cogs are aligned so that when the cogs are nearest at one magnet position, they will be slightly out of alignment at the next, as can be seen in Figure 13.15. Starting from the position shown in Figure 13.15a, when the coil connected to A-A' is energized the magnetic force pulls the cogs into the position shown in Figure 13.15b. By successively energizing A-A', B-B', C-C', and D-D', the rotor can be made to rotate completely.

Figure 13.16 illustrates two ways for controlling the sequencing of the coil energization. The diagram in Figure 13.16a is a simplified representation of the poles on the stator and the positions of the rotor. The boxes marked "Coil A" and "Coil B" are

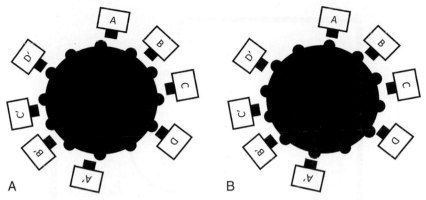

FIGURE 13.15 Schematic of a Stepper Motor.

Author drawn.

windings around the poles. When current is sent through a winding, the corresponding pole becomes magnetized. Changing the direction of the current changes the polarity (N or S) at the two ends of the pole. The simplest method for controlling a stepper motor is to activate the armature coils one at a time in sequence at some frequency. Given the rotor position shown in the diagram, if Coil A is activated so that point A is magnetic N and point A' is magnetic S then the S pole of the rotor would be attracted to position 1. If the current in Coil A is turned off and the current in Coil B is turned on so that the magnetic pole near position 3 would be N, the S pole of the rotor would be attracted to position 3. This technique gives four separate positions for the rotor in the simplified structure in Figure 13.16a. This is summarized in the table in Figure 13.16b. The numbers across the first row represent the next position on the diagram to which the rotor would move assuming the starting position is as shown in the diagram. A second common way is to activate one coil for a period, then activate that coil plus the next coil for a period, then turn off the first coil while leaving the second one on, and so on, as shown in the table in Figure 13.16c. This causes the rotor to stop between the two successive stator magnets every other period, thus giving twice as many steps per complete shaft revolution. Thus the movement of the rotor is a series of steps, typically 100 or 200 steps in real stepper motors, for a complete rotation or, equivalently, 3.6 degrees or 1.8 degrees per step. Stepper motors are designed so that these steps are uniform to within a few percent. Therefore a stepper motor, possibly with additional gearing between the shaft and the mechanical item to be physically moved, can achieve very precise and accurate motions of physical objects in the environment. On the other hand, stepper motors have lower torque, more vibration, and tend to be quite noisy compared to other DC motors. They are used in applications where precise control of the motion is required, for example, surgical robot arms.

A variety of circuits are available to control these various kinds of motors. For example, H-bridge circuits, such as the L293 series H-bridge drivers from Texas

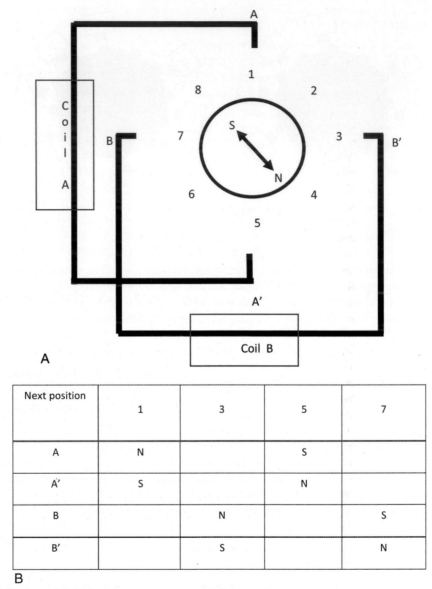

A

Next position	1	3	5	7
A	N		S	
A′	S		N	
B		N		S
B′		S		N

B

FIGURE 13.16 Successive Activations in a Stepper Motor.

Author drawn.

Instruments (TI),[4] are easily interfaced to microcontrollers and provide for reversing the current for brushless DC motors as well as power transistors to supply the necessary current. Similarly, stepper motor controller circuits, such as the DRV8885 from TI,[5] have simple interfaces to microcontrollers and provide many features such as

Next position	1	2	3	4	5	6	7	8
A	N	N		S	S	S		N
A′	S	S		N	N	N		S
B		N	N	N		S	S	S
B′		S	S	S		N	N	N

C

FIGURE 13.16 cont'd.

multiple methods for activating the coils (as described in the preceding paragraph), programmable speed, distance, and direction, and even some control over the torque.

13.7.2 Indicators and panel displays

ON/OFF and similar binary indicators are typically implemented with LED dots. These come in a variety of sizes and colors, and some models come with two colors in a single package. Most LED dots are made to operate at currents up to $20-25$ milliamps. Therefore interfacing to a microcontroller or latch requires a resistor in series to limit the current. Some special driver circuits may have the resistors built in. The brightness can be varied by either altering the voltage, which is not an option on the GPIO pins of most microcontrollers, or a technique like pulse-width modulation (PWM), described in a later section.

Simple numerical output with a small number of digits is accomplished with seven-segment digits. Figure 13.17 shows a pair of seven-segment digits mounted on a printed circuit board. Figure 13.18 shows the segment labels for the seven segments, and Table 13.1 shows which segments should be active to display each of the ten digits from 0 to 9. These displays come in two forms — positive feed (common anode) and negative feed (common cathode). In a common anode digit the common pin has positive voltage. Current is drawn through a segment, and therefore the segment lights up, by setting the corresponding segment pin to logic 0. As with LED dots the current through the segments must be limited. A seven-segment display can be driven by a dedicated GPIO port, by a latch as described in Sections 13.4 and 13.6, or by special circuits such as the SAA1064 from Phillips which has a simple serial interface to the processor, can drive up to four digits, and has built-in current limiters.

FIGURE 13.17 Two 7-Segment Digits on a Printed Circuit Board.

Picture taken by authors.

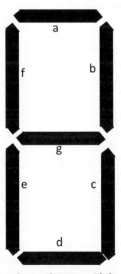

FIGURE 13.18 Segment Labels for a Seven-Segment Digit.

Author drawn.

Often an embedded system needs more than simple indicator lights and numeric display but does not need a display as big as a laptop screen. Short messages can be

Table 13.1 Active segments for the 10 digits.

Digit	a	b	c	d	e	f	g
0	1	1	1	1	1	1	0
1	0	1	1	0	0	0	0
2	1	1	0	1	1	0	1
3	1	1	1	1	0	0	1
4	0	1	1	0	0	1	1
5	1	0	1	1	0	1	1
6	0	0	1	1	1	1	1
7	1	1	1	0	0	0	0
8	1	1	1	1	1	1	1
9	1	1	1	0	0	1	1

displayed on a panel display such as an LCD display. These come in various sizes, such as 1 line and 16 characters, 2 lines with 16 or 20 characters per line, and 4 lines with 20 characters per line. Most come in packages that include the circuitry that actually drives the display itself. In many cases the display device can also be programmed to display special characters other than ordinary text. These characters can be defined by the microcontroller by writing into a special data area inside the LCD module. Interface to a microcontroller is usually in the form of a 4- or 8-bit parallel data bus or a serial connection. The typical LCD display includes commands for positioning the cursor, display backlighting, clearing the display, defining new

FIGURE 13.19 A Typical LCD Display.

Picture taken by authors.

Table 13.2 Common pins for microcontroller parallel interface.

Pin(s)	Description
DB0-DB7	8-bit bi-directional data bus
R/W	read/write — determines direction of data flow on data bus
E	data enable — determines when data is/should be on the data bus
R/S	determines if data flow is to/from data register or instruction register
GND	ground
Vcc	power

characters, shifting the display, and other operations. The microcontroller accesses these commands by writing into an instruction register inside the LCD module. Figure 13.19 shows a 2x20 LCD display panel on a project circuit board. Table 13.2 lists the common pins used for parallel interface to a microcontroller.

13.7.3 Communications circuits

We have seen that many microcontrollers have built-in communication hardware for at least some of the common communication protocols. There are also external circuits that provide more sophisticated features or higher throughput or that implement protocols that are not available on microcontrollers. We describe two such circuits here.

The PC16550 Universal Asynchronous Receiver/Transmitter[6] or equivalent is used on most laptops for the RS232 serial port. This circuit features 16-byte buffers for both input and output, software-selectable baud rates, error detection, and an interrupt signal that can be programmed to generate the interrupt when the buffers are at various levels of their capacity. For example, the circuit can be set to interrupt when the receive buffer has received 1 byte, has received 14 bytes, or is ¼ or ½ full. This is useful because it allows the processor to handle several bytes in one interrupt rather than a separate interrupt for each received byte. The disadvantage is that if the message is only a few bytes long the chip will not cause an interrupt. So the processor may have to occasionally check for new received bytes. Similar interrupt levels can be set for the output buffer. Here the issue of not getting an interrupt is not applicable because the circuit continually transmits bytes from the output buffer.

The ENC*24J600 [7] family of circuits from Microchip is a single-chip 10/100 Ethernet (see Chapter 21) controller. On the host side, it provides options for an SPI serial interface or a variety of parallel interfaces to a host processing element. For example, one of the parallel modes provides standard /RD, /WR, and ALE pins plus an 8- or 16-bit multiplexed address-data port suitable for direct connection to typical processors as external data memory. On the network side, it provides direct connection to the network with various options for handling network collisions, auto-negotiation, automatic polarity detection, padding, and many other Ethernet features. Internally the circuit has transmit and receive buffers that can be treated as random access external memory by the processing host.

13.7.4 Device drivers

A device driver is a piece of software that is called by the application software to perform operations on the device. The driver handles the low-level details, like addressing the device in either data memory space or GPIO space, toggling signals such as the read/write signals, and sending or receiving the actual data. As an example, a device driver for an LCD display might contain functions that position the cursor, turn the display on or off, write a character to the current cursor position, write a string to a particular line, etc. It is good practice to write device drivers for the devices in an embedded system. Some more sophisticated devices come with driver software. Simple devices likely do not have such off-the-shelf software. The presence of a good device driver package allows the application software to be written from a high point of view without regard to low-level details, like GPIO pin assignments or sequencing of signals to the device. Moreover, at an early stage of system development and testing, when perhaps the decisions about the platform have not yet been finalized, the device drivers isolate the application software from potential changes in the underlying hardware such as the use of a different LCD display or even a different microprocessor. If the application software was written in a high-level language and made use of such drivers, the underlying hardware and even processor platform could be changed with minimal modifications required in the application software itself; only the device drivers would need to be rewritten.

13.8 PWM for controlling motors, LEDs, etc.

An important technique for controlling simple DC motors, LED dot brightness, and similar outputs is PWM. In PWM the device is turned on and off rapidly in periodic fashion. By controlling the percentage of time that the device is on, the level of energy supplied to the device can be controlled. For many DC devices, this controls the level of operation of the device — for example, the speed of a DC motor or the brightness of an LED. There are several variations of PWM. We present the two most basic and commonly used ones.

   Simple single-wire PWM controls a single wire that makes the device run or not. For example, an LED dot is a single-wire device; one side of the LED is wired (through a resistor) to a fixed voltage (GND or power), and the other side is controlled by the microcontroller. A time is fixed for the duration of each period. During each period the device is turned on for a portion, called the duty cycle, of the period and turned off for the remainder of the period. Figure 13.20 shows three different duty cycles. When the duty cycle is higher, more energy is transferred to the device. In the case of an LED a higher duty cycle means the LED shines brighter. In the case of some DC motors a higher duty cycle means the shaft rotates faster and/or

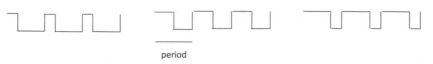

period

FIGURE 13.20 Three Duty Cycles — 25%, 50%, and 75%.

Author drawn.

with more torque. This length of the period depends on the device being controlled. For example, for controlling an LED the time for the period has to be small enough, perhaps a few milliseconds, to prevent visible flicker as the light is turned on and off. On the other hand, for a DC motor, a larger period length might be more suitable. In a heater or stove the period could be even larger, perhaps a second or more, because the heating element may not heat up properly with only very short bursts of energy.

High-end microcontrollers, like the Stellaris family, have built-in sophisticated circuitry for PWM. All that is needed is to configure the PWM control registers. In a low-end microcontroller, like the 8051, one of the timers can be used to achieve the desired duty cycle by adjusting the reload value and configuring the timer to interrupt on overflow. For example, suppose the period was to be 256 clock cycles. Recall, in the 8051 a timer increments on each clock cycle. Also, timers count up and can be configured to cause an interrupt on overflow. For a period of 256 clock cycles, an 8-bit timer could be used. The reload values would alternate between a reload that would give the amount of time for the device being on and a reload that would give the time for the device being off. For example, for a 25% duty cycle, a reload value of 192 would give 64 clock cycles before overflowing; 64 is 25% of 256. A reload value of 64 would give 192 clock cycles before overflowing; 192 is 75% of 256. Alternating between 192 and 64 gives alternating periods of 25% and 75%. Software would keep track of which reload was to be used next and whether the device should be turned on or off.

The second method applies the same concepts and techniques to devices that are controlled by two wires, such as the H-bridges used to control brushless DC motors. In such devices it is often necessary to provide a brief period when no power is applied to either side of the load. This brief period is called a deadband. Real circuits and mechanical relays do not switch on and off in zero time, and the delay in switching could allow brief periods when the power source was shorted to GND. A deadband of suitable length prevents this short circuiting by providing enough time for currently active switches to turn off before the switches that reverse the polarity on the load are switched on.

13.9 Sampling periodic analog signals

Many embedded systems applications involve the recording and/or (possibly later) reconstruction (i.e., playback) of periodic analog signals. The obvious example is the recording and playback of audio; musical performances, for example, are recorded and stored in digital format and then replayed later. In audio the sound is a periodic waveform with frequencies in the range 16 Hz to above 20,000 Hz, although the range of human hearing is typically bounded above by about 20,000 Hz. Other applications, such as radar, have periodic signals at much higher frequencies. By contrast, applications such as sensing temperature or pulse pressure measure analog signals which are not periodic or which may be periodic but at very low frequencies.

Converting periodic analog signals to digital form allows many interesting capabilities that are not possible without digitization. Storage of digitized signals is more flexible; for example, CD/DVD storage devices can be used. In music the tempo can be changed during playback without affecting the frequencies of the sound, thereby preserving the correctness of the notes. A recent development is the wireless speaker, in which the audio is transmitted wirelessly, for example, by Bluetooth, to the speaker. Digital information representing the audio (e.g., from a microphone and ADC or from a file stored on a CD) is transmitted to the speaker, where it is transformed back to analog form (i.e., audio speaker output). Many other digital processing techniques can be applied.

However, there are also issues because of the conversion to digital form and then reconversion to analog form on playback. This section discusses some of these issues. As always, our goal is to make the computer scientist or engineer aware of the issues and terminology, not to present a complete treatment of the topic. Most applications dealing with periodic analog signals require either a dedicated analog engineer or the use of off-the-shelf tools. However, the computer scientist/engineer needs to at least be aware of the issues.

Figure 13.21 shows a simple signal train in a periodic analog application. A periodic analog signal is input at the left into an ADC. The ADC is sampled by a processor at some frequency to obtain a sequence of binary numbers that represent the analog input signal at regular intervals. On playback, the processor passes these binary numbers to a DAC, usually at the same frequency, and the DAC generates analog output. These conversions produce several kinds of errors that affect the quality of the output. We now discuss these kinds of errors and describe the techniques for overcoming them.

First, the ADC circuit has a fixed resolution and can therefore only approximate the real value of the input signal to within Q volts, where Q is the voltage resolution. Q can be reduced in a particular application by increasing the resolution, but flash ADCs with higher resolution are more expensive and successive approximation

FIGURE 13.21 Simple Signal Chain From Input to Output.

Author drawn.

ADCs with higher resolution are slower. So, there is a tradeoff. In either case the processor sees a step function rather than a continuous function.

Next, recall that the typical ADC circuit samples the input voltage and then holds that voltage during the conversion. The processor, then, sees in effect a step function over a discrete sequence of time points rather than a continuous function over the continuous time domain. During the time between one conversion and the next, the value stored in the processor will be different than the value of the real signal because the input signal is changing while the value stored in the processor is fixed until the next sample is read. Moreover, the sampled voltage will likely be different than one of the 2^n values the ADC output represents. Thus, viewed from the perspective of continuous time, the input signal and the stored signal differ by an amount ranging from 0 to Q for truncating converters or $-Q/2$ to $Q/2$ for rounding converters. Figure 13.22 illustrates this difference for a 2-bit truncating converter. The curved line represents the actual signal. The dashed lines represent the digital values output by the ADC and read by the processor. The solid horizontal lines represent the voltages that the processor sees at the various points in time. The difference between the signal voltage and the voltage represented by the output of the ADC is called quantization noise. This quantization noise leads to a signal-to-noise ratio given by the formula 6.02*n decibels, where n is the number of bits of resolution.[8] Note that quantization noise is noise introduced specifically by the ADC. The signal itself may already have noise by the time it reaches the ADC input, depending on the source of the signal, its environment, and various other factors.

The next problem is aliasing. Aliasing in signal sampling means that many different periodic signals produce the same sequence of sampled digital values. Thus the processor cannot tell which signal is actually being observed, which may lead to difficulties in the signal processing algorithms. For example, Figure 13.23 shows two periodic waves being sampled at the indicated points. The waves intersect at exactly those points. A processor receiving the ADC output

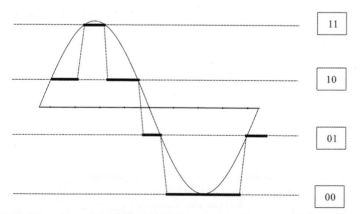

FIGURE 13.22 Illustration of the Difference Between Signal Value and ADC Output.

Author drawn.

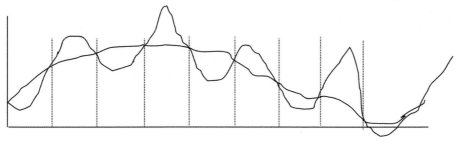

FIGURE 13.23 Two Waves That Intersect at the Sampling Points.

Author drawn.

values for those sample points would not be able to tell which of the two, or indeed which of infinitely many, curves was present at the ADC input.

One solution for the aliasing problem is to sample at higher frequencies. For example, in Figure 13.23 if the ADC were sampled twice as often every other value read by the processor would be distinct for the two curves. How fast is fast enough? There is a theoretical result, the Shannon-Nyquist Theorem,[9] which provides guidance as to how fast a signal must be sampled. This theorem states that if the input signal contains no frequencies higher than N hertz, then enough information can be obtained to completely reconstruct the signal by sampling at a frequency of 2N or higher. It should be noted that this is a theoretical result, and the proof makes use of some assumptions that are unrealistic in practice. However, in general, sampling at the Shannon-Nyquist frequency gives good results, and the Shannon-Nyquist number is a good guide for sampling frequency. The embedded systems engineers, then, have to analyze the nature of the periodic inputs to determine what are the naturally occurring frequencies in the signals and which, if any, can be removed without adversely affecting the performance of the system. For example, music contains harmonics that are higher than the 20,000 Hz limit of human hearing, but these have minimal effect on the music as heard by human audiences. Once the engineers have determined an upper limit, the sampling rate can be determined. In order to prevent higher frequency signals in the input from interfering with the

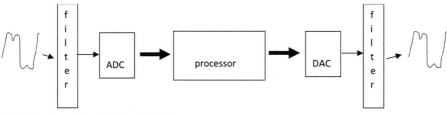

FIGURE 13.24 Signal Chain With Filters.

Author drawn.

processing, filters are inserted between the signal source and the ADC, as shown in Figure 13.24.

The sampling frequency imposes requirements on the signal processing algorithms, whether done by software or hardware. Whatever is to be done to the values read from the ADC has to be accomplished in 1/S amount of time, where S is the frequency. If the processing is nothing more than storing the values from the ADC, the requirement is fairly easy to meet. If more processing is required, for example, some kind of real-time processing of the signal, some or all of the processing may need to be done with special hardware or algorithms implemented in Field Programmable Gate Arrays. To see the nature of this problem, consider the 20,000 Hz limit for human hearing. According to the Shannon-Nyquist Theorem, such signals should be sampled at 40,000 Hz. The period for this frequency is 25 microseconds. Even in very fast microcontrollers, the amount of processing that can be done in 25 microseconds is limited.

Finally, recall that the output of the DAC is also a step function. Such an output generally needs to be "smoothed out" to produce an acceptable result in applications such as audio.

These comments lead to a system like that shown in Figure 13.24. Two filters have been added — one to condition the input signal by removing frequencies from the input signal that are too high, and one at the output of the DAC to smooth the output signal. Furthermore, we have seen that there are requirements for the processing itself based on the sampling frequency.

13.10 **Summary**

Sensing and controlling an environment is a distinguishing feature of embedded systems. In this chapter we described a variety of sensing and controlling devices, emphasizing the distinction between digital and analog devices. For analog input devices, an important issue is to calibrate readings that the processor receives with actual environmental conditions. We described several different types of ADCs and their tradeoffs. We discussed issues related to output devices, such as power for digital loads. For analog inputs and outputs, we discussed the important concept of resolution. We described how large numbers of input and output devices could be interfaced to processing elements, which have limited numbers of general-purpose I/O pins. We described a variety of input and output devices. In particular, we discussed common types of motors in embedded systems — brushed DC motors, brushless DC motors, and stepper motors. We discussed the important method of PWM for controlling analog output devices like LEDs or DC motors. Finally, we discussed the important concepts relating to discretization of analog inputs and outputs. We illustrated how quantization noise enters into a system, described the important concept of signal-to-noise ratio, and illustrated how the inclusion of filters in the sensing-processing-output chain can help overcome problems associated with noise.

We showed by example how a system could misinterpret an analog signal because the sampling rate was too low.

Problems

1. Do a web search to find three sensors that sense different kinds of environmental features. For each sensor give the following: manufacturer, what it senses, range of application values sensed, accuracy of sensing environment, output is digital or analog, output range if output is analog, and URL reference to a datasheet.

2. For each of the following tell what a suitable range of application values is and what resolution you would select for the ADC or DAC. Justify your choices.

a) A scale for weighing humans.

b) A scale for weighing meat sold at a meat market.

c) A scale used to weigh doses of medicine.

3. Draw the circuit diagram for 8 gates plus 8 latches using a pair of 138 circuits. Assume one I/O port on the processor is used for data transfer and 3 bits in a second port are used for addressing, 1 bit to indicate reading/writing, and 1 bit to indicate data is (should be) on the data lines.

4. Implement the system described in Problem 3 with 22V10 circuits instead of 138 circuits. For each 22V10 write the complete configuration file with pin assignments and equations.

5. Suppose that we are working with a successive approximation-based 4-bit A/D converter. The input voltage range extends from $V_{min} = 1$ to $V_{max} = 5$.

a) Show the input voltages corresponding to all 16 4-bit values.

b) Show the steps performed when converting the input voltage 1.75 volts.

c) Show the steps performed when converting the input voltage 3.0 volts.

6. Suppose you have a 4-bit DAC with $V_{ref} = 3.5$ volts. Calculate V_{out} for the following binary inputs:

a) 0101

b) 1100

c) 1111

7. Suppose we want to control a space heater using PWM. One of the output pins of the processing element is assigned to turn the heating coil on and off — 1 means on, 0 means off.

a) Which of the following would you use for the length L of one ON/OFF cycle — 10 microseconds, 1 millisecond, or 1 second? Explain why you selected the value you did.

b) Suppose we decide that eight levels of heat are sufficient. That is, the heating coil could be always off, on 1/8th of L, 2/8th of L, ..., on all the time. What is 1/8th of the value you chose for L in part a?

c) Suppose the processor has a counter that increments every microsecond. How many clock increments are needed to closely approximate the time you computed in part b?

   d) Is a 16-bit counter/timer sufficient to count up to the value you gave in part c?

   e) Suppose the processor could be set up to cause an interrupt every time period equal to the time you gave in part b. Suppose there is a global variable HEAT that specifies the number of periods within one ON/OFF cycle that the heating coil should be on. HEAT has integer values in the range 0–8. Write an interrupt handler to control the heating coil. Specify any additional variables global or local to the handler that you use. You may write in C code, draw a flow chart, or use any other means that can convey your algorithm.

8. For each of the following applications tell whether you would select a DC motor or a stepper motor and why.

   a) The cooling fan inside your laptop or desktop computer.

   b) The motion control for the hands of a surgical robot.

   c) Child's toy drone.

   d) Drone used for delivering packages.

   e) Robot arm used to assemble parts onto a printed circuit board.

   f) Robot arm used to assemble parts into a car on an auto assembly line.

References

[1] https://en.wikipedia.org/wiki/Brushed_DC_electric_motor.

[2] https://en.wikipedia.org/wiki/Brushless_DC_electric_motor.

[3] https://en.wikipedia.org/wiki/Stepper_motor.

[4] https://www.ti.com/lit/ds/symlink/l293.pdf.

[5] https://www.ti.com/product/DRV8885.

[6] https://www.alldatasheet.com/datasheet-pdf/pdf/9302/NSC/PC16550DN.html.

[7] https://www.microchip.com/wwwproducts/en/en022889.

[8] https://en.wikipedia.org/wiki/Signal-to-noise_ratio.

[9] https://en.wikipedia.org/wiki/Nyquist%E2%80%93Shannon_sampling_theorem.

Energy

14

14.1 Introduction

Embedded systems require energy to run. Processing elements and related circuits, communications circuits, sensors, and actuators all require energy. When the embedded system is to be used in locations where ample energy is available, energy is rarely an issue. For example, ATMs are almost always located in buildings where AC energy is present. The bridge system would always have ample energy because the motors that raise and lower the spans require it. Embedded systems in cars will have ample energy from the car's battery. When an embedded system is not used where reliable energy is available, the design team has to include an energy source in the overall system design. In this chapter we discuss four situations depending on the proximity to a reliable energy source, some alternate sources of energy, and some strategies for designing systems that are not always near reliable energy sources.

14.2 Proximity to reliable energy sources

We describe four cases depending on the proximity of the system to a reliable energy source. The first case, the simplest, includes systems that will be used in locations with reliable energy. In this case the design of the energy module for the embedded system is simple. For example, if normal AC is available, simple AC-DC converters can be used. If the reliable source is itself DC, then simple DC-DC converters would be used. The major issues are to determine the voltage(s) needed by the embedded systems and the current requirements. With this information, the implementation team can select suitable power supplies. Some embedded systems or devices are meant to be used with another device, and the other device provides the energy. For example, USB mice and other USB products intended for use with laptops and PCs can be considered to have a reliable energy source, namely, the USB port of the laptop or PC.

The second case includes systems that will not be used in locations with reliable energy but can be brought to such locations at regular intervals. Cell phones and wearable patient monitors are examples. The user can go about daily business without having to be connected to a socket but returns at regular intervals, for example, overnight, to a location with reliable energy. In these kinds of systems

Embedded System Design. https://doi.org/10.1016/B978-0-443-18470-3.00014-2

the main product would include a rechargeable battery, and the system itself would include a method for regularly recharging that battery. The product could include a secondary module specifically for recharging, or the product might make use of common recharging "stations" such as the USB ports on laptops and PCs or the recharging stations in most airport terminals. A relatively recent innovation is the portable charging power bank, a handheld device that includes a relatively large capacity battery and typically one or more USB sockets. The device can be used to recharge other battery-operated devices multiple times. For example, one power bank might hold enough energy to recharge a laptop two or three times or a cell phone eight or ten times. The main consideration for this case is how long the user should be able to stay away from the recharging station. For cell phones and patient monitoring systems, this would typically be at least one day. Circuits and batteries should be selected to provide normal operation of the product for the expected time between charges.

In the third case the product cannot be brought to a source for recharging but is easily reachable for recharging or battery replacement. Environmental sensor nodes, such as those used in agricultural or forest monitoring, fall into this class. As in the second case, a major issue is how long the system can operate on a single charge. For systems such as environmental monitors, this should be significantly more than 1 day to reduce the number of times service personnel have to travel to the system. Another issue is whether or not the system can be shut down for battery replacement. A typical sensor node can be turned off while a regular battery is being replaced. The only consequence is that for a moment or two, the sensor node will not be reporting sensor readings. For systems that should not be shut down, such as a sensor node that also controls other devices that must run continuously, the design team might consider longer-lasting batteries that are rechargeable. A charging device, such as a portable power charging bank or even a small gas-powered generator, could then recharge the system battery while the system kept operating. Another option is to allow a temporary battery to be connected to the system, after which the normal battery of the system can be removed and replaced.

The last class includes systems that are remote and not easily reachable by service personnel. An example of a system in this class is a wildlife monitoring sensor node that is attached to an animal that is to be monitored. It would be difficult or, in some cases, impossible to find the animal and hold it while the battery was replaced or recharged. Planning for the longest possible time of operation, as in the previous two cases, is critically important for this case. Where possible, processors with sleep modes should be used. Where possible, the processor should disconnect power to other devices in the system when those devices are not needed. For example, in a sensor node the power to the sensors and the communications circuit could be supplied through a transistor that is controlled by an output pin on the processor. The processor enables the transistor only when sensor readings and communication are needed. Design teams for systems in this class should also consider how energy harvesting can be used. When energy harvesting is used, the design team may consider whether the intermittent operation is possible. For example, a sensor node could have battery-level detection circuitry and detect when energy supply was low. It could shut down gracefully, saving any critical data that was needed to resume operation. When the energy harvesting had recharged the battery to a sufficient level, the node could start up again. See Section 14.4 for more information on energy harvesting.

14.3 Batteries

Readers will no doubt be familiar with the standard kinds of batteries — A/C/D cells, A/C/D cell packs mounting two or four such batteries, button batteries, and so on. There are also relatively large-capacity power banks that are normally used to recharge other devices but can also be used to power small systems. It is important to understand that battery performance can be affected by environmental conditions, such as extreme heat or cold or high humidity. How these factors affect the performance of a specific battery can usually be found in the specification sheet for that battery.

Several factors enter into the choice of a battery for a particular embedded system. Two main ones are the energy usage of the system and the time the system should operate on a single battery charge. When possible, accurate energy usage should be measured in the lab under the same environmental conditions as the system will encounter during normal usage. This measurement should be taken with the actual product, not a prototype. A prototype will likely not use all the same circuitry and devices as the final product and may not include all the software functions or operational modes such as sleep modes or the deactivation of devices in the system. If the product is used in extreme environments, then the lab environment should be adjusted as much as possible to match those extreme conditions. When lab testing is not possible, estimates can be made based on the specifications of all the devices in the system. Once the energy usage is known, a battery with sufficient capacity to supply that amount of energy over the desired length of operational time can be chosen.

14.4 Energy harvesting

There are many possible sources for harvesting energy. See [1]Ref. [1] for a comprehensive list and discussion of tradeoffs. Key issues include the reliability of the harvested source and what should happen when insufficient energy is being harvested. Solar energy can only be harvested during daylight hours, and even then, the harvesting rate varies during the day with the angle of the sun and other interfering factors such as clouds and rain. Wind may occur at any time of the day, but it is not reliable or steady. Motion can be reliable in some situations, such as river flow or offshore wave motion, but not in other cases. When possible, the design team should measure actual harvesting in the environment in which the system will be used.

Harvesting can be combined with battery storage to overcome the intermittent nature of the harvesting. The system operates on battery power, and a charging circuit is used to allow the harvesting device to pump energy into the battery. As with systems that operate only on batteries, reliable measurements of the amount of energy the system uses must be made in order to determine if harvesting or harvesting in combination with battery storage is plausible.

A design team must also plan for periods when not enough energy is available for the system to operate properly. Even when a battery is used in conjunction with harvesting, there may be extended periods when little energy is harvested and the battery eventually runs down. A battery-level detection circuit can be used to indicate when the battery is running out of energy. As noted in Section 14.2, the design team can plan for a graceful shutdown when this occurs.

The following are some of the more commonly discussed harvesting sources and issues relating to each of them.

- Solar power. Solar panels of all sizes are readily available. Figure 14.1 shows a sample small panel capable of generating ½ watt of power. The figure also shows a pen so the reader can judge its size. Small solar panels (1−2 square feet) that generate up to 15 watts at 6 volts in optimum conditions are available and could be used for small embedded systems. These are typically made by wiring several smaller panels, like those shown in Figure 14.1, together. However, the ratings for solar cell and solar panel output are for optimum conditions − full sunlight directly overhead with no clouds or other interference. Output is less during the morning and evening hours and, of course, zero overnight.

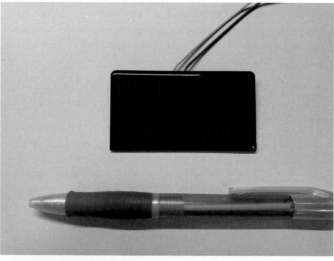

FIGURE 14.1 Small Solar Panel.

Picture taken by authors.

- Wind power. Wind may or may not be reliable depending on the location. Small wind turbines rated up to 400 watts at 12 volts are available. However, as with solar cells, the ratings are for optimum conditions, in this case, continuous wind over a speed threshold. When the wind dies down, the output is less. Propeller-type wind turbines should face into the wind for optimum performance. If the turbine cannot rotate and the wind direction changes, output will be less. Some turbine fans are designed to be omnidirectional, that is, to operate independently of the direction of the wind relative to the fan, but these may not be as efficient as the directional turbines. Figure 14.2 shows a small wind turbine mounted on a light pole.

- Water power. Water movement, when it is available, can be a relatively reliable energy source. Most rivers, for example, have relatively steady flow. Similarly, most shorelines have relatively steady wave motion. Many types of systems are available for harvesting water power. Unfortunately, few embedded systems are meant to be used solely near flowing water.

- Motion power. Motion in general can be used to harvest energy. The motion can be in the form of human motion (e.g., arm or leg swing during walking), geological motion associated with seismic events, and many others. One interesting and creative example is branch and leaf motion as the wind blows through trees,[1] which can be used in forests where the wind does not reach the forest floor where the sensor nodes are placed. In most cases such harvesting is not reliable or steady. Motion harvesting could be used in conjunction with batteries for storage or in systems that are meant to operate only sporadically when the motion is present.

FIGURE 14.2 Small Wind Turbine and Solar Panel on a Light Pole in Dominica.

Picture taken by authors.

- Thermal power. Small amounts of energy can be harvested from temperature differentials. A five-degree differential can produce 40 μW at 3 volts,[1] enough to run a small device or provide trickle charge to a battery in a system that operates sporadically.

Sources for harvesting can be combined to increase the reliability and amount of energy harvested. Figure 14.2 shows a new street light on the island of Dominica, a replacement for one destroyed in Hurricane Maria in 2017. A wind turbine at the top and a solar panel on the top side of the light collect enough energy to run the efficient LED lighting without the need for any other energy source. Dominica is an island with strong sunlight and wind almost every day, so the combination of solar and wind harvesting is an excellent choice for that location.

Energy harvesting is an ongoing area of research with many interesting and innovative ideas. One interesting avenue involves harvesting energy from photosynthesis. Researchers in England have run a small processor for 6 months using energy generated by photosynthesis from a colony of algae the size of a AA battery.[2] Energy produced by microbial fuel cells is also an active area of research, and some authors (e.g.,[3] Ref. [3]) have focused on applications in sensor networks and other embedded systems.

14.5 Design strategies

The above discussions lead to the following general design strategies for embedded systems that will be used in situations where reliable power is not always available.

- Get accurate energy usage data.
- Match computing needs to the problem. Analyze the tradeoffs between alternatives for processing elements and other circuitry. For example, more powerful processors generally use more energy, but they might get the job done more quickly, thus saving energy in the long run.
- Use sleep modes where possible.
  - Determine what percentage of time could be spent sleeping. When this percentage is nontrivial, analyze the tradeoffs between using a more sophisticated processor with sleep modes but higher energy usage versus a low-end processor that has no sleep mode but uses less energy.
  - Make sure that wake-up times are acceptable. Wake-up for periodic sensor reading in a sensor node can be slow, but wake-up for responding to an interrupt caused by an event that requires rapid response must be fast enough to compute the response in time.
- Consider separate circuits that can be depowered versus processors with built-in functions.
- When harvesting is used, get accurate data on energy harvesting in the environment in which the system will be used.

- Plan for intermittent operation, that is, plan for periods when not enough power is available in the battery and/or through harvesting.
  - Plan to shut down gracefully.
  - Note that graceful shutdown depends on the application. A sensor node could simply stop working. A patient monitoring system might take a reading of the sensors before shutting down. An application may need to save the current state of calculations if the system performs complex calculations.
  - The design team should determine whether or not the system should emit some kind of warning, such as a buzzer or vibration in a cell phone or a message from a sensor node to the base station.

14.6 Summary

In this chapter we described ways in which power can be provided to an embedded system that is deployed in a location where no reliable and continuous power source is available. The main cases involve systems that can be regularly recharged, systems that are relatively easily reachable for battery recharging or replacement, and systems that cannot be reached and must rely solely on battery power and/or harvested power. We mentioned common types of batteries and then discussed factors that could affect battery performance, an important consideration for systems that are deployed in environments with extreme conditions such as extreme temperature and humidity. We mentioned five common ways energy can be harvested — solar, wind, water, motion, and geothermal. We emphasized the importance of accurate energy consumption data. Finally, we presented some general strategies that can be applied when designing the energy portion of an embedded system.

Problems

1. Scientists have begun exploring the deepest parts of the ocean floor. See, for example,
   https://www.accuweather.com/en/weather-news/chile-deep-sea-expedition-pacific-ocean-life-atacama-trench-earthquakes-tsunamis/1161902.
   In a group or class setting brainstorm ways that sensor systems for such exploration might harvest energy and optimize operation so as to conserve energy.
2. Brainstorm ways to harvest energy in the following applications: forest monitoring, large-scale farm irrigation control, wildlife migration monitoring, and offshore wave monitoring.
3. For each of the applications in Problem 2, which of the following system features would play a significant role and why: processor sleep modes, ability to turn off sub-systems, nonvolatile memory for storing data.

References

[1] https://en.wikipedia.org/wiki/Energy_harvesting
[2] https://www.msn.com/en-us/news/technology/computer-powered-by-colony-of-blue-green-algae-has-run-for-six-months/ar-AAXbrsh?li=BBnbfcL
[3] A. Shantaram, H. Beyenal, R.R.A. Veluchamy, Z. Lewandowski, Wireless sensors powered by microbial fuel cells, Environ. Sci. Technol. 39 (2005) 5037—5042.

Hardware-software mapping

15

15.1 Introduction

The design team for an embedded system project may have proposed several different solutions for that system, and for each proposal, there could be many choices for implementing various parts. Hardware choices include low-end processors, high-end processors, field programmable gate arrays (FPGAs), off-the-shelf circuits, and specially designed application-specific circuits. If a processing element is included in a proposal, then there are choices for software, such as buy an off-the-shelf package vs. write the software in-house, whether or not to include an operating system (see Chapter 16), whether to map a specific function to software or to hardware, etc. There are many criteria for evaluating and comparing the various tentative implementations, including cost of development, cost of production of the final design, time to market, power consumption, physical size of the final product, speed and other measures of performance, and many, many more. Consider, for example, the span controller in the bridge project. Here are a variety of choices that the team could consider.

- Use a single microcontroller with sophisticated control and sensing, such as the Stellaris microcontroller, for the span module, or use several cheap micro-controllers possibly with other circuits for controlling the motor and related mechanical devices. In the second alternative, these low-end microcontrollers could include one to control the motor, one at the end of the span to sense coordination with the opposite span, one to coordinate the others and communicate with the bridge central control module, etc.
- If a sophisticated microcontroller is chosen, should all the sensing be handled by that processor, or should some of the sensing algorithms be implemented in hardware, for example, with an FPGA as discussed in Chapter 12? If the latter, should a more expensive FPGA be used and other functionalities be implemented on it?
- Should the motor control be handled by the processing element or by external circuits such as H-bridges?

Problem 1 is devoted to continuing this list as a class discussion project.

There are many methodologies and techniques that help design teams make choices. We present three commonly used ones in this chapter — task graphs, integer

Embedded System Design. https://doi.org/10.1016/B978-0-443-18470-3.00015-4

linear programming (ILP), and Pareto points and fronts. Unfortunately, unlike the case of specification and description language for which there are mature, commercially available tools, the development of general-purpose tools for hardware partitioning and hardware/software co-design remains a research problem. Many techniques have been proposed for special cases, such as systems containing a single processor or systems using one of a limited set of FPGA circuits; most of these are based on the three methodologies presented in this chapter. For an interesting discussion of the history of partitioning and co-design and predictions for the future, see Ref. [1]. For a survey of tools developed in the early 2000s in academic institutions, see Ref. [2].

15.2 Task graphs, task splitting, and task merging

An important part of mapping portions of a system design to actual hardware and software is to understand the relationship between the various tasks, in particular which tasks depend on other tasks and therefore cannot be performed until the other tasks are completed. The task dependency graph[3] is used in this kind of analysis. In a task dependency graph, each node represents one task. There is a directed edge from node T1 to node T2 if and only if task T2 depends on task T1. There are two notions of "depends." The simplest is that task T1 must be completed before task T2 starts. This may be due to output from T1 that is needed by T2, resources that are held by T1 that are needed by T2, or other reasons. The second, and more complex, notion is that T1 must produce some output which is then used by T2 and the output may be produced at any point in the execution of T1 rather than just at the end. While the second notion may sometimes be more useful than the first, the first notion is sufficient because task T1 can be split into two parts — task T1a, which is the portion of T1 that produces the output needed by T2, and task T1b, which is the portion of T1 after T1a.

Figure 15.1 shows an example task graph for the bridge project. This graph shows the tasks for the normal case of a boat approaching and passing under the bridge. The two tasks "Clear Bridge Traffic" and "Notify Operator" can be performed in parallel. No other task depends on notifying the operator, so there is no arrow leading out of that task. On the other hand, raising the span may not begin until the bridge traffic has been cleared, so "Raise Span" depends on "Clear Bridge Traffic." It makes no sense to begin looking for the boat on the other side of the bridge until at least after the spans have been raised, so in this graph, the "Sense Boat Leaving" task depends on the "Raise Span" task. Similarly, the spans should not be lowered until the boat has reached the other side, and bridge traffic should not be resumed until the spans are down again.

Figure 15.1 also illustrates how design questions can be raised and addressed at the task graph level. For example, for safety reasons the design team might require the "Notify Operator" task to be successfully completed (e.g., a message displayed on the operator's screen and the operator responded, so the system can be sure the

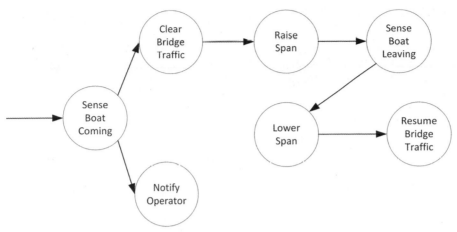

FIGURE 15.1 Simple Task Graph for the Bridge.

Author drawn.

operator is ready) before the span can be raised. Such decisions are based on the models developed for the system, like those of the earlier chapters in this book.

Figure 15.2 illustrates that tasks can be hierarchical. Clearing the ground traffic involves four smaller tasks — sounding an alarm, changing the traffic light, lowering the barriers, and checking to see if all the cars and pedestrians on the bridge are gone. Sounding the alarm, changing the traffic light, and sensing cars/pedestrians on the bridge can proceed in parallel. On the other hand, the barriers should not be lowered at least until the traffic light has turned red, so the "Lower Barrier" task depends on the "Change Traffic Light" task. The "Raise Span" task in Figure 15.1 would depend on both the "Check On Bridge Traffic" and "Lower Barrier" tasks. Note that the graph makes decisions about the order of tasks and the possibility of parallel execution explicit, which allows the design team to make informed choices. For example, the team may decide that there is no need to check for cars/pedestrians on the bridge until after the barriers have been lowered, that is, that "Check On Bridge Traffic" depends on "Lower Barrier." The design team can evaluate alternatives, such as making the tasks sequential and implemented on the same hardware platform or making them parallel and independent so they could be implemented on separate hardware platforms.

Task graphs are developed from consideration of the various use cases and scenarios. In a complex system like the bridge, there is not just a single task graph; rather, each scenario has its own set of tasks that must be completed in the order appropriate for that task. The ensemble of all task graphs gives the complete set of tasks that must be implemented.

Task graphs can be used to help select implementations. First, it may be obvious that several tasks should be implemented in the same platform. For example, the "Resume Bridge Traffic" task in Figure 15.1 would have a subtask "Lower Barrier."

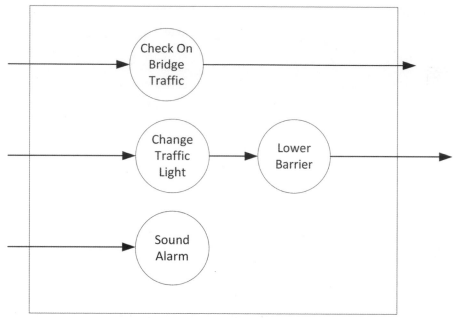

FIGURE 15.2 "Clear Bridge Traffic" Task Showing Subtasks.

Author drawn.

The two tasks "Lower Barrier" and "Raise Barrier" will be implemented on the same platform because they control the same physical device. On the other hand, separating the tasks "Lower Barrier" and "Sound Alarm" in Figure 15.2 allows these to be implemented on the same hardware platform if the gates and alarm were in an integrated configuration or on different hardware platforms if the alarm was physically separated from the gates (e.g., on the cross beam of the bridge instead of on the gate arms). The task graph may also suggest that some tasks not normally thought of as related should still be implemented in the same piece of hardware. For example, in Figure 15.1, the three tasks "Raise Span," "Sense Boat Leaving," and "Lower Span" occur in sequence. One might not originally have thought to include the sensor for telling when the boat had passed under the bridge in the same module as the span motor. However, because these three tasks occur in sequence and do not involve other tasks, on second consideration the team might consider embedding the sensor for this task together with the span motor control, both of which likely would be placed under the span and near the water. In this case, the team may map all three tasks to a single hardware platform, leading to a different solution than the one described in Chapter 3 where the downstream boat sensor was assumed in a separate location downstream.

Task graphs may include additional information about the tasks and the dependencies. Real-time requirements and associated information can be associated with individual nodes. Related information could also include items such as expected rate of arrival of various messages and any real-time constraints for processing those messages. This information can help determine the workflow in the system and the necessary processing capabilities of hardware and/or software platforms that might be used to implement the tasks. Nodes may be annotated with the shared resources that they use and even when during the task those resources are used. This kind of information can be helpful in determining whether or not to split a task or merge two tasks because of the shared resources they have in common. It is sometimes useful to group smaller tasks into a larger task while keeping individual nodes for the smaller tasks. This hierarchical structure allows for finer-grained analysis for situations where many tasks depend on the hierarchical task but depend on different parts of that task, that is, on independent subtasks of the larger task.

Several kinds of analysis can be performed using the task graph. First, requirements of the system, such as timing from start to finish or data flow through the system, can be analyzed to be sure they are met. Second, alternate divisions of the work into tasks can be proposed by either splitting or merging tasks. For example, a detailed analysis of one task T1 might show, as indicated in the previous paragraph, that the task should be split into two because a task T2 that depends on T1 can then start earlier. Or, the progression of the project from early model, as in the chapters on modeling, led to a task that on further analysis was shown to have opportunities for parallelism or refinement. If a task contains parts that can be performed in parallel, then splitting may yield a new task graph that offers more flexibility in mapping tasks to hardware. The two split tasks could be assigned to separate pieces of hardware rather than be forced onto a single piece of hardware. Occasionally, separate tasks are merged into a single task. For example, two tasks in sequence in the graph might be closely related in their functionality and use the same system information. In this case, the two tasks might be combined into a single task, thereby eliminating the communication that would be required if they were separate tasks. (Even if they were separate tasks running on the same processor, there might still be overhead in switching from the first to the second after the first task had been completed.)

Mapping tasks to hardware or software can be carried out concurrently with the above analyses, and indeed the mappings and the analyses inform each other. Knowing the workload and timing requirements for each task limits the kinds of implementations that can be considered. For example, low-end microcontrollers might be ruled out because of real-time processing requirements. On the other hand, the existence in the graph of several tasks that have some common processing for which there is off-the-shelf software might suggest merging those tasks or at least implementing them on a single high-end processing element. Or, the existence of such common functionalities might suggest implementing that functionality in hardware, such as on an FPGA, that is shared by several tasks. If that route was taken, then suitable FPGAs might have extra capacity that could be used to implement additional parts of the overall task graph. The combination of analysis of the task graph and the selection of implementations for each of the tasks is a creative process, not an algorithmic one.

15.3 Integer linear programming for finding acceptable solutions

15.3.1 Integer linear programming

ILP,[4] a special case of linear programming,[5] is a quantitative method for finding solutions to a problem that satisfies a set of constraints while optimizing some quantity. The problem is represented in the form of a set of variables, called decision variables, a set of equalities and inequalities that model the system being studied, and an objective function representing the quantity that is to be minimized. A solution is an assignment of integer values (hence the "integer" part of ILP) to the variables that satisfy all the equalities and inequalities. The equalities and inequalities are all linear (hence the "linear" part of ILP). Each alternative has a value, typically a "cost," represented by the objective function. The "cost" could be the monetary cost of the pieces used in the implementation, space used, power used, system response time, etc. The goal is to find solutions in which the total cost is less than some limit. Of course, there may be more than one solution, or there may be no solutions satisfying the cost constraint. There are powerful software packages for solving ILP problems (see Ref. [5] for a list).

In the context of mapping tasks into hardware and software, a special case of ILP, called zero-one linear programming or binary decision linear programming, is used in which the variables are allowed to take only the values 0 and 1. Variables represent concepts like "a task is implemented on an FPGA," "a task is implemented on a microcontroller," "a task is implemented in software," etc. Equalities and inequalities represent constraints, such as a task is blocked from being implemented on two different elements of some kind or on one specific kind of element, if a task is implemented in software there has to be a processor for the software to run on, etc. A solution identifies a set of components and task assignments, those whose corresponding variables are assigned the value 1, that represent a design for the embedded system satisfying the constraint represented by the objective function. If there is no solution, then no design satisfies the constraints given the proposed hardware and processor components. If there is exactly one solution, then there is only one design. If there are several solutions, then there are several possible designs that must be further analyzed to determine which is the best. We now illustrate how these variables, equalities, and inequalities can be derived from a task model of a system.

Once a task graph has been developed the design team may then propose candidates for implementing the various task nodes or combination of nodes. Hardware candidates might include circuits that the company normally has in stock, special circuits that the design team knows about or are commonly used in the application field, microcontrollers of various kinds that the team knows how to use, etc. The inclusion of processing elements presupposes that software can be purchased or developed that could execute effectively on that platform. Note that a given hardware component type could occur multiple times in a proposed solution. For example, a small microcontroller like an 8051 might be considered for implementing portions of the task graph. If some of the tasks that could be implemented on the 8051 platform are expected to be performed in physically distant locations, such as the end of the bridge span and at the motor housing mounted on the bridge pylons, then separate 8051 processors will be preferred over a single 8051 plus associated cabling. Therefore, in the ILP model we must allow for multiple copies of the various hardware components. Normally, a reasonable upper limit on how many of each type of hardware component can be determined by inspection of the graph itself. We also note that several tasks in the graph could perform the same function. For example, in the bridge main controller module, two of the tasks are to determine if there is auto traffic on the span and determine if there is pedestrian traffic on the span. These two tasks might be specified as two separate tasks in the graph, but their functionality is nearly the same and might be merged into a single task if a system was available that could recognize both kinds of activity.

15.3.2 Integer linear programming variables and equalities/ inequalities for embedded system modeling

With this much introduction, we can present some of the formal details needed to model the selection of hardware/software components to implement a task graph.

- The model needs to refer to the individual nodes in the graph. Let V be the set of names or indices of those nodes.
- Each task graph node has an associated functionality that represents what that node does, for example, sense objects in some area of the span or control a barrier. Let L be the set of these functionalities.
- Let M be the set of hardware component types that will be considered for selection. M might contain elements like low-end FPGA, high-end FPGA, special purpose off-the-shelf circuit for a particular functionality, etc.
- For each $m \in M$ the design team may have estimated a bound on the number of components of type m that should be considered. For example, the team may decide that at most three of the tasks in the graph could reasonably be implemented with low-end FPGA circuits. Therefore, for each m there is an index set J_m that identifies individual components of type m. Note that not all of these need occur in any solution identified by the ILP tool. But by identifying individual ones in J_m we allow the possibility for solutions that have one component of type m, solutions that have two components of type m, and so on.
- Like hardware components, there can be different types of processing elements, and each type may occur a bounded number of times in a potential solution. Therefore, we introduce the sets P, the set of processor types (e.g., low-end microcontroller, digital signal processing computer), and for each $p \in P$ a set K_p, the names or indices of the individual processing elements of type p.

As will be noted later in this section, other sets can be added to model additional information that might be relevant to a particular embedded system, information such as timing constraints, communication costs, etc.

The decision variables will include the following. Remember, in our context a solution will assign each of these variables to be either 0 or 1.

- $X_{v,m,k}$. This will be 1 if node v is mapped to hardware component k of type m and 0 otherwise.
- $Y_{v,p,k}$. This will be 1 if node v is mapped to processing element k of processor type p and 0 otherwise.
- $NY_{f,p,k}$. This will be 1 if software is available for processor k of type p to implement the functionality of nodes of type f and 0 otherwise.

As before, if additional information is to be encoded into the ILP model, there will be additional variables. The ones described here will be sufficient to give the reader the basic idea of how to model a problem for solution by ILP methods.

We can now consider equations and inequalities that specify properties of potential solutions. The first set of these restricts all variables to be 0 or 1. There is one set for the X variables, one for the Y variables, and one for the NY variables as follows:

$$\forall v \in V: \forall m \in M: \forall k \in J: X_{v,m,k} \leq 1; \tag{1}$$

$$\forall v \in V: \forall p \in P: \forall k \in K_p: Y_{v,p,k} \leq 1; \tag{2}$$

$$\forall l \in L, \forall p \in P: \forall k \in K_p: NY_{l,p,k} \leq 1. \tag{3}$$

The first of these, for example, says that for every task v and every hardware component type m and every individual component k of type m, variable $X_{v,m,k}$ is less than or equal to 1. A similar set of formulas with the inequality $0 \leq v$ for all variables ensures that all variables are nonnegative. The combination ensures that in any solution all variables have values zero or one.

Next, every task must be mapped to one and only one component — either a hardware component or a processor. The following set of equations, in combination with the inequalities described in the preceding paragraph, guarantee this. For every $v \in V$,

$$\sum_{m \in M} \sum_{k \in J_m} X_{v,m,k} + \sum_{p \in P} \sum_{k \in K_p} Y_{v,p,k} = 1. \tag{4}$$

Inequalities (1)–(3) ensure that any solution will assign each variable either 0 or 1. Therefore, equation (4) can be satisfied if and only if exactly one of the variables is 1 and all the others are 0, that is, task v is mapped to one and only one component.

If a task is mapped to some processing element, then software for that processing element that implements the function associated with that task must exist. This is represented by the following set of inequalities:

$$\forall l \in L, \forall v \in V \ni type(v) = l, \forall p \in P: \forall k \in K_p: NY_{l,p,k} \geq Y_{v,p,k}. \tag{5}$$

This inequality says that for any functionality l, if some task node v whose functionality is l is mapped to a processor (i.e., $Y_{v,p,k}$ is 1), then software must exist for that functionality for that processor (i.e., $NY_{l,p,k}$ is also 1).

Finally, the objective function represents some bound on the problem. For example, it could be a bound on the total cost of parts or the maximum throughput time to process an input or power consumption or any of various properties that are to be minimized or maximized. Suppose, for example, we want to minimize the cost of the parts themselves. For each hardware component and processing element, the cost for that element would have to be known. The total cost would be given by the following equation:

$$\sum_{m \in M} C_m \sum_{k \in J_1} \sum_{v \in V} X_{v,m,k} + \sum_{p \in P} C_p \sum_{k \in K_2} \sum_{v \in V} Y_{v,p,k} + C_{other} \leq \text{Budget(money)} \tag{6}$$

where C_m represents the cost of a hardware element of type m, C_p represents the cost of a processor of type p, and C_{other} represents other costs besides hardware components and processors. $X_{v,m,k}$ and $Y_{v,p,k}$ are the decision variables for mapping task nodes to hardware components and processors. In any potential solution, every decision variable has value 0 or 1, and the ones with value 1 represent the parts that are in that potential solution. The ones with value 1 (representing components included in the solution) will contribute to the total cost, and the ones with value 0 (representing components not in the solution) will contribute 0. The Budget value represents the maximum allowed cost for an acceptable design. This inequality is also part of the ILP formula set in our discussion. It ensures that solutions satisfy the budget restriction.

15.3.3 Example

We illustrate these concepts using the task graphs in Figures 15.1 and 15.2. We include the subtasks of "Resume Bridge Traffic," namely "Change Traffic Light" and "Turn Off Alarm" so that the example can illustrate some important points. (The graphs in a real bridge project would be much more complex. We keep these example graphs simple to keep the presentation relatively easier to understand.) We assume the design team has decided to implement the "Sense Boat Coming" task separately so that that module can be placed at various distances upstream from the bridge. That leaves a set of ten tasks. So, let $V = \{1, ..., 10\}$ with associations as follows:

Index	Task
1	Check on Bridge Traffic
2	Change Traffic Light (to red)
3	Lower Barrier
4	Sound Alarm
5	Raise Span
6	Sense Boat Leaving
7	Lower Span
8	Change Traffic Light (to green)
9	Raise Barrier

10 Turn Alarm Off

There are six different functionalities represented in these ten task nodes. Let $L = \{1, ..., 6\}$ with associations as follows:

Index	Task
1	Determine if there is traffic on the bridge
2	Control traffic lights
3	Control barriers
4	Control alarm
5	Control span
6	Determine if boat has passed under the bridge

The design team might guess that task 1 would require a high-end processor. A powerful high-end processor might be able to handle some additional tasks as well, but those could also be mapped to other components. On the other hand, a low-end processor or even a low-end FPGA could easily handle tasks 2 and 8 and probably also handle tasks 3 and 9 as well as tasks 4 and 10. Further, the team could decide to allow the possibility that each pair 2-8, 3-9, and 4-10 be implemented on its own platform. The team could decide that it would be easy to write software for these tasks if they are mapped onto some kind of processor. Task 6 might be accomplished with a high-end processor or a low-end processor. These comments lead the team to estimate that solutions might use as many as two high-end processors, as many as five low-end processors, and as many as three FPGAs. Thus

$M = \{1\}$, where 1 corresponds to FPGA.
$J1 = \{1, 2, 3\}$ — there could be as many as three FPGAs.
$P = \{1, 2\}$, where 1 corresponds to high-end processor, and 2 corresponds to low-end processor.
$K_1 = \{1, 2\}$ - there could be as many as two high-end processors.
$K_2 = \{1, 2, 3, 4, 5\}$ — there could be as many as five low-end processors.

Now that the various sets have been defined, we know what the decision variables will be (see Problem 4) and can write the basic equations described in Section 15.2. Equations restricting the decision variables to zero and one, the instances of inequalities (1), (2), and (3), are straightforward and are left as an exercise (see Problem 4). For each of the ten tasks, there is an equation that ensures that task is mapped to one and only one component.

$$\sum_{m \in M} \sum_{k \in J_1} X_{1,m,k} + \sum_{p \in P} \sum_{k \in K_p} Y_{1,p,k} = 1 \text{ Task 1 is mapped to one and only one}$$
component.

$$\sum_{m \in M} \sum_{k \in J_1} X_{2,m,k} + \sum_{p \in P} \sum_{k \in K_p} Y_{2,p,k} = 1 \text{ Task 2 is mapped to one and only one}$$
component.

$$\sum_{m \in M} \sum_{k \in J_1} X_{10,m,k} + \sum_{p \in P} \sum_{k \in K_p} Y_{10,p,k} = 1 \text{ Task 10 is mapped to one and only one}$$

component.

If a task is mapped to a processor, there must be software that implements the functionality of that task for the processor. For example, task 1 has functionality 1. The following equation ensures that if task 8 (Change Traffic Light to green) is mapped to high-end processor 2, then there must be software that implements functionality 2 (control traffic lights) for high-end processor 1:

$$NY_{2,1,2} \geq Y_{8,1,2}$$

Problem 4 asks the student to write additional equations of this type. Finally, the design team would decide on an objective function to minimize. Problem 4 asks the student to write an objective function based on cost of the components.

15.3.4 Adding problem-specific knowledge to the basic equations

Additional equations and inequalities may be added to the basic set to incorporate knowledge about the specific system being designed. We illustrate this with a few examples in the bridge system from Section 15.3.3.

Tasks 2 and 8 should be implemented on the same platform because those tasks control the same physical device. So, for example, if task 2 is mapped to FPGA 1, then task 8 must also be mapped to FPGA 1, and similarly for task 2 being mapped to a different FPGA or one of the low-end processors or one of the high-end processors. The following set of equations ensures that tasks 2 and 8 will be mapped to the same platform.

$$Y_{2,1,k} = Y_{8,1,k} \qquad \text{for } k = 1, 2$$

$$Y_{2,2,k} = Y_{8,2,k} \qquad \text{for } k = 1, 2, 3, 4, 5$$

$$X_{2,1,k} = X_{8,1,k} \qquad \text{for } k = 1, 2, 3$$

A similar set of equations would be required to ensure that tasks 3 and 9 were mapped to the same platform as well as tasks 4 and 10 mapped to the same platform. See Problem 4.

The design team may determine that task 1 is too complex to be implemented on any low-end FPGA or even a low-end processor because of the number of separate sensors required to check all areas for pedestrian and car traffic. Mapping task 1 to an FPGA or low-end processor can be blocked by including the following set of equations:

$$X_{1,1,1} = X_{1,1,2} = X_{1,1,3} = 0 \text{ Task 1 cannot be mapped to an FPGA.}$$

$$Y_{1,2,1} = Y_{1,2,2} = Y_{1,2,3} = Y_{1,2,4} = Y_{1,2,5} = 0 \text{ Task 1 cannot be mapped to a low-end processor.}$$

15.3.5 **Comments**

As mentioned earlier, additional information can be included as needed for a particular design problem. For example, communication costs can be estimated for the edges in the graph, and total communication time might be used in the objective function. Timing estimates for each hardware component and processor type might be given for each functionality and inequalities used to specify timing constraints on point-to-point paths in the graph. If the system has shared resources, limitations on the use of these can be represented. In each case, new variables and equalities/inequalities would be introduced. For a fuller treatment of this topic, see Ref. [6].

Such a large degree of formality may seem strange, and some of the equalities and inequalities may seem counterintuitive at first. However, remember that the reason for modeling like this is that there are powerful software tools that can find solutions for the variables and, hence, candidate solutions that satisfy the constraints. Although the general ILP problem is Non-deterministic Polynomial-time (NP) hard, there are still many packages that are able to give useful results in a large portion of the problems given to them. This is especially important for task graphs representing embedded systems that are not so simple. When a graph is small, perhaps five or ten nodes, hand analysis may lead to good solutions. Few real embedded systems have task graphs that small. Hand analysis is not feasible when there are many nodes in the graph. In such cases, the extra work to develop the ILP model pays off in the generation of optimal solutions by the ILP tools that would likely not have been discovered by hand. Further, the generation of solutions by such formal methods is quantitative and egoless. The quantitative aspect is crucial for determining that a solution really is optimal. The egoless aspect is crucial because it means solutions are found by using good engineering principles, not by who likes their own ideas the most, who has the loudest voice in the team meetings, or a host of other nonscientific or nonquantitative approaches.

15.4 **Pareto optimality**

At some point the team may have a list of several solutions, all of which meet the requirements of the problem. These may have come from analyses using such tools as ILP, as described in the previous section, perhaps with different objective functions, through team brainstorming sessions, from prior experience, or other approaches. Of course, eventually one solution must be chosen for the final implementation. (In some cases, more than one solution might be pursued with the idea of uncovering possible problems or advantages that the analysis did not make evident. However, for this section we assume the team wants to select one solution.) We present a method for narrowing the set of choices to a hopefully small set which can be studied further before making the final choice. The method is based on ideas introduced by Vilfredo Pareto,[7] an Italian engineer, economist, and sociologist, and it is also quantitative and egoless. A key feature of this method for narrowing the set of solution choices is that it does not focus on a single feature to optimize, as ILP does, but rather takes into account an arbitrary (but fixed for a given problem) set of evaluation features.

Let $S = \{s_1, ..., s_m\}$ be a set of possible solutions to the design problem for an embedded system. Let $F = \{f_1, ..., f_n\}$ be a set of features that the design team wants to focus on in selecting a good solution from S. Elements of F could be cost, power consumption, total compute time, physical size, communication costs, etc. We assume there is a function h that maps each element of S onto a vector of values in the n-dimensional space determined by F. That is, for each s in S, $h(s) = (a_1, ..., a_n)$, where a_i is the value of attribute f_i for solution s. Assume the goal is to find a solution or solutions that minimize each of these features. (Any feature f that is to be maximized can be turned into a feature to be minimized by selecting a value N for that feature that is larger than any feasible solution would display and then minimizing N-f. For example, if a goal in the bridge system was to maximize the distance D across which the boat could hear a warning horn, one could instead minimize M-D where M was, say, 5 miles.)

> **Definition 15.1** Let $x = (x_1, ..., x_n)$ and $y = (y_1, ..., y_n)$ be two distinct points in an n-dimensional ordered space. If $x_i <= y_i$ for $i = 1, ..., n$, and $x_i < y_i$ for at least one i, then x is said to dominate y, and y is dominated by x.
>
> **Definition 15.2** Let x and y be as in Definition 15.1. If x does not dominate y and y does not dominate x, then x and y are said to be indifferent to each other.

We illustrate these definitions in Figure 15.3. The definitions apply to any dimensionality, but dimensions of more than two are hard to visualize. Therefore, in Figure 15.3 we show two features — cost along the horizontal axis and energy consumption along the vertical axis. (For situations involving more than two dimensions the team would typically use software for the Pareto analysis.) Point x dominates point y, and therefore point y is dominated by point x, because x has both lower cost and lower power consumption. Point x also dominates point z because while they both have the same cost point x uses less energy. Points x and w are indifferent with respect to each other. Point x has lower cost but higher energy consumption; conversely, point w has lower energy consumption but higher cost. We can see that in the two-dimensional case, any given point divides the plane into four regions. Consider point x. The area in the quadrant above and to the right, including points on the same horizontal line as x and to the right as well as points on the same vertical line as x and above, are all the points that are dominated by x. Similarly, the points below and to the left, including the two lines but excluding x itself, are all the points that dominate x. The remaining two quadrants contain all the points that are indifferent to x.

Suppose that the point x in Figure 15.3 corresponds to a solution s_1 in S, that is $x = h(s_1)$. Let s_2 be the solution in S that corresponds to y; that is, $y = h(s_2)$. Obviously s_1 is better than s_2 in all aspects being considered. Therefore, s_2 can be eliminated from further consideration. Let s_3 be the solution that corresponds to point w. Neither s_1 nor s_3 is uniformly better than the other. Solution s_1 has lower cost but

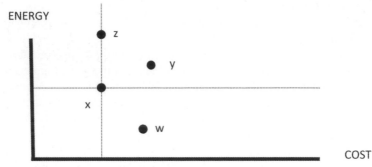

FIGURE 15.3 Comparison for Various Points on a Plane.

Author drawn.

higher energy consumption, while s_3 has lower energy consumption but higher cost. Thus, the design team would want to study and compare these two solutions further before making a final decision. These remarks lead to the following definitions.

> **Definition 15.3** Let $X = \{x_1, \ldots, x_m\}$ be a set of points in an n-dimensional space. A point x in X is Pareto optimal with respect to X if x is not dominated by any other point in X.
>
> **Definition 15.4** Let X be as in Definition 15.3. The set of Pareto optimal points with respect to X is called the Pareto front.

Figure 15.4 illustrates a set of points on a plane and shows the Pareto optimal points (the filled dots), which form the Pareto front. Figure 15.5 shows the set of all points dominated by the Pareto front in Figure 15.4.

Now let y be some point within the set of points being considered that is not in the Pareto front, and let s_y be a solution in S such that $h(s_y) = y$. If y is not in the Pareto front, then there is some point x that dominates y; that is, x is at least as good as y with respect to all features and is better for at least one feature. Let s_x

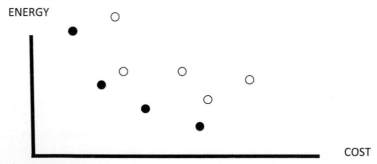

FIGURE 15.4 A Pareto Front.

Author drawn.

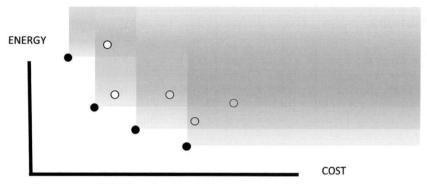

FIGURE 15.5 Area Dominated by the Pareto Front in Figure 15.4.

Author drawn.

be a solution in S such that $h(s_x) = x$. As discussed above, s_y would not be selected for implementation in the presence of a "better" solution like s_x. Therefore, s_y can be eliminated from further consideration. The team can then focus on the subset of solutions that correspond to points on the Pareto front. The team might consider additional quantitative features that were not important enough to use in the initial pruning of the solution space. It could also now consider nonquantitative criteria, such as user preferences determined by ethnographic studies, client preferences, familiarity with the components in the solution, and other human-oriented features.

15.5 **Summary**

There are many choices to be made in mapping a high-level design to specific hardware platforms and software modules. This chapter presented three common methodologies to aid in making those choices. First, the study of task graphs helps the team understand which tasks can or should be done on a single processing element and which may be split among different processing elements in the system being designed. Task graphs allow the team to study timing issues, such as end-to-end timing, and to consider which tasks might be done in software and which in hardware. We then presented two techniques for comparing specific choices of hardware and software mapping. ILP allows the team to quantitatively explore the space of choices and suggest ones that minimize a cost function. The cost function could account for a combination of features such as dollar cost of the devices, end-to-end timing, power consumption, and others. We described the kinds of equations that would be used in the ILP approach. Finally, we described Pareto analysis, by which the set of potential mappings could further be reduced to a set that could be small enough for analysis and selection of a final solution by humans. A key feature of the ILP and Pareto methods is that human ego is factored out, at least until the final selection has to be made from the solutions suggested by ILP and Pareto analysis.

Problems

1. Continue the brainstorming of ideas for the bridge project begun in the Introduction. Do the same for other modules in the bridge. Do this as a group exercise in class.

2. Modify the task graph in Figure 15.1 to handle the following scenarios. For each of your graphs discuss which tasks might be split or merged and why. Assume that once the span has started down it must go completely down before going up again.

   a) Two boats arrive from the same direction. The second boat is sensed before the first boat reaches the other side of the boat.

   b) Two boats arrive from the same direction. The second boat is not sensed until after the span starts to go down.

   c) Two boats arrive from opposite directions at about the same time.

3. Consider the following task graph with execution times indicated inside the circle for each task.

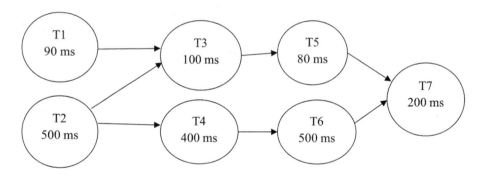

   a) What is the maximum end-to-end execution time?

   b) Which task(s) would be good candidates for splitting? What would you look for in considering whether or not to split the task?

4. Recall the example in Sections 15.3.3 and 15.3.4.

   a) How many X variables are there for this example? How many Y variables?

   b) Write the equation for task 1 being mapped to one and only one component without using the sigma notation, that is, with all the subscripts written explicitly.

   c) Write all the inequalities that indicate software is required in case task 8 is mapped to any processor.

   d) Write the equations that force tasks 3 and 9 to be mapped to the same platform.

e) Suppose the cost of an FPGA is 5, the cost of a low-end processor is 8, and the cost of a high-end processor is 20. Write the objective function giving the total cost of a design.

5. Consider a mobile robot with hands. Suppose that its activities are performed by six major tasks. The following is the description of each of the tasks, their fundamental function types, and some possible hardware that can be used:

Tasks:

Task	Task type	Description
1	vsp	vision sensing and movement targeting processing
2	psp	foot sensing and processing
3	cfm	foot movement control
4	psp	hand sensing and processing
5	chm	hand movement control
6	ccc	central control and coordination task

Candidate hardware:

- (bpkh) Bin picking robot hands (RobotIQ 2-finger Adaptive Robot Gripper 200). Assume movement control functionality is included.
- (rppf) Robot prosthetic foot (From iWalk Power foot). Assume movement functionality is included.
- (apsn) Some type of approximation sensors that can be attached to the feet and hands to determine the arrival at the part storage area and approach to the part tray.
- (dytg) Targeting system for robot movement (Teledyne DALSA: BOA 640C PRO). Assume processing software is included.
- (lmep) Stellaris embedded processor.

Suppose the following decisions have been made:

- An acceptable solution might use one or two Stellaris processors (lmep).
- The vision sensing and movement targeting function (task 1) will definitely be implemented using the Teledyne hardware (dytg).
- Task 6 must be performed on a processor.
- All other functionalities of the tasks can be implemented on either the appropriate hardware or one of the processors.

a. Based on the above information define the following sets:

$V -$

$L =$

$M -$

$K_{lemp} =$

$V \Rightarrow L$:

b. Write the set of equations that specify the acceptable choices for mapping tasks to hardware given the restrictions mentioned in the problem description. Do not use the Σ symbol; write all the terms of each equation individually.

6. Consider a set of tasks described by the following sets.

V = {1,2,3,4,5}

L = {gdt, acd, prc, dca adj}

Type: V→L be a mapping from tasks to their types, with 1→gdt, 2→adc, 3→prc, 4→dac, 5→adj.

M = {sen1, sen2, adc, dac, stp}

KP = {p1, p2}

a) Write the equations to specify the following decisions:
   a. Node 1 is mapped to hardware "sen2."
   b. Node 2 is mapped to hardware "adc."
   c. Node 3 is mapped to processor "p1."
   d. Node 4 is mapped to hardware "dac."
   e. Node 5 is mapped to hardware "stp."
   f. Task type "prc" is implemented on processor "p1."
   g. No nodes are mapped to processor "p2."

b) What are the equations that are required to ensure that each task will be implemented either in one of the hardware units or in software?

7. Pareto analysis can sometimes be used to eliminate families of alternate solutions. Suppose a design team has two options for implementing the algorithm for simple project. The first option is to use some kind of processing element; the second option is to implement the algorithm in an FPGA. Within each option, there are alternatives depending on the choice of processing element in option 1 or FPGA circuit in option 2. The figure below shows ten points in the objective space for the two different options. There are four alternatives for option 1 and six alternatives for option 2. Option 1 objective points are labeled a1−a4; option 2 objective points are labeled b1−b6. Suppose energy and speed are the only two criteria to be used in deciding on a solution.

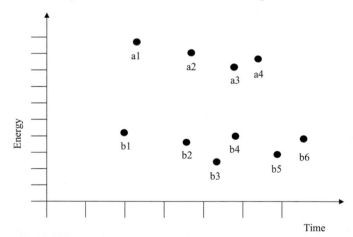

a) Draw the area of the objective space that is dominated by at least one design of option 2.

b) Is there any design belonging to option 1 that is not dominated by a design in configuration 2? If so, which one(s)?

c) Given your answer for part b., should the team continue consideration of options involving processing elements?

8. Suppose we have 12 points in an objective space of two dimensions as shown in the figure that follows. Draw a circle around the points in the Pareto-optimal set and then mark the area dominated by that set.

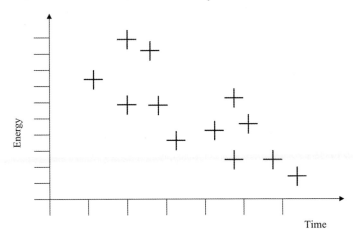

References

[1] J. Teich, Hardware/software codesign: the past, the present, and predicting the future, Proc. IEEE 100 (2012) 1411−1430.

[2] A. Gerstlauer, C. Haubelt, A.D. Pimentel, T.P. Stefanov, D.D. Gajski, J. Teich, Electronic system-level synthesis methodologies, Trans. Comput. Aided Des. Integr. Circ. Syst. 28 (10) (October 2009) 1517−1530.

[3] https://en.wikipedia.org/wiki/Dependency_graph.

[4] https://en.wikipedia.org/wiki/Integer_programming.

[5] https://en.wikipedia.org/wiki/Integer_programming.

[6] R. Niemann, Hardware/Software Co-design for Data-Flow Dominated Embedded Systems, Kluwer Academic Publishers, 1998.

[7] https://en.wikipedia.org/wiki/Pareto_efficiency.

Software

Embedded systems software has many issues that are not discussed in typical programming classes. Independent software modules run concurrently, either on the same platform or on distributed platforms. Concurrent modules running on a single platform must be scheduled so that each can complete its work on time. They must coordinate in the use of shared resources, such as shared variables and timers as described in Chapter 3, Section 3.6.2. The processing elements used in embedded systems often lack the powerful capabilities, such as advanced arithmetic, that are assumed in most high-level programming languages. Special techniques, or "tricks", may be required to accommodate this lack, contrary to general software guidelines that discourage the use of tricks and obscuring techniques in ordinary software. Operating systems that run on processing elements in embedded systems, especially the smaller processing elements, must be small and fast yet rich in features needed for embedded and real-time systems.

Part 4 focuses on concepts and techniques relating to the above issues.

Operating systems

16.1 Introduction

Unlike desktops and laptops, processors in many (if not most) embedded systems need few or perhaps even no operating system support. Operating system (OS) choices for embedded systems range from having none at all to small systems designed specifically for embedded processors to full-fledged operating systems. In this chapter we explore some of the issues relevant to making a choice about the need for OS support and whether to buy an off-the-shelf product or build your own.

16.2 Operating system features and support

OSs manage all the processes that run on the computer. They also provide high-level support for the low-level details of various parts of a system and provide easy-to-use functionality in hardware-independent forms. Figure 16.1 shows elements of a generic operating system and their relationship with application software and computer hardware.

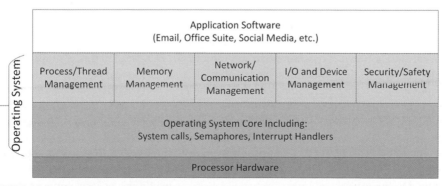

FIGURE 16.1 Elements of a Typical Operating System and Their Relationship With Application Software and Computer Hardware.

Author drawn.

Embedded System Design. https://doi.org/10.1016/B978-0-443-18470-3.00016-6

The primary function of an operating system is to manage all the processes and threads running on the computer. For example, in laptops and PCs, users may open many applications that run simultaneously. The OS controls which of these run at what times so that every application, as well as all the system processes, get adequate time to execute. In embedded systems it is often the case that processes have to be scheduled to run at particular times. (See Chapter 17 for a presentation of scheduling problems and algorithms.) For example, tasks in a smart building control system that ran on a PC would need to be executed at regular intervals — obtain temperatures in all rooms every 2 seconds, obtain energy usage every 5 seconds, update operator's panel every second, etc. The OS must arrange for all the processes for these tasks to be executed at the appropriate times. More sophisticated processing elements may have multiple CPUs, and the operating system controls the assignment of processes to those CPUs. The OS manages the sharing of system resources, such as disks and communication channels, among processes, swapping out processes that are waiting on such a resource or possibly on some other external events so that other waiting processes may use the CPU(s). The OS provides the tools for resource-sharing resources, such as semaphores (see Chapter 18), so that application developers have a uniform way of accessing the shared resources. Process management is the primary function of an OS.

Operating systems also provide memory management. For example, the general OS for a computer will provide both the internal memory management and the external mass storage memory management (e.g., file system management). In the case of embedded systems, in most cases there is no need for external mass storage, so the OS for an embedded system (if an OS is needed) mainly provides internal memory management such as cache, scratchpad, etc.

Operating systems also provide simplified and uniform interfaces between the processes and the physical devices of the system. In PCs and laptops, for example, the OS includes drivers for the hardware devices, such as disk drives and displays, which isolate the higher-level applications from having to deal with the low-level details of each individual hardware device. For example, an application that deals with files need not be coded with specific details for a specific mass storage device. Rather, the application uses high-level OS operations such as open file, close file, create file, etc., and the OS invokes the low-level device drivers for each specific mass storage device to accomplish those requests. PCs and laptops contain a large number of devices, including a variety of mass storage devices, keyboard and mouse input devices, communication devices such as serial ports and Internet cards, clocks, and many more. Devices like these can be replaced or added, and as long as the appropriate drivers are installed, applications running on that platform can access those new devices. Most embedded systems include relatively few of the kinds of devices found in PCs. For example, the span control module in the bridge project would not likely have mass storage devices, display screens, or keyboard/mouse inputs. On the other hand, other embedded systems would use at least some of these. For example, the main control module of the bridge project that oversees the whole system and provides interface to the human bridge attendant would very likely require keyboard input and may use some mass storage for saving historical information about the operation of the bridge over time. If this is implemented on a PC, the operating system will be included as part of the PC. If the engineers decide to build the main control module in-house rather than use a PC, then the question of how much OS support is needed, whether to buy or build, and many other questions will need to also be answered.

A third important feature of operating systems is that they provide security in both the operating system itself and in many of the apps that run under the OS. The major sources of security threats are email clients, browser apps, and file downloads. Few embedded systems have these. For example, the span control module of the bridge system does not have email or web browsers and does not download files for later execution. It communicates solely with the bridge main control module. If the main control module and operator interface modules are implemented as special systems rather than off-the-shelf PCs, then they might communicate only with other parts of the bridge and perhaps a central control office for the general river traffic but not the Internet or email servers.

Operating systems also provide protection against various kinds of internal problems and errors. For example, OSs usually provide safe recovery from memory errors, like overrunning the execution stack or attempting to access out-of-bounds memory. These are issues for embedded systems as well and must be handled either through the use of an OS or through extensive software testing.

Operating systems provide methods for handling interrupts and for adding new interrupt handlers when new devices are added to the system. For example, when a new device is added to a PC, the owner usually has to either download the device drivers from the web or copy them from a CD included with the device. This device-specific software will likely include interrupt handlers because the device itself will likely include interrupt capabilities. However, once an embedded system has been developed and deployed, it is highly unlikely that the system would require the addition of new devices or interrupt types and corresponding interrupt handlers. Any interrupt handlers would have been developed by the software team and included in the system at deployment whether or not an OS was included in the system. The set of devices in the system and the corresponding interrupt handlers (also called interrupt service routines or ISRs) would be fixed until, perhaps, the next system-wide upgrade to a new version. Therefore, the need for interrupts in an embedded system does not imply the need for an OS. In fact, the extra overhead of processing an interrupt through an operating system may interfere with real-time requirements for a real-time embedded system, and therefore the use of an OS may actually be a disadvantage.

16.3 Buy or build

First, we note that an embedded system may be made up of a combination of smaller subsystems. Each of those subsystems would have its own unique requirements and features. For example, in the bridge system the span controller has very limited input and output requirements — communication with the main module, input from some sensors, and outputs to control the motors that raise and lower the spans. On the other hand, the main control module would have communications with all the other subsystems as well as with the outside world (main river traffic control system, local traffic control systems of the city, weather service, etc.). The main control module might also have the more common interfaces, such as keyboard and display, for use by the human operator. Obviously, then, the decision about whether to buy an OS or not has to be made both on an individual basis for each subsystem and on the basis of how these subsystems communicate with each other.

Systems with limited inputs and outputs and non-sophisticated code would likely not need OS support, and as noted an OS may actually be a disadvantage as it requires memory and uses compute cycles. Consider a simple stop light system for controlling the lights at an intersection. Figure 16.2 shows an FSM model. There are provisions for two normal operating modes, night and day, in which the time for green in each direction can be different. For example, at night, when there is relatively little traffic, the lights can change more often so that cars don't have to wait too long. There is also a provision for an emergency signal that turns all lights to red; an emergency vehicle requests this by sending a radio signal to the system. This system uses inputs from various sensors, simple digital outputs to control the lights, and interrupts from sensors and the radio. The states are all OR states, so there are no threads and hence no need for scheduling. Drivers for interfacing with the inputs, outputs, and radio signal are easy to code. Timing can be accomplished using the counters built into most microcontrollers. The software is simple, straight-line code with a few interrupt handlers. This system would not benefit from a commercial operating system. The support required is easy to develop in-house. Similar situations include appliance controllers (unless the appliance includes Internet connectivity).

Even small embedded systems can involve features for which an operating system would be extremely useful. Consider the dashboard module of a modern car.

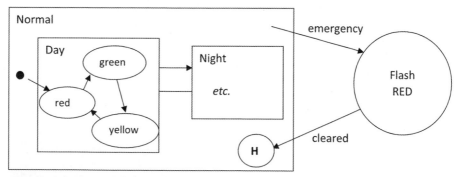

FIGURE 16.2 Stop Light Controller.

Author drawn.

This system could have many different tasks — output information to the various displays on the dashboard, monitor the GPS signals, monitor the radio controls and adjust as the user makes changes, monitor information from the engine, brakes, and various other systems, and others. Most of these are independent processes or threads. Many must be invoked periodically. For example, the GPS interface might be called at regular intervals several times a second to constantly update the position of the car. Similarly, the dashboard module may inquire about the condition of the engine, brakes, and other parts of the car at regular intervals, but each with its own period. Some other parts of the car system may generate interrupts. For example, the wireless system may generate an interrupt if the car loses wireless connectivity. So, the dashboard system has many independent tasks, many of which are periodic and require scheduling, each task with its own period, and each task with its own priority in the set of tasks. The system also has sporadic tasks, such as interrupts, and has other parts for which an OS can provide useful support. In this kind of application, an OS with proven stability and robustness would speed up the development of the system as well as make the deployed systems more robust. Systems built with multi-core processor chips would also generally need an operating system to manage the multiple cores.

Note that the OS will likely provide services for common devices and features but may not include services for all the devices included in a particular embedded system. Therefore, even if an OS is used, the team may still need to implement some drivers and special system services.

Issues that may affect the choice to buy an OS or not and to select a particular OS over another include the following.

- Cost. The cost for purchase may be a one-time cost or a per-use license. However, if the OS does not have all the required features, there will still be some in-house development costs to add on the missing pieces. The cost for developing the necessary software in-house can be figured the same way as for any software product. This would include the cost for both original development and maintenance.
- Flexibility. Can the system be maintained and extended (new features added, errors fixed, etc.) within the framework provided by the off-the-shelf OS, or will there likely be new things in future versions that go beyond the capabilities of the candidate OS?
- Space. Will the OS fit in the memory of the system and leave enough room for the rest of the software? For example, an 8051 single chip system is limited to 4K or 8K on-board program space. Some OSs, like TinyOS,[1,2] could easily fit on board and still leave most of the space for application software. More sophisticated OSs might not fit.
- Debugging tools available. Many systems are available that allow the same kind of debugging features as in typical C++ and JAVA systems. Testers can examine and change memory, set breakpoints, single step through the code, and perform many other debugging tasks. An important feature for debugging tools

used in embedded system development is the ability to count machine cycles during code execution. For example, compiler/debugger systems from Keil and Raisonance have this feature. Cycle counting gives precise measurements of execution times, an important requirement for real-time analysis and scheduling. In some cases, these debuggers require the presence of an OS; in others they are part of the compiler/assembler system.

- Configurability. As noted, most embedded systems contain few if any of the normal devices found in PCs and laptops. It is important, therefore, that the system developers be able to configure an OS to include only the features and device drivers actually needed for the system being developed. Of course, a home-built OS is completely configurable. Many off-the-shelf OSs are also configurable. A system developer uses an interface similar to the sample shown in Figure 16.3 to select the features needed from a list of all the features in that OS. Other OS features required for a chosen feature are included automatically. The interface may show additional information, such as code size for the chosen feature or total code size for all chosen features. In the case of UNIX-type systems, system developers can edit the source code, include conditional compilation commands (e.g., #ifdef and #ifndef), and use other techniques to build a UNIX system that includes only the desired functions. Note that careful coding of the application may allow the removal of portions of an OS beyond the support for hardware devices. For example, an application may be coded so as to not need dynamic memory (i.e., not use malloc/free), and in that case the part of the OS that handles dynamic memory can be removed.

Finally, we note that in-house operating systems typically take one or a combination of a limited number of forms. Two simple forms are polled loop and interrupt driven. In the polled loop form, the main control code consists of a loop in which all

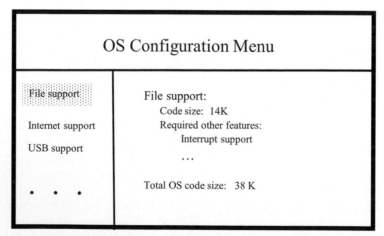

FIGURE 16.3 Sample System Developer Interface for Configuring an Operating System.

Author drawn.

the devices of the system are polled. That is, each device is read for its input and/or status, and appropriate action taken depending on the values read. At the other extreme, the system may go to sleep mode and wake up when a device causes an interrupt. This kind of control is good for systems that need to conserve energy. A system may be a combination of these two forms, polling some devices and having devices that need urgent attention when an event happens cause an interrupt.

16.4 Real-time operating system issues

Most embedded systems have real-time constraints. Therefore, the software that runs in those systems must be able to handle various aspects of time and timing. In this section we discuss several of the most important issues that must be considered.

16.4.1 Time systems

Time is important in many embedded systems. Operations in the system may need to be coordinated with real external time. For example, the street lights at many intersections change modes at various times during the day and from weekdays to weekend days. Such a system would need to sense when it was 8 pm on a weekday or that a particular day was a national holiday. Separate modules in a system may need to coordinate at specific times. For example, in a sensor network it is common for the nodes to sleep most of the time but wake up at specific times to sense and transmit data. Each node may wake up for only a few milliseconds, so it is important that they all wake up at the same time so that they receive the transmissions from the other nodes. Time stamps on data are important in many applications and are also useful for tracking performance as well as analyzing and recovering from errors.

In PCs and laptops, it is relatively easy to access current time at the millisecond resolution level from various programming languages. For example, in C/C++ the built-in functions in time.h Ref. [3] provide access to the so-called UNIX epoch time in milliseconds. However, most embedded systems are not implemented on PCs or laptops, so access to time has to be programmed in some other way such as accessing one of the international or global time systems.

There are many global time standards for measuring the day and time of day. For example, Universal Time (UT)[4,5] is a time measurement based on the earth's rotation. Variations of UT use different celestial bodies to measure the rotation. Because the earth's rotation is not constant (because of, for example, the tidal motion) and is gradually slowing down, UT measurements may have slight deviations from real time and may need occasional adjustment. UT1 is the primary universal time version, but there are others that involve more precise adjustment for variations in earth's rotation. International Atomic Time (TAI, abbreviation of the French name Temps Atomic Internationale)[6] is the average of several hundred atomic clocks around the globe. (Atomic clocks are affected by local conditions such as gravity, so taking the average of a large number of these clocks produces a more accurate and stable clock.) GPS satellites also include time stamps in their packets. Universal Time Coordinated (UTC)[5] is also an atomic-based clock, but UTC attempts to stay close to UT by adding "leap seconds" when needed (approximately every 19 months) to keep the actual date/time within 1 second of UT1. Thus, UTC suffers a discontinuity every 19 or so months. Unfortunately, these various time systems may differ slightly, and, even worse, UTC needs occasional adjustments to account for changes in the movement of the earth, on which UTC is based. However, if all subsystems within a single embedded system use the same system for measuring time of day, they should be able to coordinate.

A key question in the design of a system that uses clocks is the resolution required for the application. Many services provide updates only every second. For applications that don't require more accurate timing coordination or time stamps, this is quite sufficient. For example, the stop lights in a region that coordinate and change mode at different times of day or on weekends can easily tolerate differences up to 1 second. The lights don't all have to change within a few hundred microseconds or even milliseconds of each other. Similarly, the time stamps at, say, a secure door need to be accurate only down to the 1-second level. At the opposite end of the spectrum are applications in which microseconds make the difference between success and failure. For example, activation of the rockets that adjust the path of a spacecraft likely needs to be done within a range of a few hundred microseconds to ensure that the path of the craft is properly adjusted.

System designers and implementers also need to consider the source of the timing information and the delay in that information getting from the source into the system. This is especially important when accuracy and coordination among separate modules in the system are critical. A GPS[7] packet, for example, contains a time stamp of when that packet was sent. But the packet will not reach a GPS receiver in a particular embedded system until sometime later. This delay might only be microseconds, but if the application is trying to manage time at the microsecond level, the delay can be disastrous. Each protocol (e.g., GPS or UTC) has its own method for calculating the transmission delay, and each module in the system has to include software that computes this delay and, hence, allows accurate calculation of the real time at that receiving module. Resolutions down to 100 ns are possible from some of the global protocols (e.g., GPS) assuming the module has the appropriate software to do the computations. The module must also take into account the execution time of the software that computes the real time from the received message. Further, in GPS-based systems a common configuration is to have a separate GPS device attached to the processing element. Many GPS devices have the ability to compute the accurate real time from the GPS packets, but then this information needs to get from the GPS device into the processor. If the data path is through a slow interface, such as USB or RS232, the transmission delay can be orders of magnitude more than the 100-nanosecond resolution. Moreover, if the GPS device notifies the processor through the interrupt mechanism, there will be a delay until the process actually processes the interrupt request. Thus, in systems that require precise timing, great care must be taken in how the information is received from the outside world, how it is processed, and how it is communicated to the parts of the system that need highly accurate time information.

There are a number of other issues that vary from one global protocol to another. For example, many do not account for leap years or time zones. Some simply give elapsed time since a given starting time for that protocol. Some have limited counting range and will "overflow" at some point in the future. Some, such as UTC, cannot be used to predict elapsed time to some event in the (far) future; in the case of UTC, the issue is that the precise time of future "leap" seconds cannot be predicted accurately. The system engineers need to study the requirements of the application being designed and match those with the capabilities of the various protocols in order to make an acceptable choice.

Time information from global time services is sent out in data packets. Many of the services use the ISO 8601 time standard format.[8] See Ref. [8] for details and additional references.

16.4.2 Coordinating time among modules in a system

Many embedded systems do not need references to real time but rather simply need to coordinate. In such cases, the various modules can use their own internal clocks. However, there are issues to consider for these systems as well. First, different modules in the system can use different crystal or other time-base generators for their processors. Therefore, the processors may not all have cycle times that are the same period. For example, in a system that interfaces with musical instruments, some of the processors may use 11.0592 MHz crystals because these are convenient for generating the right serial baud rate for Musical Instrument Digital Interface (MIDI) communication, but other processors not involved in the MIDI communication may use crystals of different frequencies. The various processing elements in such a system would have difficulty coordinating at the microsecond time resolution. Even when all processing elements use the same frequency time base, there may be issues. Crystals, for example, are accurate only to a few percent, depending on how much one pays. Therefore, processors using separate crystals may have timing bases that drift relative to each other. When the elements are physically near enough, such as on the same printed circuit board, a single frequency source, such as an oscillator, can be used to drive all the elements, thus keeping their time bases exactly the same. When processors use different frequency sources, because they have to for the application or simply because they are physically separated, the above issues need to be considered. As with the use of global time sources, the major question concerns resolution. When coordination is at the 1-second level or longer (or possibly even fraction of a second), minor differences in time bases of the different system elements and modules may not be serious. Moreover, they can be overcome in a variety of ways. For example, a central module may broadcast its own time count from time to time, and the other modules update to match.

16.5 **Classification of real-time applications**

Real-time applications are those for which there are timing requirements, the failure of which means that the application cannot succeed. Desktop and laptop computers should be fast, but many, if not most, of the applications will not fail if the application takes a little extra time. For example, a word-processing application needs to be fast enough to keep up with the user's typing and to satisfy the user. However, if occasionally there was a little delay, no serious harm would be done. The user might be annoyed at having to wait a few extra seconds or even longer, but the operations being performed will still get done with no catastrophic loss. These applications are not real-time applications. Real-time applications, by contrast, will fail if the timing requirements are not met. For example, in music performance, failure to keep up with the actions of the music performers ruins the performance. It's not just that the sounds will be heard sometime later and the audience becomes a little annoyed; the performance is ruined.

Real-time applications are classified by the seriousness of failing to meet the timing requirements. Hard real-time applications are those in which failure to meet the deadline is catastrophic. The meaning of "catastrophic" can range from loss of life and/or property to unrecoverable failure of the system. An automatic braking system on a car is an example of a hard real-time system. In this system, the car is supposed to sense when an object is in the car's path and automatically apply the brakes to prevent a collision. If the system fails to react fast enough and the collision occurs, it is a catastrophe. At a minimum, there will be damage to the car and/or the object that the car hits. At a maximum, there could be loss of life if the object is a person or animal. A missile control system is another example. Failure to adjust the path of the missile in time could result in the missile landing at the wrong place, possibly killing many people. "Catastrophe" could also mean that the application fails even when there is no property damage or injury or death. For example, in a system that is supporting live music performance (e.g., recording or controlling the sound system or lights), failure to keep up with the performance means the performance is ruined. There is no property damage or injury, but the system degrades the musical performance and might as well not have been used.

Soft real-time applications are the ones that are not hard. In these systems, if the deadline is not met, the system can fail gracefully and recover. For example, a system that receives messages from a sender and has a time limit for processing and replying may miss the deadline. In that case the sender of the message will not receive the reply in time and may resend the message or take some other action. In the bridge system, if the span control module fails to receive information from the span sensors when lowering the span, the control module can stop the span and wait until the readings are received. The key point is that in these systems there are alternate actions that can be taken to avoid a disaster and even recover gracefully from the failure to meet the deadline.

There is a variety of classifications between these two extremes, such as weakly hard real-time applications or firm real-time applications. For example, in weakly hard real-time applications the system is allowed to miss a certain percentage of deadlines and still be considered to have acceptable performance. Some feedback control problems could be weakly hard problems. For example, a system that controls the steering in a car and is supposed to compute a correction every half second might be able to miss a deadline once every 5 seconds and still be able to successfully guide the car. A missed correction might be fixed by making a more drastic correction in the next few cycles, whereas after two missed corrections in a row, the car might be too far off course (e.g., off the side of the road or into the oncoming traffic lane) for any action to overcome. The design team would need to determine parameters like how many deadline misses can be tolerated and corrected for.

In real-time applications the design team has to determine the degree to which the system can fail to meet real-time constraints and still function successfully. This decision would then inform choices for hardware and software used to implement the system. The tighter the real-time constraint, the more likely the need for faster (and more expensive) hardware, more efficient data structures and algorithms, and the choice of low-level or high-level programming language.

16.6 Summary

In this chapter we described various services that operating systems provide. This knowledge helps the design team decide whether to buy an off-the-shelf operating system, use a configurable operating system that can be tailored to the specific needs of the system under design, build an operating system designed specifically for that system, or even do without any operating system at all. The chapter gave examples to illustrate when each of these options might be the best choice and a list of questions to consider in making that choice. Embedded systems are often real-time systems, so this chapter described the common time systems used throughout the world and discussed issues with coordinating time among distributed nodes in a system. Finally, this chapter described the important classes of real-time systems, those with hard real-time requirements and those with soft real-time requirements. In hard real-time systems, failure to meet the requirement may result in disaster; in soft real-time systems, that is not the case.

Problems

1. There are several operating systems designed specifically for small-to-medium processing elements such as used in embedded systems. Four such systems are TinyOS, Contiki, Windows Embedded, and the ones developed by Wind River. Search the literature and the web to find information about these OSs. Then compare and contrast them, making sure to address the following issues: size (code and RAM), thread support, configurability, language written in, target

platform(s), support for wireless communication, event handling, dynamic application loading, open source, and debugging support. Your report may be in the form of text, or a table, or a combination of text and table.

2. Regular operating systems often provide for secure data transfer, either in the OS itself or through third-party software. Such data security may or may not be important for embedded applications. For each of the following situations, tell whether or not security is important and why. If security is important, suggest a way to implement security.

   a. A wireless-sensor network monitoring temperatures in a building.

   b. A wireless sensor system monitoring a patient living at home.

   c. A door security system — records entries and failed attempts (i.e., who tried to enter and who failed), users have to enter ID.

   d. An ATM system.

   e. Internet-aware appliances (appliances that the owner can monitor and control through the Internet — e.g., rice maker that you can turn on from your office, so the rice is just cooked when you get home).

3. The UTC clock format is 8 bytes — 4 bytes representing an integer number of seconds, and 4 bytes representing a fraction of 1 second.

   a. What is the largest time in terms of years/days/hours/seconds that can be represented in this system? Do you think there are applications for which this maximum time is not a sufficient measure? If so, what are they? If not, why not?

   b. What is the smallest *non-zero* time unit that can be represented in this system? Do you think there are applications requiring more precise measure of time? If yes, what are they? If not, why not?

4. For each of the following tell if you think it is a hard real-time application or a soft real-time application. Explain your choice.

   a. MIDI record system. The system records keystrokes on the keyboard for later playback. Keystrokes must be recorded within 5 milliseconds of the actual stroke.

   b. Vehicle-counting system at an intersection. A sensor embedded in the pavement records when vehicles pass over and count the vehicles so that the system can determine how long to leave the stop lights green or red. The count must be updated within one-quarter second of the time the vehicle passes over the sensor.

   c. Security keypad reader. The system reads keystrokes on a keypad of a door security system and passes the keystrokes to a central system that verifies if a valid password has been entered. A keystroke should be transmitted to the central system within 20 milliseconds of the actual press.

5. For each of the following applications, tell whether you would buy an operating system or build whatever you needed in-house. Explain why you would make the choice you made.

   a. insulin monitor and dosage system

   b. ATM machine

   c. auto-pilot in a drone

   d. bridge operator's control panel

6. For each of the following applications, tell how accurate the timing coordination among distributed nodes should be and explain your choice. Then tell whether the UTC system described in Problem 3 can be used to represent times in that system.

   a. sensor network on a large farm

   b. nuclear particle accelerator

   c. bank system with multiple ATMs

   d. robot systems in an auto assembly line

References

[1] P. Levis, D. Gay, TinyOS Programming, Cambridge University Press, 2009, ISBN: 0521896061.

[2] http://www.tinyos.net/

[3] P.J. Plauger, Chapter 15: <time.h>. The Statandard C Labrary, Prentice-Hall. Inc., 1992, pp. 415−444.

[4] https://en.wikipedia.org/wiki/Universal_Time

[5] https://en.wikipedia.org/wiki/Coordinated_Universal_Time

[6] https://en.wikipedia.org/wiki/International_Atomic_Time

[7] E. Kaplan, C. Hegarty, Understanding GPS: Principles and Applications, second ed., Artech House, Boston, 2006, ISBN: 1580538940.

[8] https://en.wikipedia.org/wiki/ISO_8601

Scheduling

17

17.1 Introduction

As illustrated in Chapter 15, it is common for one processing element in an embedded system to implement several different tasks. For example, in the bridge project there could be a single processor that monitors all the sensors and sends signals to the various other sub-systems, such as the span controller module and the ground traffic barrier modules. This processor would have separate tasks for (1) checking the boat sensors, (2) checking ground traffic sensors, (3) computing actions for the control modules, (4) updating the operator's screen, and possibly more. Each task is performed multiple times over the operation of the system. For example, the task that monitors for boats is started, requests data from the boat sensor modules, stores the information from those sensors, and then terminates. To distinguish the generic task from individual executions of that task, the individual executions are called jobs. Thus, the bridge system has a task for updating the operator's screen, and every so often there is a new job for that task. Scheduling is the method for deciding which jobs should execute at any given time.

Tasks can be periodic or aperiodic. A task may be required to be performed at specific time intervals, or more precisely the task may have jobs that occur at regular time intervals periodic. Or, a task may be undertaken only at times determined by some external conditions — aperiodic. In the bridge project, the span sensors might report every, say, 50 milliseconds while the span is moving so that the span controller can monitor the movement of the bridge with a high degree of accuracy. Thus, at least while the span is moving, this task is periodic; every 50 milliseconds a new job for this task should be undertaken. Similarly, the update screen task might be performed every second so that the time displayed is accurate to the second. Tasks that are not periodic are aperiodic. Some aperiodic tasks are performed regularly but not with a specific period. For example, messages from the weather service may arrive regularly but at random times. Similarly, the task of computing actions for the other control modules is done regularly but only when an arriving boat is first sensed. Finally, some tasks are performed relatively rarely and are therefore called sporadic. For example, the task of reporting an error in the span motor module is only done when an error has been detected. Note that the notion of periodic or not depends on the module in which the task is running. For example, in the module

Embedded System Design. https://doi.org/10.1016/B978-0-443-18470-3.00017-8

that senses the arriving boats, checking the sensor would likely be periodic, for example, every 1 second. Assuming the sensor module sends a message to the main control module only when a boat is identified, from the point of view of the main control module sensing boat arrivals is sporadic; it occurs regularly (perhaps several times an hour) but at random times.

Part of the design process for embedded systems is to decide which tasks should be performed periodically and which should be performed aperiodically. Sometimes this decision is not so obvious and requires thought. For example, the ground traffic sensor task could be periodic or aperiodic. However, it might be expected that at times there would be many cars crossing the bridge over a brief time period — for example, during the 30-second period when a nearby stop light was green. If this task was specified to be aperiodic, perhaps causing an interrupt whenever the sensor sensed vehicles, then during certain periods the sensor module would be constantly interrupting the main process while at other times it would not be interrupting at all. The constant interruption may prevent the processor from performing other tasks. Moreover, it may not be providing any additional useful information; the processor doesn't need to be told every few milliseconds that cars are on the bridge. In fact, it might be a better idea to sense the ground traffic only when a boat is approaching. In this case, a reasonable periodic schedule seems to be preferable — check for ground traffic every, say, 1 second after a boat arrival message has been received.

An important question in scheduling is whether or not tasks in general or particular tasks can be preempted (i.e., interrupted) by other tasks. (It should be noted that preemption is different than interrupts generated by the hardware interrupt system [Chapter 10].) For example, the task that shuts down a nuclear reactor that has gone critical should not be preempted; nothing is more important than safely scramming the reactor. On the other hand, the task that updates the operator's screen in the bridge project could be interrupted by other tasks and events in the system. A few millisecond delay while the system records the arrival of a new boat, an aperiodic event, causes no harm to the operation of the bridge. Even delays from periodic events, such as checking the ground traffic sensors as in the preceding paragraph, could be acceptable; an occasional blip in the screen causes no harm, even if it does occur regularly. There are a variety of reasons for one job preempting another — a waiting job has an earlier deadline, a new job has just arrived and it has higher priority (e.g., another 50 milliseconds have passed and it's time to read the sensors again), or the operating system may simply be sharing the CPU fairly (e.g., by round-robin sharing) among the jobs and the current job has finished its current slice of CPU time. Not all operating systems support arbitrary preemption, so the engineers have to take into account the need for preemptive scheduling when selecting the hardware and related software.

Some tasks may be dependent on other tasks. For example, in the bridge project, the task that determines how the ground traffic barriers should behave is dependent on the task that checks for the presence of cars or pedestrians. The checking task must complete and return its information to the system before the control task can proceed. Other tasks may be present which do not depend on any task. The dependence or independence of the tasks plays a crucial role in scheduling.

Finally, in many cases the set of tasks and their associated properties, such as execution time and real-time requirements, may be known sufficiently at system design time to determine a complete schedule for all the tasks and their jobs when the system is being designed. This is called static scheduling. Note that in these situations task priorities may be less important. The major consideration is whether or not the tasks can be scheduled in such a way that all jobs finish by their deadline. As a simple example, suppose the bridge main processor has in normal conditions (i.e., when no boat is coming) only two tasks — update the screen every 200 milliseconds and check the upstream boat sensor every 50 milliseconds. Although somewhat artificial for this example, suppose the screen update task is required to finish within 40 milliseconds of when it starts and the checking upstream boat sensor task is required to complete within 10 milliseconds of when it starts. Suppose, further, that we have run simulations and determined that the actual time it takes to complete the screen update when there are no interruptions is 25 milliseconds; similarly, suppose our simulations show that it takes no more than 5 milliseconds to read the sensors when there are no interruptions. This situation is summarized in Table 17.1. It is easy to determine a schedule that will meet the requirements (see Figure 17.1). Assuming both tasks should start at time 0, the system simply delays updating the screen for 5 milliseconds to allow checking for the boat. This short delay does not prevent the update operation from completing before its deadline (40 milliseconds) but does ensure that the first reading of the boat sensor completes by its deadline (10 milliseconds). After the update, successive readings of the boat sensor are performed at 50, 100, and 150 milliseconds, after which the entire pattern repeats. This schedule can be built into the operating system; that is, this schedule is determined statically before the system is deployed, and the relative starting times of the various jobs are stored in a table used by the operating system to control the execution of jobs.

Not all systems can be scheduled statically. In particular, systems in which there are aperiodic tasks may not be statically schedulable. In such cases the operating system needs to dynamically determine how to order the jobs that are currently in the system. The sudden appearance and handling of an aperiodic task may require the current jobs in the system to be reordered depending on how long the aperiodic

Table 17.1 Summary of two tasks.

Task	Period	Deadline	Execution time
Update Screen	200 milliseconds	40 milliseconds after starting	25 milliseconds
Read Boat Sensor	50 milliseconds	10 milliseconds after starting	5 milliseconds

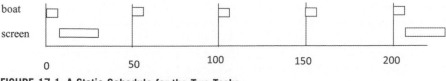

FIGURE 17.1 A Static Schedule for the Two Tasks.

Author drawn.

job takes, what the deadlines and remaining execution times are for the jobs currently in the system, and new jobs that are expected to appear soon.

Simple scheduling methods, such as round-robin and first-come-first-served, are not sufficient for real-time systems. For example, if there are several tasks in the system at a particular time round-robin scheduling will devote equal time slices to each task, thus delaying the completion of each task. The delay may push some tasks beyond their deadlines. Similarly, in first-come-first-served a newly arrived task may have a deadline that occurs before the currently executing task completes. Thus, more sophisticated scheduling algorithms are needed to ensure that all tasks complete by their deadlines.

To summarize, then, the system may have periodic tasks, aperiodic tasks, or some of each. Some or all of the tasks may be preemptable. Enough information may be known about the tasks so that a complete and acceptable schedule can be determined statically, or the operating system may need to perform dynamic scheduling. There are scheduling algorithms for various combinations of these traits, and the remainder of this chapter addresses some of the more widely used ones. There is a vast amount of literature on real-time scheduling describing all these and many other algorithms and their variations and their theoretical properties. See, for example, Refs. [1−4].

17.2 **Definitions and notation**

We use the following notation when illustrating schedules. Time is represented on the horizontal axis. When it is necessary to refer to relative times, the time axis will be marked with integers. These integers are for reference only and do not represent specific time units; they are only used to illustrate when jobs start or stop relative to each other. Tasks are drawn along horizontal lines above the timeline. Shaded rectangles along a task line represent execution times for individual jobs of a task. Up arrows represent arrival times of jobs, and down arrows represent deadlines for jobs. In some cases, a horizontal arrow is used to indicate the execution time for a task. Figure 17.2 shows a scheduling graph with two tasks. Ten job arrivals are shown for Task 1, and nine arrivals are shown for Task 2.

Most scheduling algorithms assume that for each task T_i there is an estimate of the maximum time for executing a job (i.e., an instance of that task). This is called

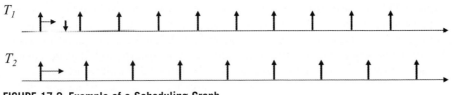

FIGURE 17.2 Example of a Scheduling Graph.

Author drawn.

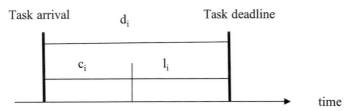

FIGURE 17.3 Illustration of Deadline, Cost, and Laxity.

Author drawn.

the cost of T_i and is denoted c_i. These costs can be determined in a number of ways, ranging from theoretical analysis of the algorithms used in T_i to the use of tools for estimating execution times, such as in Ref. [5], to actual simulation on the hardware platform that will implement the system. Note that c_i depends on the processing platform; obviously, a slower processor will have higher task costs. Next, associated with each task T_i is the deadline interval, denoted by d_i. The deadline interval comes from the real-time constraint; it is the time by which each job must finish after the time that job is received. Stated another way, it is the maximum time each job is allowed to be in the system before failing the real-time constraint for that task. The laxity for a task T_i, denoted by l_i, is the difference between d_i and c_i. Laxity represents the amount of slack time for jobs. A job might be delayed after it arrives or interrupted during its execution as long as the total delay does not exceed the laxity. In the example shown in Figure 17.3, suppose the task has laxity five. When a job of that task arrives, it could be delayed for, say, three time units and also interrupted for two time units during its execution and still meet its deadline. Laxity is used in several of the scheduling algorithms, particularly those in which preemption is allowed. Finally, if task T_i is periodic, its period is denoted by p_i.

In the next few sections we present sample scheduling algorithms for various cases of task sets. It is assumed in each case that the parameters c_i, d_i, l_i, and p_i are all known. If the tasks are not independent, then it is assumed that the dependency graph is known.

For periodic tasks the notion of a hyperperiod often plays an important role. Consider a set of tasks $\{T_i\}$ with periods $\{p_i\}$. Assume the pi are measured as integral numbers of some basic time unit so that the algorithms described later in this chapter need only deal with integers. Let H be the least common multiple (lcm) of the p_i values. H is called a hyperperiod. The hyperperiod is an important concept for periodic task sets because the pattern of arrivals and deadlines repeats every H unit of time. Thus, scheduling algorithms can focus on one hyperperiod. If an acceptable schedule is found for H, that pattern can then be repeated for all future times.

Finally, the utilization is a measure of the percentage of processor capacity that is required to handle all the tasks assigned to that processor. More specifically, the utilization is given by the formula

$$\mu = \sum_{i=1}^{n} \frac{c_i}{p_i}$$

Author drawn.

For example, suppose there are three tasks — T1 with period four and cost two, T2 with period six and cost one, and T3 with period eight and cost two. Then the utilization for this task set is

$$2/4 + 1/6 + 2/8 = 1/2 + 1/6 + 1/4 \approx 0.91667$$

Task T1 by itself uses 50% of the computing power of the processor, task T2 16.67% of the computing power, and task T3 25%. In principle, the processor would be able to handle the load, but scheduling the tasks so that each new job meets its deadline may or may not be possible with such a high load. If the system had only T1 and T2, so that the utilization was only .6667, schedules for which all jobs meet their deadline would be more likely to exist. Obviously, if the utilization is more than 1, the processor cannot possibly handle the load, and either a faster processor must be used or the tasks mapped to different processing elements.

17.3 Independent periodic tasks with preemption

When the tasks are periodic and the parameters c_i, d_i, l_i, and p_i are all known and the system allows tasks to preempt each other, several scheduling algorithms can be applied statically, that is, at system design time. We present two of these — rate-monotonic scheduling (RMS) and earliest-deadline-first scheduling. Both methods assume that the time required for a context switch when one task preempts another is negligible compared to the execution times of the tasks themselves.

17.3.1 Rate monotonic scheduling

In RMS the tasks are assigned fixed priorities in inverse order of their periods. A task with shorter period has priority higher than a task with longer period. Because the set of tasks is fixed, these priorities can be simple integers in the range 1—n where n is the number of tasks. RMS also assumes that the deadline for any task is the same as the period. That is, a job for task T must finish before the next job for T arrives. This is a minimal assumption; if jobs for T took longer than the period for T, jobs for T would just continue building up over time. In many embedded systems deadlines are shorter than the period, in which case the method described in Section 17.3.2 could be used.

Figure 17.4 shows an algorithm for the RMS method by which a schedule can be statically generated. This algorithm assumes that all the jobs run on the same processing core. In the algorithm, an event is either the arrival of a job or the finishing of a job. Jobs may not arrive every unit of time, so the variable i representing time in the for-loop is advanced as much as needed to reach the arrival or completion time of the next job. The algorithm can be extended to schedule task sets on processors which have multiple cores.[6] Recall that because we are dealing with periodic tasks only, we only need to determine the schedule for one hyperperiod. We illustrate the algorithm with the following set of tasks.

```
T1:   c1 = 1;    p1 = 2;   arrival time = 0.
T2:   c2 = 1;    p2 = 4;   arrival time = 0.5.
T3:   c3 = 2;    p3 = 8;   arrival time = 3.
```

Utilization for this set of tasks is $1/2 + 1/4 + 2/8 = 1$. We have listed the tasks in order of priority. T1 has the highest priority because it has the shortest period. T2 has the second highest priority, and T3 has the lowest priority. The hyperperiod for this task set is 8. The algorithm proceeds through time increments from 0 to the end of the hyperperiod. The notation TiJk refers to the kth job for task Ti. Table 17.2 shows the events encountered and actions specified during simulation of the algorithm.

```
RMS(task list) {

    Compute hyper-period H;
    Currently scheduled jobs   S = NULL;
    Queue of waiting jobs      Q = NULL;

    for(i=0; i<H; advance i to next event) {
        if((S!=NULL) && (currently executing job finishes at time i))  S = NULL;
        if( new jobs arrive at time i) {
            if(priority of new job > priority of currently executing job)
                Preempt current job, move it to Q.
                Schedule new job's starting time as i.
            else
                Insert new job in Q in order of priority.
        }
        if( (S==NULL)  && (Q not empty) ) {
            Remove job at front of Q.  If it had been preempted, let it continue.
            Otherwise, mark its starting time as i.
        }
    }
}
```

FIGURE 17.4 RMS Algorithm.

Author drawn.

Table 17.2 Events and actions for RMS example.

Time	T1	T2	T3	Event(s)	Notes
0	T1J1			T1J1 arrives and starts.	
0.5		T2J1		T2J1 arrives.	T1 has higher priority, so T2J1 waits in queue.
1				T1J1 finishes. T2J1 starts.	T2J1 is the only job in the queue at this point.
2	T1J2			T2J1 finishes. T1J2 arrives and starts.	The queue is empty, so the new job starts immediately.
3			T3J1	T1J2 finishes. T3J1 arrives and starts.	The queue is empty, so the new job starts immediately.
4	T1J3			T1J3 arrives. T1J3 preempts. T3J1 and starts.	T3J1 has not finished, but T1 has higher priority.
4.5		T2J2		T2J2 arrives. T1J3 continues.	T1 has higher priority. T2J2 is put in the queue in front of T3J1 because T2 has higher priority than T3.
5				T1J3 finishes. T2J2 starts.	T2J2 is at the front of the queue.
6	T1J4			T2J2 finishes. T1J4 arrives and starts.	T3J1 is in the queue, but T1 has higher priority than T3.
7				T1J4 finishes. T3J1 resumes.	T3J1 is the only job in the queue at this point.
8				T3J1 finishes.	All tasks completed their jobs on schedule within the hyperperiod.

T3J1 will finish at time 8, when the hyperperiod starts over. The schedule produced for this task set and the corresponding graph are shown in Table 17.3 and Figure 17.5.

RMS has several interesting and useful properties. First, if $\mu \leq n*(2^{1/n} - 1)$, where n is the number of tasks, then RMS is guaranteed to produce an acceptable schedule, that is, a schedule in which every job meets its deadline. If $\mu > n*(2^{1/n} - 1)$, there may or may not exist an acceptable schedule, and even if one exists RMS may not find it. Note that in order to guarantee that RMS will find a schedule there must be some slack time, i.e., time in which the processor is idle. See Problem 1 for an example of a task set which exceeds the utilization limit and for which there is no acceptable schedule.

Table 17.3 Schedule produced by RMS — table form.

Task	Job	Start/resume
T1	J1	0
T2	J1	1
T1	J2	2
T3	J1	3
T1	J3	4
T2	J2	5
T1	J4	6
T3	J1	7 (resume)

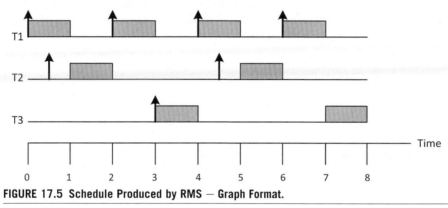

FIGURE 17.5 Schedule Produced by RMS — Graph Format.

Author drawn.

Next, if the period for each task is an integral multiple of the period for the next higher priority task, then RMS is guaranteed to produce an acceptable schedule as long as $\mu \leq 1$. (This was the case for the example earlier in this section.) For example, in the bridge project we could schedule the tasks for collecting data from the sensors and any other tasks on that processor at multiples of, say, 50 milliseconds. The ground traffic sensor task might occur every 50 milliseconds, the boat sensor task every 100 milliseconds, the weather update every 1 second, etc. Each of these tasks has a deadline equal to the period. For example, there is no need to have the sensor data in the system at any time earlier than the next scheduled reading. In this case, RMS would produce an acceptable schedule for any utilization not greater than one (assuming, of course, that context switching time was negligible). In many cases the system designers have some flexibility in assigning periods to tasks, and in such cases the periods may be chosen in such a way to reduce the slack time of the selected hardware platform. In other cases, the periods may be dictated by external requirements and, therefore, may not be arbitrarily assigned.

Finally, for the case of a single processing thread, RMS can also be shown to minimize the sum of all the slack times for individual jobs.

17.3.2 Earliest deadline first

In many cases tasks have deadlines that are less than their periods. For example, the task that checks the proximity sensor in a collision avoidance system on a car may have period 5 milliseconds but be required to complete the test in one millisecond in order to alert the braking system if an object is detected. The brakes may take an additional 5 milliseconds to engage. By ensuring that the sensor completes its task in only one millisecond (instead of 5 milliseconds, i.e., the time of the period), the system ensures that the brakes will begin to engage no more than 11 milliseconds after an object comes within range of the sensor as opposed to 15 milliseconds if the deadline for the senor task was the period (i.e., 5 milliseconds). In such cases the earliest-deadline first (EDF) algorithm is one of several algorithms that can be used. The key feature of EDF is that at any time during the operation of the system, the task that has the earliest deadline is given the highest priority. The schedule is determined (statically) by simulating the arrival and execution times in a hyperperiod and examining the deadlines as each new job arrives. A new job that has deadline earlier than the currently executing job preempts that job. The algorithm is shown in Figure 17.6. It is essentially identical to the

```
EDF(task list) {

    Compute hyper-period H;
    Currently scheduled job   S = NULL;
    Queue of waiting jobs      Q = NULL;

    for(i=0; i<H; advance i to next event) {
        if((s!=NULL) && (currently scheduled job finishes at time i))  S = NULL;
        if( new jobs arrive at time i) {
            if(deadline for new job is earlier than deadline for currently running job)
                Preempt current job, move it to Q.
                Schedule new job's starting time as i.
            else
                Insert new job in Q in order of priority.
        }
        if( (S==NULL)  && (Q not empty) ) {
            Remove job at front of Q.  If it had been preempted, let it continue.
            Otherwise, mark its starting time as i.
        }
    }
}
```

FIGURE 17.6 EDF Algorithm.

Author drawn.

RMS algorithm except for the test in the case when new jobs have arrived. In EDF, the deadlines of the new job and currently running job are compared, as opposed to the priorities in the RMS algorithm.

We illustrate with the same example as in Section 17.3.1 but with deadlines added.

```
T1:   c1 = 1;   p1 = 2;   deadline = 2;   arrival time = 0.
T2:   c2 = 1;   p2 = 4;   deadline = 2;   arrival time = 0.5.
T3:   c3 = 2;   p3 = 8;   deadline = 4;   arrival time = 3.
```

Table 17.4 shows the events encountered and actions specified during simulation of the algorithm. Table 17.5 and Figure 17.7 show the schedule produced for this example.

17.4 **Dependent periodic tasks**

When there are dependencies among the tasks in a set of periodic tasks, the problem of finding an acceptable schedule is much more difficult — in fact, NP-complete. In such cases the engineers may attempt to find a schedule by hand if the set of tasks is reasonably small. The team may decide to use a dynamic version of one of the existing algorithms. For example, it is easy to implement EDF as a dynamic scheduler that runs in the operating system. But there are no guarantees in general that tasks will always meet their deadlines. A team may try various tests to determine through simulation or emulation that the dynamic scheduler works, but there are no formal proofs for the general case of arbitrary dependent periodic task sets.

17.5 **Independent aperiodic tasks**

When tasks are aperiodic and their arrival times are not known in advance, scheduling must be done dynamically, that is, at run time. Two similar algorithms are typically used in this case — a dynamic version of EDF and Least Laxity (LL).

The dynamic EDF algorithm is almost identical to the static algorithm shown in Figure 17.6 except that the queue is maintained at run time and, of course, the output is not a table of start times. The system maintains an ordered list, Q, of jobs sorted by their deadlines, EDF in the list. When a new job arrives, its deadline is computed. If that deadline is earlier than the deadline of the currently running job, the current job is preempted and put to the beginning of Q, and the new job is started. If not, the new job is inserted into Q in order. When a job finishes execution, it is removed from the system and the job at the front of Q is started. See Problem 5 for an example. EDF can be used in systems that do not support preemption. In this case, new jobs are inserted in the queue, but the test comparing the deadline of the current job with the deadline of the new job is not performed; the current job simply continues after the new job has been inserted into Q.

Table 17.4 Events and actions for EDF example.

Time	T1	T2	T3	Event(s)	Notes
0	T1J1 D:2			T1J1 arrives and starts.	D:2 means the deadline for this job is 2.
0.5		T2J1 D:2.5		T2J1 arrives.	T1J1 has earlier deadline, so T2J1 waits in queue.
1				T1J1 finishes. T2J1 starts.	T2J1 is the only job in the queue at this point.
2	T1J2 D:4			T2J1 finishes. T1J2 arrives and starts.	The queue is empty, so the new job starts immediately.
3			T3J1 D:7	T1J2 finishes. T3J1 arrives and starts.	The queue is empty, so the new job starts immediately.
4	T1J3 D:6			T1J3 arrives. T1J3 preempts. T3J1 and starts.	T3J1 has not finished, but T1J3 has earlier deadline.
4.5		T2J2 D:6.5		T2J2 arrives. T1J3 continues.	T1J3 has earliest deadline. T2J2 is put in the queue in front of T3J1 because its deadline is earlier.
5				T1J3 finishes. T2J2 starts.	T2J2 is at the front of the queue.
6	T1J4 D:8			T2J2 finishes. T1J4 arrives. T3J1 resumes.	T3J1 has earlier deadline than T1J4.
7				T3J1 finishes. T1J4 starts.	T1J4 is the only job in the queue at this point.
8				T1J4 finishes.	All tasks completed their jobs on schedule within the hyperperiod.

Table 17.5 Schedule produced by EDF — table format.

Task	Job	Start/resume
T1	J1	0
T2	J1	1
T1	J2	2
T3	J1	3
T1	J3	4
T2	J2	5
T3	J1	6 (resume)
T1	J4	7

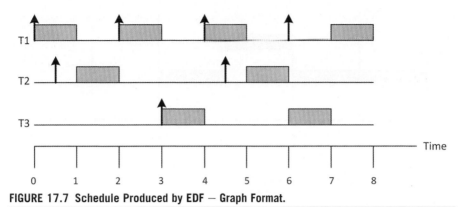

FIGURE 17.7 Schedule Produced by EDF — Graph Format.

Author drawn.

LL is very similar to EDF except that jobs are inserted into Q in order of increasing laxity. Note that the laxity decreases at each time step for every job except the currently executing job. Thus, the system has to recompute the laxities of all the jobs in the Q at each time step because laxity of the job at front may reduce to less than the laxity of the currently executing job as time goes on. See Problem 5 for an example. Recall that laxity is a measure of how much spare time there is before the deadline — the deadline minus the remaining execution time for the task. That is why the laxities for jobs in the queue continually decrease; their deadlines are getting nearer, but their remaining execution times are not changing. The laxity of the currently executing job, on the other hand, does not change; its deadline is getting nearer, but its remaining execution time is going down by the same amount of time.

Consider the picture in Figure 17.8. We have two jobs with the following statistics at time n.

```
T1:  remaining cost = 1;    deadline = n+4.
T2:  remaining cost = 3;    deadline = n+5.
```

At time n the laxities are 3 and 2. T2 would be executing. Therefore, its laxity would remain at 2, while the laxity for T1 would be decreasing. At time n+2, T1's laxity falls below the laxity of T2. T1 would then preempt T2. If preemption were not allowed and T2 were allowed to run to completion at time n+3, the laxity of T1 would have been reduced to 0. T1 could complete its execution by the deadline, but only if there were no interruptions in the processor. If, on the other hand, some external device caused an interrupt or another job arrived in the system requiring at least some small overhead for inserting into Q, T1 might miss the deadline by a small amount. LL gets around this by giving higher priority to those jobs that have the least amount of spare time. Thus, in Figure 17.8, T1 would have been granted processing time at time n+2.

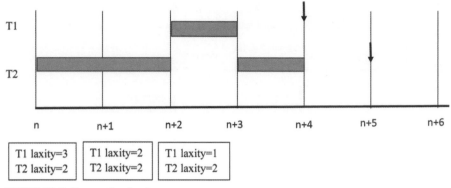

| T1 laxity=3 | T1 laxity=2 | T1 laxity=1 |
| T2 laxity=2 | T2 laxity=2 | T2 laxity=2 |

FIGURE 17.8 Decreasing Laxity.

Author drawn.

17.6 Dependent aperiodic tasks

When aperiodic tasks have dependencies, the situation is, obviously, more complicated. Individual tasks have deadlines, but the set as a whole has additional implicit deadlines. The set of jobs on which a particular job j depends must all complete in time for j to also meet its deadline. In Figure 17.9, for example, task T11 depends, either directly or indirectly, on all the tasks T1—T10. Thus, all of T1—T10 must complete by their own deadlines, if they have such, and also in time for the successive tasks up to and including T11 to complete by their corresponding deadlines. Similarly, task T10 depends on tasks T3, T4, T7, and T8. To illustrate these kinds of dependencies, recall the arrival of a boat as illustrated in Figures 15.1 and 15.2. Boat arrivals are aperiodic. When a boat arrives, it spawns four other tasks — Notify Operator, Check On Bridge Traffic, Change Traffic Light, and Sound Alarm. Change Traffic Light leads to Lower Barrier. Raise Span depends on both Check On Bridge Traffic and Lower Barrier, etc.

The dependency graph is the basis for all scheduling techniques for aperiodic dependent task sets. The two simplest techniques are as-soon-as-possible (ASAP) and as-late-as-possible (ALAP). Each of these methods forms a tree with associated time bands for the tree nodes; all the nodes in the time band k are ready for execution at time k (see Figure 17.10). ASAP generates this time-annotated tree from the independent nodes toward dependent nodes; that is, it starts with nodes that do not depend on any other tasks and then works toward the last task. ALAP works in the reverse direction. It considers the task(s) on which no other tasks depend and works backward toward the tasks that don't require input from other tasks. From the tree point of view, ASAP corresponds to traversal from the leaves (i.e., tasks that do not depend on any other tasks) to the root, and ALAP corresponds to traversal from the root (i.e., the task on which no other task depends) to the leaves.

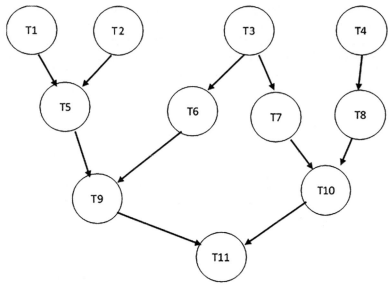

FIGURE 17.9 A Task Dependency Graph.

Author drawn.

Figure 17.11 shows the algorithms for these two approaches. The input for each algorithm includes the task dependency graph and the execution times for the tasks. The output is a schedule listing the times at which each task should start. Figure 17.10 shows the ASAP and ALAP schedules for the graph in Figure 17.9, assuming the following execution times for the tasks:

```
T1: 3    T2: 2    T3: 4    T4: 1    T5: 3    T6: 2
T7: 5    T8: 2    T9: 2    T10: 1   T11: 1
```

In Figure 17.10 we have also shown the execution times as vertical blocks so the reader can easily see that the dependencies are satisfied — no task is started before all the tasks on which it depends have finished.

For the ASAP graph, at time 0 the algorithm selects T1, T2, T3, and T4 because no other task depends on any of these. T1–T4 are scheduled to start at time 0. At time 1, only T4 has finished. T8 can now be selected because all tasks on which it depends have finished. T8 is scheduled to start at time 1. Tasks T1, T2, T3, and T8 are now scheduled. At time 2, T2 finishes. No tasks can be selected to start. T5 cannot be selected because T1 has not finished yet; T10 cannot be selected because T7 and T8 have not finished. At time 3, T1 and T8 both finish, and T5 can now be scheduled to start. At time 4, T3 finishes. Both T6 and T7 can be scheduled to start. The reader is invited to step through the rest of the algorithm to finish the ASAP schedule. The completed schedule is shown in Figure 17.10.

The total time required for all tasks will generally not be known *a priori*, so the ALAP algorithm starts a time counter at 0 and counts backward. Thus, in the loop the start times count from 0 backward. When all tasks have been scheduled, the total required time can be computed, and the start times adjusted to count forward from 0. T11 is selected because it is the only task on which no other task depends. That is, all tasks dependent on T11 (the empty set) have been scheduled to start by time 0. The cost for T11 is 1, so T11 is scheduled to start at time -1. At time -1, T9 and T10 are chosen because their dependent tasks, in this case just T11, have started by time -1. T9 is scheduled to start at time $-1 - 2 = -3$, and T10 is scheduled to start at time $-1 - 1 = -2$. The starting time t-c for task T_i ensures that the task T_i will finish by time t. At time -2, only tasks T7 and T8 have all their dependent tasks begin by time -2. T7 is scheduled to start at $-2 - 5 = -7$; T8 is scheduled to start at $-2 - 2 = -4$. The reader is invited to step through the rest of the algorithm to finish the ALAP schedule. The total time required for this schedule is, again, 11, and all the negative starting times are adjusted forward by 11. The completed schedule is shown in Figure 17.10.

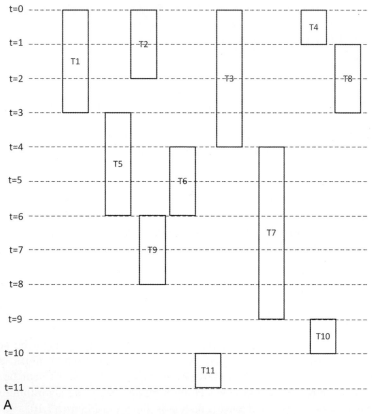

A

FIGURE 17.10 ASAP (A) and ALAP (B (below)) Schedules.

Author drawn.

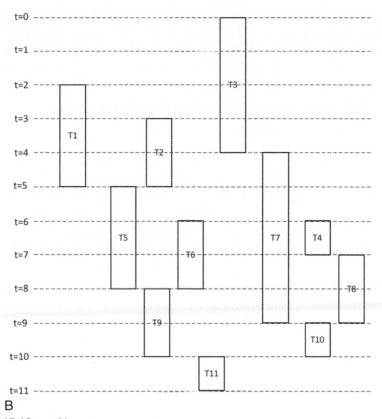

B

FIGURE 17.10 cont'd.

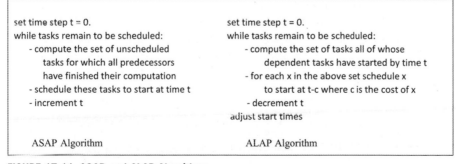

FIGURE 17.11 ASAP and ALAP Algorithms.

Author drawn.

ASAP and ALAP have an implicit assumption that is not realistic. Both assume that arbitrarily many tasks can be scheduled at any given time. This, of course, would require arbitrarily many resources, specifically arbitrarily many processing units. A simple fix when the system has a single processor is to execute the tasks scheduled to start at a given time in some arbitrary sequence. However, a more general solution to this problem is addressed in the algorithm described in the next section.

17.7 Scheduling for a fixed number of processors

Many embedded systems use multiple processing elements or processing elements that have multiple cores. This provides an additional level of flexibility in scheduling tasks. For example, for the static case jobs may be scheduled for separate processors or cores, thereby avoiding the overhead of preemption and context switching. For example, if the system has two processing cores, the static schedule in Table 17.3 can be modified to the schedule shown in Table 17.6. Preemption and context switching are completely avoided in this example, although in general this will not be the case. For the dynamic case, some algorithms use a measure called "mobility". Mobility is the difference between the start times in ASAP and ALAP. Jobs with higher mobility have more flexibility in the assignment of their start times. This flexibility could be used to adjust the start times of jobs to reduce the number of time steps in which jobs are waiting or processors are idle. See Problem 8.

The List Scheduling algorithm takes into account the number of processors available to assign tasks. The algorithm is shown in Figure 17.12. The key is to keep track of how many processors are currently being used in addition to computing which tasks are ready to run (all the tasks on which they depend have been completed). The algorithm takes the task graph ($G(V,E)$), the number of processors (B), and a priority function (u) as inputs. It returns the schedule as its answer. For each i in the loop, A_i is the set of tasks that have not already begun execution but are available to start. G_i is the set of tasks that have already begun but not yet completed; elements of G_i must continue to run on the processors where they started. If the number of elements in G_i is less than B, then some elements of A_i can be scheduled to start at that time. Elements of A_i are selected according to the priority function u.

Table 17.6 Schedule from Table 17.3 modified for two processors.

Task	Job	Start core 1	Start core 2
T1	J1	0	
T2	J1		1
T1	J2	2	
T3	J1		3
T1	J3	4	

```
List(G(V,E), B, u){
i :=0;
  repeat {
    Compute set of candidate tasks A_i;
    Compute set of not terminated tasks G_i;
    Select S_i ⊆ A_i of maximum priority r such that | S_i | + | G_i | ≤ B     (*resource constraint*)
    foreach (v_j ∈ S_i): τ (v_j):=i;     (*set start time*)
    i := i +1;
  }
  until (all nodes are scheduled);
  return (τ);
}
```

FIGURE 17.12 List Scheduling Algorithm.

Author drawn.

Consider the task graph in Section 17.6. Suppose the priority of a task is its execution time; tasks that take longer to execute have higher priority. We illustrate the first few iterations of the algorithm for the case of three processors.

i = 0. $A_0 = \{T1, T2, T3, T4\}$ $G_0 = \{ \}$ $S_0 = \{T1, T2, T3\}$

    Four tasks are available, but there are only three processors.
    The three tasks with the longest execution times are selected
    to start at time 0.

i = 1. $A_1 = \{T4\}$ $G_1 = \{T1, T2, T3\}$ $S_1 = \{ \}$

    All three tasks are still running, so no new tasks start at
    time 1.

i = 2. $A_2 = \{T4\}$ $G_2 = \{T1, T3\}$ $S_2 = \{T4\}$

    T2 has finished, so one processor is available. T1 is still
    running,
    so T5 is not available yet. Similarly, T3 is still running,
    so tasks
    T6 and T7 are not available yet. T4 is scheduled to start at time 2.

i = 3. $A_3 = \{T5, T8\}$ $G_3 = \{T3\}$ $S_3 = \{T5, T8\}$

    Tasks T1 and T4 have finished execution. T1 and T2 are now both
    done, so T5 is available. T4 is finished, so T8 is now available.
    Only one task is still running, so two tasks can be scheduled.
    Both
    T5 and T8 are scheduled to start at time 3.

i = 4. $A_4 = \{T6, T7\}$ $G_4 = \{T5, T8\}$ $S_5 = \{T7\}$

    T3 has finished, but T5 and T8 are still running. Only one new
    task can begin. Priority is determined by execution time, and
    T7 has execution time longer than T6. So, T7 is scheduled to
    start at time 4.

Table 17.7 Assignment of jobs from Section 17.6 to 3 processors.

Time	Core 1	Core 2	Core 3
0	T1	T2	T3
1	T1	T2	T3
2	T1	T4	T3
3	T5	T8	T3
4	T5	T8	T7

Table 17.7 shows the assignment of tasks to processor cores from time 0 to time 4. The reader is invited to complete the schedule.

17.8 Estimating execution times — worst-case execution time

The algorithms presented in this chapter assume, among other things, knowledge about the maximum execution time, typically referred to as the worst-case execution time (WCET), for each task. The methods for determining WCET normally produce only estimates because of issues like those noted in the next paragraph. These estimates, however, should satisfy two important properties. First, they should be safe — the estimated cost should be at least as large as the maximum execution time for any job of the task. Second, they should be tight — the estimate should not be too much larger than the actual maximum execution time. For example, estimating a cost of 2 minutes for a simple, straight-line program that executes in 50 milliseconds is safe but not tight. There are several techniques and tools used in the determination of WCETs. See, for example, Ref. [5] for an extensive treatment of this topic. In this section we discuss the basic concepts used in these tools and techniques.

As noted in Section 17.2, there are a variety of techniques for estimating the costs. However, these may not take into account a variety of issues that can affect the real execution times in fully implemented systems. For example, simulating a function on a cycle-counting simulation platform, such as the 8051 systems from Keil or Raisonance, would not factor in the processing of interrupts in a fully implemented system, where devices can cause interrupts at arbitrary times. One could artificially insert interrupts during the simulation, but if there were many sources of interrupt this process might not be feasible. A fully implemented system could contain many functions and modules executing concurrently, some of which use shared resources. Unless the entire ensemble of functions and modules is tested together in the simulation, the delays caused by requests for shared resources may be difficult to estimate. Similarly, if the platform includes cache memory, delays due to cache misses may be difficult to estimate during testing or through analysis of a single function. Some of these issues may be eliminated from the design of the system. For example, the designers may decide not to use processors with cache so that simulations of single functions could possibly lead to more accurate cost estimations. There may be a separate task devoted to processing interrupts; in this case, the interrupt function itself simply records the occurrence of the interrupt and thus imposes minimal delays on the other tasks in the schedule. The actual processing of interrupts is then treated as a regular task in the scheduling algorithm. Unfortunately, other issues may not be so easy to remove. In particular, a system whose model is a hierarchical FSM will require the use of shared resources. A more complicated shared resource, such as a mass storage device, may not be easily removable from the design.

The estimation of the costs needed for the scheduling algorithms can proceed in several phases. The first phase is an analysis of the algorithm for the task. For this phase, it is important that the maximum number of iterations of each loop should be identified. Knowing that the function executes in time O(N) will not produce a number that can be used in any of the scheduling algorithms. The N must be bounded in order to get a numeric value for WCET. Similarly, the depth of recursion for recursive functions used in the module should be bounded. (In general, real-time systems should avoid loops for which an upper bound cannot be identified. A function containing a loop which runs until some computation converges may never terminate or may take too long and make other tasks miss their deadlines. Similar remarks apply to recursive functions.) Note that determining an upper bound on loops and function calling is undecidable in general. Embedded system engineers should, therefore, take care at each step in the design process to bound these as part of the system design process, for example, as part of the UML modeling phase. In some cases, there may be natural bounds, although the design team may want to impose a limit lower than the natural bound. For example, in the bridge system there would be a maximum number of boats possible in the range of the boat sensor because of the physical size of the boats and the range limit. If the sensor had a range of, say, ½ mile, then one might estimate that at most 20 boats could be in the range of the sensor at any one time. However, in order to lower the WCET for some of the functions the design team could decide that the system will only pay attention to the nearest five boats, and this in turn could limit any loops that process waiting boats to five iterations instead of 20. In other cases, there is no natural bound, and the team must impose some limit. For example, in principle PINs could be arbitrarily long, which in turn means that checking a PIN could take an arbitrary amount of time. The team could decide that PINs should be no more than six characters, thus bounding any loop that looks at individual characters in the PIN.

Once the bounds have been determined the set of paths from function entry to termination points of the function should be enumerated. In general programming, of course, this could be extremely large, even if *a priori* upper bounds for all loops are known. However, in many embedded systems, individual tasks are relatively simple and loop bounds relatively small. Consider the various tasks for the bridge — check if there are cars or pedestrians, record the arrival of a boat and check if another boat is already present (which, as described in the previous paragraph, could be bounded to a relatively small number), etc.; the algorithms for these are quite simple and easy to analyze. A full treatment of algorithm analysis is beyond the scope of this book. We simply note that for relatively simple algorithms the analysis can be done, by hand in many cases or by tools. Note that applying the same time estimate for each iteration of a loop and multiplying by the loop limit may produce a WCET that is not as tight as it could be. Different iterations of the loop may follow different paths through the body of the loop, and these different paths could have different execution times. For example, a loop may perform one computation for even values of the loop index and a different computation for odd values. Or, a loop might perform some more complex analysis during the first few iterations of the loop and something less complex for later iterations. An example of the latter situation could occur in the bridge project; if several boats are approaching, the bridge system could perform some special operations for, say, the first two boats and simply record that the later boats were approaching.

Once the analysis of the algorithm has been done, actual cost estimates for the various platforms can be made. As noted before, these cost estimates must be made for each platform under consideration and the machine code actually generated (by a compiler or by hand). For each path, including paths obtained by unrolling any loops, the cost of executing that path is determined. This may be done by hand or by use of a cycle-counting simulator. Note that the longest path in the algorithm may not yield the maximum cost. A shorter path can contain expensive instructions (e.g., multiply/divide) or calls to functions that have long execution times. Such analysis gives a cost for each path when there are no other issues, such as cache misses or delays due to resource sharing, affecting the computation. From this set of costs, the maximum can be taken as an initial estimate of the worst-case execution time for that platform.

Finally, the estimated WCET values can be adjusted for factors that can affect the execution times. It is difficult in general to estimate how many interrupts might arrive while a particular job is executing or how many shared resource requests might result in delays. Similarly, it may not be possible to predict exactly how often shared resources might be locked by other processes in the system or how many cache misses will occur during the execution of a particular job. Further, in general these will not be the same from one job to another for the same task because the interrupts will typically not be associated with any one task nor will the set of jobs in the system for other tasks be the same for each job of a given task. One can predict the exact time of the delay for some cases. For example, the execution time of an interrupt handler can be determined. The delay for other cases, such as waiting for a shared resource to be unlocked, usually cannot be determined because the relative point in the critical section of the job that currently owns the resource cannot be determined. In these cases, one might estimate a maximum delay time. These delay times can then be used to adjust the estimated WCET to produce a safe estimate, although the revised estimate may not be as tight as one would like.

17.9 **Summary**

Embedded systems typically have to process many tasks. The sequence of tasks must be scheduled so that every task is completed within its time requirement. This chapter presents the relevant scheduling concepts and the most common techniques used to actually make schedules. The concepts include whether or not tasks arrive periodically, whether or not a running task can be interrupted (i.e., preempted) by a more urgent task, whether or not the necessary information such as arrival distributions and execution times is known *a priori*, and others. Utilization was defined, and it was shown how this could be used to determine if a proposed computing platform was fast enough to complete all tasks to be given to it. The chapter then describes the most common scheduling methods for the major classes of task sets — independent periodic tasks with preemption, independent aperiodic tasks, and dependent aperiodic tasks. The chapter then discusses scheduling when a system may have more than one, but a fixed number, of processors. Finally, the chapter closes with a discussion of ways to estimate execution for individual tasks, information that is vital for all of the algorithms presented in the chapter.

Problems

1. Suppose we have two tasks with the indicated periods and execution times:
   T1:   p=4   c=2
   T2:   p=7   c=3
   The task deadlines are the same as the periods; that is, in effect the deadline is the time at which a new job would be received. Suppose that the first job for each task arrives at time 0.
   a) Compute the average utilization and compare it to the bound for guaranteeing schedulability by the RMS algorithm.
   b) What is the hyperperiod for this set of tasks?
   c) Step through the RMS with preemption algorithm and fill in the following table. The first three lines are done to show you the format.

Time	Arrivals	Action	Reason
0	Task 1 Job 1 Task 2 Job 1	Task 1 Job 1 starts. Task 2 Job 2 put in Q.	No job was running, so one job can start. Task 1 has higher priority, so it starts and the other waits.
1		Task 1 Job 1 continues.	No new jobs have arrived.
2		Task 2 Job 1 starts.	Task 1 Job 1 has finished. No new job arrived at this time, so the task waiting in Q starts.

a) Does any job fail to meet its deadline? If so, specify which job and the time at which the deadline is passed.

b) Show the schedule produced by the EDF algorithm with preemption for this task set.

2. Three periodic tasks run on a single processor with preemption.

T1: period 4, execution time 2, first arrival time 0

T2: period 8, execution time 2, first arrival time 1

T3: period 16, execution time 4, first arrival time 4

a) Compute the utilization for this task set to two decimal places.

b) What is the hyperperiod for this task set?

c) On the diagram below show what the RMS algorithm would attempt to compute for a schedule for this task set. If the algorithm succeeds you should stop at the end of the hyperperiod. If the algorithm fails you should stop at the point of failure. Arrival times are indicated by up arrows.

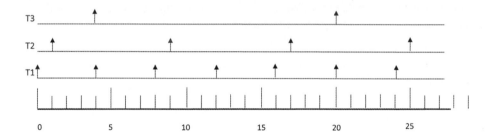

a) Based on your value for utilization in part a, would you have expected RMS scheduling to succeed? Explain your answer. Why did it succeed?

3. Three periodic tasks run on a single processor with preemption.

T1: period 3, execution time 1, first arrival time 0

T2: period 5, execution time 1, first arrival time 1

T3: period 6, execution time 2, first arrival time 1

a) What is the hyperperiod for this task set?

b) Apply the EDF algorithm to show a schedule for the hyperperiod.

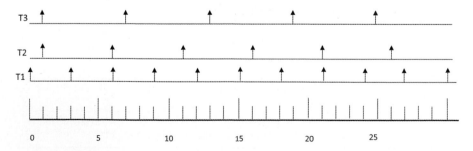

4. Repeat problem 3 with the following set of tasks.
    T1: period 3, execution time 1, first arrival time 0
    T2: period 6, execution time 2, first arrival time 0
    T3: period 8, execution time 2, first arrival time 0

5. Assume we have four tasks with arrival times, deadlines, and execution times as shown.

    T1: $A1 = 0$ $d1 = 15$ $c1 = 5$
    T2: $A2 = 2$ $d2 = 10$ $c2 = 6$
    T3: $A3 = 5$ $d3 = 6$ $c3 = 4$
    T4: $A4 = 11$ $d4 = 12$ $c4 = 8$

    a) Show a graphical representation of an EDF schedule for these tasks. Tell if any task misses its deadline.
    b) Show a graphical representation of a least-laxity schedule for these tasks. Tell if any task misses its deadline.

6. Generate ASAP and ALAP schedules for the following task set with dependencies as shown in the figure.
    T1:   c=4
    T2:   c=3
    T3:   c=2
    T4:   c=5
    T5:   c=5
    T6:   c=4

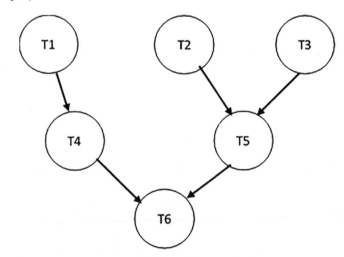

7. Consider the following task graph. The execution times and priorities are as follows:

Task	Execution time	Priority
a	2	9
b	3	8
c	1	5
d	2	4
e	3	3
f	2	5
g	1	4
h	3	6
i	2	7
j	2	6
k	2	4

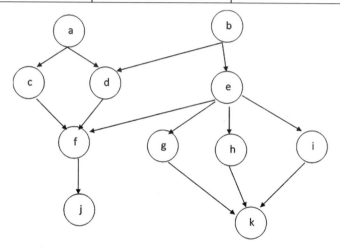

a) Apply the List Scheduling algorithm to this task graph assuming there are two processors.

b) Apply the List Scheduling algorithm to this task graph assuming there are three processors.

8. Consider the following task graph. The execution times and priorities are as follows:

Task	Execution time	Priority
a	2	6
b	1	8
c	2	4
d	1	3
e	3	7
f	1	6
g	1	2
h	1	4
i	2	5
j	2	3
k	1	1

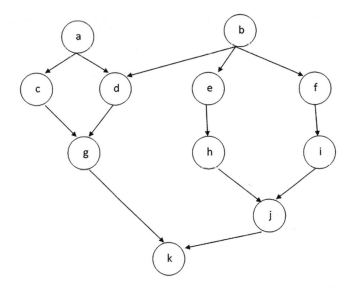

a) Apply the List Scheduling algorithm to this task graph assuming there are two processors.

b) Apply the List Scheduling algorithm to this task graph assuming there are three processors.

9. Consider the following section of code. A is an array of integers. N and j are integers. Line numbers at the left are for reference only.

```
1    j = -1;
2    do { j = j+1;
3      if( A[j] > 0 ) break;
4      g(A,j);
5    } while( j<N );
6
```

a) List all the possible execution paths when N has the value 1.

b) List all the possible execution paths when N has the value 2.

c) List all the possible execution paths when N has the value 3.

References

[1] G.C. Buttazzo, Hard Real-Time Computing Systems: Predictable Scheduling Algorithms and Applications, Springer, 1997.

[2] J.W.S. Liu, Real-Time Systems, Prentice Hall, 2000.

[3] F. Cottet, J. Delacroix, Z. Mammeri, Scheduling in Real-Time Systems, John Wiley & Sons, 2002.

[4] J. Leung (Ed.), Handbook of Scheduling: Algorithms, Models, and Performance, CRC Press, 2004.

[5] R. Wilhelm, Determining bounds on execution times, in: R. Zurawski (Ed.), Embedded Systems Handbook, CRC Press, 2006.

[6] M. Raut, M. Narnware, Analysis of rate monotonic scheduling algorithm on multicore systems, Int. J. Sci. Res. 4 (July 2015) 131−133.

Semaphores

18

18.1 Introduction

When resources are shared, there must be a way to control access to those resources. When the resources are shared among processes running on the same processing element, the common method for access control is the semaphore.[1,2] Semaphores can be used to control access to simple shared resources, such as shared variables, and to more complex shared resources such as data structures, queues, communication ports, etc.

The presence of shared resources is an important consideration in real-time systems. If one process or thread currently holds exclusive access to the shared resource, other processes and threads that need that resource are blocked. This, in turn, obviously affects the completion time of the blocked processes, possibly delaying some of them until past their deadlines. Unless handled carefully, shared resources can lead to an interesting and potentially dangerous condition called priority inversion. A low-priority process may be holding a shared resource. If a higher-priority process requests that resource, that higher-priority process is blocked; the lower-priority process continues execution, as described in Section 18.4.

This chapter addresses the issue of shared resources. It describes semaphores and how they are implemented. In these discussions we assume that the system allows higher-priority tasks to interrupt lower-priority tasks, the norm for most real-time systems.

18.2 Motivation

A simple example will illustrate the basic problem encountered when separate processes use shared resources. Suppose two processes access a shared variable as follows.

$$\text{Process 1} \quad \text{Process 2}$$

$$x = x + 1; \quad x = x - 1;$$

These processes would be running concurrently as threads on a single processor. The executions of these two threads would typically be interleaved; that is, Process 1 would execute for a while, then Process 2, then Process 1 again, etc. This leads to nondeterministic behavior. Consider the machine instructions associated with the two assignment statements.

ld x	ld x
inc	dec
st x	st x

The ld instruction moves x into the arithmetic register. The st instruction moves the contents of the arithmetic register back to x. The inc and dec instruction increments and decrements the arithmetic register, respectively. Suppose the two processes reach the assignment statements at about the same time and that x has the value 0 just before the assignment statements are executed. If Process 1 completes its assignment statement before Process 2 is allowed to execute its assignment statement, then x will have the value 1. After Process 2 executes its assignment statement, x will again have the value 0. The same result occurs if Process 2 completes its assignment statement and then Process 1 executes its assignment statement. However, if one of the processes is interrupted in the middle of the sequence of machine instructions, the result will not be 0. For example, suppose Process 1 executes the first two machine instructions, at which point the arithmetic register would contain 1. Suppose Process 1 is interrupted at that point, say by a context switch or interrupt, and assume that the arithmetic registered is saved. Suppose Process 2 is allowed to execute its assignment statement. Process 2 would first retrieve x from memory. But the memory location still contains 0 because Process 1 has not yet stored the incremented value. When Process 2 decrements and stores, the result is that the arithmetic register and memory location x both contain −1. When Process 1 is allowed to resume, the saved value, 1, is restored to the arithmetic register, and the st instruction will put that value in x. The result is that memory location x has the value 1 instead of 0. If the order of execution of the two processes is reversed — Process 2 executing its first two machine instructions, then Process 1 completing its assignment, then Process 2 resuming — the result would be −1 in memory location x. This is an example of the so-called "race condition." The result is different depending on which process wins the race of getting through the assignment statement first.

The problem is much more general than simple assignment to a shared variable. A process may have a more complicated section of code that is based on the value of the shared variable being fixed for the duration of that block of code. For example, a section of code in the bridge project may compute the expected arrival time of a boat by dividing the distance and by the current speed. If in the middle of that code another module updated the speed to 0, the division operation used to compute the arrival time would produce a machine error. Other kinds of shared resources have similar requirements. For example, a system may have three printers. Requests to print documents can be sent to any of the three that is not currently being used. The system needs to keep track of how many printers are currently being used and which ones they are. A request to print a new document when no printers are available has to be delayed until a printer becomes available; a single printer cannot be printing two jobs at the same time, with pages from the separate jobs being interspersed. The current assignment of jobs to printers must remain fixed until a job finishes, and at that point, only the information about the released printer can change. When a print job is done, the system can check if any print requests are being held. The process of checking for an available printer and assigning it to a new print request must not be interrupted by another print request. There are many similar examples in computing, embedded systems, and in general.[4] Examples include a fixed number of assembly lines in a factory, a single wireless transmitter serving multiple threads, etc.

The key to obtaining correct behavior is to ensure that modifying/manipulating values of shared resources are atomic operations, that is, once the statement is started it cannot be interrupted. Under this interpretation, there is one and only one result for the situation described in the first paragraph of this section. No matter what order the processes execute the two assignment statements, the result will always be 0 after both have been completed because the kind of interruption described in that paragraph is not allowed. Once one of the processes starts its assignment statement, the other process cannot interrupt until the first process finishes the assignment. Similarly for the printer example: the assignment of a printer to a new job and the release of a printer when its current job is done would be atomic operations. If two processes request a printer at about the same time, one process will complete its request before the other can start its request. The time during which a process must have exclusive access to a resource is called a "critical section."

18.3 Semaphores

The semaphore provides a solution to the problem illustrated in Section 18.2. Processes that need to use the resource have a very simple interface based on two semaphore functions — request the resource (the P function) and return the resource to the system (the V function). A semaphore allows processes to request exclusive access to a shared resource so that the execution of a critical section can proceed without the resource being altered by other processes in the system. It provides controlled access when there are multiple copies of the resource. Finally, it provides a mechanism for queuing processes that are waiting for a resource and wakes up waiting processes ready for resumption when a resource is available again. The concept of a semaphore in programming systems was first introduced in 1962.[3] Many forms of semaphores have been introduced over the years. We present one form as an example to illustrate the basic idea.

Each shared resource R has its own semaphore, typically denoted by S(R) or just S when the R is obvious. In the general case, S may control access to several copies of a shared resource, such as memory segments or communication channels. S contains a count n of how many resources are available to be used, which is initialized at system startup to the number of resources being controlled by S. S contains a list of processes that are blocked because they requested a copy of the resource but none was available. Initially, that list is empty. Finally, S has two functions, P and V, which are used by processes to request the resource and to release it when finished with it. (The names P and V come from the Dutch words used in Dijkstra's original paper on semaphores.) Figure 18.1 shows a generic data structure for a semaphore. Figure 18.2 shows the code for functions P and V.

Two requirements are necessary for the semaphore method to work. The first is that the decrement/increment and following test in the two semaphore functions, P and V, must not be interrupted. There can be no other modification to n between the time S.P decrements it and the time S.P tests it for being negative. Suppose, for example, a process *pr* called S.P when n was 1 and another process *pr'* called S.P after *pr* had decremented n to 0 but before it could test n for being less than 0. Process *pr'* would decrement n to −1. When process *pr* continued, the test for n less than 0 would be true and *pr* would be blocked when, in fact, it should have been granted the resource. Similar remarks hold for S.V. (Note how a computing system ensures that a section of code is atomic is beyond the scope of this text. Our purpose here is to explain how semaphores are used to ensure safe access to shared resources.) The second requirement is that the system maintains three lists for the processes and threads in that system — the list of currently running processes, the list of processes that are ready for running, and the list of processes that are blocked (i.e., cannot execute at the moment). The system blocked list would contain all the processes waiting for all the resources (i.e., the union of the waiting lists for the shared resources in the system) as well as other processes blocked for other reasons.

A process *pr* enters a critical section for a resource R controlled by semaphore S by calling S.P(). Just before leaving the critical section, *pr* calls S.V() to indicate that the resource is available again. In some cases, after gaining permission to use the resource from the semaphore, *pr* must call the system to actually be connected to the resource (or a copy of it if there are multiple copies). For example, if the system has multiple communication channels and pr has been allowed to use one by the semaphore, it may have to actually get access to an individual communication channel from the system. In such cases, *pr* must acquire the resource from the system at

```
class semaphore S {
     integer:       n      ; Number of resources currently available
     process_list:  L      ; List of processes waiting to use this resource

                    P();   ; Function to process requests for this resource
                    S();   ; Function to release an instance of this resource
}
```

FIGURE 18.1 Structure of a Semaphore S.

Author drawn.

```
S.P() {                              S.V() {
    n--                                  n++
    if(n<0) {                            if(n<=0) {
        Add the calling process to L;        Remove a process pr from L;
        Block();                             Wakeup(pr);
    }                                    }
}                                    }
```

FIGURE 18.2 Code for P and V.

Author drawn.

the beginning of the critical section and give it back to the system at the end. Note the semaphore does not assign resources to processes, only grants permission to use it. This allows the semaphore functions P and V to be very simple and fast. Figure 18.3 illustrates the general sequence of code for a process requesting use of a resource.

We now describe how a semaphore S controls permission to use the resource. To simplify the presentation, assume there is only one copy of the resource. At system startup, S.n is initialized to 1. Let *pr* be the first process to reach a critical section for this semaphore. S.n is still 1. When *pr* calls S.P(), S.n is decremented to 0. The test fails, and S.P() exits, returning to *pr*. The process performs its operations. At the end of its critical section, it calls S.V(). Suppose no other process has requested this resource, so that S.n is still 0. S.V() increments S.n, which is now 1 again. The test fails, and S.V() simply returns.

Now suppose that another process, *pr'*, calls S.P() while *pr* s is still in its critical section. S.n is decremented and becomes −1. This time the test is true, and P blocks *pr'*. Process *pr'* is suspended after the block statement in S.P(). Later, when *pr* calls

```
// Prepare to enter critical section
S.P();                     // Get permission to use
Acquire resource;          // Get connected to the resource


    ...   perform operations


Give resource back to system;  // Release resource back to system
S.V();                         //Give back permission
// Exit critical section
```

FIGURE 18.3 Code Sequence for a Process Entering a Critical Section.

Author drawn.

S.V(), S.n goes back to 0. The test is true. S.V() removes pr' from S.L and asks the system to wake it up. The system puts pr' on the list of processes ready to execute. At some later point, pr' continues execution from where it left off, namely after the block statement in S.P(). S.P() returns to pr', and pr' continues into its critical section.

Some operating systems provide semaphores. However, many embedded systems do not use off-the-shelf operating systems. In such cases where there are also shared resources, the system developers obviously have to implement appropriate semaphores. Care must be taken, then, to ensure that the P and V functions are atomic, that is, execute to completion once started. This may be accomplished by, for example, disabling interrupts that can cause context switches, for example, timer interrupts that switch context at certain time intervals.

Critical sections of code should be made as short as possible because other processes may be blocked waiting for the resource being held.

18.4 Issues with priority — priority inversion

Priorities among the processes and tasks running on a single processing element are common in embedded system. Furthermore, it is the norm for tasks with higher priority to interrupt, or preempt, running tasks with lower priority. In the bridge system, for example, it is important for the bridge to respond quickly to the arrival of a boat, and so the process that responds to signals from the boat sensors should have high priority. The process that updates the operator's display screen must also complete its task quickly. But the execution time for display update may be much longer than the deadline requirement for responding to the recognition of a new boat — perhaps 1 second for updating the screen vs. a small fraction of a second for reacting to a new boat arrival. If a boat arrives while the screen update process is in the middle of updating the screen, the low-priority update process should be interrupted to allow the high-priority boat arrival process to execute. The boat arrival process cannot wait for the update process to finish, or it may fail to meet its timing requirement. There may be many levels of priority in an embedded system. For example, in the bridge system, a third process might be used for responding to wireless messages from outside the bridge system, for example, from a central control office for the whole river or the weather service. This process may have a priority in between the priorities for the screen update and the boat response processes. The bridge system designers may decide it is more important to look at incoming wireless messages than to update the screen but less important than responding to an arriving boat. One of the aspects of system modeling and design is to determine the relative priorities of the various tasks and processes running on each processing element.

When the processes using shared resources have priorities, it is possible that processes with low priority can block processes with higher priority. When priorities exist and preemption is used, a higher-priority process will normally preempt a currently executing process with a lower priority. In the example in the preceding paragraph, if a boat arrives in the middle of updating the operator's display, the update process will be interrupted so that the urgent process may execute. However, suppose a lower-priority process, say *pr1*, is in the middle of a critical section for resource S, and the higher-priority process, *pr2*, requests that resource. *pr2* will preempt *pr1*, but when *pr2* reaches the point where it requests the resource the semaphore will block it until the lower-priority process releases that resource. This is called priority inversion — a process with low priority executes while a process with high priority waits. Figure 18.4 illustrates this situation using the example from the bridge project described in the preceding paragraph. Time is shown on the horizontal axis. Critical sections are shown as empty rectangles, and non-critical sections are shown as shaded rectangles. The time at which a process becomes active (i.e., is ready to execute) is indicated by an up arrow. The times at which a process requests or releases a resource S is indicated by S.P() and S.V(). Processes with higher normal priority are drawn above processes with lower normal priority. At time t0 the update process begins executing. At time t1 it requests and is granted a shared resource. At time t2 a boat arrives, causing the update process to be interrupted and the boat response process to begin executing. At time t3 the boat response process requests the resource that the update process already has. The boat response process will be blocked, and the update process allowed to resume. At time t4 the update process releases the resource, and the semaphore will transfer the resource to the boat response process, thereby allowing it to resume execution. At time t5 the boat response process releases the resource but continues to execute. At time t6 the boat response process completes, at which point the update process can resume and eventually finish at time t7. The period from t3 to t4 is the period of priority inversion; during this time, the higher-priority process is blocked by a lower-priority process. At times before t3 and after t4, the normal priority scheme is operational. In those times, when a higher-priority process is present, it is the one that executes.

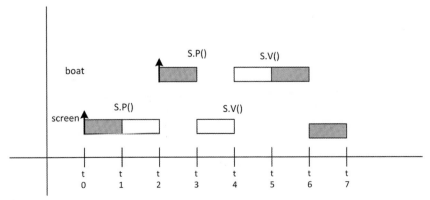

FIGURE 18.4 A Low-Priority Process Blocks a High-Priority Process.

Author drawn.

The situation can be more complicated when there are more processes and/or more shared resources. Figure 18.5 shows a situation with four processes all requiring a single resource controlled by S. Note that *pr*1 at some point is blocking all n higher-priority processes. Figure 18.6 shows a situation with three processes and two resources.

Depending on the nature of the resource and the critical sections of the processes involved, the duration of the priority inversion may be relatively short or relatively long. If, for example, the resource is a simple shared variable and the critical section of the low-priority process is a short computation, the priority inversion would only last a short time. If, however, the resource itself or the critical section using it could require a relatively long period, the delay could be long and could cause a higher-priority process to miss its deadline. For example, if the resource were a dedicated serial communication channel, it could take a relatively long period of time to complete the serial transmission of a relatively long message. A high-priority process requesting the channel would have to wait until the low-priority process using the channel completed sending the message. Although the resources used by each process are known during the design phase, it is difficult or impossible to predict what kinds of delays there might be due to priority inversion. First, the start times and request times for the processes are often random with respect to each other. For example, the operator's screen may be updated at regular intervals, but the arrival of boats is random. Second, when there are more levels of priority, the analysis becomes complex. Sometimes carefully designed simulations can help uncover potential problems. Finally, the critical sections themselves should be made as short as possible.

Preserving the integrity of the shared resource is more important than respecting the relative priorities of the processes. As noted in Section 18.2, interleaving usage

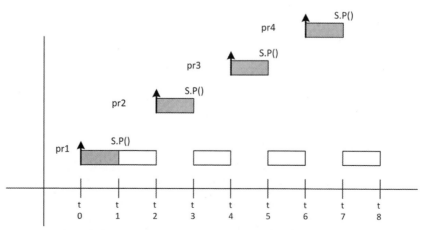

FIGURE 18.5 Multiple Processes Requesting a Single Resource.

Author drawn.

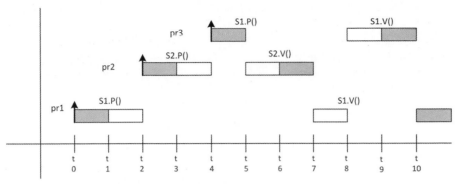

FIGURE 18.6 Three Processes Using Two Resources.

Author drawn.

of a shared resource can lead to the resource having the wrong value or in general to being in an invalid state. This, in turn, would lead to the entire embedded system being unreliable. Preventing this means that priority inversion is unavoidable. However, there are techniques that can help minimize the effects of priority inversion. The most commonly used one is priority inheritance. The priority inheritance method has the following modifications to the semaphore scheme.

1. If a process *pr3* requests a resource S and S is already granted to process *pr2*, if *pr2* has lower priority than *pr3*, then *pr2*'s priority is increased to the level of *pr3*. If *pr2* is itself blocked by another process *pr1* because of a second shared resource, *pr1* also inherits the priority of *pr3*. This transitive increase of priorities continues until a process is reached that is not blocked.

2. After a process *pr* calls S.V(), the system reduces its priority to the lowest level of any process blocked by *pr*. If no process is blocked by *pr*, its priority returns to its original level.

3. When S(V) notifies the system that a process is ready to execute again and after priorities are adjusted as in item 2, the highest-priority process is resumed.

In item 1, of course, *pr3* will still be blocked. However, *pr2* may have been preempted by a process *pr′* with priority between that of *pr3* and *pr2*. That is, there are processes *pr3*, *pr′*, and *pr2* with priorities in the order *pr3* highest, *pr′* next, and *pr2* lowest, as shown in Figure 18.7. *pr′* would have preempted *pr2* because it has higher priority than *pr2*. However, after *pr3*'s request for S is blocked, *pr2*'s priority is increased to that of *pr3*, which means *pr2* temporarily has priority higher than *pr′*. Thus, *pr2* will now preempt *pr′*. This reduces the delay time that *pr3* has to wait for S. *pr2* can finish its critical section earlier rather than waiting for *pr′* (whose priority is temporarily lower than that of *pr2*) to finish.

Priority inheritance changes the priorities of processes. Not all operating systems allow this, so if priority inheritance is to be used in some processing element of an

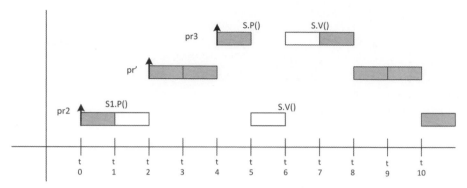

FIGURE 18.7 Two Processes Using the Same Resource and Priority Inheritance.

Author drawn.

embedded system that processing element has to either use an OS that allows priority changes or no OS at all.

It is also possible to have blocking by more than one shared resource, as illustrated in Figure 18.8. For example, *pr*1 may be using resource S1, a second high-priority process *pr*2 using resource S2, and the highest-priority process requests S1. In this case *pr*1 inherits the highest priority through the transitivity described in item 1. At time t5, the priority of *pr*1 changes to the highest level, the priority of *pr*3 because *pr*3 is blocked by *pr*1. Process *pr*2 is now blocked because its priority is less than the priority of *pr*1. At time t6, *pr*1 releases resource S1, and S1.V() returns its priority to its original value, the lowest of the three priorities in the figure. At this point, *pr*3 is marked ready for execution. It continues through its critical section, releases S1, and still continues to completion because it has the highest priority. At time t8, *pr*2 is allowed to continue. It finishes its critical section at t9 and finishes execution at t10. Finally, *pr*1 is allowed to continue its execution at t10.

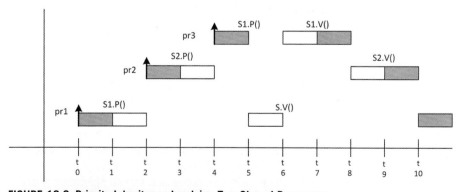

FIGURE 18.8 Priority Inheritance Involving Two Shared Resources.

Author drawn.

If pr's priority had been temporarily increased due to priority inversion, then it needs to be adjusted when it releases the resource. Its priority can be set back to the original level if no other processes are blocked by pr; otherwise, its priority is set to the highest priority of any process still blocked by pr.

Figure 18.9 shows three processes requesting the same resource but using priority inheritance. At time 3 $pr1$'s priority is temporarily increased to the level of $pr2$, and it resumes execution, still in its critical section. At time 5, $pr1$'s priority is again boosted, this time to the level of $pr3$. Again, $pr1$ resumes execution, still in its critical section. At time 6, $pr1$ completes its critical section. At this point its priority is lowered to its original value because it no longer blocks either $pr2$ or $pr3$. $pr3$ resume because it is the highest-priority process and is no longer blocked. So, priority inheritance was effective in this case in allowing the highest-priority job to continue as soon as possible. When $pr3$ finishes, $pr2$ can continue into its critical section and then into its noncritical section until it is finished. Finally, $pr1$ can resume, now in its noncritical section. We have assumed in this example that no other higher-priority processes were attempting to execute during the time period shown in the figure. If there had been other processes, the times might have been different. See Problem 8.

Priority inheritance does not solve all the problems associated with prioritized tasks in a shared-resource environment. For example, Figure 18.10 shows a situation that leads to deadlock, a situation in which none of the processes can proceed. At time t1 the screen process requests S1 and is granted access and continues to execute. At time t2 the boat process preempts the screen process. At time t3, the boat process requests a different resource, S2. It continues to execute in the critical section of S2 until it requests resource S1. At this point it is blocked because the screen process currently owns S1. The screen process is allowed to continue its execution, still in its critical section for S1. At time t5, still in the critical section for S1, the screen process requests S2. At this point neither process can continue. The boat process is blocked by the screen process because of S1, and the screen process is blocked by the boat process because of S2. Priority inheritance may be less effective when many tasks have the same priority, a situation that also leads more

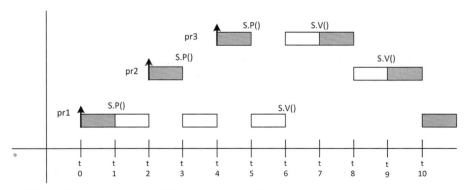

FIGURE 18.9 Three Processes Using Priority Inheritance.

Author drawn.

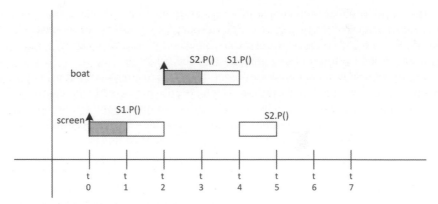

FIGURE 18.10 An Example of Deadlock.

Author drawn.

readily to deadlock. However, in many cases it is an effective solution to the problem of priority inversion.

There are other approaches to the priority inversion problem. For example, when the set of all processes and their priorities is known at system design time, a method called immediate priority ceiling can be used. In this method, each semaphore S increases the highest-priority level of any process that uses S. When S.P() is called by a process *pr* and *pr* is blocked, the process that currently holds the resource has its priority increased to the ceiling value, which may be higher than the priority of *pr*. This allows the process holding the resource to not be interrupted by other processes that request S and have higher priority. This allows fewer context switches because processes with priority between that of *pr* and the ceiling are prevented from interrupting *pr*. On the other hand, the fact that a process *pr′* might use S does not mean that every invocation of *pr′* will request S. So, immediate priority ceiling will block some executions of a process like *pr′* that actually do not need S because of the current situation in the system. There are other versions of the priority ceiling method and other approaches in general to the priority inversion problem. Each has its advantages and disadvantages. Our goal is not to present a complete study and comparison of these methods, only to make the student aware of the problem and to prepare the student to analyze a design and compare its needs with the various solution methods to select the best one.

18.5 **Summary**

Embedded systems often have shared resources such as the main processing element and its memory, which is shared among multiple tasks, and communication channels, which are shared among tasks that communicate with other nodes in a distributed system. Access to these shared resources must be carefully controlled. This chapter presents the main technique for controlling shared access — the semaphore. The chapter defines the major software concept, the critical section of a software module, and then describes the semaphore and presents the semaphore algorithms for locking a shared resource and releasing it. Systems with preemptive scheduling of tasks can suffer from an issue called priority inversion. This chapter defines priority inversion and presents a technique for overcoming it in most cases. The chapter describes situations in which priority inheritance does not work and may lead to deadlock — two tasks waiting on each other for a single resource.

Problems

1. Explain why critical sections should have as short execution times as possible.
2. The following pseudo-code represents an algorithm due to Peterson[4] for ensuring mutual exclusion of two processes from entering their critical sections. The variables p1using, p2using, and turn are global variables. The lines marked cs represent the critical sections.

```
p1using = 0;
p2using = 0;
turn ;
P1:                                     P2:
p1using = 1 ;                           p2using = 1;
turn = 1;                               turn = 2;
while( ( p2using == 1 ) && ( turn == 1 )) ;   while( ( p1using == 1 ) && (turn == 2 )) ;
cs;                                     cs;
p1using = 0 ;                           p2using = 0;
additional code;                        additional code;
```

   a) Assume the executions of P1 and P2 are interleaved line-by-line. That is, the first line of P1 is executed, then the first line of P2 is executed, then the second line of P1 is executed, etc. One execution of the while test represents one execution of that line. Thus, after P1 executes the while test one time, execution of the next line of P2 follows. Trace the execution of these two processes until they both reach their additional code.
   b) Suppose the interleaving is every two lines. That is, P1 executes the first two lines, then P2 executes its first two lines, etc. Trace the execution again until each process reaches its additional code.
   c) Suppose P1 is allowed to execute until blocked at the while statement. What happens?
   d) Suppose P2 is allowed to execute first until it is blocked at its while statement. What happens?
   e) Prove that P1 and P2 cannot both be in their critical sections at the same time. You may assume that each line is atomic; that is, each line of code completes once it is started.

   f) What is the difficulty in extending this method to more than two processes?
3. Recall the functions P and V from Figure 18.2, with class variables n and L. Consider a semaphore S governing a resource R with only one instance of the resource. Trace the schedule described in Figure 18.9. Assume S.n is 1 and S.L is empty at time t0. At each time when a call to P or V is made, trace the execution of that function and show how the values S.n and S.L change.
4. Repeat Problem 3 under the assumption that there are two instances of resource R. Assume S.n is 2 and S.L is empty at time t0.
5. Repeat Problem 3 using the schedule shown in Figure 18.6. Assume that each semaphore governs a resource with a single instance and that none of those resources is currently in use at time t0.
6. Suppose there are three tasks — T1, T2, T3 — with priorities P1, P2, P3. Suppose P1 > P2 > P3; that is, T1 has the highest priority, and T3 has the lowest priority. Each job for task T1 processes for one time unit, then enters a critical section using resource S1 for two time units, and then releases resource S1 and requires one more unit of processing to complete. Each job for task T2 follows the same pattern except that it uses resource S2 instead of S1; that is, T2 works for one unit of time, then enters a critical section for S2 for two time units, then releases S2 and works for one more time unit. The pattern for T3 is the same as for T1, with T3 also using resource S1 for two time units.
   a) Complete the timeline shown below under the assumption of *no* priority inheritance until all three tasks have finished. Job arrival times are indicated by up-arrows. Resource requests are indicated by P(Si). Use rectangles filled with gray to indicate noncritical section processing and rectangles filled with white to indicate critical section processing.

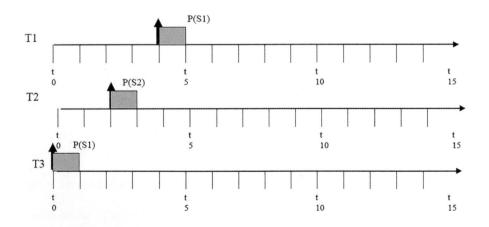

   b) Now complete the timeline assuming priority inheritance.

7. Consider three tasks with the following execution information. S1 and S2 are two separate resources. (NOTE: A process can be using both S1 and S2 at the same time.)

Name	Priority	Start time	Time at which S1 is requested	S1 critical section length	Time at which S2 is requested	S2 critical section length	Total execution time
T1	3 (H)	5			2 units after start	2	5
T2	2 (M)	2	after 1 unit of execution of S2 critical section	1	1 unit after start	4 (includes the execution time for S1)	6
T3	1 (L)	0	1 unit after start	3			5

a) Draw the schedule for these tasks assuming priority inheritance. Mark each call to a P or V function. Indicate noncritical sections with shaded rectangles and critical sections with empty rectangles.

b) Based on your schedule, answer the following questions.
   a. Does the priority of T1 change? If so, at what time points and what are the new values?
   b. Answer the question in part a. but with T2.
   c. Answer the question in part a. but with T3.

8. Suppose in the example in Figure 18.9 there had been a fourth process, say *pr4*, with priority between that of *pr2* and *pr3* (i.e., *pr4* has the second highest priority of the four). Suppose *pr4* started at time t3. Draw the new schedule assuming priority inheritance.

References

[1] https://en.wikipedia.org/wiki/Semaphore_(programming).

[2] A. Silberschatz, P. Galvin, G. Gagne, Operating System Concepts, sixth ed., John Wiley and Sons, Inc., 2003, ISBN 0-471-25060-0.

[3] E. Dijkstra, Over de sequentialiteit van procesbeschrijvingen (EWD-35), E. W. Dijkstra Archive, Center for American History, University of Texas at Austin (undated), 1962 or 1963.

[4] G.L. Peterson, Myths about the mutual exclusion problem, Inf. Process. Lett. 12 (3) (1981) 115—116.

Optimization and other special considerations

19.1 Introduction

Embedded system software often employs techniques that would not be considered in general software intended to run on PCs, laptops, and workstations. First, it is often necessary to optimize code and memory usage. The available memory on small systems is typically quite limited. Systems with tight real-time requirements must have code that runs fast. Battery-operated systems must be optimized for energy usage. There are many more reasons that may be applicable to individual systems. Second, processing elements used in embedded systems generally have a different set of capabilities than processing elements used in laptops and desktops. For example, many ARM processors have built-in features like various serial communication circuits, PWM, quadrature, and others. On the other hand, most smaller processing elements do not have floating-point arithmetic. Thus, embedded system software developers often have to use techniques that would not be considered when writing general software in a high-level language such as C++ or JAVA.

On a related note, many of the common optimizations used in embedded systems violate general principles of design. For example, in general software engineering it is advisable to avoid global variables. However, global variables are a major means of communication between states in hierarchical FSMs. Moreover, global variables provide a fast way to communicate between functions and threads, possibly allowing a system to better meet its real-time constraints. Software engineers strive in general to make their software simple and transparent, but embedded system software often needs to be more complicated to meet restrictions on the system (like limited memory) or lack of processing power and capability (like the absence of floating-point arithmetic).

In this chapter, we present two of the more common techniques used in embedded system software to get around issues like those mentioned in the preceding two paragraphs.

19.2 Fixed point arithmetic

As noted, most processing elements used in embedded systems do not support floating-point arithmetic. Even if they do, the execution times will generally be

Embedded System Design. https://doi.org/10.1016/B978-0-443-18470-3.00019-1

two to several times greater than for corresponding fixed-point operations. In some applications, only very modest fractional arithmetic is needed; an example is the case of a device dealing with dollar-and-cents monetary units. In other applications, full fractional arithmetic is needed. We illustrate in this section some techniques for dealing with fractional quantities through fixed-point arithmetic. Some of the algorithms described here are more complex than simply declaring float or double variables and using the floating-point arithmetic of typical laptop/desktop computers, and using fixed-point methods requires more thought at design time. That's the tradeoff in designing an embedded system, where cost of the hardware, energy consumption, memory usage, physical size of the circuit, etc. have to be weighed against the extra work for the software team.

The parameters of interest in our discussions are the total number, N, of digits in the number and the number, F, of fraction digits. In our discussions we do not include the sign in N. We use the notation (N,F) to indicate that a fixed-point number has N total digits and F fraction digits. For example, if the number of digits was set at four, the number 95.37 would be of form (4,2). Leading zeroes must be represented explicitly. For example, the number 7.36 in (4,2) format must be written as 0736. A large number that could not fit in the given number of digits can be approximated by a form with negative F value. For example, the decimal number 289963 could be approximated by 2899 with format (4,−2). Of course, all the numbers of the form 2899xy have the same four-digit representation, so that representation is only an approximation.

In typical binary computer arithmetic, the number of bits (i.e., binary digits) is the same in all numbers or at least one of a limited set of numbers like 16 and 32. In our discussion we will assume that all values have the same number of digits, that is, the N is the same for all values. We show most of the examples in decimal form to make the concepts and techniques more understandable. The rules are the same for binary numbers and arithmetic performed inside a computer. For example, when adding two 32-bit binary numbers of the form, say, (32,8), the sum will be a 32-bit integer of the form (32,8). If two 32-bit numbers are multiplied and they each have 24 fraction bits (i.e., are of the form (32,24)), the product will have 64 bits of which 48 will be fraction; the top 32-bit word will have 16 integer bits and 16 fraction bits. The rules and algorithms described in the following sections in decimal format carry over directly.

19.2.1 Addition, subtraction, and scalar-multiplication

In some applications, the need for fractional quantities is very simple. Consider a grocery store, in which the prices are given in terms of dollars and cents. The operations are to add dollar/cents amounts (adding up purchased items), subtract monetary amounts (a customer decides not to purchase an item, so the clerk has to subtract the price from the current total), and scalar multiplication (the customer purchases N of the same item). In a simple case like this, the quantities with fraction parts can be represented by a fixed number of digits with the understanding that there is always a decimal point between the second and third digits from the right. While we as humans may write the decimal point explicitly when doing such simple arithmetic by hand, in fact the "point" plays no role in the arithmetic itself, only in the interpretation of the result. Here are some examples written both with the decimal point as humans would write the numbers and in the form of (4,2) numbers without an explicit point as might be done in a computer. Note that in the latter form the leading zeros are written explicitly.

- Adding two prices with and without decimal point shown:

$$
\begin{array}{cc}
14.98 & 1498 \\
+7.25 & +0725 \\
\hline
22.23 & 2223 \\
\end{array}
$$

- Subtracting one price from total cost with and without decimal point shown.

$$
\begin{array}{cc}
8.95 & 0895 \\
-6.45 & -0645 \\
\hline
2.50 & 0250 \\
\end{array}
$$

- Multiplying a dollar/cents amount by a scalar with and without decimal point shown.

$$
\begin{array}{cc}
15.99 & 1599 \\
*\,5 & *\,0005 \\
\hline
79.95 & 7995 \\
\end{array}
$$

Note that arithmetic may result in overflow and underflow, just as in ordinary computer integer arithmetic. For example, with only four digits, adding 99.99 and 99.99 (i.e., 9999 and 9999) produces a result that cannot be represented in four digits. The same care as exercised in ordinary computer integer arithmetic must be applied when using integer arithmetic for fixed point values. Similarly, scalar multiplication can produce results too large to fit in the allotted space. The design team needs to analyze the range of values expected and ensure that (binary) integers will be large enough. For example, in the grocery store example 32-bit integers would surely be adequate. A 32-bit unsigned word can hold integers up to more than $4*10^9$. In the case of the grocery store, this represents amounts more than 40 million dollars. On the other hand, 16-bit words may or may not be enough. A 16-bit unsigned computer word can hold integer values up to 65,535 or dollar amounts up to \$655.35; a consumer shopping monthly and buying expensive items could conceivably have a bill more than \$656.

Finally, in applications in which the point is not always in the same relative position in the numbers, shifting will be required for addition and subtraction. Consider again decimal numbers with four digits. When adding the two numbers 90.56 and 3.752, the number 3.752 is shifted right to align the decimal points. The value 90.56 cannot be shifted left in this example because the 9 would be lost. Some accuracy in the fraction part is lost when shifting 3.752 right, but this is preferable to losing the most significant digit. In general, when adding two numbers of the form (N,F1) and (N,F2), the number with the larger fraction part is shifted right by $k = max(F1,F2) - min(F1,F2)$ positions, and the k least significant digits are lost. In the example in this paragraph, the formats are (4,2) and (4,3). The number 3.752 has the larger fraction part, so it is shifted right by $(max(2,3) - min(2,3)) = (3 - 2) = 1$ position. After shifting it will be 0375, or 3.75.

19.2.2 Multiplication with fractional parts in both numbers

Of course, there are many applications in which it is necessary to multiply and divide numbers both of which have fractional parts. Recall two basic facts from ordinary arithmetic. First, when multiplying a number with N1 digits by a number with N2 digits, the result can contain up to N1+N2 digits; if we are sure to include leading zeros, the product will be exactly N1+N2 digits and may also contain leading zeros. If the numbers of fraction digits in the two values are F1 and F2, the number of fraction digits in the product will be F1+F2. Thus, the product will have the form (N1+N2, F1+F2). If we are using computer binary words, $N1 = N2 = N$ is the word size, usually 16 or 32 bits. Then the product has the form (2*N, F1+F2).

Consider an extension to the grocery store application — computing the tax on the total bill. This requires multiplication by a fixed-point number with fraction part. We continue to use four decimal digits to represent a number. Monetary units still have two fraction digits and two integer digits. Tax rates are typically in the range of a few percent to 10 or 15%. We can therefore use four digits with the understanding that all four digits are fractions, that is, the decimal point is to the left of the first digit. The rate 11.3% (.1130) would be represented by 1130, and the rate 8.45% (.0845) would be represented by 0845. Note the use of both leading and trailing zeroes to make exactly four digits. Multiplying a monetary unit by a tax value produces a product of the form (8,6). The top four digits contain two integer digits and two fraction digits; that is, it is of the form (4,2), which is exactly the form for monetary units. This can be added to the grocery total without shifting. We illustrate with an example.

Example 19.1

Suppose the total dollar/cents amount for the groceries is $78.42 and the tax rate is 8.45%.

$$\begin{array}{cc} \$78.42 & 7842 \\ * .0845 & * 0845 \end{array}$$

$6.62649 \rightarrow \$6.63$ rounded $06626490 \rightarrow 0662 \rightarrow 0663$ after rounding

In some cases, the product has to be shifted before the result can be used in further computations. Suppose the grocery store marks up the price of its products by a factor of 2.667 over the cost the grocer pays to the distributor. The mark up can be represented as a four-digit number of type (4,3). When multiplied by a monetary value, that is, a number of type (4,2), the result is a value of type (8,5). The 8-digit product could be shifted left one digit, after which the top four digits would again have the type (4,2) and represent a monetary value as shown in Example 19.2.

Example 19.2

Suppose an item cost \$3.75, and the mark-up factor was 2.667.

\$3.75	0375
* 2.667	* 2667
\$10.00	01000125 → 10001250 → 1000

Overflow is possible with multiplication. For example, multiplying 9999 of type (4,1) by itself produces the 8-digit result 99980001 of type (8,2). The integer part of the product cannot fit into four digits. Note the top four digits, 9999, of type $(4,-2)$ could be used as an approximation to the product. Whether this was reasonable or not would depend on the application.

In applications where there is flexibility in the number of fraction digits allowed for variables, additional accuracy can be obtained by shifting resulting values to remove leading zeros and adjusting the F part accordingly. In Example 19.1, the 8-digit product could be shifted left one digit to produce 66264900 of the form (8,7). Now the top four digits represent 6.626, which is closer to the true product than 6.63. Of course, this requires additional computation at run time as well as holding F for each variable in addition to that variable's value. Thus, again there is a tradeoff, this time between run-time speed and accuracy, and the design team would need to study this tradeoff.

19.2.3 Division

Computer integer division produces a quotient with N digits and a remainder with N digits. Remember that in the notation being discussed here, both the dividend and divisor are integers. The location of the point is for human interpretation. Suppose the dividend has the form (N,F1) and the divisor has the form (N,F2). The number of fraction digits in the quotient is F1−F2. We illustrate with several examples.

Example 19.3

57.31/2.5. The fixed-point representation uses 5731 for the dividend and 0025 for the divisor. Dividing 25 into 5731 produces a quotient 229 (i.e., 0229) and remainder 6. There is one digit in the fraction part. (In this case, F1 is 2 and F2 is 1.) Therefore, we interpret the quotient, 0229, as 22.9.

Example 19.4

If the divisor in Example 19.3 were 25 instead of 2.5, the representation of the dividend and divisor would still be 5731 and 0025, respectively. The quotient is again 0229. This time there are two fraction digits because F2 is zero. So, our interpretation of the result is 2.29.

Example 19.5

Consider the difference in our representation between dividing 57.31 by 2 and dividing it by 2.0. In the first case the dividend and divisor are 5731 and 0002, respectively. The quotient in this case is 2865. F1 is two, and F2 is zero. So, in the quotient there are two digits in the fraction part. This means the value is 28.65. In the second case the divisor is 20, and the quotient is 286. There are $F1 - F2 = 2 - 1 = 1$ digits in the fraction part, which makes the value 28.6. This illustrates that trailing fractional zero digits decrease accuracy, just the opposite of multiplication where leading zeros decreased accuracy.

Example 19.6

Consider dividing 12.34 by 3.111. In the fixed-point representation, the dividend would be 1234 and the divisor 3111. The quotient is 0000, and $F1-F2$ is -1. Thus, all four digits of the quotient plus another zero are fraction. This is completely inaccurate.

Examples 19.4—19.6, especially Example 19.6, illustrate a serious deficiency with this approach to division — the smaller the dividend relative to the divisor, the more inaccurate the result. This can be overcome by additional run-time analysis, but that makes the software slower. It can also be overcome by extending the dividend to form (2N, F1+N) by adding trailing zeroes, but again this makes the basic division operation slower. In some cases, the simple method may be acceptable. Examples 19.3—19.5 illustrate that when the divisor is a relatively small integer compared to the dividend, the results are reasonably close to the correct value. A design team would again have to carefully consider the expected values and the required level of accuracy before opting for a simple solution for division.

19.2.4 Expressions involving fixed-point numbers

The rules and methods described in the preceding section can be extended to more complex expressions. In cases where no shifting is done to increase accuracy (i.e., no shifting to remove leading or trailing zeros), the type of the result of each operation will be known and can be used to determine how the software should handle the next operation in the expression. Some cases will not require any shifting. For example, suppose in the grocery store there is no sales tax on basic groceries but liquor tax on alcoholic purchases. The software might contain an expression like

$$groceryTotal + alchoholTotal * alchoholSalesTaxRate$$

Using the same types as before, (4,0) for monetary values and (4,4) for tax rates, we can determine that the product will yield an 8-digit number of the form (8,4). The top four digits are a monetary value, which can be added directly to groceryTotal. On the other hand, other cases may require shifting of values to make the points line up. For example, in the expression

$$A * B + C * D$$

The first product might be of type (N,F1) and the second of type (N,F2). If F1 and F2 are not the same, one of the intermediate values will need to be shifted before the addition as described in Section 19.2.1.

Applications that require maximum accuracy but must run on hardware without built-in floating-point arithmetic will need to have software that includes the type information for all variables and that analyzes the intermediate values obtained during the evaluation of an expression to check for leading or trailing zeros. This obviously makes the software run much slower. The design team would need to make a choice between this option and using a more expensive hardware platform.

19.2.5 Binary vs. decimal

Most computer arithmetic is performed using binary numbers. Decimal numbers that a human might enter into an application have to be converted into binary. In cases where all the numbers have the same number of fraction digits, like the grocery example in Section 19.2.1, all the values can be scaled to be integers, and there is no loss of accuracy. In cases where the fraction parts are not all the same, decimal fractions need to be converted to binary fractions. Binary fractions in general cannot represent decimal fractions exactly with even a finite number of bits much less a small number (i.e., something less than 32). For example, decimal 0.01 is an infinitely repeating binary fraction.

For a given application the design team needs to decide how accurate the decimal fractions need to be, how big the integer parts need to be, and then determine how many bits would be needed to approach that decimal accuracy. (Problem 1 asks the student to do this for a real application.) In a case like the tax rates, where there is no integer part, all the bits can be fraction bits. That is, the binary word can be interpreted as (N,N) where N is the number of bits. In cases where the integer parts can be bounded, the number of bits for the integer part can be determined, and the remaining bits can be used for the fraction part. For example, if the binary word size is 32 bits and the integer parts are never more than 255, the integer part can be represented using the top 8 bits, leaving 24 bits for fraction parts. In such cases, a table like the reader is asked to develop in Problem 2 can help the team determine how closely decimal values can be approximated.

19.3 Optimizations for loop processing

In many cases involving loops, especially nested loops, modest improvements in execution time can be made by careful organization of the loops. This can be especially effective when combined with appropriate memory organization, including the careful use of scratchpad memories. We describe a few of the common techniques.

19.3.1 Simple loop unrolling, splitting, and fusion

A simple technique is called "loop unrolling". In loop unrolling, multiple executions of a loop are combined into single executions of a larger loop, with appropriate adjustments to the loop increment and termination tests. This reduces the number of times the termination test is executed; if the termination test is non-trivial, this could save some execution time if the execution of the loop body is not already much more time consuming. If the number of loop executions is relatively small and fixed, for example always five, the body of the loop can simply be copied five times and the loop testing eliminated altogether. Of course, the tradeoff is increased code size. If memory available for code is already tight, loop unrolling may not be a possibility.

We illustrate with a number of examples.

Example 19.7

Consider a loop that initializes an array of fixed size. If the array size is a multiple of two, the elements can be initialized two at a time with the loop then executing half the number of times.

```
for(j=0; j<10; j++) A[j] = j;          for(j=0; j<10; j+=2) {
                                        A[j] = j;
                                        A[j+1] = j+1;
                                        }
```

This cuts the number of loop-termination tests in half. Also, if the system uses a cache or scratchpad memory, cache/scratchpad misses will likely be reduced because consecutive array elements are more likely to be brought into the local store together. Similar tricks can be played if the limit of the loop is a multiple of 3, multiple of 4, etc.

Example 19.8

When the loop limit is relatively small and fixed and the body of the loop is not too complex, the loop can be eliminated altogether in favor of straight-line code. Consider the problem in Example 19.7 and suppose the loop limit was 5. The following code might be preferred over a loop:

```
A[0] = 0;
A[1] = 1;
A[2] = 2;
A[3] = 3;
A[4] = 4;
```

Many compilers might even be able to optimize this further by computing the array+offset for the subscripted elements in the compiler rather than having ordinary array element address computation at run time. Another method for this would be to use a pointer and eliminate the subscript computation.

Example 19.9

Depending on the computing platform, it may be possible to replace loops that simply serve to fill memory with a particular value with a built-in instruction. For example, some processing elements have a memory-fill instruction. So, a loop that initializes an array to, say, all zero could be replaced by a single machine instruction.

In a similar vein, sometimes several loops can be merged to yield gains in efficiency. However, this has to be considered against other issues, such as cache behavior if the cache is relatively small compared to, say, the size of the arrays involved in the loops. Consider the two pieces of code shown in Example 19.10. In both cases, two arrays are initialized and then a third array is initialized to the sum of the first two. In the code on the left, this is accomplished in three separate loops, while the code on the right uses a single loop. If no cache is involved, the code on the right eliminates the overhead for two loops. It also provides some opportunity for additional optimization. For example, if the arrays were mapped into consecutive blocks of storage, a single pointer might be used to reference all three arrays, reducing the loop increment. On the other hand, if the system did include cache, the code on the right would likely incur more cache misses because each execution of the loop accesses memory from different blocks — three different arrays. The code on the left accesses nearby memory in each loop, thus potentially reducing the number of cache misses.

Example 19.10

```
for(j=0; j<N; j++) A[j] = initial-value-computation;        for(j=0; j<N; j++) {
    for(j=0; j<N; j++) B[j] = initial-value-computation;        A[j] = ... ;
    for(j=0; j<N; j++) C[j] = A[j] + B[j];                      B[j] = ... ;
                                                                C[j] = A[j] + B[j];
                                                            }
```

Loop splitting can offer significant improvement in special cases. One such special case is the need for boundary testing for multi-dimensional arrays. Consider the processing of an $N \times N$ array of pixel information. A common operation is to adjust individual pixels based on some computation involving the eight surrounding pixels. The pattern of a pixel and its surrounding pixels is shown in Figure 19.1.

One source of complexity for handling this situation is that pixels at the edge do not have eight surrounding neighbors, and pixels at the corners have even fewer surrounding pixels than those at other places on the border of the array. This is shown in the picture in Figure 19.2.

$A[i-1,j-1]$	$A[i-1,j]$	$A[i-1,j+1]$
$A[i,j-1]$	$A[i,j]$	$A[i,j+1]$
$A[i+1,j-1]$	$A[i+1,j]$	$A[i+1,j+1]$

FIGURE 19.1 A Pixel and Its Surrounding Pixels.

Author drawn.

FIGURE 19.2 The Special Areas of a Pixel Array.

Author drawn.

Straightforward code might have a simple two-level nested loop but include tests inside the loop to determine which of the nine different areas of the array was being referenced. This is required to prevent subscripts outside the appropriate range. For example, an element in the interior of the array does have eight neighbors, whose subscripts range from [i−1,j−1] to [i+1,j+1]. However, the upper left corner has subscript [0,0]; referencing an element in the row above or the column to the left is illegal. Similar remarks apply to the other shaded areas in Figure 19.2. The tests in the code of Figure 19.3 prevent the access to elements outside the array. The code in Figure 19.4 eliminates the N*N execution of the tests by splitting the nested loop

```
for(j=0; j<N; j++) {
    for(k=0; k<N; k++) {
        if( (j>1) && (j<N-1) && (k>1) && (k<N-1)) {
            // process an interior point
        }
        else if( (j>0) && (j<N-1) && (k==0)) {
            // process the left border
        }
        else if( ... ) {
            // process the right border
        }
        etc.
    }
}
```

FIGURE 19.3 Straightforward Nested Loop Code for Pixel Array.

Author drawn.

```
P[0,0] = ...;                    // Process upper left corner
P[0,N-1] = ... ;                 // Process upper right corner
P[N-1,0] = ... ;                 // Process lower left corner
P[N-1, N-1] = ... ;              // Process lower right corner
for(j=1; j<N-1; j++) {
        // Process left border
   P[j,0] = ... ;
}
etc.
```

FIGURE 19.4 Pixel Processing With Loops Split.

Author drawn.

into separate pieces of code to handle the border/corner areas. In the case of the corners, there is no looping at all; each of the four corners is handled as a special case. For the other parts of the border, the loop is a single level, not nested.

19.3.2 Memory organization for arrays and loop processing

Matrices are typically stored in memory in one of two ways — row order or column order. In row order matrix storage, the C standard, the elements are stored row by row. That is, all the elements of the first row are stored, followed by all the elements of the second row, followed by … . In column order, the FORTRAN standard, the elements of the first column are stored first, followed by the elements of the second, and so on. To the extent possible, the loops for processing matrices should be organized in a way to match the physical storage of the elements. For example, in a C program on a platform with cache memory, a loop like the following

```
for(k=0; k<N; k++)
 for(j=0; j<N; j++)
  process P[j][k] ...
```

would likely cause a high rate of cache misses because each pass through the inner loop would be accessing an element in a different row, that is, potentially in an area far enough away from the element in the previous row to cause a cache miss.

When arrays are stored in slower memory and there is scratchpad memory available, significant savings are often possible by bringing portions of the array into the scratchpad. For example, it may be possible to bring an entire row into scratchpad. If this is not possible, a second method is to bring a sub-matrix, as shown in Figure 19.5, in at a time, compute with that sub-block, and then write back out. For example, pixel adjustment as described in Example 19.10 might be done on sub-matrices. An image of size, say 1K × 1K pixels could not be held in scratchpad

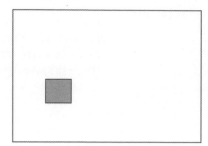

FIGURE 19.5 A Sub-Matrix of a Larger Matrix.

Author drawn.

memory, but submatrices of size, say 32 × 32 could. Copying such a submatrix into scratchpad memory, performing the adjustments in scratchpad memory, and then copying back to main memory would have lower memory access time than computing all pixel adjustments in main memory.

19.4 Summary

Embedded systems are typically real-time systems; therefore, execution speed typically plays a much more crucial role in embedded system software than in other kinds of software. This chapter describes situations in which considerations such as speed, limited memory, and simple instruction sets override some of the more common software engineering principles. The chapter then describes techniques that can improve execution speed — the use of fixed-point arithmetic when floating-point instructions are not available or take too much time and techniques for speeding up loop processing. The section on fixed-point arithmetic describes how the four floating-point arithmetic operations can be implemented using fixed-point arithmetic. Fixed-point instructions are typically much faster than floating-point instructions and are included in the instruction set for virtually every processing element. The section on loop optimization shows several techniques for splitting or combining loops that result in faster execution.

Problems

1. Data entered into and computed on tax forms are of two forms — dollar/cents amounts and fractions less than 1. For example, an annual salary might be $55,257.36, and a standard deduction might be $6,750. Fractions represent percentages, such as 7.5% (.075) for medical deductions or 33% (.33) for a tax rate. Assume all the numbers are positive, that is, the numbers are unsigned. Suppose also that dollar/cents amounts are represented as fixed-point integers

counting cents; that is, an amount like 55,257.36 would be represented by the unsigned integer 5525736.

a) Numbers (both dollar/cents amounts and fractions) could be represented as 16-bit integers or 32-bit integers. Which of these is the right choice and why?

b) The fraction values (the percentages) are all between 0 and 1. Given your choice of number of bits from part a, and assuming that the point is at the left end of the bit string, what is the representation for the following fractions?

.075 (7.5%):

.1 (10%):

.25 (25%):

2. Generate a list of the decimal equivalents of the numbers $1/2^n$ for $n = 1, 2, \ldots, 16$, that is for the binary numbers .1, .01, .001, ... .0000000000000001. Then tell how many bits you would use to represent decimal numbers that had to be accurate to one decimal place, two decimal places, three decimal places, and four decimal places. Explain your choices.

3. Consider the following numbers.

A: 67.15	D: 8517
B: 1.167	E: 7.584
C: .4673	F: 3.142

Assume we are using decimal fixed-point representation with four decimal digits.

a) For each of the variables A−F write the representation of its value and state its type (N,F).

b) Assume shifting is not done to remove leading zeros after multiplication but is done to align points for addition and subtraction. Show the individual steps in evaluating the following expressions. After each step show what is the value and the corresponding type.

    a. $A + B - C$

    b. $A * B * C + D$

    c. $A * B + C * D - E * F$

4. Repeat Problem 3.b but with shifting after multiplication to remove leading zeros.

5. Implement a class for holding numbers of arbitrary size with arbitrary number of integer and fraction bits. The class should contain data members for N (total number of bits), F (number of fraction bits, S (sign), and of course D (the actual number). Implement signed addition, subtraction, multiplication, and division. For addition, subtraction, and multiplication the number of bits in the result can be computed. Division may produce an infinite fraction part; for your class you may truncate the fraction part at some fixed number MAX of bits.

6. Name two advantages and two potential problems of loop unrolling.

7. Consider the following program:

```
int a[100];
for (i=0; i<100; i++)
{
   if ((i%2) == 0)
        a[i] = a[i]*2;
   else
        a[i] = a[i]*3;
}
```

a) Apply loop splitting to this program.

b) Use loop unrolling to eliminate the if-statement.

c) Which modified program gives better performance assuming there is no cache? Explain why.

d) Which modified program gives better performance assuming there is cache? Explain why.

Communications

Distributed embedded systems involve physically separate modules that must connect to form networks. There are many formats for networks, each with its own advantages and disadvantages that the embedded systems engineer must evaluate relative to a system under development. Separate modules send messages back and forth, and the content and format of the messages must be determined so as to satisfy both the requirements of the system (such as time, transmission speed, energy usage of the communications circuit, etc.) as well as human needs (such as being able to easily understand transmitted data streams during testing and debugging). Looking to the future, as embedded systems move into the world of the Internet of Things, messages may need to be understood by systems beyond the one under development, as described in Chapter 24.

In Part 5 we give an overview of networking and communication techniques an embedded systems engineer will need to make good decisions about the design of distributed embedded systems.

Introduction to communications and messages

20.1 Introduction

Networking and communications between modules are important parts of most embedded systems. Only small embedded systems have just a single module and no communication with the outside world beyond simple digital and analog inputs and outputs. A module in an embedded system may be running separate threads corresponding to separate blocks/processes in an Specification and Description Language (SDL) model, and these modules send messages to (i.e., communicate with) each other. A hierarchical embedded system with several physically separate modules might have wired communication channels and use standard serial communication techniques. If the modules are separated by relatively large distances, wireless communication would typically be used. In extreme cases or if the embedded system is participating in the Internet of Things (IoT), modules would communicate through the Internet. Moreover, a given embedded system might use any combination of these communication methods. For example, modern cars use wired serial buses for communication between separate modules inside the car, but they also have communications with the outside world through wireless standards such as Bluetooth.

An important special area within embedded systems and IoT is the wireless sensor network (WSN). These are networks of sensor nodes spread over relatively large (more than a few feet) areas. Examples include agricultural systems, such as irrigation and monitoring of crops, and geographical systems, such as quake detection, and animal monitoring. The individual nodes in a WSN are basic embedded systems, typically quite simple but embedded systems nonetheless. The communication between nodes in the system or between nodes and a sink or gateway is an added feature over and above the normal considerations in designing the individual nodes.

Embedded systems engineers will need to be aware of important concepts in networking and familiar with the various communications protocols in common use. These are presented in this section. This is not meant to be a complete treatment of networking or communications; that would require a course of its own. It is meant to introduce the embedded systems engineer to the most common and important topics that will be needed in designing and implementing embedded systems.

Embedded System Design. https://doi.org/10.1016/B978-0-443-18470-3.00020-8

20.2 **Messages and message passing**

Processes such as those modeled in SDL are concurrent processes that do not use shared memory. Rather, they communicate by sending messages to each other. They may be separate processes implemented on the same computing platform, or they may be processes implemented on physically separate computing platforms. In either case, once the nature of the information that has to be passed between the concurrent processes has been specified in the SDL model, the design team has to determine the precise format of the messages and decide on a number of other issues relating to how the processes coordinate.

20.2.1 **Messages and message formats**

First, designers need to decide on the content and format of the messages themselves. Here we are talking about the payload, that is, the information that one process is going to send to another process, not the extra bytes or bits that are specified by the protocol being used. The information contained in the messages should have been decided in the modeling phases of the design process. In the bridge project, for example, the early models should have determined what kinds of commands and related information the main control module sends to the other modules in the bridge and what kinds of messages those other modules send back to the main module and to each other. At the implementation stage, the designers would decide how to format the messages themselves. The options include some kind of bit/byte encoding format and a human-readable format. We illustrate the difference with sample messages in the bridge system. Suppose that the main control module will send the following kinds of messages to the span control module:

- raise to n degrees ($0 <= n <= 90$) at speed x ($0 < x <= 5$)
- lower to n degrees ($0 <= n <= 90$) at speed x ($0 < x <= 5$)
- stop
- emergency stop
- status — current position, current speed, current motor temperature, complete report, etc.

Suppose n and x are restricted to integer values.

Messages can be encoded in bit/byte streams, which are shorter than the human-readable forms described later in this section. For example, the raise and lower commands could be encoded as 3 bytes — the command (raise or lower), 1 byte specifying n, and 1 byte specifying x. The stop commands could be encoded as separate single-byte messages. The status commands could be encoded as 2 bytes — the command followed by 1 byte specifying which status item is being requested. Table 20.1 shows a possible encoding in this scheme. In the scheme shown in Table 20.1 note that the command itself uses only 2 bits of the first byte. So, for the raise and lower commands the speed parameter, x, could be packed into the upper 6 bits of the

Table 20.1 Sample message encoding scheme.

Command	Byte 1	Byte 2	Byte 3
raise n,x	0000 0000	n	x
lower n,x	0000 0001	n	x
stop	0000 0010		
emergency stop	0000 0011		
status position	0000 0100	0000 0000	
status speed	0000 0100	0000 0001	
status temperature	0000 0100	0000 0011	
status full	0000 0100	0000 0100	

command byte. That reduces those commands to 2 bytes at the expense of (quite minor) bit manipulation in the sender and receiver software.

There are many reasons an encoded format would be the format of choice. First, encoded messages are shorter by an order of magnitude or more than the human-readable form and so require less energy and time to send. This would be an important factor in a system where speed and/or energy are critical. For example, in the collision avoidance system in a car, milliseconds might make the difference between a safe stop and a collision. (A car traveling 60 miles per hour travels 88 feet per second. One-tenth of a second, or 100 milliseconds, means almost 9 feet!). In other applications transmission speed may not be critical. For the bridge, it may not be necessary for the messages to be transmitted in milliseconds or less time; the bridge span couldn't move very far in a few milliseconds anyway. A second reason the messages might be encoded is to preserve proprietary details of the product from unauthorized detection, such as electronic eavesdropping. The client may not want outsiders to be able to glean information about how the product works from the messages being sent between different processes in the system. A third reason is to preserve privacy. Privacy is particularly important in applications that involve personal information, such as health monitoring.

At the other end of the spectrum are human-readable formats for messages. These are typically represented using an XML-based markup language.[1] The messages are represented in plain text form. If the keywords are chosen carefully, the messages can be easily understood by humans. Two examples from the bridge system are shown in Figure 20.1. Obviously, messages in this format are much larger than encoded messages.

One advantage of a human-readable format is that the messages are human readable, which can be helpful during development and debugging. It can also help during normal operation because the messages between the different processes in the system can be displayed directly on the operator's console so that the operator can see what the system is trying to do. A second advantage, and perhaps the most important one, is that marked-up messages have a high degree of

<command cmd="raise">   <command cmd="report"

    <speed "3"/>

                        </command>

</command>

FIGURE 20.1 Bridge Messages in Marked-up Format.

Author drawn.

interoperability. That is, they can be understood, and therefore acted upon, by many different systems, not just the one system for which the messages have been designed. In the bridge project, there may be many entities outside the bridge that need to "listen" to the messages being sent between processes. For example, the boats themselves may have systems that could interact directly with the bridge. The government authority may be interested in logging all the activities of all the bridges on a particular section of the river. The local ground traffic system may be able to adjust traffic lights in nearby locations to divert traffic away from the blocked street when a boat is passing through. Finally, in the spirit of IoT, even more, systems that haven't been designed yet may be deployed in the future, and it may be useful or even necessary for those systems to interact with the bridge. It is unrealistic and counters to the spirit of IoT to expect all these new systems to conform to an encoding designed specifically for one kind of system known at the present time. On the other hand, with standard vocabularies, as is common with XML-based representations, it is easy for all the systems, including ones that have not been developed yet, to communicate with each other as well as to communicate internally between their own modules. A complete treatment of XML is beyond the scope of this text. But XML as a basis for message passing will be a critical technology for the future of embedded systems and the IoT, and we recommend the student become familiar with the concepts and standards.

20.2.2 Message passing

When processes are implemented on the same computing platform, message passing is relatively easy. Each channel is implemented as a queue of bytes. A process may append a set of bytes to a queue, that is, send a message to another process. The receiving process can read a set of bytes from the queue. That is, each queue has a set of producer(s) and a set of consumer(s). In the case of a Kahn model, each channel has a single producer and a single consumer. The queues themselves are shared resources on the given computer platform. If an operating system is being used, that operating system may have built-in operations for creating and managing such shared resources. If the implementers have chosen not to use an off-the-shelf operating system, they have to implement the shared resource directly, typically using semaphores as discussed in Chapter 18. The message content and format can be used to determine how much actual memory to allocate to the buffers.

When the communicating processes are on different computing platforms, one of the communication protocols (see Chapters 22 and 23) must be used to physically transfer the bytes from the sender's platform to the receiver's platform. As already noted, the actual message may be embedded inside larger packets. After the receiver gets the message, the network protocol layer(s) of the receiver side will strip off the corresponding header portion(s) of the message related to each network layer. The actual payload, that is, the message for the application, will then be received by the application to handle in the way that it needs to, for example, processing the message right away or putting it into a queue to process later.

An important decision is whether or not messages sent from one process to another need to be acknowledged by the receiving process and whether or not the sending process needs to wait for such acknowledgment. Messages are called synchronous, or blocking, if the sender is required to wait for a response from the receiver. Messages are called asynchronous, or non-blocking, if the sender does not have to wait. Figure 20.2 illustrates the difference between these two types. Blocking does provide for synchronization of activities, but it also means that some modules may be idle while waiting for a response. Therefore, designers should think carefully whether blocking is really needed or not.

When processes must coordinate, it is common to require the receiver to acknowledge at least the receipt of the message and possibly also that the receiver has taken the appropriate action and finished the request. In some cases, the sender must wait until the receiver has done something. For example, in the bridge system, when there are two spans and they are going down after a boat has passed through, the two spans need to coordinate the last few feet of travel. When one span reaches a certain point, it notifies the other span. The first span must then wait until the second span has reached the coordination point, at which time the second span acknowledges back to the first span that the synchronization point has been reached. At that time both spans may continue to move down slowly until they interlock at the bottom of their travel ranges. This kind of message passing is called synchronous or blocking communication. The sender is blocked from proceeding until an appropriate message is received back from the other process.

When such coordination is not required, the communication is called non-blocking or asynchronous. Continuing the bridge example, when the main control module sends a message to the ground traffic barrier module to lower the gates, the main control module does not need to stop and wait until the ground traffic barrier has completed the task or even acknowledged the message. The main control module can proceed with other tasks and perhaps schedule a status check for an appropriate later time, say 1 or 2 seconds later. In many cases, there is no need for any kind of acknowledgment or even status check. For example, a car

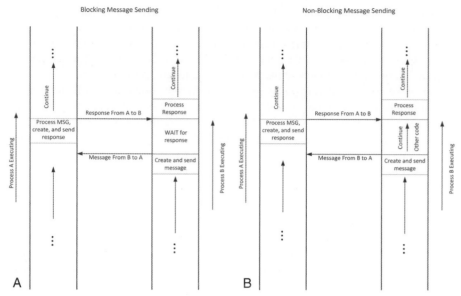

FIGURE 20.2 Illustration of Blocking vs. Non-blocking Message Passing.

Author drawn.

approaching an intersection may send information about itself to the stop-and-go light system. But the driver of the car will see whether or not the lights turn green, so there is no need for any kind of response from the stop-and-go light system back to the car.

Note that the kind of acknowledgment described in this chapter is different than the acknowledgment built into some of the communication protocols. For example, TCP/IP requires acknowledgment from the receiving machine, but this is part of the TCP/IP operation and has nothing to do with the applications (i.e., the embedded system processes) sending and receiving the messages. The TCP/IP acknowledge packet has no payload, and the only information that might be passed to the sending application is that the message successfully reached the target machine. There is no indication that the target application actually did anything with the message.

20.3 **Summary**

This chapter begins with a description of the need for messages and message passing in typical embedded systems. The chapter then illustrates two major message format schemes, bit encoded and human readable, and discusses the tradeoffs between them. Finally, the chapter discusses the issue of blocking vs. non-blocking messages.

Problems

1. For each of the following message types say whether the message should be blocking or non-blocking and explain your choice.

   a) A monitor is worn by a patient at home. The monitor collects bio-data (e.g., pulse, blood oxygen saturation, etc.) every 30 minutes and transmits that information in a message to the doctor's office.

   b) The main control module of the bridge sends messages to the River Authority every time it raises the span to allow boats to pass. The messages contain information such as how many boats, how long the bridge span was up, etc.

   c) The control module for an assembly line in a manufacturing plant sends messages to the Factory Control System requesting information about what type of product is next being assembled on that assembly line.

   d) A student sends a message to the teacher asking a question about the current homework.

2. A monitoring system for patients living at home sends hourly readings of basic bio-information (pulse, percentage blood oxygen, temperature), notifies the doctor's office immediately when one of those goes outside its acceptable range, and notifies the doctor's office immediately if it senses an emergency condition like a fall or heart attack.

   a) List the different types of messages. For each message type tell what attributes or data are associated with that message type. For each type of data tell what the range of values is.

   b) For your answer in part (a). devise a bit-packed format for the messages.

   c) For your answer in part (a). devise an XML scheme for the messages.

   d) For each of your formats (bit-packed and XML), write the complete message for the following situations:

      a. Patient has fallen.

      b. Patient's bio-information at 1 pm is pulse rate of 78, temperature of 98.1, and percentage blood oxygen of 92.

3. For each of the following applications discuss the advantages and disadvantages of bit-encoded vs. human-readable messages.

   a) Farm sensor network

   b) Building sensor network

   c) Bank system with multiple ATMs

   d) Airplane control system

   e) Missile guidance system

References

[1] https://en.wikipedia.org/wiki/XML.

Networks

21.1 Introduction

We begin this chapter with a brief history of networking. We then introduce some of the most commonly used terminologies in networking. This is followed by a discussion of the classification of networks and some of the most common network structures used for organizing the nodes in a network. Finally, we present some useful information about wired and wireless networks.

21.2 Brief history of networking

Electric/electronic networks date back to the 19th century. For example, Alexander Graham Bell was issued his patent for the telephone in 1876.[1] Bell also did work in optical communications.[1] Others were working on similar ideas at that time.

Computer networks, of course, did not appear until computers were developed. Here is a sample of early computer networks to give the reader a sense of computer networks developed over time. The Semi-automatic Ground Environment (SAGE), developed jointly by the military and IBM, was already in use in the late 1950s to connect computers monitoring and controlling radar.[2] Semi-automated Business Research Environment (SABRE) grew out of the SAGE concept through a chance meeting of an IBM employee and the president of American Airlines. By 1960 the first test SABRE system was in use by American to speed up their reservations process. Time sharing, the sharing of a single computer system by multiple users through terminals, was introduced at Dartmouth in 1964. In 1965 Western Electric introduced the first computer-controlled telephone switch. In 1969 the first four nodes of the ARPANET, which would later become the Internet, were connected. In 1973, Robert Metcalfe wrote a formal memo at Xerox PARC describing Ethernet, a networking system that was based on the Aloha network, developed in the 1960s by Norman Abramson and colleagues at the University of Hawaii.

Wireless computer networks date back as far as the 1960s. The first operational wireless computer network was the ALOHANET, designed at the University of Hawaii starting in 1969 and implemented in 1971.[3] Wireless 2G cell phone service was introduced in 1991.[3] In 1997, the IEEE introduced the 802.11 protocol for

Embedded System Design. https://doi.org/10.1016/B978-0-443-18470-3.00021-X

"Wi-Fi".[3] With the development of embedded systems and especially wireless sensor network applications during the 1990s, low-power protocols began to appear. Bluetooth and Zigbee both appeared in the 1990s and now have standards organizations. Inspired by the IEEE 802.15.4 standard in 2003 and the continuing prevalence of low-end micros that could not support standard Internet protocols yet needed to connect to the Internet, the Internet Engineering Task Force (IETF) 6LoWPAN working group was established in 2005.[4]

21.3 Basic network concepts

In this section we introduce some computer network concepts that play a special role in the design of embedded systems that require communication between modules and, in the Internet of Things (IoT) context, with other things outside the embedded system. We begin with several general definitions relating to the transmission of packets.

> **Definition 21.1** Utilization is the percentage of time a channel or other device is busy, that is, doing useful work.
>
> **Definition 21.2** Throughput is the number of packets sent through a channel per unit of time.
>
> **Definition 21.3** The response time (often referred to as the round-trip time) is the time by which a sender of a message receives a response from the intended receiver.
>
> **Definition 21.4** Delay is the amount of time it takes for a packet to pass through a channel or device.
>
> **Definition 21.5** End-to-end delay is the amount of time it takes for a packet to travel from the sender to the intended receiver.
>
> **Definition 21.6** A hop is the transmission of a packet through a single link, for example, an individual channel or a router.
>
> **Definition 21.7** Goodput is the rate in bits per second of useful information (i.e., excluding lost packets, duplicate packets, etc.) sent to an application. Goodput excludes packet overhead for the protocol being used as well as lost packets, duplicate packets, and anything that is not information to be used by the receiving application.
>
> **Definition 21.8** Latency is the minimum time for a packet to travel from the sender and be received by the receiver. It excludes any delays caused by any reason other than the speed of the links on the path.

Figures 21.1 and 21.2 illustrate some of these concepts. Figure 21.1 shows a portion of a local area network (LAN) with a router. The router has a communication channel, R, that connects to all the communication links of the devices (PCs, laptops, printers, etc.) attached to the router. When node N1 sends a packet to node N2, the packet travels through the link from N1 to the router, through the router's internal channel R, and then through the link from the router to N2. The throughput for

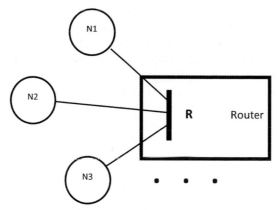

FIGURE 21.1 A Simple Network With a Central Channel.

Author drawn.

this path is limited by the throughput of the slowest link in the path. Typically, the router's internal channel would be very high speed because it has to handle traffic from many devices. The individual channels between the router and the various nodes would likely be much slower. Figure 21.2 shows two LANs connected through the Internet. A message from a node in one of those LANs must travel through its link to its local router, from the router to some node on the Internet, then through some sequence of nodes in the Internet, through a link to the router in the receiving LAN, and finally through the LAN link to the receiving node. End-to-end delay for one packet is the sum of all the time for the packet to pass through all the links and reach its destination. Note that separate packets from the sending node to the receiving node will typically not take the same path through the Internet. Packets arriving at a router may incur further delay because the receiving router is already busy working on other packets it has to process. Finally, note that packets may arrive at the destination node out of order due to different end-to-end delays for packets as they travel through different paths on the Internet.

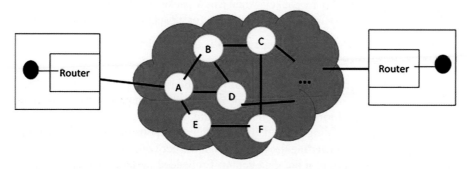

FIGURE 21.2 A Snapshot of a Network With Multiple Paths Between Nodes.

Author drawn.

Channel utilization includes both the data and the overhead for the transmission protocol. For example, IIC transmissions include at least the start event, the stop event, and an address byte, which contains the address of the other device plus the read/write bit (see Chapter 23). TCP/IP packets have several layers of information surrounding the actual data in the packet. The term "channel efficiency" is often used to refer to the amount of actual useful data sent through the channel, that is, the utilization less the overhead. Throughput for an individual channel (wired or wireless) is limited by the physical transmission speed of the channel. When the utilization is small, the throughput will be significantly less than the upper limit determined by the channel speed. If one or the other of these two measures is low, the engineers may reconsider the choice of communication link and opt for a slower but possibly lower-cost link.

Several factors affect end-to-end delay. Obviously, the channel speed is a major factor. In systems in which there is no hopping, such as wired systems like IIC and CAN or wireless systems like Bluetooth in which the devices make direct links to each other, the only other factor affecting end-to-end delay is current channel usage. Channel speed as well as the length of the wire in the case of a wired connection would be known by the system designers, so delay due to channel speed would also be known. Delay due to the channel being used by other modules in the system may not be predictable, and system designers may need to estimate average or worst-case scenarios to determine if the channel will allow the system to meet its real-time constraints. In systems where packets have to take multiple hops, additional factors come into play. Obviously, the channel speeds of all the channels on the path have to be considered. But, as already noted, individual packets may take different paths from the sender to the receiver. If all of these occur inside a given embedded system, the engineers can examine all the potential paths from any sender to any other receiver. However, when moving from the context of an individual embedded system to the context of the IoT, messages will almost surely travel outside the embedded system and into the Internet. In such cases it is almost impossible to predict end-to-end delay. Finally, we note that a router takes a certain amount of time to process each message that passes through it. Incoming messages are typically queued, and a queue may already have many packets when a new packet arrives. Thus, it is difficult to accurately predict how much time it will take for a packet to get through a router.

> **Definition 21.9** Quality of Service (QoS) is an application-specific measure of how well the system is doing what it is supposed to do.

We emphasize that QoS is an application-specific measure. Each system has requirements that must be met. These may be met even though part of the network is not working or not performing as well as it should. For example, an IoT application that is analyzing energy usage on a daily basis may still perform up to expectations even if there is a delay in getting the data through the network from the sensor nodes to the analysis application in the data center. Embedded system engineers need to understand the performance requirements at each level in the system (individual modules or nodes, network and communication protocol level, etc.) to determine how much degradation at each level can be tolerated before performance at some point in the system falls below acceptable levels.

There are several additional issues relating specifically to wireless connections due to the possible loss or duplication of packets. Packets can be lost in a variety of ways. For example, electrical disturbance, for example from high-powered machinery, in the area may interfere with the radio transmission and corrupt the bits in the packet. Or, a packet may be sent to a router whose queue is already full and therefore not able to accept another arriving packet. A third possibility is that a packet reached a node and the node failed (e.g., the battery failed) before forwarding the packet. On the other hand, in some networks packets may be duplicated during the transmission process, and the sender might receive more than one copy of a packet. This occurs, for example, in networks that broadcast packets and nodes simply forward any packets that they receive. One node may broadcast a packet, which is then received by two or three other nodes. If each of these also forwards the packet, the receiver will receive more than one copy. This leads to the following concepts.

> **Definition 21.10** The delivery ratio is the ratio of packets received to packets sent, excluding duplicates.
> **Definition 21.11** The packet loss ratio is the percent of packets lost.
> **Definition 21.12** The retransmission rate is the percentage of packets or frames that are transmitted more than once.

We make a special comment about packet delay vs. packet loss for systems with real-time constraints. If a packet is delayed so that the system cannot meet the deadline for processing that packet effectively, it is the same as if the packet were lost. For example, a traffic control system or oncoming car may send a message to a given car to maneuver to avoid a collision. If that packet is delayed so that the cars collide, the effect is the same as if the packet had been lost or never even sent. Embedded system engineers need to factor such considerations in when designing the communication component of the system.

Another important consideration for networks, especially networks with battery-operated nodes and using wireless transmission, is the question of how many nodes in the network can fail before delivery of information falls below an acceptable level. Although at first glance one might think that loss of any information would be unacceptable, there are in fact many applications where a limited amount of packet loss can be tolerated. For example, in an embedded system for monitoring soil conditions on a large farm the nodes could be distributed uniformly over the geographic area and report conditions, say, every two or four hours. Missing one report from one node can easily be tolerated because the reports from before and after the missing one can be used to make decision about irrigation, crop condition, etc. Even missing all data from a small section of the geographic area could be tolerated because this information could be approximated using data from the surrounding area. (See the section on network structures for how a situation like this — loss of data from a small geographic area — might occur depending on how the network nodes were connected.) For embedded systems in which information is transmitted around a network of nodes, the design team must consider how much information loss can be tolerated before the system functionality degrades below an acceptable level. This would affect design decisions about network structure, packet transmission strategy, quality of the batteries in a system with battery-operated nodes, whether or not to include energy harvesting capability to prolong battery life, and many other aspects of the communication and related hardware and software.

21.4 Classification of networks

Networks can be classified by geographical properties, organizational properties, and various other properties.[2] The following is a summary of the geographical classification of networks described in Ref. [2].

- Nanoscale network. This is a developing technology, but it is expected to grow in importance. As the name implies, these are networks in nanoscale distance. A major targeted application area is low-level biological sensing.
- Near-field Communication (NFC).[5] NFC involves devices that connect and communicate when brought within a very short distance, usually up to 10 centimeters, of each other. NFC can be used for contactless payment systems, ticketing, and similar activities.
- Body Area Network (BAN). This refers to networks operating within or on a single body, typically but not necessarily human. Common applications using BAN are patient monitoring, assisted living, and wearable devices.
- Personal Area Network (PAN). This refers to networks of things in close proximity to an individual, hence the name "personal". A PAN might connect a person's computer with a Personal Digital Assistant (PDA), a printer located in the same room or office, a nearby router, etc. Distances are typically up to 10 meters.
- Near-me Area Network (NAN). These are networks covering a wider area than a PAN can cover. Moreover, these tend to be *ad hoc* in nature, being created on a need basis and independent of the location of the objects. By contrast, the objects in a PAN are typically more-or-less stationary and involve a fixed set of objects. An example of a NAN (taken from Ref. [6]) is a person who lost a child and transmits a picture to other people in the area to see if anyone has seen the child. The person could be anywhere at the time (home, grocery store, amusement park), so the location is not fixed as it would be in a PAN. The network is formed just for that brief time period, after which it is no longer in existence. The other participants in the network are just the people whose devices are turned on at the moment and able to receive such messages. NANs implement one of the most important goals of the IoT, namely that devices can communicate anytime and anywhere.
- Local Area Network (LAN). These are networks distributed typically over an area such as a building. If the LAN is connected to the Internet, then all the

nodes of the LAN will share a common prefix for their URLs. In IPv4, this would be the first three octets. LANs can be wired or wireless. Examples of LANs include office buildings, factories, and smart homes.

- Wide Area Network (WAN). The WAN covers a large geographic area — a city, state, country, or even across continents. Nodes in a WAN share common URL addresses. In the IPv4 addressing scheme, the nodes in a WAN would all have the same first two octets. The actual transmission of data can be over a variety of media including, but not limited to, radio, microwave, wires, common carriers such as phone companies, and others.
- Global Area Network (GAN). These are networks covering the entire earth.

Embedded system engineers will likely work on applications that involve design of networks at the NFC, BAN, PAN, NAN, and possibly even LAN levels. One obvious example is the design and implementation of a patient monitoring system. The engineer may use off-the-shelf networking products or may for various reasons, such as cost or privacy issues, need to design and build a BAN from individual circuits. The bridge project used earlier in this book is an example where a LAN would be appropriate. Applications in which communication is over a very large distance, such as an agricultural monitoring system, will almost surely involve a LAN possibly in conjunction with a gateway with enough computing and storage capability to use off-the-shelf Internet communication. A networking technology that will play an increasingly important role in embedded systems, especially those that participate in the IoT, is cell phone networking. For example, many current patient monitoring systems have Bluetooth capable of communicating with cell phones. The sensors in and on the patient's body communicate through a BAN to a gateway node, which in turn communicates through Bluetooth to the patient's cell phone. The cell phone then communicates with the doctor's office, hospital, emergency services, etc.

Applications that use LAN or higher networks will likely use existing infrastructure and off-the-shelf software. The design issues for these applications will focus on information content and message format. Applications at the NFC, BAN, PAN, and NAN levels might require more design by the embedded system engineering team. In the next few paragraphs, therefore, we describe applications and issues for these classifications.

21.4.1 Near-field communication networks

NFC[5] involves devices that connect and communicate when brought within a very short distance, usually a few centimeters, of each other. NFC can be used for contactless payment systems, ticketing, and similar activities. NFC is relatively slow compared to most other networking technologies, typically 100–400 kbit/s; the ISO/IEC 18092 standard supports data rates of 106, 212, and 424 kbit/s. There are many applications where such speeds are perfectly adequate. The simplest NFC device can only transmit its stored information; that is, the device is read only. More complex NFC devices can read data from another NFC device in its range, and some NFC devices have the capability to write information back to a nearby NFC device. Some NFC devices are passive, that is, they have no power source and must absorb energy from the other device to which they are connected. Active devices do have their own power source.

Read-only devices can be used in applications where identification is the goal, such as in opening a locked door for an authorized person or identifying an object in an inventory application. The information on the read-only device includes an identification number that the reading device can use for checking authorization or storing in an inventory database. NFC devices that can accept new data, i.e., be both read from and written to, can be used in applications such as gift cards or transportation ticketing. When the read/write device is brought near an appropriate NFC reader, the current information on the card is read, updated, and written back to the read/write device. In some applications, both the devices read from and write to each other.

By far the most common technology for NFC is radio frequency identification (RFID). An RFID tag can be passive or active. Passive RFID tags have no internal power source. This enables passive RFID devices to take very simple form factors such as unpowered tags, stickers, or cards. When brought within range of an active RFID device, the passive device absorbs energy from the radio wave, which then allows the passive device to transmit its data. Passive RFID tags are used extensively in object identification, which is crucial for applications like inventory control or object monitoring. An RFID tag with a unique number encoded in its data is attached to an object. As the object passes an RFID reader at a known location, the tag number is read, and in this way the object and its location can be identified.

21.4.2 Body area networks

The growth in individual patient monitoring and assisted living has driven the need for special networking protocols and standards for networks attached to living beings. A BAN will typically involve several sensors, both inside and outside the body, connected with a gateway to the outside world. The gateway can be a special node connecting to a PAN or LAN, a cell phone, a nearby laptop or PC, or other similar devices. BAN devices may also include actuators, such as pacemakers or devices that dispense medicine directly into the body such as insulin pumps. In this case, two-way communication may provide for external control of the actuation, for example, external control of the medication. Connections may be wired or wireless. Connections to devices inside the body would typically be wireless, although a wired connection with a port located on the skin is possible and would allow for external power to the devices as well as normal communication. A BAN would typically be battery operated so that the person is not restricted in movement. Therefore, the devices should be as low power as possible. The very small distances allow for very low-power wireless technology to be used, although care must be taken to ensure that the radio signal is not degraded by its passage through body tissue.

BAN devices, especially ones inside the body, would typically not have much computing power because of the low-power requirements.

The FCC has dedicated the 2360–2400 MHz frequency range to medical BAN (MBAN).[7] MBAN devices using the 2360–2390 MHz band are restricted to indoor operation at healthcare facilities and are subject to registration and site approval by coordinators to protect aeronautical telemetry, which also operates in that range. Operation in the 2390–2400 MHz band is not subject to registration or coordination and may be used in all areas including residential.

Issues requiring special consideration include reliability, security, and privacy. Most BAN applications involve health, and failures may result in death or have other serious consequences. Reliability of both the hardware and software is crucial. Two reliability issues of major concern for BAN applications are power and sensor calibration. If possible, the system should predict imminent power failure of an individual device in the BAN so that the system can alert the user and possibly perform some appropriate action; for example, the system might ignore sensor readings from that device because they may not be accurate at low battery conditions. A device in the system may be able to prolong battery life by spending more time in sleep mode. This is especially true for devices that aren't monitoring continuously. Wake up might occur at specified time intervals or by some external event. For example, a fall detection sensor may be activated by vibration or vertical motion above a certain threshold, and only then would the device activate the radio component, the major power consumer. A BAN system should provide for battery recharging. Even batteries inside the body might be rechargeable through a wired port if provided, through the use of energy harvesting, or through energy transmission over radio waves as in RFID technology. Redundancy can help prevent system failure for any reason, but especially for situations in which the battery of one component fails. General issues of security and privacy apply to BAN applications because these applications involve personal data and wireless communication. Transmission ranges of the wireless components should be very small, both to prevent outside entities from stealing the information and to prevent the BAN system from interfering with other nearby systems. Conversely, a given BAN system should be as resilient as possible against interference from outside signals, both general electronic noise and malicious signals that attempt to control actuators in the system.

21.4.3 Personal area networks

PANs were developed to connect people's personal devices, such as laptops, wireless mice, PDAs, etc. The typical range is a few feet to possibly an adjoining room. PANs use both wired and wireless technology. Power is generally not an important consideration in designing these networks because either the devices have power on their own or they get power through a wired connection such as USB. Some devices may be both battery operated and wireless, such as a wireless mouse or cell phone, but typically these devices would have already had power issues handled in their own design. In any case, recharging or changing batteries in PAN applications is usually easy. PANs are dynamic; devices can enter and leave the network. But the range of device types is typically limited, known in advance, and provided for in the operating systems of typical laptops and PCs. For example, USB supports many kinds of devices, but the USB standard specifies how the USB software should handle these various devices. Bluetooth, Zigbee, and many of the other communication methods used in PANs also have standards for how to handle a wide variety but known set of device types. This is in sharp contrast to the IoT vision, in which the kinds of devices in a dynamic network may not be known or limited. A PAN would typically have at least one gateway, and in many cases there would be several devices in the network capable of independently accessing the Internet. Security is still an issue; for example, an outside entity could gain control of a wireless mouse and therefore gain control of a laptop.

21.4.4 Near-me area networks

Near-me networks are intended to operate over longer distances and in a wider variety of environments than PANs. Near-me networks are dynamic, like PANs; devices enter and leave the network. However, in this case entering and leaving the network is typically caused by the mobility of the devices, unlike the PAN case where typically the devices are stationary and just turned on or off. Currently, Bluetooth and Zigbee have the ability to recognize when similar devices have come into range and automatically connect to those devices. Some cell phone companies provide services for locating other cell phones, or even other general services like restaurants or theaters, near the current location of a cell phone user.

A major issue for near-me networking is the wide variety of communication protocols being used by the devices that are to be connected. Obviously, near-me networks would be wireless. But the different devices might use Wi-Fi, Bluetooth, Zigbee, cellular phone technology, or even line-of-sight (i.e., no obstacles between sender and receiver) methods for communication. Cell phones may subscribe to different carriers. Laptops and PDAs in the area may be connected to different LANs, so that the URLs give no clue as to the devices being near something. Thus, locating arbitrary devices nearby is a networking problem that remains to be solved.

Limited forms of near-me connectivity are feasible and can still be useful. We illustrate the range of applications of near-me networks with several examples.

- A person wants to connect to people nearby to gain or exchange some information. Typical examples mentioned in the literature include a person who lost a child or pet and wants to know if someone nearby has seen it, a person sees a restaurant and wants to know if someone nearby has experience with that establishment, and similar situations. Cell phone technology can be used to provide at least some connectivity. Cell phone carriers can provide location-based access to nearby cell phones, at least those using the same carrier. Note there may be others nearby who could provide useful information and have access to the Internet through laptops or PDAs, and the cell phone approach will not reach those people. Still, the ability to reach at least some people is useful.

- Hospital staff need access to the complete status and record for a patient when they enter the patient's room. This could involve accessing medical equipment inside the room, such as a patient monitor, and information from outside the room, such as in the hospital database. Different medical equipment could use different communication and networking technologies, unlike the situation in the previous bullet. However, the set of devices is known, so embedded system engineers could design a device that could communicate with all of them. The device would create a temporary network when the staff member enters the room and close it when the staff member leaves the room.

- A person with a medical condition wears a monitoring system, perhaps a BAN, that can detect when the person needs help. In an emergency situation the BAN should connect to any other system to get help — perhaps connect to a nearby fire department through Wi-Fi to request an ambulance, perhaps to a nearby person through their cell phone or PDA or laptop so the person could call for an ambulance, perhaps some other means. As with the second bullet point, an embedded system engineer could design a device that incorporated several currently known technologies, and that may be sufficient for the purpose of finding help for the person in need. If some new communication methodology arises, the device would need to be redesigned.

- A smart car is driven through a smart city. The car communicates with various elements of the transportation system, such as the roads or a stop light at the next intersection, to get information about traffic congestion, blockages, suggestions for alternate routes, etc. The car gets information from nearby stores and restaurants about sales or other special events. The car gets information from a nearby radio/TV station about the weather. One could imagine many other potentially useful near-me network situations that would help the driver of the car. In this case, unlike the previous bullets, the embedded system engineer may not know all the communication and networking technologies the car might encounter.

The reader can appreciate that the range of applications for near-me networks is gigantic. Note that the precision in locating a device may or may not be crucial. For example, in the case of the patient needing emergency assistance it is critical to know exactly where the patient is. In the case of person looking for a lost dog or asking about a restaurant, locating the user within a block or two would likely be adequate.

21.5 **Network topologies**

There are many ways in which a set of nodes can be connected to form a network. We present five of the most common ways for connecting computers and devices in embedded systems and discuss some of their advantages and disadvantages. The first four of these are normally static networks. That is, short of a node failing, the nodes in the network and their connections are known in advance. The last structure, the mesh, may be either static or dynamic. In particular, mesh networks allow for new nodes to enter the network and existing nodes to drop out or fail while still maintaining full or close to full network functionality. This is an important aspect of some embedded systems and IoT applications, such as animal migration monitoring, vehicle monitoring and control within a limited geographical area, and other applications in which the objects of interest move.

21.5.1 Linear networks

The devices in a linear network are connected along a single path, as shown in Figure 21.3. Depending on the network protocol being used, the number of devices may be limited to two (e.g., in RS232 serial networks) or may be significantly more than two (e.g., 127 on an IIC bus). Linear networks are wired networks and are used in both parallel and serial communications. Note that if a node on the bus fails, the remaining nodes may still function as a linear network. Other features, advantages, and disadvantages of this kind of network are highly dependent on the communication protocol being used; therefore, we defer further discussion to the section on serial communication in Chapter 23.

21.5.2 Ring networks

The devices in a ring network are connected in a circle, as shown in Figure 21.4. Each node has one connection to its predecessor in the circle and one connection to its successor in the circle. Information is transmitted in one direction only, and each device will typically have an IN socket for connection to its predecessor node and an OUT socket for connection to its successor node. Typically, each node in the ring has a processor plus some other circuitry. A node may contain only actuators which are controlled by a master node in the ring, in which case the node does not insert messages into the ring but does react to received messages that are addressed to it and does forward packets in the ring. In some devices the OUT socket may be wired directly to the IN socket. In other devices they are electrically separated, and other parts of the node (usually software) must copy messages from the IN port to the OUT port. Ring networks are typically wired networks.

FIGURE 21.3 A Linear Network.

Author drawn.

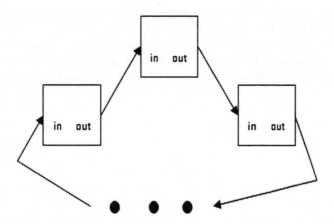

FIGURE 21.4 A Ring Network.

Author drawn.

A message that is inserted into the ring simply travels in the ring direction until either a node removes it or it reaches the node that inserted it. In the latter case, the message is removed from the ring so that it does not continue to propagate around the ring. The nodes are numbered in some way so that each node can be uniquely identified. A message may be addressed to a particular node or may be broadcast to all nodes. If a message is addressed to a particular node, it is removed from the ring when that node receives it and replaced by an acknowledge message addressed to the sender. When the original sender receives the acknowledge message, it removes that message. Note that several nodes may insert messages at the same time. An individual node that processes messages may need a queue to hold several messages while it is processing the first one.

Ring networks are simple to implement. Each node that does not contain a processor simply has circuitry that copies signals on the IN socket to the OUT socket. Each node that does contain a processor may have the IN socket wired directly to the OUT socket, but the more normal situation is that received messages are buffered internally and then copied from the buffer to the OUT socket. In both cases the node must be able to check if it is the destination for the message. In the case of a node that does not contain a processor, this would be done in circuitry, perhaps by an field programmable gate array. In nodes that contain a processor, the software checks the message destination address.

A special case of the ring structure is the token ring network. In a token ring the insertion of messages is controlled by a so-called "token". The token is typically a special message that is passed around the ring. A new message can be inserted onto the ring bus only by the node that currently has the token. If a node wants to send a message it must wait until it receives the token. At that point, it keeps the token (i.e., does not forward the "token" message) and sends its own message. When the acknowledge message is received, the node again forwards the token.

Ring networks have several advantages and one major disadvantage. The first advantage, as already noted, is that they are very simple to implement. Also, as noted in the previous paragraph, token rings have no bus contention. A corollary to this is that timing and latency are completely predictable, a critical property for real-time systems. Suppose the ring has N nodes, and the time for a packet to travel from one node to the next (including the time it takes for the processor to analyze the packet and determine to forward it) over the bus is τ. Then a message inserted onto the ring bus will return to the sender in time $N*\tau$. In a token ring, a node may need to wait $(N-1)*N*\tau$ time units before sending a packet. (Problem 1 asks the reader to derive this formula.) The embedded system engineer can use these formulas and the number of nodes in the design to determine what τ has to be in order to meet any real-time constraints for the system. Another advantage is that packet overhead can be relatively minimal because the addressing scheme for the nodes is simple. Nodes simply need to have unique numbers. If there are fewer than 256 nodes in the ring, a single byte is sufficient. The simplest packet overhead, then, consists simply of starting and stopping conditions plus one byte. If the protocol calls for, say, a byte telling the length of the message, this is just one or two more bytes. This is much simpler than the overhead for, say, TCP/IP packets, and is no more than the most efficient of the serial protocols. Unfortunately, ring networks have one serious disadvantage. If any node or link fails, the entire network fails. This almost precludes the use of ring structure in systems with battery-operated nodes (unless the application can tolerate regular network failure and the system is located in a place that is easily accessible for battery changing).

Although in principle the token ring method could be used for any network, in practice it is more useful when distances are relatively small and the number of nodes is relatively small. If there are many nodes, then as noted in the preceding paragraph there could be a long delay before a message is transferred from the sender to the receiver.

An interesting point is that the token ring network is inherently fair in the sense that no high-priority node can hog the network and block other nodes from using it. Once a node has sent a message, the token is passed to the next node and does not return until all other nodes in the network have received the token and had a chance to send a packet. On the other hand, if a node has a critical message and just missed the token, that critical message has to wait for at least $(N-1)*N*\tau$ before being sent. The wait could be significantly longer if other nodes in the ring took the token and sent their own messages. Thus, designers need to determine if there are critical messages in the application; if so, token ring may not be the right choice unless the network is relatively small.

21.5.3 Star networks

A star network consists of one central node to which are attached a number of other nodes. The other nodes do not connect directly to one another. The structure is shown in Figure 21.5. A star network would be appropriate in systems that are

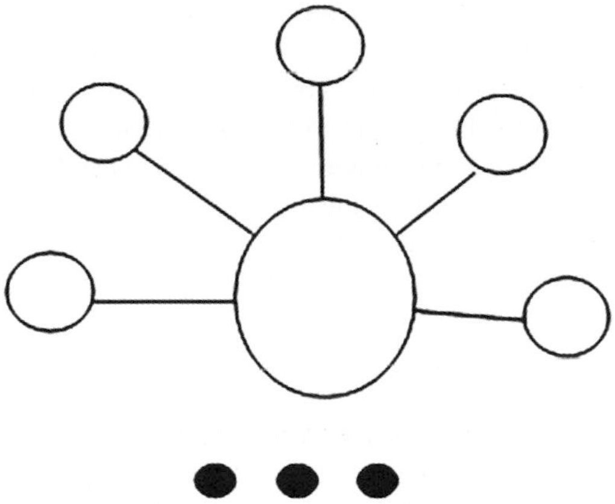

FIGURE 21.5 A Star Network.

Author drawn.

not too widely distributed and in which the nodes other than the central node do not need significant communication with each other. The central node often acts as a gateway to the Internet and/or as a data sink for any sensor nodes in the network. The bridge project could easily use a star network. The PC serving as the operator's interface and gateway to the Internet could serve as the central node of the network. Other nodes, like the ground traffic control module and the span control module would coordinate by sending messages to the central node, which would then decide what next actions to take and send corresponding messages to other nodes in the star.

Bus contention (more than one node trying to use a link at the same time) can only occur if the central node and peripheral node both try to initiate messages at the same time. This can easily be avoided by having the peripheral nodes transmit only when requested by the central node. However, this precludes a peripheral node from initiating a message, for example, to notify of an emergency. If this cannot be allowed in the system, then one of the methods for handling bus contention must be used.

Another source of delay is the fact that all traffic is routed through a single node, the central node. If many nodes are transmitting at the same time, the queue in the central node can get full and even overrun if not enough space has been allocated for it. A message that arrives in the queue has to wait until all the messages already there have been handled. If there are N peripheral nodes, if each node cannot send a second message until its previous message has been acknowledged, and if the maximum time for handling a message is τ, then the maximum waiting time in the queue is bounded by $(N-1)*\tau$. Assuming the maximum time to transmit a message between the central node and a peripheral node is τ', the maximum time for a message to reach another destination node is bounded $N*\tau + 2*\tau'$. (The student is asked to prove these limits in Problem 2.) Note that every message reaches its destination in either one hop or two hops.

One advantage of the star structure over the ring structure is that peripheral nodes and/or their links can fail and the system still continues to at least partially function. For example, in the bridge system if the ground traffic module or its link to the central node fails, the rest of the bridge can still work. In this case, perhaps the operator can call for assistance from other human workers to manually control the ground traffic, and the operator could notify the system when the ground traffic had been blocked. Of course, if the central node fails, the system as a whole fails, and it would likely be very difficult if not impossible for humans to intervene.

21.5.4 Tree networks

A tree network is a network in which the nodes form a tree and the communication links form the branches of the tree, as shown in Figure 21.6. The root node is often a gateway and/or data sink node for the network. Each node can communicate only with its parent node and its immediate child nodes. Tree networks are useful in situations where the geographical distribution of nodes covers a wide area and the positioning of the nodes does not form a regular grid. For example, in a seismic sensing system for a volcano, there may be densely populated groups of sensor nodes on different sides of the top of the volcano, where it is important to have accurate data at small distances. Each group forms one level of a tree and connects to a node further down the volcano. Several of these second-level nodes may form another level of the tree network. At the base station of the system is a single node. Another application is the monitoring of conditions in a city. Each block of the city may have a set of low-power sensor nodes, which communicate with a single medium-power node for that block. The block nodes have sufficient power to transmit further distances, perhaps to a node for a complete subdivision. The subdivision nodes can connect to higher nodes covering a wider region of the city until the root node of the network, which is the node for the entire city. Note that in this application nodes on each higher level will need to have more power to be able to transmit the longer distances. Finally, many applications have an specification and description language (SDL) model with a hierarchical structure, and it would be appropriate

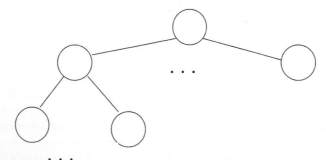

FIGURE 21.6 A Tree Network.

Author drawn.

to consider a tree network for connecting the modules in the blocks, sub-blocks, sub-sub-blocks, etc., in a way that corresponds to the logical hierarchy of the SDL block structure.

When a node generates a message destined for a node lower in the tree, the node passes the message downward to one of its child nodes. The child node similarly passes the message downward, the process continuing until the message reaches its destination. If the message is destined for a node higher up on the path to the root, the message is passed upward to the immediate parent. If the message is destined for a node somewhere else in the tree, it must travel up the tree to some node which is a common ancestor of the sender and receiver and then down again. The addressing scheme for the nodes in the tree must allow each node to determine the relative position — descendant, ancestor, or somewhere else — of the intended receiver so that the node can route the message appropriately. As with star networks, the node-to-node paths are fixed and known in advance. Also, as in star networks, bus contention on an individual link can only occur if the parent node and child node try to transmit at the same time. However, a node may receive many messages from its child nodes and parent node, so its message queue may become full and thereby delay message transmission, similar again to the situation of the central node in a star network. Indeed, a particular node along with its immediate children essentially forms a star network, with the addition of one extra link from the central node to the next higher node in the tree.

One potential problem with tree networks is that failure of a node in the middle of the tree cuts out the entire subtree below that node.

21.5.5 Mesh networks

A mesh network is a network in which the nodes can connect with each other in arbitrary patterns. Two special cases are the full mesh, in which every node is connected directly with every other node, and the grid mesh, in which the nodes are logically organized in grid fashion and each node is connected to its neighbors, four if the node is in the middle of the grid and fewer if the node is at the edge or a corner of the grid. Mesh networks can be wired or wireless. If the number N of nodes is large, it is quite expensive to wire a full mesh because the number of wires required is $N*(N-1)/2$.

Mesh networks are advantageous in a variety of situations. First, unlike the previous network structures, which are normally static, wireless mesh networks are dynamic. That is, both the nodes and the connections between nodes can change over time, a feature often referred to as "self-healing". This is essential in applications where nodes enter and leave the network (e.g., the nodes are battery operated and fail often, are located in severe environments, are located in environments subject to radio interference, are mobile and move in and out of the network area, etc.). Wireless mesh networks are also useful in applications in which the nodes are distributed over wide geographic areas and the nodes cannot conveniently be connected in a star or tree fashion. The grid mesh is convenient for wide but contiguous geographic areas in which the nodes are relatively low power and/or battery operated and therefore of limited wireless range. An example of this situation is agricultural monitoring of large farms. Each low-power node can reach its nearby neighbors, but only those nodes close to the base station for the farm need to reach that node.

Routing is a major issue in mesh networks and continues to be an active area of research. The simplest routing strategy is flooding, in which every node simply forwards any message it receives that it hasn't seen before to any other node it can reach. Obviously, this is very inefficient for several reasons. The most serious disadvantage of flooding is that it consumes much more power than other routing strategies. A second disadvantage is that the nodes have to expend computing and storage resources to keep track of messages that it has forwarded before. Along the same lines, the receiving node will generally receive many copies of each message and must remove the duplicates. A big advantage of flooding is that a large percentage of the network nodes may fail and messages still reach their destinations. As an example, consider a grid network on a farm. As long as one node N is connected to the base station and there is a path from node M to node N, a message from M can reach the base station even if almost all the nodes in the grid have failed.

More sophisticated routing methods exist. For example, a mesh network can have a special kind of message which includes the names of nodes and path information about the path those messages have taken through the mesh. These messages are broadcast at regular intervals. A node that receives such a message adds its own id to the path information and then passes the modified message along. It also uses the information in the message to update its own model of the network, thereby learning the current structure of the mesh. In some mesh networks, special nodes are configured to analyze the current mesh structure and form new path tables. These tables are then broadcast to all nodes and used to route future messages. A full treatment of routing algorithms for mesh networks is beyond the scope of this book. Our goal is to make the embedded system engineer aware of the possibilities of mesh networks.

Both Zigbee and Bluetooth support mesh networking.

21.6 Physical considerations

Embedded systems engineers need to at least be aware of certain physical considerations in implementing and deploying the network component of their design. In the case of wired networks these considerations include wire length baud rate, voltage levels, line termination, and others. On larger projects, another team member with electrical engineering expertise may oversee the implementation of the physical connections; on smaller projects, the embedded system engineer may in fact be the one to do that. In the case of wireless networks, the embedded systems design team will not be concerned with implementing the underlying transmission mechanisms; those will be built into the wireless chips selected for the system. However, other physical aspects may affect design choices made during hardware/software mapping. We describe some of these issues in the next two subsections.

21.6.1 Wired networks

Three key issues for wired connections are cable length, termination, and single vs. differential drive.

Many network protocols specify maximum cable lengths. For example, Cat6 cables for 10/100/100/BASE-T Ethernet should be no more than 100 meters for reliable transmission. For Ethernet modules separated by longer distances one or more network switches should be used. Where maximum cable lengths are not specified or are quite large, there is often a guide for matching cable length limit with the frequency of the signal to be carried. There is an inverse relationship between frequency and wire length because of the attenuation of the electrical signals in longer cables. For example, the RS485 standard for differential transmission gives guidelines as shown in Figure 21.7 for cable length vs. maximum data rate to achieve reliable signal transmission in RS485-compliant devices. In Figure 21.7, the scales in both axes are logarithmic. The practical limit for 20 megabits per second signals is about 20 feet.

Coaxial cable is commonly used for longer distances or higher-speed signals. A coaxial cable consists of a core wire of copper surrounded by an insulating layer surrounded again by a conducting layer called the shield (typically a thin layer of foil or braid) surrounded again by another insulating layer, as shown in Figure 21.8. The core conductor carries the signal. The outer conducting layer blocks electrical interference from outside the cable and is usually connected to GND at one or both ends, although care must be taken to account for ground loops.

Cable or line termination refers to treatments, usually resistors plus possibly capacitors and diodes, applied near the ends of the wire. The reader is referred to

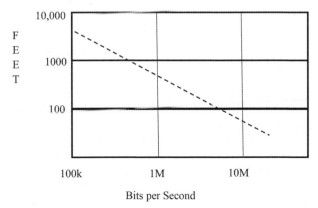

FIGURE 21.7 RS485 Cable Length Guidelines.

Author drawn.

FIGURE 21.8 Cross Section of a Coaxial Cable.

Author drawn.

Ref. [8] for an excellent treatment of termination and a host of other practical information. Termination is applied to reduce or eliminate the effect of electrical reflection in the wire. When an electrical pulse is transmitted through a wire it can be reflected in different ways depending on what is at the end of the wire. When the reflection returns back to the first end of the wire it is reflected again, although because of attenuation the second reflection will not be as strong as the first. This process repeats, producing a kind of decayed ringing on the wire. At very high frequencies, the duration of noticeable ringing can be nearly as long as the pulses themselves, causing the intended receiving circuit to misinterpret the signal. Figure 21.9 shows an example of how such reflections might affect the transmitted signal at the receiver end of the wire.

Figure 21.10a shows series termination, the most common termination configuration for a single, end-to-end wire link, that is, a wire connecting a single sender to a single receiver. Note that the resistor in series termination is placed close to the sender device. The value of the resistor plus the impedance of the driver inside the sender circuit should equal the impedance of the wire. (The impedance of the driver and of the wire can be obtained from the manufacturers of those products.) There will be no impedance mismatch where the resistor connects to the wire leading to the receiver. There will be a mismatch at the receiver, so there will be a

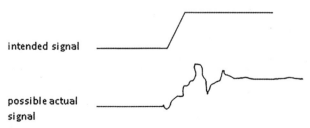

FIGURE 21.9 Intended vs. Actual Received Signal.

Author drawn.

FIGURE 21.10A Series Termination.

Author drawn.

reflection. However, this reflection will be absorbed by the resistor, so there will be no ringing. This is a simple scheme, easy to implement, and adds only a single new component to the design. The resistor does slow the rise and fall times (the slew rates) of pulses, so care needs to be taken for very high-frequency signals. Serial termination is suitable for end-to-end connections such as the TTL/RS232/RS485 serial lines.

Figure 21.10b shows a termination configuration, called parallel termination, for cases when there are many senders and/or receivers connected to the wire. The wire is terminated at one end through a resistor to ground. This design also adds only a single component. However, current flows through the resistor any time when the line is at a positive voltage. Hence, this design uses more energy, which is a distinct disadvantage for embedded systems, especially battery-operated ones. Figure 21.10c shows a variation, called Thevenin (or Thevenin equivalent circuit), in which a pair of resistors is used connecting the wire to both ground and the power supply voltage. The sum of the two resistors should equal the impedance of the line so that there is no impedance mismatch at the point where the resistors connect to the wire. This keeps the wire at a voltage between ground and power and makes it somewhat easier for devices attached to the wire to drive pulses. However, current always flows through one or the other or both of the resistors. This form of termination is often used for wires connecting multiple devices, such as IIC or CAN serial lines.

Figure 21.10d shows the common termination method for differential drive. Note that many differential receivers have the terminating resistor built into the circuit, eliminating the need for an external resistor.

FIGURE 21.10B Parallel Termination to GND.

Author drawn.

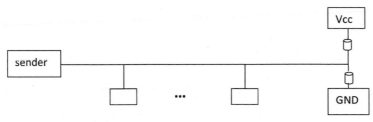

FIGURE 21.10C Thevenin Termination.

Author drawn.

FIGURE 21.10D Termination for Differential Drive.

Author drawn.

Finally, Figure 21.10e shows the so-called fail-safe termination scheme. This would be used for long cables in environments susceptible to extreme electrical interference, such as near heavy magnets that are switched on and off or in places where lightning might strike. The diodes prevent voltages lower than ground or higher than power voltage from propagating on the line.

Differential drive is a technique for sending signals long distances. Differential drive uses two wires per signal. One wire carries the signal itself, and the other wire carries the signal inverted. The receiving end compares the two voltages and outputs logic 1 if the positive line has higher voltage than the inverted line and logic 0 otherwise. This process of comparing the voltages produces a very clean signal on the output side of the voltage comparator. Figure 21.11 shows a pulse on the two wires leading in to a differential drive receiver and the comparator output. The signals at the inputs of the comparator can be quite messy, but still the comparator output is clean. It is common to use matched chipsets, for example, the 26LS31/32 pair, for

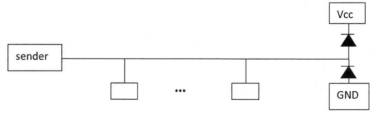

FIGURE 21.10E Fail-safe Termination.

Author drawn.

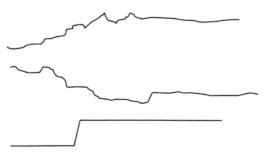

FIGURE 21.11 Differential Drive Signals and Comparator Output.

Author drawn.

the driver end and the receiver end. USB also uses differential drive. It is common to use twisted pair cables for differential drive. The positive and inverted signal wires are wrapped around each other except where they connect to the sender and receiver circuits. This twisting means that any external electrical interference will be felt in the same way on both the positive and inverted signals, and thus the difference in voltage will remain the same. This makes differential drive over twisted pair very immune to external interference.

21.6.2 Wireless networks

Embedded system engineers generally would not have to worry about the actual transmission details of a wireless network. The transmission through the air would already be built into any wireless circuits selected. The main issues for the embedded system engineer, then, are distance, power, and whether or not line of sight can be used.

For end-to-end communication when the line of sight between the devices will always be open, one choice for the physical communication is infrared, as is used in TV remote controls. Infrared offers high reliability and high data speed at low cost and low power over short to medium distances. However, it is severely impacted by poor air quality such as fog, rain, snow, pollution, and anything else in the air space between the sender and receiver. It is useful in scenarios where the distances are small and there are other factors preventing wired or radio transmission. Examples include LAN-to-LAN over short distances such as inside a building, inter-circuit communication in a small enclosure, crossing a road or other geographic obstacle when installing wires is impractical or blocked for other reasons such as right-of-way, etc.

For general wireless communication, radio transmitters and receivers are used. Radio transmission does not require line-of-sight clearance. Radio waves will travel through obstacles between the sender and receiver, although at the expense of signal degradation. There are now several protocols specifically for wireless computer networking — Wi-Fi, Bluetooth, Zigbee, 6LoWPAN, etc. See Chapter 23 for more information about these protocols. Distance and the presence of intermediate obstacles are the major issues for consideration. The low-power protocols for computer networking have limited range, typically in the 10—20 meter range for indoor communication through walls and up to 1000 or more meters for outdoor communication with no intermediate obstacles. Off-the-shelf circuits include all the radio functionality and often also include an antenna. Radio signals are susceptible to magnetic interference. The signals can also be degraded by reflections from nearby surfaces, such as buildings, interior walls, etc., that result in the signal being received from multiple paths with the multiple signals out of phase. Another problem is the so-called hidden-node problem,[9] in which a receiving node B is between two transmitting nodes, A and C, as shown in Figure 21.12. If both A and C are transmitting on the same frequency, the signals received by B will interfere with each other. Most of the solutions proposed in the literature for these various problems, such as

FIGURE 21.12 Hidden Nodes.

Author drawn.

increasing the power or using directional antennas or moving the nodes, may not be feasible in embedded systems. For example, in an embedded system for monitoring migration of animals in the wild, the nodes will be battery operated, so increasing the power consumption will decrease the life of the node. The animals are already moving and may cause hidden node problems from time to time in arbitrary ways. Using directional antennas is out of the question because the animals will not always be facing in the right directions.

21.7 Summary

This chapter begins with a brief history of computer networking. The chapter then presents major concepts concerning network performance. The chapter then describes major network classifications relevant to the design of embedded systems, with more detailed discussion of NFC networks, BANs, PANs, and NANs. The major network topologies — linear, ring, star, tree, and mesh — are described. The chapter discusses the tradeoffs of these various topologies vis-à-vis embedded system applications. Finally, issues regarding the physical transmission of signals, both wired and wireless, are presented. Common problems with wired transmission are described, and common termination methods for overcoming those issues are presented. Similarly, a few of the more common issues regarding wireless transmission are described.

Problems

1. Derive the formula for worst-case time in a token ring. HINT: the worst case is the node just missed the token and every other node is also waiting to send a packet.
2. Prove the bounds on maximum waiting time in the queue and maximum time for a message to reach its destination node mentioned in paragraph 3 of Section 21.5.3 for star networks. Assume that processing messages in the queue is the highest priority process in the central node. That is, any other process running on the central node is interrupted if there is a message in the queue.
3. In a tree, a simple addressing scheme is that all messages go up to the root and then down to the receiver. Discuss the timing of such a scheme and also the benefits and disadvantages.

4. Which network structure would you use in each of the following situations and why?
   a) High-rise building?
   b) Fjords or similar "canyon" type geographies?
   c) ATM?
   d) Car?
   e) The bridge example used in this text?
5. Discuss Quality of Service requirements for each of the following applications. Compare your answers in group discussions with the whole class of study groups.
   a) Agricultural monitoring. On a farm information about soil conditions is sent to a central server every 15 minutes.
   b) Patient monitoring. Patient information (pulse, O_2 saturation, etc.) is sent to a hospital every 5 minutes.
   c) ATM. Information is sent from the ATM to the bank and from the bank to the ATM when people are using the ATM.
6. For each of the following applications tell which network topology you think is most appropriate and why.
   - A lab with various equipment that is all connected to a PC.
   - A system that monitors biological information for an individual cow so that the farmer knows the optimal time for milking and can adjust the feeding regimen.
   - A system that collects information generated by the monitoring systems in the previous bullet from all the cows on a farm.
   - A security system for an individual door.
7. A BAN meant for monitoring human patients has the following sensors:
   - A blood sugar monitor.
   - A pulse monitor.
   - A gate monitor for monitoring how many steps the patient takes during the day.
   - A position monitor to monitor how much time the patient is standing of lying down.

   Each monitor sleeps as much as it can to conserve energy. For each monitor tell if the wake up should be period or event drive. If periodic, suggest a reasonable period and justify your choice. If event driven, explain what event or events cause the wake up.
8. Consider a 4 × 4 grid mesh. Suppose the node in the upper left corner sends a packet to the node in the lower right corner. Assume each node checks to see if it has seen that packet earlier before sending it on to its neighboring nodes.
   a) Describe how the packet flows through the network.
   b) How many copies of the packet are received by the target receiver?

References

[1] https://en.wikipedia.org/wiki/Alexander_Graham_Bell.

[2] https://en.wikipedia.org/wiki/Computer_network.

[3] https://en.wikipedia.org/wiki/Wireless_network.

[4] http://www.eetimes.com/document.asp?doc_id=1278812.

[5] https://en.wikipedia.org/wiki/Near-field_communication.

[6] https://en.wikipedia.org/wiki/Near-me_area_network.

[7] https://www.fcc.gov/document/fcc-dedicates-spectrum-enabling-medical-body-area-networks.

[8] H. Johnson, M. Graham, High-Speed Digital Design: A Handbook of Black Magic, Prentice Hall, 1993, ISBN 10: 0133957241.

[9] https://en.wikipedia.org/wiki/Hidden_node_problem.

The Internet

22

22.1 Introduction

Embedded systems often need to communicate with the world outside the system itself. Examples include the bridge system, which may communicate with the local smart city or the weather service, the BAN for a patient monitoring system, which communicates with the doctor's office or may need to go on the Internet in case of an emergency, and many others. In some cases, the embedded system contains a PC with all the Internet connectivity built in; for example, the bridge system might have a PC at the operator's station. Other embedded systems may not have any computing element capable of supporting a full-blown operating system with built-in Internet connectivity; the BAN patient monitoring system with a very low-end microprocessor as the gateway is an example of this case. In the latter case, the gateway will need hardware and software designed and implemented by the embedded system engineers. In this chapter we describe basic concepts of the Internet and give an overview of the three most common protocol families used to access the Internet. We illustrate the application of these concepts and techniques with a simple example showing steps a design team might take to design and implement Internet accessibility into a system with a very low-end processing element as the gateway.

The Open Systems Interconnection (OSI)[1] model and the TCP/IP protocol family[2,3] both define layers that separate the various functionalities that are used in transmitting messages. OSI defines seven layers, and TCP/IP defines four layers. The highest layer in each model includes the applications with which the users interact directly. Successively lower layers describe operations that are progressively closer to the actual transmission of data between nodes on a network. Each of the layers in each of the models is described in more detail in the following two sections. Figure 22.1 shows how the layers of OSI and TCP/IP relate.

22.2 The Open Systems Interconnection model

The OSI model[1] is a model, not a protocol. However, it serves as a general guide for how data should flow between an application in a device and the external connection

Embedded System Design. https://doi.org/10.1016/B978-0-443-18470-3.00022-1

OSI	TCP/IP
Application Presentation Session	Application
Transport	Transport
Network	Internet
Data Link Physical	Network Access

FIGURE 22.1 OSI vs. TCP/IP.

Author drawn.

of that device to the outside world. Figure 22.2 shows the model in the context of a PC. The model specifies seven layers. Each layer isolates the layer above from having to handle details closer to the actual physical transmission, as described more fully in the following paragraphs. At the top level, the application layer, this means that application developers can write software that can access the Internet no matter what kind of physical connection is used at the device's ports; application developers do not need to know the details of all the various transmission methods that currently exist or will be developed in the future. Similarly, engineers who write the drivers for

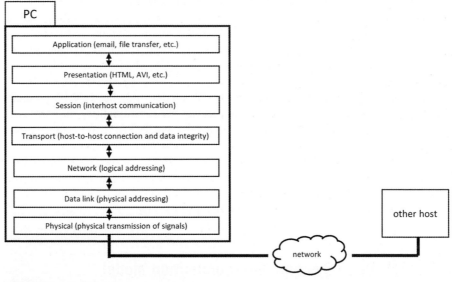

FIGURE 22.2 The OSI Model in a PC.

Author drawn.

the devices that connect to the outside world, that is, that occupy the OSI physical layer, need not be concerned with the nature of the data that is transmitted or received, for example, text or video or audio, etc., or how that data will be used. This separation into layers provides for interoperability, a necessary feature for the success of the Internet.

The OSI application layer facilitates communication between lower layers and the actual applications, providing high-level services for those applications such as Domain Name Service (DNS), File Transfer Protocol (FTP), Post Office Protocol (POP), and other services. Having these services in a separate layer and built in to the operating system relieves application programmers from having to know about such details or to modify the application software as new developments in these services are implemented. The application layer also manages Internet connections for separate portions of an application, called application entities, that communicate with different targets on the Internet. For example, an online ordering system would have an application entity that interacts with the inventory database, an application entity that interacts with the billing database, etc.

The presentation layer focuses on translating data from application layer formats to formats that are transmitted over the Internet and *vice versa*. Two common translations occurring in this layer are encryption/decryption and compression/decompression. Continuing the online ordering example, the login information (user id and password) should be encrypted before being sent out over the Internet. On the other hand, the part number and quantity being ordered may not need to be encrypted. The two application entities would have generated the raw text, but the encryption would be handled by the presentation layer. The presentation layer also provides for simple data translation such as serialization of structured data or between character representations such as EBCDIC, ASCII, and the more recent international language character sets.

The session layer handles the connection between one host and another host. It provides the services that initiate a connection, manage the connection, and terminate the connection. Management issues include recovering or restarting a connection that has been broken and authentication of the other host.

The transport layer provides for reliable transmission and reception of byte sequences across the Internet. This layer verifies that the byte sequence to be passed up to the session layer and ultimately up to the application in the receiving host is the same as the byte sequence transmitted from the application in the sending host. This is typically done by checksums. The transport layer in the sending host computes a checksum and includes that in the byte stream. The receiving host computes the checksum of the received byte stream and compares it to the one computed by the sending host. Note that the nature of the data — text, video stream, encrypted data, etc. — is of no concern in this layer. The only concern is that the byte stream sent was accurately received. The transport layer also manages the splitting of longer byte sequences into smaller packets that can be handled by the transport protocol being used for this connection and the reconstruction of received packets into the correct order before being sent to the session layer.

The network layer is responsible for routing messages from the transport layer to appropriate paths through the Internet. The network layer determines how to get the packet to its destination. If the packet has to be routed to a different network, for example, if the sending and receiving hosts are on different wide-area networks, the network layer would determine an intermediate node for the first hop. The network layer of that node would then determine the next node, etc. The network layer does not check for reliable transmission, only that the packet gets sent out. Reliability is checked at the transport layer, not the network layer.

The data link layer manages transfer between two hosts that are directly connected, such as over an ethernet link. This layer handles access to the physical medium, such as checking if the physical link is already being used, and the transfer of data to and from the physical device that actually transmits or receives signals. This layer also checks for errors in the physical transmission of signals.

The physical layer focuses on the transformation of logical bits into the physical signals of the medium and *vice versa* — voltages for wired media and radio signals for wireless media. The physical layer is also concerned with general features of media transmission such as baud rates, timing characteristics, idle vs. busy states, full/half duplex, etc. In the case of wired media, the physical layer also deals with the configuration of the connectors to which the wires are attached.

PCs and laptops provide a multitude of devices at the physical layer. The operating systems on those machines provide the services at all the OSI layers, including device drivers for the devices at the physical layer. Many operating systems for small processing elements do not have support for some or all of the OSI levels. For embedded systems using those processing elements, the engineers will need to include additional circuitry for the physical layers and software to implement the higher layers. The OSI model can be used as a guide for this, especially if the node is to be used as a gateway for the system to the Internet.

22.3 Transport Control Protocol and Internet Protocol

Transport Control Protocol (TCP)[2] and Internet Protocol (IP)[3] are two widely used protocols for Internet communication. TCP functions mostly in the OSI Transport Layer, although some of TCP's functions, such as gracefully closing a broken connection, are modeled at the Session Layer in OSI. IP functions at the Network Layer of the OSI model. These are actual protocols (or more precisely, families of protocols), not just models. Each one specifies the details of how an Internet connection should work at the associated level. An embedded system design team would need to understand at least the basics of IPs like TCP and IP if it was designing a system in which a low-end processing element was used as a gateway and had to be programmed for Internet connectivity. We describe some of the basics for each of these protocol families in the following sections. Each protocol has many additional features that are not described here. Our goal is to make the student aware of the basic concepts so that, whatever IP is chosen for a project, the student will be able to easily learn the required protocol and then implement any required parts on the small processing elements as needed.

22.3.1 **Transport Control Protocol**

The main functions of the TCP protocol are to manage host-to-host connections over an IP network and to reliably transmit and receive byte streams. Managing a connection includes opening the connection (i.e., establishing a connection with an application on another machine), closing the connection when the applications are through communicating, attempting to reconnect if the connection is broken, and other similar activities. Reliable transmission and reception of byte streams include error checking received data, receiving acknowledgment that the other machine has successfully received a transmission and retransmitting if no acknowledgment is received within a specified time, partitioning a long stream being sent into smaller packets that are acceptable to the IP layer and the physical transmission devices and reforming received packets into correct order before being passed to the application on this machine, controlling the flow of packets across the connection, and others. Note that the extra computation to ensure reliability, proper ordering of received packets, and possible requests for retransmission may introduce significant delays in the communication. This may be a problem for communications that have to satisfy real-time constraints, such as audio and video streaming. There are other OSI Transport Layer protocols, for example, User Datagram Protocol (UDP),[4] that are better for real-time applications.

Table 22.1 lists the fields contained in a TCP packet and their corresponding lengths. The fields are described in more detail in the following bullet list.

* Source and Destination Ports. Each application running on a computer is assigned a port number for TCP use. Common applications have corresponding common port numbers — for example, 21 is the standard port number for FTP,

Table 22.1 Summary of fields in a TCP packet.

Field name	Length in bits
Source port	16
Destination port	16
Sequence number	32
Acknowledge number	32
Data offset	4
Reserved (should all be 0)	3
Flags	9
Window size	16
Checksum	16
Urgent pointer	16
Additional options	0—320 (must be multiple of 32)
Payload	(See bullet list below.)

110 for POP, 25 for SMTP, etc. This allows several applications to be communicating through TCP/IP at the same time. When a message is received, TCP uses the destination port number to route the payload to the appropriate application. An application in an embedded system would be assigned a port number by the design team. This would be placed in the source port field when that application sent a message across the Internet to another system. Conversely, that other system would use the assigned port number in the destination port field when it sent messages to the embedded system application. An embedded system might have several applications running concurrently, corresponding perhaps to concurrent processes in the UML and/or FSM models of the system. For example, the gateway in a BAN for patient monitoring might have a process for handling regular patient reports and a second process for handling emergency situations, each of which sent and received messages through the Internet. Each of these processes would have its own port number.

- Sequence Number. Long messages may need to be split into segments that can be handled by the lower levels of the protocol stack. The sequence number field is used to number the segments so that they can be reassembled in the proper order at the destination.
- Acknowledge Number. TCP is a reliable transmission protocol. One of the techniques it uses to guarantee reliable delivery is to have the destination machine acknowledge receipt of each packet sent to it. There are two methods used to determine that a packet has not been acknowledged and should be retransmitted. The simplest is the timeout approach. An estimate of the time by which acknowledgment should be received is made when a packet is transmitted. If acknowledgment is not received by the timeout, the packet is retransmitted. In the second approach, the receiver watches for gaps in the sequence of received packets. If the receiver has received all packets from $1-N$ and the next received packet has sequence number higher than $N+1$, say $N+3$, then packets $N+1$ and $N+2$ may be lost. In this case, the receiver uses N for the acknowledged number in acknowledging packet $N+3$, and the sender will know that packets $N+1$ and $N+2$ may be lost. Of course, they might simply be taking longer to reach the destination, so the sender will wait until it has received several acknowledgments, typically three or more, before retransmitting. Note that receipt of an acknowledgment only means that the target machine has received the packet in its TCP layer; the packet may not have been delivered to the application yet.
- Data Offset. The number of 32-bit words before the payload starts. This allows for variable amounts of additional options to be included in the packet.
- Reserved. These three bits are reserved for future use. They should all be 0.
- Flags. There are nine flags. Three of these are used to allow the application to respond to Internet congestion. An additional three flags are the SYN flag, used to open a connection, the FIN flag, used to close it, and the RST flag, used to reset it. (See the following paragraph for more details about these operations.) The remaining three flags in this field are URG, indicating the Urgent Pointer is relevant, ACK, indicating that the Acknowledge field is relevant, and PSH,

indicating that any data collected so far in the TCP protocol should be pushed to the application without waiting for additional packets.

- Window Size. This field specifies the size of the buffer that TCP uses to collect data being received. A sender should not send more packets than the target receiver can hold. A receiver can stop the sender from transmitting by making this field 0 in its latest acknowledgment. The ability of the TCP protocol to buffer multiple received packets for a particular application allows more efficient use of the Internet. A sender does not need to wait for acknowledgment of each packet before sending more packets. If the receiver's buffer is large enough, the sender might even be able to transmit a long message without waiting for any acknowledgments. In addition, some buffer space is necessary to hold packets that are received out of order.
- Checksum. This is a standard checksum for a packet and is used to detect errors in the received data.
- Urgent Pointer. If the URG flag is set, this pointer tells where the end of the urgent data is in the payload. This urgent data is pushed immediately up to the application rather than being buffered like ordinary data.
- Additional Options. There are a variety of additional options, the scope of which is beyond this brief introduction. These additional options are encoded in the Additional Options area.
- Payload. The data being sent by the application or that is to be received by the application is included at the end of the TCP packet.

A TCP connection has to be opened before information can flow between the two associated applications, and when the connection is no longer needed, it should be closed. The TCP layer on any host machine monitors the IP layer for incoming messages that request initiation of a connection. A TCP connection is initiated by one host sending an SYN packet (a packet with the SYN flag set to 1) to the other host. When the other machine receives the SYN packet it does two things. First it sets its sequence number for this connection to the sequence number in the packet. In this way the two ends of the connection have coordinated sequence numbers. Second it sends an SYN-ACK packet back to the initiating host. Finally, the initiating host sends an ACK packet back to the other host so that both hosts can be sure the connection has been established. Closing a TCP connection is done similarly except that there is an extra FIN transmission. One of the connected hosts sends a FIN packet (a packet with the FIN flag set to 1) to the other host. The other host acknowledges with a FIN-ACK, indicating that it is ready to close the connection. The other host then sends a FIN packet to the terminating host, which the terminating host then acknowledges. Thus, there are four packets sent. Each host sends a FIN packet, and each host acknowledges to the other that it is closing the connection.

22.3.2 Internet Protocol

The function of the IP is to route packets out into the Internet so they can begin their journey to their destinations. Packets from TCP or UDP or other transport layer protocols are embedded into the IP packets as the payload. The IP protocol does not guarantee reliable communication. There is no IP acknowledgment from the destination machine. (Of course, once the message is received in the transport layer of the target machine, the transport layer protocol may form an acknowledge message. But this happens at the transport layer of the target machine, not the IP layer.) IP communication is deemed "best-effort delivery". A node along the path from source to destination may drop a packet if that node detects that the packet has been corrupted, the Internet traffic is too clogged at that point, or a variety of other reasons. A given packet may travel through many routers and networks on its way to its destination, and two IP packets from the same TCP or UDP message may not take the same path through the Internet. IP communication is connectionless in the sense that the two end machines do not form an established connection prior to communication. There is no initiation request and acknowledgment between the two end machines, as there is in TCP.

There are two main versions of the IP protocol — the original IPv4[5] and the more recent IPv6.[6] The major difference is that addresses in IPv4 are 32 bits while addresses in IPv6 are 128 bits. The enlarged address space was made necessary because nearly all the addresses in the IPv4 version were used by 2011.[7] Aside from the change in the size of the addresses, there were significant changes in the packet format between the two versions. Many fields in the IPv4 format were dropped and new fields added. The IPv4 header includes interesting fields that illustrate some issues involved in Internet communication, so we present that format in the following table and bullet list.

Table 22.2 lists the fields contained in an IPv4 packet and their corresponding lengths. The fields are described in more detail in the following bullet list.

- Version. This field distinguishes between IPv4, IPv6, and other IP protocols. For IPv4 these four bits are 0100, that is, the number 4.
- IHL. This is the number of 32-bit words in the header. This allows for up to four 32-bit words to be included in the Additional Options field.
- DSCP. These 6 bits have been used in different ways over the years. One of these ways is to indicate a priority, for example, best-effort, priority, critical, etc.
- ECN. These are available to indicate congestion conditions in the network.
- Total Length. The total length of the packet, including header and payload.
- Identification. The sequence number of the original transport layer message has been segmented.
- Flags. The first bit is reserved and should be 0. The second bit is the Don't Fragment (DF) flag. It indicates to nodes on the path that this packet cannot be split. If splitting is required for the node to forward the packet, the packet is dropped. The third bit is the More Fragments (MF) flag. If a packet has been split, this flag is 1 for all but the last segment.
- Fragment Offset. This gives the position of this fragment in a very long message.
- Time to Live. It is possible for an IP packet to travel in a loop through the network, that is, to be forwarded by a node and eventually come back to that

Table 22.2 Summary of fields in an IPv4 packet.

Field name	Length in bits
Version	4
Internet Header Length (IHL)	4
Differentiated Service Code Point (DSCP)	6
Explicit Congestion Notification (ECN)	2
Total Length	16
Identification	16
Flags	3
Fragment Offset	13
Time to Live	8
Protocol	8
Header Checksum	16
Source IP Address	32
Destination IP Address	32
Additional Options	0–128 (must be a multiple of 32)
Payload	(See bullet list below.)

node. Thus, in principle, a packet could take arbitrarily many hops and possibly never reach its destination. This field places a limit on either the time in seconds or the number of hops before the packet is dropped. The most common measure is number of hops.

- Protocol. There are many transport layer protocols that use IP. This field tells which one created this message.
- Header Checksum. This is a checksum for the header. It does not include any of the payload. It is the responsibility of higher-level protocols to check for validity of the data in the payload.
- Source and Destination IP Addresses. These are the IP address of this machine and the IP address of the machine to which the packet is being sent.
- Additional Options. IP supports many additional features and options. These are indicated in the next four 32-bit words if this packet is using any of those features or options.
- Payload. This is the data received from the TCP or UDP or other transport layer protocol.

IP packets are passed down to the Data Link layer of the OSI model and from there down to an actual physical device that sends bit streams out of the machine and into the network. The details at these layers depend on the actual transmission medium (wire, radio, optical, etc.), and a survey of these is beyond the scope of this book. These devices and their drivers would be built into a laptop or PC. For a low-end microprocessor used as a gateway in an embedded system, the design team would need to find suitable hardware, buy or implement the drivers for it, and format the IP packets for transmission over that physical link.

22.3.3 **Example**

We illustrate the steps an embedded system engineer might take in the design and implementation of the Internet communication in a system using a low-end micro-controller as the gateway to the Internet. The system is a BAN for patient monitoring and medication. The design presented here is not the only solution for this system. For example, the Internet connectivity could be implemented on the patient's PC, and the connection between the BAN and the PC could be a specially designed private network. We present the following solution so that we can illustrate how an embedded system might implement the TCP/IP protocols on a low-end processing element.

The system is supposed to take readings of sensors around the body at regular intervals and transmit that information to a PC in the doctor's office. The doctor's office can send messages to the patient system changing the interval depending on the patient's situation; for example, the period might be 30 minutes, but if the readings have been stable for the past 24 hours, the doctor's office might change the period to 60 minutes. Suppose also that the doctor's office PC can request information about current medication dosages and send information back to the patient monitoring system to adjust those dosages. The system monitors its administration of medicines and notifies a local pharmacy when it's time for refills. Further, the patient monitoring system can detect emergency situations (e.g., patient passed out, fell, etc.) and broadcast a message over the Internet to nearby hospitals and ambulance services. The gateway is chosen to be a microcontroller with no operating system but with a Wi-Fi circuit for connecting to the patient's laptop. The IPv4 version of IP is chosen as the IP, and TCP is chosen for the transport layer protocol.

Suppose the FSM model of the system running on the gateway included three concurrent modules — one for the regular reporting, one for the medication dosage control, and one for emergency response. (There may have been others, but they are of no concern for this example.) The software for the gateway, then, includes three modules corresponding to the three AND super-states of the FSM model. These three modules are the applications in the TCP protocol, and the team would assign a port number to each of them. This port number is used as the source port when messages are transmitted from the gateway to the Internet, and conversely the PC in the doctor's office or pharmacy would need to know these port numbers in order to send messages to the gateway. Note that communication is two-way between the doctor's office and each of the reporting and medication applications but only one-way for the emergency application.

The design team would have to assign an IPv4 address to the gateway. This address would be a local address on the same local area network (LAN) as the patient's PC. The software implementing TCP/IP on the gateway would need to know the IPv4 address of the PC in the doctor's office, the one in the pharmacy, etc., and use those IPv4 addresses in the packets that it sent out. Further, the software would have to use the Internet broadcast IP address for the emergency system broadcast of an emergency request message. An application would be developed to run on the PC in the doctor's office. This application would need an assigned port number, and the gateway software would need to use this port number when sending messages to the doctor's office. Conversely, the application in the doctor's office PC would need to use the port numbers for the modules in the gateway when sending messages back to the patient system.

Because of the simplicity of the software running on the gateway, the IP and TCP protocols could be combined into a single software module. Similarly, the OSI session, presentation, and application layers could be merged. Thus, each application would form a message, encrypt the message, and then pass the encrypted message plus the application's port number and the destination IPv4 address to the TCP/IP module. That module would form a complete TCP/IP message and send it to the Wi-Fi circuit for transmission to the patient's PC and from there into the Internet. Conversely, when the Wi-Fi circuit has received a string of bytes forming a complete incoming TCP/IP packet, the TCP/IP module would extract the payload and port number and pass the message to the application module, which would perform any required decryption and forward to the appropriate application. Note some communications circuitry may provide some of these services, and it is up to the engineer to understand which services are provided by the chosen circuitry and which need to be implemented by the development team.

22.4 **The ethernet protocol**

Ethernet[8] is a family of protocols that has evolved over time. First introduced in 1973, it has become widely used in the commercial sector during the 1980s. It has been governed by IEEE 802.3 standards since 1983. Ethernet protocols apply to the OSI data link (ethernet Media Access Control [MAC]) and physical (ethernet PHY) layers. Ethernet is used for LANs and small networks such as those within a building. Ethernet connectivity has become one of the key infrastructure technologies of the modern Internet. Ethernet would be a good candidate for the connectivity in embedded systems for home or office applications and other applications where the distances are up to 100 meters if in wired networks or up to 2 kilometers in fiber optic networks. In addition, repeaters, wireless adapters, routers, and bridges[9] allow ethernet to be used over longer distances or in applications where wiring between all devices in the system is not feasible.

Ethernet was originally designed as a linear network using coaxial cable and CSMA/CD (see Section 23.4, Chapter 23) for handling collision. As the number of devices on ethernet networks increased, performance degradation due to collisions became a problem. This led to the development of switches (see next paragraph) that greatly reduced or even eliminated collision. Nowadays, the wired connections are made using twisted pair cables and 8P8C (8 position, 8 contact) connectors, such as the RJ45 connector common in telephones, allowing for full-duplex transmission. Speeds up to 400 GBS are possible depending on the transmission medium (copper or fiber optic) and the distances. Many high-end processing elements, such as the Luminary family of processors, have built-in ethernet sections that implement both the MAC and PHY ethernet layers. There are also inexpensive (less than $10) chipsets readily available for embedded system engineers to design an ethernet add-on for low-end processing elements.

To reduce or solve the collision problem, low-cost devices such as bridges and, later, switches are used. Each of these devices has several ethernet ports. A computer would no longer be connected to every other computer on the network. Rather, the computer would be connected to a switch, for example. This connection is point-to-point and full duplex, so there are no collisions on this link. The switch spreads the connection over its other ports. For example, if the switch had eight ports, one would be used to connect to the computer, and the other seven would connect to other parts of the network. See Figure 22.3 for how switches isolate individual computers from the general network. In this figure the solid bumps on the switch rectangles represent ports and the arrows represent wired connections to other devices (PC or another switch). If any of the other ports are connected to multiple devices, those ports may experience collision. In ethernet terminology, each port is its own collision domain. Because these collision domains are smaller than the whole network, the probability of collision is reduced. Moreover, the switch handles collisions without the need for action by the computer attached to it. It is common to include enough switches in the network so that every port is connected only to a computer or a single other switch (see Problem 1), eliminating collisions altogether, an important consideration for real-time applications. It is also common to use different ports in the switch to connect to devices with different speeds, one port being for low-speed devices, another for high-speed, etc.

Switches perform two operations that help improve network performance but that are not performed on bridges. First, a switch remembers the addresses of packets

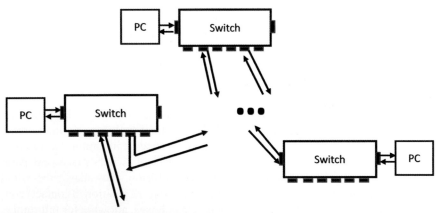

FIGURE 22.3 An Ethernet Network With Switches.

Author drawn.

sent through it. When first turned on the switch has no record of addresses, and it forwards all packets received at one port out to all its other ports. However, the switch remembers the source address for each packet received on each port. In the future, if the switch receives a packet, it checks if it knows the port associated with the target address. If so, it only forwards the packet out to the correct port. Over time, a switch will learn all or almost all the addresses of devices on the network and is therefore very efficient at routing packets to the correct port. This greatly reduces network traffic. Second, switches that use the store-and-forward technique receive and store an entire packet before forwarding it. These switches perform various tests on packets, such as being corrupted or smaller than the minimum size, and delete bad packets. (The alternative to store-and-forward, called cut-through, routes a packet to the appropriate port or ports as soon as the destination address in the packet has been received. The cut-through approach decreases the packet delay in the switch at the expense of failing to detect bad packets.) Some more sophisticated switches also perform some functions at higher OSI levels. A router performs all the operations of a switch but also includes connections to other networks such as other wide-area networks.

Ethernet packets, or frames, have two formats, one at the MAC level and one at the PHY level. The fields in a MAC frame are shown in Table 22.3. Addresses in ethernet packets are MAC addresses. These are 48-bit numbers assigned uniquely to (and hard-wired into) individual network interface controllers (e.g., the NIC card in a laptop) that connect directly to the physical layer of the Internet. MAC addressing is an OSI data link layer phenomenon, as opposed to URL addressing used at the OSI application layers and the IPv4/IPv6 addressing used at the OSI network layer. The MAC frame is embedded into a PHY frame, whose format is shown in Table 22.4.

The fields are described in more detail in the following bullet list.

- The preamble is a sequence of alternating 1s and 0s that allows other ethernet devices connected to the transmitting device to synchronize their clocks. The preamble consists of seven 0xAA bytes in sequence.
- The start frame delimiter is the byte 0xAB. The hardware uses this last byte to synchronize byte timing.

Table 22.3 Summary of fields in an ethernet MAC frame.

Field name	Length in bytes
MAC destination address	6
MAC source address	6
802.1Q tag (optional)	4
Ethertype or length	2
Payload	46–1500
CRC	4

Table 22.4 Summary of fields in an ethernet PHY frame.

Field name	Length in bytes
Preamble	7
Start frame delimiter (SFD)	1
MAC frame	64—1522
Interpacket gap	12

- MAC destination and source addresses are the 48-bit MAC addresses of the device generating the physical level transmission and the device that is supposed to receive it.
- The 802.1Q field is an optional field used to indicate a virtual LAN.
- Ethertype has two mutually exclusive uses. Values 1500 or less indicate the length of the payload. Values 1536 or above are used to indicate which protocol is used in the payload.
- The payload is the stream received from the OSI network layer.
- CRC is a 32-bit cyclic redundancy check.
- The interpacket gap is required to allow receiving devices to process the packet. The transmitting device is required to transmit 96 bits of idle state.

Wi-Fi was developed as a wireless alternative to ethernet for physical layer Internet connectivity. Wi-Fi is discussed along with other wireless protocols in Chapter 23, Section 23.3.1.

22.5 Summary

Embedded systems, especially those destined to participate in the Internet of Things, often need to communicate with other systems and entities through the Internet. So, it is important for embedded system designers and engineers to understand the capabilities and requirements of The Internet. This chapter presents the two major Internet models — the OSI model and the TCP/IP model. The layers in each model are described, and issues relating to those layers in the design of an embedded system are noted. In particular, it is noted that lower-level processing elements without significant operating system support would require additional hardware and/or software to allow the system to communicate over the Internet. The details provided in this chapter would allow embedded system engineers to implement the required pieces. The discussion of TCP/IP includes an extended example illustrating the steps the design and implementation teams would need to take. The chapter closes with a presentation on the ethernet protocol, the most common method for implementing LANs. Many embedded systems take the form of a LAN.

Problems

1. Consider the BAN for patient monitoring and medication described in the example in Section 21.3.3. Suppose the port number assigned to the monitoring application in the gateway is 36, and the port number for the application in the PC in the doctor's office is 91. Suppose further that the IPv4 address of the gateway is 210.57.2.30 (i.e., the first byte of the IPv4 address is 210, the second 57, etc.), and the IPv4 address of the PC in the doctor's office is 147.95.78.20. Assume that all messages transmitted back and forth between the gateway and the doctor's office are small and will never be split or fragmented. Assume neither of TCP nor IP will use any extra options. The gateway is sending the following report to the doctor's office:

   "id=192547,p=78,o=98,s=137"

   (The message indicates this is the patient whose id is 192547, the pulse is 78, the oxygen saturation is 98%, and the blood sugar level is 137.)
   a) Look up the detailed description of the TCP flags[3] and tell what values each should have in this message.
   b) Look up the detailed description of the IP DSCP flags[4] and tell what values each should have for this message.
   c) Based on your answer for part a, write out the full TCP header excluding the checksum field for this message.
   d) Based on your answer for part b, write out the full IP header excluding the checksum field for this message. Assume Time-to-Live is set to the maximum.

2. Suppose we are to design a network for devices in a lab. Suppose each device has an ethernet port. Suppose we use switches with eight ports.
   a) Suppose the lab has six devices. Which network topology (Section 21.6, Chapter 21) would most likely be used? Draw the network.
   b) Suppose the lab has 50 devices. Draw a suitable network showing the number of switches that are used and how the devices are connected to the switches.
   c) Suppose the lab had one computer that collected data from and controlled all other devices in the lab. Suppose the number of devices could increase arbitrarily. What network topology would you use for this situation? Describe an algorithm for adding new devices into that network structure.

3. Tell at which OSI layer each of the following happens:
   a) Determine if there is an error in a packet.
   b) Determine that the packet target is outside the local network.
   c) Open a session and connect to another machine.
   d) Generate wireless signals.
   e) Hold a message because the device is currently transmitting another message.

References

[1] https://en.wikipedia.org/wiki/OSI_model.
[2] https://en.wikipedia.org/wiki/Transmission_Control_Protocol.
[3] https://en.wikipedia.org/wiki/Internet_Protocol.
[4] https://en.wikipedia.org/wiki/User_Datagram_Protocol.
[5] https://en.wikipedia.org/wiki/IPv4.
[6] https://en.wikipedia.org/wiki/IPv6.
[7] https://en.wikipedia.org/wiki/IPv4_address_exhaustion#Address_depletion.
[8] https://en.wikipedia.org/wiki/Ethernet.
[9] https://en.wikipedia.org/wiki/Network_switch.

Low-level communication protocols

23.1 Introduction

A communication protocol is the specification of relevant details for some aspect of how messages get transmitted. A protocol might focus on the physical transmission of signals. For example, protocols for wired connections between devices might specify cable lengths, baud rates, and electrical characteristics of the signals and the circuits. A protocol might focus on the data format. For example, it might specify the maximum length of a message or the format of information within a sequence of bytes. A protocol might specify how a channel is shared among multiple users or a variety of other aspects of the communication. In this chapter we describe some of the most common communication protocols. This book is not about communication protocols, so the descriptions given here are meant only to acquaint the student with the major protocols and make the student aware of the issues associated with protocols in general. Some guidance is given as to when each protocol might be appropriate for a particular embedded system. The goal is to prepare the student for selecting an appropriate set of protocols for a given project and then, if necessary, designing and implementing the necessary hardware and software.

We begin the presentation with a discussion of the most common model of the Internet and the most common protocol used for Internet communication. We then focus on lower-level communication schemes, including wired and wireless, used to connect individual nodes in an embedded system. We finish with a discussion of collision, a common problem with shared channels, and methods to handle it.

23.2 Common serial protocols for wired connections

In wired serial transmission, data is sent one bit at a time. The following are common features of a wired serial protocol.

- Different voltages on the data wire are used to indicate a 0-bit or a 1-bit.
- The rate at which the bits are sent is called the baud rate. In some protocols the baud rate can vary over a range but must be fixed during one transmission event. In other protocols, for example, IIC, the time for each bit is determined by a separate wire in the cable that carries a clock signal.

Embedded System Design. https://doi.org/10.1016/B978-0-443-18470-3.00023-3

- Because data is sent only one bit at a time, only one wire or two wires are needed for data.
- During some time periods, no data is being sent on the wires, a condition called idle. Therefore, most protocols require some means to indicate when a transmission event is starting.
- Normally some time period between two transmissions is required for the wire(s) to settle into the idle state and the receiver to accept the transmission. Some protocols specify one or two stop bits for this purpose.
- Because only one bit is sent at a time, the bits are sent either most-significant bit (MSB) first or least-significant bit (LSB) first.
- Parity is an option in some protocols. Even parity means the number of 1 bits in the message is even; odd parity means the number of 1 bits is odd. Parity is used to detect some errors in transmission. If a serial connection is using odd parity and a packet with an even number 1 bits is received, the receiver knows there was an error in transmission. Parity requires an extra bit in the transmission, and the sender sets that bit to either 0 or 1 to make the message itself match the chosen parity. In some protocols the stop bit is used for this purpose.

Each protocol has its own additional special features. Figure 23.1 shows a sample serial transmission of the byte $3A_H$ with LSB first and even parity. Time increases from left to right. So, at the beginning (i.e., at the left end) the signal is idle. Then the start bit occurs, followed by bit 0, etc.

There are many serial transmission protocols. We present here a few of the most commonly used ones. Our goal is to make the student aware of the variety of serial protocols currently used and expose the student to the issues involved in selecting a protocol appropriate for an application and then implementing it on the chosen platforms. Further, many microcontrollers do not have built-in serial capability or do not have the ones deemed most suitable by the design team. In such cases, I/O pins can be used for the signals, and the protocol implemented through software. So, it is important to understand the low-level details of the protocols such as message format and timing.

23.2.1 TTL serial protocols

Perhaps the simplest serial protocol is the one used in many microprocessors, including, for example, the 8051. It is an end-to-end or point-to-point protocol.

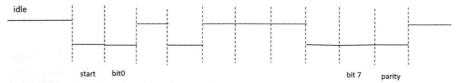

FIGURE 23.1 Sample Serial Transmission of 3AH in RS232 Protocol.

Author drawn.

That is, exactly two devices communicate over this kind of serial line — one device at each end of a cable. 1 byte is transmitted at a time, so a multibyte application message requires multiple serial transmissions, one for each byte of the application message. The following are the major specifications for this protocol.

- The cable connecting the two ends has a wire for each direction, that is, a wire for the first node to send data to the second and a wire for the second node to send data to the first. This is called full duplex connection, and full duplex connections can send data in both directions at the same time. (Note, some other serial protocols may use a single wire for both directions, called half duplex. In this case only one node can be transmitted at a time.)
- The TTL protocol does not specify minimum or maximum baud rates. The maximum rate would be determined by the particular processor used and, of course, the length of the cable. As noted, longer cables cannot carry higher-speed signals reliably.
- One start bit. One or two stop bits, typically selectable under software control by setting some configuration register.
- The format of a 1-byte transmission is the start bit, 8 data bits, and the stop bit(s). The order of the bits within the payload depends on the microcontroller being used. In the 8051 family it is LSB.
- Transmission is asynchronous, so each processor must have its own clock. The processors at the two ends must be programmed to have the same baud rate. Note that because the two processors have separate clocks, some additional measures must be used to overcome the problems associated with the clocks themselves not being synchronized and being out of phase. See the paragraph following this bullet list.
- Parity is not specified but can be programmed through software by controlling the stop bit. For example, on the 8051 the sender software will set a bit in a control register to 0 or 1 as needed to obtain the correct parity, and the receiver can test the stop bit to check the parity.
- The voltage in the wires is the same as the operating voltage of the microcontroller, typically 5 V or 3.3 V. Low voltage is logic 0, and high voltage is logic 1.
- Idle state is high voltage. The start bit must pull the wire to logic 0, that is, low voltage.

The pattern in Figure 23.1 represents a 1-byte transmission using this protocol.

In asynchronous serial transmission, the devices at the ends of the cable each have their own clocks. These clocks may not be exactly the same frequency; for example, minor variations in crystals of nominally the same frequency can lead to clocks that are a fraction (or possibly more) different. Even if the clocks had exactly the same frequency, the devices themselves may be powered up at different times or, if powered up at the same time, require different amounts of time to start up. Therefore, the clocks may be out of phase. Figure 23.2 illustrates this, showing two clocks that are 180 degrees out of phase. For any reasonable length cable, the time for the pulse to travel from the sender to the receiver (perhaps a few nanoseconds) is

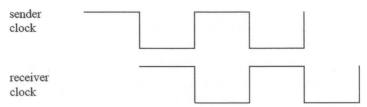

FIGURE 23.2 Two Clocks 180 Degrees Out of Phase.

Author drawn.

completely ignorable relative to the time per bit (typically on the order of milliseconds). Suppose the sender initiates each bit on the falling edge of its clock and the receiver samples the data line on the rising edge of its clock. If the clocks are 180 degrees out of phase, as shown in Figure 23.2, the receiver would be sampling the data line at exactly the point in time when the sender may be trying to change the signal for the next bit. This situation will certainly lead to errors. Note that if the receiver was sampling on the falling edge of its clock, the same problem would occur if the clocks were in phase.

The desired situation is that the receiver samples the data line at about the middle of the time period for each bit, no matter whether the clocks are in phase or out of phase. A simple yet elegant solution is for the receiver to use a clock that is a multiple of the baud rate. The typical multiple is 16, leading to the so-called 16× method. Figure 23.3 illustrates the 16× method. When the receiver senses the data line going from idle to start bit, it counts 8 of its 16× clock periods and then samples the data line. (In some implementations, the receiver samples at the 7th, 8th, and 9th 16× clock points for greater reliability.) Regardless of the phase relation, the sample point in the receiving device will be close to the middle of the time period for that bit. Even if the sender and receiver clocks have slightly different frequencies, the cumulative error after 10−11 bits (start bit, 8 data bits, 1−2 stop bits) will still not put the sample point of the last bit very far from the middle of the time period for that bit.

23.2.2 RS232 protocol

The RS232 protocol has many features in common with the simple TTL protocol − point-to-point transmission, one start bit, 1−2 stop bit(s), 16× sampling, and full

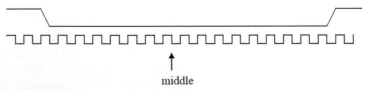

middle

FIGURE 23.3 Sampling With 16× Receiver Clock.

Author drawn.

duplex. Parity is optional, but if it is selected then the frame for 1 byte contains an additional bit other than the start, data, and stop bits. Line voltages range typically from −12 V to +12 V. Negative voltages represent logic 1, and positive voltages represent logic 0. Line idle is represented by logic 1, and the start bit is represented by logic 0. Baud rates can run typically up to 56K. Cable lengths can be up to 50 feet or more, but longer cables require extra care for reliable transmission. Simple RS232 transmission is asynchronous — the processors at the ends of the cable each have their own clocks.

The RS232 protocol dates from the early 1960s and was originally designed as a communication mechanism between mainframe computers, printers, modems, and other such equipment. In order to accommodate the additional features of these devices, the RS232 protocol has several other features, such as a signal for a modem to inform its host processor that there is an incoming call or a signal from a slow device like a printer to inform its host that it is ready to receive more data. A simple cable that does not use any of these features may have only three wires — send, receive, and common GND. The full cable may have up to 11 signals and use 25-pin connectors at the ends.

Many embedded systems use both microcontrollers with built-in TTL serial and communication to PCs and other devices that use simple asynchronous RS232. There are many circuits available, such as the MAX 232 circuit, that can translate between the voltage levels of these two protocols, thus allowing a very simple interface.

23.2.3 Inter-integrated circuit (I^2C) protocol

The I^2C (also written as IIC) protocol is significantly different than the TTL and RS232 protocols. I^2C is not point-to-point; rather, up to 127 different devices can be connected to one I^2C bus (although in practice because of address collision, the number of devices in typical applications is much lower). Each I^2C device has a 7-bit address in the range 1−127. I^2C is a synchronous protocol; there is a common clock signal (SCL). There is a single data line (SDA) even though data can flow from any device on the bus to any other device on the bus. Frames can contain arbitrarily many data bytes, as opposed to TTL and RS232 in which a frame contains exactly 1 byte. Each byte in a frame has an acknowledge bit (ACK). For each byte transfer, the eight data bits are sent by one device and the ACK bit is sent by the device receiving the eight data bits. This allows, among other things, for the device initiating a transfer to ascertain that the device with which it is trying to communicate is actually on the bus and active. Some I^2C devices, called bus masters, can initiate bus events. Other devices, called slaves, can only respond when they are addressed by a master. Figure 23.4 shows an overview of an I^2C bus.

Figure 23.5 shows how bus events are started and stopped. In the idle state both SCL and SDA are logic 1. A frame is started by a master device pulling SDA low while SCL remains high, an event called the START condition. All the devices on the bus will recognize this as the start of a bus frame. The frame is terminated by

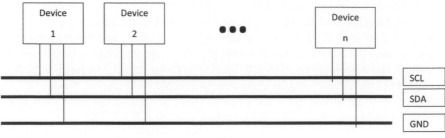

FIGURE 23.4 A Typical I²C Bus Configuration.

Author drawn.

FIGURE 23.5 I²C Start (Left) and Stop (Right) Conditions.

Author drawn.

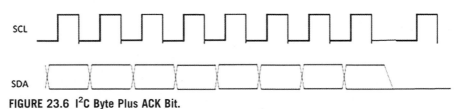

FIGURE 23.6 I²C Byte Plus ACK Bit.

Author drawn.

a STOP condition in which the master pulls the SDA line from low to high while SCL is high. After the STOP condition, the bus becomes idle, and any master can initiate a new bus frame. During the remainder of the frame the master generates the SCL signal, except for so-called clock stretching described in a later paragraph. Bytes are sent to MSB first. After the 8 bit is transmitted, the receiving device should generate the ACK bit during the ninth clock cycle by pulling the SDA line to logic 0 (i.e., GND). The SDA line is allowed to change when SCL is low and is sampled when SCL is high. There can be arbitrarily many bytes transferred in a single frame. Figure 23.6 shows the structure of 1 byte with an ACK bit and the clock stretched between the last data bit and the ACK bit.

The first byte of the frame contains the 7-bit address of the device with which the master is trying to communicate followed by a single bit to indicate whether the master wants to send data (logic 0) to the other device or receive data (logic 1) from the other device. This is followed by an ACK bit from the target device. If the addressed device is on the bus and able to communicate, that device will pull SDA low during the ninth clock period (the ACK period). If the master does not detect a low during that clock period, then the addressed slave device is assumed to be absent or not ready and the frame will be aborted. Note that the master controls SDA during the first eight of these clock periods, while the slave controls SDA during the ninth clock period. If the master indicates that it will write to the slave device, then the master will send additional bytes. For each byte, the master will control the SDA line for eight clock cycles, and the slave will control for the ninth (ACK) clock cycle. If the slave does not pull SDA low for the ACK bit, it means the slave is not able to accept more bytes at that time. If the master had indicated in the first byte that it wanted to read data from the slave device, then the master generates SCL, but the slave controls SDA for the first eight clock cycles of each data byte transfer, and the master then responds with an ACK signal. When the master does not want to receive more bytes, it leaves SDA at logic 1 during the ninth clock cycle.

A variation on the basic frame format is the repeated START. In this scenario, the master will not issue a STOP condition after the end of the data bytes. Instead, the master issues another START condition to start a new frame. In this way, the master maintains control of the bus rather than having the possibility that another master on the same bus can get control.

The SDA and SCL lines have an interesting property that is different from TTL and RS232 lines. I^2C devices are supposed to use open-drain circuitry to connect to these lines. Open-drain circuitry allows one device to pull the line high while another device pulls it low without causing a short circuit and damaging the circuitry. In this kind of situation, the wire itself will have the low voltage level. Typical I^2C devices can detect when they are trying to pull the line high while another device is trying to pull the line low. This is used in two different ways — bus arbitration and clock stretching.

First, an I^2C bus can have more than one master device. It is possible, therefore, that more than one device may try to gain control of the bus (i.e., signal a START condition) at about the same time, a situation called bus contention. At some point in the bus frame one transmitting device will try to send a logic 0 (drive SDA low) while another device tries to send logic 1 (hold SDA high). As noted, in this situation SDA will stay at logic 0. The device that is trying to set SDA high will notice that SDA is different than expected and will then stop operation. This situation can occur during the first byte of the frame when the masters are sending the device address and read/write bit. If the two masters are addressing two different slave devices, then the one sending out the higher address will abort its frame because it will try to transmit a 1 bit while the master sending the lower address will be sending a 0 bit. If the two masters are addressing the same slave device but one is trying to read (1) and the other trying to write (0), the master trying to write will gain control of the bus, and the one trying to read will abort its event. If both masters are accessing the same device with a read operation, assuming the two masters use the same clock frequency, both masters will successfully read the same data unless one master is trying to read fewer bytes. If both masters are trying to write to the same device, then the master that tries to write a data bit 1 first will lose control of the bus and abort its event. Note, in this case the device itself will correctly receive the frame from the master that maintained control of the bus.

The second way that open-drain is used effectively is so-called clock stretching. The master device in a bus event generates the SCL signal, but its driving circuitry is open-drain. A device that is slower may hold SCL low without damaging the master device circuitry. This allows the slower device extra time to drive SDA if the master is reading the device or to sample and hold the bit if the master is writing to the device. This feature allows devices with a variety of speeds to coexist on the same bus.

I^2C device addresses are usually built into the devices themselves with some flexibility for adjusting the address through the device pins. For example, the PCF8591 ADC/DAC has the top four of the seven address bits built into the device — 1001. The bottom three bits are determined by three of the device pins. Strapping one of these pins to GND makes the corresponding address bit 0, while strapping it to power makes the corresponding address bit 1. Thus, a single I^2C bus could have up to eight of these devices. Still, the limit of 127 addresses on a single I^2C bus is very restrictive considering there are thousands of I^2C devices on the market. It is not uncommon for an embedded system to have more than one I^2C bus to avoid address contention; multiple buses also allow for the separation of fast and slow devices.

Although multiple masters on a single bus are allowed, a common configuration is to have a single master with the remaining devices all slave devices. In this case, the master could be a processing element, like a microcontroller, and the remaining devices be sensors, controllers, or other kinds of devices that are polled by the microcontroller. The microcontroller need not have an I^2C address because no other device can initiate a bus event and try to access the microcontroller. In this simple case, the microcontroller will dedicate two pins to the SDA and SCL lines and will need to control these lines by software. Few microcontrollers have open-drain I/O pins, so clock stretching would not be possible. Therefore, the microcontroller software must account for the speeds of the devices on the bus and manipulate SCL accordingly. There are circuits, such as the PCF 8485, that provide 8-bit interface to a microcontroller and handle all the operations on SDA and SCL as well as bus error checking, programmable SCL speeds, and many other features. These circuits usually can be configured to generate an interrupt to the processor on the completion of each byte transfer. Some more recent microcontrollers, such as the ARM family of microcontrollers, have built-in I^2C capability, and the use of the corresponding I/O pins is managed by writing to configuration registers, as discussed in Chapter 10.

The operating speeds are typically 0–100 KHz, although later revisions of the protocol allow for bit speeds up to 5 MHz. Note that this is the bit speed. Considering that each frame starts with an address byte and each byte must have an acknowledge bit, the byte transfer speed can be much lower than the byte transfer rate of the TTL protocol operating at the same bit speed. For example, even if the frame has only 1 data byte, the bus event must include one address byte plus its acknowledge bit and then the data byte and its acknowledge bit for a total of 18 bits, not counting the START and STOP conditions.

Because of the open-drain format for SCL and SDA and the limit on capacitance (400 pF) for these two signals, cable lengths are limited to a few meters. Also, pull-up resisters are required to maintain the logic 1 level when the bus is idle. Thus, the I^2C approach is useful mainly for small systems — a single printed circuit board or a system with a few such boards closely connected on, say, a small motherboard.

There is a large variety of I^2C devices including ADC, DAC, memories, LCD displays, switches, and many other kinds of devices. In most cases the messages that are exchanged between the devices on an I^2C bus are relatively short — perhaps a few bytes. However, an interesting feature of the I^2C protocol is that messages can be arbitrarily long. This means that the I^2C protocol is suitable for applications in which data is streamed, albeit at relatively slower speeds. Examples of such applications include file transfers where the speed of the transfer is not critical or the transfer of large amounts of sensor data.

23.2.4 Controller area network protocol

The controller area network (CAN) protocol also allows multiple nodes, including multiple masters, to exist on a single bus. It differs from I^2C, and TTL and RS232, in several significant ways. First, the number of devices on the bus can be significantly more than 127. The base CAN protocol has 11 bits for device ids, and the extended format has 29. Second, the CAN protocol has a built-in integrity check in the form of a cyclic redundancy check (CRC) field. CRC integrity checking is much more robust than the simple parity check allowed in TTL and RS232 protocols. Finally, the payload is limited to 0—8 bytes. There are also significant differences in the physical transmission layer. Unlike I^2C devices, CAN devices are typically expected to have some computing power as well as other capabilities such as sensing and controlling. Figure 23.7 shows the standard model of a CAN

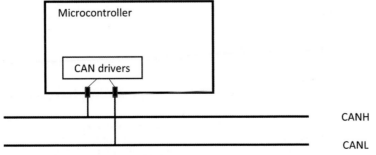

FIGURE 23.7 Structure of a Typical CAN Node.

Author drawn.

node. CAN was originally designed for and is used most extensively in the automotive industry. It has been adapted to other control-intensive applications, such as elevator systems. In such applications, the messages are relatively short, so the streaming capability of the I^2C protocol is not relevant. CAN buses use two wires which carry the data signal, one called CANH (CAN high) and the other called CANL (CAN low). As noted in Chapter 21, differential drive can significantly reduce or eliminate signal degradation due to electrical noise near the bus, especially if the signals are carried over twisted pair, shielded cable. This makes the CAN protocol especially useful for applications like cars, factory floors, and other applications with electrically noisy environments.

There are four types of CAN frames — base data frame, extended data frame, error frame, and overload frame. The format of a CAN base frame is shown in Table 23.1. In the bus idle state, the data line is logic 1 (also called "recessive" in the CAN standards and literature). A node, S, starts a frame by pulling the data line to logic 0 (called "dominant" in the CAN standards and literature). The following 11 bits give the id of the node, T, with which S is trying to communicate. This is followed by a single bit, the remote transmission request (RTR) bit (logic 1 if S is requesting data from T, logic 0 if S is sending data to T). Next is a single bit, the identifier extension (IDE) bit (logic 0 for base format, logic 1 for extended format). The following bit is reserved for future use and should be logic 0. The next 4 bits specify the number of data bytes in the message. This should be a number in the range 0—8. Larger numbers can be inserted here, but CAN devices will not accept more than 8 data bytes. (Note, later versions of the CAN standard, such as CAN FD, allow payloads up to 64 bytes, but not all CAN devices can accept such messages.) If S is requesting data from T (RTR is logic 1), the number of data bytes

Table 23.1 CAN base frame format.

Bit(s)	Purpose	Value
0	Frame beginning	0
1—11	Target node id	Address of target CAN node
12	Remote transmission request	0 for write, 1 for read
13	Extension	0 if base CAN frame, 1 if extended CAN frame
14	Reserved	0
15—18	Number of data bytes (N)	0—7
19 − K	Data	N data bytes
K+1 − K+15	Cyclic redundancy check	15-bit cyclic redundancy value
K+16	CRC delimiter	1
K+17	ACK	Acknowledge bit
K+18	ACK delimiter	1
K+19 − K+25	End of frame	1111111

*(Note: K = 8 * N + 18)*

should be zero because S is not sending any data to T. The next bytes are the actual data. This is followed by a 15-bit CRC and a single logic 1 bit for spacing the CRC from the ACK bit. In the ACK bit position S would write logic 1 while T may write logic 0. As in the I²C protocol, this allows S to know that T is on the bus and able to communicate. (The logic 1 bit after the CRC allows time for T to prepare to drive the data line to logic 0.) There is a single bit (ACK delimiter) of logic 1 and, finally, 7 bits of logic 1 to terminate the frame. In addition, there are at least three logic 1 bits to separate one frame from the next frame. The extended data format has extra bits as follows: a substitute remote request (SRR) bit, 18 bits of extended id, and an extra reserved bit.

The CAN specification does not provide for a signal representing a clock. Therefore, each node will typically have its own internal clock, and all the nodes must use the same clock frequency. To compensate for phase shift among the clocks and minor variations in individual clocks, a mechanism similar to the 16× method for TTL and RS232 serial protocols is used. Each node divides the time for 1 bit into a number of equal-time periods, called "quanta" in the CAN standards and literature. This number need not be 16 but should be sufficiently high to allow for the phases and adjustments to be described in this paragraph. Figure 23.8 shows a typical bit period with 16 quanta. Within 1 bit period there are four portions. The first portion is for synchronization, as described in the next paragraph. The second phase allows for bus delay. The boundary between the third and fourth portions is used to set the sampling point. The CAN standard does not specify exactly how many quanta are in each portion, and many devices allow these to be adjusted to suit the needs of the application.

Synchronization is accomplished in two ways. When a node starts a frame by driving the data line to logic 0 from the idle state, all other nodes synchronize their internal counting for bit periods. This is called hard synchronization. As the transmission of the frame continues, each time the data line transitions from logic 1 to logic 0, each node on the bus compares its internal counter to see if it is in sync with the expected transition. If not, the node adjusts its counter accordingly. This is called resynchronization. (The details of how a node accomplishes this are not specified by the CAN standards and are left to the manufacturers of individual CAN devices.) The CAN protocol has an interesting feature that ensures continued

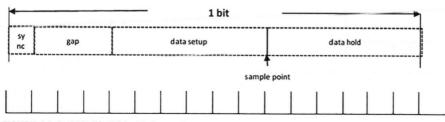

FIGURE 23.8 CAN Bit With 16 Quanta.

Author drawn.

synchronization. After any sequence of 5 bits of the same logic value, a bit of opposite value is inserted. This ensures that there will be resynchronization transitions on the data line, even if the message is mostly logic 1 bits or logic 0 bits. The stuffed bits are not part of the message and are removed by the receiving node. Thus, the actual physical frame may be longer than the logical frame. This feature of resynchronization allows the nodes to remain in synch despite minor variations in their internal clocks. More importantly, it allows a receiving node to resynchronize with the arbitration winner when two or more nodes try to initiate a frame at the same time.

As in the I^2C protocol, the CAN standard specifies that when two or more nodes are trying to drive the bus at the same time, any such node that tries to drive a logic 1 while some other node is trying to drive a logic 0 will lose control of the bus, that is, lose arbitration. Because node ids in a CAN bus must be unique and data is sent MSB first, when two nodes try to gain control and are addressing two distinct target nodes, bus arbitration will occur during the 11 (or 29) bits of the id section of the frame. This has an interesting consequence in those nodes with smaller ids that have higher priority because during the transmission of the id, the higher id number will cause a 1 bit on the data line before the one with the lower id number. One aspect of the design of systems using CAN buses is to carefully assign node ids with this priority in mind. If two nodes try to gain access to the bus at the same time and for the same target node (i.e., same id), the node sending a data frame will win arbitration over the node sending a request frame because the data frame has 0 for the RTR bit.

There are two basic CAN protocols — high-speed (up to 5 MB/second or more) and low-speed (up to 125 KB/second). The high-speed protocol uses a single pair of wires for CANH and CANL in a linear bus format terminated at both ends with a 120-ohm resister between the two wires, as shown in Figure 23.9. This termination means that when no attached circuit is driving the wires, the voltages will float to approximately the same value. Circuits interpret a voltage difference less than

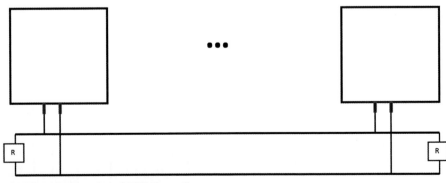

FIGURE 23.9 High-Speed CAN Network.

Author drawn.

0.5 volts as logic 1. When a circuit wants to send a logic 0, that circuit drives the CANH line with a voltage close to Vcc and the CANL line with a voltage close to GND. Circuits interpret a voltage difference more than +2 V as logic 0. See Figure 23.10.

The low-speed CAN protocol allows for more complex network structures, such as star-shaped networks or even clusters of sub-networks connected on a top-level CAN bus. In these cases, the line termination occurs at the CANH and CANL pins on each circuit, with the total termination resistance about 100 ohms. See Figure 23.11. Because the two wires are not connected directly by resisters, the circuits must actively drive the wires to produce logic 1, as shown in Figure 23.12.

The CAN protocol is useful for systems in which messages are relatively short, cable lengths are no more than 40 meters for 1 Mbit/s transmission speeds (or longer at slower speeds), and/or the environment can be electrically noisy.

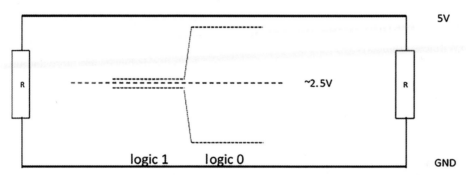

FIGURE 23.10 High-Speed CAN Logic 1 and 0 Signals.

Author drawn.

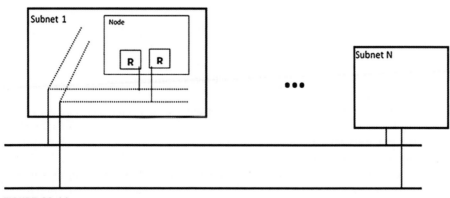

FIGURE 23.11

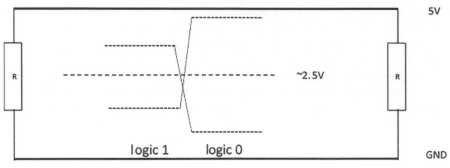

FIGURE 23.12 Low-Speed CAN Logic 1 and 0 Signals.

Author drawn.

23.3 Common low-power wireless protocols and technologies for computer networks

Wireless connectivity is useful for situations in which wiring is not possible, practical, or economical. This includes systems in which the distances are large and in which, therefore, cabling would be expensive. It also includes systems being added to existing infrastructure, such as existing building, in which it would not be economically feasible to run new cables through existing wires. Other situations include severe environments in which cables might degrade over time, rough environments where vibration and other environmental factors might cause connections to come loose, and many others.

Wireless communications have some common features that are either not present in wired systems or are different than in wired systems. First, point-to-point communication is not possible in wireless communication. A transmitter sends a radio signal out, and any radio receiver in range will receive that signal. Some wired protocols, like IIC and CAN, are also not point-to-point; other wired protocols, notably ethernet and TTL/RS232, are. Because wireless communication cannot be point-to-point, wireless packets must always include a header section that includes at least the address of the target radio receiver. Next, wireless connectivity is susceptible to eavesdropping because, again, any receiver in range of the transmitter will receive the signal. This raises the security risk of wireless communication. This is different than in wired systems, where an eavesdropper has to either be connected to the wire or at least be physically close (e.g., have a current sensor wrapped around the wire). Similarly, wireless communication is susceptible to interference, either accidental or malicious. Nearby devices, such as other radio systems or heavy machinery that emits electromagnetic energy, can interfere with the radio signal, similar to static in a regular radio. An attacker may generate purposeful radio interference that maliciously changes the broadcast data. A third issue for wireless communication is the "hidden-node" problem, described in Chapter 21, Section 21.6.2. There are no hidden nodes on a wired bus. In Figure 21.12 of Chapter 21, Section 21.6.2, there is a collision at node B, but neither of the nodes A and C can detect it. If two nodes on a wired bus try to use the bus at the same time, a collision will occur. In most wired protocols collisions can be detected, and at least one and in some cases both the nodes will abort the transmission.

An embedded system engineer would normally not be concerned with the physical aspects of transmitting radio waves through the air or how a transmission is started or stopped (start/stop conditions). These would be built into the circuits. Aspects of concern include baud rates, power consumption, ranges, and how the range is affected by intervening objects such as walls. In the sections that follow the baud rates are for raw bits. Throughput has to take into account the raw bit rate and the relative sizes of the header and the payload, as in wired protocols that are not point-to-point. Ranges are for individual links — one radio transmitter to receivers in the range with no obstacles in the way. For protocols like Bluetooth and Zigbee, it is common to use networks of devices based on that protocol to extend the one-link range. Range is affected by obstacles between a transmitter and receiver, such as walls that can absorb some of the radio signal, and reflections from nearby obstacles which can cause the receiver to receive two slightly out-of-phase copies of the original signal. The choice of antenna will also usually make a significant difference, and chip makers often recommend an antenna to go with the radio chip. An embedded system engineer may want to know the radio frequencies used by the circuits in case other parts of the embedded system or the environment in which it is deployed also generate radio waves. The engineer would select a protocol that allowed a different carrier frequency to reduce interference.

Range, baud rates, and power consumption are continually improving as circuitry improves. The values mentioned in the following sections are based on standards and circuits at the time of the writing of this book. Embedded system engineers involved in selection of networking technologies should review the standards and available circuitry at the time a system is being designed to determine the latest values.

The following presentations are meant to introduce basic concepts for the selected protocols that an engineer would consider in choosing which one to use for a given project. They are not meant to be complete tutorials; such tutorials could easily occupy a whole book. Implementation using one of the protocols would require detailed knowledge about the method that is not relevant to selecting that method over the others. For example, programming a Zigbee node requires knowledge about Zigbee profiles and details about Zigbee Device Objects, but that knowledge would not participate in choosing Zigbee over Bluetooth or Wi-Fi.

23.3.1 Wi-Fi

Wi-Fi[1] was developed as a wireless alternative to ethernet for use as communication links in local area networks and the Internet. It is based on the IEEE 802.11 family of standards. The Wi-Fi Alliance[2] is a nonprofit organization that establishes standards for Wi-Fi communication and certifies that products meet minimal standards. The 802.11 frame format is similar to the ethernet frame format at the data link layer, which makes integration of Wi-Fi and ethernet together into local area networks and the Internet relatively easy. Wi-Fi addresses are 48-bit MAC addresses, the same as ethernet addresses. Wi-Fi has evolved over many years, as Table 23.2 indicates.

Because Wi-Fi uses radio transmission methods, the power is limited by government regulations such as Federal Communications Commission (FCC) rules. A common limit is 100 mW. This is less than a cell phone but more than other low-power networking protocols such as Bluetooth and Zigbee. Power consumption is an issue for battery-operated systems, so there would need to be a compelling need for the advantages of Wi-Fi over other options for such a system. Range and, to some extent baud, rate are dependent on power.

Wi-Fi ranges vary from 20 meters to many miles depending on the radio power, the type of antenna, and the presence or absence of objects between a transmitter and a receiver. Most Wi-Fi devices use omnidirectional antennas so that they can connect to other Wi-Fi devices in any direction. This would be crucial in an application like home control, where the devices would be spread in all directions around the home. Directional antennas can increase the range by focusing all the radio energy in one direction. If the receiver also uses a directional antenna, the range can be up to 20 miles or more. This could be useful in an application like agricultural monitoring, where a number of nodes may be spread around the farm but one node has to communicate with a central data depository several miles away. Access points and routers are also frequently used to both increase the range and provide local area networking. An access point connects several Wi-Fi devices. The individual devices may be far away from each other as long as they are within the range of the access point. A router is an access point that also provides IP routing and often one or more ethernet connections. Many Wi-Fi chipsets include moderate computing power and memory (e.g., a 32-bit microprocessor with 4 or 8 MB flash memory) which includes IP services and possibly also TCP/UDP services. Many of these also include sleep modes for power reduction.

Table 23.2 Versions of Wi-Fi.

Version	IEEE standard	Baud rates (MBs)	Year adopted	Carrier frequencies (GHz)*
1	802.11b	1–11	1999	2.4
2	802.11a	1.5–54	1999	5
3	802.11g	3–54	2003	2.4
4	802.11n	72–600	2009	2.4, 5
5	802.11ac	433–6933	2014	5
6	802.11ax	600–9608	2019	1.6, 2.4, 5

*Carrier of frequencies .9, 5.9, and 60 GHz are also used in special circumstances.

Wi-Fi channels are half-duplex; devices communicate in only one direction at a time. Wi-Fi uses collision avoidance to share the channels. A device listens to see if another radio is broadcasting before attempting to transmit.

23.3.2 Bluetooth

Bluetooth[3] is a wireless networking technology with a family of protocols, or standards as they are called in the Bluetooth community. It is designed for applications requiring local networking, possibly including mobile devices, but not requiring access to the Internet. Sample applications include home control, wireless mice and other PC/laptop accessories, wireless speakers, and other personal area network applications. It was originally meant as a wireless replacement for the wired RS232 protocol, a point-to-point communication protocol. It has since evolved to allow local networks, called piconets in the Bluetooth terminology, of up to eight devices. It is based on the IEEE 802.15.1 standard, and the Bluetooth Special Interest Group is responsible for establishing Bluetooth-specific standards. Bluetooth Low Energy[4] is a low-power version useful for battery-operated and other low-power devices.

Bluetooth standards specify five classes of devices, shown in Table 23.3. The power level for each class is the maximum level allowed for that class. Devices that do not provide that level of power (e.g., the battery is running low) will have shorter range. Intervening objects and antenna choice will also impact the range. Finally, some devices in a particular class may not reach the upper limit; an embedded system engineer should read the specification sheet for the device carefully to determine not only the class but the actual range of an individual device. The power levels are set by design rather than being limited by government regulation. For example, a wireless mouse should not have range more than a few feet, otherwise it will interfere with nearby laptop users. On the other hand, a wireless speaker system should have a range of up to, say, 10 meters so that the speakers can be placed apart for good listening. The classes provide the embedded system designer with a useful guide in selecting Bluetooth devices for a given application.

Bud rates for Bluetooth devices are in the 1−3 MBS range. Bluetooth Low Energy, starting with Bluetooth Version 5.0 in 2016, provides for alternative baud rates

Table 23.3 Bluetooth classes.

Class	Maximum power (mW)	Range (meters)	Sample application
1	100	100	Building control
1.5	10	20	Home control
2	2.5	10	Lab equipment
3	1	1	Handsfree Bluetooth in cars
4	.5	.5	Computer mouse

at the expense of range. The maximum baud rate is 2 MBS, but 5.0 provides for baud rates as low as 125 KBS with greatly extended range. This makes BLE Version 5.0 applicable in a broad range of situations. Applications involving large amounts of data or streaming but over relatively short distances can use a high-speed BLE device. Applications that do not involve large amounts of data, such as sensor nets, can use lower-power devices spread over larger areas.

Bluetooth devices can form ad hoc networks, called piconets, of up to eight devices. (Larger networks are possible through special techniques.) The network itself automatically designates one device, usually the one that started the networking process, to be the piconet master. Devices may change roles, with a different device taking over as master, in various circumstances such as the current master leaving the network. All communications are initiated by the master, thus avoiding collisions caused by multiple devices attempting to transmit at the same time. Data is transmitted in time slots of 625 microseconds. The master communicates during the first half of each slot, and another device communicates in the second half. The master polls the other devices in the piconet so that each other device gets a chance to use the network.

Bluetooth radios operate in the 2.400–2.485 GHz range. This range is divided into 79 sub-channels (40 sub-channels for BLE). The devices use a technique called frequency hopping spread spectrum (FHSS)[5] to continuously change the carrier frequency. This reduces the risk of interference from some nearby static radio signal and also reduces the risk of eavesdropping. It also reduces the risk of collision with other nearby Bluetooth piconets.

Bluetooth specifies a large number of profiles. A profile contains parameters and other information about a specific kind of device such as a computer mouse, audio headset, speaker, game console, video display, home automation, and control. There are hundreds of standard profiles. Part of the initial handshaking when two devices connect is the exchange of profile ids. This allows each connecting device to know what kind of device the other one is without having to exchange whole profiles or extensive amounts of data. This will become especially important as the Internet of Things evolve, where all kinds of devices are expected to dynamically connect and communicate with each other. A device can have more than one profile; for example, a device might be a handsfree control device and use both the handsfree profile and the control profile. Devices may refuse connections to another device if the second device is of the wrong type. A simple example is a speaker, which should only connect to audio streaming devices. The speaker would normally refuse to connect to, say, a computer mouse.

Bluetooth devices can automatically detect other Bluetooth devices within range. Connections can then be made either completely autonomously or after various levels of authorization from a user. The former is an important aspect of the Internet of Things but also includes a security risk through connection to completely unknown devices. The latter is generally more secure but is not feasible in situations where a user cannot interact with the system. The low-level details of the pairing process are not of concern to the embedded system engineer and are presented here only to set the context for issues that are of concern.

- Normally a device must be in "discoverable" mode to be detected. Exceptions can occur if another device already knows the MAC address of the first device and usually involve a malicious attack.
- The device in "discoverable" mode broadcasts information about itself such as its type, name, and services and possibly optional additional information such as the manufacturer name.
- A second device responds.
- The first device sends a passkey to the second device. The passkey may be built into the device or provided through interaction with a user.
- The second device sends a passkey to the first device, a kind of double authentication.
- If the passkeys match, the connection is established.

Two issues of concern to the embedded system engineer are discoverable vs. nondiscoverable mode and the generation of passkeys. As noted in the previous paragraph, normally a Bluetooth device cannot be discovered if it is not in discoverable mode. It is important to note that a Bluetooth device can be power-up and not be discoverable. This can be important in a system that is not supposed to attempt connections at certain points of its operation. For example, a robot that operates in a factory and the factory's nearby surroundings might be allowed to connect to devices inside the factory as it operates near those devices but not allowed to connect to (unknown) devices outside the factory when the robot is outside. The robot could change modes as it exited and reentered the building.

The second issue of concern is the level of user interaction in the generation of passkeys and the associated level of security. Passkeys are four- or six-digit numbers used to allow a connection and to generate the encryption keys used for the connection. The passkey must be the same in two devices to allow Bluetooth connection. If a device is intended only to be connected to a known set of other devices, as in the factory robot example in the previous paragraph, the passkey can be built into the robot and all the other devices with which it is intended to connect. Many commercial devices use default built-in passkeys, such as 0000 or 1234. Systems that have input means can allow a user to participate in the interaction. The simplest method is for the device to request user permission. In this case a default or built-in passkey is used. Some information is displayed to the user, such as the requesting device name or passkey, and the user simply needs to press a button to accept the pairing request. If both devices have key input, users can agree on the passkey and enter it into each device when prompted. The user key entry approach has several variations. For example, a device with a display unit could display the other device's passkey and request the user to reenter it as a means of authentication. The design team would need to decide on what level of user interaction is feasible and desirable. In the case of, say, the factory robot, it would likely not be feasible to require user intervention as the robot navigated around the factory. In the case of a laptop, cell phone, or other devices with full keyboard and display capability, user interaction is obviously feasible but may not be desirable. For example, a laptop should be able to connect to a mouse or printer without bothering the laptop user.

Security has always been an issue with Bluetooth. Early versions of Bluetooth had very little security. In 2008 the National Institute of Standards published guidelines for Bluetooth security. The more recent versions of Bluetooth use encryption with the encryption key based on the passkey. However, there are still a number of security weaknesses such as eavesdropping and even message modification. Embedded system designers must assess the level of security needed and provide any additional security within the application itself (e.g., at the application or presentation layers in the OSI model).

23.3.3 Zigbee

Zigbee[6] is a low-power, low-bandwidth wireless protocol family designed for personal area networks (PANs) and similar applications where low baud rates are acceptable and power consumption is a major concern. A typical application is home sensing and control. The volume of data being sensed (temperatures in various rooms, open/closed state of doors and windows, etc.) is quite small, and the transmission of commands (turn a light on or off, sound an alarm, etc.) is also quite small. It is based on IEEE 802.15.4 standard, and the Zigbee Alliance[7] is responsible for establishing Zigbee-specific standards.

Zigbee ranges vary from 10 to 100 meters. Indoor ranges typically vary from 10 to 20 meters depending on intervening walls and other obstacles. Outdoor line-of-sight range can be as much as 150 meters if extra power is used for the radio. The Zigbee protocol supports star, tree, and mesh networking. Each link can be 10−100 meters or more, so the network as a whole could cover quite a large area. Baud rates are 20−250 KBS. Zigbee radios operate in 2.4−2.4835 GHz band with 16 channels and use spread spectrum frequency hopping. Some countries outside the US also have special frequencies below 1 GHz but with much lower raw through-the-air data rates.

There are three kinds of Zigbee devices − Zigbee controllers (ZC devices), Zigbee routers (ZR devices), and Zigbee end devices (ZED devices). The ZED can only communicate with its immediate neighbor typically its parent node. It cannot forward messages. The radio portion of a ZED can be off except when the ZED wants to send information to its parent. A sensor node would typically be a ZED. When the node senses a change in its sensors, it can wake up to radio and transmit the new data. ZED nodes also periodically wake up the radio and send a "check-in" message to see if there are any messages from other nodes in the network targeted for that ZED. ZEDs consume very low amounts of energy compared to ZCs and ZRs because the radio can be off most of the time. ZR devices can forward messages (as well as perform their own function such as sensing or controlling). These devices could be used at the interior nodes of a network (e.g., the nonleaf nodes in a tree network or nonperimeter nodes in a mesh network). They would also typically be used for actuator nodes in a sensor/actuator network. ZR devices need to have at least their radio receivers operating continuously so that they can monitor for incoming messages, either messages that have to be forwarded or messages asking the node to change the state of its actuators. ZC devices initiate the formation of the network, store network configuration information, store information about what kinds of devices are in the network and what services they provide, and store and distribute security keys. A Zigbee network has exactly one ZC device.

There are two network modes in Zigbee — beacon and nonbeacon. In a beacon network, one ZR device broadcasts a message periodically. For network speed of 250 KBS, the period can range from 15.36 milliseconds to 251.66 seconds. Any other node in the network turns its radio off between beacons, which greatly extends the battery life of battery-operated nodes. When the beacon wakes up the network, nodes communicate with each other. Beacon operation is particularly useful for sensor networks because the sensor nodes could store the sensor readings but only turn the radio on at the beacon time. It may not be inappropriate for networks with actuators because commands to change an actuator state would have to wait for the next beacon, which might not come within the real-time requirement for the actuator to respond to situations. Timing is an issue with beacon networks. Each node has its own clock, so the timing is asynchronous. A node should wake up perhaps a short time before the end of a beacon period to ensure that it does not accidentally miss the beacon because its clock is a bit slow. In nonbeacon networks, ZC and ZR devices typically always have their radio receivers on to monitor for incoming messages. In these networks it may be possible for multiple Zigbee devices to be ready to transmit at the same time. Zigbee uses collision avoidance; each device checks to see if another device is broadcasting on a frequency before trying to transmit on that frequency itself. An application in which actuators have to respond to changes in sensors within a short period of time would use the nonbeacon format. Sensor nodes can immediately broadcast changes in their sensor value(s) without waiting for a beacon, and the messages will be immediately forwarded by any intervening node in the network until they reach appropriate actuator node.

Like Bluetooth, the Zigbee Alliance has defined a large set of profiles. Each profile includes characteristics of the device and a list of the services provided. For example, a SWITCH profile would indicate that the object has ON/OFF capability and that it responds to commands to turn ON or turn OFF. A LEVEL profile would indicate that the object can function at different levels and that it responds to commands to change the level. A Zigbee device might have several profiles. For example, the fan motor for an HVAC system might include both the SWITCH profile and the LEVEL profile. The fan can turn on and off, but when it is on it can run at different speeds. The Zigbee standard allows manufacturers to define their own profiles and include those in a Zigbee device.

Zigbee networks are also dynamic. A ZC node initiates the formation of a network. The ZC node could store specific MAC addresses and broadcast messages requesting devices with those addresses to join the network. In this way, access to the network is completely controlled. The ZC node could also broadcast a general message, forwarded through the ZR nodes already in the network, requesting any device within range to respond. Other Zigbee devices may respond by sending out their own MAC addresses and other information about themselves, including their PAN ID (PID) or Extended PAN ID (EPID). The ZC node can decide whether or not to allow the other node to join based on all this information.

Zigbee uses 128-bit symmetric encryption. The encryption key can be hard coded into the devices that will form the network if the network is to be static, that is, all the devices that will ever be allowed to join the network are already known. More commonly, the ZC node has a list of keys or a method to dynamically generate such keys. The chosen key would then be passed to nodes as they joined the network. Note that this implies there is a brief period when new nodes are joining when security may be compromised.

23.3.4 Ipv6lowPAN

6LowPan (IPv6 over Low-power Wireless Personal Area Network)[8] is a modified version of Ipv6 that allows small devices with limited computing power to connect to the Internet in a way compatible with Ipv6. This is accomplished mainly through compression techniques applied to the standard Ipv6 headers. 6LowPAN is designed to operate over IEEE 802.15.4 networks. Fragmentation is used to allow standard Ipv6 packets, which must be at least 1280 octets, to be transmitted over 802.15.4 channels, where the packet size is 127 octets and these packets include significant overhead octets. Although designed to allow small nodes to connect to the Internet, there are many challenges in making this happen. In addition to the issues about header format and packet fragmentation, there are issues about differing address formats in Ipv6 and 802.15.4, associated issues with routing, and device discovery, to name just a few of the difficulties. Still, 6LowPAN may provide the means for reaching the IoT vision of arbitrary things being able to connect through the Internet as well as directly with each other.

23.4 Contention and collisions

When more than one node on a bus or radio frequency can initiate an event, the possibility that several will attempt to gain control of the bus or channel at the same time exists, a situation called contention. In this section, we describe three of the most common techniques for dealing with or avoiding contention — priority-based arbitration, carrier sense multiple access (CSMA), and time division multiple access (TDMA). TDMA is relatively easy to implement, although coordinating the timing may require some care. Priority-based arbitration and CSMA transmission normally require extra hardware for collision detection and possibly also additional software support but can lead to better utilization of the bus or channel. Our goal in this section is to make the student aware of various techniques so that appropriate selections can be made for a given project.

We begin this discussion with a brief description of how collisions can actually be detected on a wired bus, that is how devices on a bus can determine when another device is also trying to use the bus. We then discuss the three methods mentioned in the preceding paragraph for either avoiding collisions or arbitrating among competing devices for which one gets control and what the others must do to gain control later.

23.4.1 **Collision detection and/or avoidance**

Although knowledge of how collisions are detected is not likely to affect any embedded system design decisions, the reader may be interested to know how it is possible. In the case of wired buses, collision can be detected by use of a certain kind of circuitry called open-drain. The internal details of how the transistors are used are of interest only from an electrical engineering perspective. The key property from the point of view of collision detection is that some circuits on the bus may have pins set to logic 1 while others have pins set to logic 0 without damaging any of the circuits. The circuit uses an open-drain drive to connect one of its output pins to the bus. It also includes a sensor to tell if the voltage on that pin is positive or not. See Figure 23.13. The circuit can then determine if it is trying to drive a high voltage (typically logic 1) onto the bus while another device is trying to drive a low voltage (logic 0). The device trying to drive logic 1 would know there is a collision and could stop trying to transmit.

In the case of wireless transmission, the simple use of different frequencies by different transmitting devices can help avoid collision. Although the radio signals are mixed in the air, if a receiver is tuned to the frequency of its corresponding sender, it can filter out the other radio signals and receive only the one meant for it. Some radio receivers can listen to multiple frequencies and detect which ones are broadcasting. As noted in Section 23.3, Bluetooth and Zigbee use this along with frequency hopping spread spectrum to attempt to avoid collisions. In this approach, the transmission frequency changes regularly, usually hundreds of times a second, through a fixed set of frequencies, a process called frequency hopping. The chance that another device would be transmitting at the same time and with

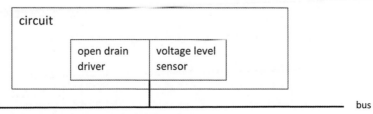

FIGURE 23.13 Open Drain Output Pin With Voltage Sensor.

Author drawn.

the same frequency signal is therefore quite small. The hopping sequence is usually fixed or based on a random sequence known to both the transmitter and the potential receivers. So, once the connection is established, that is, once a receiver has recognized a broadcast meant for it and on a particular frequency, that receiver can hop through the frequency sequence the same as the sender.

23.4.2 Priority-based arbitration

One method for bus arbitration is to assign the devices on the bus a fixed priority. As with all fixed priority schemes, higher-priority devices may starve lower-priority devices. Still, for networks with only a small number of nodes, this may be an acceptable method. The designers of a particular embedded system would need to analyze the expected and worst-case network traffic and determine if a fixed priority scheme could be implemented that meets real-time constraints for all the nodes in the network, even nodes with the lowest bus priority.

A simple method to achieve a fixed priority scheme is to use a central one-level bus arbiter circuit. This circuit has a single input for receiving requests for the bus and a single output to indicate bus access is granted. All devices connect to the bus request line using open drain outputs. The bus grant signal is daisy-chained through the devices. The first device has a grant input pin connected directly to the bus arbiter grant output. This device then has a separate grant output pin that connects to the grant input pin on the next device. This arrangement continues to the end of the chain of devices. The configuration is shown in Figure 23.14. Each device must have three I/O pins dedicated to bus arbitration. This can easily be accomplished in even the lowest microcontrollers.

In a central one-level system, when no device is requesting/using the bus, the bus request line is logic 1, and the bus grant output from the bus arbiter is logic 0. A device requesting access to the bus pulls its request line low. Because the request lines for the devices are open drain, this does not cause damage to other devices which are not requesting the bus and whose pins are attempting to drive a high signal. When the bus arbiter receives a request, it waits a short time in case other devices also request access to the bus. It then sets its grant output to logic 1. A device in the chain that did not request the bus passes along the logic 1 signal. A device that did request

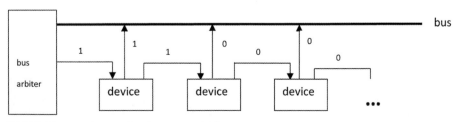

FIGURE 23.14 A Central One-Level Bus Arbiter.

Author drawn.

the bus takes control of the bus and outputs logic 0 on its grant output pin. The first device in the chain that had requested the bus will see a 1 on its grant input pin; other devices further down the chain will see 0 on their grant input pins. In this way, the device closest to the arbiter circuit gets control of the bus. Thus, priority is determined by distance from the arbiter circuit and is, of course, therefore fixed priority. Figure 23.14 shows the case where the second and third devices had both requested the use of the bus. The second device gains control.

More complex bus arbiter circuits have separate request and grant lines, one for each device on the bus. These kinds of bus arbiters can implement many kinds of priority schemes, including for example round robin, fixed, and programmable. Of course, they require many more pins and much more wiring between devices.

Some serial transmission protocols, such as I^{2}C and CAN use a distributed bus arbitration scheme based on the open drain property. For example, in the CAN protocol the first 11 bits after the start bit form the address of the target device being addressed. If two devices, S1 and S2, attempt to begin a transmission at the same time and they are addressing two separate devices, say D1 and D2, the message targeting the device with the larger address will lose control of the bus. The larger address will have its earliest 1 bit before the smaller address. When this is detected, the sender transmitting to the target with the larger address will stop its transmission. Neither CAN nor I^{2}C protocols specify how the nodes that lost arbitration eventually gain access to the bus.

23.4.3 Carrier sense multiple access

One family of protocols that specifies methods for distributing access to the bus is the carrier sense multiple access (CSMA) family of protocols.[9] There are many variations of CSMA, such as CSMA/CD (carrier sense multiple access with collision detection), CSMA/CA (carrier sense multiple access with collision avoidance), and different methods for specifying how nodes that lost arbitration should attempt to gain access again. The common features of these variants are that (1) each node senses the bus before attempting to gain control and (2) when a collision occurs there is a prescribed method for how long the node should wait before trying again.

CSMA specifies several options for when a collision occurs. A node that has lost arbitration can continue to monitor the line and attempt to resend its packet as soon as the line becomes idle. This approach has the advantage that if no other node is waiting to transmit, the delay is minimized. On the other hand, if several nodes are waiting, they will all attempt to gain access at about the same time, and collision will occur again. Therefore, in networks where nodes transmit frequently there may be many collisions, and some nodes may be starved if they keep losing arbitration. A second approach is that the node losing arbitration waits a random amount of time and tries again. The node may, of course, be blocked again if the bus was still being used or another node gained access while the node was waiting. However, if several nodes were blocked it is less likely that they will all try to gain access at the same time, thus reducing the chance for collision after the current message is finished.

The disadvantage of this approach is that if no other node is waiting to send, the one node that is waiting will likely wait longer than necessary. A third approach is for a supervisory node to assign an order for nodes to gain access. Alternatively, the nodes can be assigned fixed priorities, and after the completion of one transmission the nodes waiting to use the bus broadcast their priorities on the bus. If a node detects a request from a higher-priority node, it waits again. Methods, such as those described in Section 23.4.1, can be used for this arbitration phase.

CSMA typically maintains a high level of throughput on the network. On the other hand, when priority is involved in selecting the next node to transmit, nodes with low priority can be starved. Also, it is generally not possible to compute *a priori* bounds on the time it takes for a message that is ready in one node to successfully reach its destination. As noted before, this is a serious drawback for real-time systems because it prevents obtaining accurate timing estimates for communication.

23.4.4 Time division multiple access

The TDMA protocol[10] avoids both collisions and starvation at the cost of throughput in the network. The TDMA protocol works as follows. First, all the nodes on the network must use the same clock — either a common clock or their own clocks with some method for synchronization. Second, time on the bus is divided into bus frames, which are distinct from message frames from individual nodes. A bus frame has a time slice for each node on the network and a global starting condition. Each time slice may itself have structure, for example, have a period for payload and a period providing a gap between that slice and the next one. There may be additional portions of time in the bus frame for further synchronization, spacing between node slices, and other purposes. Figure 23.15 shows the basic structure of a bus frame. As an example, a bus frame might use 4 bytes for the starting synchronization and 4K bytes for each slice. The nodes are numbered 0-$(n-1)$. Node j can control the bus during slice j and must not drive the bus at any other time.

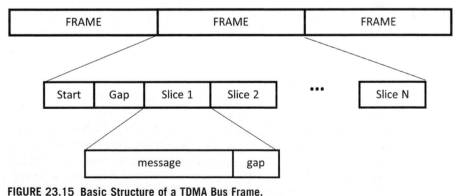

FIGURE 23.15 Basic Structure of a TDMA Bus Frame.

Author drawn.

In TDMA a node can begin transmitting a message as soon as that message is ready and that node's next time slice occurs, leading to easy analysis of the time required for messages to reach their destinations. As noted before, this is especially important in real-time systems. A major disadvantage is that if only a small percentage of the nodes are transmitting at a given time the bus has a high level of idle time and thus a low level of throughput because most of the time slices are not being used.

23.5 Summary

Communication among elements in a distributed embedded system is typically handled through one of a variety of low-level wired or wireless serial communication protocols. This chapter presents a discussion of a select set of these protocols that illustrate the wide range of physical and nonphysical aspects of low-level protocols in general. The features that define a serial protocol are described. A sample of the most commonly used wired serial protocols is then described, and advantages and disadvantages of each are noted. This presentation would help designers and implementers choose a particular one for a given system under design or to quickly understand a new protocol and determine if it was a good choice. The chapter gives a similar discussion and comparison of the most commonly used wireless protocols. Two major issues concerning the physical transmission of signals in a network — contention and collision — are described, and common solutions for handling these are presented.

Problems

1. Describe five features that a protocol might specify.
2. For each of the following tell if you would use parallel, wired serial communication, or wireless communication and why.
   a) Communication between a processor and devices inside a PC.
   b) Communication between a processor and devices inside an ATM.
   c) Communication between the main module and the other modules in our bridge system.
   d) Communication between the various modules in an elevator system in a four-story building.
   e) Communication between the various modules in an elevator system in a 100-story building.
3. List five common features in protocols for wired serial communication. Tell how each of these is specified for each of RS232, IIC, and CAN serial protocol.
4. Suppose the message "Hi" is to be transmitted from one device to another. Describe the sequence of bits for each of RS232, IIC, and CAN protocol. Where necessary, you can make up addresses for the sender and intended receiver.

5. In an ATM, a processor communicates with a network interconnect (NIC) device, a keypad device, a money dispenser device (actually moves bills to the out slot for the user to take), and a monitor device that monitors how many bills are left in the ATM storage. A single serial bus is to be used for communication among these devices.

   a) Explain why TTL and RS232 are not appropriate for this application.

   b) To which of the devices would you assign high priority, and to which would you assign low priority? Explain why you made your choices.

   c) Give your answers to part (b), how would you assign addresses to the devices if the serial protocol was CAN? Explain your choice.

6. A patient monitoring system includes some sensors implanted inside the patient's chest and some sensors worn on the outside of the body. Sensors take readings every five minutes or compute average performance over five-minute periods (e.g., a sensor node for the heart might detect how many anomalies occurred over each five-minute period.). One of the devices outside the body, the data sink, collects sensor data from all the sensors and stores it for daily transmission to the doctor's office. The transmission to the doctor's office is handled by the patient's cell phone; once a day the data sink communicates with the cell phone to upload the collected data. All communication between sensor nodes and with the cell phone is by Bluetooth.

   a) Which class of Bluetooth should be used and why?

   b) Should the nodes in the system be able to connect with other Bluetooth devices outside the system? Explain why you chose your answer.

   c) Assuming the nodes of the system should not be allowed to connect to other Bluetooth devices, what Bluetooth feature can be used to prevent such connections?

   d) If the system was also supposed to monitor for emergency situations and call for help when an emergency occurred, how would any of your answers to parts (a)–(c) change?

7. Suppose Zigbee was used in the patient monitoring system instead of Bluetooth.

   a) For simple monitoring without emergency detection, which Zigbee device types should be used for the sensors and the data sink?

   b) Should the network use a beacon or not? Explain your answer.

   c) If the system is supposed to detect emergencies, how would your answers to parts (a) and (b) change?

8. Which of the following applications could use the Zigbee beacon method for controlling network traffic? Explain your answers by estimating an acceptable latency.

   a) Controlling the flaps on the wings of a modern jet.

   b) Controlling the heating/cooling switches in a refrigerated transport vehicle for transporting food.

   c) Networking the individual sub-systems in the bridge example from earlier chapters.

9. A winery uses automation to control the aging process of its wines. Wine is stored in large vats. An aging room contains a 10×10 grid of vats; that is, there are 10 rows of vats, each row with 10 vats. The vats are spaced five meters apart in each grid direction. Each vat has a sensor that measures acidity and other details of the liquid inside that vat. Each aging room has a control node that monitors the condition of all the vats in that room and controls heating/air-conditioning and humidifiers in that room. Design a Zigbee network for this application. Specify the type for each device in the network. Specify whether the network would use a beacon or not, and explain your choice.

10. Draw a diagram of a bus arbiter with four levels and four devices. How could such a device be used in networks with more than four nodes? (HINT: use cascading)

11. Suppose we have a network with four nodes on a TDMA bus. Each node is assigned one slice in the frame period — slice 1 to node 1, slice 2 to node 2, etc. Suppose each slice is able to hold 1000 bytes of information, not including the gap and guard time. Below is a sequence of frames and an indication of when the processes are ready to send data.

   a) Fill in the time slices with the bytes of the files from the corresponding processes that are being transmitted in that frame. The first one has been done so you can see the format.

Frame sync	Frame gap	slice 1	slice 2	slice 3	slice 4

Frame 0		empty	empty	empty	empty

Process 2 is ready to transmit a file of 6356 bytes.

Frame 1		empty	bytes 0–999	empty	empty

Process 4 is ready to transmit a file of 256 bytes.

Frame 2					

Process 3 is ready to transmit a file of 2374 bytes.

Frame 3					

Frame 4					

Frame 5					

Frame 6					

Frame 7					

b) Suppose that the bus did not use TDMA but only allowed one process to send data at a time. Also, suppose that once a process started to transmit a file, that process kept the bus until the file transfer was complete. Assume that one frame was 4000 bytes; that is, the frame is still the same size as in the first part of this question. Finally, assume that the processes generate the same files at the same times as before. Fill in the frames below indicating which process was using the bus and which bytes were being transmitted.

Frame 0	empty

Process 2 is ready to transmit a file of 6356 bytes.

Frame 1	empty

Process 4 is ready to transmit a file of 256 bytes.

Frame 2	empty

Process 3 is ready to transmit a file of 2374 bytes.

Frame 3	empty

Frame 4	empty

12. Review Section 4.4 and Figure 4.4 of Chapter 4. Let B1 be the barrier module, B2 be the light module, and B3 be the main control module. Suppose the channel between the main control module and the ground traffic module carries signals of type light message and barrier message. Suppose the channel uses the TDMA protocol with two time slots per frame, each slot 64 bytes. Slot 1 is assigned to module Ba, and slot 2 is assigned to module B2. For each of the following situations tell which message is placed in the main control module receiving queue first.

a) At frame N module B2 generates a message with 200 bytes, and at frame N+1 module B1 generates a message of 32 bytes.

b) At frame N module B2 generates a message of 100 bytes and module B1 generates a message of 200 bytes.

c) At frame N module B2 generates a message of 128 bytes and module B1 generates a message of 64 bytes.

References

[1] https://en.wikipedia.org/wiki/Wi-Fi.
[2] https://www.wi-fi.org/.
[3] https://en.wikipedia.org/wiki/Bluetooth.
[4] https://en.wikipedia.org/wiki/Bluetooth_Low_Energy.
[5] https://en.wikipedia.org/wiki/Frequency-hopping_spread_spectrum.
[6] https://en.wikipedia.org/wiki/Zigbee.
[7] https://zigbeealliance.org/.
[8] https://en.wikipedia.org/wiki/6LoWPAN.
[9] https://en.wikipedia.org/wiki/Carrier-sense_multiple_access.
[10] https://en.wikipedia.org/wiki/Time-division_multiple_access.

Cloud vs. edge vs. local computing

24.1 The cloud

Advances in networking and the development of cloud computing present new dimensions in the design of embedded systems. The development of the cloud allows designers much more flexibility in choices about where computation is done and where data is stored and processed, but it also introduces other issues concerning questions of privacy, trust, ownership of data, and others. (For a more detailed discussion of these latter issues, see Chapter 26.)

A cloud is a network of high-powered computing and data storage platforms. It may be public or private. Public clouds offer services to the general community for a price. Private clouds are used only by other entities in the enterprise that owns that cloud. Clouds receive data and requests for computation from smaller platforms and return results to those platforms. An embedded system, for example, could submit a request to a cloud to perform some complex analysis that was beyond the computing capabilities of the processing element(s) in that embedded system. The sensors in embedded systems connect the cloud hierarchy to the real physical world and are referred to as the edge. Edge computing refers to computation performed in the embedded systems and possibly in nearby computers. For example, the embedded systems and workstations in an automated factory perform edge computation. They are very close to the edge. There may be additional levels of computer platforms between the low-level embedded system and a cloud. These are often referred to as the fog. Platforms in the fog might be modest computing devices, such as PCs and workstations, that have additional computation, data storage, and knowledge access capabilities beyond that in the edge computers. Figure 24.1 shows the edge-fog-cloud hierarchy. Chapter 25 presents a more detailed discussion of models of this hierarchy.

Embedded system designers can now incorporate more complex and time-consuming computations into the system being designed by arranging for those computations to be done on platforms outside the embedded system itself. Similarly, designers can plan for their systems to collect much more data because that data can be stored in the cloud, that is, stored outside the embedded system. Further, because of improvements in networking and the development of cloud services, designers may consider advanced features for a system that would have been hitherto

Embedded System Design. https://doi.org/10.1016/B978-0-443-18470-3.00024-5

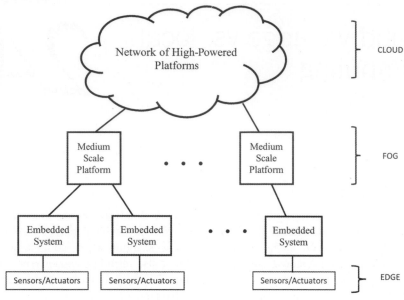

FIGURE 24.1 Illustration of Cloud, Fog, and Edge.

Author drawn.

impossible because of limitations on the computational and storage components inside the system itself. For example, the components of a farm irrigation system may not have enough storage and computing power to do complex chemical analysis from the sensor readings of its sensor nodes and may not even have that kind of power in a local PC used as a base station for the farm network. Before cloud computing had been developed, such systems would have simply not had that capability. Such a system can now be connected to the cloud which can easily perform such complex analyses. Finally, the designers of a system may now consider additional capabilities that would not normally have been considered in the design of the system itself. Considering the farm irrigation system again, prior to cloud computing the designers of a farm irrigation system may never have considered using economic factors in determining irrigation and fertilization schedules. Now, however, such additional knowledge can easily be accessed and used to control the farm more intelligently.

In this chapter we present basic concepts about cloud computing. Cloud computing in general could easily fill an entire course or more. Our goal here is to make embedded systems designers aware of what the cloud can do for an embedded system and what the design team should consider when looking at potential use of the cloud for a given design.

24.1.1 Characteristics of the cloud

The National Institute of Standards and Technology of the U.S. Department of Commerce lists the following five properties as "essential characteristics" of cloud computing.[1] We describe each feature and mention why it would be important for an embedded system.

- On-demand self-service. An entity should be able to access the services at any time and without the need for human intervention. Most embedded systems run for long periods at a time, often 24/7, and operate autonomously or nearly autonomously. If a service required human approval, it would severely limit the utility. A huge amount of data generated by embedded systems need to be uploaded without intervention or delay. Most embedded systems also have some real-time requirements, often quite tight, so any computation that is to be done in the cloud and returned for use by the embedded system must be done without the delay imposed by human intervention. An example of this kind is real-time facial recognition for a security system that should unlock doors for people waiting to enter an area.
- Broad network access through standard protocols. Entities of all types, such as PCs and cell phones and microcontrollers with attached wireless circuits, should be able to reach the cloud anywhere and anytime that normal network connectivity is available. Many embedded systems are stationary, but many others are mobile. In both cases, the system should be able to reach the cloud through normal network protocols.
- Resource pooling and elasticity. Cloud providers should pool their resources and dynamically allocate them to multiple clients as needed to meet demand. It would normally appear to a cloud user as though there were arbitrarily many resources. While this does not relate directly to the operation of an embedded system, it does lead to better cloud performance and, therefore, better service to an embedded system using cloud resources.
- Rapid elasticity. "Capabilities can be elastically provisioned and released, in some cases automatically, to scale rapidly outward and inward commensurate with demand. To the consumer, the capabilities available for provisioning often appear to be unlimited and can be appropriated in any quantity at any time".[1]
- Measured service. The amount of resources used by any individual entity is monitored and can also be controlled or limited. Again, while this does not relate directly to the operation of an embedded system using the cloud, it can provide useful information to the owners of that embedded system about how the system is interacting with cloud and in what ways (e.g., simple data storage, processing, bandwidth, and active user accounts).

There are three main ways that cloud providers provide service to users[1,2]

- by providing basic computing and storage platforms (Infrastructure-as-a-Service, IaaS),
- by providing computing platforms and associated development tools (Platform-as-a-Service, PaaS),
- and by providing fully developed software applications (Software-as-a-Service, SaaS).

An IaaS vendor provides basic hardware, such as computing platforms and mass data storage, to client. Clients write their own software, which then runs on the hardware provided by the IaaS vendor. Some embedded systems generate large amounts of data that must be stored outside the system itself, as we have already seen. Other embedded systems might benefit from specialized, perhaps even proprietary, software that would be written by the company designing the embedded system but would require much more powerful processing elements than were designed into that embedded system. A company that sold such an embedded system could purchase services from an IaaS vendor and offer cloud data storage and computing to its clients as part of the embedded system product. An example of this kind of situation is a specialized bio-monitoring system that generates large amounts of sensor data and uses specialized proprietary software to analyze that data.

A PaaS service provides the infrastructure and also development services and tools such as programming languages and development tools, libraries of common software, database services, web services, networking services, etc. A small embedded system design company, such as a small start-up, may not be able to afford the sophisticated and powerful computers and development tools needed for developing the applications to run in the cloud; a PaaS vendor could provide those development tools and then provide the infrastructure to run the applications.

Finally, a SaaS vendor provides infrastructure as well as a collection of standard software applications such as statistical analysis software or relational database applications. Many embedded systems do not need specialized software, only general software, and companies selling those kinds of embedded systems could use a SaaS vendor rather than having to buy their own computer equipment and pay licensing fees for the corresponding software. General health monitoring and smart cities are examples of embedded systems that would likely need only general software application and mass data storage. For example, the embedded systems distributed throughout a smart city (traffic monitors at intersections, bridge systems if the city had a river, energy monitors in buildings, etc.) would provide huge amounts of data to the cloud, which could then perform ordinary statistical analyses using standard statistical packages.

Cloud computing may be purchased from a public vendor or provided privately by the company requiring the benefits of cloud computing. For example, a company that designs bridge systems and sells them all over the world, or perhaps even its parent company, may be large enough to afford the purchase of equipment to form its own cloud. Such a large company may be able to gain some financial benefit by spreading the cost of its private cloud over many different embedded systems that it sells and also providing only those cloud services that it actually needs. The company would also have complete control over its cloud, whereas public cloud vendors exercise that control over the public clouds. On the other hand, launching, maintaining, and continuously updating a cloud requires considerable investment, so only major entities like large corporations or governments would generally take this approach. A cloud service can be part private and part public, a so-called hybrid cloud service. In the hybrid model, the company builds proprietary services and services that may need high-speed response into a private cloud and then connect that private cloud to a public cloud vendor to handle non-proprietary and other functions that do not require fast turn-around.

24.1.2 Benefits of cloud computing

There are many advantages to cloud computing in general and for embedded systems in particular. As already noted, cloud computing may make feasible features that would be impossible or prohibitively expensive in a stand-alone embedded system. The advantages stem to a large extent from economies of scale — large companies that provide cloud services to thousands of clients have the money to invest in resources, both human and hardware/software, to do things that small companies that design, implement, and maintain embedded systems cannot. The following is a list of some of the most important ones along with a brief discussion of how they are relevant to embedded system design.

- Store massive amounts of data. A modern car can generate gigabytes of data per day.[3] Similar applications, such as airplane monitoring systems, generate similar huge amount of data. Obviously, such large amounts of data cannot be stored inside the embedded system itself. And even if it could, doing so would make that data unavailable to powerful analysis software available in the cloud or at other places on the web. The capability of storing collected data outside an embedded system itself increases the flexibility in generating the specification for that system.
- Perform difficult or intense short-term computations. In many embedded systems the computing platforms are relatively simple in order to reduce the overall cost of the system. A simple sensor node, for example, could not include a workstation as its computing element because the node normally should be small and often has to run on battery power. Features that require bursts of complex computation, such as floating-point arithmetic and numerical analysis, can be added to the embedded system by having those computations performed in the cloud and the results returned to the embedded system assuming that the embedded system can tolerate the delay in receiving the results.
- Perform long-term calculations and analyses. Software in the cloud can analyze data collected over a long period and from multiple sources in ways that individual embedded systems cannot. An individual farm or even local community of farms cannot do the kind of analysis that can be done for agricultural information collected from a whole state over, say, one or more years. An individual car might monitor its parts for wear or improper performance, but only the cloud (perhaps a private cloud operated by the car manufacturer) can analyze data for the entire fleet to identify possible weaknesses in the car design. Embedded system designers need to be aware that data collected from the system being designed may be used by entities outside that system.

- Provide better security. Cloud providers can invest heavily in security, while small design companies cannot. For embedded systems that collect sensitive data, this reduces the need for designing security at the local level.
- Provide global access to data. Large companies using cloud data storage and computing may have many offices in widespread locations, many of which need to use the data being collected by embedded systems. On the other hand, data may need to be used by different organizations; for example, data collected from patient monitoring systems and other health monitoring systems used by the Centers for Disease Control and Prevention (CDC) and the World Health Organization (WHO).
- Allow design teams to focus on the application rather than on infrastructure and related issues. A team designing an embedded system that depends, in part, on common computing paradigms may incorporate cloud computing to handle those common aspects, thereby reducing the complexity and cost of the elements of the embedded system itself.

The advantages do not come without a cost. Here are some of the tradeoffs to be considered in embedded systems designs that might make use of cloud computing.

- Cloud services cost money. The cloud adds another choice in the specification and high-level design. Company management and the high-level design team need to work together to evaluate the benefits of cloud services and the increased capabilities they can add to the system being designed vs. the overall cost of both development of the system and unit cost of each deployed product.
- There is a time delay for cloud services that are used in the operation of the embedded system itself. A request from an operational embedded system to have the cloud perform some computation and return the result must be sent through the Internet to reach the cloud service. The cloud provider considers current usage by all its clients in deciding when to allocate resources to that request. After the request has been satisfied, the result must be sent back through the Internet to reach the embedded system. All of these take time. In some cases, this delay can be tolerated. For example, a farm system that controls watering and fertilization doesn't need to know the exact amount of fertilizer to apply within some tight time restriction; several minutes or even hours might be ok. A door security system that asks for a person to be identified before unlocking the door can't wait that long.
- The ownership of the data sent into the cloud is a serious issue. The owners of an embedded system that sends data into the cloud may lose control over that data. See the section on big data in Chapter 26 for a more detailed discussion of this issue.
- Connection to the cloud requires connectivity to the Internet. For embedded systems that are not near wired connections, this requires wireless communication. Even for systems that already have wireless communication,

communicating with the cloud would use more energy and thus place additional burden on the power supply.

24.2 Issues for embedded system design

We illustrate the extended range of choices available because of the cloud with an example. Consider a small-to-medium size company designing a door security system for buildings. Entrance through doors is controlled using some biometric measurement, for example, fingerprint. A record of who passed through the door is maintained.

- A simple design for individual doors with only a limited number of people allowed access could consist of a medium-sized memory, for example, a memory key, to store the fingerprints, a fingerprint scanner, and a medium-scale processing element capable of reading and writing to the memory key and performing the calculations necessary to compare a scan with fingerprints on the memory key. Security officers could pull the memory key and read it into a handheld device to retrieve the record of people who passed through the door. Such a simple system would be relatively inexpensive and not require hardwired or wireless connectivity to any device not part of the door.
- A more sophisticated system might handle an entire building. Each door could have a simple system consisting of a low-end (and therefore cheap) microcontroller and a scanner. The microcontroller simply scans the fingerprint reader and sends the scan to a PC that monitors all the doors in the building. From the point of view of an individual door, the building PC might be considered an edge device. The building PC has the database of all the fingerprints of people with permissions and the doors each one is allowed to pass through. The building PC also maintains the record of all permissions and denials of permission. The individual nodes at the doors are cheaper and simpler, although they do now require connectivity, most likely wireless, to the building PC.
- A variation on the previous system is to allow at least some doors to open for anyone who, say, does not have a criminal record. The building PC may use the Internet to access a regional database to determine if someone has a criminal record. Such a regional database is an edge system relative to the building as a whole.
- Finally, suppose the system is to be used by a large corporation with many buildings in many different locations. The system is to keep the entire history of every building and every door. Statistical analysis of what kinds of people (staff, maintenance, scientists, etc.) used what kinds of doors (supply room doors, lab doors, etc.) so that the corporation could optimize the property that it owns and how that property is used. Further, information could be used in special cases, for example, if supplies were stolen. This is full cloud computing, making use of

mass storage and high-powered computing platforms to perform sophisticated analyses.

Each of these options is more sophisticated and also more costly than the previous one. Engineers could present the alternatives and the associated added features and costs to management of the company that will make security systems, who would then evaluate the marketability of the options and match that with the company's business model.

To summarize, the choices for the product specification team and the design team include, among others, the following.

- Which computations required for the basic operation of the product do not have tight real-time constraints and can therefore possibly be done at the edge or in the cloud? Removing those computations from inside the product to the edge or cloud could reduce the need for sophisticated and powerful processing elements inside the product, thereby reducing the complexity and unit cost of the product. Does there exist software available in the cloud through a SaaS provider that performs the required functions or can be adapted to perform them?
- Conversely, are there additional features that could be incorporated into the product if cloud computing were included in the design? How much complexity and cost, for example, for added communications circuitry, would be incurred if the product were designed to make use of the cloud? Would the extra energy consumption to communicate with the cloud be offset by energy savings in local computation? Would those additional features make the product more profitable? Would there then be benefits like those mentioned in the previous bullet point?
- Which type of cloud service (IaaS, PaaS, SaaS) is most suitable for application to the product being designed? What are the costs for these services? Will clients who buy the product be able to afford those services?
- Related to the above, can the company selling the product launch its own cloud service to serve the clients who buy the product (and possibly other clients buying different products)?
- How do non-technical issues, such as those described in Chapter 26, affect decisions about whether or not to use cloud computing?

24.3 Summary

In this chapter we described the main characteristics of the cloud and cloud computing — on-demand service, mass storage, access through standard protocols, resource pooling and elasticity, and measured service. We described the three main ways cloud providers provide service — IaaS, PaaS, and SaaS. The IaaS mode mostly just makes sophisticated hardware available to clients. The PaaS mode provides hardware plus software tools for clients to use in developing their own applications. The SaaS mode provides software packages to clients. We mentioned tradeoffs in using public vs. private clouds. We described major benefits clouds provide to clients — mass storage, the ability to perform complicated and expensive computations that are not feasible on the client's own hardware, the ability to perform long-term analysis of data collected from the client's own systems, the ability to access data from anywhere in the world, and the ability of a design team to focus on application-specific issues while leaving more general aspects of the system being designed to the cloud. We also described possible disadvantages to cloud use — the added cost, added delay in sending data to the cloud and waiting for the response, and ownership of data sent to the cloud. We illustrated with a specific sample embedded system, a door security system, and different scenarios in which the designers might or might not use various features of the cloud.

Problems

1. For each of the following applications, have a group or class brainstorming session to discuss the questions posed in Section 24.2.
   a. The bridge system.
   b. A patient monitoring system.
   c. A smart home system.
   d. A farm monitoring and watering/fertilizing system.
   e. A car monitoring system.
2. For each of the applications mentioned in Problem 1, based on your discussions which kind of cloud service (IaaS, PaaS, SaaS) would be appropriate and why?
3. For each of the applications listed in Problem 1, assuming the product does use cloud computing tell if a private cloud might be feasible.

References

[1] P. Mell, T. Grance, The NIST Definition of Cloud Computing (Technical report), National Institute of Standards and Technology: U.S. Department of Commerce, September 2011. https://doi.org/10.6028/NIST.SP.800-145. Special publication 800-145.
[2] https://en.wikipedia.org/wiki/Cloud_computing.
[3] F. Richter, Big Data on Wheels, Digital image, February 9, 2017. https://www.statista.com/chart/8018/connected-car-data-generation/. Accessed November 24, 2019.

The Internet of Things

6

The Internet of Things (IoT) envisions embedded systems that were designed independently and without knowledge of one another to dynamically connect and disconnect during operation in opportunistic ways not foreseen by the designers of any one of the individual systems. In the future, cars might temporarily connect to street lights as they drive through the city, allowing both the car and the city to make more informed decisions about traffic flow and control. Patient monitoring systems might temporarily connect to various medical institutions, such as hospitals or doctor' offices or pharmacies, as the patient travels. There are many research issues to be solved, both technical and social, before IoT becomes a reality, but the future will almost surely include some form of IoT. This final part of the text introduces the reader to the two current formal models of IoT and to the major social issues facing the acceptance of IoT by general society.

Reference models for the Internet of Things

25.1 Introduction

Standardized models for computing applications have played critical roles in advancing the development of useful systems that can work with each other. Perhaps the most important and well-known of these in the computer field are the models for the Internet communication, such as the seven-layer Open Systems Interconnection (OSI) model[1] described in Chapter 22. Such models provide guidelines for developing software and related systems that interoperate with each other across programming languages and computing and networking platforms. A good model provides both generality and flexibility. Generality allows the model to be used as a guide for all applications in the intended area. Flexibility allows freedom to implement the features of the model in ways that are most appropriate and efficient for a particular application while still meeting the specifications given in the model.

The IoT World Forum and INTEL have each proposed a reference model for the Internet of Things (IoT). These models will be important guides to designers of embedded systems for preparing their systems for participation in the IoT and ensuring compatibility with the future IoT standardizations. Note that IoT models include embedded systems in the lower layers but also include high-level aspects such as big data analysis and business planning. We introduce these two models in the next two sections and discuss some of the pros and cons of each model as they apply to the design of embedded systems, part of the foundation of the IoT. These models may serve as guides for teams designing and implementing their own IoT applications.

25.2 The IoT World Forum model

The IoT World Forum[2] has proposed a seven-level vertical reference model.[3] The lowest level contains the "things", and the highest two levels contain the business applications and the software and human collaboration needed for business decision making and enterprise resource planning (ERP). Levels in between manage the transfer of data through the system. Note that the seven levels in the IoT World Forum Reference Model are not to be confused with the seven layers in the OSI

Embedded System Design. https://doi.org/10.1016/B978-0-443-18470-3.00025-7

model; in fact, the OSI layers, as well as layers in other network models, would occur in the communication level (Level 2) of the IoT World Forum model. Figure 25.1 shows the seven levels of the model. Embedded system engineers would be most concerned with the first three levels — the things, communication, and perhaps fog computing. However, knowledge about the potential usage of data that is sent up from an embedded system into, say, the cloud and about where and why information might come down to the embedded system can help the design

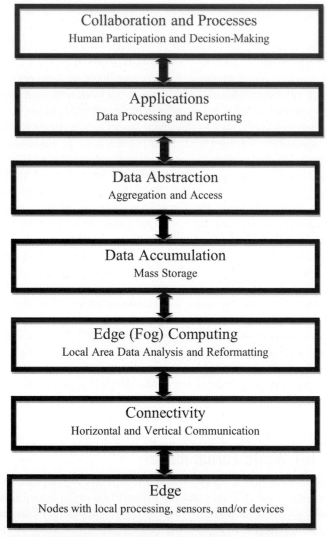

FIGURE 25.1 The Seven Levels of the IoT World Forum Reference Model.

Author drawn.

team make informed choices about how that particular embedded system should or should not connect to the general outside world. In Chapter 26 we discuss some of the choices that face embedded system engineers as we describe various issues relating to the IoT.

We describe the individual levels in more detail in the following paragraphs.

Level 1, the Edge, consists of the things that can generate data and the things that can act on the physical world, that is, sensors and actuators. It is important to note that this level also contains "Intelligent Edge Nodes", that is, nodes that have computing power to respond rapidly to local situations. So, a sensor node that contained a small microcontroller plus some sensors and/or actuators would be an intelligent edge node. These kinds of edge things can perform computation, but in the IoT World Forum model these computations are for internal operation, in contrast to the kind of computation performed in Level 3 in this model. An edge node can generate data, typically from sensors, and can perform actions in its environment through its actuators, typically on/off switches, analog devices, motors, and other such mechanisms. The node can transmit data on its own to the communication level or hold it until it receives a request from the communication level. The node can perform an action either by its own choice or in response to a command from the communication level. The node can perform local transformations on data such as converting an analog value from a sensor to digital form or converting a digital value into an analog form for one of its analog actuators. It can translate local data into different ranges, for example, translate an 8-bit number from an analog temperature sensor to a value representing degrees centigrade. Beyond these capabilities the model places no other restrictions on what a Level 1 thing is. It could be a microchip sensor or a whole car or even something larger. It could be stationary or mobile. As long as it can generate data and respond to messages received from the networking level, it is an edge node.

Level 2, Connectivity, handles vertical and horizontal communication issues. In the vertical direction, the communication level handles the transmission of data from Level 1 to Level 3 and vice versa as well as information from one Level 1 node to another Level 1 node (in which case the information travels up to the communication level and then back down to the edge level again). The horizontal direction includes the transfer of information across network protocols, switching and routing, the delivery of information reliably, maintaining security at the network level, etc. Level 2 does not include communication, which is strictly internal to the edge device, such as a CAN bus connecting two modules within a single embedded system like the system in a modern automobile. The proposal in Ref. [2] emphasizes the use of existing networking protocols and systems but does acknowledge that the proliferation of new Level 1 devices and their forms of communication may require new paradigms.

Level 3, Fog Computing, is mainly devoted to analysis and processing of data for passage to the higher levels and to decision making that must be done close to real time. Data from different sources may need to be brought into a common format. Some data may not be relevant to higher levels, and some data may best be aggregated to reduce the volume before being passed up to Level 4. Some combinations of data might trigger an event that requires communication and coordination with other parts of the IoT in a relatively short time. For example, a temperature in a single room that exceeds a threshold might require turning on the air conditioner in that room, a trivial decision that can be made in the sensor/actuator node in that room alone without any data communication through Level 2 to Level 3. On the other hand, rising temperatures in many rooms in the building may trigger a call to maintenance or even to the fire department, the kind of decision that the individual node in an individual room cannot make. Level 3 is where such non-trivial data analysis is introduced. The goal is to have such decisions made as quickly as needed, which requires computation relatively close to Level 1.

Levels 4—7 address the storage and use of data that is not required to be done in real time. These would typically not be of immediate concern to the designers of an embedded system, except possibly for the actual storage of data being generated by the system (i.e., Level 4). Levels 4 and 5 are responsible for the actual storage of data, including transformation of information into forms suitable for storing in databases, decisions on how and where to store data (in a single repository, distributed database, general cloud, etc.), whether or not data needs to be online, etc. Levels 6 and 7 are where long-term data analysis occurs, with applications occurring in Level 6 and human participation occurring in Level 7. Again, the designers of a particular embedded system might be interested to know that the data generated by their system would be analyzed by high-level management, but that knowledge would have little effect on the design of the system itself.

It should be noted that these are meant as logical levels, not necessarily physical levels. Nowadays many processor chips incorporate onboard communication such as wireless networking. Consider a wireless sensor/actuator network. Each node is an independent embedded system, albeit a very simple one. As such, each node in the network is a Level 1 thing in the IoT World Forum model; it can send data to and receive requests and commands from the Internet. However, obviously every node includes the Level 2 functionality because each node at least has the capability to communicate directly with other nodes on the Internet. Moreover, if one of the nodes includes some data storage and higher-level data analysis, that node would include Level 3 features. In a case like this, the model can be used as a guide for organizing the software, keeping the sensing/actuating parts of the software together perhaps in one software module while isolating the message formatting and packet construction in a separate software module and, in the case of the data storage node, isolating the data storage and analysis software modules from the remainder of the software in that node.

Embedded systems are often hierarchical, containing sub-systems that are themselves complete embedded systems perhaps even with networking capability. This raises other questions in relation to the IoT World Forum model. Both the system as a whole and some of the sub-systems might be considered as separate Level 1 nodes. The communication between these separate sub-modules would be considered as internal communication from the point of view of the overall embedded system but as Level 2 functionality from the point of view of a collection of individual

Level 1 nodes. The embedded system designers might reconsider whether or not individual sub-modules would be allowed to communicate outside the system. This may simplify the way the whole embedded system interacts with the world and may improve the ability to maintain security and privacy.

25.3 The INTEL model

INTEL has also proposed a reference model.[4] The INTEL reference model has several points of view, ranging from the highest levels relating to business planning to the lowest levels that address things like sensors and actuators and their control.

Figure 25.2 shows the highest-level view of the IoT. This view focuses on the control and management involved in collecting data from the IoT and using it to make business decisions. The business and application layers are where human interaction with the IoT takes place. The remaining layers in the center column are the runtime tools that manage the flow of data. As in the IoT World Forum model, security pervades all levels, as indicated on the right. However, the INTEL reference model also proposes a set of tools, indicated on the left, to be used by developers in designing and implementing items at each of the levels.

Of more interest to embedded system engineers are the data flow view and the notion of a thing. Figure 25.3 shows an abstraction of the data flow view from the INTEL proposal (Figure 3 in Ref. [4]). It represents a picture of pieces of an enterprise and how data, control, management, and security might flow between those pieces. The pieces themselves include the embedded systems and other things in that enterprise, in-house data processing and decision management, and possible third parties with an interest in that enterprise. (Note that in the INTEL model third parties might share data but do not share security or control.) The "things" in the box on the left-hand side of the diagram include embedded systems of the kind discussed in this book as well as simpler (perhaps even "dumb") objects like radio frequency identification (RFID) tags and barcodes. Some smart things may communicate data and security/management information with each other directly, as indicated by the lines inside the box on the left. Other things act as gateways to the Internet infrastructure.

Figure 25.4 shows more detail for the INTEL notion of a typical thing. A thing may contain the following pieces.

- Sensors and/or Actuators. A thing may have one or the other or both. One might even consider some things to have neither. For example, bar codes have been considered important early parts of the IoT because they were used to identify the objects to which they were attached. However, as the IoT develops, most of the things will have one or more sensors, one or more actuators, or both.
- The presence of sensors or actuators implies the presence of hardware and/or software for handling those. There would be modules for ingesting and

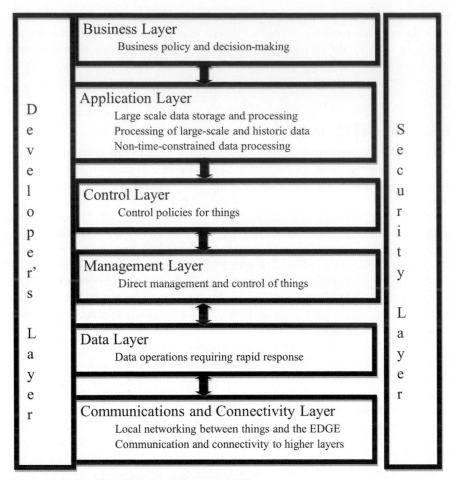

FIGURE 25.2 The INTEL High-level View of the IoT.

Author drawn.

processing data from sensors. This might require, among other things, analog-to-digital conversion (ADC), scaling or reformatting data received from the sensors, aggregation, annotating data with time stamps or other annotations, filtering out outliers, and other operations. Modules associated with actuators might include, for example, digital-to-analog conversion (DAC), software for reverse scaling, etc.

- Protocol Abstraction and Management Layer. The INTEL reference model proposes that a thing isolates the details of operation and interface for sensors and actuators from the rest of the system. This allows other parts of the software running in a thing and even software in other parts of the IoT, for example, in other things or in the enterprise cloud, to issue requests to the sensors and

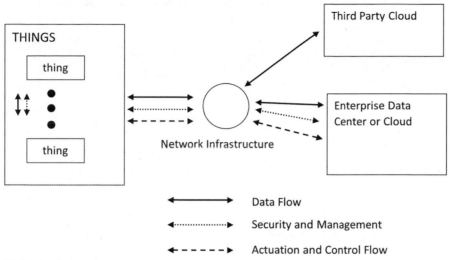

FIGURE 25.3 Overview of Data Management and Control Flow in an Enterprise.

Author drawn.

actuators without having to know specifically how they work. This is consistent with the vision of the IoT that things will be able to coordinate and cooperate in often unanticipated ways.

- Storage. A thing may have minimal storage, modest amounts of non-volatile storage, or perhaps even some mass storage. An RFID tag, for example, might be thought of as having no storage at all beyond the bytes that are programmed into it.

- Thing/Device Management. This would ordinarily be the main software that runs when the device is turned on. The INTEL reference model makes a clear distinction between this software and various other pieces of software that run on the device, such as the Protocol Abstraction and Management software. This separation ensures a high degree of modularity. This software would interpret messages from the outside, form messages such as data and alerts to be transmitted to the outside, recognize events that could be handled locally by the thing's own actuators, handle error conditions, and perform similar functions.

- Analytics and Machine Learning. The INTEL reference model acknowledges that many things even today have the ability to analyze data and make decisions about what kinds of actuation should be done. It also anticipates that in the future more and more devices will be able to learn over time and adjust their behavior.

- Security. The INTEL reference model specifically indicates that security should be included. This would include, among other things, authentication of messages received, authentication of the senders of those messages, and encryption of messages being sent to the Internet.

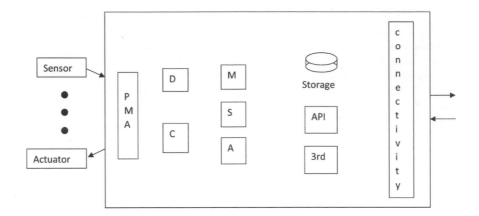

- Sensor – a sensor, including associated hardware such as ADC.
- Actuator – an actuator, including associated hardware such as DAC.
- PMA – Protocol Abstraction and Management Layer.
- D – data ingestion.
- C – control to actuator(s).
- M – device/thing manager.
- S – security software.
- A – analytics and learning software.
- Storage – local storage for raw and/or processed data.
- API – APIs.
- 3rd – 3rd party software.
- Connectivity – connection to other things and/or the internet.

FIGURE 25.4 A Typical "Thing".

Author drawn.

- Application Programming Interface. Smart things may contain software related in an auxiliary way to the functioning of the thing. For example, a door security system might include face recognition software. A gateway may include software for preparing data for transmission into the Internet and then actually transmitting it.
- Third-Party Business and Application Agent.
- Internet Connectivity. This could be either wired or wireless.

25.4 Summary

Similar to the case of the Internet, the IoT has models of its structure. This chapter presents the two main models of the IoT — the IoT World Forum model and the INTEL model. For each model, the presentation illustrates how model concepts in each layer relate to issues that embedded system designers and engineers would need to consider. The "things", that is, what comprises the bottom layer in each model, are embedded systems and their components. The higher layers address issues like communication among things, data flow, analysis of data from multiple things, and others. Embedded system designers and engineers should take these issues into consideration so that the system being designed will be prepared for potential future participation in the IoT.

Problems

1. For each of the following applications describe the elements of that application that might be found in each of the seven layers of the IoT World Forum model. Then discuss your answers in your study group or in the class as a whole.

    a) Community monitoring. Individual home systems monitor various aspects of the home and communicate with the homeowner, local police, local fire, and local medical emergency in case of detected anomaly. Information from the homes in a geographical area may be aggregated by higher government services to analyze for patterns of crime, patterns of health issues, etc.

    b) Intelligent traffic control. The system monitors traffic at critical points in a city. Information is used to control traffic lights and provide information to drivers to help ease traffic congestion. Information collected from throughout the city is used to inform traffic planning, the improvement of roads, and various other planning activities.

    c) Community energy. Monitors in individual buildings collect information about energy usage. This information is aggregated by the local energy providers. Information about geographical areas of the city is used to plan future expansion of energy production and suggest areas that need energy improvements (e.g., more insulation in buildings, search for energy leakage, etc.).

2. Do the same but using the INTEL model.

References

[1] https://en.wikipedia.org/wiki/OSI_model.

[2] http://www.iotwf.com.

[3] A. El Hakim, Internet of Things (IoT) System Architecture and Technologies, White Paper. 10.13140/RG.2.2.17046.19521. 2018. Available for download at https://www. researchgate.net/publication/323525875_Internet_of_Things_IoT_System_Architecture and_Technologies_White_Paper.

[4] https://www.intel.com/content/www/us/en/internet-of-things/white-papers/iot-platform-reference-architecture-paper.html.

IoT issues

26

26.1 Introduction

Complete coverage of the issues associated with Internet of Things (IoT) systems would not be possible in one or even several books. Our purpose in this chapter is to introduce the reader to some of the major problems and issues so that an embedded system design team can consider them during the design and development of an embedded system. For example, knowing that the system might interact with IoT in the future might lead the team to decide to include security as a process somewhere in the system, which may lead to the decision to include at least one medium power processor in the system. Or, the team may decide not to allow interaction with the outside world (i.e., not to allow participation in the IoT, or to be a completely closed system). We focus on six major issues — what are things, scale, security, heterogeneity, connectivity, and analysis of massive amounts of data. There are other issues, of course, and most of the issues associated with IoT are still in the research stage. However, embedded systems engineers will certainly face these issues in their careers, so we believe even this brief introduction will be useful.

26.2 Things

Although the notion of what a "thing" is may seem obvious, in the IoT world the concept has much broader meaning than just physical things. Of course, most things in IoT will be physical — vehicles, appliances, humans, other animals, assembly lines, etc. However, many things in the IoT will be virtual. For example, code running on a processor may be considered a thing capable of identifying itself, taking measurements (e.g., of its own performance), and actuating other things that control its environment, such as controlling the wireless module to conserve energy. Other examples of virtual things include the stock market and even the weather. Embedded system engineers who want to make their systems compatible with future developments of the IoT should keep in mind the breadth of things that the system might eventually interact with.

We have already noted the range of capability of things. Simple things can identify themselves. More sophisticated things can perform operations that range from

Embedded System Design. https://doi.org/10.1016/B978-0-443-18470-3.00026-9

simple sensing and reporting of conditions in their environments to activating controls that affect their environments to analysis of the situation in their environments and even intelligent decision making. A thing may be quite complex, for example, an entire embedded system, and have other things as its parts.

The set of things has hierarchical structure based on class and sub-class, known in the AI community as the ISA (IS-A) hierarchy. For example, an ambulance is an emergency vehicle, which in turn is a vehicle. A stretcher may also be considered an emergency vehicle in some contexts. A health-monitoring system that calls for help in an emergency could issue a call for an ambulance in some contexts or a stretcher in other contexts. Making a decision in this situation requires some level of intelligence, either built into the system or at least available to the system through some kind of query mechanism. Embedded system engineers designing new systems should consider to what extent their systems may in the future choose or need to interact with other systems in a way that requires such intelligence and decide to either build it into the system (which affects the decision about the kind of processing power to include) or to provide some means of accessing the required intelligence by reaching outside the system. Similarly, individual objects may include other things as parts, the so-called HASA (HAS-A) relationship in AI. A car is a thing. It has a steering sub-system, which is itself another thing. Cooperative control among different things in the IoT may require knowledge about such structure in a way similar to the above example about the ISA relationship.

Each type of thing has its own kind of data. Data can be digital or analog and can provide discrete measurements, such as the current temperature, or have streaming forms, such as video.

Things have life spans, just as humans do. Things are born (i.e., created) and die (i.e., destroyed). Things that transmit data to the outside world will have persistence in the form of the historical data that is kept about that object in various repositories, such as the cloud. Things may also enter and leave the Internet, that is, come into and go out of connectivity. Mobile things may enter and leave areas where Internet access is available. Battery-operated things may have their batteries go dead and later be replaced. Failure to communicate with a thing does not mean that the thing has died.

Each thing that is to be part of the IoT will need a name so that it can be referenced and located. The industry has implemented standards for naming objects and an Object Naming Service (ONS), which is an extension to the Domain Naming Service (DNS) already in use on the Internet. In many cases, things will communicate with each other directly without the need for searching for a communication path. For example, two cars approaching each other may recognize each other as soon as they come within range of their respective wireless communication circuits. In other cases, a system may need to use the ONS to locate an object with which it is trying to establish a link. For example, the base station of an animal migration monitoring system will need a locator service when trying to establish a link to a node attached to an animal that is moving, much the same way that cell phone systems have to search for a number being called. IPv6 will play a crucial role in naming things in the IoT. IPv4 is capable of referencing only about 4.3 billion distinct addresses. The number of connected things surpassed that level early in this century.

26.3 Scale

The anticipated scale of devices and data on the IoT is not of direct concern to embedded system engineers during the design and implementation of a particular product, for example, the bridge. However, scale is one of the major issues discussed in the current literature on IoT, so we introduce a few comments about it here.

The first issue of scale is the sheer number of devices. As noted in Chapter 1, estimates of the number of IoT-connected devices by the year 2020 range up to 50 billion. Moreover, the number of devices will continue to grow, perhaps doubling every few years. IPv4 is already insufficient to address all the connected devices. In an embedded system, on the other hand, the number of devices is typically fixed or at least grows at only very slowly compared to the IoT. That number may be quite small, for example, five or six sensors in a bio-monitoring system, or fairly large, for example, hundreds or even thousands in a large agricultural system monitoring and controlling hundreds or thousands of acres of farmland. Still, it would not be on the order of billions of devices. The number of devices in a given embedded system may grow. For example, the agricultural control system may be designed so that new sensor/controller modules can easily be added in case the farmer buys additional land. Or, an existing embedded system design could be upgraded with a new kind of sensor/actuator as technology advances; for example, a 2.0 version of the bridge system might add stress sensors to monitor the metal in the bridge spans and supports. But these kinds of growth are quite small compared to the doubling or tripling of devices every few years foreseen for the IoT. The design team should consider if the system should be allowed to expand the number of internal devices and if it should be allowed to interact with external devices. In the latter case, should the type of external device be set during the design process, as in the agricultural monitoring system example earlier in this paragraph, or should the system be prepared to interact with arbitrarily many devices of arbitrary types?

The second issue of scale in IoT is networking. Billions of devices are expected to communicate on the Internet, and those billions of devices will be using a variety of networking protocols. This is in stark contrast to an individual embedded system, say S, in which the networking structure and protocol is completely defined. It may be a wired structure, for example, a CAN bus in a car or appliance, or a wireless protocol, for example, Bluetooth for networking the sensor/actuator modules in an irrigation system. But once the decision has been made during the design of S, the internal structure and protocol for S is fixed, at least until a new version of the system is designed. However, in the spirit of IoT, it might be assumed that at some time in the future S would communicate with entities outside S in ways that were not envisioned during the design process. The embedded system engineers should consider this possibility and either decide not to allow it or to provide some hooks through which such future communication might be implemented.

The third issue of scale in IoT is data. Again, in an individual embedded system, the size and nature of the data would be understood in the early stages of modeling. The design team would have selected processing hardware capable of handling that data within the real-time constraints of the system. And, of course, the size of the data for that system would be minuscule compared to the size of the data being generated in the IoT. For example, the bridge system might generate a few hundred or thousand bytes of data every minute or two — a handful of sensor readings every few seconds, perhaps a video of the approaching boat traffic, etc. A modern car can generate gigabytes of data per day.[1] Both of these are trivial compared to all the data from all the cars, monitoring stations, and other related objects being uploaded to the cloud every day. The analysis of "big data" is an active area of research and a critical area for the IoT. For individual embedded systems, the nature and size of the data is typically not so large and can be managed with existing techniques. However, the design team may want to consider whether or not the information from inside the embedded system should ever be exported and, if so, how the team can make the system's data more useful to the IoT and the outside world in general.

26.4 Heterogeneity of things

Heterogeneity of things refers to the vast number of different kinds of things that are expected to participate in the IoT. Many kinds of things are already connected to the Internet — cars, humans (through bio-monitoring systems), appliances, etc. Many kinds of things already exist but have not yet connected or are just beginning to be connected — roads, buildings, clothing, etc. As new products are developed, completely new kinds of things will eventually participate in the IoT — things that don't even exist now. We have already seen in the introduction to this chapter and in earlier sections of the book a sample of the many different kinds of things — vehicles, soil sensors, biosensors, appliances, our bridge, etc.

How can one thing understand messages received from other things so that it can respond appropriately? For example, a car may receive a message with one of the message bytes having the value 50. That message may have come from another car, with the value 50 meaning the other car is approaching at 50 mph. But if the message had come from a stop light instead, the value 50 could mean 50 seconds before the light turns red. Or, the message may have come from the road, and the value 50 represents the recommended maximum speed for that road in the current weather conditions. Or, the message may have come from a nearby store, and the value 50 means there is a 50% sale on car-related items that the driver may want to take advantage of. All these scenarios are possible, even likely, in the vision of IoT. The embedded systems incorporated into things of one kind will be developed by experts knowledgeable about that kind of thing independent of other kinds of things with which the application might connect in the future IoT. The experts in each area will use their own knowledge and language in developing and implementing their systems. How, then, can all these different kinds of things understand each other?

One solution is to use mark-up languages for messages and standard dictionaries, such as is done on the Internet with HTTPS and in publishing with mark-up standards for math, chemistry, physics, etc. See Refs. [2, 3] for background on mark-up languages and the use of namespaces in marked-up files. Continuing the example from the previous paragraph, the message might have been the following.

```
<message xmlnamespace="www.embsysstandards.org/trafficcontrollers">
<stoplight id="159.30.180.21">
<eastbound light="green" timeleft="50">

   ...

</stoplight>
</message>
```

Mark-up languages provide many advantages in general and also in situations where there is heterogeneity. Assuming the names and other mark-up are chosen reasonably well, mark-up files are human readable. While not of direct benefit to the things, this can make development of the languages and namespaces easier and can often be useful in developing and debugging new (embedded) systems. Obviously they facilitate interoperability because along with the corresponding standard namespaces they provide the context by which one system can understand messages from arbitrary other systems. This includes a proper understanding of both domain-specific information, such as about cars or bio-sensing, and general information, such as the variety of formats for numbers. However, marked-up files also have serious disadvantages. First, they are obviously much larger than encoded files, typically by at least an order of magnitude or more. Second, they are meant to be readable by arbitrary other systems, so the information is completely insecure. If the message is about the weather or about the time left before the stop light changes, the lack of security is not a problem and, in fact, is a benefit. If the message contains bio-information about a person, then security is an important concern to prevent personal information from being disclosed to unauthorized systems.

A special consideration for embedded systems with real-time constraints is the amount of time required to parse incoming messages. For messages in a marked-up format, this includes the time to tokenize and parse the text and the time to retrieve the namespaces being referenced. To avoid Internet access for namespace retrieval, embedded systems can maintain local copies of time-critical namespaces or even build the recognition of names for time-critical messages into the code. For example, a car has time constraints for reacting to messages from other cars, stop lights, the road, etc. Recognition of names and parameters for messages from these sources can be built into the code. On the other hand, messages that are not time critical, such as advertisements from nearby stores, can use the normal namespace retrieval mechanism through the Internet. It would not be a disaster if the driver of the car missed one sale.

Another consideration for embedded systems engineers is where such mark-up should be added to messages being sent out or be parsed for messages coming in. Many things in the IoT have little or no computing power, as already noted. Radio frequency identification (RFID) tags might be configured to send marked-up text if the message was small enough, but RFID tags cannot send large numbers of bytes. Motes and other small sensor nodes also do not have enough computing power to handle any but the most trivial mark-up, and this would reduce battery life for those nodes running on battery power. One approach is to configure the embedded system as a private local network and identify one node as the gateway to the outside world. During the design process, then, the embedded system engineers would decide how much communication with the outside world would be allowed and select a hardware platform strong enough to handle the expected message traffic.

26.5 Security, privacy, and trust

Security refers to the property that the system is protected against unauthorized access. Such access includes reading information from the system, using the system (either for its intended purpose or some other purpose), and modification. Privacy refers specifically to protecting information from unauthorized access. Trust refers to the system believing that users of the system are authorized and that they are who they say they are. The term "users" refers to both humans and any other entity outside the system itself. Each of these terms may be applied to the system as a whole or to parts of the system. For example, in our bridge system we expect that no outside entity other than authorized bridge operators and the local traffic control system may access the bridge system or any part of it. On the other hand, an ATM cannot prevent arbitrary people from pressing keys on the machine, but the id/password mechanism prevents unauthorized access to inner parts of the system.

Most embedded systems are closed or nearly closed. The interface between the system and the outside world is precisely defined by the messages that can be sent in or out of the system, and this is done during the early stages of the design as the Unified Modeling Language, Specification and Description Language, and other models of the system are developed. For example, the bridge system has well-defined connections to the outside world, perhaps through a gateway implemented on the main control computer. Information from outside the bridge system may come in and may be authenticated at the gateway. Information from inside the system, such as sensor readings or current operations like span going up, can be sent out of the system, but the kinds of such information would all be determined at system design time. In the original concept of the bridge control system, it probably would not be expected that the motor itself would communicate with the world outside the bridge. The IoT changes all that. One of the goals of the IoT is that things communicate with each other on a need basis and that things dynamically form new connections. In current cars, the steering system may accept commands from the steering wheel or parking module. But in the future, it may be sent messages from other things, such as other cars or even the road itself, to avoid a collision or even just to move to another, less crowded route to the car's destination. Of course, this leads to security threats. The car may also receive steering commands from car thieves or kidnappers. A particularly dangerous case of this kind of security threat is software updates; a malicious outside entity could command a unit to accept a software patch that was not valid. How can one embedded system know that the other thing is really what it says it is? Embedded systems designers, therefore, need to consider how their systems might connect to the IoT in the future and plan for an appropriate level of security and the mechanisms to enforce it.

Protection from unauthorized access by external things may be easier to accomplish in systems in which the communication is wired instead of wireless. Access to the Internet could then be completely disallowed or at least focused through a single gateway. For example, a car would likely have wired communication between its submodules like steering, brakes, carburation, etc., using a CAN bus. Perhaps only the main control module has the ability to connect wirelessly. The system designers, then, can select a hardware platform for this gateway that has sufficient power to include security checks. Communication between, say, other cars or the road can then be checked by the gateway before being forwarded to submodules like steering and brakes. Security in wireless modules is more problematic. Many embedded system modules have too little computing power to handle security checking. A module like that with actuators could be compromised into performing some deleterious action by a malicious attacker. Even if the module has no actuators and only sends data to other parts of the system, an attacker may intercept and alter the data to either corrupt the embedded system as a whole or trick it into doing something bad.

Privacy will become an important issue as more and more embedded systems participate in the IoT. It is easy to build privacy into a closed system. System designers can determine in the early stages which parts of the system need to know about private information and which do not. As an example, consider a bio-monitoring system. Of course, emergency services need to know which patient has just displayed symptoms of a heart attack and where that patient is located. On the other hand, such information would not be needed by local health officials monitoring the general health of the population. Related to this last point is the fact that IoT envisions possible future networking that may not have been anticipated at the time a particular embedded system was developed. For example, the designers of the bio-monitoring system may not have planned to share information beyond the patient's doctor and local emergency services. The doctor may later decide or be compelled to share information with other agencies, such as local health officials or the World Health Organization. In some cases, the embedded system designers can implement measures that will lessen the possibility of privacy violations. For example, smart electric meters are being used more and more to make the power system more efficient. However, unauthorized people could break into the communications link to monitor individual homes and determine, for example, when a home may be empty by observing significantly lower power usage. If the meter averaged power usage over, say, an hour, it would be more difficult for eavesdroppers to determine when an individual homeowner was away for a local errand, such as shopping. If the information from all the smart meters in an area such as a block or apartment building was aggregated, it would be difficult for eavesdroppers to tell even if an individual unit were empty for longer periods, such as the family on a vacation. The system designers would need to analyze whether either or perhaps both of these approaches can still meet the information requirements of the entire electrical distribution system and be implementable with an acceptable cost. The point is that the designers need to think about possible future connections to the IoT and how information can or should not be made available outside the original embedded system.

Many of the existing security techniques may not be feasible for particular embedded systems or may go against the IoT vision of dynamic networking. Consider the following well-known techniques.

- Firewalls.[4] This is easy to implement and may be appropriate for embedded systems that are not meant to participate in the IoT. However, firewalling does go against the IoT vision of arbitrary groups of things dynamically connecting in an opportunistic way.
- Access control.[5] Generally, blacklisting will require much more memory than is available on smaller modules. This could be used if the embedded system had a gateway module with sufficient memory.
- Encryption.[6] This could be a useful technique for protecting data from snoopers, but again, small modules will likely not have the computing power needed to implement good encryption. If the embedded system's internal communication was over a wired protocol so that internally the data was protected and private, a reasonably powerful gateway module could be used to provide strong encryption before data was transmitted outside the system.

An additional challenge in selecting a security system for battery-operated systems is to implement a method that will not require too much energy.

In addition to electronic security issues, embedded systems have physical security issues. For example, ATM security has been compromised by thieves who simply steal the entire ATM. Physical concerns go beyond simply protecting against malicious behavior. A sensor node in an agricultural monitoring system needs to be protected against rain and sun exposure or it will fail soon after it is deployed.

Security and IoT have conflicting goals. Security wants to limit access to protect the system. The IoT wants things to be open to arbitrary hook-ups with other things. Embedded system engineers will need to strike an appropriate balance between these two conflicting goals in order to make new systems that meet their needs and yet have acceptable levels of security and privacy.

26.6 **Connectivity**

In Chapters 22 and 23 we described the most common communication protocols. There are many other Internet protocols, and this illustrates another serious issue for IoT, namely the variety of networking protocols. In a single embedded system, the designers would likely focus on one or maybe two connectivity methods, and the system implementers could easily implement the protocols and any transformation mechanisms needed to make the different protocols work with each other. However, the vision of the IoT is that systems that have been developed quite independently can connect with each other in opportunistic ways. The designers of one embedded system cannot predict which kinds of other systems their system will try to connect with or what the protocols of the other systems might be. In the future, new protocols might be developed and new systems deployed using those protocols. Embedded systems that are meant to participate in the IoT will almost surely need a reasonably powerful gateway capable of handling the heterogeneity of networking protocols. An important research topic in IoT is how, if at all, to overcome the heterogeneity of networking protocols so that arbitrary things can dynamically connect with each other.

Another issue in IoT is that of reaching other things that a particular thing knows about. One thing, say T1, might have already established a relationship with and know the name or IP address of another thing, say T2. However, many things are highly mobile in the IoT and can travel hundreds or even thousands of miles. If T1 wants to communicate with T2 but T2 is not in direct range of T1's radio, T1 needs to invoke some service to locate T2. This is rather like the situation with cell phones. When one cell phone is used to call another, the phone system has to first locate where the second phone is.

26.7 **Issues regarding big data and data ownership**

How to deal with "big data"[7] is a recent research problem. As can be seen from Section 26.3, the amount of data in the IoT will be many orders of magnitude larger than in any individual database, such as the government's database on citizens or a credit card company's database on its members. The development of the cloud[8] makes it possible to store and analyze such huge amounts of data. This leads to interesting questions for embedded systems engineers and new possibilities for things in the IoT to do their jobs better. Where should data be stored? Where should computation be done? How can a particular embedded system take advantage of data and computing power in the cloud? Embedded systems are just the edge applications and data generators; real power comes when those systems can invoke intelligence and the processing power in the cloud/fog to make better decisions and provide better service. The intelligence comes, in part, from high-powered computing applied to massive amounts of data. IoT value comes, then, from the combination of edge and cloud/fog computing, not one or the other but both together.

We have already seen how data and computation can be shared and distributed over nodes in an embedded system which is itself a network. For example, a gateway node can provide storage for data collected from simple sensor nodes and provide computational power to analyze that data and to control its transmission outside the system. The gateway can provide storage and computing power that individual nodes cannot. The sensor and actuator nodes can be thought of as being at the edge of the embedded system, connecting to the physical world, while the gateway is at the center of the system, providing data storage and computation as well as the link to the outside world. In a similar way, in the vision of the IoT embedded systems are at the edge of the cloud, connecting to the physical world. The cloud will collect data from embedded systems (i.e., the IoT edge nodes), store it, and perform potentially massive computations on those data. Not only can the cloud store more data and perform more computation, but it can also combine data from different sources and can therefore generate useful knowledge that no single embedded system could possibly generate. For example, an agricultural system could collect data about soil moisture, temperature, daily sunlight, etc., for a particular farm. It might even receive information from the weather service about predicted rainfall or temperature changes and adjust its watering schedule. In contrast, the cloud could collect data from thousands of individual farm systems and combine that with historical data about crop yields under different conditions of weather and fertilization as well as expected consumer needs and wants throughout the world to generate guidance for individual regions or even countries about what to plant, when to plant, and which crops to plant. This is well beyond the capabilities of any individual farm-embedded system and perhaps even beyond the dreams of the engineers who designed that system.

The question of how such huge amounts of data are stored and processed is the topic of a recent research activity called "big data". The general questions concerning big data are beyond the scope of this book and are not of direct concern to the embedded system engineer. However, there are related issues that are important to the design of embedded systems. Some of these, such as privacy and security, we have already seen. We now consider one more question that might be relevant to the design of individual embedded systems — ownership of data.

Ownership of data passed into the cloud[9] is a thorny, perhaps even legal, issue that has yet to be adequately addressed, much less solved. Does the system that generated data and passed it into the cloud retain any rights or control over that data? Who has a right to use data in the cloud and for what purposes? Obviously, data that is considered to be private should not be passed into the cloud or at least not passed in without appropriate hiding of the private nature of the data. However, designers of embedded systems of the future should consider what kinds of data generated by the system under design could be useful to other embedded systems and should therefore be sent into the cloud, even at the risk of losing control of that data. In what ways can the data be processed before being sent to the cloud to preserve privacy and yet still be useful to society? A major goal of the IoT, and of cloud computing as well, is to improve society. Designers of individual embedded systems will need to study the balance between privacy for their users and the potential benefit to society as a whole.

26.8 Summary

Embedded systems and their components can be considered as the "things" in either of the two models described in the previous chapter. Therefore, it is important for embedded system designers and engineers to be aware of IoT issues. This chapter presents some of the issues that will be major topics of discussion on the IoT for the foreseeable future. Some of these issues will impose requirements on individual embedded systems; examples of these issues include connectivity, security, big data, and cloud computing. Other similar issues, such as the precise nature of "thing" or the scale of the IoT, may not impose immediate requirements during the design of an embedded system but is important for design teams to be aware of.

Problems

1. For each of the following applications write a 3- to 4-page discussion of the issues presented in this chapter. Discuss your write-up with your study group or the class as a whole.

   a) World Health Organization. Information about individual patients (from hospital/doctor files, personal health monitors, etc.) is aggregated for analysis and detection of epidemics and for long-term planning for world health.

   b) The community monitoring application described in the preceding chapter problem set.

   c) The traffic control application described in the preceding chapter problem set.

   d) The community energy application described in the preceding chapter problem set.

2. Hold a study group or class discussion about privacy in the presence of ubiquitous monitoring. What are the advantages of ubiquitous monitoring of people and things, the disadvantages, the dangers, and the risks?

3. In a group or class brainstorming session, list other things that each of the following things might communicate with in the future that the original designers of the given thing might not have thought of.

   a) A car.

   b) A smart home appliance.

   c) A bridge.

   d) A watch.

   e) A desk lamp.

4. Hold a study group or class discussion about data ownership for each of the following. Discuss different kinds of data that the thing could generate, different kinds of external entities that might reasonably claim ownership, different kinds of external entities that should not be allowed access to that data, etc.

References

[1] Richter, F., Big data on wheels. Digital image, 2017. https://www.statista.com/chart/8018/connected-car-data-generation/. (Accessed November 24, 2019).

[2] https://en.wikipedia.org/wiki/XML.

[3] https://en.wikipedia.org/wiki/XML_namespace.

[4] https://en.wikipedia.org/wiki/Firewall_(computing).

[5] https://en.wikipedia.org/wiki/Access_control.

[6] https://en.wikipedia.org/wiki/Encryption.

[7] https://en.wikipedia.org/wiki/Big_data.

[8] https://en.wikipedia.org/wiki/Cloud_computing.

[9] https://en.wikipedia.org/wiki/Big_data_ethics.

Index

Note: Page numbers followed by f indicate figures, t indicate tables, and b indicate boxes.

A

Actuators, 12–13
ALOHA Network system, 11, 55, 395–396
Analog inputs
    bits and binary numbers, 255–256
    flash, 256–257
    internal structure, 256
    microphone, 255
    potentiometers, 255
    resolution, 256
    sensor output voltage, 255
    speed, 256
    successive approximation approach (SAR),
        257–258, 258f
    temperature measurement, 255
Analog outputs
    DC motors, 259–260
    digital-to-analog converters (DACs), 260–261
    embedded system design, 259–260
Analog-to-digital converters (ADCs), 251
Aperiodic tasks, 327–328
ARM Cortex-M3 Processor, 213f
ARPANET, 395
Arrival time, 175
As-late-as-possible (ALAP) schedule, 340–344,
        343f
As-soon-as-possible (ASAP) schedule, 340–344,
        343f
AT45DB161D memory circuit, 226–228, 227f
Automated teller machine (ATM)
    communications link failure, 150
    human error, 151

B

Backward reasoning, 157
Barrier control, 196f
Bathtub Curve Model, failure rate, 145f
Batteries, 285
Battery-operated systems, 371
Beacon network, 457
Behavioral models, 42–43, 164–165
Big data, 499–501
Binary numbers, 377
Bluetooth
    classes, 453, 453t
    connections, 454–455
    discoverable vs. nondiscoverable mode, 455

Bluetooth (*Continued*)
    frequency hopping spread spectrum (FHSS), 454
    passkeys, 455–456
    piconets, 454
    profile, 454
    sample applications, 453
    security, 456
Body area network (BAN), 400, 402–403
Bridge Barrier Control FSM (BARRIER), 65f
Bridge Downstream Boat Sensor (DSSEN), 66f
Bridge Light Control FSM (LIGHT), 65f
Bridge system
    bridge operator, 29
    cars and boats, 29
    cars/pedestrians crossing, 29f
    inspector, 29
    output signals generation, 31
    partially open state, 28f
    pedestrians, 29
    repairmen, 29
    robustness
        environmental parameters, 142b
        incorrect input handling, 143b–144b
        local power failure, 144b
        pedestrians walk, 142b–143b
    sample top-level architecture, 196f
    stakeholders, 31–32
    sub-contractor, 30–31
    use case analysis
        diagrams, 35, 36f
        product design, 40
        sequence diagrams, 35–40, 37f
        walk-through process, 34
    use cases and scenarios, 32–34
Bridge Traffic Sensor FSM (TrSENSOR), 65f
Bridge Upstream Boat Sensor (USSEN), 66f

C

Cable/line termination, 413–414
Cache memory, 230–231
CAN (Controller Area Network) protocol, 11–12
    bit period with 16 quanta, 447, 447f
    buses, 445–446
    frames, 446–447, 446t
    high-speed protocol (CANH), 448–449
    vs. inter-integrated circuit (I^2C) protocol,
        445–446

CAN (Controller Area Network) protocol
    (*Continued*)
  low-speed CAN protocol (CANL), 449, 450f
  node structure, 445f
  vs. RS232 protocol, 445–446
  synchronization, 447–448
  vs. TTL serial protocols, 445–446
Carrier sense multiple access (CSMA), 458–459,
    461–462
Client-oriented evaluation, 167
Cloud computing
  benefits of, 473–475
  broad network access, 471
  characteristics, 470–473
  edge computation, 469
  embedded system design issues, 475–476
  fog computation, 469
  hybrid model, 472–473
  infrastructure-as-a-service (Iaas), 472
  measured service, 471
  on-demand self-service, 471
  platform-as-a-service (Paas), 472
  private clouds, 469
  public clouds, 469
  rapid elasticity, 471
  resource pooling and elasticity, 471
  software-as-a-service (SaaS), 472
Coaxial cable, 413, 414f
Cognitive issues, 164
Colorblind, 164
Colored predicate/transition Petri Net
  data types, 121
  Petri Net modeling, 120
  place/transition list, 122t–124t
  TDMA protocol, 121, 121f
Computer networks, 11–12
Concurrent systems
  multiple signal arrival at same time, 73–74
  StateMate semantics, 72–73
Condition/event Petri Net
  conditions, 92–93
  events, 93
  firing, 93
  flow relations, 93
  physically separated modules, 93–94
Controller area network (CAN) protocol
  bit period with 16 quanta, 447, 447f
  buses, 445–446
  frames, 446–447, 446t
  high-speed protocol (CANH), 448–449
  vs. inter-integrated circuit (I^{2}C) protocol,
    445–446

Controller area network (CAN) protocol
    (*Continued*)
  low-speed CAN protocol (CANL), 449, 450f
  node structure, 445f
  vs. RS232 protocol, 445–446
  synchronization, 447–448
  vs. TTL serial protocols, 445–446

D

DACs (digital-to-analog converters), 251
  output, 260
  resistors, 260–261
  thermometer-coded, 260–261
  types, 261f
Data ownership, 499–501
Deadlock, 366f
Decimal numbers, 377
Dependent aperiodic tasks, 340–344
DES (discrete event simulation). *See* Discrete
    event simulation (DES)
Deterministic finite-state machines (FSMs), 55
Diamond property, 110
Differential drive termination, 416f
Digital input device
  application standpoint, 251–252
  electrical standpoint, 251–252
  electronic circuits, 253–254
  key debounce circuit, 254f
  mechanical buttons and switches, 254
  opto-isolator, 252–253
  single pole input devices, 252, 252f
  transistor transistor logic (TTL) circuit, 251–252
Digital outputs, 259
Digital-to-analog converters (DACs), 251
  output, 260
  resistors, 260–261
  thermometer-coded, 260–261
  types, 261f
Discrete event sequence, 176
Discrete event simulation (DES)
  events and event queues, 175–176
  finite state machine (FSM)
    BARRIER transitions, 183
    initial event queue, 182
    internal state transitions, 180
    LIGHT and TrSENSOR transitions, 182–183
    time specification, 181
    walkthrough specific times, 180
  message sequence chart
    actors behavior, 178
    event queue, 179–180
    internal and external event time, 178–179

Discrete event simulation (DES) (*Continued*)
  main module, 178
    timing information, 178
  Petri net, 183–184
  time, 176–177
Domain naming service (DNS), 492–493

E

Earliest-deadline first (EDF) algorithm, 336–337
Economist Intelligence Unit (EIU), 6–7
Edge computation, 469
Electrically erasable programmable read-only
    memory (EEPROM), 229
Electric/electronic networks, 395
Embedded system development process
  vs. simple software design, 16
  software development life cycle (SDLC), 13–16
  waterfall process
    analyze requirements, 18
    collect requirements, 17–18
    deploy and test, 19
    design, 18
    implement and test, 19
    prototype, 18–19
Emulation, 174–175
Encryption, 498
Energy
  batteries, 285
  design strategies, 288–289
  harvesting
    motion power, 287
    solar power, 286, 286f
    thermal power, 288
    water power, 287
    wind power, 287
  reliable energy sources
    cell phones and patient monitoring systems,
      283–284
    environmental monitors, 284
    proximity, 283
    wildlife monitoring sensor, 284–285
EPROM (erasable programmable read-only
    memory), 229
Erasable programmable read-only memory
    (EPROM), 229
Esthetics and issues, 155, 166
Ethernet protocol
  fields, 433–434, 433t–434t
  frames, 433
  LANs and small networks, 431
  switches, 432–433, 432f
Evaluation process, 155, 167

Event, 175
Event time, 175

F

Face recognition software, 80
Fail-safe termination scheme, 416, 416f
Field-programmable gate arrays (FPGAs), 10
  algorithms, 239
  complex programmable logic devices (CPLDs),
    237
  logic blocks, 237
  low-end CPLD genre
    ATF 22V10 DIP circuit, 240–242
    chip-select signals generation, 240–242
    clock cycle, 245–246
    clock feature, 242–243
    internal flip-flops, 242–243
    sensor, 243f–244f
    transitions and output values, 244, 245t
  SENSING state, 246
  and system-on-a-chip (SOC), 237–238
FIFOs (First In First Outs), 83–84
Finite-state machines (FSMs)
  acceptors and transducers, 48–51
  deterministic behavior, 55
  discrete event simulation (DES)
    BARRIER transitions, 183
    initial event queue, 182
    internal state transitions, 180
    LIGHT and TrSENSOR transitions, 182–183
    time specification, 181
    walkthrough specific times, 180
  in embedded systems
    boat sensing module, 51–52
    graphical representation, 52
    symbol, 51–52
    top-level bridge system, 52t
  graphical representation, 49f
  hierarchical. *See* Hierarchical finite-state ma-
    chines (FSMs)
  non-deterministic, 55
  refining and correcting, 53–54
  single-processor model, 79
  timed, 56–58
  transducer, 50–51
Firewalls, 498
First In First Outs (FIFOs), 83–84
First stage modeling
  ATM system, 26
  bridge system. *See* Bridge system
  case development and analysis, 42
  participants, 25–26

First stage modeling (*Continued*)
  phone system, 26—27
  unified modeling language (UML), 26, 42
  universal design, 41—42
Fixed point arithmetic
  addition, 372—374
  binary computer arithmetic, 372
  binary numbers, 377
  decimal numbers, 377
  division, 375—376
  expressions, 376—377
  floating-point arithmetic, 371—372
  fraction digits, 372
  multiplication with fractional parts, 374—375
  scalar-multiplication, 372—374
  subtraction, 372—374
Flash analog-to-digital converters (ADCs),
      256—257, 257f
Flash memory, 229
Forward reasoning, 157
FPGAs (field-programmable gate arrays). *See*
      Field-programmable gate arrays (FPGAs)
Frequency hopping spread spectrum (FHSS), 454
FSM (finite-state machines). *See* Finite-state
      machines (FSMs)

G

General system memory, 230f
Generic embedded system, 193f
Global area network (GAN), 401
Ground traffic process, 83f

H

Hardware, 193f, 194—195, 239
Hardware-software mapping
  hardware choices, 291
  integer linear programming, 296—302
  Pareto optimality, 302—305
  span controller, 291
  task dependency graph
    analysis, 295
    bridge project, 292, 293f
    "clear bridge traffic" task, 293, 294f
    complex system, 293
    hardware/software mapping, 295
    implementations, 293—294
    notions, 292
    real-time requirements, 294—295
Hearing impairment, 164
Heterogeneity of things
  mark-up languages, 495
  messages received, 494—495

Heterogeneity of things (*Continued*)
  namespaces, 495—496
  radio frequency identification (RFID) tags, 496
Hierarchical finite-state machines (FSMs)
  OR super-state
    anomalous situation/error, 60—61
    open span, 61f
    sub-states, 59
    transitions out, 61—62, 61f
    TV set, 60
  AND super-state
    Bridge Barrier Control FSM (BARRIER), 65f,
        67, 69
    Bridge Downstream Boat Sensor (DSSEN),
        66f
    Bridge Light Control FSM (LIGHT), 65f, 68
    bridge normal operation, 63—64, 63f
    Bridge Traffic Sensor FSM (TrSENSOR), 65f,
        67—68
    Bridge Upstream Boat Sensor (USSEN), 66f,
        69
    entrance mechanisms, 62—63
    multiple signal arrival at same time, 73—74
    Span Control FSM (SPAN), 64, 64f, 71
    StateMate semantics, 72—73
    variables and timers, 62
High-Speed CAN Network, 448—449, 448f
Human-computer interface, 151

I

ILP (integer linear programming). *See* Integer
      linear programming (ILP)
Immediate priority ceiling, 366
Independent aperiodic tasks, 337—339
Infrastructure-as-a-service (Iaas), 472
Integer linear programming (ILP)
  equalities and inequalities, 296—299
  hardware component, 296—297
  non-deterministic polynomial-time (NP), 302
  problem-specific knowledge, 301
  zero-one linear programming, 296
Interfacing devices
  573 circuit configured, 264f
  generic configuration, 264
  GPIO pins and ports, 261—262
  573 latch/gate circuit, 262f
  output latch, 264—265
  processor, 263—264
  sensors and actuators, 263—264
Inter-integrated circuit (I^2C) protocol
  acknowledge bit (ACK), 442—443
  bus configuration, 442f

Inter-integrated circuit (I^{2}C) protocol (*Continued*)
  clock stretching, 444
  common clock signal (SCL), 441–442
  microcontroller, 444
  operating speeds, 444–445
  PCF8591 ADC/DAC, 444
  single data line (SDA) event, 441–442
  start (left) and stop (right) conditions, 442f, 443
Internal memory, 207–208
Internet
  BAN patient monitoring system, 421
  ethernet protocol, 431–434
  internet protocol, 427–429
  open systems interconnection (OSI) model,
    421–424
  transport control protocol (TCP), 425–427
Internet of Things (IoT) systems
  computer networks, 11–12
  vs. embedded systems, 7–8
  generic format, 2, 2f
  health monitoring, 4
  INTEL model
    analytics and machine learning, 487
    application programming interface, 488
    data flow view, 485
    highest-level view, 485, 486f
    protocol abstraction and management layer,
      486–487
    security, 487
    sensors and actuators, 485–486
    smart things, 485
    storage, 487
    thing/device management, 487
  inventory control, 3
  issues
    big data and data ownership, 499–501
    connectivity, 499
    heterogeneity of things, 494–496
    privacy, 497–498
    protection, 497
    scale, 493–494
    security, 496
    things, 491–493
  microprocessors, 9–10
  projects, 20
  radio frequency identification (RFID) and bar
    codes, 1–2
  safety and security, 5
  sensors and actuators, 12–13
  smart agriculture, 3–4
  smart buildings and homes, 4
  smart city, 4–5

Internet of Things (IoT) systems (*Continued*)
  smart electrical grid, 4
  smart objects, 1–2
  transportation, 4
  vision for, 3
  World Forum model
    communication level, 483
    data storage, 484
    edge, 483
    fog computing, 483–484
    long-term data analysis, 484
    seven levels, 482f
    wireless sensor/actuator network, 484
Internet protocol (IP)
  destinations, 427–428
  IPv4 packet, 428–429, 429t
  versions, 428
Interrupt system, 199–203
  compare instruction, 201–202
  Intel 8051 and TI Stellaris family, 202–203
  interrupt handlers, 202
  interrupt process, 199–200
  interrupt source, 200–201
  jump_positive instruction, 201–202
  priority scheme, 202
  pseudomachine code, 201
IoT (Internet of Things) systems. *See* Internet of
    Things (IoT) systems

L

Linear networks, 406, 406f
List Scheduling algorithm, 344, 345f
Local area network (LAN), 396–397, 400–401
Loop processing
  loop unrolling, 378
  memory organization, 381–382
  pixel array
    loops split, 381f
    special areas, 380f
    straightforward nested loop code, 380f
Low-level communication protocols
  contention and collisions
    carrier sense multiple access (CSMA),
      461–462
    detection and avoidance, 459–460
    priority-based arbitration, 460–461
    time division multiple access (TDMA),
      458–459, 462–463
  physical signal transmission, 437
  wired serial transmission
    controller area network (CAN) protocol,
      445–449

Low-level communication protocols (*Continued*)
    inter-integrated circuit (I^2C) protocol,
        441–445
    RS232 protocol, 440–441
    TTL serial protocols, 438–440
    wired serial protocol, 437–438
    wireless communications
        bluetooth, 453–456
        features, 450–451
        Ipv6lowPAN, 458
        Wi-Fi, 451–453
        Zigbee, 456–458

M

Manual dexterity impairment, 164
Mean down time (MDT), 140
Mean time between failures (MTBF), 140
Mean time to failure (MTTF), 140–141
Mean time to repair (MTTR), 140
Medical body area network (BAN), 403
Memories
    logical-level issues, 229–232
        cache memory, 230–231
        memory management units (MMUs), 232
        scratchpad memory, 231
    physical-level issues
        onboard *vs.* offboard memory, 225–226
        serial *vs.* parallel access, 226–228
        volatile *vs.* non-volatile memory, 228–229
Memory management units (MMUs), 232
Mesh networks, 411–412
Messages and communication
    formats
        human-readable formats, 389–390
        main control module, 388
        marked-up format, 390f
        sample message encoding scheme, 389t
    module, 387
    passing
        blocking/synchronous, 391
        Kahn model, 390–391
        non-blocking/asynchronous, 391–392
    wireless sensor network (WSN), 387
Microcontrollers, 197–198, 198f
Microprocessors, 9–10, 198–199
Miniature mechanical switch, 253f
M2M World of Connected Services, 6f
Modest-sized system, 195–196
Module-to-module fault dependency, 149–150
Motion power, 287
Motors
    brushed DC motor, 266f, 267

Motors (*Continued*)
    brushless DC motors, 267–268
    circuits, 269–271
    magnets, 266
    stepper motor, 268, 269f–270f
Multiply-accumulate (MAC) instruction,
    215–216, 216f

N

Nanoscale network, 400
Near-field communication (NFC) networks,
    400–402
Near-me area network (NAN), 400, 404–405
Networks
    body area network (BAN), 402–403
    channel efficiency, 398
    classification, 400–405
    definition, 396
    end-to-end delay, 398
    history, 395–396
    local area network (LAN), 396–397
    near-field communication (NFC) networks,
        401–402
    near-me area networks, 404–405
    packet duplication/loss, 399
    personal area networks (PANs), 403–404
    physical considerations
        wired networks, 413–417
        wireless networks, 417–418
    topologies, 405–412
        linear networks, 406, 406f
        mesh networks, 411–412
        ring network, 406–408, 407f
        star network, 408–410, 409f
        tree network, 410–411, 410f
Nonbeacon network, 457
Non-deterministic finite-state machines (FSMs),
    55
Non-deterministic polynomial-time (NP), 302
Non-volatile memory, 228–229

O

Object naming service (ONS), 492–493
Offboard memory, 225–226
Onboard memory, 225–226
Open systems interconnection (OSI) model, 481
    application layer, 423
    data link layer, 424
    management issues, 423
    network layer, 424
    in PC, 422f
    physical layer, 424

Open systems interconnection (OSI) model
(*Continued*)
presentation layer, 423
session layer, 423
vs. TCP/IP, 422f
transport layer, 423
Operating systems
configurability, 318, 318f
cost, 317
dashboard module, 316–317
debugging tools, 317–318
elements, 313, 313f
flexibility, 317
hardware devices, 314–315
high-level operations, 314–315
interrupt handling, 315
low-level device drivers, 314–315
main control module, 315–316
memory management, 314
real-time operating system issues. *See* Real-time
operating system issues
resource-sharing resources, 314
security threats, 315
space, 317
Stop Light Controller, 316, 316f
subsystem, 315–316
Optimizations
embedded system software, 371
fixed point arithmetic, 371–377
loop processing, 377–382
Opto-isolator, 252–253, 253f
OSI (open systems interconnection) model. *See*
Open systems interconnection (OSI)
model
Output devices
communications circuits, 274–275
device drivers, 275
indicators and panel displays
common pins, 274t
LCD display, 272–274, 273f
LED dots, 271
7-segment digits, 271, 272f
motors, 266–271

P

PAN (personal area networks), 400, 403–404
Pareto optimality, 302–305, 304f
Periodic analog signals sampling
aliasing, 278–279
digitized signals, 277
higher resolution, 277–278
processor, 278

Periodic analog signals sampling (*Continued*)
Shannon-Nyquist theorem, 279–280
simple signal train, 277, 277f
Periodic task, 327–328
Personal area networks (PANs), 400, 403–404
Petri Net
colored predicate/transition Petri Net
data types, 121
Petri Net modeling, 120
place/transition list, 122t–124t
TDMA protocol, 121, 121f
condition/event, 92–94
coordination, 91
discrete event simulation (DES), 183–184
place/transition, 94–108
predicate/transition, 120–121
time, 128f
clock state, 126
firing semantics, 127
function f, 126
marking, 127
notations, 127
reachability graph, 126
real-world actions, 124–125
simulation test, 128
transition, 127–129
Phone system, 26–27
Piconets, 454
Place/transition Petri Net, 99t, 104t
bridge system, 101–102, 103f
boat movement, 105
light module, 105–106
span module, 105
transition sequence, 106–107
definition, 94–95
graph, 94–95
incidence matrix for, 114–115
industrial car assembly line, 95–96, 96f
invariants and vectors, 118–120
mutual exclusion mechanism, 98
reachable markings
boundedness, 111
diamond property, 110
graph, robot example, 110–111
incidence matrix, 115–117
liveness properties, 113
robot assembly line simulation, 112
satisfying conditions, 110
transitive closure, 109–110
two-robot working process, 112–113, 112f
real capacity, 109
real-life systems, 108

Place/transition Petri Net (*Continued*)
structural properties, 118
Time Division Multiple Access (TDMA)
network, 100f
two-robot system, 98, 98f
Platform-as-a-Service (Paas), 472
Priority inheritance, 364–366, 365f
processes, 365f
same resource, 364f, 365
semaphore modification, 362–363
shared resources, 364–366, 364f
Private clouds, 469
Processing elements
functional features, 208–209
internal memory, 207–208
interrupt system, 199–203
compare instruction, 201–202
Intel 8051 and TI Stellaris family, 202–203
interrupt handlers, 202
interrupt process, 199–200
interrupt source, 200–201
jump_positive instruction, 201–202
priority scheme, 202
pseudomachine code, 201
microcontrollers, 197–198, 198f
microprocessors, 198–199
nonfunctional features
debuggers, 210
form factor, 209
off-the-shelf single-board systems, 209–210
price, 210
power control and sleep modes
deep sleep modes, 204–205
energy consumption, 203
processor chip, 204
sensor application, 204
shallow sleep modes, 204–205
voltage scaling, 205
wireless sensor node deployment, 203
wireless transmission of data, 203–204
sample processors
8051 family, 210–212
Stellaris family, 212–215
special purpose processors
hardware implementations, 216–217
multiply-accumulate (MAC) instruction, 215–216, 216f
raster operations pipeline, 215
TS320 family, 218
very-long instruction word (VLIW) operations, 217–218
start-up times, 218–220

Processing elements (*Continued*)
ramp-up period, 218–219, 219f
Stellaris processors, 218
stop-and-go light, 219–220
timers and counters
counting examples, 206
magnetic switches, 206
registers, 206–207
rotating devices, 206
software, 205–206
TimerInc, 207
timing examples, 206
Programmable read-only memory (PROM), 228–229
Program status word (PSW), 201
Public clouds, 469
Pulse width modulation (PWM), 9
deadband, 276
duty cycles, 275–276, 276f
high-end microcontrollers, 276
single-wire PWM controls, 275–276

R

Radio frequency identification (RFID), 402, 496
Random access memory (RAM), 207–208
Rapid application development (RAD), 15
Rate monotonic scheduling (RMS)
algorithm, 333, 333f
events and actions, 333, 334t
ground traffic sensor task, 335
higher priority task, 335
schedule produced, 335f, 335t
Read-only memory (ROM), 228
Real-time operating system issues
classification, 322–323
coordinating time, 321
feedback control problems, 322–323
hard real-time applications, 322
soft real-time applications, 322
time systems
programming languages, 319
sensor network, 319
system designers and implementers, 320–321
Universal Time (UT), 319–320
word-processing application, 322
RFID (radio frequency identification), 402, 496
Ring networks, 406–408, 407f
RMS (rate monotonic scheduling). *See* Rate monotonic scheduling (RMS)
Robustness, 141–144

Round-robin scheduling, 330
RS485 cable length guidelines, 413, 413f
RS232 protocol, 440 441

S

SABRE (semi-automatic business research environment), 11, 395
Safety and robustness design
  behavioral modeling, 137—138
  bridge system, 138
  design principles
    behavioral model, 149
    diagnosis and repair, 151
    fault-containment regions, 150
    faults propagation limitation, 149—150
    human-computer interface, 151
    human input, 151
    whole system failure, 149
  earlier design steps, 137
  failure rates, 138—139
    Bathtub Curve Model, 145, 145f
    counteraction, 148
    human intervention, 148
    and lifetimes, 145—146
    mechanical switch, 145
    nonvolatile memory circuits, 145
    postdeployment testing, 146
    redundancy, 147—148
    subsystem, 148—149
    switch, 146
  faults, 138—139
  fault tolerance, 137
  principles for, 146—151
  reliability
    mean down time (MDT), 140
    mean time between failures (MTBF), 140
    mean time to failure (MTTF), 140—141
    mean time to repair (MTTR), 140
    probability, 139—140
  robustness, 141—144
Scheduling method
  aperiodic tasks, 327—328
  cost and laxity, 330—331
  dependent aperiodic tasks, 340—344
  dependent periodic tasks, 337
  first-come-first-served, 330
  fixed number of processors, 344—346
  graph, 330, 331f, 335f
  ground traffic sensor task, 328
  hyperperiod, 331—332
  independent aperiodic tasks, 337—339
  independent periodic tasks

Scheduling method (*Continued*)
  earliest-deadline first (EDF) algorithm, 336—337
  rate monotonic scheduling (RMS), 332—336
  periodic task, 327—328
  processor, 327
  round-robin scheduling, 330
  static scheduling, 329
  utilization, 332
  worst-case execution time (WCET), 346—348
Scratchpad memory, 231
SDL (Specification and Description Language).
  See Specification and Description Language (SDL)
SDLC (Software development life cycle). *See*
  Software development life cycle (SDLC)
Semaphores
  code sequence, 358—359, 359f
  decrement/increment, 358
  functions, 357
  P and V functions, 360
  priority inversion
    immediate priority ceiling, 366
    priority inheritance, 364—366, 365f
  shared resource, 357—358
  structure, 358f
Semi-automatic business research environment (SABRE), 11, 395
Semi-automatic ground environment (SAGE) system, 11, 395
Sensors, 12—13
Sequence diagrams
  annotations, 37—38
  boat crossing, 35—36, 37f
  Bridge Span, 36—37
  Control Unit, 36—37
  refinements and requirements, 38—40
Serial peripheral interface (SPI), 11—12, 226—228
Shannon-Nyquist theorem, 279
Shared resources
  assignment statements, 356
  control access, 355
  machine instructions, 356
  shared variable, 355—357
Simple embedded system, 8f
Smart agriculture, 3—4
Smart buildings and homes, 4
Smart city, 4—5, 5f
Smart electrical grid, 4
Software-as-a-Service (SaaS), 472
Software development life cycle (SDLC), 13
  continuous integration, 15

Software development life cycle (SDLC) (*Continued*)
  incremental development, 15
  prototyping, 14—15
  rapid application development (RAD), 15
  spiral development process, 16
  waterfall development method, 15—16
Solar power, 286, 286f
Span Control finite-state machines (SPAN), 64f
Specification and Description Language (SDL)
  behavioral specification
    computation, 81—82
    generic data types, 82
    ground traffic process, 82, 83f
    hierarchical structure, 81, 81f
    notations, 81—82
  communication, 82—84
    First In First Outs (FIFOs), 83—84
    signals, 82—83
    synchronization, 82—83
  communication delays, 84—85
  distributed systems, 80—84
  Kahn process networks, 85
  messages, 80
  wait function, 86
Star network, 408—410, 409f
State invariant, finite-state machines (FSMs), 56—57
StateMate semantics, 72—73
Static scheduling, 329, 330f
Stellaris family
  additional GPIO pins, 213—214
  ARM Cortex-M3 Processor, 213f
  GPIO and I/O pins, 214
  hardware features, 212
  standard ARM instructions, 214—215
Stepper motor, 268, 269f
Successive approximation approach (SAR), 257—258, 258f

T

TCP (transport control protocol). *See* Transport control protocol (TCP)
Testing process
  behavioral models, 171
  discrete event simulation (DES). *See* Discrete event simulation (DES)
  emulation, 174—175
  simulation
    bridge behavioral model, 171—174
    robustnes, 173—174

Testing process (*Continued*)
    stimuli, 173
    timing issues, 174
  test case generation
    brainstorming, 185
    concurrency issues, 186
    internal models, 185
    principles and guidelines, 186—188
    random number generators, 186
TDMA (time division multiple access) network, 458—459, 462—463
  colored predicate/transition Petri Net, 121, 121f
  Place/transition Petri Net, 100f
Thermal power, 288
Thevenin termination, 415
Timed finite-state machines (FSMs), 56—58
  abstract model, 56
  state invariant, 56—58
  timers, 56
  timing requirement, 56
Time division multiple access (TDMA) network, 458—459, 462—463
  colored predicate/transition Petri Net, 121, 121f
  Place/transition Petri Net, 100f
Timed Petri Net
  clock state, 126
  firing semantics, 127
  function f, 126
  marking, 127
  notations, 127
  reachability graph, 126
  real-world actions, 124—125
  simulation test, 128
  transition, 127
Transport control protocol (TCP)
  acknowledge number, 426
  checksum, 427
  data offset, 426
  FIN packet, 427
  flags, 426—427
  functions, 425
  payload, 427
  sequence number, 426
  source and destination ports, 425—426
  SYN packet, 427
  Urgent Pointer, 427
  window size, 427
Tree network, 410—411, 410f
TTL serial protocols, 438—440
Two-robot working process, 112—113, 112f

U

Unified modeling language (UML), 42
Unified modeling process (UMP), 42
Universal Time (UT), 319—320

V

Validation
    esthetics, 166
    evaluation, 167
    human interfaces
        group icons, 163
        highly usable products, 162f
        learnability, 163
        operability, 163
        understandability, 162—163
        usability, 162
    installability and maintainability, 165—166
    portability, 166
    properties of interest, 156—157
    requirements, 155—156, 161
    universal access, 164—165
Verification, 155
    properties of interest, 156—157
    reasoning techniques
        backward reasoning, 157, 160—161
        case analysis, 157—158
        conditions and actions, 159t
        counterexamples, 158
        forward reasoning, 157, 160
        induction proof process, 158
        meaning of states, 159t
        modified bridge control FSM, 158—159,
            158f
Very-long instruction word (VLIW) operations,
    217—218
Volatile memory, 228—229

W

Waterfall development method, 15—16
Water power, 287
Wide area network (WAN), 401
Wi-Fi, 451—453
Wind power, 287
Wired networks
    cable/line termination, 413—414
    coaxial cable, 413, 414f
    differential drive termination, 416—417, 416f
    fail-safe termination scheme, 416
    intended *vs.* actual received signal, 413—414,
        414f
    parallel termination, 415, 415f
    RS485 cable length guidelines, 413, 413f
    series termination, 414—415
    Thevenin termination, 415, 415f
Wireless networks, 417—418
Wireless sensor network (WSN), 3—4, 387
Worst-case execution time (WCET), 346—348

X

Xilinx Zynq-7000 All Programmable System,
    238f
XML-based markup language, 389

Z

Zigbee
    devices, 456—457
    encryption key, 458
    home sensing and control, 456
    indoor ranges, 456
    network modes, 457
    outdoor line-of sight range, 456
    profiles, 457
    ZC node, 457—458